FEDfind:*

Your Key to Finding
Federal Government
Information

A Directory of
Information Sources,
Products and Services

Richard J. D'Aleo

Foreword by Senator William Proxmire

Illustrated by Carol S. Ratkus

Helping you be "information efficient"
and competitive
in the "information communications age"*

because

The future belongs to the "information efficient."*

ICUC Press

* A trademark of ICUC Press

NOTICES

Information sources, products and services included in FEDfind were selected on their perceived value to its readers by the author and he receives no compensation from any organization cited in the book.

Every effort was made to obtain reliable and up-to-date information. The book is current as of February 1986. The author assumes no legal responsibility for the completeness, accuracy or continued availability of material cited in this book.

Copyright 1986 by Richard J. D'Aleo
All Rights Reserved
Printed in the United States of America

No part of this book may be used or reproduced in any manner whatsoever without written permission of the publisher except in the case of brief quotations embodied in critical articles, reviews, notices or announcements.

ICUC Press, P.O. Box 1447, Springfield, VA 22151 (703/323-8065)

First Edition published in 1982. Second Edition 1986.

International Standard Book Number: 0-910205-03-5 $17.95
International Standard Book Number: 0-910205-02-7 (pbk.) $9.95

Library of Congress Cataloging-in-Publication Data

D'Aleo, Richard J., 1943–
  FEDfind: your key to finding federal government information

  Includes index.
  Summary: A directory of information sources and publications by or about the federal government, including private sector sources of such products or services.
  1. United States—Government publications—Bibliography. 2. United States—Politics and government—Bibliography. 3. United States—Politics and government—Information services—United States. [l. United States—Politics and government—Bibliography. 2. United States—Politics and government—Information services. 3. United States—Government publications—Bibliography] I. Ratkus, Carol S., ill. II. Title.
Z1223.Z7D3 1986 [J83]   015.73053   85-27267
ISBN 0-910205-03-5
ISBN 0-910205-02-7 (pbk.)

To my mother

Summary Table of Contents

Federal Organizations Abbreviations Index 6
Table of Contents 7
List of Figures 15
Foreword 17
Preface 19
Acknowledgements 21
How to Use *FEDfind* 23

Part I—The Organization and Its People

Chapter 1   Federal Government Organization 31
    2   Directories 41
    3   Civilian Personnel Management 55

Part II—The Branches and Selected Activities

Chapter 4   Legislative Branch 75
    5   Judicial Branch 105
    6   Executive Branch Overview 125
    7   Executive Office of the President 135
    8   Executive Branch Departments 145
    9   Executive Branch Agencies 227
    10   The Budget Process 309
    11   Program Administration and Evaluation 325
    12   Statistical Programs 335
    13   Science and Technology 349
    14   Federal Procurement and Business Information 359
    15   Mapping, Charting and Geologic Activities 379

Part III—Primary Publishers

Chapter 16   Government Printing Office 389
    17   National Technical Information Service 409
    18   General Accounting Office 421
    19   Selected Private Sector Publishers 429

Appendices
   A   Public Access Laws 435
   B   Paperwork Reduction Act of 1980 441
   C   Ethics in Government Act 443
   D   Computerized Information Resources 445
   E   Research and Document Retrieval Services 449
   F   Foreign Embassies 451

Publisher Order Forms 459

Subject-Organization-Publisher Index 471

Federal Organizations Abbreviations Index

ABMC	234	FHLBB	254	NOAA	163
ACDA	298	FJC	123	NRC	281
ACIR	231	FLC	101	NSC	142
AID	6	FLICC	101	NSF	278
Amtrak	277	FLAA	255	NTIS	164
ARC	235	FMC	256	NTSB	280
BJS	200	FMCS	257	OMB	141
BLS	207	FS	213	OPD	142
CBO	96	FTC	259	OPIC	284
CCR	238	GAO	97	OPM	283
CDC	189	GPO	98	ORSIP	192
CEA	142	GSA	260	OSHA	208
CEQ	143	HHS	185	OSHRC	282
CFA	239	HUD	193	OSTP	143
CFTC	240	IAF	262	OTA	102
CIA	237	ICC	263	PADC	287
CPSC	241	IDCA	301	PBGC	288
CRS	100	INS	202	PCC	285
CS	179	IRS	224	PCPFS	290
DOD	167	ITA	163	PHS	189
DOE	181	ITC	302	PRC	289
DOL	205	LC	98	PTO	164
DOT	215	LSC	264	RRB	291
DTIC	174	MSPB	304	SBA	295
EEOC	245	NAL	154	SEC	292
EIA	183	NARA	267	SOI	124
EOP	135	NASA	265	SRS	157
EPA	243	NBS	163	SSA	191
ERIC	179	NCES	179	TVA	297
ERS	152	NCHS	190	U.N.	214
FAA	217	NCLIS	270	USCG	219
FBI	201	NCPC	269	USDA	147
FCA	247	NCUA	271	USGS	198
FCC	248	NEA	272	USIA	299
FCIC	250	NEH	272	USPS	305
FDA	190	NIE	179	USRA	307
FEC	251	NIH	191	VA	308
Fed	258	NLM	191	WHO	141
FEMA	252	NLRB	274		
FERC	253	NMB	276		

Table of Contents

Summary Table of Contents 5
Federal Organizations Abbreviations Index 6
List of Figures 15
Foreword 17
Preface 19
Acknowledgements 21
How to Use *FEDfind* 23

Part I—The Organization and Its People

Chapter 1 Federal Government Organization 31
                Government Information Sources 31
                Federal Executive Boards 36
                Agency Annual Reports 36
                Private Sector Products and Services 36
                Federal History 40

Chapter 2 Directories 41
                The Federal Environment 41
                Legislative Branch 47
                Executive Branch 49
                Judicial Branch 52
                Foreign Affairs 52
                Directories of Directories 53

Chapter 3 Civilian Personnel Management 55
                Civilian Personnel Operations 55
                Labor-Management Relations 63
                Merit Systems Protection 64
                Management References 65
                Employment Information 67
                News Publications 73

Part II—The Branches and Selected Activities

Chapter 4 Legislative Branch 75
                Organization and Operation of Congress 76
                Congressional District Information 80
                Senate Rules and Procedures 82
                House Rules and Procedures 83
                How a Bill Becomes Law 84
                Legislative Proceedings 87

    The Congressional Scene 90
    Biographies 92
    Computerized Information Resources 93
    Legislative Branch Organizations 95
     Architect of the Capital 95
     Congressional Budget Office 96
     Copyright Royalty Tribunal 97
     General Accounting Office 97
     Government Printing Office 98
     Library of Congress 98
      Center for the Book 100
      Congressional Research Service 100
      Federal Library and Information Center
       Committee 101
      National Referral Center 101
     Office of Technology Assessment 102
     United States Botanic Garden 102
    Executive Branch Policy Directive 103

Chapter 5 Judicial Branch 105
    The U.S. Court System 105
    Legal Research Guides 108
    The Constitution 108
    The Supreme Court 110
    Judicial Procedures and Prosecution 113
    United States Code and Statutes 114
    Periodicals Covering the Courts 116
    Biographies 118
    Computerized Information Resources 118
    Judicial Branch Organizations 119
     The Supreme Court of the United States 119
     Lower Courts 119
     National Courts 121
     Administrative Office of the United States
      Courts 122
     Federal Judicial Center 123
    Subject Bibliographies 124

Chapter 6 Executive Branch Overview 125
    Federal Register System 125
    The Federal Register 128
    Code of Federal Regulations 130
    Periodicals Covering Executive Branch
     Activities 132
    Biographies 133

Chapter 7 Executive Office of the President 135
    The American Presidency 135
    Presidential Documents 138
    Executive Office of the President Publications .. 140
    Computerized Information Resources 141

Executive Office of the President Divisions 141
   The White House Office 141
   Office of Management and Budget 141
   Council of Economic Advisors 142
   National Security Council 142
   Office of Policy Development 142
   Office of the United States Trade
      Representative 143
   Council on Environmental Quality 143
   Office of Science and Technology Policy 143
   Office of Administration 143
Office of the Vice President of the United
   States 144

Chapter 8 Executive Branch Departments 145
   Department of Agriculture 147
   Department of Commerce 159
   Department of Defense 167
      Department of the Air Force 171
      Department of the Army 172
      Department of the Navy 173
      Defense Technical Information Center 174
      Department of Defense Agencies and Joint
         Service Schools 174
   Department of Education 177
   Department of Energy 181
   Department of Health and Human Services 185
   Department of Housing and Urban
      Development 193
   Department of the Interior 195
   Department of Justice 199
   Department of Labor 205
   Department of State 211
   Department of Transportation 215
   Department of Treasury 221

Chapter 9 Executive Branch Agencies 227
   ACTION 229
   Administrative Conference of the United States . 230
   Advisory Commission on Intergovernmental
      Relations 231
   Agency for International Development 232
   American Battle Monuments Commission 234
   Appalachian Regional Commission 235
   Board for International Broadcasting 236
   Central Intelligence Agency 237
   Commission on Civil Rights 238
   Commission on Fine Arts 239
   Commodity Futures Trading Commission 240
   Consumer Product Safety Commission 241

Environmental Protection Agency 243
Equal Employment Opportunity Commission ... 245
Export-Import Bank of the United States 246
Farm Credit Administration 247
Federal Communications Commission 248
Federal Deposit Insurance Corporation 250
Federal Election Commission 251
Federal Emergency Management Agency 252
Federal Energy Regulatory Commission 253
Federal Home Loan Bank Board 254
Federal Labor Relations Authority 255
Federal Maritime Commission 256
Federal Mediation and Conciliation Service 257
Federal Reserve System 258
Federal Trade Commission 259
General Services Administration 260
Inter-American Foundation 262
Interstate Commerce Commission 263
Legal Services Corporation 264
National Aeronautics and Space Administration . 265
National Archives and Records Administration . 267
National Capital Planning Commission 269
National Commission on Libraries and
   Information Science 270
National Credit Union Administration 271
National Foundation on the Arts and the
   Humanities 272
National Labor Relations Board 274
National Mediation Board 276
National Railroad Passenger Corporation 277
National Science Foundation 278
National Transportation Safety Board 280
Nuclear Regulatory Commission 281
Occupational Safety and Health Review
   Commission 282
Office of Personnel Management 283
Overseas Private Investment Corporation 284
Panama Canal Commission 285
Peace Corps 286
Pennsylvania Avenue Development Corporation 287
Pension Benefit Guaranty Corporation 288
Postal Rate Commission 289
President's Council on Physical Fitness and
   Sports 290
Railroad Retirement Board 291
Securities and Exchange Commission 292
Selective Service System 294
Small Business Administration 295
Smithsonian Institution 296
Tennessee Valley Authority 297

United States Arms Control and Disarmament
    Agency 298
United States Information Agency 299
United States International Development
    Cooperation Agency 301
United States International Trade Commission .. 302
United States Merit Systems Protection Board .. 304
United States Postal Service 305
United States Railway Association 307
Veterans Administration 308

Chapter 10 The Budget Process 309
            General Information 309
            Executive Preparation and Submission 314
                Policy Directives 314
                OMB Technical Staff Papers 317
                Budget Documents, Fiscal Year 1987 318
            Congressional Budget Process 321
            Implementation and Control 322
            Review and Audit 324

Chapter 11 Program Administration and Evaluation 325
            Policy Directives 326
            Congressional Sourcebook Series 327
            Program Catalogs 328
            Program Operations 331
            Program Evaluation 331

Chapter 12 Statistical Programs 335
            Central Coordinating Office 336
            Statistics—Future, Present and Past 337
            Selected Information Resources 338
            Subject Bibliographies 344
            Independent Organizations 345

Chapter 13 Science and Technology 349
            General Guides 349
            Resource Guides and Catalogs 350
            Current Awareness Products 353
            Foreign Technology Developments 355
            Computerized Information Resources 356
            Small Business Innovation Research Program .. 357
            Subject Bibliographies 358

Chapter 14 Government Procurement and Business
            Information 359
            Policy Directives 359
            Government Procurement 362
            Government Procurement References 362
            Government Procurement Periodicals 369
            Business Information Resources 371

	Exporting Information References 374
	Exporting Information Periodicals 376
	Computerized Information Resources 377
	Subject Bibliographies 378
Chapter 15	Mapping, Charting and Geologic Activities 379
	Policy Directive 379
	Map Collections 381
	Cartographic Data and Topographic Maps 381
	Nautical Charts 384
	Aeronautical Charts 385
	Defense Mapping Agency Products 385
	Geological Information 387

Part III—Primary Publishers

Chapter 16	Government Printing Office 389
	Publications Catalogs and Services 389
	Subject Bibliographies 396
	Federal Depository Library System 402
Chapter 17	National Technical Information Service 409
	More About NTIS 411
	Current Awareness Products 414
	Annual Indexes 414
	Special Bibliographies 415
	Computer/Automation Related Products 416
	Federal Machine-Readable Data 417
	Specialized Programs and Products 417
Chapter 18	General Accounting Office 421
	Organization and Operations 421
	Identifying GAO Publications 425
	GAO Legal Decisions and Opinions 426
	GAO Bibliographies 427
Chapter 19	Selected Private Sector Publishers 429
	American Enterprise Institute 429
	Brookings Institution 430
	Bureau of National Affairs, Inc 430
	Cato Institute 430
	Center for Strategic and International Studies .. 430
	Chamber of Commerce of the United States 431
	Channing L Bete Co, Inc 431
	Claritas Partners 431
	Commerce Clearing House, Inc 431
	Common Cause 432
	Congressional Information Service, Inc 432
	Congressional Quarterly Inc 432

Table of Contents 13

The Heritage Foundation 432
Hoover Institution 432
Institute for Policy Studies 433
The Lawyers Co-Operative Publishing Co 433
National Academy of Public Administration 433
Northeast-Midwest Institute 433
Prentice-Hall, Inc 433
Public Citizen 434
The Rand Corporation 434
The Roosevelt Center 434
West Publishing Co 434

Appendices
  A Public Access Laws 435
      Freedom of Information Act 436
      Privacy Act of 1974 438
      Government in the Sunshine Act 439
      Federal Advisory Committee Act 439
  B Paperwork Reduction Act of 1980 441
  C Ethics in Government Act 443
  D Computerized Information Resources 445
  E Research and Document Retrieval Services 449
  F Foreign Embassies 451

Publisher Order Forms
  GPO Order Forms
    GPO Order Form 459
    GPO Subscription Order Form 461
    GPO Subject Bibliography Order Form 462
  NTIS Order Form 465
  GAO Order Form 469

Subject-Organization-Publisher Index 471

List of Figures

I-1	The Successful Information Hunt With FEDfind	24
1-1	Federal Government Organization Chart	32
1-2	Standard Federal Regions Map	34
1-3	Federal Executive Boards	37
3-1	Numbers of Federal Government Employees	56
3-2	Steps to a Civil Service Job	68
3-3	U.S. Government Organizations With Positions Outside the Competitive Civil Service	69
4-1	House and Senate Committees	77
4-2	How a Bill Becomes a Law	85
4-3	Legislation Tracking Directory	86
5-1	The United States Court System	106
5-2	United States Code Titles	115
5-3	The Thirteen Federal Judicial Circuits	120
6-1	Federal Rulemaking Process	126
6-2	Code of Federal Regulations Titles	131
7-1	Executive Office of the President	136
10-1	The Federal Budget-Making Process	310
10-2	Congressional Budget Timetable	311
10-3	Summary of Receipts and Outlays of the U.S. Government, Fiscal Year 1985 (in millions)	312
11-1	Budget Functional Categories	325a
14-1	GSA Business Service Centers	363
15-1	Selected List of Types of Maps Published by Government Agencies	380
16-1	Government Printing Office (GPO) Bookstores	390
16-2	Priority Announcements Lists	392
16-3	Subject Bibliographies	397
16-4	Regional Depository Libraries	403
17-1	Subject Classification Schemes	410
17-2	NTIS Promotional Items	412
18-1	GAO Issue Areas by Lead Division	422
C-1	Code of Ethics for Government Service	444

Foreword

The Federal Government employs more than two million people. Among that number, the citizen can find experts on every subject from aardvarks, a type of anteater, to zymurgy, a branch of applied chemistry.

The key word, however, is "find." Those two million people work for a bewildering array of departments, agencies, bureaus and commissions. Merely listing the acronyms for agencies within the Department of Defense, as an example, takes several pages of small print.

Citizens facing this maze for the first time are likely to come away frustrated. After perhaps five telephone calls, they are referred back to the number they first called. Down goes the receiver with a bang and a muffled curse!

The result: distrust of the Federal Government and Federal employees. A government based on the consent of the governed, as ours is, cannot function successfully in that environment.

That is why a good guide to the Federal Government is extremely useful to all who deal with that sprawling enterprise. And that is what Mr. D'Aleo has prepared. *FEDfind* starts with that indispensable tool, an organization chart. Then for each branch of Government and for each executive agency it lists: a summary of what the agency does, key offices within the agency, other sources of information about the agency, and telephone numbers.

These telephone numbers are a gold mine. For each agency, Mr. D'Aleo has listed the numbers that will be most helpful to those searching for general information. In addition, he has listed the numbers for offices that provide more specific information to those citizens who know generally what they are looking for.

FEDfind also lists key information sources about each agency. These include helpful material published by the agency on publications available, services provided, contract opportunities, and how to do business with the agency. This information is usually free, but most citizens do not know it is widely available.

The telephone listings and the other sources of information will help citizens to find the answers to 99 percent of the questions usually asked. The other one percent may be unanswerable, even by the Federal Government.

The Federal Government is not a mysterious, distant presence, more to be feared than used. Yet many citizens approach the Government with trepidation. Such anxiety helps explain the growth of the lobbying business. Lobbyists act as intermediaries between the Federal Government and citizens and make a bundle of money while doing so. It is to their advantage that the Government remain a mystery.

But we still have the most open government in the world. Foreign journalists working in Washington, even those from other democracies, are astonished at how easy it is to get information from the Federal Government. The same holds true for citizens who can find their way through the bureaucratic maze. *FEDfind* will help you do just that.

Use this book and get to know your Government. After all, you pay for it.

William Proxmire
U.S. Senator

Preface

A popular Government, without popular information, or the means of acquiring it, is but a Prologue to a Farce or a Tragedy; or, perhaps both. Knowledge will forever govern ignorance: And a people who mean to be their own Governours, must arm themselves with the power which knowledge gives.

James Madison (1822)

Ever since entering Government service twenty years ago, I have had a strong desire to learn about U.S. Government activities, programs and information resources. It has been a difficult, but challenging task to learn about the multitude of activities devoted to the collection, processing and dissemination of information to use fully the vast information holdings of the Federal Government. But persistence and patience paid off as I mastered the pathways through the "Washington information maze."

The key to finding the information I need, when I need it, is to know which Federal office to write or call, or which information product or service to use. We do not usually gain access to information directly, but rather through the use of "finding aids" that direct us to the information we need.

FEDfind is a catalog of such "finding aids" to information by and about the Federal Government, including private sector products and services. With *FEDfind* you can identify the information source, product or service that is appropriate to meet your specific needs, and thereby help yourself become "information efficient" in your dealings with or about the Federal Government, or in other fields about which the Government publishes material.

*   *   *

The continuing viability and success of the United States of America as a democratic form of government depends on an informed citizenry. The principle of equal and ready access by the public to information collected, compiled, produced and published by the Federal Government—in any format—has been considered the cornerstone of our system and an imperative of a free society that must not be taken for granted. After all, the more citizens know about their Government, the more likely they are to get actively involved in its affairs. And that can only mean one thing: a better Government for all of us.

In a democracy it is the ability of the individual to use Government information—and not in one's access to it—that should count. Otherwise a gap—based on ability to pay—between information "haves" and "have-nots" evolves. Such a gap unfairly limits individual opportunity and competitiveness in our free and democratic society.

It is my hope that *FEDfind* and successor related information products will help prevent such an "information gap" from evolving. *FEDfind* was created to help make the Federal Government understandable and its information accessible to its citizens. Complementing the library community, it helps the public be "information efficient" in its access to information it needs, when needed. I hope that the synergism created between *FEDfind* and the library community will enable citizens to gain access to Federal Government information so that they may participate fully and effectively in our democratic government.

Acknowledgments

This book would not have been possible if it were not for the help and cooperation of many people. Individuals from all the organizations cited in the text generously gave of their time and expertise to assist me in providing accurate and complete information. Only a few are mentioned here, but only for lack of space, not for lack of gratitude.

A number of chapters were reviewed and suggestions made by following individuals: Leon Brody, "Civilian Personnel Management"; Katherine Wallman, "Statistical Programs"; Edward Lehmann, "Science and Technology"; Charles McKeown, Mary Lee O'Brien, Susan Tomlin and June Malina, "Government Printing Office"; Walter Finch and his staff and Ruth Smith, "National Technical Information Service"; and Laura Kopelson, "General Accounting Office."

Special thanks go to the staff of the Government Printing Office's Records Branch for their help with the bibliographic information in the hundreds of GPO citations included throughout the text. Thanks to Records Branch chief Thomas Downing and the librarians of the Bibliographic Control Section, lead by Linda Dobb, Amy Fleischman, Ginny Snider and Glenn Lewis. Also, thanks to the staff of Congressman Stan Parris for its invaluable assistance during my research.

I am especially indebted to Irene Saunders Goldstein for her editing and word processing skills and for her many constructive ideas in critiquing this book; to Ellen Law for her review of the final manuscript; and to Carol Ratkus for the cover art and numerous illustrations that help the reader capture the feel of how important information is to the workings of the Federal Government.

I owe special gratitude to my wife, Anne, for her years of support and patience during the writing and publishing of this book.

How to Use *FEDfind*

> Knowledge is of two kinds. We know a subject ourselves, or we know where we can find information upon it.
>
> James Boswell, *Life of Johnson* (1775)

Using *FEDfind* is as easy as 1-2-3. You simply:

1. **Identify** an appropriate information source, product or service using the Subject-Organization-Publisher Index, Federal Organizations Abbreviations Index or Table of Contents.

2. **Contact, obtain or access** the resource, as applicable.

3. **Use** the information obtained to meet your needs.

The only information you can use is the information you can find. The Federal Government annually spends billions of taxpayer dollars collecting, compiling, producing and publishing information. To get your money's worth, you need help. *FEDfind* will help you be successful in your hunt through the "Washington information maze" to find the Federal Government information you need, when you need it (Figure I-1).

For products or services that cost money, consider first contacting your library to see if it has the item or an acceptable alternative. (Regional Depository Libraries [see Figure 16-4] are one place to consider; they are a part of the Federal Depository Library System described in Chapter 16, "Government Printing Office.") Otherwise, order the item directly from the publisher. If you need more details, simply write or telephone for promotional material or a sample copy.

An important strategy to keep in mind when turning to the Government itself for help is that nearly all Federal organizations operate public information offices that are intended to assist the "outsider" identify and access information. The most up-to-date information on a specific topic may be available only from an agency itself, because it might not yet be—nor might it ever be—published. These programs are identified for each organization under the headings "Key Offices and Telephone Numbers" and "Key Information Resources." Chapters 4 through 9 include these types of information for the legislative (Chapter 4), judicial (Chapter 5) and executive branches (Chapters 6 through 9), respectively. For information on specific publications, it is often necessary to contact the Federal organizations individually. For additional directory publications, see Chapter 2.

Figure I-1. The Successful Information Hunt With *FEDfind*

Key to *FEDfind* Listings

Listings are of two basic kinds: those for products and services, and those for information sources (Federal Government organizations).

A complete product or service listing includes: name of the product or service; a brief non-evaluative description; the publication date (including the month of the edition for recurring documents); frequency of issue; pagination; price; order number, stock number (S/N), international standard book number (ISBN) or international standard serial number (ISSN); in parenthesis the Superintendent of Documents catalog number or Library of Congress card number; and the publisher's name, address and telephone number.

A complete Federal Government organizational listing (information source) includes: name of the organization; its commonly-known abbreviation, if applicable; a brief mission statement with selected associated activities cited (for more detailed information, consult the *U.S. Government Manual* as described in the Chapter 1 section, "Government Information Sources"); its fiscal year 1985 (October 1, 1984 through September 30, 1985) budget, number of paid civilian employees and the percentages that each comprise of the total Federal budget ($936,809 million) and civilian work force (2,950,332), the latter as of January 1, 1985; the *Code of Federal Regulations* (CFR) Title, Subtitle or Chapter in which an agency appears; "Key Offices and Telephone Numbers," including the organization's headquarters address; and "Key Information Resources." The latter are products or services, many **FREE**, that provide details on the information resources of the organization.

A negative [-] "net budget outlay" indicates that an agency received more money, usually for property sold or services rendered, than it spent on its operations. The sources—and the chapters in which they are described—for the basic agency budget outlay amounts, civilian personnel counts and CFR references, respectively are: *Final Monthly Treasury Statement of Receipts and Outlays of the United States Government (For Fiscal Year 1985)*, Chapter 10; *Organization of Federal Executive Departments and Agencies* (data as of January 1, 1985), Chapter 1; and the *CFR Index and Finding Aids,* "Alphabetical List of Agencies Appearing in the CFR" (as of September 13, 1985), Chapter 6.

Note: Before placing a telephone call to a headquarters office in Washington, DC, check your local telephone directory under "United States Government" for a possible local department or agency office.

The following information will facilitate your use of the "Key Offices and Telephone Numbers" section. A complete listing includes:

General Information
This is usually the switchboard telephone number.

Personnel Locator

Public/Consumer Information
Includes toll-free telephone numbers.

Procurement Information
Headquarters procurement office. Enquire of individual offices for possible "Contracting Guides."
Office of Small and Disadvantaged Business Utilization (OSDBU), if any.
Office of the headquarters "Competition Advocate." Federal agencies' purchases totaled more than $182 billion in fiscal year 1984, almost one-fifth of the Federal budget. The Government's procurement data system (see Chapter 14) reported that about 40 percent of this total was awarded competitively. The *Competition in Contracting Act of 1984* requires that an advocate for competition be established in each executive branch agency and in each procuring activity within an agency. The advocate for competition is responsible for challenging barriers to and promoting full and open competition in the agency's procurement. As of January 1986, each agency must submit an annual report to Congress that specifies the agency's plans to increase competition and to reduce non-competitive contracts, and that summarizes the competition advocate's accomplishments during the previous fiscal year. Each agency must also enter into the Federal Procurement Data System information on its competitive and non-competitive procurement actions (other than small purchases).

Press Inquiries
The office that provides liaison with the media.

Other Key Offices (names indicated may not be official agency titles)

Agency Committee Management
The office that manages the agency's Federal advisory committees. See Appendix A for information on the *Federal Advisory Committee Act*.

Congressional Liaison/Legislative Affairs
The office that provides liaison with Congress.

Ethics in Government Act
See Appendix C for information on this law.

Fraud, Waste and Mismanagement Hotline

The telephone number of the office to report any case of fraud, waste or mismanagement that you have witnessed or know of, that if corrected, would promote the integrity, economy or efficiency of the Federal Government. They're your tax dollars, and you can make a difference! For agencies that do not have a hotline, the telephone number provided is that of the General Accounting Office (GAO)—the investigative arm of Congress. GAO will contact the appropriate agency office and will follow the case to ensure that it is appropriately reviewed or investigated.

Freedom of Information/Privacy Act

See Appendix A for additional information on these laws.

General Counsel

This is the law office of the agency.

Library

Generally this is the reference desk for those agencies that have libraries.

Paperwork Reduction Act (IRM/ADP)

See Appendix B for additional information on this law that relates to information resources management (IRM) and automated data processing (ADP).

Personnel

This is the telephone number of the headquarters personnel office.

Statistical Information

For executive branch departments only, the name of the statistical component from which more information may be obtained.

Library Directories

The following publications may be useful in identifying libraries that have materials by or about the Federal Government. Contact the publishers for details on their reference works.

A Directory of U.S. Government Depository Libraries

(See Chapter 16, "Government Printing Office," section on the "Federal Depository Library System" for further information.)

Federal Library Resources: A User's Guide to Research Collections
Science Associates/International, Inc.
1841 Broadway
New York, NY 10023
(212) 265-4995

Directory of Government Document Collections and Libraries
(Compiled by the Government Documents Round Table of the American Library Association)
Congressional Information Service, Inc.
4520 East-West Highway, Suite 800-DM
Bethesda, MD 20814
(800) 638-8380
(301) 654-1550 in Maryland

Libraries and Reference Facilities in the Area of the District of Columbia
(Compiled for the American Society for Information Science)
Knowledge Industry Publications, Inc.
701 Westchester Avenue
White Plains, NY 10604
(800) 248-5474
(914) 328-9157 in New York State

The following sources may be helpful in identifying and using materials relevant to Federal Government information resources.

Subject Guide to U.S. Government Reference Sources

A guide to print and nonprint reference sources produced by the Federal Government. It includes seminal, historical and other key works in a four-part arrangement—General Reference Sources, Social Sciences, Science and Technology and Humanities. Emphasis is on materials that are accessible through purchase, loan, depository library collections, requests for single free copies or database searches. It may be used as a companion to *Government Reference Books*, a guide to U.S. Government reference materials, published biennially by the same publisher. 1985, 2nd ed. 365pp. $40.00. ISBN 0-87287-496-6. (85-10120) Libraries Unlimited, P.O. Box 263, Littleton, CO 80160; (303) 770-1220.

Introduction to United States Public Documents

An introduction to the basic sources of information that comprise the bibliographic structure of Federal Government publications. It includes chapters on such subjects as the Government Printing Office, the depository library system, technical report literature and materials of the legislative branch. 1983, 3rd ed. 309pp. Cloth, $28.50, ISBN 0-87287-359-5; paper, $19.50, ISBN 0-87287-362-5. (82-22866) Libraries Unlimited, see entry above.

Documents to the People

Documents to the People (DTTP) is the official publication of the American Library Association (ALA) Government Documents Round Table (GODORT). It provides current information on government publications, technical reports and maps at the Federal, State, local and foreign levels; on related government activities; and documents librarianship. DTTP is published quarterly in March, June, September and December. ISSN 0091-2085. It is sent free to ALA/GODORT members. Subscriptions are available to non-members on a per volume (annual) basis for $15.00 prepaid, made payable to "ALA/GODORT," sent to Distribution Manager Jean Kellough, Documents Division, Sterling C. Evans Library, Texas A&M University, College Station, TX 77843; (409) 845-2551.

Part One

Chapter 1
Federal Government Organization

The basic organizational structure of the Federal Government is specified in the first three articles of the *United States Constitution*: the legislative, executive and judicial branches, respectively. The framers of the Constitution created the powers of each branch to interrelate and overlap—thus providing checks and balances among them. The chart on the following page shows the more important organizational components of the Government. The sources described in this chapter provide the basis for a comprehensive understanding of the structure, responsibilities and activities of the Federal Government.

The information resources described in this chapter are organized under the following headings:

- Government Information Sources
- Federal Executive Boards
- Agency Annual Reports
- Private Sector Products and Services
- Federal History

Government Information Sources

Title 5, United States Code: Government Organization and Employees

The title of the *Code of Federal Regulations* (CFR) that presents the general and permanent rules governing the executive departments and agencies, and employees of the Federal Government is prepared by the House of Representatives Committee on Post Office and Civil Service. The document is divided into three parts: The Agencies Generally, Civil Service Functions and Responsibilities, and Employees. The third section provides information on general provisions, employment and retention, employee performance, pay and allowances, attendance and leave, labor-management and employee relations, and insurance and annuities. Sold as part of Volume 1 of the CFR, which includes Titles 1-6. 1983. 1,258pp. $22.00. GPO S/N 052-001-00209-1. (Y 1.2/5:982/v.1) See the GPO order form.

United States Government Manual 1985/86

The official annual handbook on the Federal Government, this publication provides information on the programs, activities, functions, organization and

32 FEDfind

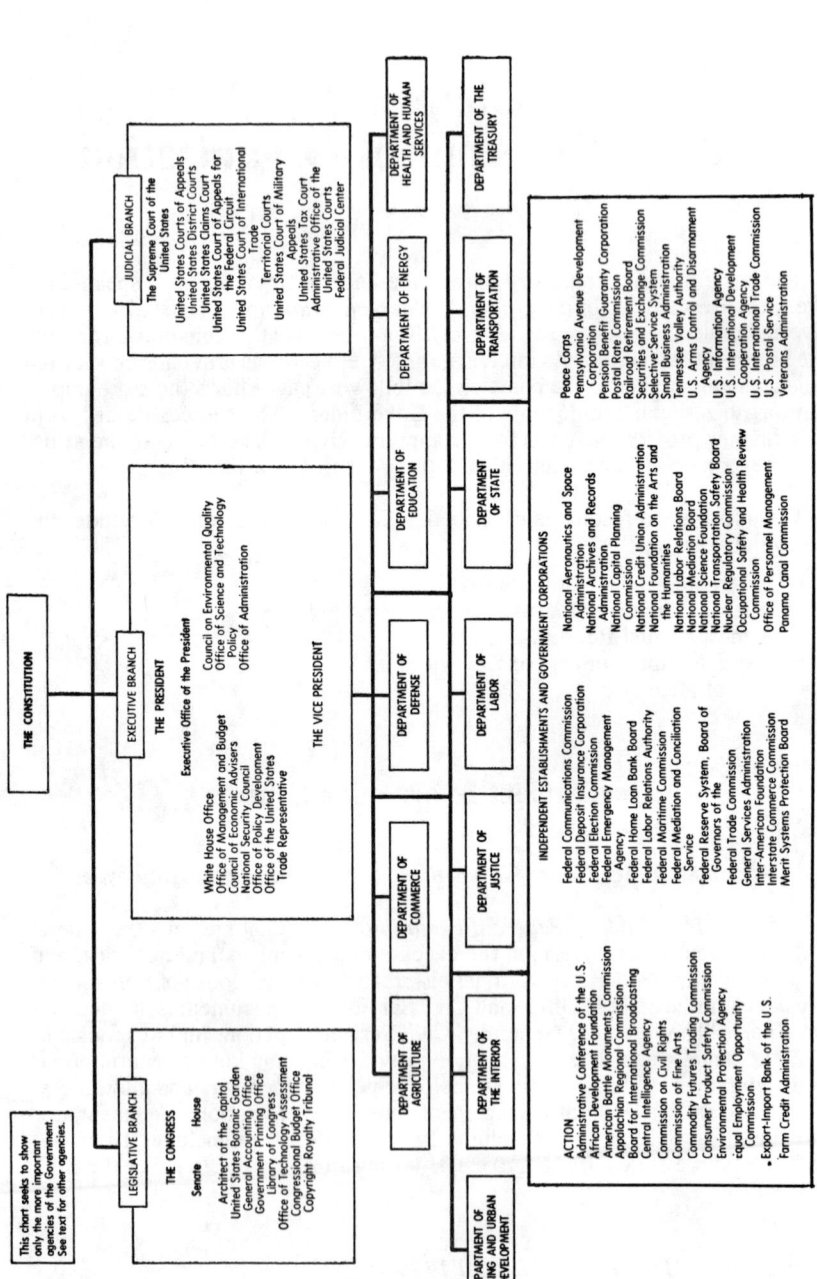

(Source: The U.S. Government Manual 1985–86)

Figure 1-1. Federal Government Organization Chart

principal officials of the agencies of the legislative, executive and judicial branches. The manual also includes information on quasi-official agencies, international organizations in which the United States participates, and boards, committees and commissions. September 1985. 935pp. $15.00. GPO S/N 022-003-01118-8. (AE 2.108/2:985-86) See the GPO order form.

Federal Advisory Committees—Annual Report

The activities, status and changes in the composition of Federal advisory committees are covered in this annual report of the President to the Congress. A Federal advisory committee, as defined by the Federal Advisory Committee Act, is any committee, board, commission, council, conference, panel, task force, or other similar group, established for the purpose of obtaining advice or recommendations on issues or policies for any agency or the President. It is prepared by the General Services Administration (GSA), as required by the *Federal Advisory Committee Act* (Public Law 92-463). The report lists all advisory committees in existence at the end of the fiscal year (September 30) with the responsible agency indicated; Presidential Advisory Committees at the end of the year; and all advisory committees initiated, in existence and terminated during the year; alphabetically by agency. May 1985. 131pp. **FREE**. Committee Management Secretariat (CBC), GSA, Washington, DC 20405; (202) 523-4884.

Standard Federal Regions

This Executive Office of the President (EOP) Office of Management and Budget (OMB) Circular No. A-105 formally establishes ten standard Federal regions, uniform regional boundaries, and common regional office headquarters locations, as a long-range goal for all Federal domestic agencies. Standard regions were introduced to promote more systematic coordination among agencies and Federal-State-local governments and for securing management improvements and economies through greater interagency and intergovernmental cooperation. The circular also provides guidelines for establishing or realigning field structures, regional offices and sub-regional structures. Figure 1-2 provides a map showing the standard boundaries. 1974. 9pp. **FREE**. EOP Publications, 726 Jackson Place NW, Room 2200, Washington, DC 20503; (202) 395-7332.

Organization of Federal Executive Departments and Agencies

Published annually, this is a chart that shows the major organizational divisions and personnel strengths of the executive departments and independent agencies and commissions, including the Executive Office of the President, as of January 1 of the publication year. A table is included that provides work force totals of organizational components for the current year, previous year, and 10 and 20 years past. For the current year work force, a breakdown is made of eemployees inside and outside the United States. March 1985. $1.00. Out-of-print. GPO S/N 052-070-05921-4. (Y 4.G 74/9:Ex 3/984).

Federal Civilian Work Force Statistics, Monthly Release

This monthly periodical presents employment information on the Federal civilian work force based on reports submitted by each department and agency.

34 FEDfind

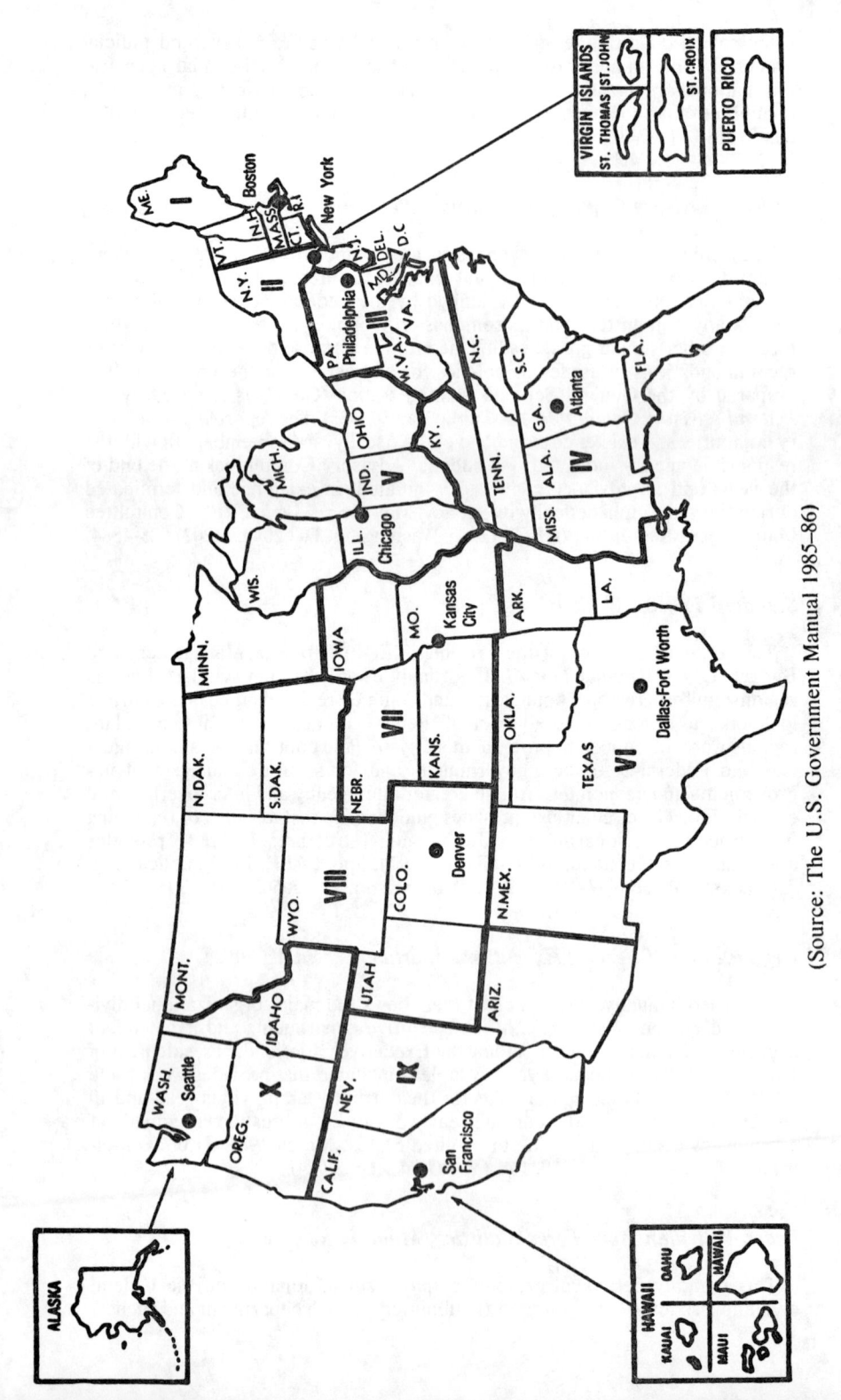

(Source: The U.S. Government Manual 1985–86)

Figure 1-2. Standard Federal Regions Map

Federal Government Organization   35

Current employment data by branch, agency and location; 13-month trends of employment, payroll and turnover; and accession and separation rates are summarized in detailed statistical tables. Narrative analyses highlight each month's most important developments. Monthly employment data are occasionally supplemented by reports from other periodic surveys on the occupational, geographic, and wage and salary characteristics of Federal civilian employees. A "Data Source and Definition" section provides details on the method of data collection and definitions of the classifications used in this publication. Subscription price: $24.00 a year. Single copy price: $3.75. GPO List ID FCW. (PM 1.15:) See the GPO subscription order form.

United States Government Policy and Supporting Positions

More commonly known as the "Plum Book," this 1984 edition lists the top positions in the United States Government outside the competitive civil service. The positions include those to which appointments are made by the President, as well as top level executive and managerial positions of the Senior Executive Service (SES). Many incumbents in the positions listed serve at the pleasure of the agency head because the positions' excepted status reflects such considerations as confidentiality, advocacy of administration programs, or policy-making duties. Issued every four years with responsibility alternating between the Senate Governmental Affairs Committee (this edition) and the House Government Operations Committee. March 1985. 270pp. $9.00. GPO S/N 052-070-05960-5. (Y 4.G 74/9:S.prt.98-286) See the GPO order form.

Federal Executive Boards

The Federal Executive Boards (FEB) consist of the heads of Federal field offices in 26 metropolitan areas. FEBs were established to improve internal Federal management practices, provide a central focus for Federal participation in civic affairs in major metropolitan centers of Federal activity, serve as a means for disseminating information within the Federal Government and for promoting discussion of Federal policies and activities of importance to all Federal executives in the field. The FEBs carry out their functions under the supervision and control of the Office of Personnel Management (OPM). Figure 1-3 provides the addresses and telephone numbers of the FEBs. Federal Executive Associations, Councils or Committees have been established in more than 100 other metropolitan areas. They perform functions similar to the FEBs, but on a lesser scale of organization and activity. For further information, contact the FEB nearest you or the Office of Regional Operations, OPM, 1900 E Street NW, Room 5532, Washington, DC 20415; (202) 632-5544.

Agency Annual Reports

Nearly all Federal Government departments, agencies and commissions publish annual reports. They summarize the functions, activities, programs and organizational changes of the organization—normally over a fiscal year (October 1-September 30). The reports are designed primarily for oversight elements of Congress and the executive branch and focus on how well organizations have fulfilled their missions for the year. The information in the reports is of interest to anyone who wants to understand an agency as it currently operates. A list of these reports and their prices may be obtained **FREE** by requesting the *Annual Reports* subject bibliography (SB-118) from the Government Printing Office (GPO). While annual reports are sold by the GPO, organizations usually keep a supply on hand. Booklets become available during the period January-May, depending on the time required for preparation of each individual publication. Enquiries may be made of the public affairs or press office. Most of the annual reports may be obtained using the GPO Standing Order Service (see Chapter 16, GPO section on "Publications Catalogs and Services").

Private Sector Products and Services

Encyclopedia of Governmental Advisory Organizations

A reference guide to the activities and personnel of more than 4,790 current and historical groups that advise, or have advised, the President and various Federal departments and agencies. Each entry includes up to 14 points of information, including name, address, telephone number, executive secretary, history and authority, program, membership, staff, subsidiary units, publications and reports, and meetings. The material is organized into 10 subject areas, from agriculture to transportation. 1985, 5th ed. 1,133pp. $425.00. Subscription to inter-edition supplements, *New Governmental Advisory Organizations*: $325.00. Gale Research Co., Book Tower, Detroit, MI 48226; (800) 223-GALE or (313) 961-2242.

Federal Government Organization 37

Albuquerque-Santa Fe, NM
Federal Executive Board
U.S. Forest Service
U.S. Department of Agriculture
P.O. Box 793
Albuquerque, NM 87102
(505) 842-3300

Atlanta, GA
Federal Executive Board
Richard B. Russell Federal Building
75 Spring Street SW, Room 844
Atlanta, GA 30303
(404) 221-4400

Baltimore, MD
Federal Executive Board
Federal Building 31 Hopkins Plaza,
Room 1021
Baltimore, MD 21201
(301) 962-4047

Boston, MA
Federal Executive Board
John F. Kennedy Federal Building
Room 2411
Boston, MA 02203
(617) 223-6830

Buffalo, NY
Federal Executive Board
c/o U.S. Department of Housing and
Urban Development
107 Delaware Avenue
Buffalo, NY 14202
(716) 846-5733

Chicago, IL
Federal Executive Board
230 S. Dearborn, Room 3744
Chicago, IL 60604
(312) 353-7280

Cincinnati, OH
Federal Executive Board
John Weld Pack Federal Office
Building
550 Main Street, Room 1116
Cincinnati, OH 45202
(513) 684-2101

Cleveland, OH
Federal Executive Board
A.J. Celebreeze Federal Building
1240 E. 9th Street, Room 747
Cleveland, OH 44199
(216) 522-7086

Dallas-Fort Worth, TX
Federal Executive Board
1100 Commerce Street, Suite 6F45
Dallas, TX 75242
(214) 767-0767

Denver, CO
Federal Executive Board
Denver Federal Center
P.O. Box 25405
Denver, CO 80225
(303) 236-7411

Detroit, MI
Federal Executive Board
McNamara Building
477 Michigan Avenue, Room 956
Detroit, MI 48226
(313) 226-3534

Honolulu, HI
Federal Executive Board
300 Ala Moana Boulevard
Box 50268
Honolulu, HI 96850
(808) 433-5716

Figure 1-3. Federal Executive Boards

Houston, TX
Federal Executive Board
2515 Murworth, Suite 112
Houston, TX 77054
(713) 660-4092

Kansas City, MO
Federal Executive Board
315 W. Pershing Road, Room 525
Kansas City, MO 64108
(816) 374-2973

Los Angeles, CA
Federal Executive Board
P.O. Box 1109
Los Angeles, CA 90053
(213) 688-7138

Miami, FL
Federal Executive Board
Federal Office Building
51 S.W. First Avenue, Room 927
Miami, FL 33130
(305) 350-4344

Newark, NJ
Federal Executive Board
970 Board Street, Room 1434B
Newark, NJ 07102
(201) 645-6217

New Orleans, LA
Federal Executive Board
701 Loyola Avenue, Room 4024
New Orleans, LA 70113
(504) 589-2438

New York, NY
Federal Executive Board
c/o Office of Personnel Management
26 Federal Plaza, Room 29-108A
New York, NY 10278
(212) 264-1890

Philadelphia, PA
Federal Executive Board
William J. Green, Jr., Federal Building
600 Arch Street, Room 1204
Philadelphia, PA 19106
(215) 596-6858

Pittsburgh, PA
Federal Executive Board
Federal Building
1000 Liberty Avenue, Room 611
Pittsburgh, PA 15222
(412) 644-4309

Portland, OR
Federal Executive Board
Federal Building
1220 S.W. Third Avenue, Room 1776
Portland, OR 97204
(503) 221-3010

St. Louis, MO
Federal Executive Board
1520 Market Street, Room 2025
St. Louis, MO 63103
(314) 425-6312/894-4601

San Francisco, CA
Federal Executive Board
Box 36017
415 Golden Gate Avenue
San Francisco, CA 94120
(415) 556-2991

Seattle, WA
Federal Executive Board
GSA Center
Auburn, WA 98002
(206) 442-0420

Twin Cities (Minneapolis-St. Paul), MN
Federal Executive Board
510 Bishop Henry P. Whipple
Federal Building
Fort Snelling
Twin Cities, MN 55111
(612) 725-3687

Figure 1-3. Federal Executive Boards (Continued)

Federal Organization Service—Civil

This subscription service provides a looseleaf binder containing 120 uniform, fold-out organizational charts of all executive departments except the Department of Defense, plus major independent agencies and Congress. Each chart provides the names, offices, telephone numbers, and responsibilities of high level civilian Federal employees. It is indexed by name and subject key words. The service provides updated material every six weeks. Also included with the subscription are bulletins on personnel and organizational changes and a telephone reference and research service. Subscription price: $325.00 a year. Carroll Publishing Co., 1058 Thomas Jefferson Street NW, Washington, DC 20007; (202) 333-8620.

Federal Organization Service—Military

A subscription service in looseleaf form of 116 uniform, fold-out organizational charts of more than 1,400 military departments and offices are provided. The service covers the Departments of Defense, Army, Navy and Air Force. Each chart provides the names, titles, offices, telephone numbers and responsibilities of the military establishment. It is indexed by name and program. The service provides updated material every six weeks. Also included with the subscription are bulletins on personnel and organizational changes and a telephone reference and research service. Subscription price: $500.00 a year. Carroll Publishing Co., see entry above.

U.S. Army—Navy—Air Force and Government Organization Chart Service

This subscription service provides organization charts of U.S. military organizations, commands, activities, laboratories, and nearly every Federal Government organization—executive and legislative branch and quasi-official agencies. The service covers more than 625 organizations and is updated every 90 days. Subscription price: $350.00 a year. U.S. Organization Chart Service, P.O. Box 1335, La Jolla, CA 92038; (619) 454-3711.

Government Agencies

An encyclopedia, edited by Donald R. Whitnah, that contains more than 100 profiles of Federal Government bodies including Cabinet-level departments, bureaus, commissions, Government corporations and quasi-government entities. Each essay, written by a scholar, presents a historical overview of the agency, evaluates its past performance and enumerates its current objectives. The book covers some defunct bodies, particularly those of the New Deal era. Included are four appendices: a chronology of the creation of agencies, an alphabetic listing of government entities, a genealogy of agencies and an organizational chart of various umbrella departments. Indexed by name and subject. 1983. 683pp. $49.95. ISBN 0-313-22017-4. (82-15815) Greenwood Press, P.O. Box 5007, Westport, CT 06881; (203) 226-3571.

Federal History

Directory of Federal Historical Programs and Activities

The Society for History in the Federal Government, the American Historical Association and the National Coordinating Committee for the Promotion of History jointly published this directory of Federal historical programs. The directory is organized into three sections: a program list, a name index and a grade survey. The program list is arranged by department or agency. Each entry for a major program or office includes a brief program description, the name of the head of the program with mailing address and telephone number, and a roster of current personnel. Entries for subordinate offices and for field programs include the same information except for the program description. 1984, 2nd ed. 86pp. $7.00 prepaid. American Historical Association, Publications Sales Department, 400 A Street SE, Washington, DC 20003; (202) 544-2422.

The Federalist

A bimonthly newsletter of the Society for History in the Federal Government, this publication reports on the organization's activities and related information. The Society is a nonprofit professional organization whose purpose is "to encourage, promote, and foster historical, archival and other related activities of the United States Government." The newsletter is available, along with a copy of the directory cited above, as part of the Society's $12.00 a year membership fee. P.O. Box 14139, Washington, DC 20044.

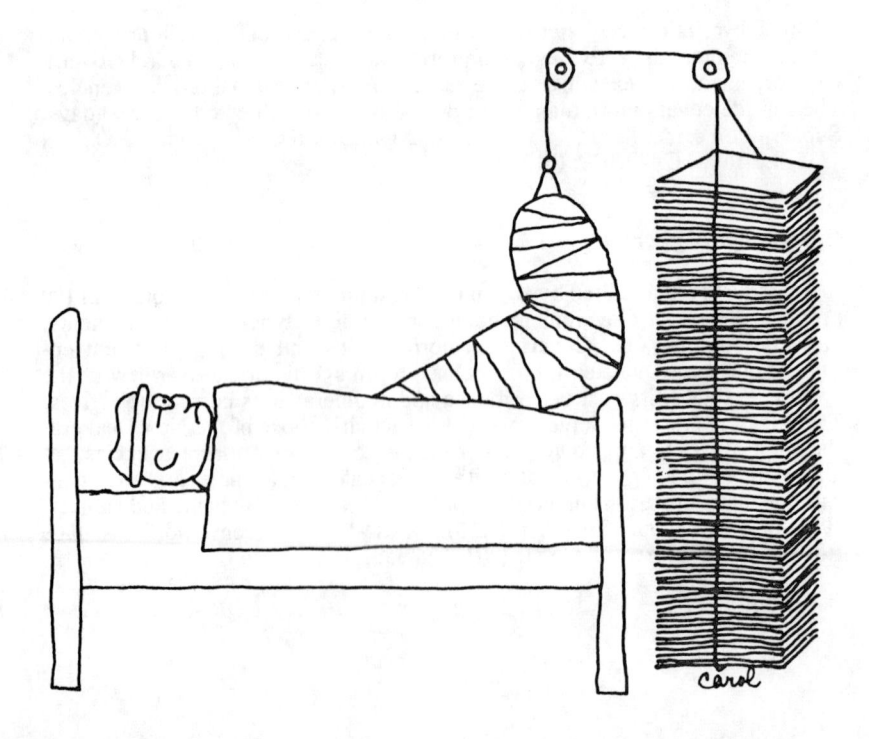

Chapter 2
Directories

Individuals associated with the operations of the Federal Government—both inside and outside the bureaucracy—are generally open about their activities and are willing to share information. The difficulty is in locating the right person or office to help access the desired information, or to provide a reference to appropriate materials. This chapter identifies many of the available guides to individuals and organizations that make information gathering more efficient.

"Key Offices and Telephone Numbers" are listed for Federal organizations in Chapters 4 through 9. This includes information sources for the legislative (Chapter 4), judicial (Chapter 5) and executive branches (Chapters 6 through 9), respectively. These information sources are intended to assist you in identifying and accessing information quickly—when you need it.

There are many more publications produced by the Government than are cited in this chapter. Omitted are those publications that cover individual departments and agencies. The Government Printing Office (GPO) makes available **FREE** a subject bibliography (SB) entitled *Directories and Lists of Persons and Organizations* (SB-114) listing publications for sale. See the GPO subscription order form.

The information resources described in this chapter are organized under the following headings.
- The Federal Environment
- Legislative Branch
- Executive Branch
- Judicial Branch
- Foreign Affairs
- Directories of Directories

The Federal Environment

The Capital Source

A semiannual directory of names, titles, addresses and telephone numbers of people and organizations in the Nation's Capitol. Tabbed sections cover branches of the Federal Government; foreign embassies and local government; major corporations, think tanks, unions and interest groups; trade associations, law firms, ad agencies and public relations firms; and national, foreign and local media. April 1986. approx. 130pp. $15.00. National Journal Inc., 1730 M Street NW, Suite 1100, Washington, DC 20036; (800) 424-2921 or (202) 857-1400.

Directory of Key Government Personnel

A pocket-sized directory of key executive, legislative, judicial and regulatory officials of the Federal Government. The directory includes the names, titles, addresses and telephone numbers of more than 2,000 officials. Also included is a chapter on "Forms of Address and Salutations." Compiled and edited by Amy Hardwick. Biennial, 1985–86 edition August 1985. 135pp. Single copy **FREE** with a self-addressed 5" × 7-1/2" envelope with 90 cents postage. Each additional copy is $5.00, plus 90 cents postage for each copy ordered. Hill and Knowlton, Inc., 1201 Pennsylvania Avenue NW, Suite 700, Washington, DC 20004; (202) 638-2800.

Directory of Public Information Contacts

This annual directory lists the names, addresses and telephone numbers of U.S. Government agencies' press and public affairs officials. It also includes a section on information contacts at foreign embassies in Washington. Compiled and edited by Daniel H. Schurz. Copies of this publication are available to members of the press, government public affairs officers, and others in the public affairs and public relations community. Requests should be in writing on your letterhead. January 1986. 79pp. **FREE** to qualified individuals. Martin Marietta Corp., Attn: Public Relations, 6801 Rockledge Drive, Bethesda, MD 20817.

Federal Fast Finder

A directory that provides telephone numbers of more than 1,000 Federal Government departments, agencies, boards and commissions. It is arranged by key words, e.g., safety—all offices whose title includes the word "safety" appear together. Included also are addresses of major offices in the three branches; telephone numbers of recorded messages that provide up-to-the-minute highlights; and toll-free "hotlines." Spring 1986, 8th ed., 77pp. $10.00. Washington Researchers Publishing, 2612 P Street NW, Washington, DC 20007; (202) 333-3533.

Federal-State-Local Government Directory 1986

The Federal Government section of this biennial directory provides information about the people and organizations that make up the Federal environment. This includes the Reagan White House and Cabinet secretaries (with photos and brief biographies); other agency heads; Senate and House Members (with photos and biographies) and top staffers, committees and subcommittee memberships; selected media, including political cartoonists; selected public opinion polls; Congressional District maps; state chairpersons of the Democratic and Republican Parties; and political think tanks. 1986. 1,200pp. $49.95 + $2.50 shipping. Braddock Publications, Inc., 1001 Connecticut Avenue NW, Suite 210, Washington, DC 20036; (202) 296-1317.

Hudson's Washington News Media Contacts Directory 1986

A subscription service guide to the Washington, D.C. press corps, this directory lists approximately 3,000 news outlets (bureaus, newspapers, news services, radio/TV, magazines, newsletters, syndicates) and more than 3,200 correspondents and editors. The material is organized into 25 categories, e.g., newspapers, radio-TV and periodicals. An index lists each publication, bureau or station in alphabetical order; it also lists the assignments of correspondents of the major news bureaus. A special subject index presents specialized magazines, newsletters, and periodicals by subject area. January 1986. (68-22594) Revisions are issued in April, July, and October. Subscription price: $90.00 a year. Hudson's Associates, 44 W. Market Street, Rhinebeck, NY 12572; (914) 876-2081.

Almanac of Federal PACs

Every political action committee (PAC) that contributes $50,000 or more to Federal candidates during an election cycle is listed, together with a profile description of its sponsors—corporations, labor unions, trade and professional groups, ideological organizations and single-issue pressure groups. Each listing includes a Federal Election Commission computer identification number for easy access to the PAC's latest contribution data, along with an election-by-election overview of the PAC's overall political finance performance. Background information is based on documents filed at such agencies as the Securities and Exchange Commission and the Department of Labor. Edited by Ed Zuckerman. 1986. approx. 400pp. $49.50. Amward Publications, Inc., 824 National Press Building, Washington, DC 20045; (202) 628-6710.

PACs Americana

A directory of non-party political action committees (PACs), this publication provides information on 2,400 PAC sponsors, their 4,300 PACs, and the sponsors' legislative and economic interests. One section lists the 93 major interest categories identifying PACs within each category. The alphabetical listing of all 3,100 non-party PACs includes names and acronyms, sponsor's name and address, PAC treasurer and/or contact person, and a breakdown of PAC contributions by campaign type. February 1986. approx. 1,200pp. $225.00. ISBN 0-942236-00-9. Sunshine Services Corp., 325 Pennsylvania Avenue SE, Washington, DC 20003; (202) 544-3647

Public Interest Profiles

The 1986-87 edition updates and revises information on the nation's key public interest organizations. For each of the more than 250 public interest organizations, it contains addresses and telephone numbers; key staff members; staff size; current budget; scope of activity; basic purpose; method of operation; political orientation; name, content, and frequency of newsletter; history of group; board membership; funding sources; future agenda; and an analysis of the effectiveness of the organization. Biennial, Spring 1986. approx. 650pp. Enquire for price information. Foundation for Public Affairs, 1255 23rd Street NW, Suite 750, Washington, DC 20037; (202) 872-1750.

Researcher's Guide to Washington Experts

This guide lists more than 13,000 individuals who are Federal data experts. Included are the expert's name, title, subject areas of expertise, mailing address and telephone number. A cross-referenced index of more than 12,000 subject headings makes it possible to identify experts in one area from more than one organization. Spring 1986, 8th ed. 420pp. $85.00. ISBN 0-934940-23-1. (80-54598) Washington Researchers Publishing, 2612 P Street NW, Washington, DC 20007; (202) 333-3533.

The Social List of Washington D.C.

An annual directory and subscription service, commonly known as "The Green Book," lists those considered to be the Washington elite according to strict social protocol. Subscribers may call regarding the latest updates and changes in Government officials and diplomatic groups, addresses of prominent new arrivals in Washington, changes of address, etc. A special section covers official precedence, proper address of officials and diplomats, the written invitation and correct procedure at social functions. The advisory services of the publisher and staff are available to subscribers. Assistance in the seating of small luncheons and dinners in accordance with "who outranks whom" is provided as part of the subscription. Subscriptions are available only to those individuals listed in the directory and selected other Government and business officials. September 1985. The Social List of Washington, Inc., 3930 Knowles Avenue, Suite 302, Kensington, MD 20895; (301) 949-7544.

Washington Information Directory 1986-87

This annual directory of executive, legislative and private organizations is organized by major subject areas, rather than by Federal Government or private organization name. For each of the more than 5,000 information sources, the directory provides the name, address and telephone number of the organization, as well as the name of an individual to contact for further information. There is also a description of the role played by each organization within the context of the subject area. Organizations may appear in as many subject areas as appropriate. There are two indexes—subject and agency/organization—bibliographies and appendices. June 1986. approx. 1,000pp. $49.95. ISBN 0-87187-370-2. (75-646321) Congressional Quarterly Inc., 1414 22nd Street NW, Washington, DC 20037; (202) 887-8620.

Washington Information Workbook

A companion publication to the *Researcher's Guide to Washington Experts*, this workbook identifies the major Federal departments and agencies and targets prime information sources. It also explains how to use the Freedom of Information Act (see Appendix B), information clearinghouses and Capital Hill. Chapters include coverage of the Library of Congress, statistical sources, trade and professional associations, Federal document rooms and libraries, document retrieval companies, recorded messages from Washington, and the art of obtaining information. Spring 1986, 8th ed. 550pp. $75.00. ISBN 0-934940-22-3. (80-54599) Washington Researchers Publishing, 2612 P Street NW, Washington, DC 20007; (202) 333-3533.

Duke's Washington Pocket Directory 1986

Subtitled "A Citizen's Guide to Major Government Offices and Information Services," this annual publication covers the three branches of the Federal Government. In addition to an introduction, the directory is divided into the following major sections: Federal Information Centers, Consumer Information Guide, Government Job Information, Congress, White House, Supreme Court, Federal Agencies/Offices, State-by-State Listing, and a Washington Tourist Guide. April 1986. 162pp. $9.95. ISBN 0-942008-35-9. WANT Publishing Co., 1511 K Street NW, Washington, DC 20005; (202) 783-1887.

The Washington Lobbyists & Lawyers Directory

This directory provides information about more than 10,000 lobbyists and lawyers. It is divided into an index and a cross-index. First is an alphabetical list of lobbyists and lawyers, identifying their employers. Second, all of the data contained in the first section is reversed. Here, listed in alphabetical order are all the law firms and lobbying organizations, complete with a local Washington address and telephone number. With each entry appear the names of each lobbyist or lawyer working for that office. In the case of law firms and other organizations that hire out their lobbying services, the entries also include a list of clients the directory's compilers have been able to discover. Spring 1986. approx. 300pp. $45.00. Communications Service, 121 4th Street SE, Washington, DC 20003; (202) 544-8792.

Washington 85

An annual directory that includes information on approximately 3,000 institutions, firms, companies, governmental offices and representational bodies, and other organizations that are important to one aspect or another of the Nation's capital. The publication is intended to be a guide to the power structure of Washington, i.e., a directory of significant public and private institutions of the metropolitan area and the people who lead them. For each of the more than 15,000 individuals listed, titles, addresses and telephone numbers are included. In addition to being identified with their organization's listing, the individuals appear in an alphabetical index where all affiliations and positions of each individual are grouped. June 1985. 729pp. $40.00. ISBN 0-910416-55-9. ISSN 0083-7393. Columbia Books, Inc., 1350 New York Avenue NW, Suite 207, Washington, DC 20005; (202) 737-3777.

Washington Representatives 1985

An annual directory of nearly 10,000 lobbyists, legal advisors, government affairs consultants and other representatives of public interest and consumer groups, trade and professional associations, corporations, labor unions, State and city governments, foreign governments, special issue organizations, political action committees and more. It is organized into two alphabetical cross-referenced lists: The Representatives—their names, addresses and telephone numbers, prior Government service and dates of registration as lobbyists or foreign agents; and Organizations Represented—their Washington addresses and telephone numbers, names and titles of their representatives and a description of their activities and interests. Included also are subject and country-of-origin indexes. March 1985. 639pp. $45.00. ISBN 0-910416-54-0. Columbia Books, Inc., see entry above.

46 **FEDfind**

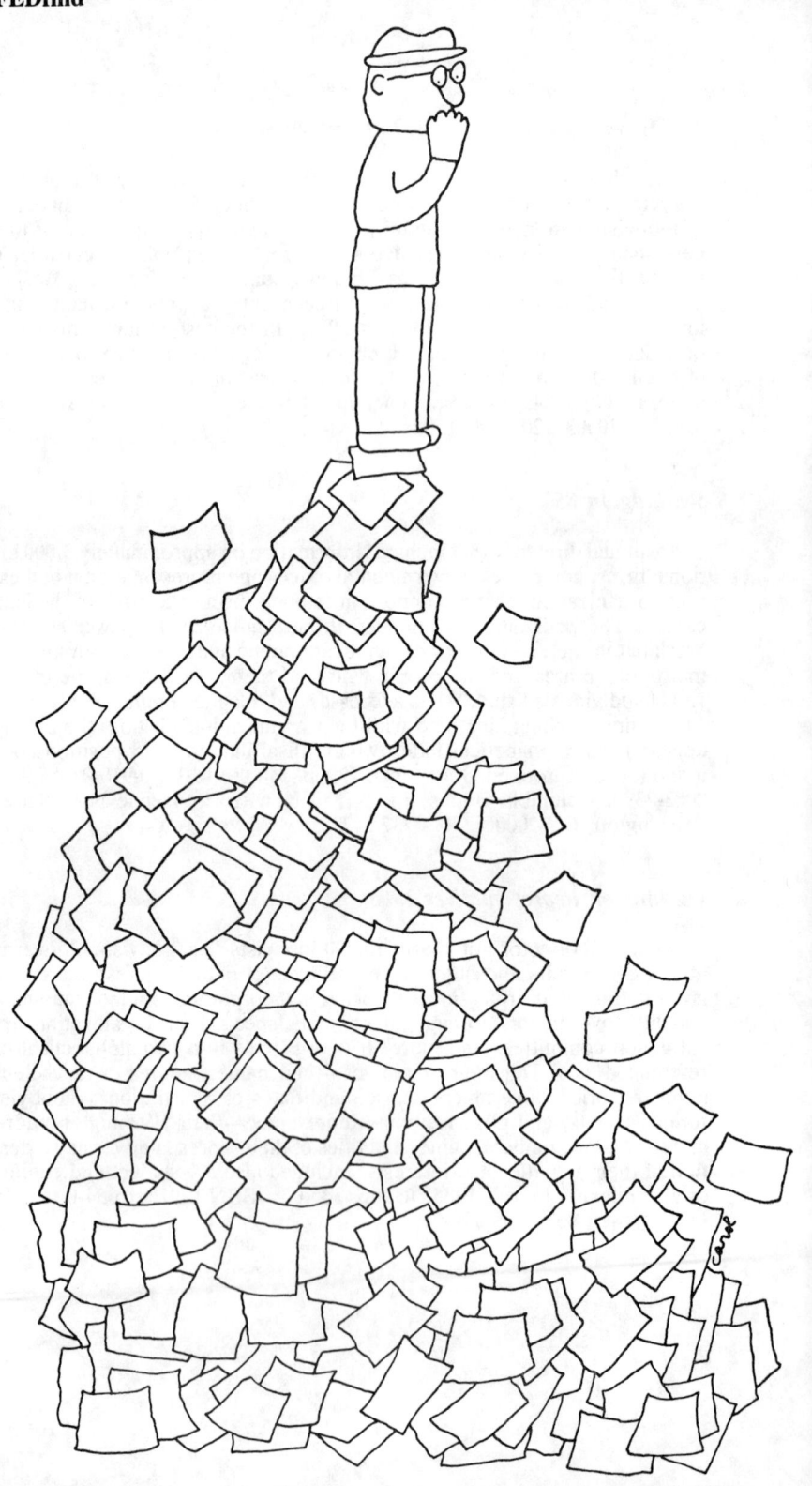

Legislative Branch

Advance Locator for Capitol Hill

This annual directory is a pre-publication supplement to the 1986 Congressional Staff Directory (see entry below) that includes an update on entries for Members, their staffs and their districts. January 1986. 448pp. $12.00. ISBN 0-87289-063-5. Congressional Staff Directory, Ltd., P.O. Box 62, Mount Vernon, VA 22121; (703) 765-3400.

Capital Guide

Prepared annually by the United States League of Savings Institutions, this guide contains a complete listing of the Members of Congress—with biographical information and photographs—and the membership of Senate and House committees. The names of the administrative and legislative assistants and the appointment secretary for each Member of Congress is included. There is also an alphabetical list of executive departments, select independent and regulatory agencies, with key officials' names, titles and telephone numbers. The Depository Institutions Deregulation Committee and the Federal Home Loan Bank Board are highlighted. Comb-binding. March 1986. approx. 350pp. $10.00. United States League of Savings Institutions, Attn: Order Processing Department, 111 E. Wacker Drive, Chicago, IL 60601; (312) 644-3100.

Congressional Directory 1985–86

The *Congressional Directory*, published for each Congress, provides information on all three branches of the Federal Government. Primarily, it includes biographies of current Members of Congress, home State and Washington, DC-area addresses and committee information. The Senators and Representatives are listed by State, in alphabetical order by name, and by term of service. The Directory also includes a listing of all Federal departments and agencies, including addresses, telephone numbers, and names and titles of key officials. Biographies of Supreme Court Justices and judges of the other U.S. courts are also provided. Other information includes the names of members of the press allowed in the galleries at the Capitol, addresses of international organizations, diplomatic representatives to the United States, maps of each State's congressional districts, and an extensive index. The Directory is available in three formats. May 1985. 1,228pp. Paper, $13.00, GPO S/N 052-070-05994-0; cloth, $17.00, GPO S/N 052-070-05995-8; cloth with thumb index, $21.00, GPO S/N 052-070-05996-6. (Y 4.P 93/1:1/99-1/cloth) See the GPO order form.

Congressional Handbook

An annual pocket-sized directory, this publication lists Members of Congress alphabetically and by State delegation and committee assignments. It also includes rosters for all standing committees. April 1985. 88pp. $3.00. Chamber of Commerce of the United States, Attn: Publications Fulfillment Department, 1615 H Street NW, Washington, DC 20062: (301) 468-5128.

Congressional Pictorial Directory, 99th Congress

This directory—published for each Congress—includes photographs of the President, Vice President and all Members of the Congress. It identifies the Member's political party, number of the term being served and district represented. There is a list of State delegations, list of Senators, Representatives, Delegates and Resident Commissioner of each State and their home post offices and political parties. Arrangement is first alphabetically by State, then numerically by district; and alphabetically by last name. January 1985. 209pp. Paper, $6.00, GPO S/N 052-070-05992-3; cloth, $10.00, GPO S/N 052-070-05993-1. (Y 4.P 93/1:1 p/99/paper) See the GPO order form.

Congressional Staff Directory

This annual directory concentrates on the staff who work for Senators, Congressmen, committees, subcommittees and other offices of the legislative branch. It provides their office room numbers, telephone numbers and committee assignments. Biographical information is provided for Members of Congress and key staff members. The directory includes lists and indexes, such as cities and towns in Members' districts, and district and State offices of Members. April 1986, 28th ed. 1,232pp. $45.00. ISBN 0-87289-061-9. Congressional Staff Directory, Ltd., P.O. Box 62, Mount Vernon, VA 22121; (703) 765-3400.

Congressional Yellow Book

A looseleaf directory of Members of Congress, their committees, administrative and leadership offices, caucuses and key staff aides, this publication also includes listings for the various components of the legislative branch: Congressional Budget Office, General Accounting Office, Government Printing Office, Library of Congress, Office of Technology Assessment and others. Updated in its entirety four times a year. Subscription price: $107.00 a year, plus $8.00 postage and handling. The Washington Monitor, Inc., 1301 Pennsylvania Avenue NW, Suite 1000, Washington, DC 20004; (202) 347-7757.

The U.S. Congress Handbook 1986: 99th Congress (Second Session)

This annual publication lists the Members of Congress alphabetically with their photographs, biographies, committee and subcommittee memberships. Staff aides such as administrative, legislative and press are listed. State office locations are given for each Member and, where available, names of persons in charge. Also included are articles on how a bill moves through the legislative pipeline, powers of Congress, tips on writing a Member, Blacks in Congress, rating Members of Congress and more. March 1986. Single copy price: $6.95; discounts on two or more copies. The U.S. Congress Handbook, P.O. Box 566, McLean, VA 22101; (703) 356-3572.

Directories 49

Executive Branch

Country Experts in the Federal Government

This publication gives the name, address, telephone and room numbers of some 1,000 country experts and 300 regional experts who cover more than 200 countries. It includes the "home" agency of each expert, such as the Department of State, Department of Agriculture, Agency for International Development, Bureau of Mines or Department of Energy. In addition, the Washington address and telephone numbers of each foreign embassy are given. Spring 1986, 8th ed. 68pp. $40.00. ISBN 0-934940-26-6. Washington Researchers Publishing, 2612 P Street NW, Washington, DC 20007; (202) 333-3533.

Directory of Federal Audit and Inspector General Organizations

A guide to Federal audit organizations prepared by the General Accounting Office (GAO), this book was designed to aid in the development of intergovernmental cooperation by facilitating the interchange of information among audit and investigative groups. Included is information on 56 organizations—staffed by some 21,445 professionals—directly involved in the audit of Federal funds, and information on investigative groups in the Offices of Inspector General as well as some external audit organizations. 1985, 5th ed. 102pp. **FREE**. See the GAO order form.

Directory of Federal Contract Audit Offices

Compiled by the Defense Contract Audit Agency (DCAA), this two-volume directory was designed to assist in identifying the location and cognizance of Federal audit offices. Volume 1 contains basic information regarding office location (i.e., office and agency name, address and telephone numbers), hours of operation, management officials and general audit cognizance. Volume 2 is an alphabetical listing of Defense and non-Defense Department contractors that have been audited by the DCAA, based on assigned audit cognizance or arrangement that have been made for audit of contracts awarded by other organizations. Looseleaf for updating. 1982. Volume 1, 314pp., $10.00. Out-of-print. GPO S/N 008-007-03247-0; Volume 2, 436pp., $10.00, GPO S/N 008-007-03248-8. (D 1.46:5100.6/2/v.1, v.2) See the GPO order form.

Executive Bio-Pictorial Directory 1985

A biennial guide that provides photographs and brief biographies of approximately 500 key officials in the Reagan Administration, this edition includes the Reagan White House and top staff, Executive Office of the President, executive departments and agencies, and commissions. Also, congressional leadership, the Smithsonian Institution, and other select institutions are included. October 1985. 270pp. $29.95 + $2.50 shipping. Braddock Publications, Inc., 1001 Connecticut Avenue NW, Suite 210, Washington, DC 20036; (202) 296-1317.

Federal Executive Directory

Published six times per year, this directory includes information on the Cabinet departments, independent agencies and commissions of the executive branch and the Congress. Each division, branch, section and office is accompanied by the name of the individual who (permanently or temporarily) fills the position. Its more than 82,000 entries are divided into four color-coded and cross-referenced sections: alphabetic—a listing of names and telephone numbers; organizational for congressional, and organizational for executive branch—includes every unit, section, branch, division or office, along with the address of each; and key word—lists individuals by subject. Subscription price: $140.00 per year. Carroll Publishing Co., 1058 Thomas Jefferson Street NW, Washington, DC 20007; (202) 333-8620.

Federal Regional Executive Directory

A directory that lists Federal employees of the executive, legislative and judicial branches of the U.S. Government who are based outside the Washington, DC area, its more than 73,000 entries are divided into four color-coded, line-by-line cross-referenced sections (alphabetical, organizational, geographic [city with State] and functional). Updated twice a year. Subscription price: $125.00 per year. Carroll Publishing Co., see entry above.

Federal Regulatory Directory

This directory is designed to provide answers and explanations to questions about which agency does what in the area of regulation. Major sections include a history of Federal Government regulation, including new proposals currently before Congress; an analysis of the future of the regulatory process; profiles of the major regulatory agencies including their organization and functions by department, responsibilities and enforcement powers, staff and telephone numbers, regional and area offices; lists of data, reports and key publications available from major agencies; descriptions of other agencies and departments and small units with regulatory powers, many not usually thought of as regulators; and two indexes cross-referenced by agency/subject and personnel. By using the index alone, all the offices, agencies, and personnel that regulate any topic may be identified, e.g., housing, food, energy, product safety, etc. 1986, 5th ed. 893pp. $49.95. ISBN 0-87187-362-1. (79-644368) Congressional Quarterly Inc., 1414 22nd Street NW, Washington, DC 20037; (202) 887-8620.

Federal Staff Directory 1986

An annual directory that contains information on executive branch personnel, this publication provides information on more than 27,000 Federal Government executives—mostly GS-16 and above—giving titles, organizations, addresses and telephone numbers. The book provides biographical briefs on key officials and a key word subject index. November 1985. 1,344pp. $45.00. ISBN 0-87289-062-7. Congressional Staff Directory, Ltd., P.O. Box 62, Mount Vernon, VA 22121; (703) 765-3400.

Federal Yellow Book

A looseleaf directory of more than 31,000 Federal employees in the White House, the Executive Office of the President, the Federal departments and agencies and regional offices nationwide. Structured by organization, the directory includes names, titles, addresses, and room and telephone numbers. Updates are issued six times a year and constitute at least two complete revisions in every 12-month period. Subscription price: $130.00 a year, plus $12.00 postage and handling. The Washington Monitor, Inc., 1301 Pennsylvania Avenue NW, Suite 1000, Washington, DC 20004; (202) 347-7757.

Industry Analysts in the Federal Government

This document identifies more than 100 Federal experts who are specialists in specific industries. The book is arranged by Standard Industrial Classification Codes (industry and product) to aid in identifying the name, address, and telephone number of a given professional who may provide data or sources for a given industry. These analysts are associated with the Department of Commerce, particularly the Bureau of the Census. Spring 1986, 8th ed. 61pp. $30.00. ISBN 0-934940-27-4. Washington Researchers Publishing, 2612 P Street NW, Washington, DC 20007; (202) 333-3533.

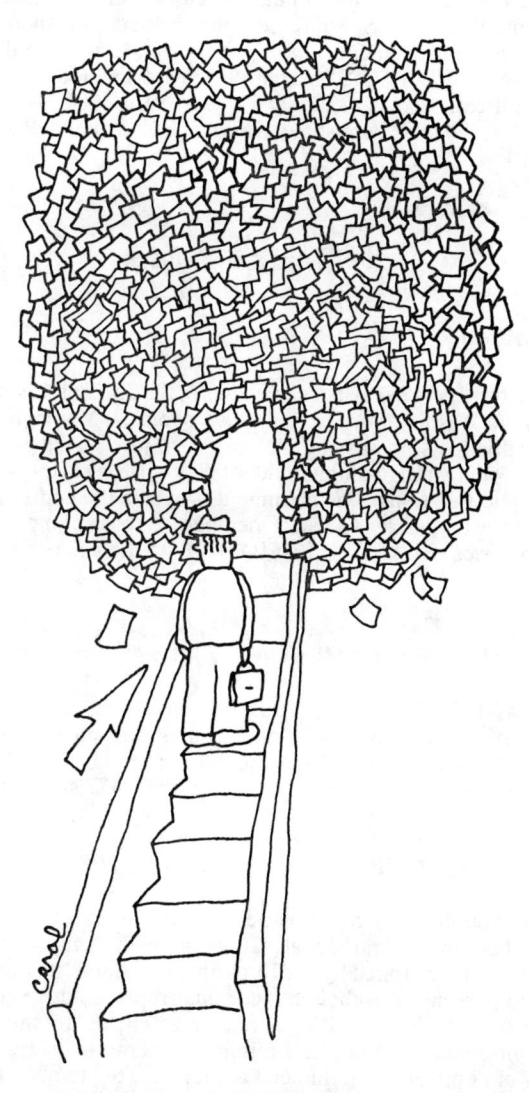

Judicial Branch

United States Court Directory 1985

An annual looseleaf directory that provides the mailing addresses and telephone numbers of the Federal courts. For each court, it provides—as appropriate—the names of judges, magistrates, Federal public defenders, chief probation officers and clerks. The directory is organized by type of court within geographic area. September 1985. 269pp. $12.00. GPO S/N 028-004-00062-1. (Ju 10.17:985-2) See the GPO order form.

Want's Federal-State Court Directory

The Federal section of this annual directory includes names, addresses and telephone numbers of U.S. Supreme Court Justices and all lower Federal court judges (including special courts such as the Tax Court and the Claims Court), clerks of the court and U.S. magistrates. Also included are U.S. Attorneys, probation officers and bankruptcy judges. April 1986. 140pp. $16.95. ISBN 0-942008-36-7. WANT Publishing Co., 1511 K Street NW, Washington, DC 20005; (202) 783-1887.

Foreign Affairs

Diplomatic List

This quarterly periodical lists the names of the diplomatic staffs of all missions in and around Washington, D.C. and their spouses. Members of the diplomatic staff are individuals possessing diplomatic status. These persons—with some exceptions—enjoy full immunity under the provisions of the Vienna Convention on Diplomatic Relations. The document provides the addresses and telephone numbers of the embassies and staff members. Subscription price: $14.00 a year. Single copy price: $3.75. GPO List ID DIPL. (S 1.8:) See the GPO subscription order form.

Employees of Diplomatic Missions

Known as the "White List," this quarterly publication is a listing of the employees of foreign missions in and around Washington, D.C. It is arranged alphabetically by country. Subscription price: $13.00 a year. Single copy price: $3.50. GPO List ID EDMI. (S 1.8/2:) See the GPO subscription order form.

Foreign Consular Offices in the United States 1985

An annual publication that provides a complete and official list of the foreign consular offices in the United States, together with their jurisdictions and recognized personnel. Compiled by the Department of State, it is intended for organizations and persons who deal with consular representatives of foreign governments. It was designed with particular attention to the requirements of government agencies, State tax officials, international trade organizations, chambers of commerce and judicial authorities. September 1985. 95pp. $3.50. GPO S/N 044-000-02081-5. (S 1.69/2:985) See the GPO order form.

Directories of Directories

Guide to U.S. Government Directories

This two-volume guide is an annotated directory of more than 1,600 directories published by the U.S. Government, including directories published as parts of other Government publications. Subject areas of these directories range from dance touring companies, local planning agencies, and school districts to hazardous waste management facilities, organizations providing Hispanic speakers, and owners of nuclear power plants. Each directory is described in terms of information coverage, scope, arrangement, SuDocs number, indexing and how to obtain a copy. Compiler Donna Rae Larson. Volume 1: 1970-1980. 1981. 208pp. $55.00. ISBN 0-912700-63-7. Volume 2: 1980-1984. 1985. 232pp. $55.00. ISBN 0-89774-162-5. Oryx Press, 2214 North Central at Encanto, Phoenix, AZ 85004; (800) 457-ORYX or (602) 254-6156.

U.S. Government Directories, 1970-1981

A selected, annotated bibliography that describes 575 Federal depository library titles. It is organized by subject and lists both directories and publications with directory-type information published by Federal agencies. Subject area coverage includes guides to areas and places, associations and organizations, businesses and industries, Government agencies, individuals and more. Each section is arranged by Government Printing Office Superintendent of Documents (SuDocs) number. Among other data, information in the following areas are provided: first date of publication and last date (if applicable), number of volumes, issuing agency, number of pages, serials information, format (if other than paper) and frequency of publication. Compiled by Constance Staten Gray. 1984. 270pp. $35.00. ISBN 0-87287-414-1. (83-26801) Libraries Unlimited, P.O. Box 263, Littleton, CO 80160; (303) 770-1220.

54 FEDfind

Chapter 3
Civilian Personnel Management

The Office of Personnel Management (OPM) is the Federal civilian personnel agency. This agency is generally responsible for the Government's personnel management system, which includes such tasks as: job classification, pay and benefits administration, evaluation of agency personnel programs, training, recruiting and examining, personnel investigations and executive development. OPM administers Federal employee retirement and insurance programs, and provides management leadership in labor relations and affirmative action. It develops personnel policies governing civilian employment in executive branch agencies and in certain agencies of the legislative and judicial branches. The executive branch departments and agencies have their own personnel policies in addition to those published by OPM. Each organization also has its own merit promotion and affirmative action plans.

The members of the military are managed by the policies developed by the Department of Defense (DOD) and its service components—the Air Force, Army, Navy and Marine Corps. Figure 3-1 provides a summary of the numbers of civilian and military personnel within the Federal establishment.

In addition to the information presented in this chapter, the Government Printing Office (GPO) makes available **FREE** two subject bibliographies (SB) in this area that cite publications for sale. These are *Labor-Management Relations* (SB-64) and *Office of Personnel Management Publications* (SB-300). See the GPO subscription order form.

The information resources described in this chapter are organized under the following headings.

- Civilian Personnel Operations
- Labor-Management Relations
- Merit Systems Protection
- Management References
- Employment Information
- News Publications

Civilian Personnel Operations

Federal Personnel Manual

The *Federal Personnel Manual* (FPM) is the official publication of the Office of Personnel Management that contains instructions to other agencies on matters of personnel management. It is used to identify the various laws, rules, regulations,

Executive Office of the President	1,618
Executive Departments	1,767,414
Department of Agriculture	119,763
Department of Commerce	34,984
Department of Defense	1,061,836
Office of the Secretary of Defense	88,672
Department of the Air Force	248,756
Department of the Army	383,027
Department of the Navy	341,381
Department of Education	5,140
Department of Energy	16,699
Department of Health and Human Services	141,948
Department of Housing and Urban Development	12,108
Department of the Interior	74,225
Department of Justice	61,858
Department of Labor	19,137
Department of State	24,837
Department of Transportation	63,236
Department of the Treasury	131,643
Independent Agencies	1,125,531
ACTION	507
Administrative Conference of the United States	21
Advisory Commission on Intergovernmental Relations	38
American Battle Monuments Commission	404
Appalachian Regional Commission	7
Board for International Broadcasting	18
Commission of Fine Arts	7
Commodity Futures Trading Commission	538
Consumer Product Safety Commission	567
Delaware River Basin Commission	2
Environmental Protection Agency	12,650
Equal Employment Opportunity Commission	3,231
Export-Import Bank of the United States	367
Farm Credit Administration	311
Federal Communications Commission	1,999
Federal Deposit Insurance Corporation	5,076
Federal Election Commission	251
Federal Emergency Management Agency	2,766
Federal Home Loan Bank Board	1,533
Federal Labor Relations Authority	321
Federal Maritime Commission	231
Federal Mediation and Conciliation Service	356
Federal Mine Safety and Health Review Commission	50
Federal Reserve System (Board of Governors)	1,591
Federal Trade Commission	1,433
General Services Administration	29,678

Figure 3-1. Numbers of Federal Government Employees

Civilian Personnel Management 57

Inter-American Foundation	67
International Development Cooperation Agency	5,141
Interstate Commerce Commission	1,025
Merit Systems Protection Board	450
National Aeronautics and Space Administration	21,876
National Capital Planning Commission	50
National Credit Union Administration	600
National Foundation on the Arts and the Humanities	587
National Labor Relations Board	2,646
National Mediation Board	55
National Science Foundation	1,890
National Transportation Safety Board	336
Nuclear Regulatory Commission	3,578
Occupational Safety and Health Review Commission	86
Office of Personnel Management	6,588
Overseas Private Investment Corporation	156
Panama Canal Commission	8,070
Peace Corps	1,129
Pennsylvania Avenue Development Corporation	35
Postal Rate Commission	64
Railroad Retirement Board	1,577
Securities and Exchange Commission	2,040
Selective Service System	308
Small Business Administration	5,083
Susquehanna River Basin Commission	26
Tennessee Valley Authority	32,824
U.S. Arms Control and Disarmament Agency	241
U.S. Commission on Civil Rights	254
U.S. Information Agency	8,369
U.S. International Trade Commission	444
U.S. Postal Service	714,054
Veterans Administration	241,929
Total, Executive Branch	2,894,563
Total, Legislative Branch	38,598
Total, Judicial Branch	17,171
Total, Civilian Work Force	2,950,332
Total, Military Personnel	2,138,332
Air Force	598,538
Army	780,674
Navy	561,479
Marine Corps	197,641
Total, Civilian and Military Personnel	5,088,664

(Source: Organization of Federal Executive Departments and Agencies, 1985.)

Figure 3-1. Numbers of Federal Government Employees—Continued

policies and instructions pertinent to personnel administration. The FPM consists of a basic manual and 27 separate supplements. The basic manual provides general policies and requirements of the U.S. Government in personnel management. The supplements are designed to provide specialists with detailed information in particular areas. Subscription service includes supplements, letters and bulletins issued irregularly. The *Basic Federal Personnel Manual* subscription price from the Government Printing Office (GPO) is $917.00. GPO List ID FPMBC. Listed below are the various "FPM Supplements," their subscription prices, and GPO List IDs. (PM 1.41/3: supplement number) See the GPO subscription order form.

271-1 *Development of Qualification Standards:* $4.25; FPMQS
271-2 *Tests and Other Applicant Appraisal Procedures:* $4.50; FPMAP
292-1 *Personnel Data Standards:* $57.00; FPMPD
293-31 *Personnel Records and Files:* $65.00; FPMPR
296-33 *Guide to Processing Personnel Actions:* $235.00; FPMGP
298-1 *The Central Personnel Data File:* $29.00; FPMCP
298-2 *The 113 Summary Data Reporting System:* $41.00; FPMSD
305-1 *Executive Resources Management:* $13.00; FPMEE
335-1 *Evaluation of Employees for Promotion and Internal Placement:* $25.00; FPMEP
337-2 *Library of Rating Schedules:* $26.00; FPMLS
339-31 *Reviewing and Acting on Medical Certificates:* $13.00; FPMRM
410-1 *Model Control System for Long-Term Training:* $32.00; FPMMC
451-1 *Incentive Awards:* $18.00; FPMIA
512-1 See *Job Grading System for Trades and Labor Occupations* later in this section.
532-1 *Federal Wage System:* $125.00; FPMCF
532-2 *Federal Fund Wage System—Non-Appropriated Employees:* $70.00; FPMWS
711-1 *Labor-Management Relations Program Provisions and Technical Guidance:* $29.00; FPMMR
731-1 *Determining Suitability for Federal Employment:* $22.00; FPMDS
792-1 *Occupational Health Services for Federal Civilian Employees:* $15.00; FPMDH
792-2 *Alcoholism and Drug Abuse Program:* $10.00; FPMDA
831-1 *Retirement:* $130.00; FPMR
870-1 *Life Insurance:* $61.00; FPMLI
890-1 *Federal Employees Health Benefits:* $140.00; FPMHB
910-1 *National Emergency Readiness of Federal Personnel Management:* $12.00; FPMNE
990-1 *Civil Service Laws, Executive Orders, Rules and Regulations:* $135.00; FPMLR
990-2 *Hours of Duty, Pay, and Leave, Annotated:* $27.00; FPMDL
990-3 *National Emergency Standby Regulations and Instructions, Personnel and Manpower:* $8.50; FPMES

Civilian Personnel Law Manual

Issued by the Office of General Counsel, General Accounting Office (GAO), this manual is comprised of four separately bound titles and an introduction that reviews the legal entitlements of Federal employees. Included is an overview of the statutes and regulations that give rise to those entitlements. These entitlements cover the following areas: Title I—Compensation, Title II—Leave, Title III—Travel, and Title IV—Relocation. Supplements are issued annually. 1983, 2nd ed. 1,502pp. **FREE**. (GA 1.14:C 49/983) See the GAO order form.

Handbook of Occupational Groups and Series of Classes Established Under the Federal Position-Classification Plan

This subscription handbook presents the occupational structure of the jobs in the U.S. Government subject to the Classification Act of 1949. The *Handbook* consists of four parts: (1) an introduction explaining certain basic position-classification principles, the occupational code, the coverage of the document, and the procedure for keeping it up to date; (2) an outline of the position-classification groups and specific job series; (3) definitions of the occupational groups and specific job series; and (4) an alphabetical index to the definitions of the occupational groups and specific job series. Subscription price: $120.00 for an indeterminate period. GPO List ID HOGC. (PM 1.8/2:) See the GPO subscription order form.

Handbook X-118

This subscription handbook, officially entitled *Qualification Standards for White Collar Positions Under the General Schedule*, provides the qualification standards for each occupation in the General Schedule. The *Handbook* is maintained by the Office of Personnel Management and is applicable to those Government agencies with positions under the Classification Act of 1949. Also known as the "Qualifications Standards," the manual describes examination requirements for the various positions in the civil service. Subscription price: $80.00, which includes the *Handbook* reprinted through the most current transmittal and monthly revised pages for an indeterminate period. GPO List ID HX118. (PM 1.8/3:X-118) See the GPO subscription order form.

Position Classification Standards for Positions Under the General Schedule Classification System

The Classification Act of 1949 directed that standards be published for the classification of civil service positions covering occupations common to Federal agencies. This subscription service contains all position classification standards developed by the Office of Personnel Management as of the date of purchase. Bimonthly changes, for an indeterminate period, are provided as they occur. Selected individual standards are sold separately with varying prices. Subscription price: $230.00. GPO List ID PCS. (PM 1.30:) See the GPO subscription order form.

Instructions for the Factor Evaluation System

The Factor Evaluation System (FES) is a method of assigning grades in the classification of nonsupervisory positions, GS-1 through GS-15 under the General Schedule (GS). Under the FES, positions are placed in grades on the basis of their duties, responsibilities, and the qualifications required as evaluated in terms of the following nine factors common to nonsupervisory positions in GS occupations: (1) knowledge required by the position, (2) supervisory controls, (3) guidelines, (4) complexity, (5) scope and effect, (6) personal contacts, (7) purpose of contacts, (8) physical demands, and (9) work environment. This booklet describes levels for each of the factors and point values for these levels. It serves as the basic framework for FES, and in FES classification standards and guides. GS position grades are determined through use of the procedures set forth in this document. 1977. 52pp. $4.50. Out-of-print. GPO S/N 006-000-00991-3. (CS 1.39/a:E 11).

How to Write Position Descriptions Under the Factor Evaluation System

This guide explains how to write position descriptions (PD) in the format required by the Factor Evaluation System (FES). A PD is the official record of the work assigned by management to an employee. It is to be used for jobs in the U.S. Government's General Schedule (GS) that are classified under FES position classification standards. 1979. 32pp. $3.75. GPO S/N 006-000-01054-7. (PM 1.8:P84) See the GPO order form.

Job Grading System for Trades and Labor Occupations (Blue Collar)

Designated as FPM (Federal Personnel Manual) Supplement 512-1, this subscription outlines the most common method of grading, titling and coding the various Federal jobs in trades and labor occupations. It carries out the principles and concepts of the Coordinated Federal Wage System by providing uniformity and equity in grading and paying Federal blue-collar employees. The system covers jobs in the executive agencies and applies to most trades and labor jobs outside the Postal Service that are paid from appropriated funds. The basic guidelines for determining trades or labor jobs (and for distinguishing them from General Schedule [GS] jobs) appear in the introduction to the *Position Classification Standards for Positions Under the General Schedule*, Section IV, "Guidelines for the Determination of Trades, Crafts, or Manual-Labor Positions." Individual job standards are sold on a single copy basis; however, other parts of the subscription service are not sold separately. Back issues, including the individual job standards, are furnished to all new subscribers. Subscription price: $100.00 for an indeterminate period. GPO List ID JGTL. (PM 1.41/4:512-1/rep) See the GPO subscription order form.

Digest of Significant Classification Decisions and Opinions

A quarterly periodical designed to assist in increasing the level of classification consistency in Federal position descriptions, this digest presents some key classification decisions by the Office of Personnel Management (OPM). Digested decisions highlight a specific problem or troublesome classification factor, and briefly describe OPM's rationale for resolving the problem. The *Digest* is not a classification standard, and the items in it cannot be used in lieu of current OPM classification standards and guides. Subscription price: $12.00 a year. Single copy price: $4.50. GPO List ID DSCDO. (PM 1.40:) See the GPO subscription order form.

Federal Employees' Almanac 1986

This annual reference is aimed at Federal and U.S. Postal Service workers. It contains facts and features on such topics as performance appraisal systems, life and health insurance benefits, retirement programs, job rights, collective bargaining rights, equal employment rules, injury compensation benefits, appeals and grievance procedures, take-home pay tables, overseas job opportunities, part-time work programs, Government employee hot-lines for complaints and advice. January 1986, 33rd ed. $3.50 per copy; discounts on orders of six or more copies. ISBN 0-910582-05-X. Federal Employees' News Digest, Inc., P.O. Box 7528, Falls Church, VA 22046; (703) 533-3031.

Federal Personnel Guide 1986

This fourth annual edition includes expanded sections on reduction-in-force, reinstatement, furloughs, and other subjects of current interest and concern to Federal employees. It contains detailed pay tables that reflect deductions for Federal income taxes and retirement, along with sections on merit pay, promotions, leave, labor management relations, unemployment compensation, retirement, equal employment opportunity, and other subjects of interest to the Federal worker. January 1986. $3.00; discounts are available on orders of five or more. ISSN 0163-7665. Federal Personnel Publications, P.O. Box 274, Washington, DC 20044; (703) 532-1631.

Federal Personnel Management Service

A microfilm information service containing the entire Office of Personnel Management (OPM) *Federal Personnel Manual*, FPM supplements and letters, OPM bulletins, Federal Labor Relations Authority and Merit Systems Protection Board documents, and a variety of Federal personnel management standards. The standards consist of the following publications: Handbook of Occupational Groups, Position Classification Standards, Factor Evaluation System, Job Grading System, and Qualification Standards X-118 and X-118C. The service is available on either 24X microfiche or 16mm microfilm cartridges and is updated every 15 or 30 days. Enquire for price information. Information Handling Services, 15 Inverness Way East, Englewood, CO 80150; (800) 525-7052 or (303) 790-0600.

Personnel Literature

This is a selected list of books, pamphlets and other publications acquired by the library of the Office of Personnel Management. Periodical articles, unpublished dissertations and microfilms are also listed. Published monthly, with an annual index, it includes items on such personnel management subjects as performance evaluation, productivity, executives, employee training and development and labor-management relations. Coverage is not limited to Federal personnel management; it also includes State and local governments, foreign governments and private organizations. Arrangement is by general subjects; each entry is analyzed in descriptive terms. Subscription price: $23.00 a year. Single copy price: $2.00. Annual index: $5.50. GPO List ID PLM. (PM 1.16:) See the GPO subscription order form.

Fed Facts

Fed Facts is a series of pamphlets prepared by the Office of Personnel Management that provide information regarding various aspects of Federal employment. Those titles currently available from GPO include their respective price and GPO S/N. Other titles are made available in Federal personnel offices. (PM 1.25: number in the series) See the GPO order form.

Fed Facts 1   *The Incentive Awards Program*
Fed Facts 2   *Political Activity of Federal Employees*
Fed Facts 3   *The Civil Service Recruitment System*
Fed Facts 4   *Financial Protection for Federal Employees*
Fed Facts 5   *The Federal Merit Promotion Policy*
Fed Facts 6   *Serving the Public: The Extra Step.* $1.75. 006-000-01176-4.
Fed Facts 7   *The Federal Wage System*

Fed Facts 8   *Meeting Your Financial Obligations.* $2.00. 006-000-01165-9.
Fed Facts 9   *Maternity Benefits for Federal Employees*
Fed Facts 11 *Actions for Unacceptable Performance and Adverse Reactions*
Fed Facts 12 *The Displaced Employee Program*
Fed Facts 13 *Reductions in Force in Federal Agencies*
Fed Facts 14 *Reemployment (Restoration) Rights of Federal Employees Who Perform Duty in the Armed Services*
Fed Facts 15 *Federal Labor Relations*
Fed Facts 16 *Pay Under The General Schedule*
Fed Facts 17 *The Cost of Living Allowance for Federal Employees.* $1.75. 006-000-01265-5.
Fed Facts 18 *The Intergovernmental Mobility Program*
Fed Facts 19 *How Your GS Job is Classified and the Classification Appeals System.* $2.00. 006-000-01263-9.
Fed Facts 20 *Merit System Principles and Prohibited Personnel Practices*
Fed Facts 21 *Performance Appraisal*
Fed Facts 22 *Reduction in Force Benefits Guide*
Fed Facts 23 *Severance Pay. $2.00.* 006-000-01276-1.
Fed Facts 24 *Furlough. $1.75.* 006-000-01293-1.

Federal Trainer

Issued quarterly by the Office of Personnel Management, this publication contains news and features pertaining to programs for training Federal employees. Subscription price: $12.00 a year. Single copy price: $2.25. GPO List ID FEDT. (PM 1.19/3:) See the GPO subscription order form.

Spotlight on Affirmative Employment Programs

A quarterly magazine published by the Office of Personnel Management, this periodical describes current activities and programs in the area of affirmative employment. Subscription price: $11.00 a year. Single copy price: $3.00. GPO List ID SOAEP. (PM 1.18/3:) See the GPO subscription order form.

Labor-Management Relations

Guide to the Federal Service Labor-Management Relations Statute

This Federal Labor Relations Authority booklet provides guidelines to Federal sector labor law. Designed to assist employees, unions, and agencies, the booklet contains a nontechnical, detailed summary of the statute. It also explains the Authority's structure and, where applicable, refers the user to the specific statutory or regulatory section. 1984. 54pp. $2.00. GPO S/N 063-000-00021-3. (Y 3.F 31/21-3:8 F 31) See the GPO order form.

FLRA Reports of Case Decisions, FSIP Releases and Administrative Law Judge Decisions of the FLRA

The Federal Labor Relations Authority (FLRA) administers the law that protects the right of Federal employees to organize, bargain collectively, and participate through labor organizations in decisions that affect them. The Federal Services Impasses Panel (FSIP), an entity within the FLRA, provides assistance in resolving negotiation impasses between agencies and unions. The decisions of these two bodies are published as a subscription item. Subscription price: $100.00 a year. GPO List ID FLRAR. (Y 3.F 31/21-3:) See the GPO subscription order form.

Federal Labor Relations Reporter

The FLRR is a monthly looseleaf service, including both current reports and back volumes, that provides information on all third-party rulings in the area of Federal labor-management relations since the inception of Executive Order 11491 in 1970. All cases are summarized and indexed. The first binder of the FLRR reports decisions of the Federal Labor Relations Authority, the Federal Service Impasses Panel, private interest arbitration panels, the Comptroller General, and the Federal courts. The second binder provides indexed reports on available Federal sector arbitration awards, and reports appeals of arbitration awards that cite back to appeal decisions in the first binder. This avoids the problem of relying on decisions that may have been overturned. Subscription price: $475.00 a year. LRP Publications, 1725 K Street NW, Suite 702, Washington, DC 20006; (202) 833-1122.

The Federal Labor-Management and Employee Relations Consultant

Published by the Office of Personnel Management, this biweekly newsletter reports on Federal labor-management relations. It is intended to inform management, staff, union officials and arbitrators of new developments in the field. Feature areas include: The Arbitration Roundtable, The Labor-Management Forum, and Bookshelf. Subscription price: $28.00 a year; no single copies sold. GPO List ID FLMC. (PM 1.13:) See the GPO subscription order form.

Federal Civil Service Law and Procedures

This basic guide, edited by Ellen M. Bussey, describes the provisions of current Federal law and how the various appeal processes in the system operate and interrelate. Authorities in the field of Federal personnel law tell what is required in the event a personnel action is contemplated, taken or contested. It describes types of personnel actions that may be challenged; helps the reader assess the legitimacy of a case; and explains what, when and where to file an appeal. Supplementary information includes addresses of national and field offices, forms required for personnel actions or appeals from actions, texts of relevant statutes and a Table of Cases. 1984. 362pp. $25.00. ISBN 0-87179-448-9. BNA Books, 300 Raritan Center Parkway, C. N. 94, Edison, NJ 08818; (201) 225-1900.

Merit Systems Protection

Digest

This is a monthly publication that contains summaries and listings of current decisions issued by the United States Merit Systems Protection Board. The cases that are summarized are organized by such subject categories as: adverse actions, jurisdictions, particular employment categories, performance related actions, reductions in force, remedies, retirement, special counsel, suitability and fitness for duty examinations, mootness, practice and procedures. Subscription price: $21.00 a year. Single copy price: $2.00. GPO List ID DIG. (MS 1.11:) See the GPO subscription order form.

Federal Merit Systems Reporter

In looseleaf form, this monthly service covers all final decisions, opinions, and orders of the U.S. Merit Systems Protection Board (MSPB) since its creation under the Civil Service Reform Act of 1978. It also provides coverage of appeals from MSPB decisions to the Federal courts and to other administrative bodies. Each significant decision of the MSPB is summarized and indexed. All major decisions are reproduced in full text. In addition to case listing by parties and subject, the FMSR also contains a "Citation Tracker" for tracing the subsequent history of each case reported, as well as a "Statute/Regulation Tracker" that allows for research by specific statutory or regulatory provision. Each issue also contains a listing of MSPB decisions pending on appeal to the courts. Subscription price: $475.00 a year. LRP Publications, 1725 K Street NW, Suite 702, Washington, DC 20006; (202) 833-1122.

United States Merit Systems Protection Reporter

This subscription service covers the activities of the Merit Systems Protection Board (MSPB). It includes reports on MSPB decisions of hearings on charges of wrongdoing, employee appeals, corrective and disciplinary actions and special studies conducted by the board to maintain the integrity of the merit systems. A summary of each opinion is provided at the beginning of the full text. Enquire for price information. West Publishing Co., P.O. Box 64526, St. Paul, MN 55164; (612) 228-2500.

Management References

Federal Manager's Guide to Washington

Intended for Federal managers newly assigned to the Nation's Capital, this guide presents information about its laws, procedures, traditions, and institutions. On the personal side, it describes schools, hospitals, taxes, and even how to get a driver's license. The first section contains chapters entitled: Civil Service Reform and Reorganization, Making Policy, Knowing Your Organization, Special Concerns (e.g., conflict of interest; financial reporting requirements; Privacy, Government in the Sunshine, and Freedom of Information Acts), and Managing the Organization. The chapters contained in Section 2 are: Benefits, Why Protocol, Welcome to Washington, and Useful Telephone Numbers. 1980. 73pp. $4.75. Out-of-print. GPO S/N 006-000-01224-8. (PM 1.8:M 31/5).

The Federal Managers Quarterly

The official publication of the Federal Managers' Association (FMA), this periodical—along with the FMA's *Directory of Federal Managers Association*, the semimonthly *Congressional Actions* newsletter, *Congressional Handbook* and *Political Action Guide*—is available with membership in the FMA. For further information, contact the FMA, 2300 S. 9th Street, Suite 511, Arlington, VA 22204; (703) 892-4408.

Management

Published quarterly by the Office of Personnel Management (OPM), this magazine provides explanations of personnel management policy and reading of general interest to Government managers. Each issue contains four or five features on timely subjects, along with continuing coverage of current legal decisions, legislation, State and local notes, and summaries of personnel and general management reading and developments that affect U.S. Government management. Subscription price: $13.00 a year. Single copy price: $3.50. GPO List ID CSJ. (PM 1.11/2:) See the GPO subscription order form.

Manager's Handbook

Produced by the Office of Personnel Management, this handbook is a guide for Federal managers. It is a composite of questions and recommendations for handling hundreds of management related situations. It contains chapters on personnel management resources, hiring the right person for the job, classifying jobs, performance appraisals, training, compensation, incentive awards, performance and conduct, occupational safety and health, attendance and leave, benefits programs, affirmative employment, labor-management relations, appeals and grievances, ethics, improving productivity, and Senior Executive Sservice (SES)/executive development. Most of the material is based on laws, regulations, and administrative procedures that provide the framework for Federal personnel management. Where appropriate, a primary reference is given at the beginning of each chapter to indicate where more detailed information may be found within the Federal Personnel Manual System. In addition, footnotes and selected bibliographies are provided for those who may seek further information on a specific aspect of personnel management. 1981. 304pp. $7.00. Out-of-print. GPO S/N 006-000-01230-2. (PM 1.8:M 31/981).

Developing Executive and Management Talent: A Guide to OPM Courses, Fellowships, and Developmental Assignments

This booklet describes Office of Personnel Management (OPM) courses, fellowships, and developmental assignment programs appropriate for executive, management, and professional staff development. The courses listed in the publication are offered by the two primary training groups within OPM: the Executive Personnel and Management Development Group and the Workforce Effectiveness and Development Group. The booklet contains the following information on most courses and programs: level of executive, management, or professional staff development; length; location; description; special eligibility requirements, where appropriate; nomination procedures, where appropriate; executive and managerial competencies; the training source address and telephone number for additional information. Registration instructions, course dates, and costs are available from the training source. 1980. 63pp. $5.00. Out-of-print. GPO S/N 006-000-01189-6. (PM 1.8:Ex 3).

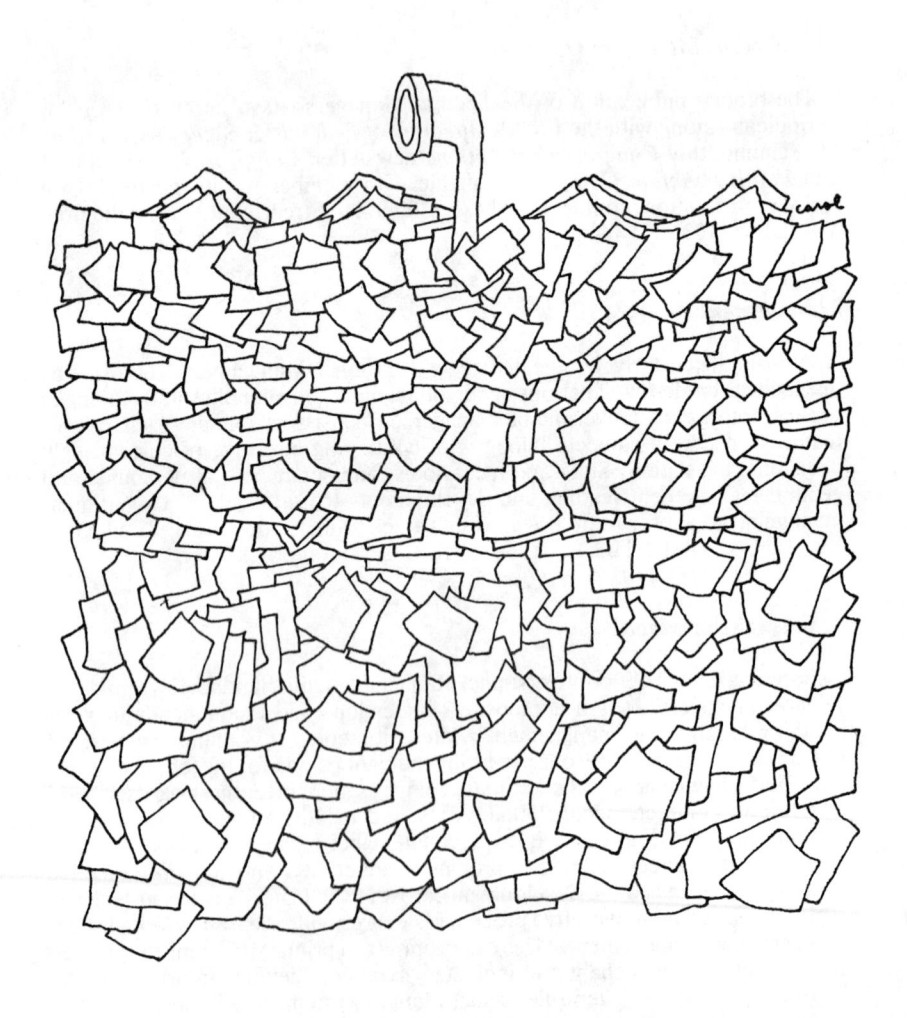

Employment Information

Job Employment Basics and References

Most Federal Government jobs are part of the competitive civil service. To get one of these jobs, you must prove yourself qualified, sometimes by taking a written test given by either the Office of Personnel Management (OPM) or by a Federal agency under the direction of the OPM. You then may compete with other applicants for a job. Figure 3-2 provides an overview of the steps in getting a competitive civil service job.

OPM accepts applications for Federal employment, other than "Excepted Service" positions (see below), based on the current and projected hiring needs of Government agencies. After you apply, OPM examiners evaluate your application to see whether you are qualified for the kind of work you want. If you are qualified, your name goes on a list with the names of other people who are qualified for the same kinds of jobs. When Government hiring officials have vacancies, they may ask OPM for the names of people qualified to fill the jobs. The best qualified applicants' names are referred from OPM lists for hiring consideration by the agency. Your chances of being hired depend on your qualifications, how fast vacancies are occurring in the area where you want to work, the number of qualified applicants who want the same kind of job, and the salary level you say you will accept.

Many factors affect whether Government agencies will be hiring and the number of jobs of various types they will fill. Among them are such factors as current policy and program priorities, budget and workload levels, labor market conditions and rates of turnover.

When there are enough qualified applicants on its lists, OPM stops accepting applications. Also, because Government hiring needs vary by location, you might be able to apply for a certain type of job in one place, but not in another.

Veterans of the armed forces are given some degree of preference in appointments to Federal Government jobs. If you are a veteran, contact OPM for details.

Some Federal organizations are excluded from the competitive civil service. They are known as "Excepted Service" agencies. These organizations fill their positions through their own hiring systems. Figure 3-3 provides a list of these Excepted Service organizations, along with addresses of their respective personnel offices. OPM does not supply information or application forms for jobs in these organizations. If you are interested in a job with one of these organizations, you must contact that organization directly.

For information on competitive service job opportunities contact one of the OPM area offices or Federal Job Information Centers listed in your telephone directory under "United States Government." OPM also provides Federal employment information to State Job Service (State Employment Security) offices, and for college-entry jobs, to college placement offices. In addition, many Federal agencies recruit directly for their own vacancies and provide information if contacted directly.

68 FEDfind

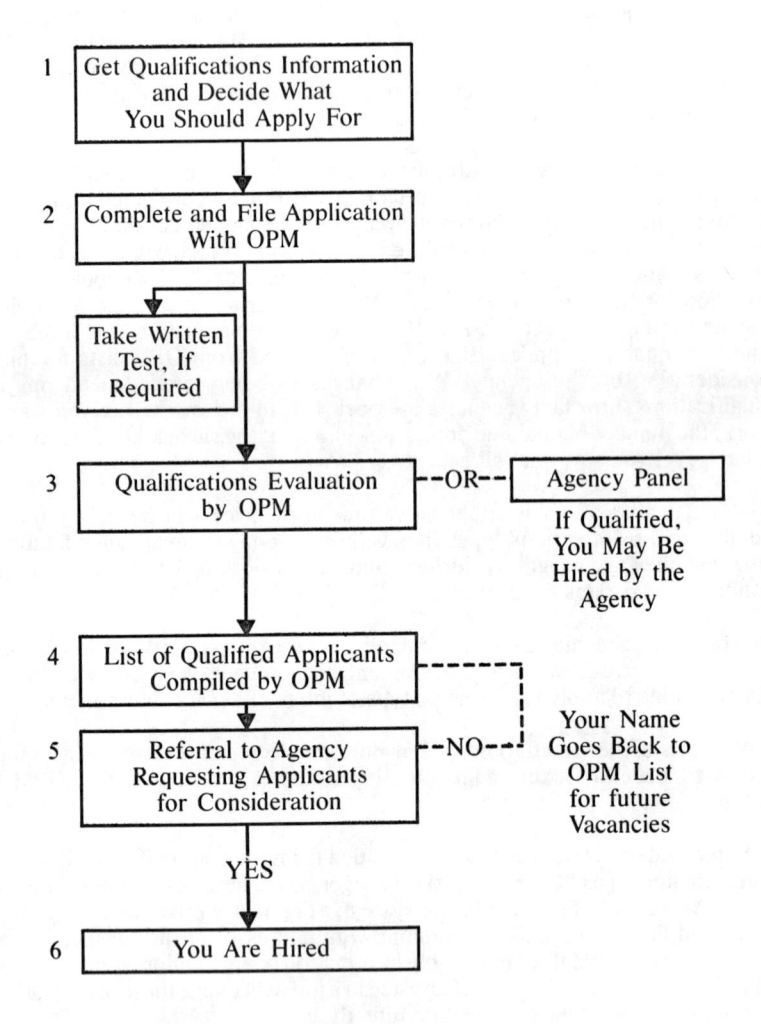

```
1  Get Qualifications Information
   and Decide What
   You Should Apply For
           │
           ▼
2  Complete and File Application
   With OPM
           │
           ▼
   Take Written
   Test, If
   Required
           │
           ▼
3  Qualifications Evaluation  --OR--  Agency Panel
   by OPM                              If Qualified,
                                       You May Be
                                       Hired by the
                                       Agency
           │
           ▼
4  List of Qualified Applicants
   Compiled by OPM          ┐
           │                │
           ▼                │      Your Name
5  Referral to Agency  --NO--┘    Goes Back to
   Requesting Applicants           OPM List
   for Consideration               for future
           │                       Vacancies
          YES
           ▼
6  You Are Hired
```

Figure 3-2. Steps to a Civil Service Job

Defense Intelligence Agency
Civilian Personnel Division
Pentagon
Washington, DC 20301

Federal Bureau of Investigation
10th Street and Pennsylvania Avenue NW
Washington, DC 20535

Federal Reserve System, Board of Governors
20th Street and Constitution Avenue NW
Washington, DC 20551

General Accounting Office
441 G Street NW, Room 4650
Washington, DC 20548

International Development Cooperation Agency
320 21st Street NW
Washington, DC 20523

National Security Agency
Fort Meade, MD 20775

U.S. Nuclear Regulatory Commission
Division of Organization of Personnel
Personal Resources and Employment Branch
Washington, DC 20555

Postal Rate Commission
Administrative Office, Room 500
2000 L Street NW
Washington, DC 20268

U.S. Postal Service
(Contact your local Postmaster.)

Tennessee Valley Authority
Division of Personnel
Chief, Employment Branch
Knoxville, TN 37902

United States Mission to the United Nations
799 United Nations Plaza
New York, NY 10017

Veterans Administration, Department of Medicine and Surgery
Employment inquiries should be sent to VA Medical Centers nationwide.

Judicial Branch of the Government (except the Administrative Office of the United States Courts and the United States Customs Court)
Apply to the individual office with the job you are interested in.

Legislative Branch of the Government (includes Senators' offices, Representatives' offices, the Library of Congress, and the Capitol, but not the Government Printing Office)
Apply to the individual office with the job you are interested in.

Figure 3-3. U.S. Government Organizations With Positions Outside the Competitive Civil Service

Working for the USA

This booklet describes briefly the Federal Civil Service system. Topics covered include the competitive service, how jobs are filled, employment requirements, benefits, pay schedules and probationary periods. 1982. 26pp. $3.50. Out-of-print. GPO S/N 006-000-01297-3. (PM 1.10:BRE-37/2).

Local Federal Job Opportunity List

The Local Federal Job Opportunity List (FJOL) provides basic information on those competitive examinations for which job applications are being accepted and tells where to obtain additional information, including application forms. This listing is based on projected Federal hiring needs, and is not a list of job openings. The listings in the Local FJOL are used to fill jobs located in the Washington, DC metropolitan and Atlantic overseas areas. Available at Office of Personnel Management area offices, State employment and college placement offices.

Senior Executive Service Vacancy Announcements

The Senior Executive Service (SES) is a corps of men and women who administer Federal programs at the top levels of the U.S. Government. This periodically updated listing, compiled by the Office of Personnel Management, provides information on SES position vacancies. Each Federal agency establishes the qualifications necessary for its SES positions, accepts and considers applications and makes selections. **FREE.** OPM List 294. Available at OPM area offices.

How to Get a Federal Job or Survive a RIF

This guide, written by David Waelde, explains the details and mechanics of Federal job openings, application procedures, career advancement, and reduction-in-force (RIF) related survival techniques. It is primarily designed for a person who either wants a civil service job or who wants to get ahead in the system. In so doing, the guide provides an overview of Federal hiring and promotion practices. 1984, 5th edition. 250pp. $15.00. Federal Research Service, Inc., P.O. Box 1059, Vienna, VA 22180; (703) 281-0200.

The 171 Reference Book

A guide by Patricia B. Wood to writing a Standard Form 171 (SF 171) for Federal Government employment or advancement, the book provides step-by-step instructions for completing the SF 171, including 225 "buzz words," master pages of expanded 171 experience blocks, instructions for completing a Supplemental Qualifications Statement (SQS), such as Knowledge, Skills and Abilities (KSA), sample 171s for various fields, and more. 1984. 131pp. $15.95 plus $1.50 for postage and handling. Workbooks, Inc., c/o The Resume Place, Inc., 810 18th Street NW, Washington, DC 20006; (202) 737-8637. Phone orders: (617) 264-4771.

Federal Career Opportunities

A biweekly compilation of current General Schedule (GS) professional and semi-professional vacancies (GS-5 and above) within Federal agencies in Washington, D.C., nationwide and overseas. The publication provides the information necessary for applicants to apply for each vacancy: job title, GS series and grade, vacancy/announcement number, closing data, address to which a Government resume application (Form SF-171) should be forwarded, and, if available, a personal contact and telephone number. Single copy price: $6.50, $6.76 for Virginia residents. Subscription rate for six biweekly issues: $36.00. Federal Research Service, Inc., P.O. Box 1059, Vienna, VA 22180; (703) 281-0200.

Federal Jobs Digest

A biweekly compilation of civil service professional job openings in the executive and legislative branches, including every area of the country and overseas. The opportunities on Capitol Hill are appointed positions on congressional staffs. Included in the initial six biweekly issues subscription is a Federal Job Kit that includes the Federal job application form (SF-171) and a 10-page booklet with instructions for preparing the application. Subscription price for six biweekly issues, including the above items: $29.00. Federal Jobs Digest, 325 Pennsylvania Avenue SE, Washington, DC 20003; (800) 543-3000.

National and Federal Legal Employment Report

A monthly listing of Federal attorney and law-related job vacancies in Washington, D.C., throughout the United States and abroad. Included for each job vacancy listing are position title, job series, and grade organization and location; announcement number, closing date, description of the position, and application submission details. It also includes a section called "JOBWATCH" that provides current information on matters related to employment in legal areas of the Government. Subscription prices: three months, $30.00; six months, $50.00; one year, $90.00. Federal Reports Inc., 1010 Vermont Avenue NW, Suite 408, Washington, DC 20005; (202) 393-3311.

Landing a Legal Job

A booklet to assist attorneys, recent law school graduates and law students in completing the various tasks associated with seeking employment in the legal field. The first seven chapters roughly parallel the sequence of tasks that virtually all jobhunters must address, from "Assessing Potential Careers" to "Following Up An Interview." The eighth focuses on landing a legal position with the Federal Government. This includes an explanation of the Federal hiring process and how to prepare the Federal job application form (SF-171) and lists many law-related positions available to those with legal training. 1985. 40pp. $9.95. Federal Reports Inc., see entry above.

Summer Legal Employment Guide

An annual guide for law students listing summer opportunities with the U.S. Government and other organizations. It is produced by the American Bar Association (ABA), in conjunction with Federal Reports. 1986 ed., September 1985. 16pp. $7.95. Federal Reports Inc., see entry above.

Capitol Jobs: An Insider's Guide to Finding a Job in Congress

This book provides information for congressional job seekers on the process of finding and getting a job working for the Congress. It includes descriptions of typical jobs as well as insight into how congressional offices operate, and tips on how to determine who makes the hiring decisions in each office. Chapters provide help in identifying the right jobs, writing a resume and cover letter, and getting through a congressional job interview. Included also are explanations of how Congress works, how a bill becomes law, and how to understand "Hillspeak." Appendixes include tips on "where to meet Hill types," descriptions of ethics laws and job "perks" for congressional staffers, key Capitol Hill telephone numbers, and other information useful to a job seeker. This book was written by Kerry Dumbaugh and Gary Serota, both veterans of Capitol Hill. A 1986 edition is planned. 1983. 120pp. $5.95 + $1.00 postage and handling. ISBN 0-9605750-4-9. Tilden Press, 1737 DeSales Street NW, Suite 300, Washington, DC 20036; (202) 638-5855.

News Publications

Federal Career Insights

A monthly newsletter that analyzes issues that affect the Federal career employee such as pay, benefits and retirement programs; interprets new rules and regulations, policy changes, legal decisions and what they mean to the Federal employee; and examines topics that are important to the Federal professional such as training opportunities, management techniques and other career development information. Subscription price: $67.00 a year. Federal Research Service, Inc., P.O. Box 1059, Vienna, VA 22180; (703) 281-0200.

Federal Employees' News Digest

A weekly newsletter, edited by Joseph Young, covering news associated with Federal employment activities and issues. Subscription price: $32.00 a year. ISSN 0430-1692. Federal Employees' News Digest, Inc., P.O. Box 7528, Falls Church, VA 22046; (703) 533-3031.

Federal Times

A weekly newspaper that addresses the events and issues related to the activities of the U.S. Government. Subscription price: $36.00 a year. Army Times Publishing Co., Springfield, VA 22159; (703) 750-2000.

FPG Weekly News Up-Date

A weekly newsletter that covers events dealing with compensation, benefits, organization and other matters of current interest to Federal employees. Subscription price: $25.00 a year. ISSN 0745-841X. Federal Personnel Publications, P.O. Box 274, Washington, DC 20044; (703) 532-1631.

74 FEDfind

Part Two

Chapter 4
Legislative Branch

Article 1, Section 8 of the Constitution of the United States defines the powers of Congress: to assess and collect taxes; to regulate commerce, both interstate and foreign; to coin money; to establish post offices and post roads; to establish courts inferior to the Supreme Court; to declare war; and, to raise and maintain an army and navy. Congress is further empowered: "To provide for calling forth the Militia to execute the Laws of the Union, suppress Insurrections and repel Invasions; . . . and To make all Laws which shall be necessary and proper for carrying into Execution the foregoing Powers." This chapter includes information resources related to the legislative branch and the process by which laws are enacted. Also included is a description of the various organizational elements of the legislative branch, along with addresses, telephone numbers and key information resources.

The Government Printing Office (GPO) makes available **FREE** a subject bibliography (SB) of publications for sale entitled *Congress* (SB-201). See the GPO SB order form.

The information resources described in this chapter are organized under the following headings.

- Organization and Operation of Congress
- Congressional District Information
- Senate Rules and Procedures
- House Rules and Procedures
- How a Bill Becomes Law
- Legislative Proceedings
- The Congressional Scene
- Biographies
- Computerized Information Resources
- Legislative Branch Organizations
    Architect of the Capital
    Congressional Budget Office
    Copyright Royalty Tribunal
    General Accounting Office
    Government Printing Office
    Library of Congress
        Congressional Research Service
        Federal Library and Information Center Committee
        National Referral Center
    Office of Technology Assessment
    United States Botanic Garden
- Executive Branch Policy Directive

Organization and Operation of Congress

In addition to the publications described in this section, Figure 4-1 is provided to help you obtain the most current information available from the congressional organizations listed.

Capitol Hill Manual

This handbook, written by Frank Cummings, explains the political and procedural course through which a legislative proposal must be steered to become a law. It also deals with power centers in Congress, money bills and nonlegislative activities in Capitol Hill offices. The book was designed for use by congressional and executive agency staff members, lobbyists, the media, D.C. corporate executive and trade association congressional liaisons. 1984, 2nd ed. 338pp. $25.00. ISBN 0-87179-355-5. BNA Books, 300 Raritan Center Parkway, C. N. 94, Edison, NJ 08818; (201) 225-1900.

CIS Legislative Histories Annual 1984

A guide to some 275 public laws enacted in 1984, this publication cites relevant publications in each law's history, including the slip law, bills, Presidential messages and statements, hearing testimony, committee reports and prints, House and Senate documents, debate from the *Congressional Record* and more. Also included is a summary of each law's major provisions, and subject, public law names and bill number indexes. Annual, June 1985. 807pp. $175.00. ISBN 0-88692-049-3. (79-158879) Congressional Information Service, Inc., 4520 East-West Highway, Suite 800, Bethesda, MD 20814; (800) 638-8380 or (301) 654-1550.

Congress and Its Members

Members of Congress wear two hats—a Washington hat and an at-home hat. This book explains how the legislative branch operates and how Members manage both roles. The authors, Roger H. Davidson and Walter J. Oleszek of the Congressional Research Service, consider topics such as leadership and parties, campaigns, committees, staffs, lobbies and the decision-making process. 1985, 2nd ed. 477pp. $19.95 (cloth), ISBN 0-87187-345-1; $14.95 (paper), ISBN 0-87187-325-7. (85-463) CQ Press, 1414 22nd Street NW, Washington, DC 20037; (202) 887-8620.

Congressional Procedures and the Policy Process

This book describes the organization, rules and procedures of the U.S. House of Representatives and the Senate. It examines how the contemporary Congress makes laws and how its rules and procedures shape public policy. By Walter J. Oleszek of the Congressional Research Service. 1984. 289pp. $16.95 (cloth), ISBN 0-87187-318-4; $10.95 (paper), ISBN 0-87187-281-1. (83-20860) CQ Press, see entry above.

Senate Committees

Agriculture, Nutrition and Forestry (SR-328A) .... (202) 224-2035
Appropriations (SD-118) .... (202) 224-3471
Armed Services (SR-222) .... (202) 224-3871
Banking, Housing and Urban Affairs (SD-534) .... (202) 224-7391
Budget (SD-621) .... (202) 224-0642
Commerce, Science and Transportation (SD-508) .... (202) 224-5115
Energy and Natural Resources (SD-360) .... (202) 224-4971
Environment and Public Works (SD-410) .... (202) 224-6176
Finance (SD-219) .... (202) 224-4515
Foreign Relations (SD-440) .... (202) 224-4651
Governmental Affairs (SD-340) .... (202) 224-4751
Judiciary (SD-224) .... (202) 224-5225
Labor and Human Resources (SD-428) .... (202) 224-5375
Rules and Administration (SR-305) .... (202) 224-6352
Small Business (SR-428A) .... (202) 224-5175
Veterans' Affairs (SR-414) .... (202) 224-9126

House Committees

Agriculture (1301 LHOB) .... (202) 225-2171
Appropriations (H218 CAP) .... (202) 225-2771
Armed Services (2120 RHOB) .... (202) 225-4151
Banking, Finance and Urban Affairs (2129 RHOB) .... (202) 225-4247
Budget (214 HOB Annex #1) .... (202) 226-7200
District of Columbia (1310 CHOB) .... (202) 225-4457
Education and Labor (2181 RHOB) .... (202) 225-4527
Energy and Commerce (2125 RHOB) .... (202) 225-2927
Foreign Affairs (2170 RHOB) .... (202) 225-5021
Government Operations (2157 RHOB) .... (202) 225-5051
House Administration (H326 CAP) .... (202) 225-2061
Interior and Insular Affairs (1324 LHOB) .... (202) 225-2761
Judiciary (2137 RHOB) .... (202) 225-3951
Merchant Marine and Fisheries (1334 LHOB) .... (202) 225-4047
Post Office and Civil Service (309 CHOB) .... (202) 225-4054
Public Works and Transportation (2165 RHOB) .... (202) 225-4472
Rules (H312 CAP) .... (202) 225-9486
Science and Technology (2321 RHOB) .... (202) 225-6371
Small Business (2361 RHOB) .... (202) 225-5821
Standards of Official Conduct (HT-2 CAP) .... (202) 225-7103
Veterans' Affairs (335 CHOB) .... (202) 225-3527
Ways and Means (1102 LHOB) .... (202) 225-3625

Figure 4-1. Senate and House Committees

Senate Select Committees

Aging (SD-G33) .... (202) 224-5364
Ethics (SH-220) .... (202) 224-2981
Indian Affairs (SH-838) .... (202) 224-2251
Intelligence (SH-211) .... (202) 224-1700

House Select Committees

Aging (712 HOB Annex #1) .... (202) 226-3375
Children, Youth and Families (385 HOB Annex #2) .... (202) 226-7660
Hunger (507 HOB Annex #2) .... (202) 226-5470
Intelligence (H405 CAP) .... (202) 225-4121
Narcotics Abuse and Control (234 HOB Annex #2) .... (202) 226-3040

Joint Committees

Economic (SD-G01) .... (202) 224-5171
Library of Congress (SR-305) .... (202) 224-0291
Printing (SH-818) .... (202) 224-5241
Taxation (SD-204) .... (202) 224-5561

Location of Buildings

SD—Dirksen Senate Office Building, 1st and C Streets NE
SH—Hart Senate Office Building, 2nd and C Streets NE
SR—Russell Senate Office Building, 1st and C Streets NE
CHOB—Cannon House Office Building, 1st and Independence Avenue SE
LHOB—Longworth House Office Building, Independence and New Jersey Avenue SE
RHOB—Rayburn House Office Building, Independence and South Capitol Street SW
HOB Annex #1—New Jersey Avenue and C Street SE
HOB Annex #2—2nd and D Streets SW
CAP—The Capitol Building

Correspondence to members and committees of Congress may be sent c/o either the U.S. House of Representatives, Washington, DC 20515 or U.S. Senate, Washington, DC 20510. U.S. Capitol Switchboard (202) 224-3121.

Figure 4-1. Senate and House Committees—Continued

Guide to Congress

A reference on the origins, history, organization and working procedures of Congress, the guide explains congressional powers, pay, campaign financing, lobbying and ethics. This edition includes information on the revised committee structure and the increased power of subcommittees, campaign finances and the rise of political action committees (PACs), and congressional economic policy making. 1982, 3rd ed. 1,185pp. $100.00. ISBN 0-87187-239-0. (82-14148) Congressional Quarterly Inc., see entry above.

Congressional Publications: A Research Guide to Legislation, Budgets, and Treaties

This work is a research guide to how information in general—and printed matter in particular—is transmitted to, within, and by the U.S. Congress. Congressional publications are presented in the context of the whole legislative process. The publication begins with an examination of the nature of congressional authorship and provides an overview of the flow and control of information in the legislative environment. It then describes the political setting and presents a systematic account of the legislative process, explores background studies prepared by and for legislative committees, analyzes the key role of committees as workshops and conduits of information, describes House and Senate chamber proceedings, analyzes a public budget as a political document and explains the treaty-making process. 1983. 195pp. $22.50. ISBN 0-87287-358-7. (82-18652) Libraries Unlimited, P.O. Box 263, Littleton, CO 80160; (303) 770-1220.

Congressional Roll Call 1984

An annual chronology and analysis of votes in the House and Senate, this edition covers the second session of the 98th Congress. It is indexed so you may determine how a particular Member of Congress voted on key issues. February 1985. 225pp. $14.95. ISBN 0-87187-347-8. (72-77849) Congressional Quarterly Inc., 1414 22nd Street NW, Washington, DC 20037; (202) 887-8620.

Porter's Guide to Congressional Roll Call Votes

A source of information for roll call votes in the House and Senate. Each vote is annotated to clarify the significance of the bill, amendment or resolution. A subject index is included to eliminate the need for knowledge of the formal title of the bill. 1983 House, 1983 Senate, 1984 House, 1984 Senate. Single volume, $80.00; two volumes or more, $72.50 each. The publisher also provides legislative monitoring, roll call vote tracking and analysis, opposition research, legislative histories and computer system evaluation. Legislative Information Group, 1718 Connecticut Avenue, Suite 310, Washington, DC 20009; (301) 270-8939.

The Intern Resource Guide

This manual, written by Sue Grabowski, is designed for use by interns and other congressional employees who have responsibility for legislative research, monitoring and tracking. 1980. 48pp. $5.00. Congressional Management Foundation, 333 Pennsylvania Avenue SE, Washington, DC 20003; (202) 546-0100.

Setting Course: A Congressional Management Guide

This manual, edited by Burdett A. Loomis of the Congressional Management Project, is designed to assist a first-term Member of Congress in becoming an effective manager of his or her office. The book includes guidance in setting up an office, planning and handling information. 1984. 265pp. $10.00. The American University, Ward Circle Building, Room 201, Washington, DC 20016; (202) 885-3848.

Storming Washington: An Intern's Guide to National Government

A booklet, by Stephen E. Frantzich, to help undergraduate students decide whether a Washington internship should be part of their undergraduate experience and to make the most of the experience, should they pursue it. The publication provides tools for competent observation and analysis in the Federal Government environment. 1986, 2nd ed. approx. 52pp. $3.00. ISBN 0-915654-72-5. American Political Science Association, 1527 New Hampshire Avenue NW, Washington, DC 20036; (202) 483-2512.

The United States Congress: A Bibliography

This reference provides bibliographic listings of books, articles, essays, dissertations, theses and periodicals with material on the Senate and House of Representatives published in English in the last 200 years. More than 5,000 citations are classified according to 14 major topics. By Robert U. Goehlert and John R. Sayre. 1982. 376pp. $50.00. ISBN 0-02-911900-6. Macmillan Professional and Library Services, 100B Brown Street, Riverside, NJ 08075; (800) 257-5755 or (609) 461-6500.

Vital Statistics on Congress, 1984-1985

Statistical information on Members of Congress, elections, campaign finance, committees, staff and operating expenses, workload, budgeting and voting alignments is presented in this book. Most tables include information that goes back several decades or more so that changes and trends may be seen. Compiled by Norman J. Ornstein, et al. 1984. 261pp. $19.95 (cloth), ISBN 0-8447-3560-4; $9.95 (paper), ISBN 0-8447-3564-7. American Enterprise Institute, 1150 17th Street NW, Washington, DC 20036; (800) 424-2873 or (202) 862-5869.

Congressional District Information

In addition to the following references that provide information on congressional districts, information on Members of Congress and the social, economic and political climate of the States and congressional districts may be found in the *Almanac of American Politics* and *Politics in America*, described in the "Biographies" section of this chapter.

Congressional District Atlas: Districts of the 99th Congress

Prepared by the Bureau of the Census, this biennial atlas presents maps showing boundaries of congressional districts for the 99th Congress of the

United States, 1985–86. It includes listings that identify the congressional districts in which counties and incorporated municipalities within each State are located. Maps are provided for the District of Columbia, Puerto Rico and outlying areas. The atlas is issued periodically, usually whenever a number of States has changed congressional boundaries because of a decennial census reapportionment, a State initiative or court-ordered redistricting. Supplements will be printed if any States redistrict for the 100th Congress. 1985, 10th ed. 583pp. $15.00. GPO S/N 003-024-06132-5. (C 3.62/5:985) See the GPO order form.

Congressional Districts in the 1980s

A guide to congressional districts, this book presents their key political, social and economic characteristics. Descriptive and statistical profiles are presented for each State and congressional district. The reapportionment and redistricting process that followed the 1980 census is described for each State. Additional information for each district includes lists of universities, newspapers, commercial television stations, military installations, nuclear power plants and industries. 1983. 632pp. $95.00. ISBN 0-87187-264-1. (83-18988) Congressional Quarterly Inc., 1414 22nd Street NW, Washington, DC 20037; (202) 887-8620.

Congressional District Profiles, 98th Congress

This Bureau of the Census report supplements and serves as a national summary for *Congressional Districts of the 98th Congress*, described below. This report provides a brief profile of each district and a means of comparing districts. Tables include population by age, sex and race; family income; poverty; employment; and housing. 1983. 58pp. $3.50. Out-of-print. GPO S/N 003-024-05769-7. (C 3.223/12:80-S1-11).

Congressional Districts of the 98th Congress

A Bureau of the Census publication issued as a series of separate State reports, this item presents 1980 population and housing data by congressional district. Information on States affected by redistricting for the 99th Congress has been revised. Prices vary for each State report. See the GPO order form.

Congressional District ZIP Codes: 99th Congress

Section 1 is a list—by congressional district—that indicates ZIP codes within that district; Section 2 is arranged in ZIP code order and indicates the congressional district in which each is located. Information on any State may be ordered separately. Prices vary for each State report. Tyson Capitol Institute, 7735 Old Georgetown Road, Bethesda, MD 20814; (301) 652-4185.

The Historical Atlas of United States Congressional Districts, 1789-1983

This atlas presents the history of representation in Congress for every city, county and State since 1789. Part I provides the history, development and theory of geographical representation in Congress, and explains how the atlas may be used as a tool by researchers, students and teachers. The heart of the book, Part

82   **FEDfind**

II, contains 97 national-scale maps of the 1st through the 97th Congress, with lists of the representatives of each district. Part III provides a history of changing State congressional boundaries from admission to present and an alphabetical list of every individual who ever served in the House of Representatives and the session of Congress served. 1982. 302pp. $150.00. ISBN 0-02-920150-0. (82-70583) Macmillan Professional and Library Services, 100B Brown Street, Riverside, NJ 08075; (800) 257-5755 or (609) 461-6500.

Senate Rules and Procedures

These publications provide authoritative information on current and historical practices and precedents in the U.S. Senate.

Enactment of a Law: Procedural Steps in the Legislative Process

Prepared by the Parliamentarian of the Senate, this document describes in detail the legislative process in terms of the procedural steps by which a bill may become a law. It discusses the composition and powers of the Congress and the origin of legislative ideas. It also traces the path an idea takes on its way to becoming a law. Included are examples of bills, acts, reports and conference reports. 1979. 28pp. $3.50. GPO S/N 052-071-00580-3. (X 96-1:S.doc.15) See the GPO order form.

Senate Legislative Procedural Flow (and Related House Action) (Bills, Resolutions, Nominations and Treaties)

The material in this publication was originally intended as a flow diagram explaining the legislative process for use in the LEGIS (Legislative Information and Status System) computer system. The path of a bill from its introduction to its public distribution as a law is followed through the Senate, the House of Representatives, the conference committee and the President. Treaties and Presidential nominations are likewise examined in their progression to ratification and confirmation, respectively. 1978. 98pp. $4.75. GPO S/N 052-002-00033-8. (Y 1.3:L 52/978) See the GPO order form.

Senate Manual

Prepared at the beginning of each Congress by the Senate Committee on Rules and Administration, this manual contains the standing rules, orders, laws and resolutions affecting the Senate. It also includes historical lists of Senators by State and year of election, Cabinet members, and Supreme Court Justices. It is issued each Congress as Senate Document No. 1. 1984. 887pp. $14.00. GPO S/N 052-071-00677-0. (Y 1.1/3:98-1) See the GPO order form.

Senate Procedure: Precedents and Practices

This is a compilation of the rules of the Senate, portions of laws affecting Senate procedure, rulings by the Presiding Officer and established practices of the Senate. An appendix includes suggested forms for various procedures, e.g., filing motions or filing conference reports. 1981. 1,339pp. $15.00. GPO S/N 052-071-00623-1. (Y 1.1/3:97-2) See the GPO order form.

House Rules and Procedures

These publications provide authoritative information on current and historical practices and precedents in the U.S. House of Representatives.

Constitution, Jefferson's Manual and Rules of the House of Representatives of the United States

Prepared for each Congress by the Parliamentarian of the House, this manual contains the fundamental source material for parliamentary procedure used in the House of Representatives, 99th Congress. In addition to the Constitution and *Jefferson's Manual*, it includes principal rulings and precedents, the history and jurisdiction of each legislative committee and other matters. 1985. 1,147pp. $19.00. GPO S/N 052-071-00686-9. (Y 1.1/7:98-277) See the GPO order form.

Deschler's Precedents of the United States House of Representatives

Lewis Deschler, Parliamentarian of the House during 1928–1974, was authorized by public law to compile a comprehensive collection of the parliamentary precedents of the House of Representatives. These volumes set forth and analyze precedents from 1936 through the first session of the 93rd Congress (1973). When completed, the series is expected to include eight to ten volumes. All but Volume 6 is out-of-print.

- Volume 1, Chapters 1–6. 1977. 662pp. $10.00. GPO S/N 052-001-00125-7. (X 94-2:H.doc.661/v.1)
- Volume 2, Chapters 7–9. 1977. 888pp. $12.00. GPO S/N 052-001-00144-3. (X 94-2:H.doc.661/v.2)
- Volume 3, Chapters 10–14. 1979. 729pp. $13.00. GPO S/N 052-001-00156-7. (XTH94-2:H.doc.661/v.3)
- Volume 4, Chapters 15–17. 1981. 953pp. $20.00. GPO S/N 052-001-00157-5. (XTH94-2:H.doc.661/v.4)
- Volume 5, Chapters 18–20. 1982. 550pp. $16.00. GPO S/N 052-001-00189-3. (XTH94-2:H.doc.661/v.5)
- Volume 6, 1983. 732pp. $21.00. GPO S/N 052-001-00208-3. (X 94-2:H.doc.661/v.6)

Procedure in the United States House of Representatives, 97th Congress: A Summary of the Modern Precedents and Practices of the United States House, 86th Congress–97th Congress

Formerly known as Deschler's *Procedures*, this one-volume publication is a summary of procedures of the House. Prepared by the Parliamentarian of the House, it also provides a condensed version of the modern precedents of the House from the 86th through the beginning of the 97th Congress. 880pp. $14.00. Out-of-print. GPO S/N 052-001-00207-5. (Y 1.2:P 94/2).

Gavel to Gavel

Intended for viewers of the House of Representatives proceedings carried by the Cable Satellite Public Affairs Network (C-SPAN), this guide provides a practical, simplified explanation of the various aspects of observing the activities of the House on television. By Alan Green and Bill Hogan. 1982. 40pp. Single copy **FREE**. The Benton Foundation, 1776 K Street NW, Suite 900, Washington, DC 20006; (202) 429-7350.

C-SPAN Update

A weekly newspaper of the Cable Satellite Public Affairs Network (C-SPAN), a private and non-profit cable cooperative, that includes articles and schedule information. The core of C-SPAN's programming is its live, gavel-to-gavel coverage of the House of Representatives, whenever it is in session. C-SPAN also televises congressional hearings, major conventions, press conferences, public issues forums, National Press Club addresses and a variety of special events taking place in Washington, DC and around the country. Subscription price: $12.00 a year. ISSN 0746-3812. C-SPAN, P.O. Box 75298, Washington, DC 20013; (202) 737-3220.

How a Bill Becomes Law

Described here are publications that focus on the path of legislation through Congress. Figures 4-2 and 4-3 depict, respectively, how a bill becomes a law, and the key offices, addresses and telephone numbers helpful in tracking legislation.

How Federal Laws Are Made

A step-by-step description of the Federal lawmaking process, this guide follows the law-making process from introduction of a bill in Congress, to enactment into law, to the issuance of agency regulations. A special section describes the executive and congressional budget process. Also included are guides to the use of the *U.S. Code*, *Congressional Record*, *Federal Register* and *Code of Federal Regulations*; a telephone directory of House and Senate committees and other congressional and *Federal Register* numbers; and a section on how to follow Federal laws and regulations. 1985. 135pp. $10.95. ISBN 0-942008-38-3. WANT Publishing Co., 1511 K Street NW, Washington, DC 20005; (202) 783-1887.

How Our Laws Are Made

Prepared by the House of Representatives, this booklet provides a plain-language explanation of the Federal lawmaking process, from the origin of an idea for a legislative proposal through its publication as a statute. 1980. 79pp. $4.50. GPO S/N 052-071-00617-6. (X 96-2:H.doc.352) See the GPO order form.

Legislative Branch 85

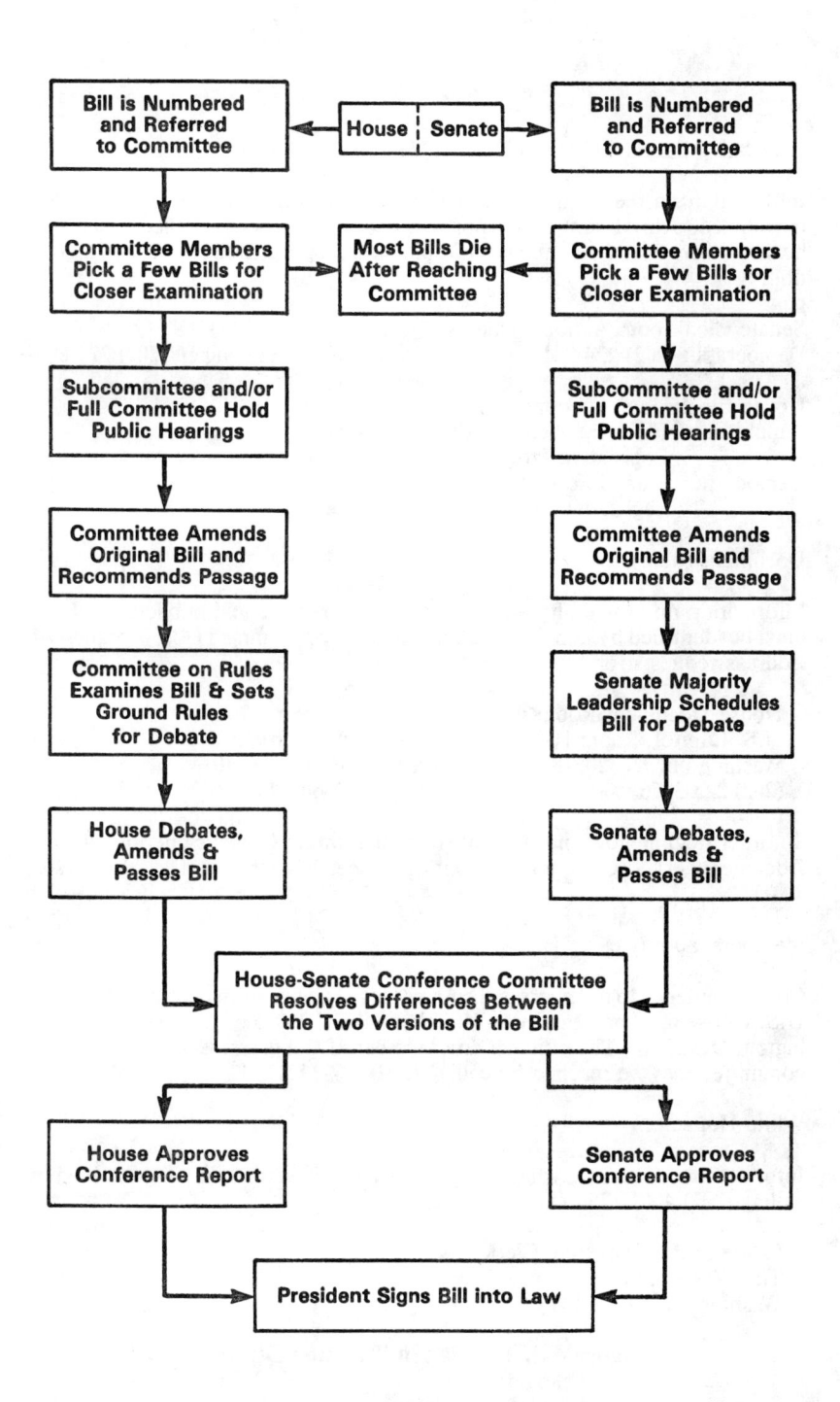

```
         ┌─────────────┐                    ┌─────────────┐
         │Bill Numbered│◄──House│Senate──►  │Bill Numbered│
         │and Referred │                    │and Referred │
         │to Committee │                    │to Committee │
         └──────┬──────┘                    └──────┬──────┘
                ▼                                  ▼
      ┌──────────────┐   ┌──────────────┐   ┌──────────────┐
      │Committee     │──►│Most Bills Die│◄──│Committee     │
      │Members Pick  │   │After Reaching│   │Members Pick  │
      │Few Bills     │   │Committee     │   │Few Bills     │
      └──────┬───────┘   └──────────────┘   └──────┬───────┘
             ▼                                     ▼
      (Subcommittee Hearings) ... (continues down both sides)
```

House Path	Senate Path
Bill is Numbered and Referred to Committee	Bill is Numbered and Referred to Committee
Committee Members Pick a Few Bills for Closer Examination	Committee Members Pick a Few Bills for Closer Examination
Subcommittee and/or Full Committee Hold Public Hearings	Subcommittee and/or Full Committee Hold Public Hearings
Committee Amends Original Bill and Recommends Passage	Committee Amends Original Bill and Recommends Passage
Committee on Rules Examines Bill & Sets Ground Rules for Debate	Senate Majority Leadership Schedules Bill for Debate
House Debates, Amends & Passes Bill	Senate Debates, Amends & Passes Bill

House-Senate Conference Committee Resolves Differences Between the Two Versions of the Bill

| House Approves Conference Report | Senate Approves Conference Report |

President Signs Bill into Law

Figure 4-2. How a Bill Becomes Law

Legislative Status Office: (202) 225-1772

Information on the status of legislation in either the House or Senate, when introduced, a brief summary, sponsors and cosponsors, whether Committee hearings have been held, number of Committee reports, and any related legislation.

Senate Cloakroom Announcements
Democratic: (202) 224-8541   Republican: (202) 224-8601

House Cloakroom Announcements
Republican: Floor Information, (202) 225-7430
             Legislative Program, (202) 225-2020
Democratic: Floor Information, (202) 225-7400
             Legislative Program, (202) 225-1600

Document rooms:

Information on availability and copies of bills, reports and public laws. Laws must be identified by number, and a self-addressed, gummed label is requested. Address requests for copies to:

House Document Room   Senate Document Room
U.S. Capitol, Room H-226   Hart Building, Room B-4
Washington, DC 20515   Washington, DC 20510
(202) 225-3456   (202) 224-7860

To order documents from the Government Printing Office: Superintendent of Documents, U.S. Government Printing Office, Washington, DC 20402; (202) 783-3238

Members' addresses:

Correspondence to members and committees of Congress may be sent c/o either U.S. House of Representatives, Washington, DC 20515 or U.S. Senate, Washington, DC 20510. The office of any Member of Congress, Committee or Subcommittee may be reached by calling (202) 224-3121.

White House:

Information concerning when a bill was signed or vetoed may be obtained by calling (202) 456-2226 or by writing to:

Office of the Executive Clerk
The White House
Washington, DC 20500

Figure 4-3. Legislation Tracking Directory

Legislative Proceedings

The following items are useful in tracking the proceedings of the Senate and the House of Representatives.

Congressional Record

The edited transcript of Senate and House floor proceedings, this document includes conference reports, extensions of remarks, the numbers and short titles of bills with a statement of their background and purpose, floor speeches and an index. Further, it highlights and summarizes the body of the text in the back of each document. The "Daily Digest" section summarizes selected floor and committee actions, as well as lists scheduled hearings. An index is issued every two weeks and includes a history of bills and resolutions introduced in both chambers. Published daily when Congress is in session. Subscription price: $218.00 a year. A special six-month subscription is available for $109.00. Single copy price: $1.00. GPO List ID CR. (X/a.:) See the GPO subscription order form.

Congressional Record Abstracts—Master and Topical Editions

A publication issued every day following a meeting of Congress. It provides a topical index to, and abstract of, material appearing in the *Congressional Record* under 350 index terms grouped into 40 major subject and format sections. Each issue includes a subject finder guide. For more specific information needs, the publisher prepares topical abstracts covering energy, national defense, foreign affairs and ecology. Customized service is available. Annual subscription prices: master edition, $725.00; four topical editions, $495.00, $525.00, 495.00, and $495.00, respectively. Prices on selected profiles provided on request. Microfiche copies of the *Record* are available daily for $385.00 a year. It is available online through DIALOG and SDC. National Standards Association, 5161 River Road, Bethesda, MD 20816; (800) 638-8094 or (301) 951-1305.

Congressional Monitor

A daily report that provides a detailed schedule of congressional action on the floors of the House and the Senate and in committees and subcommittees. Coverage includes the agenda for the current week's congressional hearings and witness lists, as well as *Congress Daily*, a brief analysis of the previous day's action and a look at the next day. A weekly supplement, *Congress in Print* (available separately at $165.00 per year) lists printed committee hearings, reports, prints and staff studies released during the week. The basic service includes a telephone information service and a 24-hour tape recording featuring highlights of the day's activities on Capitol Hill. Subscription price: $887.00 a year. The weekly version of this daily is the *Weekly Congressional Monitor*. It lists every committee and subcommittee hearing scheduled for the week, and for two to three months in advance. Subscription price: $425.00 a year. The *Congressional Record Scanner*, a daily listing under basic subject categories of all items appearing in the *Congressional Record*, is available for an additional $414.00 a year. Congressional Quarterly Inc., 1414 22nd Street NW, Washington, DC 20037; (202) 887-8620.

Calendars of the U.S. House of Representatives and History of Legislation

Prepared by the Clerk of the House, this weekly is issued every Monday while Congress is in session. It lists all House and Senate bills on which some action has been taken, provides a history of these bills, lists the status of all bills in conference and provides a table that summarizes the status of major bills. A weekly subject index is also included. Subscription price: $162.00 per session of Congress, no back issues furnished, and only the final issue of a session is sold on a single copy basis. GPO List ID CUSHR. (Y 1.2/2:) See the GPO subscription order form.

Digest of Public General Bills and Resolutions

Prepared by the Congressional Research Service, a division of the Library of Congress, this subscription publication consists of cumulative issues, including a final issue upon adjournment of Congress. It provides brief accounts of public bills and resolutions introduced in Congress and gives status of bills acted upon and enacted. It is indexed by public law number, sponsor, subject, title and bill number. Subscription price: $43.00 per session of Congress. Single copies vary in price. GPO List ID DPGB. (LC 14.6:) See the GPO subscription order form.

Major Legislation of the Congress

The Congressional Research Service (CRS), a division of the Library of Congress, prepares this subscription publication that summarizes selected major legislation of the current Congress by subject and includes background on the issue, information on the content, and the status of major bills affecting that issue. The information is extracted from issue briefs prepared by CRS. The service consists of approximately 10 irregularly-published issues per Congress (two-year period). Subscription price: $30.00 per Congress. Single copies vary in price. GPO List ID MLC. (LC 14.18:) See the GPO subscription order form.

CIS/Index

The monthly Congressional Information Service, Inc.'s *CIS/Index* provides summaries of congressional hearings, committee prints, reports, documents and special publications. It includes an annual cumulation—arranged by committee—that summarizes these publications. Included are indexes by subject, name, witness, title, bill number, report and document numbers, and in the annual volume, by public law number. Full-text microfiche reproductions of publications covered by the *Index* are available. Subscription rates available upon request. Congressional Information Service, Inc., 4520 East-West Highway, Suite 800, Bethesda, MD 20814; (800) 638-8380 or (301) 654-1550.

CCH Congressional Index

This looseleaf service reports the status of all pending legislation. Included are indexes by subject, sponsor, and companion and identical bill number. Congressional actions on reorganization plans, treaties and nominations are indicated. The counts on roll call and recorded teller votes are given by party, with a list of Members who did not vote with the majority of their party. Measures enacted are indexed by public law number, bill number, subject and sponsor. A chronological list of measures vetoed is provided. Another chronological list of hearings by committee indicates whether the transcript has been prepared. Published weekly while Congress is in session. Enquire for price information. Commerce Clearing House, Inc., 4025 W. Peterson Avenue, Chicago, IL 60646; (312) 583-8500.

Congressional Quarterly Weekly Report

Each issue reports on all major legislative action, the President's legislative proposals and analyses of the Supreme Court's decisions, as well as covers political and lobbying activities. A quarterly index by names and subjects is prepared for all preceding issues during the year. The annual *Congressional Quarterly Almanac* is also included. Subscribers also gain telephone access to CQ's Research Department. Questions of fact on politics, Congress, the Federal Government and national issues are provided at no charge. Subscription price: $839.00 a year. Special rates are available to government agencies and public libraries; call (202) 887-8620 for details. Congressional Quarterly Inc., 1414 22nd Street NW, Washington, DC 20037; (202) 887-8620.

The Congressional Scene

The following periodicals cover legislative and policy making matters and activities of the Congress.

Campaigns & Elections

"The Journal of Political Action" is a quarterly source of information on campaign strategies, tactics and technologies. It provides articles on managing volunteers, raising and spending money and how to deal with the regulatory aspects of campaigning and electioneering. A special feature entitled "Campaigns & Computers" discusses what to buy and what to rent for automated direct mail, campaign polling and budgeting. Subscription price: $48.00 a year. Campaigns & Elections, 1331 Pennsylvania Avenue NW, Washington, DC 20004; (202) 244-8959.

Campaign Practices Reports

A biweekly newsletter and reference service that covers events that affect campaign law and finance, this newsletter includes information on campaign practices and finance issues and developments affecting them. The reference service, updated monthly, provides a complete text of all laws, rules, guidelines and advisory opinions issued from the Federal Election Commission, Congress or the courts. Subscription price: $399.00 a year; newsletter only, $256.00 a year. Congressional Quarterly Inc., 1414 22nd Street NW, Washington, DC 20037; (202) 887-8620.

CongresScan

This subscription service reports on current congressional publications about legislative issues and how to obtain them. It includes an annual guide to more than 500 reports (organized by subject) and monthly updates for a year. The congressional publications selected for inclusion focus on issues important to business; they analyze issues, review bills, identify key players, discuss pros and cons, report major events and list resources. The service is designed to help identify emerging issues, track legislation, prepare position papers and speeches. Subscription price: $240.00 a year. Policy Analysis Co., Inc., 1090 Vermont Avenue NW, Suite 1000, Washington, DC 20005; (202) 682-1682.

Congressional Digest

Each issue features a pro/con discussion of a current legislative problem, such as space weapons policy, criminal sentencing policy and Federal budget deficit. An overview of each issue precedes the discussions and notes recent congressional action. Issued 10 times per year; yearly index published with the December issue. Subscription price: $22.00 a year, single copy price: $2.50. Congressional Digest Corp., 3231 P Street NW, Washington, DC 20007; (202) 333-7332.

Congressional Insight

This weekly newsletter analyzes the pressures, people and politics that affect Capitol Hill decisions. It identifies the important legislative work planned for the following week and month, and includes key legislation being marked up in committee, who is supporting it and who is fighting it. Subscription price: $258.00 a year. Congressional Quarterly Inc., 1414 22nd Street NW, Washington, DC 20037; (202) 887-8620.

Legislative Branch 91

National Journal

Articles in this weekly magazine provide commentaries on activities of Congress, the White House and executive agencies. Features such as "At a Glance" provide a checklist of major issues. Other columns such as "Washington Update" and "Opinion Outlook" report on trends and policies in the Federal Government and politics. Includes semiannual indexes. Enquire for price information. National Journal Inc., 1730 M Street NW, Suite 1100, Washington, DC 20036; (800) 424-2921 or (202) 857-1400.

Private Bills

Private bills pertain to particular groups or individuals. Issued irregularly. Subscription price: $375.00 per session of Congress. No single copies sold or back issues furnished. GPO List ID PRB. (X 99-1:Priv. bill) See the GPO subscription order form.

Public Bills, Resolutions and Amendments

Public bills are those that, if enacted into law, would affect people in general or affect Government organization. This subscription service provides copies of bills, resolutions and amendments that are proposed in Congress. Subscription price: $7,957.00 per session of Congress. No single copies or back issues furnished. GPO List ID PBRA. (X 99-1:Pub. bill) See the GPO subscription order form.

Public Laws

A public law, often referred to as a slip law, is the initial publication of a Federal law upon enactment and is printed as soon as possible after approval by the President. With a public law number assigned, the document is added to the U.S. Statutes at Large. Margin notes, U.S. Code classifications, approval dates and legislative history references are also indicated. Issued irregularly. Subscription price: $104.00 per session of Congress. Single copies vary in price. GPO List ID P9901. (GS 4.110:99/) See the GPO subscription order form.

Reports on Public Bills

This subscription service provides the congressional reports issued on public bills. Irregularly issued. Subscription price: $1,098.00 per session of Congress. No single copies, or back issues furnished. GPO List ID RPUB. (X 99-1:) See the GPO subscription order form.

Roll Call: The Newspaper of Capitol Hill

Published every Thursday while Congress is in session, this publication provides human interest stories and information on social events involving Members of Congress and staff. It also highlights legislative activity. The column "Congressional Casualty List" provides a cumulative listing of Members who have died, announced retirement, resigned, were defeated in a primary election or regular election, or are seeking other office. Subscription price: $15.00 a year. Roll Call, 236 Massachusetts Avenue NE, Suite 204, Washington, DC 20002; (202) 546-3080.

Biographies

The Almanac of American Politics 1986

This biennial almanac, written by Michael Barone and Grant Ujifusa, is a guide to American politics, giving facts and figures about Congressional and State Districts, Senators, Representatives and State Governors. The book describes how the politicians won their offices, the nature of their constituencies, their votes on key issues and the ratings they receive from organizations across the liberal-conservative spectrum. Also included is information on the impact of the 1980 census on reapportionment and redistricting, and major changes in national demographics that would influence American politics in the 1980s. July 1985. 1,423pp. $34.95 (cloth), $28.95 (paper), plus $2.00 per volume for postage and handling. ISBN 0-89234-030-4 (cloth), 0-89234-031-2 (paper). National Journal Inc., P.O. Box 6159, Washington, DC 20044; (800) 424-2921 or (202) 857-1491.

Politics in America 1986

A biennial guide, this book provides profiles on each Senator and Representative, information on their past campaigns and where they stand on issues. The book evaluates the performance of each Member of Congress, both in Washington and at home in the district or State—including legislative influence, personal style and effectiveness in working with colleagues and for constituents. Beyond the personal profiles, the book describes each State and Congressional District—the political heritage, ethnic makeup, constituent concerns and other factors that influence who is elected to Congress. Edited by Alan Ehrenhalt. August 1985. 1,758pp. $29.95. ISBN 0-87187-375-3. (85-12777) Congressional Quarterly Inc., 1414 22nd Street NW, Washington, DC 20037; (202) 887-8620.

Members of Congress Since 1789

A volume of basic biographical data on all persons who have served in Congress, this book includes Members elected to the 99th Congress, 1985–86. The book contains summary and statistical material about membership, including age, religion, occupations, women and black Members, turnover and shifts between chambers. The more than 11,000 brief biographies of individuals include birth and death dates, party affiliation, State, years of congressional service and major offices held. 1985, 3rd ed. 192pp. $10.95. ISBN 0-87187-335-4. (84-27504) Congressional Quarterly Inc., see entry above.

Biographical Directory of the American Congress, 1774–1971

This directory lists, by Administration or Congress, every member of the Administrations of George Washington through Richard Nixon's First Administration, plus Members of Congress from the Continental Congress (1774) to the 91st Congress (1969–71). It includes more than 10,800 individual biographies in alphabetical order. All entries include places and dates of birth, summaries of education, capsule histories of nonpolitical careers, political campaigns and elections, household moves, post-elective careers, places and dates of death, and places of interment. 1971. 1,972pp. $40.00. GPO S/N 052-071-00249-9. (X 92-1:S doc 8) See the GPO order form.

Guide to Research Collections of Former United States Senators, 1789–1982

The U.S. Senate will commemorate its 200th anniversary in 1989. The first in a series of bicentennial publications, this guide was developed to facilitate research into the history of the Senate and its former members. It contains detailed information on location and contents of former members' research collections. Housed in approximately 350 publicly accessible repositories across the nation, these collections include personal papers, portraits, photographs, oral history transcripts and memorabilia. The entries in the main body of the guide are arranged alphabetically by member. Each citation includes the name and location of the repository followed by a description of its holdings for the particular Senator. Appendices list collections by repository and Senators alphabetically by State, with information on party membership, other major offices held, and birth and death dates. 1983. 324pp. **FREE**. Historical Office, U.S. Senate, Washington, DC 20510; (202) 224-6900.

Computerized Information Resources

The following are commercially available computer-based information systems that relate to the legislative branch and its activities. For more information on online sources, see Appendix D, Computerized Information Resources.

The Bill Text Tracking System

An automated online service that provides the current language of any bill or resolution before Congress, including the latest amendments. A keyword searching feature lets you access the text of any bill or resolution by entering any word or phrase that may appear in the text. For further information, contact Washington On-Line, 507 8th Street SE, Washington, DC 20003: (202) 543-9101.

Congressional Liaison System

The Congressional Liaison System (CLS) is an assembly of 35 programs and 50 databases that operate on an IBM personal computer or IBM-compatible equipment. CLS's information includes biographies of all Members of Congress and their staffs, as well as listings of 3,000 members of the executive branch; tallies, summary vote reports, sponsors, cosponsors and amendment descriptions of floor votes for both houses (updated daily); political action committee (PAC) information, including current campaign contributions, and the names and addresses of PAC treasurers and contacts; media profiles including listings of contacts at newspapers, television and radio stations in the Nation's top 214 metropolitan areas; and profiles of the nearly 300 committees and subcommittees, including members by rank and seniority, biographies of senior staff members, and committee jurisdictions. Some examples of analyses that may be performed include: define groups of Members by specific criteria or characteristics; develop ratings on Members by comparing actual voting records to an "ideal" record; or define groups of Members by specific criteria or characteristics. The CLS may be used in stand-alone applications or in a multi-user local area network. For further information, contact Lobbyist Systems Corp., 1919 Pennsylvania Avenue NW, Suite 702, Washington, DC 20006; (202) 429-0652.

Electronic Legislative Search System

The Electronic Legislative Search System (ELSS) is the automated online teletype service offered by Commerce Clearing House, Inc. (CCH), to monitor bills and actions taken on them in the 50 States and the U.S. Congress. ELSS allows you to search for a bill or series of bills by subject, bill sponsor, actual bill number or by an action code that denotes action taken on a particular bill(s). A synopsis of each bill is provided, as well as the name of the legislator(s) who introduced the bill. For further information, contact CCH, 4025 W. Peterson Avenue, Chicago, IL 60646; (312) 583-8500.

LEGI-SLATE

LEGI-SLATE is the Washington Post Company's computer-based online service that provides daily updated information on congressional and regulatory activity. Examples of reports available from the system include information on new bills introduced on selected subjects; changes in bill status; committee schedules, including witness lists; cosponsors added or withdrawn from selected bills; news about selected bills or issues from the *Electronic Washington Post*, *National Journal* and *Congressional Quarterly's Weekly Report*; votes on selected bills or issues, and how selected members voted; and *Federal Register* announcements with full text online. For further information, contact LEGI-SLATE, Inc., 111 Massachusetts Avenue NW, Suite 520, Washington, DC 20001; (202) 898-2300.

P.C. Facts U.S. 99th Congress Diskettes

A set of two IBM-PC compatible diskettes to support interaction with the Congress. One diskette includes the software to produce custom reports and update any of the congressional information in the product's database. The second diskette includes the following information for each member of the Senate and House of Representatives: party affiliation, Washington, DC mailing address and telephone number, State district office mailing addresses and telephone numbers, and committee assignments. $45.00. Micro Mega Corp., P.O. Box 150067, Nashville, TN 37215; (615) 292-4005.

Politics On-Line

Politics On-Line (POL) is an online information service of Public Affairs Information (PAI) that covers both Federal and State legislative activities. The service provides information on the more than 7,000 State legislators and 535 Members of Congress. POL includes a directory of State elected officials, Members of Congress and their staffs that gives names, addresses, titles and telephone numbers; political action committee (PAC) contributions data from the Federal Election Commission; daily *Congressional Record* and *Federal Register* abstracts. Still more information is being added to expand POL's library of political databases. For further information, contact PAI at 1000 Potomac Street NW, Suite 401, Washington, DC 20007, (202) 342-3950; or 2900 14th Street, Sacramento, CA 95814, (916) 444-0840.

SCORPIO

The Subject-Content-Oriented-Retriever-for-Processing-Information-On-Line (SCORPIO) was developed for the Congressional Research Service (CRS)

SCORPIO offers access to a number of machine-readable files, such as the Bibliographic Citation File, a file in the areas of public policy and current affairs that lists periodical articles, pamphlets, and U.S. Government and United Nations publications; and the Legislative Information Files, which are an automated version of the CRS *Digest of Public General Bills and Resolutions*. The system is available **FREE** to the public only at the Library of Congress Computer Catalog Center. The Library also offers **FREE** classes on using its online computer catalog, plus user manuals to help researchers learn to use the system. For further information, write the General Reading Rooms Divisions, Library of Congress, Washington, DC 20540.

Washington Alert Service

The Washington Alert Service is a computer-based online information service of seven databases operated by Congressional Quarterly Inc. (CQ). The databases include Congressional Schedules—committee and floor schedules for up to three months in the future, updated daily; Legislative Action—news highlights, plus day-by-day summaries of floor actions; Bill Status—chronologies of all bills introduced, including a history of their movement through the legislative process, their current status and the identities of all cosponsors; CQ Analysis—reports on legislation, politics and elections available before publication of *CQ's Weekly Report*; Congressional Documents—a listing of newly released Senate, House and joint committee reports, prints and hearings, as well as General Accounting Office reports and new public laws; Floor Votes—all roll-call votes taken by House and Senate, including CQ's captions summarizing the issues; and Member Profiles—CQ's biographies of Members of Congress including background data, political style, committees, election returns and financing, key votes and ratings, and congressional district descriptions and data. For further information, contact CQ, 1414 22nd Street NW, Washington, DC 20037; (202) 887-6353.

Legislative Branch Organizations

In addition to the Senators, Representatives and their staffs and committees that make up the Congress, there are a number of other organizations that are part of the legislative branch. Fiscal year 1985 budget for the legislative branch, $1,610 million or 0.17% of the total Federal budget; 38,598 paid employees, or 1.31% of the total civilian work force.

Architect of the Capitol

The Architect of the Capitol administers the structural, mechanical and domestic care and maintenance of the U.S. Capitol Building, the 209 acres of Capitol grounds, the Library of Congress Buildings, the U.S. Supreme Court Building, the House and Senate office buildings, and a number of other legislative branch facilities. This office also makes arrangements for ceremonies held in the Capitol Building and on the grounds. For further information, contact the Office of the Architect of the Capitol, U.S. Capitol Building, Washington, DC 20515; (202) 225-1200.

Congressional Budget Office

The Congressional Budget Office (CBO) was created by the Budget and Impoundment Control Act of 1974 (Public Law 93-344) that established procedures by which the Congress considers and acts upon the annual Federal budget. This process enables the Congress to develop an overview of the Federal budget and to determine the appropriate level of Federal revenues, spending, and debt, and the size of the deficit or surplus. The CBO, a non-partisan organization, provides Congress with basic budget data and with analyses of alternative fiscal, budgetary and programmatic policy issues. Specific responsibilities of the CBO include estimating the five-year budgetary costs of proposed legislation, tracking Congressional budgetary actions against budget targets preset in concurrent resolutions (scorekeeping), forecasting economic trends and alternative fiscal policies, analyzing programmatic issues that affect the Federal budget, analyzing the inflationary impact of proposed legislation, and preparation of an annual report on major budgetary options. The office does not make recommendations on policy. Rather, it presents Congress with options for consideration and the budgetary ramifications of those options.

Key Offices and Telephone Numbers

Address: 2nd and D Streets SW, Washington, DC 20515

General Information	(202) 226-2621
Public/Consumer Information	
Office of Intergovernmental Relations	(202) 226-2600
Procurement Information	
Budget and Finance Office	(202) 226-2609
Press Inquiries	
Office of Intergovernmental Relations	(202) 226-2600
Other Key Offices	
Congressional Liaison/Legislative Affairs	(202) 226-2600
Ethics in Government Act	(202) 632-7642
Fraud, Waste and Mismanagement Hotline	(800) 424-5454
In the Washington, DC area	(202) 633-6987
General Counsel	(202) 226-2633
Library	(202) 226-2635
Personnel	(202) 226-2628
Publications	(202) 226-2809
Statistical Information	(202) 226-2840

Key Information Resources

The *CBO List of Publications* and their booklet *CBO Responsibilities and Organization* are available **FREE** from the Office of Intergovernmental Relations. Also, the Government Printing Office (GPO) has a **FREE** subject bibliography (SB) entitled *Congressional Budget Office Publications* (SB-282) of documents for sale by the GPO. See the GPO SB order form.

Copyright Royalty Tribunal

The Copyright Royalty Tribunal makes determinations concerning the adjustment of copyright royalty rates for records, jukeboxes and certain cable television transmissions. The Tribunal distributes cable television and jukebox royalties deposited with the Register of Copyrights; in cases of controversy among claimants, the Tribunal determines the distribution of the royalties. The Tribunal also establishes—and makes determinations concerning—terms and rates of royalty payments for public broadcasting stations' use of published nondramatic compositions and pictorial, graphic and sculptural works. For further information, contact the Copyright Royalty Tribunal, 1111 20th Street NW, Room 450, Washington, DC 20036; (202) 653-5175.

General Accounting Office

The General Accounting Office (GAO), the investigative arm of Congress, provides independent audits of Federal Government agencies, their programs and activities. Its basic functions are to assist the Congress, its committees and its Members in carrying out their legislative and oversight responsibilities, consistent with GAO's role as an independent, apolitical agency in the legislative branch; to carry out legal, accounting, auditing and claims settlement functions with respect to Federal Government programs and operations as assigned by Congress; and to make recommendations designed to provide for more efficient and effective Government operations. For details on GAO and its information resources, see Chapter 18, General Accounting Office.

Key Offices and Telephone Numbers

Address: 441 G Street NW, Washington, DC 20548

General Information	(202) 275-2812
Personnel Locator	(202) 275-5067
Public/Consumer Information	
Office of Public Information	(202) 275-2812
Telephonic Device for the Deaf (TDD)	(202) 275-5184
Procurement Information	
Office of Acquisitions Management	(202) 275-3550
Press Inquiries	
Office of Public Information	(202) 275-2812
Other Key Offices	
Congressional Liaison/Legislative Affairs	(202) 275-5388
Ethics in Government Act	(202) 632-7642
Fraud, Waste and Mismanagement Hotline	(800) 424-5454
In the Washington, DC area	(202) 633-6987
General Counsel	(202) 275-5207
Library (Technical)	(202) 275-5180
Library (Law)	(202) 275-5560
Paperwork Reduction Act (ADP/IRM)	(202) 275-8688
Personnel	(202) 275-6092
Publications (see GAO order form for mail order)	(202) 275-6241

Government Printing Office

The Government Printing Office (GPO) serves as the principal publisher for agencies of the Federal Government. GPO invites bids from commercial suppliers on a wide variety of printing and binding services, awards and administers contracts, and maintains liaison between ordering agencies and contractors. It prepares catalogs and distributes and sells, through mail orders and GPO bookstores, approximately 16,000 different publications that originate in the agencies of all three branches of the Government. GPO also administers the Depository Library Program through which selected Government publications are made available in libraries throughout the country. For details on GPO and its information resources, see Chapter 16, Government Printing Office.

Key Offices and Telephone Numbers

Address: 710 N. Capitol Street NW, Washington, DC 20401

General Information	(202) 275-2051
Personnel Locator	(202) 275-3648
Public/Consumer Information	
Legislative Liaison/Public Affairs Office	(202) 275-3204
Procurement Information	
Printing Procurement Department	(202) 275-3774
Materials Management Department	(202) 275-2761
General Procurement Department	(202) 275-2470
Press Inquiries	
Legislative Liaison/Public Affairs Office	(202) 275-3204
Other Key Offices	
Congressional Liaison/Legislative Affairs	(202) 275-2894
Ethics in Government Act	(202) 632-7642
Fraud, Waste and mismanagement Hotline	(800) 424-5454
In the Washington, DC area	(202) 633-6987
General Counsel	(202) 275-2758
Library Programs Service	(202) 275-1114
Personnel	(202) 275-2951
Publications (see GPO order forms for mail order)	(202) 783-3238

Library of Congress

The Library of Congress (LC) is the Nation's library. Its services extend not only to Members, committees and staffs of the Congress, but to the executive and judicial branches of the Federal Government, to libraries throughout the Nation and the world, and to scholars, researchers, artists and scientists who use its resources. Through the Congressional Research Service (CRS), the library serves as the research and reference arm of the Congress (see the section on CRS that follows). The Library's extensive collections are universal in scope. They include books on every subject and a multitude of languages. Other collections include music manuscripts; maps and views; photographic records from the daguerreotype to the latest news photos; recordings, including folksongs and other music, speeches and poetry readings; prints, drawings and posters; government documents, newspapers and periodicals from all over the world; and motion pictures, microforms, and audio and video tapes. Admission to the various research facilities of the Library is free.

Legislative Branch 99

While the Library of Congress exists primarily to serve the needs of Members of Congress and thereafter the needs of Federal Government and other libraries, general reference and information assistance is also provided to people who have exhausted other information resources available to them.

Part of the responsibility of the Library of Congress is to support local, state, academic and other libraries by giving them the first opportunity to serve their clientele, since they are often able to be more responsive to local information needs than the Library of Congress. The staff of these libraries know that they may turn to the Library of Congress for help on questions requiring access to its collections.

People who have fully used their local and regional resources may seek assistance from the Library of Congress, confident that it will respond to them insofar as time and resources allow.

While working at the Library of Congress, the public has access to computer terminals tied into several of the databases developed by the Library. Trained staff members provide instruction in the use of these terminals and on the substance and characteristics of the various databases. Currently, access to the Library's databases is available to the public only through the terminals located on the Library's premises and is not available through remote or dial-up terminals.

Key Offices and Telephone Numbers

Address: 101 Independence Avenue SE, Washington, DC 20540

General Information and Personnel Locator	(202) 287-5000
Public/Consumer Information	
Information Line Recording	(202) 287-6400
Copyright Public Information Office	(202) 287-8700
Procurement Information	
Procurement and Supply Division	(202) 287-8605
Press Inquiries	
Information Office	(202) 287-5108
Other Key Offices	
Congressional Liaison/Legislative Affairs	(202) 287-6577
Ethics in Government Act	(202) 632-7642
Fraud, Waste and Mismanagement Hotline	(800) 424-5454
In the Washington, DC area	(202) 633-6987
General Counsel	(202) 287-6316
Library (Telephone Reference)	(202) 287-5522
Personnel	(202) 287-6080
Publications (Catalog of LC Books)	(202) 287-5093

Key Information Resources

The following booklets are available **FREE** from the Information Office: *Services to the Nation, The Library of Congress*; *Public Services in The Library of Congress, Locations and Hours of Opening*; *The Library of Congress, Services to Publishers*; *Library of Congress, Tips for Students*; and a summary sheet, *The Library of Congress Classification System*. A list of *Library of Congress Publications in Print*, many of which are of interest to the general public, is available **FREE** from the Central Services Division, Library of Congress, Washington, DC 20540. A monthly *Calendar of Events* that lists programs and exhibits at the Library of Congress may be requested from the same office.

The Cataloging Distribution Service (CDS), for a fee, will prepare a bibliographic listing based on a search of virtually every data element on the traditional Library of Congress catalog card. For further information, contact Customer Services Section, CDS, Library of Congress, Washington, DC 20541, and ask for their CDS Retriever Service.

Library of Congress
Center for the Book

The Center for the Book was established by law in 1977 to stimulate public interest in books and reading to encourage the study of books and the printed word. Its symposia, projects and publications are made possible by tax-deductible contributions from individuals and corporations. For further information and a publications list, contact the Center for the Book, Library of Congress, Washington, DC 20540; (202) 287-5221.

Library of Congress
Congressional Research Service

The Congressional Research Service (CRS), a division of the Library of Congress, is a legislative support arm of the Congress. It conducts research, analyzes legislation and provides information at the request of committees, Members of Congress and their staffs. The CRS makes such research available without partisan bias. Because all inquiries are confidential, CRS staff are not permitted to divulge which Members or committees have requested information from CRS on particular topics. Not all CRS reports are individualized for Members' requests. CRS publishes such items as "Issue Briefs," "Info Packs" and "Research Guides" on topics of general interest to Congress. Information products published by CRS are cited in its annual volume *Subject Catalog of CRS Reports in Print*, its semiannual supplement, and a monthly document, *Update*. These indexes and most of the publications they cite are available only through your Senator or Representative. Contact your Member of Congress by mail at U.S. House of Representatives, Washington, DC 20515 or U.S. Senate, Washington, DC 20510, or through the U.S. Capitol switchboard, (202) 224-3121.

CRS studies and reports published by authority of Congress come in various forms, including committee prints, published hearings of congressional committees, and those that were inserted into the *Congressional Record* at the request of a Member. Many of these documents may be obtained from the Government Printing Office (GPO); some are available from the committees responsible for particular prints or hearings. A bibliography of *CRS Studies in the Public Domain* is available as a semi-annual subscription service from GPO, $4.25 a year; single copy price, $2.50. GPO List ID CRSSC. (LC 14.20:) See the GPO subscription order form.

The monthly *Congressional Research Service Review* is a professional journal that includes articles intended to provide the congressional community, others in government and the general public with articles on public policy issues. Subscription price: $16.00; single copy price: $1.75. GPO List ID CRSR. (LC 14.19:) See the GPO subscription order form.

Library of Congress
Federal Library and Information Center Committee

The Federal Library and Information Center Committee (FLICC), formerly the Federal Library Committee (FLC), is a focal point for cooperation and action within the Federal library and information community. The Committee makes recommendations on Federal library and information policies, programs and procedures to Federal agencies and to others concerned with libraries and information centers. It serves as a forum to consider issues and policies that affect Federal libraries and information centers, needs and priorities in providing information services to the Government and the Nation, and efficient and cost-effective use of Federal library and information resources and services. The FLICC promotes improved access to information, continued development and use of the Federal Library and Information Network (FEDLINK), research and development in the application of new technologies to Federal libraries and information centers, improvement in the management of Federal libraries and information centers, and relevant educational opportunities. For further information, contact FLICC, Library of Congress, Washington, DC 20540; (202) 287-6055.

Library of Congress
National Referral Center

The National Referral Center of the Library of Congress is a **FREE** referral service that directs those with questions concerning any subject to organizations that can provide the answers. A subject-indexed, computerized file of approximately 13,000 organizations (i.e., information resources), is maintained for this purpose. Included for each organization is its special fields of interest and the types of information service it is willing to provide. Requests for referral service may be made by letter, telephone or in person (call for appointment). The Center invites organizations that have information in specialized fields to participate as information resources. For further information, ask for their **FREE** descriptive flyer and *Titles Available in the WHO KNOWS? Series*. Telephone inquiries should be directed to (202) 287-5670 for referral service or to schedule visits; (202) 287-5680 for registration of information resources; or (202) 287-5683 for information about the center's publications or database developments. Correspondence should be addressed to National Referral Center, Library of Congress, Washington, DC 20540.

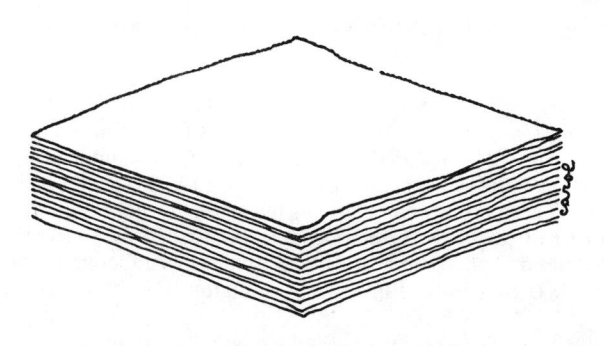

Office of Technology Assessment

The Office of Technology Assessment (OTA) is a non-partisan, analytical support agency that provides the Congress with objective analyses of emerging—often highly technical—issues of the 20th Century. It explores complex issues involving science and technology and provides Congress with both policy options and the potential consequences of adopting each option. OTA does not advocate particular policies or actions, but points out their pros and cons, along with the facts associated with each. The OTA staff plans, directs and drafts all assessments. It draws extensively on the broad technical and professional resources of the private sector, including universities, research organizations, industry and public interest groups.

Key Offices and Telephone Numbers

Address: 600 Pennsylvania Avenue SE, Washington, DC 20510

General Information	(202) 226-9241
Personnel Locator	(202) 224-8713
Public/Consumer Information	
Congressional Relations and Public Affairs	(202) 224-9241
Procurement Information	
Administration Office	(202) 226-2146
Press Inquiries	
Press Officer	(202) 226-2115
Other Key Offices	
Congressional Liaison/Legislative Affairs	(202) 226-2115
Ethics in Government Act	(202) 632-7642
Fraud, Waste and Mismanagement Hotline	(800) 424-5454
In the Washington, DC area	(202) 633-6987
Library	(202) 226-2160
Personnel	(202) 224-8713
Publishing Office	(202) 224-8996

Key Information Resources

Booklets entitled: *What OTA Is, What OTA Does, How OTA Works*; *OTA List of Publications* and *Assessment Activities* are available **FREE** from the Publishing Office. The booklet *Assessment Activities* provides announcements of recently published reports; notices of publications in press; brief summaries of current work projects, organized by OTA division and program, and the dates currently projected for publication; and lists of selected publications of interest.

United States Botanic Garden

The U.S. Botanic Garden collects, cultivates and grows the various vegetable products of the United States and other countries for exhibition and display to the public and for study material for students, scientists and garden clubs. The entire collection of the Garden includes more than 10,000 species and varieties of plant growth. There are special displays during most months of the year in its conservatory near the U.S. Capitol and at its nursery in Anacostia, DC. For further information concerning the U.S. Botanic Garden, contact the Architect of the Capitol, U.S. Capitol Building, Washington, DC 20515; (202) 225-1200.

Executive Branch Policy Directive

Legislative Coordination and Clearance

This Office of Management and Budget (OMB) Circular No. A-19 outlines procedures for the coordination and clearance by OMB of agency recommendations on proposed, pending and enrolled legislation. The circular also provides instructions on the timing and preparation of agency legislative programs. All executive branch agencies are subject to the provisions of the circular, except those agencies specifically required by law to transmit their legislative proposals, reports or testimony to the Congress without prior clearance. 1979. 32pp. **FREE**. EOP Publications, 726 Jackson Place NW, Room 2200, Washington, DC 20503; (202) 395-7332.

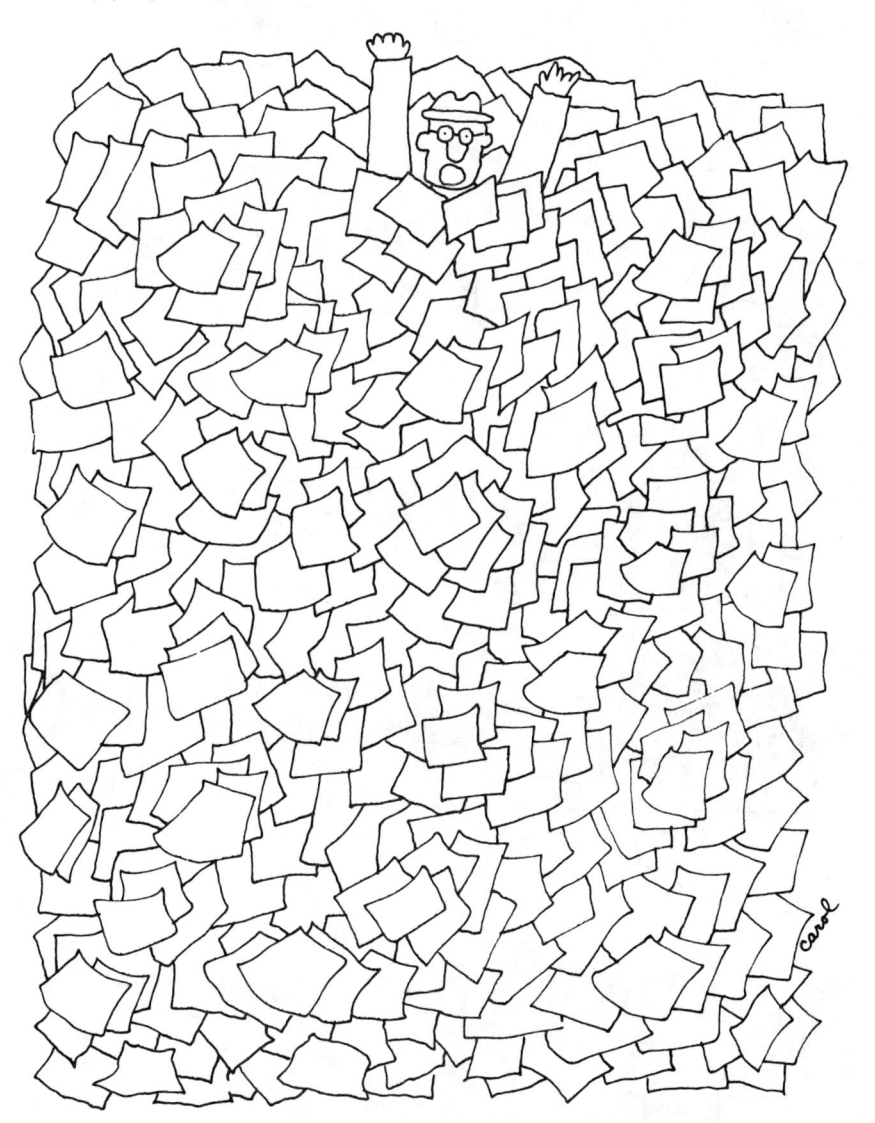

104 **FEDfind**

Chapter 5
Judicial Branch

Under the Constitution of the United States of America, the judicial power is vested in the Supreme Court and such inferior courts as the Congress may from time to time "ordain and establish." As such, the judicial branch is a coequal and independent branch of the Federal Government. Since the founding of the Nation, the Congress has developed a system of courts, depicted in Figure 5-1, that could be considered the most comprehensive in the world. In this chapter, information resources related to the Federal court system and its operations are described. Also included is a description of the various organizational elements of the Federal system, along with addresses and telephone numbers for further information.

The information resources described in this chapter are organized under the following headings.

- The U.S. Court System
- Legal Research Guides
- The Constitution
- The Supreme Court
- Judicial Procedures and Prosecution
- United States Code and Statutes
- Periodicals Covering the Courts
- Biographies
- Computerized Information Resources
- Judicial Branch Organizations
    The Supreme Court of the United States
    Lower Courts
    National Courts
    Administrative Office of the United States Courts
    Federal Judicial Center
- Subject Bibliographies

The U.S. Court System

The United States Courts: Their Jurisdiction and Work

An introduction to the U.S. system of courts—including State courts—and how they function, this brochure was prepared for the Committee on the Judiciary, House of Representatives. 1985. 23pp. **FREE**, supplies limited. Administrative Office of the United States Courts, Office of the Director, Washington, DC 20544; (202) 633-6097.

106 **FEDfind**

```
                    SUPREME COURT
                    OF THE UNITED STATES
                           │
        ┌──────────────────┴──────────────────┐
   United States Courts of Appeals      United States Court of Appeals
        12 Circuits                        for the Federal Circuit
```

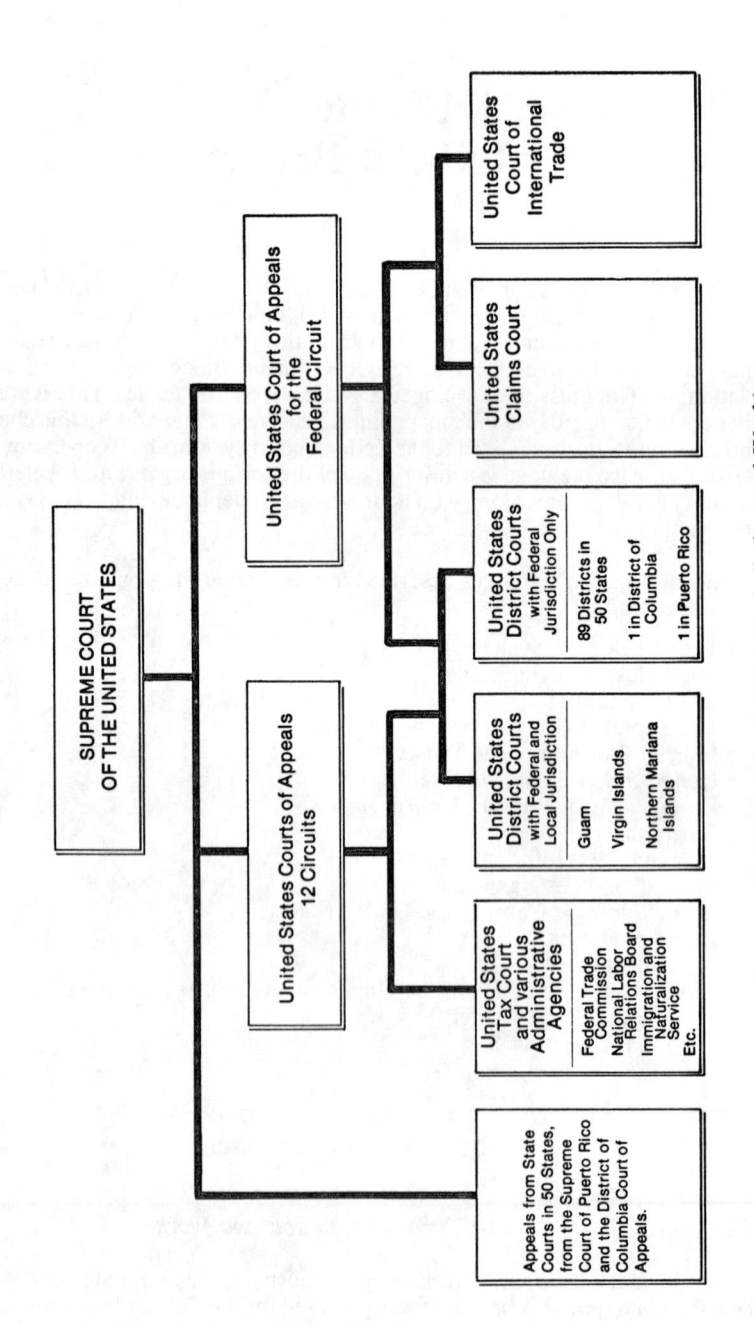

- Appeals from State Courts in 50 States, from the Supreme Court of Puerto Rico and the District of Columbia Court of Appeals.
- United States Tax Court and various Administrative Agencies
  - Federal Trade Commission
  - National Labor Relations Board
  - Immigration and Naturalization Service
  - Etc.
- United States District Courts with Federal and Local Jurisdiction
  - Guam
  - Virgin Islands
  - Northern Mariana Islands
- United States District Courts with Federal Jurisdiction Only
  - 89 Districts in 50 States
  - 1 in District of Columbia
  - 1 in Puerto Rico
- United States Claims Court
- United States Court of International Trade

(Source: The U.S. Courts: Their Jurisdiction and Work)

Figure 5-1. The United States Court System

Guide to the Federal Courts

An introduction to the U.S. court system and its operations. It describes the relationships among the courts in the Federal system, including the U.S. Supreme Court and lower Federal courts, and various special courts such as the Court of Claims and the Tax Court. The guide explains the litigation process of a Federal court case by use of examples. A glossary of terms is included. 1984. 102pp. $9.95. ISBN 0-942008-06-5. WANT Publishing Co., 1511 K Street NW, Washington, DC 20005; (202) 783-1887.

Proceedings of the Judicial Conference and the Annual Report of the Director—Administrative Office of the United States Courts

An annual report on the business of the courts and the activities of the Administrative Office of the United States Courts as submitted by the Director for the twelve month period ended June 30, 1985. The report consists of four subdivisions: Judicial Business, Judicial Administration, Judicial Appropriations and Expenditures, and the reports of the courts on the Equal Employment Opportunity Program of the Judicial Conference. Appended are detailed statistical analyses of the workload of the Federal courts during the reporting period. October 1985. 620pp. $12.00. GPO S/N 028-004-00060-5. (Ju 10.1/2:985) See the GPO order form.

Management Statistics for United States Courts

This annual publication presents statistics on the workload of the Federal courts. One page is devoted to each district and appeals court, detailing statistical data on docket conditions for the fiscal years ending June 30, 1980-1985. Detailed explanations are provided for the data included in the statistical profiles of the appeals and district courts. Court workload figures are divided by the number of authorized positions or panels of judges to permit comparison between courts of different sizes. October 1985. 129pp. FREE. Administrative Office of the United States Courts, Statistical Analysis and Reports Division, Washington, DC 20544; (202) 633-6094.

Federal Judiciary Almanac

A directory of information on each of the Federal courts. The publication includes an alphabetical State-by-State listing of each court; biographical information on each sitting Federal judge; maps of the circuits, districts and divisions; statistics on caseloads; addresses and telephone numbers of key court personnel; and a demographic breakdown of the regions from which juries are drawn. Compiled by W. Stuart Dornette and Robert R. Cross. 1984. 1,087pp. $75.00. ISBN 0-471-80269-7. (83-21880) Wiley Law Publications, P.O. Box 1777, Colorado Springs, CO 80901; (201) 469-4400.

Legal Research Guides

Finding the Law: A Workbook on Legal Research for Laypersons

An introduction to legal research, this book's focus is on Federal law with a mention of State and municipal sources. Intended for employees of the Bureau of Land Management, Department of the Interior who deal with laws and regulations in their daily work, it is equally valuable to the general public. An introductory section defines the nature of American law. Sections on statutory and case law explain the procedures and publications concerned with legislative law, administrative regulations and court cases. The final section covers digests, citators, encyclopedias, dictionaries, periodical indexes and similar finding tools. An in-depth biblography is included for works covered in the main body. 1982. 283pp. $8.50. Out-of-print. GPO S/N 024-011-00148-4. (I 53.2:L 41)

Fundamentals of Legal Research

The successor to the fourth edition of *Pollack's Fundamentals of Legal Research*, this is a detailed guide to in-depth legal research. It includes research in Federal legislation and administrative—or regulatory—law. By J. Myron Jacobstein and Roy M. Mersky. 1985, 3rd ed. 717pp. $22.95. ISBN 0-88277-245-7. (85-12952) The Foundation Press, Inc., 170 Old Country Road, Mineola, NY 11501; (516) 248-5580.

The Legal Research Manual

A step-by-step guide to basic legal research, this manual explains how to gather and evaluate the facts; identify the legal issues; find the law; read and analyze the law; and determine whether the law in question is still valid. It also includes flow charts, diagrams and checklists of research and analysis steps; an introduction to the basics of computerized legal research; and a summary overview of civil procedure. By Christopher G. and Jill Robinson Wren. 1983. 197pp. $8.95 + $1.90 postage and handling. ISBN 0-89579-185-4. (83-9955) A-R Editions, Inc., 315 W. Gorham Street, Madison, WI 53703; (608) 251-2114.

The Constitution

Constitution of the United States of America, As Amended

Prepared under the direction of the House Committee on the Judiciary, this booklet includes the text of the Constitution with all 26 amendments, together with ratification notes. It also contains information regarding the five proposed amendments adopted by the Congress but not ratified by three-fourths of the States. There is a detailed analytical index of the Constitution and the 26 amendments, with references to articles, sections, and clauses. 1977. 79pp. $4.50. GPO S/N 052-071-00545-5. (X 95-2:H.doc.256) See the GPO order form.

The Constitution of the United States of America: Analysis and Interpretation

Prepared by the Congressional Research Service, Library of Congress, this volume and supplement sums up the most important rulings under each appropriate constitutional clause. A 1986 edition is planned. 1973. Out-of-print. 1980 supplement, 360pp. $9.00, GPO S/N 052-071-00645-1. (X 96-2:S.doc.64) See the GPO order form.

The Constitutional Law Dictionary

This dictionary focuses on concepts of constitutionalism, words and phrases common to constitutional law and leading decisions rendered by the Supreme Court of the United States. In addition to definitions—each followed by a paragraph of "Significance"—the dictionary includes an initial chapter on constitutionalism, chapter-by-chapter overviews for each amendment presented, and a chapter of definitions of more than 100 legal words and phrases. By Ralph C. Chandler, Richard A. Enslen and Peter G. Renstrom. Volume 1, Individual Rights, 1984. 460pp. $47.50. ISBN 0-87436-031-5. Volume 2 will cover Governmental Powers. ABC-Clio, P.O. Box 4397, Santa Barbara, CA 93140; (800) 422-2546 or (805) 963-4221.

Reforming American Government: The Bicentennial Papers of the Committee on the Constitutional System

Undertaken by the Committee on the Constitutional System, this is an assessment of the U.S. Constitution in connection with the document's approaching bicentennial anniversary (1987). The Committee is a non-partisan and non-governmental group of some 200 prominent citizens. The book includes both a discussion of the problems of modern governance and an assessment of various proposed reforms. Included for each proposal is draft language and an assessment of "pros and cons." Edited by Donald L. Robinson. 1985. 300pp. $35.00, cloth, ISBN 0-8133-7059-0; $13.95, paper, ISBN 0-8133-7114-7. Westview Press, 5500 Central Avenue, Boulder, CO 80301; (303) 444-3541.

This Constitution

In commemoration of the bicentennial of the U.S. Constitution in 1987, the American Historical Association and the American Political Science Association (APSA) have undertaken a joint effort—"Project '87." In addition to organizing scholarly conferences on the Constitution, awarding research grants and fellowships, and producing television programs, Project '87 publishes this quarterly magazine. The magazine features articles on constitutional issues, annotated original documents, and information about bicentennial grants, events, publications and media programs. Subscription price: $10.00 a year for individuals, $16.00 for institutions. Project '87, APSA, 1527 New Hampshire Avenue NW, Washington, DC 20036; (202) 483-2512.

The Supreme Court

Guide to the U.S. Supreme Court

This work combines history, biography, political science and constitutional law into a reference volume on the Supreme Court. The history, decisions and procedures are presented in numerous sections on the Court and the Federal system, the Court and individual rights, origins and development of the U.S. Supreme Court 1789–1979, pressures on the Court, members of the Court, appendices, and case and subject indexes. 1979. 1,022pp. $95.00. ISBN 0-87187-184-X. (79-20210) Congressional Quarterly Inc., 1414 22nd Street NW, Washington, DC 20037; (202) 887-8620.

A Reference Guide to the United States Supreme Court

A general reference work that examines the various aspects of the Supreme Court: its origins, history, structure, functions, activities, decisions and influences. Its five sections include an introduction that chronicles the history of the Court and its role in modern America; three thematic sections on Federal constitutional powers, Federal-State authority and the protection of individual rights; and a landmark decisions section that examines more than 300 key decisions by the Court. A biography section profiles every Justice who ever sat on the Court. Edited by Stephen P. Elliott. 1986. 544pp. $50.00. ISBN 0-8160-1018-8. Facts on File, Inc., 460 Park Avenue South, New York, NY 10016; (800) 322-8755 or (212) 683-2244.

Individual Slip Opinions of the U.S. Supreme Court

The Court's opinions as announced from the bench are provided. Issued irregularly. Subscription price: $172.00 a term of the Court; single copies vary in price. GPO List ID SCISO. (Ju 6.8/b:) See the GPO subscription order form.

Preliminary Prints of the U.S. Supreme Court

These official reports of the Supreme Court include all opinions with syllabi, names of counsel, indexes, tables of cases and other editorial additions. Issued irregularly. Subscription price: $56.00 per term of the Court; single copies vary in price. GPO List ID SCPP. (Ju 6.8/a:) See the GPO subscription order form.

Supreme Court Reporter

A semimonthly service during the term of the Court that provides both full majority and dissenting opinions of current decisions in the form of advance sheets. The accumulated advance sheets are ultimately bound into permanent volumes. Enquire for price information. West Publishing Co., P.O. Box 64526, St. Paul, MN 55164; (800) 328-9352 or (612) 228-2973.

Judicial Branch 111

U.S. Supreme Court Bulletin

Issued weekly when the Court is in session, this publication reproduces the full text of opinions and actions announced by the Supreme Court during the previous week. It also includes the Court's tentative "Argument Schedule" and "Status Table" of each docketed case. Subscription price: $370.00 per session. Commerce Clearing House, Inc., 4025 W. Peterson Avenue, Chicago, IL 60646; (312) 583-8500.

United States Supreme Court Decisions

This book, written by Nancy A. Guenther, is an index to literature about Supreme Court decisions. It indexes approximately 600 books and 320 periodicals published between 1960 and 1980. Case name and subject indexes supplement the chronological listing of Supreme Court decisions that spans 1798 through 1980. The indexes list both plaintiffs and defendants. Book and periodical references are cited for the decisions in the chronological listing. 1983, 2nd ed. 864pp. $52.50. ISBN 0-8108-1578-8. (82-10518) Scarecrow Press, Inc., P.O. Box 4167, Metuchen, NJ 08840; (201) 548-8600.

United States Reports

This is a series of volumes of cases adjudged in the U.S. Supreme Court. Contact the Government Printing Office (GPO) for information on which volumes are currently available. (Ju 6.8:) See the GPO order form.

Decisions of the United States Supreme Court

For each term of the U.S. Supreme Court beginning in 1963, a separate volume has been prepared with summary descriptions of the cases considered. Also included are how each case came before the Court, facts involved, issues presented, holding of the Court with reason, concurring and dissenting views outlined and a listing of the litigants' attorneys in each case. (64-17924) Inquire for prices of individual volumes. The Lawyers Co-operative Publishing Co., Aqueduct Building, Rochester, NY 14694; (716) 546-5530.

Complete Oral Arguments of the Supreme Court of the United States

Presented in this work are the oral arguments of the counsel for each party as they appeared before the Court to convince the Justices of the merits of their cases. Justices have the opportunity to confront each counsel, to query or analyze, support or criticize, to confirm or dispel any individual or collective doubts concerning the facts of each case and the positions of the opposing sides. Microfiche, with printed index. Retrospective Series: 1953 Term–1968 Term, $1,750.00; 1969 Term–1979 Term, $2,970.00; 1980–1983 Terms: $375.00 per term; 1984 Term: $425.00. University Publications of America, 44 N. Market Street, Frederick, MD 21701, (800) 692-6300 or (301) 694-0100.

Judicial Procedures and Prosecution

Rules of Practice and Procedure: United States Tax Court

These rules govern the practice and procedure in all cases and proceedings in the U.S. Tax Court. In those instances where there is no applicable rule or procedure, the Court or judge before whom the matter is pending may prescribe the procedure, in light of current Federal rules of civil procedure to the extent that they are adaptable to the matter at hand. 1983. 161pp. $4.50. GPO S/N 028-005-00150-1. (Ju 11.8:983) See the GPO order form.

Federal Rules of Evidence

The rules of evidence for use in proceedings in the courts of the United States and before U.S. magistrates, as promulgated and amended by the U.S. Supreme Court to August 1, 1985, are presented in this publication. Prepared by the Committee on the Judiciary, House of Representatives. As stated in the forward, the purpose of these rules is to "secure fairness in administration, elimination of unjustifiable expense and delay, and promotion of growth and development of the law of evidence to the end that the truth may be ascertained and proceedings justly determined." 1985. 35pp. $1.00. GPO S/N 052-070-06070-1. (Y 4.J 89/1:R 86/985) See the GPO order form.

Federal Rules of Appellate Procedure, With Forms

The Federal rules of appellate procedure, as promulgated and amended by the U.S. Supreme Court, to October 1, 1985, together with the forms adopted by the Court are presented in this publication. Prepared by the Committee on the Judiciary, House of Representatives, in response to the need for an official up-to-date document containing the latest amendments. Where a rule was amended, a reference to the citation and effective date of the amendment is included. 1985. 45pp. $1.25. GPO S/N 052-070-06073-5. (Y 4.J 89/1:Ap 4/2/985) See the GPO order form.

Manual for Administrative Law Judges

This manual is written with "the typical formal administrative proceeding" in mind. It includes sections designed for special types of cases, such as short cases with few parties and issues, and long technical cases with many parties or issues or both. It provides guidelines for formal administrative proceedings and a discussion of the expanding functions of administrative law judges. Commissioned by the Administrative Conference of the United States, this manual provides a special section on judicial writing. 1982. 171pp. $5.50. GPO S/N 052-049-00013-0. (Y 3.Ad 6:8 J 89/98) See the GPO order form.

Rules of Civil Procedure for the United States District Courts, With Forms

The rules of civil procedure for U.S. district courts together with forms are presented. These rules and forms were promulgated and amended by the U.S.

Supreme Court as of August 1, 1985. Prepared by the Committee on the Judiciary, House of Representatives, in response to the need for an official up-to-date document containing the latest amendments. Where a rule was amended, a reference to the citation and effective date of the amendment is included. 1985. 114pp. $3.00. GPO S/N 052-070-06072-7. See the GPO order form.

Rules of Criminal Procedure for the United States District Courts, With Forms

The rules of criminal procedure for the U.S. district courts together with forms are presented. These rules and forms were promulgated and amended by the U.S. Supreme Court as of August 1, 1985. Prepared by the Committee on the Judiciary, House of Representatives, in response to the need for an official up-to-date document containing the latest amendments. Where a rule was amended, a reference to the date the amendment was promulgated and the date the amendment became effective is included. 1985. 50pp. $1.50. GPO S/N 052-070-06071-9. See the GPO order form.

Proving Federal Crimes

A looseleaf reference manual for Federal prosecutors, this publication includes legal summaries of cases and precedents relating to the acquisition, use and misuse of evidence, as well as the laws of evidence. Indexes for statutes and rules, appellate and civil procedure, criminal procedure and Federal rules of evidence are provided. 1980. 271pp. $20.00. GPO S/N 027-000-00903-4. (J 1.8/2:P 94/4) Supplement 1, intended for insertion in the preceding manual, contains two chapters— "Joinder and Severance" and "Trial by Jury"—as well as a revised and expanded index. 1981. 64pp. $5.50. GPO S/N 027-000-01090-3. Supplement 2 contains revisions of various chapters in the basic manual where there have been significant decisions by the U.S. Supreme Court and the courts of appeals. Also includes a new section on "Speedy Trials." 1981. 100pp. $6.00. GPO S/N 027-000-01151-9. See the GPO order form.

Manual for Courts-Martial, United States, 1984

This manual contains the rules for courts-martial, military rules of evidence, punitive articles and nonjudicial punishment procedures. It includes appendices with forms for legal counsel and the uniform code of military justice. In looseleaf form, punched for 3-ring binder. 1984. 848pp. $13.00. GPO S/N 008-000-00403-0. (D 1.15:984) See the GPO order form.

United States Code and Statutes

United States Code

The United States Code (USC) is an official U.S. Government publication comprised of fifteen volumes that contain all Federal laws in force as of the time of publication. It is organized by subject (titles), Figure 5-2, and includes general and name indexes. Details on the contents and pricing of each volume may be obtained from the Government Printing Office (GPO). Set $661.00. GPO S/N 652-001-00237-1. See the GPO order form.

1. General Provisions
2. The Congress
3. The President
4. Flag and Seal, Seat of Government and the States
5. Government Organization and Employees
*6. [Surety Bonds]
7. Agriculture
8. Aliens and Nationality
9. Arbitration
10. Armed Forces
11. Bankruptcy
12. Banks and Banking
13. Census
14. Coast Guard
15. Commerce and Trade
16. Conservation
17. Copyrights
18. Crimes and Criminal Procedure
19. Customs Duties
20. Education
21. Food and Drugs
22. Foreign Relations and Intercourse
23. Highways
24. Hospitals and Asylums
25. Indians
26. Internal Revenue Code
27. Intoxicating Liquors
28. Judiciary and Judicial Procedure
29. Labor
30. Mineral Lands and Mining
31. Money and Finance
32. National Guard
33. Navigation and Navigable Waters
@34. [Navy]
35. Patents
36. Patriotic Societies and Observances
37. Pay and Allowances of the Uniformed Services
38. Veterans' Benefits
39. Postal Service
40. Public Buildings, Property, and Works
41. Public Contracts
42. The Public Health and Welfare
43. Public Lands
44. Public Printing and Documents
45. Railroads
46. Shipping
47. Telegraphs, Telephones, and Radio Telegraphs
48. Territories and Insular Possessions
49. Transportation
50. War and National Defense; and Appendix

*This title has been superseded by the enactment of Title 31.
@This title has been superseded by the enactment of Title 10.

Figure 5-2. United States Code Titles

United States Code Annotated

The U.S. Code Annotated (USCA) provides all Federal statutes (in 50 titles and 8 index volumes), including all court constructions of the statutes. Editorial features include: notes on court decisions, histories of statutory provisions that may help determine the intent of the Congress in passing a certain law, cross references to related and qualifying laws, and a popular name table to locate a law if only the popular name is known. Each volume is kept up-to-date by an annual supplement and pamphlets published during sessions of Congress. A master index provides access to statutes by subject. Details on the prices of each statute volume and indexes may be obtained from West Publishing Co., P.O. Box 64526, St. Paul, MN 55164; (800) 328-9352 or (612) 228-2973.

United States Code Service

The U.S. Code Service supplements the actual language of the Federal statutes, which are a part of the service. These include references to the *Code of Federal Regulations*; reprints of rules of practice of major administrative agencies; case notes for cases that meaningfully construe or interpret the statute; history of each section together with amendment notes tracing development of the law; and cross-references to secondary authorities of broad use and acceptance. An illustrative brochure, including a list of titles and sample pages of coverage along with prices and terms, is available on request. The Lawyers Cooperative Publishing Co., Aqueduct Building, Rochester, NY 14694; (716) 546-5530.

United States Statutes at Large

These bound volumes, issued annually, contain all public and private laws and concurrent resolutions enacted during a session of Congress, reorganization plans, proposed and ratified amendments to the Constitution, and Presidential proclamations. Included also are "finding aids," which include a guide to legislative history with each public law and proposed or ratified constitutional amendments and indexes. Details on the contents and pricing of each volume may be obtained from the Government Printing Office (GPO). See the GPO order form.

How to Find U.S. Statutes and U.S. Code Citations

Originated and prepared by the Office of the Federal Register, National Archives and Records Administration, this pamphlet is designed to assist individuals searching for laws both in the *United States Statutes at Large* and in the *United States Code*. A research procedure chart is used to enable the user to obtain up-to-date and accurate citations. 1980, 4th ed. 13pp. $1.25. Out-of-print. GPO S/N 022-00-00082-1.

Periodicals Covering the Courts

United States Law Week

A general law service, this publication provides weekly notification of important Federal and State court decisions, Federal agency rulings, procedural rules promulgated by the U.S. Supreme Court and Federal statutes. It provides digests of court opinions, agency rules and brief descriptions of important developments of the week. The service reports on every Supreme Court case on the appellate docket—from initial docketing to final disposition—including full text and digests of opinions that are mailed to subscribers on the day they are handed down. Supreme Court coverage also includes reporting of important cases awaiting decision, coverage of oral arguments in important cases, and a year-end review, broken down by subject matter, of the preceding term's work. Two filing binders are furnished, one for general law and the other for Supreme Court materials, each indexed. Enquire for price information. Bureau of National Affairs, Inc., 1231 25th Street NW, Washington, DC 20037; (800) 372-1033; in Maryland, (800) 352-1400; in DC, 258-9401.

United States Tax Court Reports

A monthly subscription item, this publication provides a consolidation of U.S. Tax Court decisions for the previous month. Subscription price: $35.00 a year. Single copy price: $4.25. GPO List ID TAC. (Ju 11.7/a 2:) See the GPO subscription order form.

Federal Filings Alert

This is a weekly nationwide listing of selected civil actions filed in Federal district courts. The focus is on such areas as antitrust/unfair trade, copyright/patent/trademarks, labor, product liability and securities. It provides docket information on each case reported. This enables one to obtain, through the appropriate court, the complaint (the first document filed in a Federal court case) as well as other documents filed. Subscription price: $228.00 a year. WANT Publishing Co., 1511 K Street NW, Washington, DC 20005; (202) 783-1887.

Biographies

Judges of the United States

A directory of biographical sketches of the more than 2,600 judges who have served in the courts of the United States through December 1981, this book was prepared under the auspices of the Bicentennial Committee of the Judicial Conference of the United States that was constituted as part of the celebration of the Declaration of Independence. The directory provides information and insights into the wide variety of regional, educational and ethnic backgrounds of Federal judges. As each new Federal judge is confirmed, information is collected that will appear in periodical revisions. 1983, 2nd ed. 700pp. $20.00. Out-of-print. GPO S/N 028-004-00056-7. (Ju 10.2:J 89/4/983)

The Justices of the United States Supreme Court

Edited by Leon Friedman and Fred L. Israel, this five-volume set includes essays on Supreme Court Justices for the period 1789 through 1978. All the contributors are legal scholars and/or practicing attorneys and have selected important opinions of the Justices to illustrate themes in their essays. 1980. 3,900pp. (paper) $100.00. ISBN 0-87754-130-2. (69-13699) Chelsea House Publishers, 133 Christopher Street, New York, NY 10014; (800) 523-0458 or (212) 924-6414.

Computerized Information Resources

The following are commercially available computer-based information systems that relate to the judicial branch and its activities. For more information on online sources, see Appendix D, Computerized Information Resources.

LEXIS

LEXIS is a computer-assisted legal research system by Mead Data Central. It allows for full text searching of Federal law libraries including among them tax, securities, trade regulation, bankruptcy, patent and trademark, copyright, communications, labor and contracts law. For further information, contact Mead Data Central, P.O. Box 1830, Dayton OH 45401; (800) 227-4908.

WESTLAW

WESTLAW is the West Publishing Company's computer-assisted legal research system. A variety of Federal law and related information is available on such topics as the U.S. Code, decisions of the U.S. Tax Court and Tax Court memorandum decisions, the Internal Revenue Code, and the full text of West's *Supreme Court Reporter*. Special interest libraries include securities, antitrust and business regulation, labor, Federal Government contracts, patent, trademark, copyright, communications and admiralty. For further information, contact West Publishing Co., P.O. Box 64526, St. Paul, MN 55164; (800) 328-0109 or (612) 228-2450.

Judicial Branch Organizations

The business of all the Federal courts described here—except the United States Court of Military Appeals and the United States Tax Court, which are not administered as part of the Federal judicial system—is discussed in detail in the text and tables of the *Annual Report of the Director of the Administrative Office of the United States Courts*. Information on this publication is provided in the discussion of the Administrative Office of the United States Courts later in this section. Fiscal year 1985 budget for the judicial branch is $996 million or 0.10% of the total Federal budget; 17,171 paid employees, or 0.58% of the total civilian work force.

The Supreme Court of the United States

This is the highest court of the United States of America. It consists of nine Justices appointed for life by the President, with the advice and consent of the Senate. One Justice is designated the Chief Justice, while the others are Associate Justices. The term of the Court begins, by law, on the first Monday in October each year and continues as long as business before the Court requires—usually until about the end of June. Six members constitute a quorum. Approximately 5,000 cases are passed upon each term.

Key Offices and Telephone Numbers

Address: 1 First Street NE, Washington, DC 20543

General Information	(202) 479-3000
Clerk of the Court	(202) 479-3011
Library, Reference	(202) 479-3177
Library, Records and Briefs	(202) 479-3186

Lower Courts

United States Courts of Appeals

The intermediate appellate courts in the United States judicial system are the courts of appeals in 13 circuits (see Figure 5-3). A disappointed suitor in a district court usually has a right to have the decision of the case reviewed by the court of appeals of his or her circuit. In addition to appeals from the district courts, the courts of appeals receive many cases to review actions of the Tax Court and various Federal administrative agencies for errors of law. The decisions of the courts of appeals are final, except as they are subject to discretionary review or appeal in the U.S. Supreme Court.

United States District Courts

The district courts are the trial courts of general Federal jurisdiction. Each State has at least one district court, while some larger States have as many as four. There are 89 district courts in the 50 States, plus one each in the District of

120 FEDfind

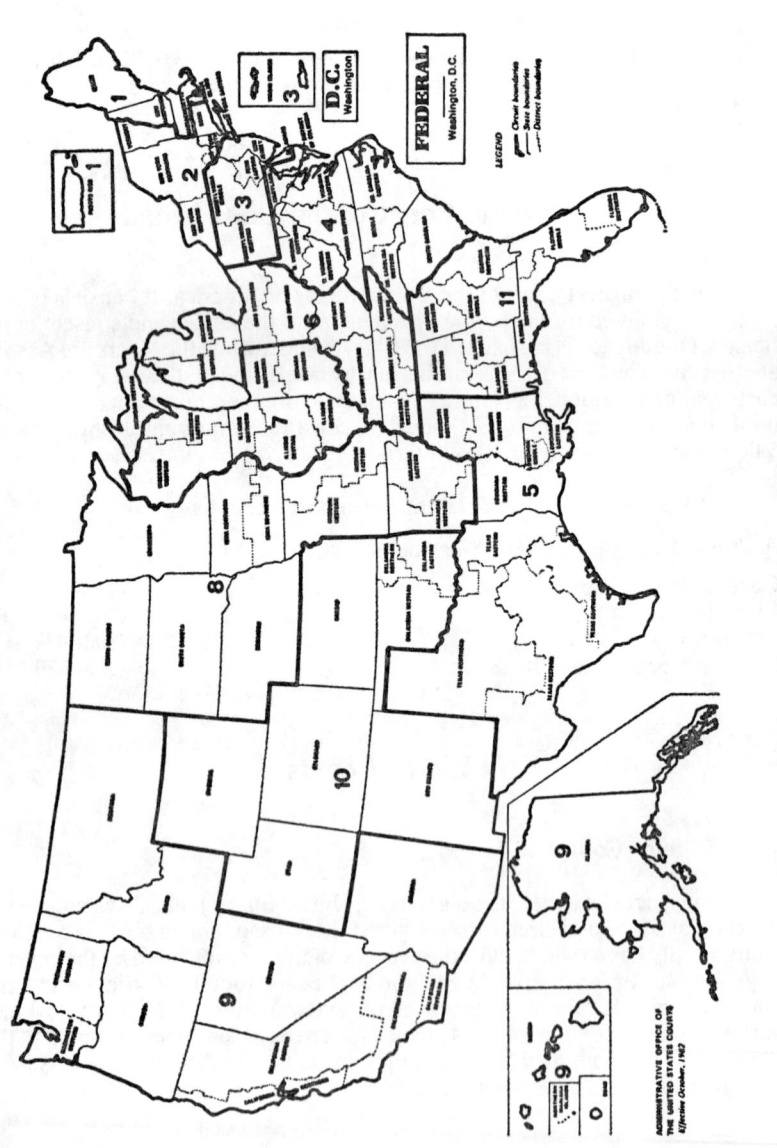

(Source: The U.S. Courts: Their Jurisdiction and Work)
Figure 5-3. The Thirteen Federal Judicial Circuits

Columbia, Guam, Puerto Rico, the Virgin Islands and the Northern Mariana Islands. A district court may have several divisions and several locations where the court may hear cases. Cases from the district courts are reviewed by the applicable United States court of appeals, except that injunction orders of special three-judge district courts and certain decisions holding acts of Congress unconstitutional may be appealed directly to the Supreme Court.

National Courts

In addition to the Supreme Court, the United States courts of appeals and district courts, there are a number of special courts that deal with particular types of cases. Appeals from decisions of these courts may ultimately be reviewed in the Supreme Court.

Temporary Emergency Court of Appeals

This court has exclusive jurisdiction of all appeals from district courts in cases arising under economic stabilization laws. It consists of eight district and circuit judges designated by the Chief Justice. For further information, contact the Clerk, Temporary Emergency Court of Appeals, United States Courthouse, Washington, DC 20001; (202) 535-3390.

United States Court of Appeals for the Federal Circuit

This court was created in 1982 by merging the former United States Court of Claims and the United States Court of Customs and Patent Appeals into one court. As such, the court hears appeals in patent, copyright and trademark cases from any district court, all appeals from the United States Claims Court and the United States Court of International Trade, and certain other appeals. The judicial business of the courts of appeals is conducted through courts located in the principal cities in each circuit. For further information, contact the Clerk, United States Court of Appeals for the Federal Circuit, 717 Madison Place NW, Washington, DC 20439; (202) 633-6550.

United States Claims Court

This court has jurisdiction to render money judgments upon any claim against the Federal Government wherein the Congress has waived the sovereign immunity of the United States. Aliens and their governments may also bring suits in this court, provided the courts of their nations give U.S. citizens the same privilege. Judgments are subject to appeal to the U.S. Court of Appeals for the Federal Circuit. The court is composed of 16 judges appointed by the President and confirmed by the Senate for 15 years, one of whom is designated as the chief judge by the President. For further information, contact the Clerk, United States Claims Court, 717 Madison Place NW, Washington, DC 20005; (202) 633-7257.

United States Court of International Trade

Cases that involve international trade and customs duties are the focus of this court's activities. Most of its cases involve controversies concerning the classification and valuation of imported merchandise. The U.S. Court of Appeals for the Federal Circuit hears all appeals from this court. The court consists of nine judges appointed by the President for life. For further information, contact the Clerk, United States Court of International Trade, 1 Federal Plaza, New York, NY 10007; (212) 264-2814.

United States Court of Military Appeals

This is the final appellate tribunal to review court-martial convictions of all the services. The court consists of three civilian judges appointed by the President for 15-year terms. For further information, contact the Clerk, United States Court of Military Appeals, 450 E Street NW, Washington, DC 20442; (202) 272-1448.

United States Tax Court

A special court that decides controversies between taxpayers and the Internal Revenue Service, this court hears cases that involve alleged underpayment of Federal income, gift and estate taxes. All decisions other than small tax cases are subject to review by the courts of appeals. The court is composed of 19 judges who are appointed by the President for terms of 15 years. For further information, contact the Administrative Office, United States Tax Court, 400 Second Street NW, Washington, DC 20217; (202) 376-2751.

Administrative Office of the United States Courts

This organization performs the administrative duties for the Federal court system. Among other duties, the office prepares and submits to Congress the budget for the courts; receives reports from and exercises some supervision over the clerical staffs of the courts, probation officers, bankruptcy judges, United States magistrates, reporters and other court personnel; audits and disburses money for the operation of the courts through the United States marshals; compiles and publishes statistics on the volume and distribution of business in the courts; supplies a professional secretariat and legal and statistical services to committees of the Judicial Conference of the United States; and conducts studies of court procedures for the Judicial Conference, as well as for other interested groups including committees of the Congress.

Key Offices and Telephone Numbers

Address: 811 Vermont Avenue NW, Washington, DC 20544

General Information	(202) 633-6097
General Counsel	(202) 633-6127
Legislative Affairs	(202) 633-6040
Library and Legal Research Services	(202) 633-6314
Personnel	(202) 633-6113
Statistical Analysis and Reports Division	(202) 633-6094

Key Information Resources

The Statistical Analysis and Reports Division (SARD) collects, analyzes and publishes data on the workload of the Federal courts. The preliminary *Annual*

Report of the Director, published in September, excludes the Proceedings of the Judicial Conference and is available **FREE** by contacting the SARD. The final *Annual Report*, published in January, is available from the Government Printing Office (GPO). See the GPO order form for information. All other publications, listed below, are available from SARD. Most of the reports are supplied **FREE**; others, however, are limited and are available on loan for 30 days. All annual reports are for years ending June 30, unless otherwise noted.

Annual Report of the Director
Federal Court Management Statistics
Grand and Petit Juror Service in U.S. District Courts
Federal Offenders in U.S. District Courts
Federal Judicial Workload Statistics
Report on Applications for Orders Authorizing or Approving the Interception of Wire or Oral Communications (calendar year report)
U.S. District Courts:
  Civil and Trials—Statistical Tables, 1970–1979
U.S. District Courts:
  Criminal Statistical Tables, 1970–1979
U.S. District Courts:
  Bankruptcy Statistical Tables, 1970–1979
Courts of Appeals:
  Workload Statistics for the Decade of the 1970's
Glossary of Terms Used in the Federal Courts
Index of City and Town Locations Within County and State
Requests for Fees & Expenses Under the Equal Access to Justice Act
Sentences Imposed Chart
Pictorial Summary

Federal Judicial Center

The Federal Judicial Center (FJC) furthers the development and adoption of improved judicial administration in the Federal courts of the United States. As such, the FJC is the research, development and training arm of the courts, which comprise probation offices and appellate and district courts, as well as the U.S. Supreme Court. The work of the Center revolves around the four divisions that are listed below. The Chief Justice of the United States is the chairperson of the Center's Board, which also includes the Director of the Administrative Office of the United States Courts and six judges elected for four-year terms by the Judicial Conference of the United States.

Key Offices and Telephone Numbers

Address: 1520 H Street NW, Washington, DC 20005

General Information	(202) 633-6011
Continuing Education and Training Division	(202) 633-6332
Innovations and Systems Development Division	(202) 633-6361
Inter-Judicial Affairs and Information Services Division	(202) 633-6347
Research Division	(202) 633-6326
Personnel and Budget Office	(202) 633-6321

Key Information Resources

The Center's annual *Catalog of Publications*, published in January, describes reports of research and analysis performed by or for the FJC, as well as products of Center seminars and workshops conducted for various judicial branch personnel. Their *Annual Report*, published in August, summarizes the Center's activities and describes the work projected through the end of the next fiscal year. Both publications are available **FREE** from the Center's Information Services Office.

Subject Bibliographies

Most of the judiciary-related publications for sale by the Government Printing Office (GPO) may be identified using the following subject bibliographies (SB), available **FREE** from the GPO. See the GPO SB order form.

- Board of Tax Appeals and Tax Court Reports (SB-67)
- Courts and Correctional Institutions (SB-91)
- United States Code (SB-197)
- United States Court of Claims Reports (SB-174)
- United States Reports [Supreme Court] (SB-25)
- U.S. Court of Customs and Patent Appeals Reports and U.S. Court of International Trade (SB-52)

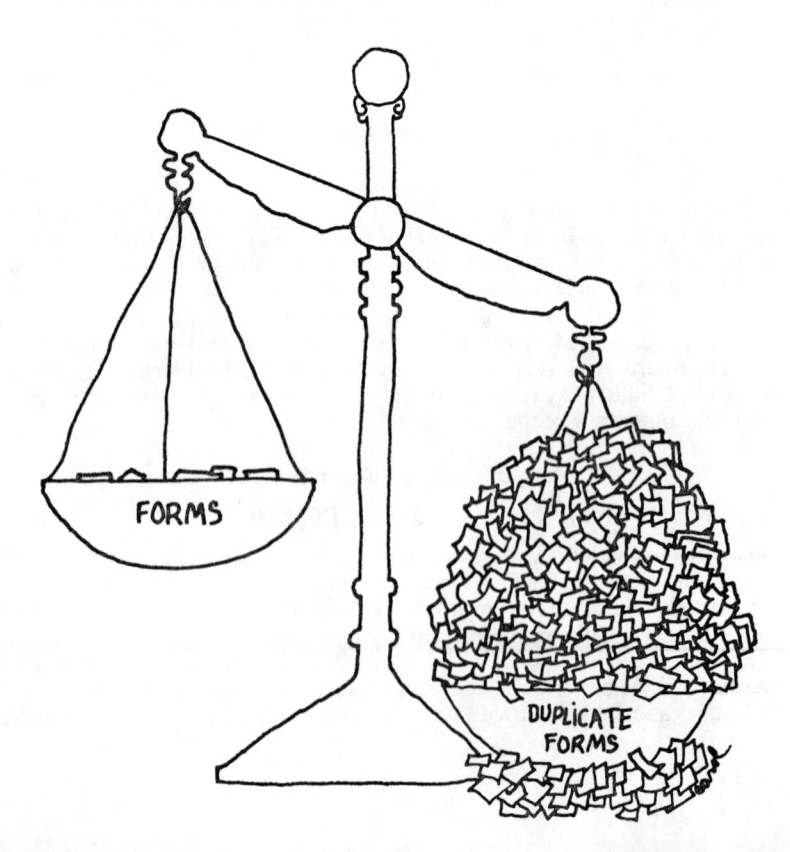

Chapter 6
Executive Branch Overview

The executive departments and agencies of the U.S. Government were developed to administer the laws of the Nation. Agencies in the executive branch may be created by statute, reorganization plans, internal departmental reorganizations, or, in some cases, by Presidential directive. Regulatory commissions are independent agencies established by Congress to regulate an aspect of the United States' economy. These and other so-called independent agencies in fact are not independent of the U.S. Government, since they are subject to the laws enacted by Congress and executed by the President. Numerous publications and services describe these organizational entities and their missions and functions—many of which are described in this chapter.

The information resources described in this chapter are organized under the following headings.
- Federal Register System
- The Federal Register
- Code of Federal Regulations
- Periodicals Covering Executive Branch Activities
- Biographies

Federal Register System

The Federal Register System is comprised primarily of two major publications—the daily *Federal Register* (FR) and the annually-revised *Code of Federal Regulations* (CFR). These two publications together provide an up-to-date version of any regulation. To understand the system one must understand each separate publication as well as the relationship between them. Figure 6-1 depicts the basic rulemaking process along with key offices and telephone numbers associated with the process.

List of Libraries That Have Announced Availability of Federal Register and Code of Federal Regulations

This is an annual list of libraries where the *Federal Register* and *Code of Federal Regulations* are available for examination free of charge. April 1985. 12pp. **FREE**. Office of the Federal Register, National Archives and Records Administration, Washington, DC 20408; (202) 523-5240.

126 FEDfind

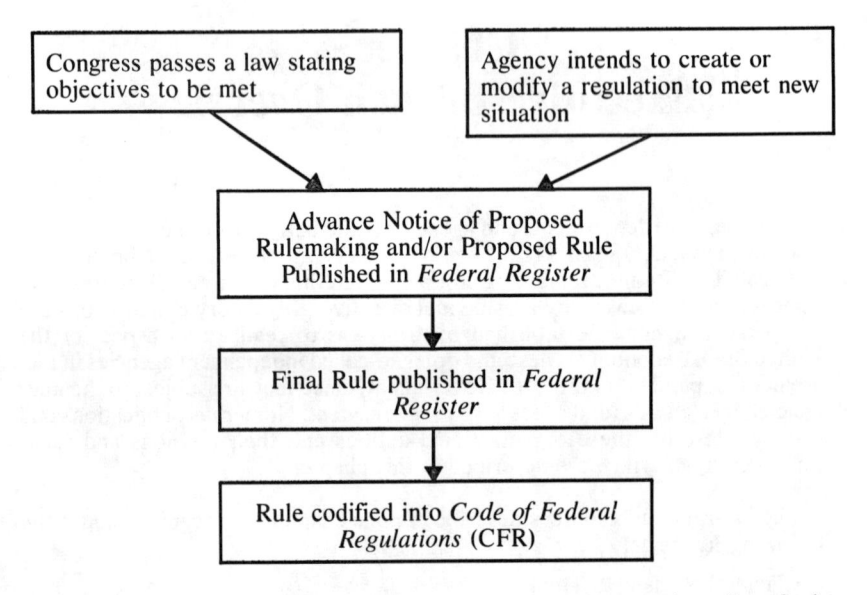

```
┌─────────────────────────────┐     ┌─────────────────────────────┐
│ Congress passes a law stating│     │ Agency intends to create or  │
│ objectives to be met         │     │ modify a regulation to meet new│
│                              │     │ situation                    │
└─────────────────────────────┘     └─────────────────────────────┘
                    ↘               ↙
              ┌─────────────────────────────────┐
              │ Advance Notice of Proposed       │
              │ Rulemaking and/or Proposed Rule  │
              │ Published in Federal Register    │
              └─────────────────────────────────┘
                              ↓
              ┌─────────────────────────────────┐
              │ Final Rule published in Federal  │
              │ Register                         │
              └─────────────────────────────────┘
                              ↓
              ┌─────────────────────────────────┐
              │ Rule codified into Code of Federal│
              │ Regulations (CFR)                │
              └─────────────────────────────────┘
```

The Reader Aids section of the daily *Federal Register* carries a list of telephone numbers for information and assistance regarding Office of the Federal Register publications and programs. To contact this office, write or call, Office of the Federal Register, National Archives and Records Administration, Washington, DC 20408; (202) 523-5240. Appearing every Monday is a CFR checklist that provides current prices and revision dates for each CFR volume.

Figure 6-1. Federal Rulemaking Process

Executive Branch Overview   127

A Guide to Federal Agency Rulemaking

Prepared by the Administrative Conference of the United States, this guide is primarily designed as a tool for agency rulemakers and the administrative bar. It is also useful to individuals who want a clear and comprehensive understanding of the process by which rules are made and tested. This includes anyone who participates in, reviews or monitors agency rulemaking. (A rule is "an established standard, guide or regulation; a principle or regulation set up by authority; prescribing or directing action on forbearance" according to *Black's Law Dictionary*. After statutory law, it is the most visible manifestation of the power of the State.) The guide provides an integrated view of the many requirements that apply to rulemaking. It includes discussion of significant issues and developments pertaining to rulemaking. A detailed table of contents and a chapter-by-chapter bibliography are included to help users locate topics and sources of additional information. 1983. 322pp. $5.50. GPO S/N 052-003-00923-4. (Y 3.Ad6:8 R86) See the GPO order form.

The Federal Register: What It Is and How To Use It

This handbook provides guidelines for using the *Federal Register* and related publications, an explanation of how to solve a sample research problem and a discussion of how the consumer can be a participant in the regulatory process. The guide is prepared by the Office of the Federal Register, National Archives and Records Administration. 1985. 113pp. $4.50. GPO S/N 022-003-01116-1. (AE 2.108:F 31) See the GPO order form.

Federal Register: Document Drafting Handbook

Prepared by the National Archives and Records Administration, Office of the Federal Register, this handbook is designed to help Federal agencies prepare documents for publication in the *Federal Register*. It provides details on regulatory development procedures, document format and publication. The information is presented in a functional manner, divided into sections that allow the user to identify necessary information. A revised edition is to be published in 1986. 1980. 66pp. $5.00. GPO S/N 022-001-00138-4. (GS 4.107/a:D659) See the GPO order form.

Federal Register Thesaurus of Indexing Terms

This thesaurus is a basic indexing vocabulary for Federal regulations published in the *Federal Register* and the *Code of Federal Regulations*. There are two sections to the thesaurus—an alphabetical list of all indexing terms with a series of notations under each term to refer users to preferred or related terms, and a grouping of terms under 19 broad subject categories that allows the user to determine the existing thesaurus terms for each broad subject. 1983. 27pp. FREE. Office of the Federal Register, National Archives and Records Administration, Washington, DC 20408; (202) 523-5240.

The Federal Register

Federal Register

The official daily publication that provides a uniform system for publishing Presidential and executive agency documents, these papers include Executive orders and proclamations as well as rules, proposed rules and notices of Federal agencies. The proposed rules section invites citizens or groups to participate in consideration of the proposed rule through the submission of written data, views, or arguments and, on occasion, oral presentation. In addition, the *Federal Register* publishes nonregulatory, public interest announcements such as advisory committee meetings, grant application deadlines and availability of environmental impact statements. Subscribers automatically receive the monthly *Federal Register Index* and the *Code of Federal Regulations, LSA, List of CFR Sections Affected*. Issued daily Monday through Friday, except on legal holidays. Subscription price: $300.00 a year. Single copy price: $1.50. A special six-month subscription is available at $150.00. GPO List ID FR. A microfiche (24X) edition is also available. Subscription price: $145.00 a year. Single copy price: $1.50. Special six-month subscription: $72.50. GPO List ID MFFR. (AE 2.106:) See the GPO subscription order form.

Federal Register Index

A monthly collection of material published in the daily *Federal Register*. Each issue is cumulative. The December issue serves as the annual issue and covers the period January 1–December 31. Entries are found primarily under the names of the issuing agencies. Significant subjects are noted as cross-references. Subscribers to the *Federal Register* receive the service automatically as part of that subscription. Subscription price: $22.00 a year. No single copies sold. GPO List ID FRSU. (AE 2.106:) See the GPO subscription order form.

Federal Register Abstract Master Edition

A publication issued each day following a meeting of Congress, it includes all items published in the *Federal Register* in abstract form separated into more than 31 major topic divisions and more than 350 subject headings. It provides summary descriptions of all proposed and final regulations, references to affected sections of the *Code of Federal Regulations*, notices of meetings, hearings, and departmental and agency actions. The abstracts include dates, docket numbers and other citations. Customized service is available; a user may request specific information from pre-selected subject headings. Subscription price for the master edition: $725.00 a year. Prices on selected profiles provided on request. A microfiche copy of the *Register* is available at $250.00 a year. National Standards Association, 5161 River Road, Bethesda, MD 20816; (800) 638-8094 or (301) 951-1305.

Federal Register Abstracts

The above database is available in machine-readable form for specialized user applications. Computer software support is provided to customize all or any portion of the file to the user's retrieval system. Pricing for this service is available on request, see entry above.

CIS Federal Register Index

This Congressional Information Service, Inc. (CIS) weekly publication is a finding aid to the *Federal Register*. It indexes all rules, proposed rules, announcements and Presidential documents in each daily *Federal Register*. A detailed subject index lists all new items under as many headings as appropriate. In addition to Federal agencies, programs and authorizing legislation, the *Federal Register Index* lists new announcements under geographic place names, names of individuals and organizations, chemical substances, industries, professions and other subjects. An index by *Code of Federal Regulations* (CFR) section numbers indicates what type of change was made or proposed to a CFR section. An index by agency docket number shows where to find *Federal Register* items concerning a particular docket number. Also included is a Calendar of Effective Dates and Comment Deadlines. This is a summary of effective dates of final rules, comment deadlines, and hearing and reply dates. Subscription to the FRI includes monthly, quarterly and semiannual cumulative issues. Subscription price: $595.00 a year. CIS, 4520 East-West Highway, Suite 800, Bethesda, MD 20814; (800) 638-8380 or (301) 654-1550.

Code of Federal Regulations

Code of Federal Regulations

The *Code of Federal Regulations* (CFR) is an annually revised codification of the general and permanent rules published in the *Federal Register* by the executive departments and agencies. The CFR is divided into 50 titles (see Figure 6-2) that represent broad areas subject to Federal regulation. Each title is revised at least once each calendar year. The CFR is kept up-to-date by the individual issues of the *Federal Register* and *Code of Federal Regulations, LSA, List of CFR Sections Affected*. Therefore, the *Federal Register* and the CFR must be used together to determine the latest version of any given rule. Each CFR title includes an alphabetical listing by agency of subtitle and chapter assignments in the *Code of Federal Regulations*. Issued irregularly. Sold in both paperback (approximately 175 books) and microfiche (1,200 fiche). Paperback subscription price: $595.00 a year; GPO List ID CFR86. (GS 4.108:) Single copies vary in price. Microfiche (24X) subscription price: $185.00 a year; single copy price: $3.75; GPO List ID CFRM6. (GS 4.108: MF/) See the GPO subscription order form.

Code of Federal Regulations, LSA, List of CFR Sections Affected

A monthly listing of amendatory actions published in the *Federal Register*, entries indicate the nature of changes, such as revision, removal or correction. The December issue is the Annual for CFR Titles 1–16; the March issue is the Annual for Titles 17–27; the June issue is the Annual for Titles 28–41; and the September issue is the Annual for Titles 42–50. Subscribers to the *Federal Register* receive this publication as part of their subscription. Subscription price: $24.00 a year. No single copies sold. GPO List ID LCS. (GS 4.108/3:) See the GPO subscription order form.

CFR Index and Finding Aids

The *Code of Federal Regulations* (CFR) index and finding aids volume is revised twice a year as of January 1 and July 1. It contains a subject/agency index for rules currently codified in the CFR; a list of agency-prepared indexes appearing in individual CFR volumes; a table of laws and Presidential documents cited as authority for regulations currently codified in the CFR; a list of acts requiring publication in the *Federal Register*; a list of CFR titles, chapters, subchapters and parts; and an alphabetical list of agencies that appear in the CFR. 1985. 1,050pp. $18.00. GPO S/N 822-004-00046-6. (GS 4.108:ind./985) See the GPO order form.

Index to the Code of Federal Regulations

With its thesaurus of approximately 20,000 terms, this annual index to the CFR provides a controlled system of subject access to Federal regulations, regardless of the CFR titles in which the information appears. The index also provides access to Federal regulations based on the geographic area affected, using a two-part index that covers independent political and geographic entities. One section covers cities, counties, States and regions of the U.S., along with countries, continents and regions of the world. Another section provides access to specific

1. General Provisions
2. [Reserved]
3. The President
4. Accounts
5. Administrative Personnel
6. [Reserved]
7. Agriculture Treasury
8. Aliens and Nationality
9. Animals and Animal Products
10. Energy
11. Federal Elections
12. Banks and Banking
13. Business Credit and Assistance
14. Aeronautics and Space
15. Commerce and Foreign Trade
16. Commercial Practices
17. Commodity and Securities Exchanges
18. Conservation of Power and Water Resources
19. Customs Duties
20. Employees' Benefits
21. Food and Drugs
22. Foreign Relations
23. Highways
24. Housing and Urban Development
25. Indians
26. Internal Revenue
27. Alcohol, Tobacco Products and Firearms
28. Judicial Administration
29. Labor
30. Mineral Resources
31. Money and Finance: Treasury
32. National Defense
33. Navigation and Navigable Waters
34. Education
35. Panama Canal
36. Parks, Forests and Public Property
37. Patents, Trademarks and Copyrights
38. Pensions, Bonuses and Veterans' Relief
39. Postal Service
40. Protection of Environment
41. Public Contracts and Property Management
42. Public Health
43. Public Lands: Interior
44. Emergency Management and Assistance
45. Public Welfare
46. Shipping
47. Telecommunications
48. Federal Acquisition Regulations System
49. Transportation
50. Wildlife and Fisheries

Each volume of the CFR is revised at least once each calendar year and issued on a quarterly basis approximately as follows:

Titles 1-16, January 1
Titles 17-27, April 1
Titles 28-41, July 1
Titles 42-50, October 1

The appropriate revision date is printed on the cover of each volume. Each year's cover is a different color for quick reference.

Figure 6-2. Code of Federal Regulations Titles

rivers or bodies of water, parks, monuments, military installations, Indian reservations and similar federally administered properties named in the text of the CFR. For the year 1984, published October 1985. 4 vols., 4,257pp. $730.00. Congressional Information Service, Inc., 4520 East-West Highway, Suite 800, Bethesda, MD 20814; (800) 638-8380 or in Maryland (301) 654-1550.

Unified Agenda of Federal Regulations

This semiannual publication describes new regulations under development and existing regulations under review within each agency of the Federal Government. It is prepared by the Regulatory Information Service Center (RISC) of the Office of Management and Budget (OMB). Each "agenda" description includes—at a minimum—the following information: title, agency contact, effects on small business and other entities, *Code of Federal Regulations* citation, legal authority, an abstract and a timetable. Actions for each agency or subagency are grouped together. Within each agency grouping, entries are listed by type of action in the following order: current and projected rulemakings, reviews of existing regulations and completed actions. Contact the National Technical Information Service (NTIS) for availability and price of the April or October editions. See the NTIS order form.

Periodicals Covering Executive Branch Activities

National Journal

The *National Journal* is a weekly subscription publication that examines Government activities. Each issue includes articles that range from an explanation of the mechanics of the Federal Government to in-depth analyses of emerging trends and issues. The former includes outlines of the positions, strategies and tactics of the players in the Administration, Congress, agencies and special interest groups. An "At a Glance" section tracks the progress of 20 important issues confronting Congress and the White House in brief weekly capsules. A weekly "People" section is a source for following the movements of key policy people in government, business, labor, interest groups and media. An "Update" column covers developments in policy and politics in brief. A digest of significant studies, surveys and statistics is provided in the "InfoFile" section. Individuals and interest groups who want to present position papers on current issues may do so in the "Policy Forum" department. Extra services are included with the subscription. Subscribers may call the research desk for answers to questions on the status of bills, congressional votes, Government documents and previous articles. Twice a year, subscribers receive cumulative indexes to all subjects, people and organizations discussed in the *National Journal*. White House and Congressional telephone directories are sent out periodically to subscribers. Enquire for price information. National Journal, Inc., 1730 M Street NW, Suite 1100, Washington, DC 20036; (800) 424-2921 or (202) 857-1400.

Regulation

This bimonthly magazine covers regulatory activity of all kinds—legislative, judicial and administrative—whether directed at economic, political, social or cultural affairs. In addition to its general informational purpose, it is designed to foster a systematic analytic approach to regulation by examining policy choices and implications of regulations. It is intended not only for Government officials, but also for those with an interest in the policy process associated with regulation. Subscription price: $24.00 a year; single copy price: $5.00. American Enterprise Institute, 1150 17th Street NW, Washington, DC 20036; (800) 424-2873 or (202) 862-5870.

Biographies

Biographic information can also be found in a number of the publications described in Chapter 2, Directories.

Political Profiles

These presidential profiles are published every four years prior to the presidential election. The profiles feature exclusive interviews with the candidates and their families, comprehensive political and personal biographies, issue stances on more than 100 current topics, key staffers' names and more. Profiles prepared for the 1984 election include John Glenn, Gary Hart, Walter Mondale and Ronald Reagan. 1984. 32pp. $3.00 each. Political Profiles, Inc., 209 C Street NE, Washington, DC 20002; (202) 544-3833.

Biographical Directory of the United States Executive Branch, 1774–1977

This directory provides biographical sketches of Presidents, Vice Presidents and Cabinet leaders confirmed by the Senate. Appendices include Cabinets of all Presidents, and other government service, education, birth state, etc., of persons listed. 1977, 2nd ed. 503pp. $55.00. ISBN 0-8371-9527-6. Greenwood Press, P.O. Box 5007, Westport, CT 06881; (203) 226-3571.

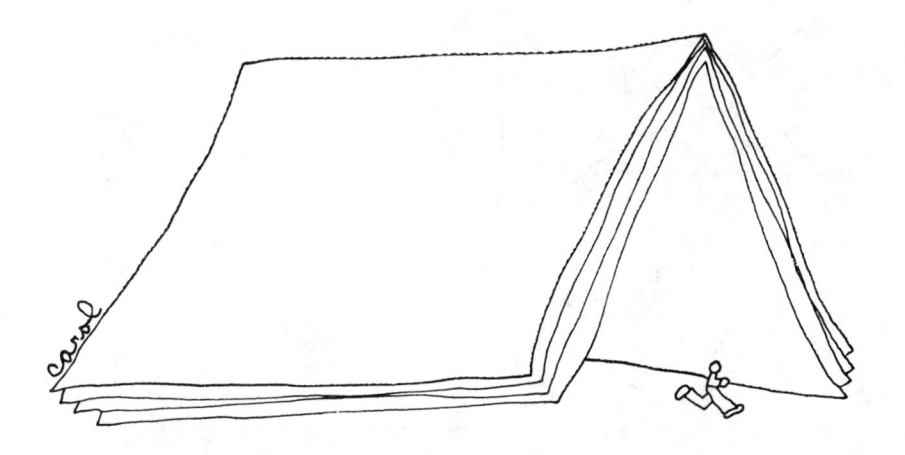

134   **FEDfind**

Chapter 7
Executive Office of the President

Under the authority of the Reorganization Act of 1939, various Federal Government agencies were consolidated under a new umbrella—the Executive Office of the President (EOP). Since then, Presidents have used Executive orders, reorganization plans and legislative mandates to reorganize the EOP to make its composition compatible with the goals and management style of their own administrations. The EOP currently consists of nine divisions that assist the President in the management of the executive branch and advise the President on a variety of issues. Figure 7-1 presents an organizational chart that shows the current structure of the EOP.

The information resources described in this chapter are organized under the following headings.

- The American Presidency
- Presidential Documents
- Executive Office of the President Publications
- Computerized Information Resource
- Executive Office of the President Divisions
  The White House Office
    Office of Management and Budget
    Council of Economic Advisors
    Council of Environmental Quality
    National Security Council
    Office of Policy Development
    Office of the United States Trade Representative
    Office of Science and Technology Policy
    Office of Administration
- Office of the Vice President of the United States

The American Presidency

In addition to the documents described below, the Government Printing Office (GPO) makes available **FREE** a subject bibliography (SB) of publications for sale entitled *Presidents of the United States* (SB-106). See the GPO SB order form.

The American Presidency: A Historical Bibliography

A bibliography of the more than 3,000 abstracts of articles, such topics are covered as lives of the presidents, presidential elections and the growth of the

136　FEDfind

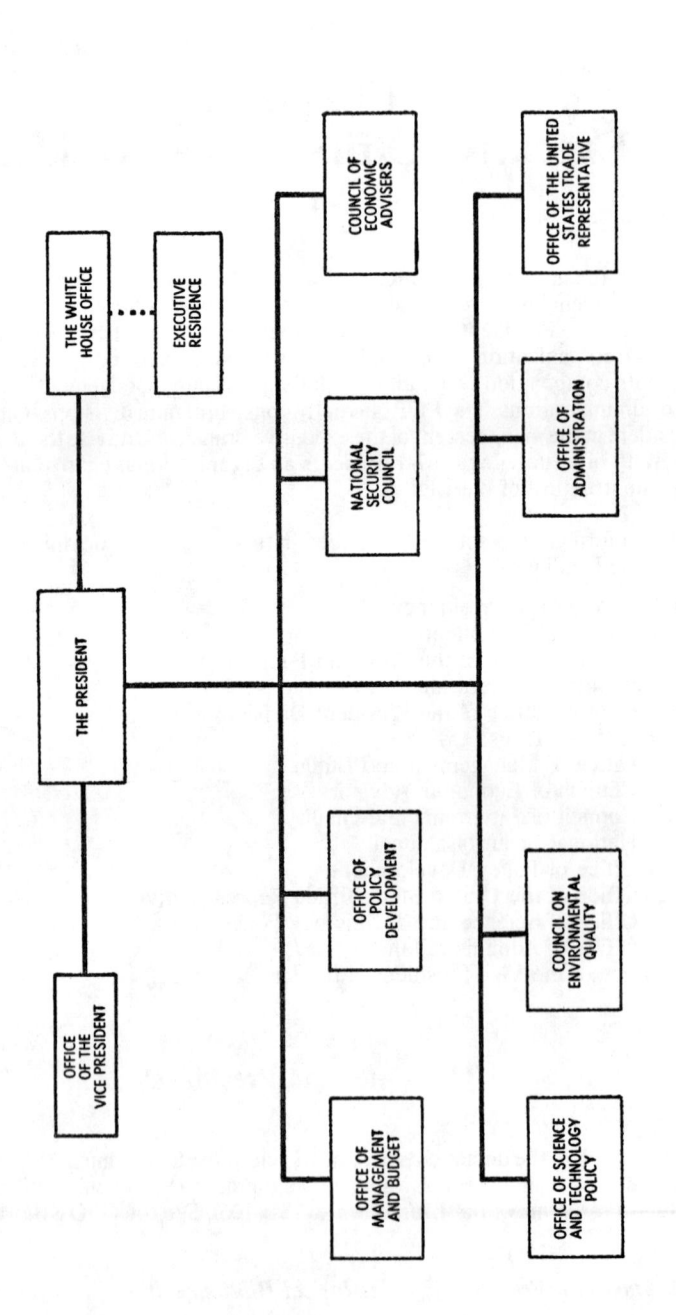

(Source: The U.S. Government Manual 1985–86)

Figure 7-1. Executive Office of the President

executive branch of the Federal Government—including the vice presidency and related departments. 1984. 376pp. $64.00. ISBN 0-87436-370-5. ABC-Clio, P.O. Box 4397, Santa Barbara, CA 93140; (800) 422-2546 or (805) 963-4221.
The Complete Book of U.S. Presidents

This book, written by William A. DeGregorio, includes a section on each president from Washington to Reagan covering each man's career before the presidency, his appointments to the Cabinet and the Supreme Court (with discussions of each appointee), the States added to the Union and the amendments added to the Constitution during his tenure, what was said and written about him, what he said and wrote, his upbringing, relatives, education, early romances, military service and more. A bibliography on each President is also included. 1984. 691pp. $22.50. ISBN 0-934878-36-6. (83-23201) Dembner Books, 80 Eighth Avenue, New York, NY 10011; (212) 924-2525.

Facts About the Presidents

This book is a compendium of facts and anecdotes about every President from George Washington to Ronald Reagan. Part 1 consists of 40 chapters—one for each President; each includes data about their lives, families, careers and administrations. Part 2 assembles this information so that comparisons may be made of Presidents' backgrounds and accomplishments. Also included are facts about the Presidency, party alignments of each Congress, names of Cabinet members, electoral and popular votes from every election, an alphabetical list of all Presidential candidates, etc. 1981, 4th ed. 456pp. $32.00. ISBN 0-8242-0612-6. (81-7537) Supplement to the 4th ed., 1985. 12pp. $3.00. ISBN 0-8242-0709-2. The H.W. Wilson Co., 950 University Avenue, Bronx, NY 10452; (800) 367-6770 or (800) 462-6060 in New York.

A Guide to Manuscripts in the Presidential Libraries

A description and index to more than 4,600 manuscript collections, microfilm and oral histories from the seven Presidential libraries in the National Archives system. For each library is included the names of directors, hours of operation and other information for use by researchers and visitors. The libraries are the Herbert Hoover, Franklin D. Roosevelt, Harry S. Truman, Dwight D. Eisenhower, John F. Kennedy, Lyndon B. Johnson and Gerald R. Ford. 1985. 475pp. $90.00. ISBN 0-934631-00-X. Research Materials Corp., P.O. Box 243, College Park, MD 20740; (301) 552-2622.

The Inaugural Addresses of the Presidents of the United States, 1789–1985

A volume of the complete and unabridged inaugural addresses from George Washington's first to Ronald Reagan's second inauguration. 1985. 192pp. $29.95. ISBN 0-932037-00-3. (84-72691) American Inheritance Press, 2314 Arctic Avenue, Atlantic City, NJ 08401; (609) 344-0383.

The Presidency: A Research Guide

This research guide describes primary and secondary resources on the subject of the U.S. Presidency. Written by Robert U. Goehlert and Fenton S. Martin, this guide is divided into four sections. "The Institution of the Presidency" provides data on Presidential papers, the *Federal Register* system, statutes and administrative laws. "The Oval Office" focuses on the Presidency from the perspective of the individual. The section details locations of papers and publications of specific Presidents and the Presidential library system. The third part concentrates on campaigns and elections. The last section describes the methodology of Presidential research. Here the authors provide tips on how to develop topics, as well as how to design and conduct a search strategy. Included in its 26 appendices are sources of Presidential documents, actions, speeches, messages and proclamations; terms of office by year and Congress; election statistics sources; and tables of research operations for secondary sources that locate references for specific types of data. 1984. 341pp. $28.50. ISBN 0-87436-373-X. (84-6425) ABC-Clio, P.O. Box 4397, Santa Barbara, CA 93140; (800) 422-2546 or (805) 963-4221.

Presidential Also-Rans and Running Mates, 1788–1980

Written by Leslie H. Southwick, this political/biographical reference book provides convention and election facts, followed by entries on the 88 major party and significant third-party nominees who never served as President. Also included are biographical details and bibliographies with each entry. 1984. 736pp. $49.95. ISBN 0-89950-109-5. (83-25577) McFarland & Co., Inc., Publishers, P.O. Box 611, Jefferson, NC 28640; (919) 246-4460.

The Presidents: A Reference History

A compendium of 35 biographies edited by Henry F. Graff, this book covers every President through Jimmy Carter. Each Presidential administration is analyzed in terms of the social, political, economic and foreign policy decisions and their effects on domestic and foreign affairs. Selected bibliographies are provided for further study. 1984. 700pp. $65.00. ISBN 0-684-17607-6. (83-20225) Charles Scribner's Sons, Order Department, Front and Brown Streets, Riverside, NJ 08075; (800) 257-5755 or (609) 461-6500.

Presidential Documents

Weekly Compilation of Presidential Documents

A periodical that provides full texts of the President's public speeches, statements, messages to Congress, news conferences, personnel appointments and nominations, and other Presidential materials released by the White House, it carries a Monday dateline and covers materials released during the preceding week. Each issue includes an index and a cumulative index to prior issues. Separate indexes are published quarterly, semiannually and annually. Also included are lists of legislation approved by the President and nominations submitted to the Senate, a checklist of White House press releases, and a digest of other Presidential activities and White House announcements. For a sample copy write to Director, Office of the Federal Register, National Archives and Records Administration, Washington, DC 20408. Subscription price: $64.00 a year (nonpriority), $101.00 a year (priority); single copy price: $1.75. GPO List ID PD. (AE 2.109:) See the GPO subscription order form.

Codification of Presidential Proclamations and Executive Orders

A source of proclamations and Executive orders that have general applicability and continuing effect, each codified document is assigned to one of 50 chapters that represent broad subject areas similar to the title designations of the *Code of Federal Regulations* and the *United States Code*. Incorporated into each proclamation and Executive order are all amendments in effect on the most recent revision date. It includes documents issued or amended during the period January 20, 1961 through January 20, 1985. $10.00. GPO S/N 022-002-00110-1. See the GPO order form.

Public Papers of the Presidents of the United States

This series supplies in chronological order the papers of the Presidents back to Herbert Hoover (1929–33), excluding those of Franklin D. Roosevelt. The latter are included in a privately published series of 13 volumes entitled *The Public Papers and Addresses of Franklin D. Roosevelt*, edited by Samuel I. Rosenman. Included are public speeches and remarks, messages to the Congress and public statements and letters. Beginning with the Carter administration, the series includes all materials contained in its companion publication, the *Weekly Compilation of Presidential Documents* described above. For a list of the more than 50 volumes in the series including ordering information, contact the Office of the Federal Register, National Archives and Records Administration, Washington, DC 20408; (202) 523-5240.

Executive Office of the President Publications

A Guide to Publications of the Executive Office of the President—Cumulative

Publications issued by the divisions of the Executive Office of the President (EOP) address a broad range of subjects relating to the policy aspects of the executive branch. A cumulative issue that includes citations issued during the first administration of President Reagan—January 20, 1981–December 31, 1984—is available. Publications are grouped by the sponsoring EOP division and ordering information is provided for each publication. 1985. 5pp. **FREE**. A quarterly document is also issued that provides a cumulative list of publications issued by the divisions of the EOP since January 1985. EOP Publications, 726 Jackson Place NW, Room 2200, Washington, DC 20503; (202) 395-7332.

Revised Table of Contents, Index and Rescinded Office of Management and Budget (OMB) Circulars and Federal Management Circulars Under OMB Jurisdiction

Office of Management and Budget (OMB) circulars communicate instructions and information to executive branch departments and establishments. The terms "departments and establishments" include any executive department, independent commission, board, bureau, office, agency, Government-owned or controlled corporation, or other establishment of the Government, including regulatory commission or board, and also the municipal government of the District of Columbia, but do not include the legislative or judicial branches of the Government. The provisions of any circular, except as otherwise specified in the circular, are to be observed by every such department or establishment insofar as the subject matter pertains to its affairs. A bulletin series is used in conjunction with the circular series when the nature of the subject matter requires single or one-time action or is of a transitory nature. This document includes an index to the current OMB circulars as of June 1984. 19pp. **FREE**. EOP Publications, see entry above.

Information Collection Report: OMB Control of Programs

A monthly report that outlines the Office of Management and Budget's (OMB) paperwork clearance decisions for the preceding month, highlighting those actions that are deemed to be "particularly significant or controversial." This includes information on the total number of information requests reviewed by OMB, the number disapproved, the number withdrawn by the sponsoring agencies and the number approved. For proposals considered "significant," the report provides brief synopses of the purposes of each information collection proposal and of OMB's action. Subscription price: $35.00 a year. Single copy price: $5.00. OMB Watch, 2001 O Street NW, Washington, DC 20036; (202) 659-1711.

White House Weekly

This weekly newsletter covers the happenings inside the White House. Subscription price: $295.00 per year. Feistritzer Publications, 1901 Pennsylvania Avenue NW, Suite 707, Washington, DC 20006; (202) 463-8344.

Executive Office of the President

Inside the Administration

A biweekly report on the Executive Office of the President and Cabinet chiefs, it covers economic, regulatory and management policies in such areas as taxes, the environment, energy, labor, competition, Federal procurement and paperwork. Subscription price: $465.00 a year. Inside Washington Publishers, P.O. Box 7167, Washington, DC 20044; (800) 424-9068 or (202) 347-1941.

Computerized Information Resources

The following is a commercially available computer-based information system that relates to the activities of the Executive Office of the President. For more information on online sources, see Appendix D, Computerized Information Resources.

White House News Service

The White House News Service (WHNEWS) is a general interest wire service that provides information from the White House Press Office, Office of the Vice President, Office of the First Lady, Office of Management and Budget and the National Security Council. WHNEWS supplies the full text of news releases, speeches, personnel announcements, legislation, fact sheets, transcripts, disaster statements and other public information. Also included is the daily feature, "Today at the White House," which lists the public schedule of meetings and briefings at the White House. Available through ITT Dialcom, Inc., 1109 Spring Street, Suite 410, Silver Spring, MD 20910; (301) 588-1572.

Executive Office of the President Divisions

The White House Office

The White House Office (WHO) serves the President in the performance of the many activities and duties incident to his or her immediate office. The staff of the President facilitates and maintains communication with the Congress and its individual Members, the heads of executive departments and agencies, the press and other information media, and the general public. The various Assistants to the President are personal aides and assist the President in such matters as he or she may direct. For further information, contact WHO, 1600 Pennsylvania Avenue NW, Washington, DC 20500; (202) 456-1414.

Office of Management and Budget

The Office of Management and Budget (OMB) is primarily responsible to assist the President develop and maintain an effective Federal Government by reviewing organizational structure and management procedures of the executive branch to ensure that they produce the intended results. In addition the OMB assists the President in preparing the Federal budget and formulate the fiscal program of the Government; supervise and control the administration of the budget; perform evaluations of Federal Government programs; clear and coordinate departmental advice on proposed legislation and recommendations for Presidential action on bills passed by the Congress; and assist in the development of regulatory reform proposals and in programs for paperwork reduction, especially reporting burdens on the public. Through its Office of Federal Procurement Policy (OFPP), the OMB also provides overall direction of procurement policies, regulations and procedures for the agencies of the executive branch. For further information, contact OMB, Executive Office Building, Washington, DC 20503; (202) 395-3080.

Council of Economic Advisors

The Council of Economic Advisors (CEA) analyzes the national economy and its various segments; advises the President on economic developments; appraises the economic programs and policies of the Federal Government; recommends to the President policies for economic growth and stability; and assists in the preparation of the annual economic report of the President to Congress. The Council consists of three members appointed by the President by and with the advice and consent of the Senate. One of the members is designated by the President as Chairperson. For further information, contact CEA, Old Executive Office Building, Washington, DC 20500; (202) 395-5084.

National Security Council

The National Security Council (NSC) advises the President with respect to the integration of domestic, foreign and military policies relating to national security. Its chairman is the President and statutory members are the Vice President and the Secretaries of State and Defense. The Chairman of the Joint Chiefs of Staff is the statutory military advisor to the Council and the Director of Central Intelligence is its intelligence advisor. For further information, contact NSC, Old Executive Office Building, Washington, DC 20506; (202) 395-4974

Office of Policy Development

The Office of Policy Development (OPD)—formerly the Domestic Policy Staff—assists the President in the formulation, coordination and implementation of economic and domestic policy. OPD also serves as the policy staff for the President's various Cabinet Councils. For further information, contact OPD, 1600 Pennsylvania Avenue NW, Washington, DC 20500; (202) 456-6405.

Office of the United States Trade Representative

The Office of the United States Trade Representative (USTR) is responsible for setting and administering overall U.S. trade policy. The USTR is headed by the United States Trade Representative, a Cabinet-level official with the rank of ambassador, who is directly responsible to the President. The Trade Representative supervises and coordinates U.S. foreign trade policy and has policy and negotiating responsibility for direct investment, trade commodities and energy, export expansion and East-West trade. In addition, the Trade Representative conducts U.S. affairs relating to the General Agreements on Tariffs and Trade (GATT). For further information, contact USTR, 600 17th Street NW, Washington, DC 20506; (202) 395-3230.

Council on Environmental Quality

The Council on Environmental Quality (CEQ) develops and recommends to the President national policies to improve environmental quality; performs a continuing analysis of changes and trends in the national environment; reviews and appraises programs of the Federal Government to determine their contributions to sound environmental policy; conducts studies, research and analyses relating to ecological systems and environmental quality; and assists the President in the preparation of the annual environmental quality report to the Congress. For further information, contact CEQ, 722 Jackson Place NW, Washington, DC 20006; (202) 395-5700.

Office of Science and Technology Policy

The Office of Science and Technology Policy (OSTP) provides the President with scientific, engineering and technological analysis and judgment regarding major policies, plans and programs of the Federal Government. The OSTP also advises the President on scientific and technological aspects of national concern, including the economy, national security, health, foreign relations and the environment; evaluates the scale, quality and effectiveness of Federal science and technology efforts; and assists the President in coordinating Federal research and development programs. For further information, contact OSTP, New Executive Office Building, Washington, DC 20506; (202) 395-4692.

Office of Administration

The Office of Administration (OA) provides administrative support and services to all Executive Office of the President divisions, except those services that are in direct support of the President. The services provided by the OA include information, personnel and financial management; data processing; library services; records management; and general office operations, such as non-Presidential mail, messenger service, printing, procurement and supply services. For further information, contact the Office of Administration, Old Executive Office Building, Washington, DC 20500; (202) 456-7052.

Office of the Vice President of the United States

In addition to his or her role as President of the Senate, the Vice President is empowered to succeed to the Presidency, as set forth in the Constitution and its amendments. The executive functions of the Vice President include participation in Cabinet meetings and, by statute, membership in the National Security Council and the Board of Regents of the Smithsonian Institution. For further information, contact the Office of the Vice President, Executive Office Building, Washington, DC 20501; (202) 456-2326. For Vice Presidential schedule information, call (202) 395-4245.

Chapter 8
Executive Branch Departments

The laws of the U.S. Government are administered by the thirteen executive departments and their respective agencies, along with numerous independent organizations (described in Chapter 9). A brief description of the mission and selected activities of each organization is included.

Also provided are the departments' budgets for fiscal year 1985 (ended September 30, 1985) and the number of civilian personnel assigned as of January 1985. Percentages for each figure are provided to help you better appreciate the relative resources (dollars and people) used by each department to accomplish its mission.

The "CFR *(Code of Federal Regulations)* reference" cites where detailed information on the department may be found. (The *United States Government Manual* may be consulted for more detailed information concerning the programs and activities of each department, as well as their respective agencies.)

Provided also are the sections "Key Offices and Telephone Numbers" and "Key Information Resources." These are designed to help you find the information you need quickly and are described in the Introduction, "How to Use *FEDfind*."

Following each department guide is a description of its respective component agencies, including the address and telephone number of its headquarters public information office. Check your local telephone directory under "United States Government" to see if a local department/agency office is located near you.

Listed below are the thirteen departments described in this chapter.
- Department of Agriculture
- Department of Commerce
- Department of Defense
- Department of Education
- Department of Energy
- Department of Health and Human Services
- Department of Housing and Urban Development
- Department of the Interior
- Department of Justice
- Department of Labor
- Department of State
- Department of Transportation
- Department of the Treasury

146 **FEDfind**

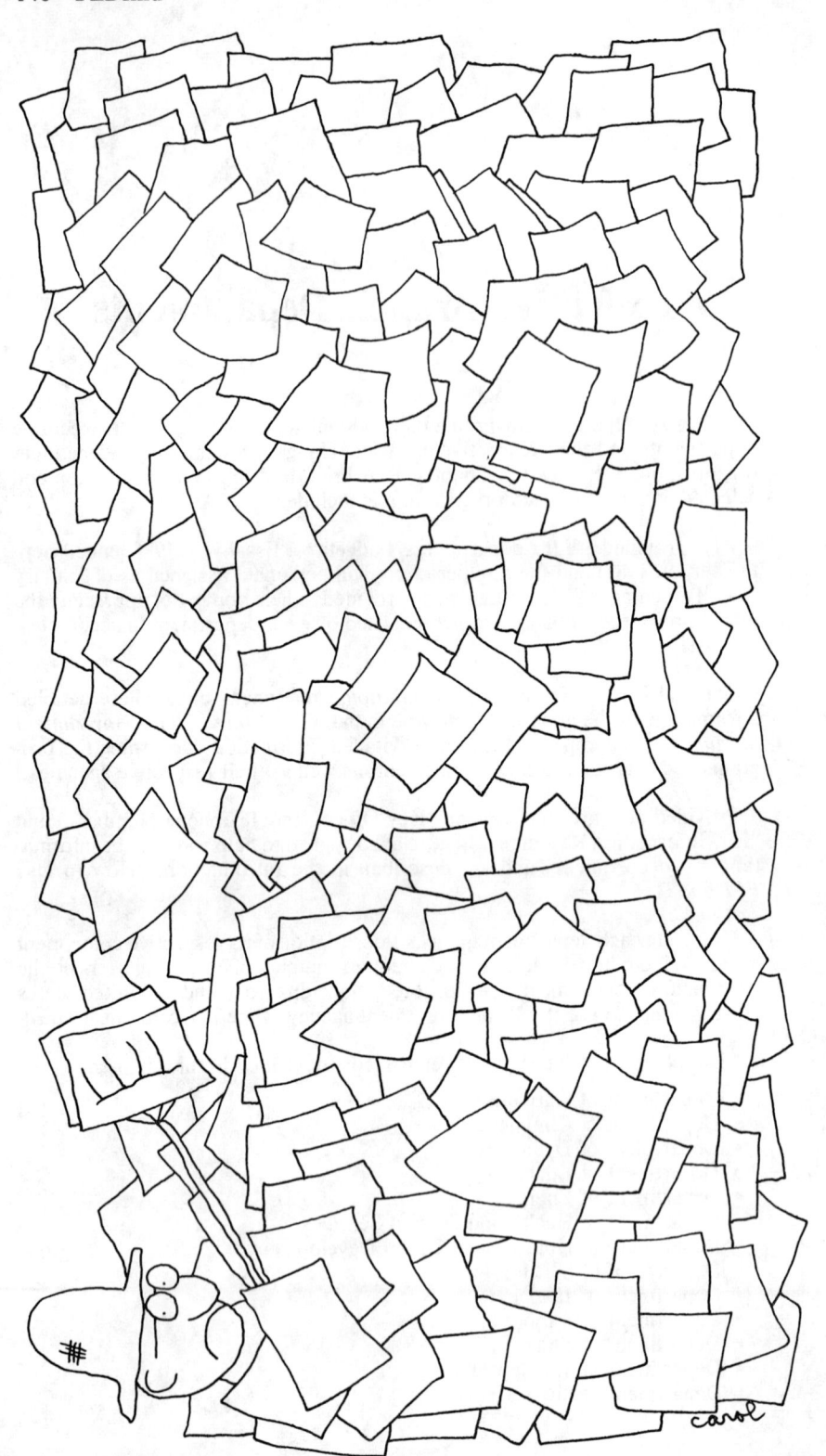

Department of Agriculture

The U.S. Department of Agriculture (USDA) works to improve farm income, expand overseas markets for farm products and assure consumers of an adequate food supply at reasonable prices. The Department helps to safeguard the wholesomeness of the food supply through inspection of food processing plants and voluntary food grading services. It provides nutrition education and food assistance programs. USDA research activities focus on animal production, plant and animal diseases and pest controls, crop production, marketing and the use of agricultural products, nutrition, food safety and forestry. The Department also works to enhance the environment and to maintain the Nation's production capacity by helping landowners protect the soil, water and forests, and to conserve energy. Rural development, credit assistance and conservation programs are elements in USDA national growth policies. Fiscal year 1985 budget of $49,596 million, or 5.29% of the total Federal budget; 119,763 paid employees, or 4.06% of the total civilian work force. (CFR reference: Title 7) For information on individual components of USDA, see the component descriptions below.

Key Offices and Telephone Numbers

Address: 14th Street and Independence Avenue SW, Washington, DC 20250

General Information	(202) 447-2791
Personnel Locator	(202) 447-8732

Public/Consumer Information

Office of Information	(202) 447-2791
Meat and Poultry Hotline	(800) 535-4555
In the Washington, DC area	(202) 447-3333

Procurement Information

Procurement Office	(202) 447-3037
Office of Small and Disadvantaged Business Utilization	(202) 447-7117
Competition Advocate	(202) 447-7117

Press Inquiries

Office of Information	(202) 447-4026
News features and highlights recording	(202) 488-8358

Other Key Offices

Agency Committee Management	(202) 447-3291
Congressional Liaison/Legislative Affairs	(202) 447-2798
Ethics in Government Act	(202) 447-3585
Fraud, Waste and Mismanagement Hotline	(800) 424-9121
In the Washington, DC area	(202) 472-1388
Freedom of Information/Privacy Act	(202) 447-8164
General Counsel	(202) 447-2571
Library (National Agricultural Library, see entry below)	(301) 344-3755
Paperwork Reduction Act (ADP/IRM)	(202) 447-2118
Personnel	(202) 447-5625

Statistical Information, see the Statistical Reporting Service and Economic Research Service below

Key Information Resources

Available **FREE** from the Office of Information are: *How to Get Information from the United States Department of Agriculture*, *Your USDA*, *List of Available Publications of the USDA*, *Services Available Through the USDA* and *Natural Disaster Assistance Available from the USDA*.

Department of Agriculture Telephone Directory

Contact the Government Printing Office (GPO) for information on the most current edition.

USDA Online

A computerized information service that gives access to USDA's original national and many regional news releases, crop reports, outlook and situation summaries, a daily agricultural news digest, a weekly farm newsletter, and more. For further information, contact the Federal Systems Division, ITT Dialcom, Inc., 1109 Spring Street, Suite 410, Silver Spring, MD 20910; (301) 588-1572.

USDA EDI

The USDA's Electronic Dissemination of Information (EDI) service makes available for further dissemination such information as USDA market reports, crop and livestock statistical reports, economic outlook and situation reports, foreign agricultural trade leads, export sales reports, world agricultural round-ups and USDA news releases. Users of the system are generally organizations that further distribute USDA information, such as commercial electronic information and videotex services, publishers, news services, farm organizations and trade associations. For further information, contact Martin Marietta Data Systems, 6303 Ivy Lane, Greenbelt, MD 20770; (301) 982-6792.

USDA Subscription Services

The following is a list of USDA subscription services available from the GPO. For more detailed information, including order forms, consult the USDA publications list cited above or *Government Subscription Services* (Price List 36), available **FREE** from the GPO. See the GPO subscription order form.

    Accepted Meat and Poultry Equipment
    Agricultural Economics Research
    Agricultural Outlook
    Agricultural Research
    Chemistry Laboratory Guidebook
    Crop Reporting Board Reports
      Agricultural Prices
      Catfish
      Cattle
      Celery
      Cold Storage
      Crop Production
      Dairy Products
      Egg Products
      Eggs, Chickens and Turkeys
      Grain Stocks
      Hogs and Pigs
      Livestock Slaughter
      Milk Production
      Non-Citrus Fruits and Nuts

    Peanut Stocks and Processing
    Potatoes and Sweet Potatoes
    Poultry Slaughter
    Rice Stocks
    Vegetables
Economic Indicators of the Farm Sector
Extension Review
Family Economics Review
Farmer Cooperatives
Farmline
Fire Management Notes
Food and Nutrition
Food News for Consumers
Foreign Agricultural Trade of the United States
Foreign Agriculture
List of Materials Acceptable for Use on Systems of REA Electrification Borrowers
List of Materials Acceptable for Use on Telephone Systems of REA Borrowers
Meat and Poultry Inspection Directory
Meat and Poultry Inspection Manual and Compilation of Meat and Poultry Inspection Issuances
Meat and Poultry Inspection Regulations
National Food Review
Outlook and Situation Reports
    Cotton and Wool
    Dairy
    Feed
    Fruit
    Inputs
    Livestock and Poultry
    Oil Crops
    Outlook for United States Agricultural Exports
    Rice
    Sugar and Sweetener
    Tobacco
    Vegetable
    Wheat
    World Agriculture
    World Agriculture Regional Supplement
Rural Development Perspectives
Soil and Water Conservation News
Tree Planters' Notes
World Agricultural Supply and Demand Estimates

Agricultural Cooperative Service

The Agricultural Cooperative Service (ACS) provides research, management and educational assistance to cooperatives to strengthen the economic position of farmers. It also collects and publishes statistics regarding the role and scope of cooperative activity in U.S. agriculture. For further information, contact ACS, USDA, Washington, DC 20250; (202) 447-8353.

Agricultural Marketing Service

The Agricultural Marketing Service (AMS) administers standardization, grading, inspection, market news, marketing orders, research and regulatory programs. AMS grade standards exist for more than 300 agricultural products. The Service provides current, unbiased information to producers, processors and distributors to aid in the orderly marketing and distribution of farm commodities. Regulatory activities of the AMS are designed to protect producers, handlers and consumers of agricultural commodities from financial loss or personal injury resulting from careless, deceptive or fraudulent marketing practices. (CFR reference: Title 7, Chapters I, IX, X, XI) For further information, contact the Information Officer, AMS, USDA, Washington, DC 20250; (202) 447-8999.

Agricultural Research Service

The Agricultural Research Service (ARS) conducts basic, applied and developmental research in animal and plant protection and production; the use and improvement of soil, water and air; the processing, storage and distribution of farm products; and human nutrition. The research applies to commodities, natural resources and geographic, climatic and environmental conditions. (CFR reference: Title 7, Chapter V) For further information, contact the Information Staff, ARS, USDA, Beltsville, MD 20705; (301) 344-2264.

Agricultural Stabilization and Conservation Service

The Agricultural Stabilization and Conservation Service (ASCS) administers commodity and related land use programs designed to achieve voluntary production adjustment, as well as price, market and farm income stabilization. Commodity stabilization is provided through commodity loans, purchases and payments to eligible producers. The commodities within ASCS' purview are wheat, corn, cotton, soybeans, peanuts, rice, tobacco, milk, wool, mohair, barley, oats, sugarbeets, sugarcane, grain sorghum, rye and honey. The ASCS also provides natural disaster assistance to agricultural producers and certain emergency preparedness activities. (CFR reference: Title 7, Chapter VII) For further information, contact the Information Division, ASCS, USDA, P.O. Box 2415, Washington, DC 20013; (202) 447-5237.

Animal and Plant Health Inspection Service

The Animal and Plant Health Inspection Service (APHIS) conducts regulatory and control programs to protect and improve animal and plant health. In cooperation with State governments, this agency administers Federal laws and regulations pertaining to animal and plant health and quarantine, humane treatment of animals, and the control and eradication of pests and diseases. It also inspects and certifies domestic plants for export, administers a law that licenses veterinary biological products for their safety and effectiveness, and enforces animal welfare and horse protection acts. (CFR references, Titles and Chapters: 7, III; 9, I, III) For further information, contact the Legislative and Public Affairs Staff, APHIS, USDA, Washington, DC 20250; (202) 447-2511.

Commodity Credit Corporation

The Commodity Credit Corporation (CCC) is a Government-owned and operated corporation. It finances the farm programs and is authorized to support prices of agricultural commodities through loans, purchases, payments and other operations, in order to maintain adequate supplies of agricultural commodities and to aid in their distribution. The Corporation buys goods for sale to other Government agencies, foreign governments and various relief and rehabilitation agencies. (CFR reference: Title 7, Chapter XIV) For further information, contact the Information Division, CCC, USDA, P.O. Box 2415, Washington, DC 20013; (202) 447-4785.

Cooperative State Research Service

The Cooperative State Research Service (CSRS) administers Federal formula and grant funds to land-grant colleges and universities, State agricultural experiment stations, schools of forestry, colleges, universities and other research organizations. Through its competitive grants program, CSRS funds basic research in selected high-priority areas related to food production—photosynthesis, nitrogen fixation, genetic engineering and biological stress, for example—and human nutrition. (CFR reference: Title 7, Chapter XXXIV) For further information, contact the Office of the Administrator, CSRS, USDA, Washington, DC 20250; (202) 447-4423.

Economics Management Staff

The Economics Management Staff develops economic and statistical analyses to evaluate complex domestic and foreign agricultural problems and issues. The Staff reviews and evaluates recommendations submitted by Agriculture Department agencies, task forces and study groups for their impact upon the agricultural economy. It also analyzes the economic policy implications of legislative proposals of the Department. For further information, contact Information Division, Economics Management Staff, USDA, Washington, DC 20250; (202) 786-1515.

Economic Research Service

The Economic Research Service (ERS) conducts research on domestic and foreign agricultural economics. The Service analyzes factors affecting agriculture, farm productivity, financing, use of resources and potentials of rural areas; evaluates marketing potentials and development, and marketing costs; studies U.S. trade in agricultural products and the role of agriculture in economic development of other nations; and issues outlook and situation reports, commodity projections, price spreads and analyses of U.S. farm commodity programs. For further information and a copy of their **FREE** *Information Contacts* and *Reports*, contact the Information Division, ERS, USDA, Washington, DC 20250; (202) 786-1515.

Extension Service

The Extension Service is the primary educational arm of the Department of Agriculture. Federal, State and local governments share in financing and conducting cooperative extension educational programs to help farmers, processors, handlers, farm families, communities and consumers apply the results of food and agricultural research. Major program areas include more efficient production and marketing of agricultural products, natural resource management, 4-H youth development, nutrition, and community and rural development. For further information, contact the Director, Information and Communications, Extension Service, USDA, Washington, DC 20250; (202) 447-3029.

Farmers Home Administration

The Farmers Home Administration (FmHA) provides loans for ownership and operation of family-size farms and ranches. These loans enable owners or tenant-operators access to agricultural credit who are unable to get credit from other sources at reasonable rates and terms. FmHA also makes emergency disaster loans to help farmers and ranchers recover from natural disasters, as well as loans for soil and water conservation and pollution abatement. (CFR reference: Title 7, Chapter XVIII) For further information, contact the Office of Legislative Affairs and Public Information, FmHA, USDA, Washington, DC 20250; (202) 447-4323.

Federal Crop Insurance Corporation

The Federal Crop Insurance Corporation (FCIC) insures farmers against loss of crop investment due to adverse weather conditions including drought, excessive rain, hail, wind, hurricanes, tornadoes and lightning. It also covers unavoidable losses due to insect infestation, plant disease, floods, fires and earthquakes. Participation in the program is voluntary and the producer pays a premium for the protection. (CFR reference: Title 7, Chapter IV) For further information, contact the Office of Congressional and Public Affairs, FCIC, USDA, Washington, DC 20250; (202) 447-3287.

Federal Grain Inspection Service

The Federal Grain Inspection Service (FGIS) is responsible for the inspection and weighing of grain and other assigned commodities. The Service administers a nationwide system of official, private and State grain inspection agencies. The FGIS also establishes and maintains U.S. standards for grain and grain products. (CFR reference: Title 7, Chapter VIII) For further information, contact the Information Specialist, FGIS, USDA, Washington, DC 20250; (202) 475-3367.

Food and Nutrition Service

The Food and Nutrition Service (FNS) administers programs to make food assistance available to people who need it. These programs are operated in cooperation with States and local governments. FNS food assistance programs include food stamps; supplemental food for women, infants and children; school lunch; school breakfast; special milk; child care, summer feeding and other child nutrition and family food assistance programs. (CFR reference: Title 7, Chapter II) For further information, contact the Public Information Office, FNS, USDA, 3101 Park Center Drive, Alexandria, VA 22302; (703) 756-3276.

Food Safety and Inspection Service

The Food Safety and Inspection Service (FSIS) administers the Federal meat and poultry inspection program to provide for the safe, wholesome and truthful labeling of these products. Federal inspection is provided for products processed by plants that ship in interstate and foreign commerce. (CFR reference: Title 9, Chapter III) For further information, contact the Director of Information and Legislative Affairs, FSIS, USDA, Washington, DC 20250; (202) 447-7943.

Foreign Agricultural Service

The Foreign Agricultural Service (FAS) regulates imports and promotes overseas sales for United States agricultural products. It serves as a basic source of information to U.S. agriculture on world crops, policies and markets; administers agricultural import regulations; assists in the export of U.S. farm products; represents U.S. agriculture in foreign trade matters; administers export credit programs and the reporting of export sales. (CFR reference: Title 7, Chapter XV) For further information, contact the Information Division, FAS, USDA, Washington, DC 20250; (202) 447-3448.

Forest Service

The Forest Service manages 190 million acres of the National Forest System. Its programs are concerned with wilderness management, forest engineering and management, planning, wildfire prevention and suppression, mining, land reclamation and reforestation. Forest Service activities focus on timber production, outdoor recreation, habitat for fish and wildlife, watershed protection and livestock grazing. Other aspects of its work include the marketing and utilization of forest products, resource surveys, urban forestry and pollution. The Forest Service also provides incentives—such as the production and distribution of seedling planting stocks—to stimulate the growth of State, county, municipal and community forests. (CFR reference: Title 36, Chapter II) For further information, contact the Information Office, Forest Service, USDA, P.O. Box 2417, Washington, DC 20013; (202) 447-3760.

Graduate School

The Graduate School, U.S. Department of Agriculture, is a nonprofit, self-supporting school for adults. The Graduate School's mission is to improve Government services by providing continuing education and training opportunities for Government employees and agencies. The school does not grant degrees, but does provide planned sequences of courses leading to certificates of accomplishment in a number of occupational and career fields important to the Government. For further information, contact the Information Office, Graduate School, USDA, 600 Maryland Avenue SW, Washington, DC 20024; (202) 447-4419.

Human Nutrition Information Service

The Human Nutrition Information Service (HNIS) performs research, provides technical assistance and disseminates information on human nutrition. The Service measures food consumption and dietary levels of the population, develops standard reference tables on the nutritive values of foods, and develops materials to aid the public in meeting dietary needs, with emphasis on good nutrition. For further information, contact the HNIS, USDA, Hyattsville, MD 20782; (301) 436-7725.

National Agricultural Library

The National Agricultural Library (NAL) specializes in information on agriculture and subjects supporting agricultural research. Its collection is comprised mainly of agricultural science materials, but also includes materials on technical agriculture, farming, veterinary science, entomology, botany, forestry, soil science, food and nutrition, agricultural products, rural sociology, economics, and statutes and laws pertaining to agriculture. Certain bibliographic resources are available through computerized online database services. The library is the coordinator and primary resource for the national network of State land grant and field libraries and serves as the U.S. center for an international agriculture information system. For further information, contact the NAL, USDA, Beltsville, MD 20705; (301) 344-3755.

Office of Consumer Advisor

The Office of Consumer Advisor (OCA) coordinates Department of Agriculture actions on problems and issues of importance to consumers. The Office represents the Department in policy discussions related to consumer issues before Congress or in meetings with other departments and agencies in various public forums. For further information, contact the OCA, USDA, Washington, DC 20250; (202) 382-9681.

Office of Energy

The Office of Energy develops and coordinates Department of Agriculture energy-related programs that may affect agriculture and rural America. Included are issues that deal with agricultural energy use and agricultural impacts of energy development and use. (CFR reference: Title 7, Chapter XXIX) For further information, contact the Office of Energy, USDA, Washington, DC 20250; (202) 447-2634.

Office of Grants and Program Systems

The Office of Grants and Program Systems (OGPS) administers a program of competitive extramural grants to promote research in food, agriculture and related areas. Eligible parties include State agricultural experiment stations, colleges and universities, other research institutions and organizations, Federal agencies, private organizations or corporations, and individuals. (CFR reference: Title 7, Chapter XXXII) For further information, contact the Office of the Director, OGPS, USDA, Washington, DC 20250; (202) 475-5720.

Office of International Cooperation and Development

The Office of International Cooperation and Development (OICD) coordinates the Department's international training and technical assistance programs. The Office also sponsors international research projects and scientific and technical exchanges with other nations on topics of interest to U.S. farmers and agribusiness. The Office provides planning and analysis support to encourage private agribusiness to become involved in development work overseas. (CFR reference: Title 7, Chapter XXII) For further information, contact the Information Staff, OICD, Washington, DC 20250; (202) 475-4071.

Office of Rural Development Policy

The Office of Rural Development Policy (ORDP) develops and oversees implementation of rural development programs. The Office coordinates rural programs with other Agriculture Department and Federal agencies in the areas of historic preservation, health, elderly needs, transportation, housing, voluntarism and private sector initiatives. ORDP serves as a staff to various national committees, working groups and advisory boards concerned with rural development. The work of ORDP is carried out with State and local governments, regional bodies and their national representatives. For further information, contact the Office of the Director, ORDP, USDA, Washington, DC 20250; (202) 382-0044.

Office of Transportation

The Office of Transportation (OT) is responsible for services and research activities relating to the transportation of farm products, commodities and equipment. This includes representation of agricultural and rural transportation interests before regulatory bodies. For further information, contact the OT, USDA, Washington, DC 20250; (202) 447-3963.

Packers and Stockyards Administration

The Packers and Stockyards Administration is responsible for enforcing the *Packers and Stockyards Act*. This Act is an antitrust law intended to maintain effective competition and fair trade practices in livestock, meat and poultry for the protection of livestock and poultry producers. (CFR reference: Title 9, Chapter II) For further information, contact the Information Specialist, Packers and Stockyards Administration, USDA, Washington, DC 20250; (202) 382-9528.

Rural Electrification Administration

The Rural Electrification Administration (REA) is a credit agency that assists rural electric and telephone utilities in obtaining financing. REA assistance may take the form of loans from REA, guarantees of loans made by others, or REA approval of security arrangements. (CFR reference: Title 7, Chapter XVII) For further information, contact the Public Information Office, REA, USDA, Washington, DC 20250; (202) 382-1255.

Soil Conservation Service

The Soil Conservation Service (SCS) conducts a national soil and water conservation program in cooperation with landowners and operators, in local soil and water conservation districts and with other government agencies. With the help of landowners and operators, the SCS inventories and assesses soil, water and plant resources, as well as applies conservation practices to reduce soil erosion, and to maintain land productivity. The agency also administers the Great Plains conservation program and assists landowners and local groups in resource conservation and development projects. (CFR reference: Title 7, Chapter VI) For further information, contact the Public Information Staff, SCS, USDA, P.O. Box 2890, Washington, DC 20013; (202) 447-4543.

Statistical Reporting Service

The Statistical Reporting Service (SRS) prepares official Agriculture Department data and estimates of production, supply, prices and other information necessary for orderly operation of the U.S. agricultural economy. The reports include statistics on field crop, fruits and vegetables, cattle, hogs, sheep, poultry and related commodities or processed products. Other estimates concern prices received by farmers for products sold and prices paid for commodities and services, indexes of prices received and paid, parity prices, farm employment and farm wage rates. Available **FREE** is their *Information Contacts, Crop Reporting Board Catalog* and *Preparing Crop and Livestock Estimates* from the SRS Publications Office, USDA, Washington, DC 20250; (202) 447-4020.

World Agricultural Outlook Board

The World Agricultural Outlook Board coordinates the Agriculture Department's information gathering and dissemination on developments in domestic and international agriculture. The Board chairs interagency commodity estimates committees; leads interdepartmental research on weather, climate and remote sensing; and performs assessment of the impact of weather on agriculture. For further information, contact the Information Officer, World Agricultural Outlook Board, USDA, Washington, DC 20250; (202) 447-5447.

FEDfind

Executive Branch Departments 159

Department of Commerce

The Department of Commerce encourages, promotes and serves the United States' economic growth, international trade and technological advancement. The programs of the Department offer assistance and information in the following areas: help increase exports and prevent unfair foreign trade competition; provide social and economic statistics and analyses for private and public users; provide research and support for the increased use of scientific, engineering and technological development; grant patents and register trademarks; provide assistance to promote domestic economic development; improve understanding of the Earth's physical environment and oceanic life; promote travel to the United States by residents of foreign countries; and assist in the growth of minority businesses. Fiscal year 1985 budget of $2,140 million, or 0.23% of the total Federal budget; 34,984 paid employees, or 1.19% of the total civilian work force. (CFR reference: Title 15) For information on individual components of the Department of Commerce, see the component descriptions below.

Key Offices and Telephone Numbers

Address: 14th Street between Constitution Avenue and E Street NW, Washington, DC 20230

General Information and Personnel Locator	(202) 377-2000
Public/Consumer Information	
Office of Public Affairs	(202) 377-4901
Office of Consumer Affairs	(202) 377-5001
Office of Business Liaison, Roadmap Program	(202) 337-3176
Divers Alert Network Hotline	(919) 684-8111
For general information	(919) 684-2948
Tariff and trade information recording	(301) 921-3200
Procurement Information	
Procurement Operations Office	(202) 377-5555
Office of Small and Disadvantaged Business Utilization	(202) 377-1472
Competition Advocate	(202) 377-2773
Press Inquiries	
News Division	(202) 377-4901
Economic news recording	(202) 393-4100
News highlights recording	(202) 393-1847
Weekly feature recording (Friday evenings)	(202) 393-4102
Other Key Offices	
Agency Committee Management	(202) 377-4951
Congressional Liaison/Legislative Affairs	(202) 377-3663
Ethics in Government Act	(202) 377-5387
Fraud, Waste and Mismanagement Hotline	(800) 424-5197
In the Washington, DC area	(202) 377-2495
Freedom of Information/Privacy Act	(202) 377-3271
General Counsel	(202) 377-4772
Library	(202) 377-2161
Paperwork Reduction Act (ADP/IRM)	(202) 377-1296
Personnel	(202) 377-3827

Statistical Information, see the Bureau of the Census and Bureau of Economic Analysis below

Key Information Resources

Available **FREE** from the Office of Consumer Affairs is the *Inventory of U.S. Department of Commerce Consumer Services*. Available **FREE** from the Office of Business Liaison is its *Business Services Directory*.

Department of Commerce Telephone Directory

Contact the Government Printing Office (GPO) for information on the most current edition.

Commerce Publications Update

A biweekly subscription service that includes a listing of all publications and press releases issued by the Department during the preceding two-week period. It also highlights Commerce publications of special interest and provides, as released, the latest figures in key areas of business and economic activity, such as personal income, consumer prices, employment and housing. Subscription price: $31.00 a year. Single copy price: $1.50. GPO List ID CPU. (C 1.24/3:) See the GPO subscription order form.

Department of Commerce Subscription Services

The following is a list of Commerce Department subscription services available from the GPO. For more detailed information, including order forms, consult *Government Subscription Services* (Price List 36), available **FREE** from the GPO. See the GPO subscription order form.

Business America
Business Conditions Digest
Census Final Reports
Census Preliminary Reports
Classification Definitions (Patents)
Commerce Business Daily
Commerce Publications Update
Construction Reports
Construction Review
Current Business Reports
Current Business Reports: Monthly Wholesale Trade, Sales and Inventories
Current Construction Report: Residential Alterations and Repairs (C-50)
Current Housing Reports
Current Housing Reports H-130, Market Absorption of Apartments
Current Industrial Reports
Current Population Reports
Daily Weather Maps, Weekly Series
Data User News
Export Administration Regulations
Fishery Bulletin
Foreign Economic Trends and Their Implications for the United States
Foreign Trade Reports
Governments Quarterly Report
Journal of Research of the National Bureau of Standards
Manual of Classification [Patent Office]
Manual of Patent Examining Procedure
Manual of Regulations and Procedures for Federal Radio Frequency Management
Marine Fisheries Review
Mariners Weather Log
Monthly and Seasonal Weather Outlook

NOAA
Oceanographic Monthly Summary
Official Gazette of the United States Patent and Trademark Office: Patents
Official Gazette of the United States Patent and Trademark Office: Trademarks
Overseas Business Reports
Patent and Trademark Office Notices
Quarterly Financial Report for Manufacturing, Mining and Trade Corporations
Report on Cotton Ginnings by Counties
Report on Cotton Ginnings by States
Schedule B
Survey of Current Business
Trade and Employment
Trademark Manual of Examining Procedure

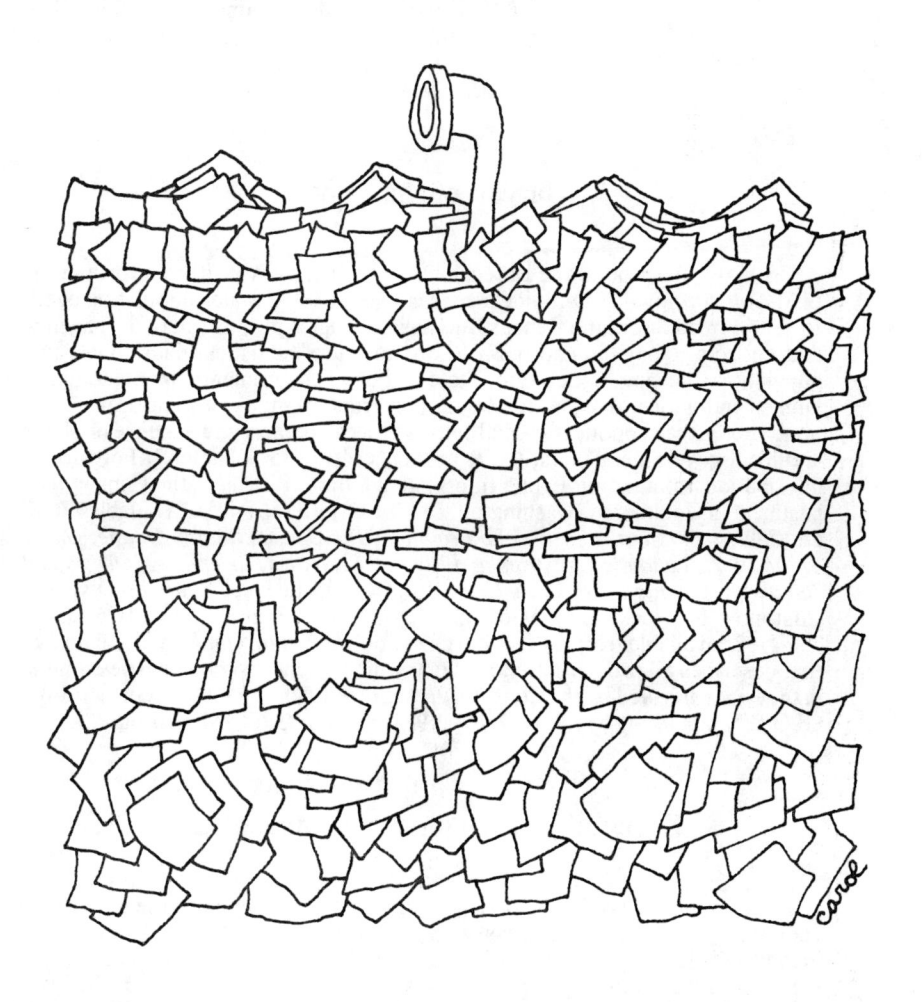

Bureau of Economic Analysis

The Bureau of Economic Analysis (BEA) provides analysis and research related to the preparation and interpretation of the economic accounts of the United States. These accounts provide a quantitative view of the economic process in terms of the production, distribution and use of the Nation's output. The accounts consist of national income and product accounts summarized by gross national product, wealth accounts, inter-industry accounts of the interrelationships among industrial markets, regional accounts and U.S. international transactions accounts. The BEA also prepares analyses—based on national economic accounts—of other measures of business activity, including various tools for forecasting economic developments, such as surveys of investment outlays and plans of U.S. business, econometric models of the U.S. economy, and a system of leading, coincident and lagging economic indicators. (CFR reference: Title 15, Chapter VIII) For further information, contact the Public Information Office, BEA, Department of Commerce, Washington, DC 20230; (202) 523-0777. Available **FREE** from this office are the *BEA Catalog of Publications and Computer Tapes* and *BEA Telephone Contacts for Data Users*.

Bureau of the Census

The major function of the Bureau of the Census, as explicitly set forth in the *U.S. Constitution,* is to provide a census of the United States population every 10 years. In addition, the Census Bureau is a general-purpose statistical agency that collects, tabulates and publishes a variety of statistical data concerning population, housing, agriculture, State and local governments, manufacturers, mineral industries, distributive trade, construction industries and transportation. The Bureau conducts special censuses at the request and expense of States and local government units. (CFR reference: Title 15, Chapter I) For further information, contact the Public Information Office, Bureau of the Census, Department of Commerce, Washington, DC 20233; (301) 763-4051. Available **FREE** are *Census Bureau Programs and Products*, *The Census Bureau Online*, *Guide to the 1982 Economic Censuses and Related Statistics*, *Reference Sources* and *Telephone Contacts for Data Users* from the Data User Services Division, Customer Services, Bureau of the Census, Washington, DC 20233: (301) 763-4100. Available from GPO is the *Census Catalog and Guide 1985*, an annual that describes all products (reports, maps, microfiche, computer tapes, online data services) issued by the Census Bureau since 1980. June 1985. 360pp. $13.00. GPO S/N 003-024-06331-0. (C 3.163/3:985) See the GPO order form.

Economic Development Administration

The Economic Development Administration (EDA) supports the long-range economic development of areas with severe unemployment and low family income problems. EDA programs include public works grants, economic adjustment assistance grants, guarantees of leases for private industry and of private loans for industrial and commercial facilities and working capital, and technical, planning and research assistance for areas designated as Redevelopment Areas. (CFR reference: Title 13, Chapter III) For further information, contact the Assistant for Public Affairs, EDA, Department of Commerce, Washington, DC 20230; (202) 377-5113.

International Trade Administration

The International Trade Administration (ITA) conducts programs involving export administration and regulates aspects of international trade relating to imports, exports and foreign trade zones. Through its overseas posts and district offices across the United States, ITA serves as a link between U.S. suppliers and foreign buyers and as a promoter of U.S. exports in foreign markets. The ITA also addresses problems that arise in marketing in specific countries and regions, and in exporting from the standpoint of specific industrial sectors. (CFR references, Titles and Chapters: 15, III; 19, III) For further information, contact the Office of Public Affairs, ITA, Department of Commerce, Washington, DC 20230; (202) 377-3808.

Minority Business Development Agency

The Minority Business Development Agency (MBDA) develops and coordinates programs for minority business enterprise. Management and technical assistance is provided to minority firms through a network of local business development organizations funded by the Agency. Specialized business assistance is available to firms that exhibit growth potential, that demonstrate current growth, or that are in high technology sectors of the economy. For further information, contact the Office of Public Affairs, MBDA, Department of Commerce, Washington, DC 20230; (202) 377-1936.

National Bureau of Standards

The National Bureau of Standards (NBS) supports the advancement and strengthening of the Nation's science and technology and facilitates their application for public benefit. To this end, the NBS conducts research and provides a basis for the Nation's physical measurement system, scientific and technological services for industry and government, U.S. involvement in domestic and international product standardization activities, and technical services promoting public safety. (CFR reference: Title 15, Chapter II) For further information, contact the Research Information Center, NBS, Department of Commerce, Gaithersburg, MD 20899; (301) 921-2318.

National Oceanic and Atmospheric Administration

The mission of the National Oceanic and Atmospheric Administration (NOAA) is to explore, map and chart the global ocean and its living resources and to describe, monitor and predict conditions in the atmosphere, ocean, sun and space environment. Among its principal functions, NOAA reports the weather of the United States and its possessions and provides weather forecasts, issues warnings of destructive natural events such as hurricanes, tornadoes and floods, and provides special services in support of aviation, marine activities, agriculture, forestry, urban air-quality control and other weather-sensitive activities. (CFR references, Titles and Chapters: 15, IX; 50, II-IV) For further information, contact the Office of Public Affairs, NOAA, Department of Commerce, Washington, DC 20230; (202) 377-4190.

National Technical Information Service

The National Technical Information Service (NTIS) is the central source for the public sale of U.S. Government-sponsored research, development and engineering reports, as well as foreign technical reports and other analyses prepared by national and local government agencies, their contractors or grantees. NTIS is the central source for Federally-generated machine-readable data files. The Service manages the Federal Software Center. NTIS also acquires generally unpublished foreign technology reports of potential interest to U.S. industry, promotes U.S. Government-owned patents for licensing by U.S. manufacturers, and operates the Center for Utilization of Federal Technology (CUFT) that provides U.S. industry with information on selected Federal technology with potential practical value. For further information, contact NTIS, 5285 Port Royal Road, Springfield, VA 22161; (703) 487-4600. See Chapter 17, "National Technical Information Service," for a detailed description of its information products and services.

National Telecommunications and Information Administration

The National Telecommunications and Information Administration (NTIA) develops policy for the Department of Commerce in the areas of information, telecommunications and associated industries. NTIA also provides policy and management for Federal use of the electromagnetic spectrum and telecommunications facilities grants to public service users. (CFR reference: Title 15, Chapter XXIII) For further information, contact NTIA, Department of Commerce, Washington, DC 20230; (202) 377-1832.

Patent and Trademark Office

The Patent and Trademark Office (PTO) administers the patent and trademark laws. The Office examines applications for three kinds of patents: design patents (issued for 14 years), plant patents (issued for 17 years) and utility patents, including reissue patents (issued for 17 years). The issuance of a patent by the PTO provides the inventor with exclusive rights to its use for the specified length of time. Trademarks are examined by the PTO for compliance with various statutory requirements to prevent unfair competition and consumer deception. Registration of a trademark is for 20 years, with renewal rights. (CFR reference: Title 37, Chapter I) For further information, contact the Office of Public Affairs, PTO, Department of Commerce, Washington, DC 20231; (703) 557-3428.

United States Travel and Tourism Administration

The United States Travel and Tourism Administration (USTTA) establishes and carries out national tourism policy, the primary objectives of which are to foster the contribution of tourism and recreation industries to the U.S. economy, eliminate unnecessary trade barriers to the U.S. tourism industry, and assist in the collection, analysis and dissemination of tourism data. USTTA conducts a marketing program to expand tourism to U.S. destinations. (CFR reference: Title 15, Chapter XII) For further information, contact USTTA, Department of Commerce, Washington, DC 20230; (202) 377-3811.

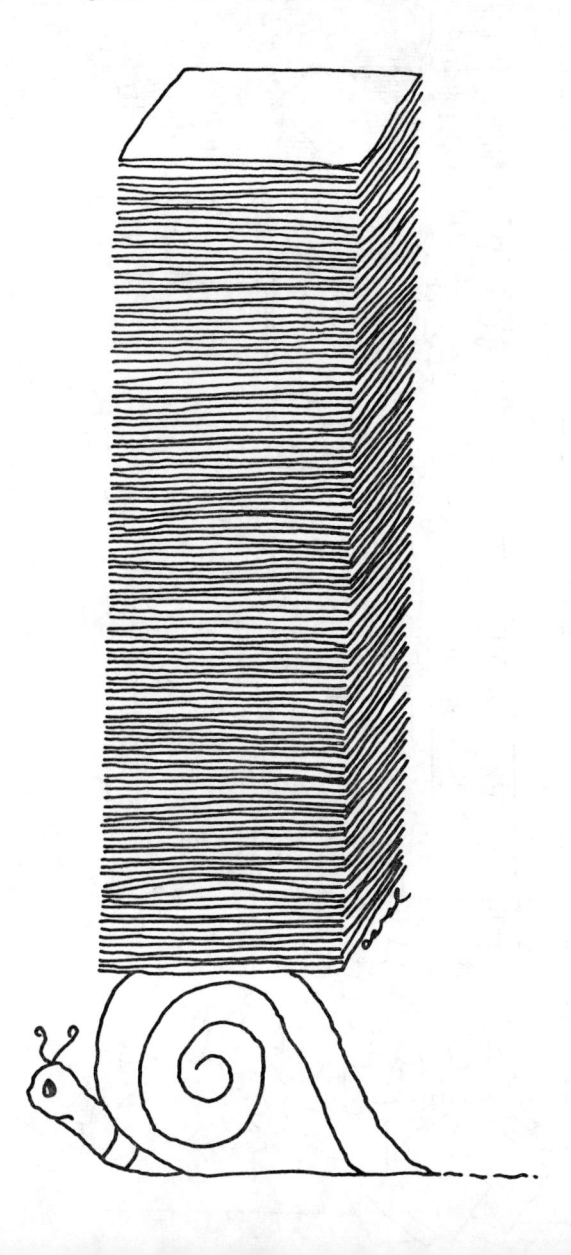

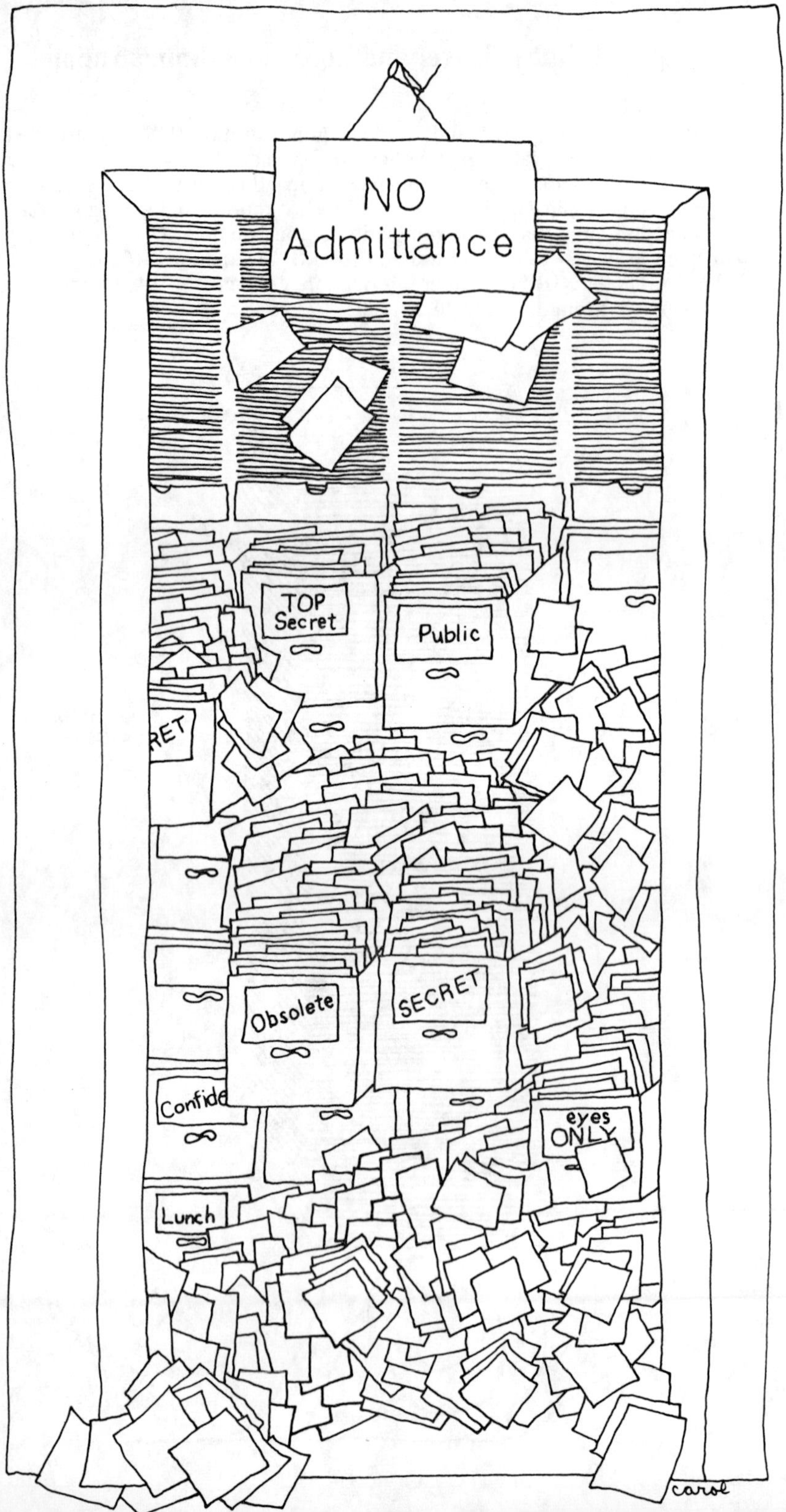
NO Admittance
TOP Secret
Public
RET
Obsolete
SECRET
Confide
eyes ONLY
Lunch
carol

Department of Defense

The Department of Defense (DOD) provides military forces needed to deter war and protect the security of the United States. The Department includes the separately organized military departments of Army, Navy (including the Marine Corps) and Air Force, the Joint Chiefs of Staff, the unified and specified combatant commands, and various defense agencies established for specific purposes. Fiscal year 1985 budget of $262,898 million, or 28.06% of the total Federal budget; 1,061,836 paid employees, or 35.99% of the total civilian work force. (CFR reference: Title 32) For information on individual components of the Department of Defense, see the component descriptions below.

Key Offices and Telephone Numbers

Address: The Pentagon, Washington, DC 20301

General Information and Personnel Locator	(202) 545-6700
Public/Consumer Information	
Office of Public Affairs	(202) 697-5737

Procurement Information
Selling to the Military, the DOD *Small and Disadvantaged Business Utilization Specialists* and other DOD procurement-related publications are described in Chapter 14, "Government Procurement and Business Information." For the telephone number of a "Competition Advocate," contact the DOD procurement facility with which you are doing or plan to do business.

Press Inquiries

Armed Forces News Branch	(202) 697-5131
Defense News Branch	(202) 695-0192

Other Key Offices

Agency Committee Management	(202) 695-4281
Congressional Liaison/Legislative Affairs	(202) 695-2503
Ethics in Government Act	(202) 695-4436
Fraud, Waste and Mismanagement Hotline	(800) 424-9098
In the Washington, DC area	(202) 693-5080
Freedom of Information/Privacy Act	(202) 697-1180
General Counsel	(202) 695-3341
Library	(202) 697-4301
Paperwork Reduction Act (ADP/IRM)	(202) 695-3237
Personnel (Office of the Secretary of Defense)	(202) 697-4211
Statistical Information	(202) 695-0192

Key Information Resources

Available **FREE** from the Government Printing Office (GPO) are subject bibliographies (SB) on *Armed Forces* (SB-131), *Military History* (SB-98) and *National Defense and Security* (SB-153). See the GPO SB order form.

Defense Almanac

An annual publication that provides an overview of the Department of Defense (DOD). It is issued as the September issue of the periodical *Defense*, for sale by the Government Printing Office. The 1985 issue contains sections entitled: Evolution of the National Defense Structure, DOD at a Glance, Organization, Total Force, Money, People, Training, Weapon Systems and Combat Forces, Force Locations, International Security Relationships, Conflicts and Casualties, Defense Presence by State, Military Installations and Properties. September 1985. 51pp. Single copy **FREE**. Armed Forces Information Service, 1735 N. Lynn Street, Room 210, Arlington, VA 22209; (202) 696-5294.

Department of Defense Telephone Directory

A triannual document that includes an alphabetical directory of DOD (including Army, Navy, and Air Force) personnel, and a classified section by agency, for the Washington, DC metropolitan area. Subscription price: $19.00 a year. Single copy price: $9.00. GPO List ID TDD. (D 1.7:) See the GPO subscription order form.

Research Guide to Current Military and Strategic Affairs

A guide to sources on worldwide military and strategic affairs. Both basic and specialized sources are provided in each topic area, along with suggestions for advanced research. The first part describes tools that are most useful, most easily accessible and broadest in scope. A separate section describes the U.S. Government documents system and introduces hundreds of publications issued by Federal Government agencies. By William M. Arkin. A second edition is planned for late 1986 or 1987. 1981. 232pp. $9.95 (paper), $19.95 (cloth). Institute for Policy Studies, 1901 Q Street NW, Washington, DC 20009; (202) 234-9382.

How to Get It—A Guide to Defense-Related Information Resources

A guide to identify or acquire Government published or sponsored documents, maps, patents, translations, databases, specifications or standards and other resources of interest to the defense community. It is prepared by the Defense Technical Information Center (DTIC). The entries are arranged alphabetically, in a single list, by document type, source, acronym, series designation or short title. Each entry consists of an identification of the item and detailed acquisition information such as source, order forms to use, cost, where indexed and telephone numbers for additional information. Included is a glossary and a bibliography. 1982. 531pp. $40.95. Available from DTIC to registered DTIC users; available for public sale through the National Technical Information Service (NTIS). NTIS order number AD-A110000. See the NTIS order form.

Department of Defense Dictionary of Military and Associated Terms

A dictionary of common terms established for use by all Department of Defense components that will use the terms and definitions so designated without alteration. The dictionary has been approved for U.S. Government interdepartmental usage, as well as established for use by member nations of the Inter-American Defense Board and the North Atlantic Treaty Organization. Punched for 3-ring looseleaf binder. 1984. 414pp. $12.00. GPO S/N 008-004-00020-0. (D 5.12:1/11) See the GPO order form.

Air Force, Army and Navy Times

Each of these three independent weekly newspapers covers events and issues related to each respective Service. The *Navy Times* also covers Marine Corps and Coast Guard stories. Subscription price: $42.00 a year for each. Army Times Publishing Co., Springfield, VA 22158; (703) 750-8920.

Military Personnel Publications

Uniformed Services Almanac, *Reserve Forces Almanac*, *National Guard Almanac* and *Retired Military Almanac* are annual reference books that provide information on pay, promotion and benefits for personnel in each respective category. Published annually January through March. $4.25 each, quantity discounts available. Uniform Services Almanac, Inc., P.O. Box 76, Washington, DC 20044; (703) 532-1631.

Department of Defense Subscription Services

The following is a list of Defense Department subscription services available from the GPO. For more detailed information, including order forms, consult *Government Subscription Services* (Price List 36), available **FREE** from the GPO. See the GPO subscription order form.

- Air Defense Artillery
- Air Force Comptroller
- Air Force Engineering and Services Quarterly
- Air Force Journal of Logistics
- Air Force Law Review
- The Air Reservist
- Air University Review
- Airman
- All Hands
- Approach
- The Army Lawyer
- Army Logistician
- Army Research, Development and Acquisition
- Army Trainer
- Civilian Manpower Statistics
- Combat Crew
- Companies Participating in the Department of Defense Subcontracting Program
- Defense Contract Audit Manual
- Defense 86
- Defense Management Journal
- Defense Standardization and Specification Program Policies, Procedures and Instructions (Manual DoD 4120.3-M)
- Department of Defense Index of Specifications and Standards
- Department of Defense Telephone Directory
- Direction (The Navy Public Affairs Magazine)
- Directory of DCAA Offices
- DOD FAR Supplement
- DOD Hazardous Materials Information System: Hazardous Item Listing, DoD 6050.5-L
- Driver, The Traffic Safety, etc.
- Engineer

Faceplate
Fathom
Federal Supply Classification Listing of DoD Standardization
    Documents
Federal Supply Code for Manufacturers, U.S. and Canada
Flying Safety
Global Autovon Telephone Directory
Instrument Flying
Joint Travel Regulations
The Mac Flyer
Maintenance
Marines
Master Cross Reference List
MECH
Medical Service Digest
Military Intelligence
Military Law Review
Military Manpower Statistics
NATO Supply Code for Manufacturers (Excluding U.S. and Canada)
Naval Aviation News
Naval Military Personnel Manual
Naval Research Reviews
The Navigator
Navy Civil Engineer
ONR Far East Scientific Bulletin
Parameters: Journal of the United States Army War College
Prime Contract Awards
Prime Contract Awards by State
Prime Contract Awards in Labor Surplus Areas
Program Manager, The Journal of the Defense Systems Management
    College
PS, The Preventive Maintenance Monthly
The Reporter
Selected Medical Care Statistics
Soldiers
Surface Warfare Magazine
TAC Attack
Translog
United States Army Aviation Digest
United States Government's Preferred Products List
United States Navy Medicine
Worldwide Manpower Distribution by Geographical Areas
Worldwide United States Active Duty Military Personnel Casualties

Department of the Air Force

The United States Air Force (USAF) provides an air force that, in conjunction with the other armed forces, is capable of preserving the peace, security and defense of the United States. (CFR reference: Title 32, Chapter VII)

Key Offices and Telephone Numbers

Address: The Pentagon, Washington, DC 20330

General Information	(202) 545-6700
Personnel Locator	
Civilian	(202) 695-4582
Military	(202) 695-4803
Public/Consumer Information	
Office of Public Affairs	(202) 697-1128
Procurement Information, see DOD listing above	
Press Inquiries	
Media Relations Division	(202) 695-5554
Other Key Offices	
Agency Committee Management, see DOD listing above	
Congressional Liaison/Legislative Affairs	(202) 697-8153
Ethics in Government Act	(202) 697-0941
Fraud, Waste and Mismanagement Hotline	(800) 538-8429
In Virginia	(800) 468-6661
Freedom of Information/Privacy Act	(202) 695-4992
General Counsel	(202) 697-0941
Library, see DOD listing above	
Paperwork Reduction Act (ADP/IRM)	(202) 695-4440
Personnel (Headquarters)	(202) 697-9117
Statistical Information, see DOD listing above	

Key Information Resources

In addition to the materials cited above, there is available **FREE** the subject bibliography (SB) *Air Force Manuals* (SB-182). See the GPO SB order form.

Department of the Army

The United States Army provides the armed forces that focus on land operations. The Army also administers programs aimed at improving waterway navigation, flood and beach erosion control and water resource development. The Army supports the National Civil Defense Program, provides military assistance to Federal, State and local government agencies. (CFR references, Titles and Chapters: 32, V: 33, II; 36, III)

Key Offices and Telephone Numbers

Address: The Pentagon, Washington, DC 20310

General Information	(202) 545-6700
Personnel Locator: Military and Key Civilian	(202) 695-5110
Public/Consumer Information	
Office of Public Affairs	(202) 694-0739
Procurement Information, see DOD listing above	
Press Inquiries	
Media Inquiry Branch	(202) 697-7589
Other Key Offices	
Agency Committee Management, see DOD listing above	
Congressional Liaison/Legislative Affairs	(202) 697-6767
Ethics in Government Act	(202) 697-4807
Fraud, Waste and Mismanagement Hotline	(800) 446-9000
In Virginia	(800) 572-9000
Freedom of Information/Privacy Act	(202) 325-6163
General Counsel	(202) 697-9235
Library, see DOD listing above	
Paperwork Reduction Act (ADP/IRM)	(202) 325-6183
Personnel (Headquarters)	(202) 695-2963
Statistical Information, see DOD listing above	

Key Information Resources

In addition to the materials cited above, there are available **FREE** the subject bibliographies (SB) *Army Technical and Field Manuals* (SB-158) and the *United States Army Corps of Engineers* (SB-261). See the GPO SB order form.

Department of the Navy

The United States Navy provides armed forces to maintain freedom of the seas. The Marine Corps component of the Navy supports the seizure or defense of advanced naval bases. (CFR reference: Title 32, Chapter VI)

Key Offices and Telephone Numbers

Address: The Pentagon, Washington, DC 20350

General Information and Personnel Locator	(202) 545-6700
Public/Consumer Information	
Public Inquiries and Research Branch	(202) 695-0965
Navy Recruiting Information Center	(800) 327-NAVY
U.S. Naval Observatory master clock time recording	(202) 653-1800
Procurement Information, see DOD listing above	
Press Inquiries	
News Desk	(202) 697-5342
Other Key Offices	
Agency Committee Management, see DOD listing above	
Congressional Liaison/Legislative Affairs	(202) 695-5276
Ethics in Government Act	(202) 694-1994
Fraud, Waste and Mismanagement Hotline	(800) 522-3451
In the Washington, DC area	(202) 433-6743
Freedom of Information/Privacy Act	(202) 697-1459
General Counsel	(202) 694-1994
Library	(202) 433-4131
Paperwork Reduction Act (ADP/IRM)	(202) 695-0103
Personnel (Headquarters)	(202) 696-4567
Statistical Information, see DOD listing above	

Key Information Resources

In addition to the materials cited above, there are available **FREE** the subject bibliographies (SB) *Naval Facilities Engineering Command Publications* (SB-219), *U.S. Naval History* (SB-236) and *Naval Personnel Bureau and Naval Education and Training Command Publications* (SB-173). See the GPO SB order form.

Defense Technical Information Center

The Defense Technical Information Center (DTIC), formerly the Defense Documentation Center (DDC), is a component of the Department of Defense (DOD) scientific and technical information program. DTIC contributes to the management and conduct of defense research and development efforts by providing access to and transfer of scientific and technical information for DOD personnel, DOD contractors and potential contractors, and other U.S. Government agency personnel and their contractors. The mission of DTIC is to help others exploit the contents of its collection of information to answer the three basic questions related to research, development, test and evaluation (RDT&E) activities of the DOD. These questions are: (1) What research is being planned? (2) What research is currently being performed? and (3) What results were realized by completed research?

The general public can gain access to DTIC information as it releases unclassified/unlimited technical reports and bibliographic information through the National Technical Information Service (NTIS), see Chapter 17. DTIC documents released to NTIS are indexed in NTIS's *Government Reports Announcements and Index* and are available online through the NTIS Bibliographic Data Base. Information on unclassified/unlimited research-in-progress, part of the DTIC's DOD Work Unit Data Base, may be obtained in summary form from NTIS.

A complete description of DTIC programs is available in their information packet, available **FREE** from DTIC. For further information, including the information packet, contact DTIC, Office of User Services (DTIC-B), Building 5, Cameron Station, Alexandria, VA 22304; (202) 274-7633.

Department of Defense Agencies and Joint Service Schools

In addition to the three military departments, various agencies have been established within the Department of Defense to serve specific functions. These agencies, along with their addresses and telephone numbers, are listed below.

Armed Forces Staff College (AFSC) Norfolk, VA 23511	(804) 444-5231
Armed Services Board of Contract Appeals (ASBCA) Hoffman Building II200 Stovall Street Alexandria, VA 22332	(202) 325-9070
Defense Advanced Research Projects Agency (DARPA) 1400 Wilson Boulevard Arlington, VA 22209	(202) 694-5469
Defense Communications Agency (DCA) 8th Street and S. Courthouse Road Arlington, VA 22204	(202) 692-0018
Defense Contract Audit Agency (DCAA) Cameron Station, Building 4 Alexandria, VA 22304	(202) 274-6785

Defense Institute of Security Assistance (513) 255-5850
Management (DISAM)
Wright-Patterson Air Force Base, OH 45433

Defense Intelligence Agency (DIA) (202) 697-8844
The Pentagon
Washington, DC 20301

Defense Investigative Service (DIS) (202) 475-0966
1900 Half Street SW
Washington, DC 20324

Defense Legal Services Agency (DLS) (202) 695-3341
The Pentagon
Washington, DC 20301

Defense Logistics Agency (DLA) (202) 274-6000
Cameron Station
Alexandria, VA 22314

Defense Mapping Agency (DMA) (202) 653-1478
U.S. Naval Observatory, Building 56
Washington, DC 20305

Defense Nuclear Agency (DNA) (202) 325-7095
Washington, DC 20305

Defense Security Assistance Agency (DSAA) (202) 695-3291
The Pentagon
Washington, DC 20301

Defense Systems Management College (DSMC) (703) 664-2790
Fort Belvoir, VA 22060

Department of Defense Computer Institute (DODCI) (202) 433-3000
Washington Navy Yard, Building 175
Washington, DC 20374

DOD Motion Media Depository (714) 382-7047
DAVCOM Division, Building 248
Norton Air Force Base, CA 92409

DOD Still Media Depository (202) 433-6009
Anacostia Naval Station, Building 168
Washington, DC 20374

Industrial College of the Armed Forces (ICAF) (202) 475-1832
Fort Lesley J. McNair
4th and P Streets SW
Washington, DC 20319

National Defense University (NDU) (202) 475-0811
Fort Lesley J. McNair
4th and P Streets SW
Washington, DC 20319

National Security Agency/Central Security   (301) 688-6311
Service (NSA/CSS)
Fort George G. Meade, MD 20755

The National War College (NWC)   (202) 475-1776
Fort Lesley J. McNair
4th and P Streets SW
Washington, DC 20319

Strategic Defense Initiative Organization (SDIO)   (202) 653-0057
Washington, DC 20301
Uniformed Services University   (301) 295-3030
of the Health Sciences (USUHS)
4301 Jones Bridge Road
Bethesda, MD 20814

Department of Education

The Department of Education establishes policy and administers Federal assistance to education. This includes programs in special education and rehabilitation; bilingual education; elementary and secondary education; vocational and adult education; and postsecondary education. It also has certain responsibilities for four federally-aided corporations: the American Printing House for the Blind, Gallaudet College, Howard University, and the National Technical Institute for the Deaf. Fiscal year 1985 budget of $16,682 million, or 1.78% of the total Federal budget; 5,140 paid employees, or 0.17% of the total civilian work force. (CFR reference: Title 34) For information on individual components of the Department of Education, see the component descriptions below.

Key Offices and Telephone Numbers

Address: 400 Maryland Avenue SW, Washington, DC 20202

General Information and Personnel Locator	(202) 245-3192
Public/Consumer Information	
Office of Public Affairs	(202) 245-8601
Federal Financial Aid Student Information Center	(301) 984-4070
Information Clearinghouse on Bilingual Education	(800) 336-4560
In the Washington, DC area	(703) 522-0710
Procurement Information	
Contracts Operations Division	(202) 732-2520
Office of Small and Disadvantaged Business Utilization	(202) 245-9582
Competition Advocate	(202) 245-9582
Press Inquiries	
News and Information Division	(202) 245-8564
Other Key Offices	
Agency Committee Management	(202) 245-6081
Congressional Liaison/Legislative Affairs	(202) 245-8280
Ethics in Government Act	(202) 732-2603
Fraud, Waste and Mismanagement Hotline	(800) 646-8005
In the Washington, DC area	(202) 755-2770
Freedom of Information/Privacy Act	(202) 245-8907
General Counsel	(202) 732-2600
Library	(202) 254-5060
Paperwork Reduction Act (ADP/IRM)	(202) 732-2174
Personnel	(202) 245-8366

Statistical Information, see Center for Statistics below

Key Information Resources

Available **FREE** is *Publications of the U.S. Department of Education* from the Editorial Policy Division, Office of Public Affairs, Department of Education, 400 Maryland Avenue SW, Washington, DC 20202; (202) 245-8601.

The Government Printing Office (GPO) makes available **FREE** the following subject bibliographies (SB): *Adult Education* (SB-214), *Educational Statistics* (SB-83), *Elementary Education* (SB-196), *Financial Aid to Students* (SB-85), *Foreign Education* (SB-235), *Higher Education* (SB-217), *Reading* (SB-164), *Secondary Education* (SB-68) and *Vocational and Career Education* (SB-110). See the GPO SB order form.

Department of Education Telephone Directory

Contact GPO for information on the most current edition.

The Student Guide—Five Federal Aid Programs

A guide that describes Federal student college aid programs and how to apply for them. 1986. 46pp. **FREE**. Federal Student Aid Programs, Dept. DEA-87, Pueblo, CO 81009.

American Education

A monthly publication, except August/September and January/February, that covers preschool-to-adult education, new research and demonstration projects, major education legislation, school and college bond data, grants, loans, contracts and fellowships. Subscription price: $23.00 a year. Single copy price: $2.50. GPO List ID AMED. (ED 1.10:) See the GPO subscription order form.

American Rehabilitation

A quarterly publication of the Rehabilitation Services Administration, this magazine comments on all aspects of life affecting handicapped people and brings program, treatment, news, and legislative and technical matters of interest to a wide range of professional and consumer groups. Subscription price: $11.00 a year. Single copy price: $3.00. GPO List ID ARHB. (ED 1.211:) See the GPO subscription order form.

Resources in Education

A monthly publication that provides up-to-date information about educational research sponsored by the Bureau of Research, Office of Education. Designed to keep teachers, administrators, research specialists, the public and others in the educational community informed about the latest significant findings from educational research. Subscription price: $56.00 a year. Single copy price: $8.50. GPO List ID RIE. (ED 1.310:) See the GPO subscription order form.

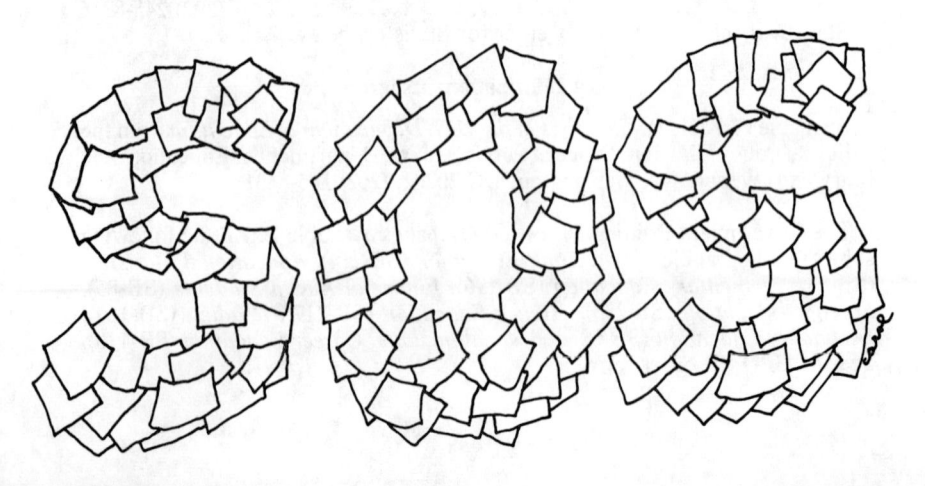

Center for Statistics

The Center for Statistics (CS), formerly the National Center for Education Statistics (NCES), collects and disseminates statistical information on the condition of education in the United States. The Center analyzes and reports the meaning and significance of these statistics and other data related to education in the United States and in other nations. CS also assists State and local education agencies in improving their statistical systems. Other responsibilities of CS include performing studies to develop and implement a national vocational education data system, conducting a continuing survey of the supply and demand for educational personnel, and producing profiles on the degree to which States are achieving equalization of resources for elementary and secondary education. Available **FREE** from CS are *Selected Publications from CS* and *CS Directory of Computer Tapes*. For further information, contact CS, 1200 19th Street NW, Washington, DC 20208; (202) 254-6057.

National Institute of Education

The National Institute of Education (NIE) directs a nationwide program of research and development in the field of education. Its aim is to create networks among those who conduct research and those who use it—from policymakers to school principals and teachers to the Nation's students and their parents. NIE-sponsored research focuses on issues and educational needs that include effective schools, literacy and instruction in basic skills, technology in education, and the need for more emphasis on science and mathematics education. The Institute supports research through requests for proposals, which deal with specific needs; grants competitions, which cover broad problem areas; and the NIE unsolicited proposals program, which seeks to encourage participation in educational research and development by qualified persons and groups not usually involved in research. For further information, contact NIE, 1200 19th Street NW, Washington, DC 20208; (202) 254-5740.

National Institute of Education
Educational Resources Information Center

The Educational Resources Information Center (ERIC) is a national information system that provides access to descriptions of exemplary programs, research and development efforts, and related information that may be used in developing more effective educational programs. ERIC consists of a central Federal Government office that makes policy, funds and monitors the entire system; 16 subject-specialized "clearinghouses" that collect and analyze the literature and produce information products; a central "ERIC Document Reproduction Service," and a commercial publisher that produces the various ERIC publications. Available **FREE** is *A Pocket Guide to ERIC, How to Use ERIC* and *ERIC Clearinghouses*. For further information, contact ERIC, 1200 19th Street NW, Washington, DC 20208; (202) 254-5500.

180 **FEDfind**

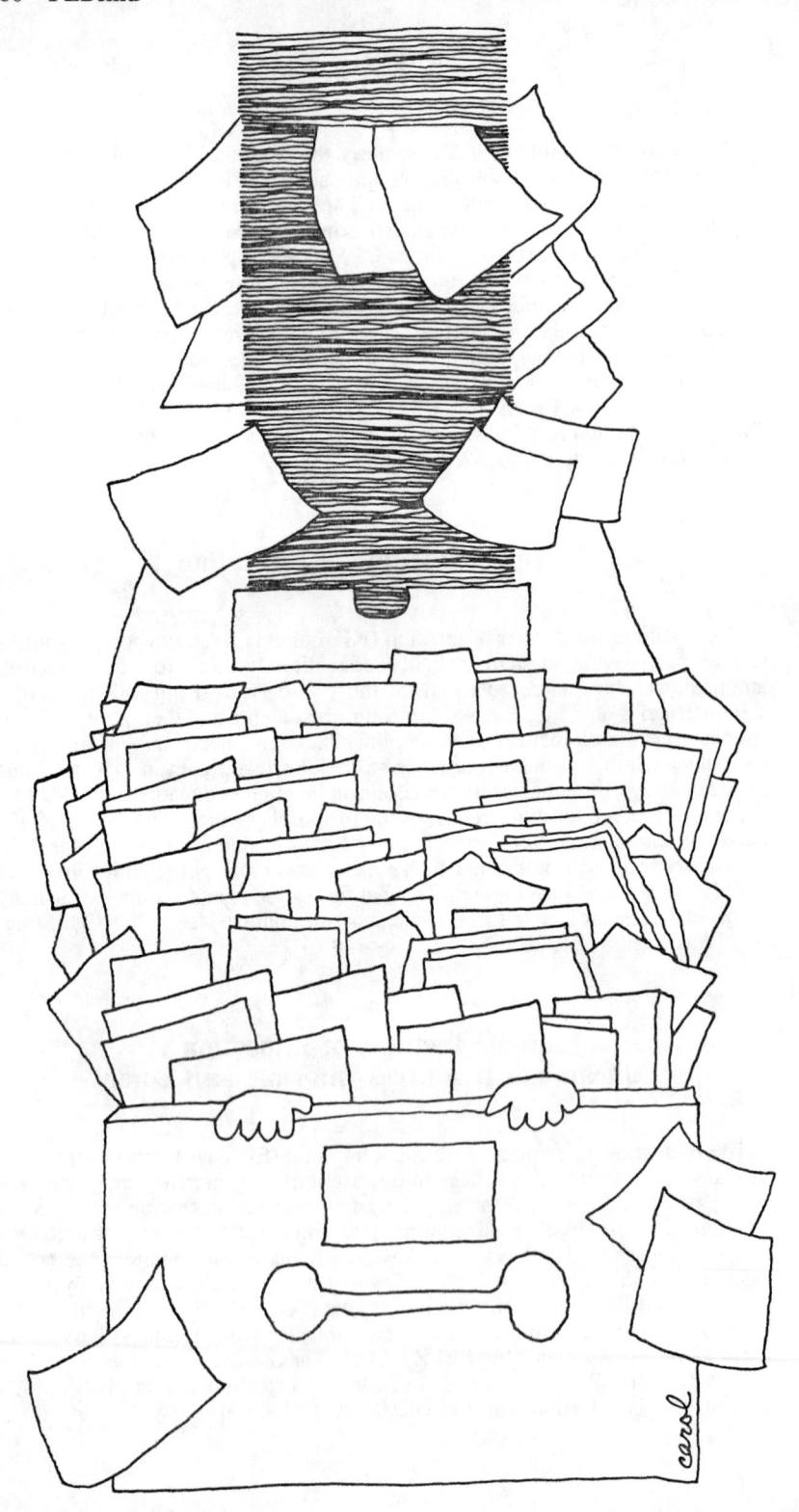

Department of Energy

The Department of Energy (DOE) coordinates and administers energy functions of the Federal Government. It is responsible for long-term, high-risk research and development of energy technology; the marketing of Federal power; energy conservation; the nuclear weapons program; energy regulatory programs; and a central energy data collection and analysis program. Fiscal year 1985 budget of $10,186 million, or 1.09% of the total Federal budget; 16,699 paid employees, or 0.57% of the total civilian work force. (CFR references, Titles and Chapters: 10, II, III, X; 41, 109) For information on individual components of the Department of Energy, see the component descriptions below.

Key Offices and Telephone Numbers

Address: 1000 Independence Avenue SW, Washington, DC 20585

General Information and Personnel Locator	(202) 252-5000
Public/Consumer Information	
Office of Public Affairs	(202) 252-5575
Conservation and Renewable Energy Inquiry and Referral Service	(800) 523-2929
In Pennsylvania	(800) 462-4983
In Alaska and Hawaii	(800) 233-3071
Minority Energy Information Clearinghouse	(202) 252-5876
Procurement Information	
Procurement Office	(202) 252-8228
Office of Small and Disadvantaged Business Utilization	(202) 252-8203
Competition Advocate	(202) 252-9077
Press Inquiries	
Press Services Division	(202) 252-5810
Other Key Offices	
Agency Committee Management	(202) 252-8990
Congressional Liaison/Legislative Affairs	(202) 252-5468
Ethics in Government Act	(202) 252-8665
Fraud, Waste and Mismanagement Hotline	(202) 252-4073
Toll Free, call GAO	(800) 424-5454
Freedom of Information/Privacy Act	(202) 252-8618
General Counsel	(202) 252-5281
Library	(202) 252-9534
Paperwork Reduction Act (ADP/IRM)	(202) 252-5940
Personnel	(202) 252-8536
Statistical Information, see Energy Information Administration below	

Key Information Resources

The *Energy Information Directory* and *EIA Publications Directory* are available **FREE** from the Energy Information Administration, see below.

Available **FREE** from the Government Printing Office (GPO) are the following subject bibliographies (SB): *Atomic Energy and Nuclear Power* (SB-200), *Energy Conservation and Research Technology* (SB-306), *Energy Management for Consumers and Business* (SB-303), *Energy Policy, Issues and Programs* (SB-305), *Energy Supplies, Prices and Consumption* (SB-304) and *Solar Energy* (SB-9). See the GPO SB order form.

Department of Energy Telephone Directory

Contact GPO for information on the most current edition.

Department of Energy Subscription Services

The following is a list of Department of Energy subscription services available from the GPO. For more detailed information, including order forms, consult the *Government Subscription Services* (Price List 36), available **FREE** from the GPO. See the GPO subscription order form.

Coal Distribution
DOE This Month
Electric Power Monthly
Electric Power Quarterly
Energy Abstracts for Policy Analysis
Energy Related Laboratory Equipment
Energy Research Abstracts
Monitor
Monthly Energy Review
Natural Gas Monthly
Nuclear Safety, A Bimonthly Technical Progress Review
Petroleum Marketing Monthly
Petroleum Supply Monthly
Quarterly Coal Report
SERI Technical Report Desktop Library
Short-Term Energy Outlook
Weekly Coal Production
Weekly Petroleum Status Report

Economic Regulatory Administration

The Economic Regulatory Administration (ERA) regulates the supply, pricing and distribution of crude oil, natural gas liquids and petroleum products. It is responsible for the administration and enforcement of programs dealing with the pricing, allocation and import/export of various oil and gas products; conversion of oil- and gas-fired utility and industrial facilities to coal; regional coordination of electric power system planning; energy conservation standards; and national energy emergency and contingency planning. The ERA takes part in proposing, negotiating and implementing United States international energy agreements. For further information, contact the Director of Management Services, ERA, DOE, 1000 Independence Avenue SW, Washington, DC 20585; (202) 252-4241.

Energy Information Administration

The Energy Information Administration (EIA) collects, processes and publishes data in the areas of energy production, demand, consumption, distribution, reserves and technology. It provides the data and associated analyses to public and private users. EIA analyses are prepared on long-term energy trends, the economic impact of energy trends on regional and industrial sectors, competition within the energy industries, and the capital/financial structure of energy companies. Available **FREE** are the *EIA Publications Directory* and the *Energy Information Directory* from the National Energy Information Center, EI-20, EIA, 1000 Independence Avenue SW, Washington, DC 20585; (202) 252-8800.

Technical Information Center

The DOE Technical Information Center collects and indexes worldwide scientific and technical information in the area of energy. The Center also collects and archives DOE-generated energy information products. The information is distributed to Federal agencies and their contractors, colleges and universities, and State energy offices. Available **FREE** is the *Technical Information Center's Products and Services* brochure and *Contacts* list. For further information, contact the Customer Services Division, Technical Information Center, P.O. Box 62, Oak Ridge, TN 37831; (615) 576-1541.

FORMS
5500
5503
5329
5498
001
5529
EXTRAS
LUNCH
5501
MISC.
carol

Department of Health and Human Services

The Department of Health and Human Services (HHS) administers programs concerned with the health, welfare and income security of the Nation's people. This is accomplished primarily through the activities of its six operating divisions: Health Care Financing Administration, Office of Child Support Enforcement, Office of Community Services, Office of Human Development Services, Public Health Service, and Social Security Administration. Fiscal year 1985 budget of $315,553 million, or 33.68% of the total Federal budget; 141,948 paid employees, or 4.81% of the total civilian work force. (CFR reference: Title 45) For information on individual components of HHS, see the component descriptions below.

Key Offices and Telephone Numbers

Address: 200 Independence Avenue SW, Washington, DC 20201

General Information and Personnel Locator	(202) 245-6296

Public/Consumer Information

Office of Consumer Affairs	(202) 634-4140
Cancer Information Service	(800) 4-CANCER
In Hawaii: Oahu	(808) 524-1234
In Alaska	(800) 638-6070
In the Washington, DC area	(202) 636-5700
Child abuse hotline	(800) 421-0353
In California	(800) 352-0386
National Health Information Clearinghouse	(800) 336-4797
In Virginia	(703) 522-2590
National Runaway Switchboard	(800) 621-4000
Surgical opinion hotline	(800) 638-6833
In Maryland	(800) 492-6603

Procurement Information

Procurement Office	(202) 245-6313
Office of Small and Disadvantaged Business Utilization	(202) 245-7300
Competition Advocate	(202) 245-8771

Press Inquiries

News Division	(202) 245-6343

Other Key Offices

Agency Committee Management	(202) 426-2753
Congressional Liaison/Legislative Affairs	(202) 245-7644
Ethics in Government Act	(202) 475-0150
Fraud, Waste and Mismanagement Hotline	(800) 368-5779
In Maryland only	(800) 638-3986
Freedom of Information/Privacy Act	(202) 472-7453
General Counsel	(202) 245-7741
Library	(202) 245-6791
Paperwork Reduction Act (ADP/IRM)	(202) 245-6396
Personnel	(202) 245-3244

Statistical Information, see the National Institutes of Health's National Center for Health Statistics and the Social Security Administration's Office of Research, Statistics and International Policy below

Key Information Resources

Health Information Resources in the Federal Government

Compiled by the staff of the National Health Information Clearinghouse (NHIC), the directory includes selected Federal and federally-sponsored health information resources that the NHIC staff have found useful in responding to health inquiries. The directory provides a central source of information for each agency or department cited. The entries are arranged alphabetically by principal keyword, e.g., the National Institute of Allergy and Infectious Diseases is listed under the keyword "allergy." Each entry presents the information necessary to contact the resource and describes the major services and activities. Any known limitations, such as restrictions on use, audience or charges for services, are stated. The NHIC is a service of the Office of Disease Prevention and Health Promotion of the Public Health Service. The directory also includes organization and subject indexes. 1985, 3rd ed. 34pp. **FREE**. NHIC, P.O. Box 1133, Washington, DC 20013; (800) 336-4797, (703) 522-2590 in Virginia.

Department of Health and Human Services Subscription Services

The following is a list of HHS subscription services available from the Government Printing Office (GPO). For more detailed information, including order forms, consult the *Government Subscription Services* (Price List 36), available **FREE** from the GPO. See the GPO subscription order form.

Abridged Index Medicus
ADAMHA News
Aging
Alcohol Health and Research World
Approved Prescription Drug Products (With Therapeutic Equivalence Evaluations)
Cancer Treatment Reports
Children Today
Current Awareness in Health Education
Environmental Health Perspectives
FDA Consumer
FDA Enforcement Report
Focal Points
Grants Administration Manual
Health Care Financing Review
Health Sciences Audiovisuals
Health Sciences Serials
Index Medicus
Journal of the National Cancer Institute
Medicare Carriers Manual, Part B, Claims Process, Part 3, HCFA Publication #14-3
Medicare Home Health Agency Manual, HCFA Publication #11
Medicare Hospital Manual, HCFA Publication #10
Medicare Intermediary Manual, Part A, Claims Process, Part 3, HCFA Publication #13-3
Medicare Provider Reimbursement Manual, HCFA Publication #15-1
Medicare Skilled Nursing Facility Manual, HCFA Publication #12
Monthly Benefit Statistics
Morbidity and Mortality Weekly Report

Executive Branch Departments   187

National Drug Code Directory
National Library of Medicine Audiovisuals Catalog
National Library of Medicine, Current Catalog
NIOSH Manual of Analytical Methods, Third Edition
Physical Fitness/Sports Medicine
Psychopharmacology Bulletin
Public Health Reports
Quarterly Public Assistance Statistics
Recombinant DNA Technical Bulletin
Registry of Toxic Effects of Chemical Substances
Research Resources Reporter
Schizophrenia Bulletin
The Ship's Medicine Chest and Medical Aid at Sea
Social Security Bulletin
Social Security Rulings on Federal Old-Age, Survivors, and Disability, etc.

Health Care Financing Administration

The Health Care Financing Administration (HCFA) oversees the Medicare and Medicaid programs and related Federal medical care quality control staffs. The Medicare program is the Federal health insurance program for persons over 65 years of age and certain disabled persons. HCFA develops and implements policies, procedures and guidance related to program recipients, the providers of services such as hospitals, nursing homes, physicians and contractors that process the claims. The Medicaid program, through grants to States, provides medical services to those who cannot afford adequate medical care. (CFR reference: Title 42, Chapter IV) For further information, contact the Office of Public Affairs, HCFA, 330 Independence Avenue SW, Washington, DC 20201; (202) 245-6113.

Office of Child Support Enforcement

The Office of Child Support Enforcement (OCSE) provides leadership in the planning, development, management and coordination of the Department's Child Support Enforcement programs and activities. These programs require States to enforce support obligations owed by absent parents to their children by locating absent parents, establishing paternity when necessary and obtaining child support. (CFR reference: Title 45, Chapter III) For further information, contact the Public Inquiries Office, OCSE, 6110 Executive Boulevard, Rockville, MD 20852; (301) 443-5327.

Office of Community Services

The Office of Community Services (OCS) administers the Community Services block grant and discretionary grant programs and manages the Community Service transition project grants. (CFR reference: Title 45, Chapter X) For further information, contact the Office of the Director, OCS, 200 Independence Avenue SW, Washington, DC 20201; (202) 475-0373.

Office of Human Development Services

The Office of Human Development Services (HDS) provides human services programs for the elderly, children and youth, families, Native Americans, persons living in rural areas, handicapped persons and public assistance recipients. (CFR reference: Title 45, Chapter XIII) For further information, contact the Office of Public Affairs, HDS, 200 Independence Avenue SW, Washington, DC 20201; (202) 472-7257.

Public Health Service

The Public Health Service (PHS) promotes the protection and advancement of the Nation's physical and mental health. The PHS does this through the activities of organizations described below. (CFR reference: Title 42, Chapter I) For further information, contact the PHS, 200 Independence Avenue SW, Washington, DC 20201; (202) 245-6296 or 5600 Fishers Lane, Rockville, MD 20857; (301) 443-2404.

Public Health Service
Agency for Toxic Substances and Disease Registry

The Agency for Toxic Substances and Disease Registry (ATSDR) administers programs designed to protect the public health and worker safety and health from exposure and adverse health effects of hazardous substances in storage sites or released in fires, explosions or transportation accidents. To accomplish its mission, the agency collects, analyzes and disseminates information relating to serious diseases and mortality relating to human exposure to toxic or hazardous substances; maintains a listing of areas closed to the public or otherwise restricted in use because of toxic substance contamination; and provides medical, epidemiological and technical advice to protect individuals in instances of exposure or potential exposure to hazardous substances. For further information, contact ATSDR, 1600 Clifton Road NE, Atlanta, GA 30333; (404) 452-4113.

Public Health Service
Alcohol, Drug Abuse and Mental Health Administration

The Alcohol, Drug Abuse and Mental Health Administration (ADAMHA) deals with health problems and issues associated with the use and abuse of alcohol and drugs and with mental illness and mental health. The Service conducts and supports research on the biological, psychological, behavioral and epidemiological aspects of alcoholism, drug abuse, and mental health and illness, along with research on treatment delivery and prevention services. The information it gathers and analyzes is provided to the public and to the scientific community. For further information, contact the Division of Communications and Public Affairs, ADAMHA, 5600 Fishers Lane, Rockville, MD 20857; (301) 443-3783.

Public Health Service
Centers for Disease Control

The Centers for Disease Control (CDC) administer programs for the prevention and control of diseases and other preventable conditions and for responding to public health emergencies including environmental, chemical and radiation. The CDC directs and enforces foreign quarantine activities and regulations. The Center also conducts research and develops occupational safety and health standards through its National Institute for Occupational Safety and Health (NIOSH). For further information, contact the CDC, 1600 Clifton Road NE, Atlanta, GA 30333; (404) 329-3286.

Public Health Service
Food and Drug Administration

The purpose of the Food and Drug Administration (FDA) is to protect the public against impure and unsafe foods, drugs and cosmetics and to regulate hazards involved with medical devices and radiation. To accomplish its mission, the FDA regulates, inspects, tests, sets standards for and licenses the manufacture of biological products shipped in interstate or foreign commerce; sets standards for, monitors the quality of, and regulates labeling of all drugs for human use; develops regulations for the composition, quality, nutrition and safety of foods, food additives, colors and cosmetics, and inspects processing plants; sets standards for safe limits of radiation exposure; evaluates the safety of veterinary preparations and devices; and develops policy for and evaluates the safety, efficacy and labeling of medical devices. (CFR reference: Title 21, Chapter I) For further information, contact the Office of Consumer Affairs, FDA, 5600 Fishers Lane, Rockville, MD 20857; (301) 443-3170.

Public Health Service
Health Resources and Services Administration

The Health Resources and Services Administration (HRSA) fosters the improvement of health services for the people of the United States and develops health care and maintenance systems to meet the needs of individuals at all levels of society. To accomplish this, HRSA supports efforts to integrate health services delivery programs with public and private health financing programs; administers the health services block grants, categorical and formula grant-supported programs; provides technical assistance for modernizing or replacing health care facilities; and supports activities to improve the education, training, distribution, supply, use and quality of the Nation's health care personnel. For further information, contact the Office of Communications, HRSA, 5600 Fishers Lane, Rockville, MD 20857; (301) 443-2086.

Public Health Service
National Center for Health Statistics

The National Center for Health Statistics (NCHS) collects, analyzes and disseminates health statistics on vital events and health activities to reflect the health status of people, health needs and health resources. The Center conducts surveys on a continuing basis in such areas as health costs, insurance coverage, nutritional status, the supply of health manpower, prevalence of chronic diseases, disability, basic morbidity and mortality data, and utilization of health services. The Nation's official statistics on births, deaths, marriages and divorces are developed from NCHS' vital statistics program. Available **FREE** are the *Catalog of Publications of the NCHS* and *Public Use Data Tapes from the NCHS*. For further information, contact the Scientific and Technical Information Branch, Division of Data Services, NCHS, 3700 East-West Highway, Hyattsville, MD 20782; (301) 436-8500.

Public Health Service
National Institutes of Health

The National Institutes of Health (NIH) conduct and support biomedical research into the causes, prevention and cure of diseases. Each of its major components, focuses on a specific medical area. For further information, contact NIH, 9000 Rockville Pike, Bethesda, MD 20205; (301) 496-4000. For a **FREE** copy of the *NIH Publications List*, write to the Editorial Operations Branch, NIH, Building 31, Room 2B03, Rockville, MD 20892.

Public Health Service
National Institutes of Health
National Library of Medicine

The National Library of Medicine (NLM) is the world's largest research library in a single scientific or professional field. The library collects materials exhaustively in all major areas of the health sciences and, to a lesser degree, in such areas as chemistry, physics, botany and zoology. The Library's resources and information services are available to public and private organizations and individuals. The Library's computer-based Medical Literature Analysis and Retrieval System (MEDLARS) and TOXLINE (toxicology information online) provide online bibliographic access to the Library's store of biomedical information. Available **FREE** are *NLM Publications*, *NLM Users Guide*, and the fact sheet *NLM*. For further information, contact the Office of Inquiries and Publications Management, NLM, 8600 Rockville Pike, Bethesda, MD 20894; (301) 496-6308.

Social Security Administration

The Social Security Bdministration (SSA) administers a national program of contributory social insurance whereby employees, employers and the self-employed pay contributions that are pooled in special trust funds. When earnings stop or are reduced because the worker retires, dies or becomes disabled, monthly cash benefits are paid to the worker or his/her beneficiary. Principal SSA programs include the Old Age Survivors and Disability Insurance program, Aid to Families with Dependent Children, and the Supplemental Security Income program. (CFR references, Titles and Chapters: 20, III; 45, IV) For further information, contact the Office of Field Operations, SSA, 6401 Security Boulevard, Baltimore, MD 21235; (301) 594-2520.

Social Security Administration
Office of Research, Statistics and International Policy

The Office of Research, Statistics and International Policy (ORSIP) develops and conducts the SSA's research and statistical program. It conducts research on income security, redistributive efforts on the economy of social security benefits and financing, and the adequacy of cash benefits. Statistical data and studies carried out or funded by ORSIP appear in a vriety of publications. These include a number of statistical releases, the monthly research and statistical journal *Social Security Bulletin* (published by the Government Printing Office), monographs, and note and technical paper series. Available **FREE** is the *ORSIP Publications Catalog* from ORSIP, 1875 Connecticut Avenue NW, Room 921, Washington, DC 20009; (202) 673-5576.

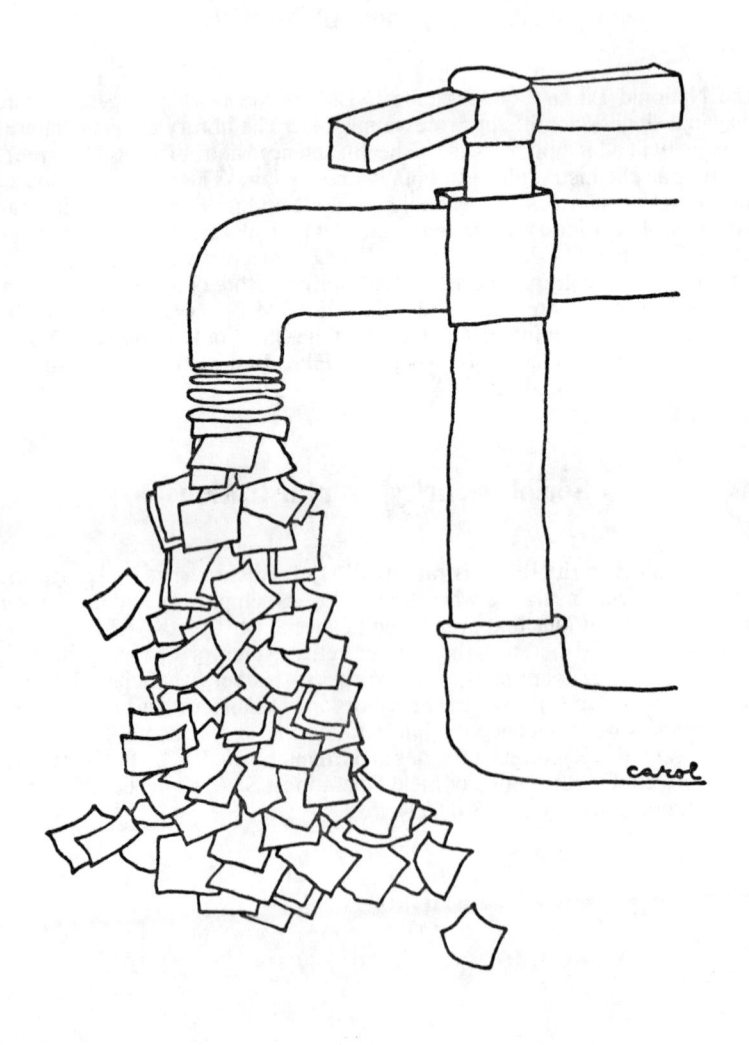

Department of Housing and Urban Development

The Department of Housing and Urban Development (HUD) is responsible for programs concerned with housing needs, fair housing opportunities, and improving and developing the Nation's communities. To accomplish its purpose, HUD administers mortgage insurance programs, a rental subsidy program for lower income families and programs that aid in neighborhood rehabilitation and preservation of urban areas. HUD also protects home buyers by regulating certain types of housing and real estate activities. This includes mobile home standards, interstate land sales registration and real estate settlement procedures. Fiscal year 1985 budget of $28,671 million, or 3.06% of the total Federal budget; 12,108 paid employees, or 0.41% of the total civilian work force. (CFR reference: Title 24)

Key Offices and Telephone Numbers

Address: 451 7th Street SW, Washington, DC 20410

General Information and Personnel Locator	(202) 755-5111
Public/Consumer Information	
Office of Public Affairs	(202) 755-6980
Program Information Center	(202) 755-6420
Housing discrimination complaints	(800) 424-8590
In the Washington, DC area	(202) 426-3500
Procurement Information	
Office of Procurement and Contracts	(202) 755-5290
Office of Small and Disadvantaged Business Utilization	(202) 755-1428
Competition Advocate	(202) 755-6945
Press Inquiries	
Office of Public Affairs	(202) 755-6685
Other Key Offices	
Agency Committee Management	(202) 755-5123
Congressional Liaison/Legislative Affairs	(202) 755-7380
Ethics in Government Act	(202) 755-7137
Fraud, Waste and Mismanagement Hotline	(202) 472-4200
Toll Free, call GAO	(800) 424-5454
Freedom of Information/Privacy Act	(202) 755-6685
General Counsel	(202) 755-7244
Library	(202) 755-6370
Paperwork Reduction Act (ADP/IRM)	(202) 755-6940
Personnel	(202) 755-5500
Statistical Information	(202) 755-6373

Key Information Resources

Programs of HUD

A catalog of HUD programs categorized into community planning and development, housing, public and Indian housing, fair housing and equal opportunity, policy development and research, Government National Mortgage Association (GNMA), access to housing for the handicapped, and solar energy and energy conservation bank. Entries for each program description includes, as appropriate: nature of program, grantee eligibility, funding distribution, legal authority, administering office, information sources, current status and scope of program. 1985. 116pp. **FREE**. Office of Public Affairs, HUD, 451 7th Street SW, Washington, DC 20410; (202) 755-6980.

HUD USER: A Guide to Research Information Services

A brochure describing HUD USER, an information service that provides access to research information in housing and urban topics. The HUD USER database includes information on building technology, community development, energy conservation and utilization, housing assistance programs, services for the elderly and handicapped, and neighborhood rehabilitation and conservation. **FREE**. Also available **FREE** is the *HUD USER Publications List and Order Form*. HUD USER, P.O. Box 280, Germantown, MD 20874; (301) 251-5154.

Minimum Property Standards

A subscription service that consists of a basic manual and quarterly revisions for an indeterminate period, punched for 3-ring looseleaf binder. Volume II, Multifamily Housing, includes standards relating to durability, energy, the elderly and the handicapped. Subscription price: $35.00. GPO List ID MPS02. (HH 1.6/9:M 91/984) See the GPO subscription order form.

Department of the Interior

The Department of the Interior is responsible for nationally-owned public lands and natural resources. This includes fostering wise use of the Nation's land and water resources, protecting fish and wildlife, preserving the environmental and cultural values of the national parks and historical places, and providing for the enjoyment of life through outdoor recreation. The Department assesses the Nation's energy and mineral resources and works toward their best development in the interests of the country and its people. The Department also has certain social and economic responsibilities for American Indians, Alaska Natives and for people who live in Island Territories under U.S. administration. Fiscal year 1985 budget of $4,828 million, or 0.52% of the total Federal budget; 74,225 paid employees, or 2.52% of the total civilian work force. (CFR reference: Title 43) For information on individual components of the Department of the Interior, see the component descriptions below.

Key Offices and Telephone Numbers

Address: C Street between 18th and 19th Streets NW, Washington, DC 20240

General Information	(202) 343-1100
Personnel Locator	(202) 343-7220
Public/Consumer Information	
Office of Public Affairs	(202) 343-6416
Procurement Information	
Office of Acquisition and Property Management	(202) 343-3433
Office of Small and Disadvantaged Business Utilization	(202) 343-8493
Competition Advocate	(202) 343-5830
Press Inquiries	
Office of Public Affairs	(202) 343-3171
News features recording	(202) 343-3020
Other Key Offices	
Agency Committee Management	(202) 343-4863
Congressional Liaison/Legislative Affairs	(202) 343-7693
Ethics in Government Act	(202) 343-5916
Fraud, Waste and Mismanagement Hotline	(800) 424-5081
In the Washington, DC area	(202) 343-2424
Freedom of Information/Privacy Act	(202) 343-6191
General Counsel	(202) 343-4423
Library (Natural Resources Library)	(202) 343-5815
Paperwork Reduction Act (ADP/IRM)	(202) 343-6194
Personnel	(202) 343-2154
Statistical Information, contact appropriate public affairs office	

Key Information Resources

For information on publications, contact the individual bureau's or office's public affairs office provided with each component description. Information regarding bibliographies on selected subjects is available from the Natural Resources Library Information Services Branch.

Department of the Interior Subscription Services

The following is a list of subscription services available from the Government Printing Office (GPO). For further information, including order forms, consult *Government Subscription Services* (Price List 36), available **FREE** from the GPO. See the GPO subscription order form.

Decisions of the Department of the Interior
Duck Stamp Data
Earthquake Information Bulletin
Fish Health News
Land and Water Conservation Fund Grants Manual
New Publications: Bureau of Mines
Preliminary Determination of Epicenters
Sport Fishery Abstracts
Wildlife Review

Department of the Interior Telephone Directory

Contact the GPO for information on the most current edition.

Bureau of Indian Affairs

The Bureau of Indian Affairs (BIA) fosters the development of Indian and Alaskan Native people to manage their own affairs under the trust relationship with the Federal Government. This includes seeking to provide adequate educational opportunities, to promote social welfare and to develop and implement programs for economic advancement. The BIA also acts as trustee for lands and moneys held in trust by the United States. (CFR references, Titles and Chapters: 25, I; 41, 14H) For further information, contact the Office of Public Affairs, Bureau of Indian Affairs, Washington, DC 20240; (202) 343-7445.

Bureau of Land Management

The Bureau of Land Management (BLM) is responsible for the management of 284 million acres of public lands. Resources managed by the Bureau include timber, hard minerals, oil and gas, geothermal energy, wildlife habitat, endangered plant and animal species, rangeland vegetation, recreation and cultural values, wild and scenic rivers, designated conservation and wilderness areas, and open space. BLM programs are intended to provide for the protection, orderly development and use of public lands and resources. (CFR reference: Title 43, Chapter II) For further information, contact the Office of Public Affairs, BLM, Washington, DC 20240; (202) 343-5717.

Bureau of Mines

The Bureau of Mines primarily conducts research to provide the technology for the extraction, processing, use and recycling of the Nation's nonfuel mineral resources to help ensure adequate supplies for the national security of the United States. The Bureau also collects, compiles, analyzes and publishes statistical and economic information on all phases of nonfuel mineral resource development, including exploration, production, shipments, demand, stocks, prices, imports and exports. (CFR reference: Title 30, Chapter VI) For further information, contact the Office of Technical Information, Bureau of Mines, Washington, DC 20241; (202) 634-1004.

Bureau of Reclamation

The Bureau of Reclamation has the responsibility to locate, construct, operate and maintain works for the storage, diversion and development of water resources for the reclamation of arid and semi-arid lands in the Western States. Reclamation projects include municipal and industrial water supply, hydroelectric power generation, irrigation water service, flood control, water quality improvement, wind power and solar power research, and river regulation and control. Through contracts with project beneficiaries, the Bureau arranges for partial repayment to the Government. (CFR reference: Title 43, Chapter I) For further information, contact the Office of Public Affairs, Bureau of Reclamation, Washington, DC 20240; (202) 343-4662.

Minerals Management Service

The Minerals Management Service (MMS) assesses the nature, extent, recoverability and value of leasable minerals on the Outer Continental Shelf. The Service provides for the inventory, development and recovery of mineral resources; utilization of available and safe technology; and fair financial returns to the Federal Treasury for produced commodities. (CFR reference: Title 30, Chapter II) For further information, contact the Office of Public Affairs, MMS, Washington, DC 20240; (202) 343-3983.

National Park Service

The National Park Service administers the Federal national parks, monuments, historic sites and recreation areas. The Park Service relates the natural values and historical significance of these areas to the public through talks, tours, films, exhibits and publications. The Service also operates campgrounds and other visitor facilities and provides for lodging, food and transportation services in many areas. (CFR reference: Title 36, Chapter I) For further information, contact the Office of Public Affairs, National Park Service, Washington, DC 20240; (202) 343-7394.

Office of Surface Mining Reclamation and Enforcement

The Office of Surface Mining Reclamation and Enforcement (OSMRE), in conjunction with State governments, regulates strip mining and reclamation of land previously damaged by strip mining. Major activities relate to development of national policy for the conduct of surface mining control and reclamation program; reviews of State programs; and provision of technical assistance through its field offices and technical centers. (CFR reference: Title 30, Chapter VII) For further information, contact the Office of Public Affairs, OSMRE, Washington, DC 20240; (202) 343-4719.

United States Fish and Wildlife Service

The U.S. Fish and Wildlife Service helps preserve, protect and enhance the Nation's fish and wildlife resources and their habitats. This includes wild birds, endangered species, certain marine mammals and inland sport fisheries. Within this framework, the FWS maintains a refuge system, fish hatcheries and research laboratories. It is also responsible for monitoring the land and water environment for pesticides, heavy metals and thermal pollution and performing environmental impact assessments as related to fish and wildlife populations. (CFR reference: Title 50, Chapters I, IV) For further information, contact the Office of Public Affairs, U.S. Fish and Wildlife Service, Washington, DC 20240; (202) 343-5634.

United States Geological Survey

The U.S. Geological Survey (USGS) identifies the Nation's land, water, energy and mineral resources; classifies federally-owned lands for minerals and energy resources and water power potential; investigates natural hazards such as earthquakes, volcanoes and landslides; and conducts the National Mapping Program (see Chapter 15, "Mapping, Charting and Geologic Activities"). To accomplish these functions the USGS prepares maps, collects and interprets data on mineral and water resources, performs fundamental and applied research in the sciences and techniques involved, and publishes and disseminates the results of its investigations in maps and reports. (CFR reference: Title 30, Chapter IV) For further information, contact the Public Affairs Office, USGS, 119 National Center, Reston, VA 22092; (703) 860-7444.

Department of Justice

The Department of Justice serves as legal counsel for the citizens of the United States. Its primary roles are protection against criminals and subversion, ensuring competition in the Nation's free enterprise system, and enforcement of drug, immigration and naturalization laws. The Department also plays a role in protecting citizens through its efforts for effective law enforcement, crime prevention, crime detection, and prosecution and rehabilitation of offenders. The Attorney General, as head of the Department, directs the Government in legal matters generally, as well as those of the U.S. attorneys and U.S. marshals in the various Federal judicial districts around the country. Fiscal year 1985 budget of $3,518 million, or 0.38% of the total Federal budget; 61,858 paid employees, or 2.10% of the total civilian work force. (CFR reference: Title 28) For information on individual components of the Department of Justice, see the component descriptions below.

Key Offices and Telephone Numbers

Address: Constitution Avenue and 10th Street NW, Washington, DC 20530

General Information and Personnel Locator	(202) 633-2000

Public/Consumer Information

Office of Public Affairs	(202) 633-2007
National Center for Missing and Exploited Children	(800) 843-5678
In the Washington, DC area	(202) 634-9836
National Criminal Justice Reference Service	(800) 851-3420
In the Washington, DC area	(301) 251-5500
Justice Statistics Clearinghouse	(800) 732-3277
In the Washington, DC area	(301) 251-5500
Juvenile Justice Clearinghouse	(800) 638-8736
In the Washington, DC area	(301) 251-5500

Procurement Information

Procurement Office	(202) 633-2728
Office of Small and Disadvantaged Business Utilization	(202) 724-6271
Competition Advocate	(202) 272-8360

Press Inquiries

Office of Public Affairs	(202) 633-2007

Other Key Offices

Agency Committee Management	(202) 633-3101
Congressional Liaison/Legislative Affairs	(202) 633-2141
Ethics in Government Act	(202) 633-3101
Fraud, Waste and Mismanagement Hotline	(202) 633-3365
Toll free, call GAO	(800) 424-5454
Freedom of Information/Privacy Act	(202) 724-7400
General Counsel	(202) 633-2057
Library	(202) 633-3775
Paperwork Reduction Act (ADP/IRM)	(202) 633-4292
Personnel	(202) 633-2096

Statistical Information, see the Bureau of Justice Statistics below

Key Information Resources

Department of Justice Subscription Services

The following is a list of Justice Department subscription services available from the Government Printing Office (GPO). For further information, including order forms, consult the *Government Subscription Services* (Price List 36), available **FREE** from the GPO. See the GPO subscription order form.

Antitrust Division Manual
Drug Enforcement
Federal Probation: A Journal of Correctional Philosophy and Practice
FOIA Update (Freedom of Information Act Update)
Immigration and Naturalization Service Code Operating Instructions, Regulations and Interpretations
INS Reporter
Interim Decisions of the Department of Justice
Justice Assistance News
United States Attorney's Manual

Bureau of Justice Statistics

The Bureau of Justice Statistics (BJS) collects, analyzes, publishes and disseminates statistics on victims, criminal offenders and operation of justice systems at all levels of government throughout the United States. BJS provides State and local statistical and operating agencies with financial and technical support. The Bureau also develops national policy on issues such as data privacy, confidentiality and security, and the interstate exchange of criminal records. Available **FREE** from this office are *How to Gain Access to BJS Data* and the *BJS Bulletin—Telephone Contacts*. For further information, contact BJS, 633 Indiana Avenue NW, Washington, DC 20531; (202) 724-6100.

Bureau of Prisons

The Bureau of Prisons is responsible for the custody and care of those persons convicted of Federal crimes. It operates a nationwide system of maximum, medium and minimum security prisons and community program offices. The community program offices, along with contract halfway houses, help in the transition of Federal prisoners back into society after they have served their sentences. (CFR reference: Title 28, Chapter V) For further information, contact the Public Information Office, Bureau of Prisons, 320 1st Street NW, Washington, DC 20534; (202) 724-3198.

Drug Enforcement Administration

The Drug Enforcement Administration (DEA) is the lead Federal agency in enforcing narcotics and controlled substances laws and regulations. The primary responsibilities of DEA include investigation of major narcotics violators who operate at interstate or international levels; enforcement of regulations governing the legal manufacture, distribution and dispensing of controlled substances; management of a national narcotics intelligence system; coordination with Federal, State and local law enforcement authorities and with counterpart agencies abroad; and training, scientific research and information exchange in support of drug traffic prevention and control. (CFR reference: Title 21, Chapter II) For further information, contact the Office of Public Affairs, DEA, 1405 I Street NW, Washington, DC 20537; (202) 633-1469.

Executive Office for Immigration Review

The Executive Office for Immigration Review includes the Board of Immigration Appeals and the Office of the Chief Immigration Judge. The Office is completely independent of the Immigration and Naturalization Service (INS), the body charged with the enforcement of the immigration laws. The Board of Immigration Appeals is a quasi-judicial body that hears appeals from decisions entered by district directors of the INS and by immigration judges. Decisions of the Board are binding on all INS officers and immigration judges unless modified or overruled by the Attorney General, and are subject to judicial review by the Federal courts. The Office of the Chief Immigration Judge is responsible for the general supervision and direction of the immigration judges in the performance of their duties. For further information, contact the Administrative Officer, Executive Office for Immigration Review, 5203 Leesburg Pike, Suite 1609, Falls Church, VA 22041; (202) 756-6171.

Federal Bureau of Investigation

The Federal Bureau of Investigation (FBI) is the principal investigative arm of the Department of Justice. It is responsible for gathering and reporting facts, locating witnesses, and compiling evidence in matters in which the Federal Government is, or may be, a party. The FBI investigates all violations of Federal laws with the exception of those that have been assigned to some other Federal agency. Its jurisdiction includes espionage, sabotage and other domestic security matters; kidnapping, extortion; bank robbery; interstate transportation of stolen property; civil rights matters; interstate gambling violations; narcotics violations; fraud against the Federal Government; and assault or killing the President or a Federal officer. For further information, contact the FBI, 9th Street and Pennsylvania Avenue NW, Washington, DC 20535; (202) 324-3000.

Foreign Claims Settlement Commission of the United States

The Foreign Claims Settlement Commission is a quasi-judicial Federal agency authorized by specific legislation to determine claims of United States nationals for loss of property in specific foreign countries. These losses are the result of nationalization of property by foreign governments or from damage and loss of property as a result of military operations during World War II. Also, the Commission has determined claims of U.S. military and civilian personnel who have been held in a captured status during World War II or the Korean or Vietnam conflicts. (CFR reference: Title 45, Chapter V) For further information, contact the Office of the General Counsel, Foreign Claims Settlement Commission of the United States, 1111 20th Street NW, Washington, DC 20579; (202) 653-5883.

Immigration and Naturalization Service

The Immigration and Naturalization Service (INS) administers the immigration and naturalization laws as they relate to the admission, exclusion, deportation and naturalization of aliens. Specifically, INS inspects aliens to determine their admissibility into the United States; adjudicates requests of aliens for benefits under the law; guards against illegal entry into the United States; investigates, apprehends and removes aliens in this country who are in violation of the law; and examines alien applicants wishing to become U.S. citizens. (CFR reference: Title 8, Chapter I) For further information, contact the Office of Information, INS, 425 I Street NW, Washington, DC 20536; (202) 633-4316, 4330 or 4354.

International Criminal Police Organization —United States National Central Bureau

The International Criminal Police Organization—United States National Central Bureau (INTERPOL-USNCB) promotes mutual assistance among law enforcement authorities worldwide in the prevention and suppression of international crime. INTERPOL-USNCB serves as the United States' liaison to INTERPOL. INTERPOL-USNCB provides a communications link among the United States, other INTERPOL member countries and INTERPOL headquarters, and enables State and local police organizations and Federal law enforcement agencies to obtain the assistance of foreign law enforcement authorities. For further information, contact INTERPOL-USNCB, Washington, DC 20530; (202) 272-8383.

Justice System Improvement Act Agencies

The Justice System Improvement Act (JSIA) agencies' programs provide assistance to State and local criminal justice organizations. The Office of Justice Assistance, Research and Statistics (OJARS) coordinates the activities of and provides staff support to the Bureau of Justice Statistics (BJS), the National Institute of Justice (NIJ) and the Office of Juvenile Justice and Delinquency Prevention (OJJDP). BJS is described separately above because of its importance as a principal statistical collection agency. The NIJ supports research into crime, criminal behavior and crime prevention. The OJJDP operates programs to deter juvenile delinquency and improve State and local juvenile justice programs. For further information, contact the Office of Congressional and Public Affairs, Office of Justice Programs, 633 Indiana Avenue NW, Washington, DC 20531; (202) 724-7782.

United States Marshals Service

The U.S. Marshals Service provides support and protection to the Federal courts, including judges, attorneys and jurors; apprehends Federal fugitives; operates the witness security program, providing for the safety of endangered witnesses; transports Federal prisoners; and executes arrest warrants. The Marshals Service also is responsible for the prevention of civil disturbances and restoration of order in riot or mob-violence situations. For further information, contact the Office of Congressional and Public Affairs, U.S. Marshals Service, One Tysons Corner Center, McLean, VA 22102; (703) 285-1131.

United States Parole Commission

The U.S. Parole Commission grants, denies or revokes parole for eligible Federal offenders. The Commission also supervises paroled or otherwise released offenders until the expiration of their terms. For further information, contact the Office of the Chairman, U.S. Parole Commission, 5550 Friendship Blvd., Chevy Chase, MD 20815; (301) 492-5990.

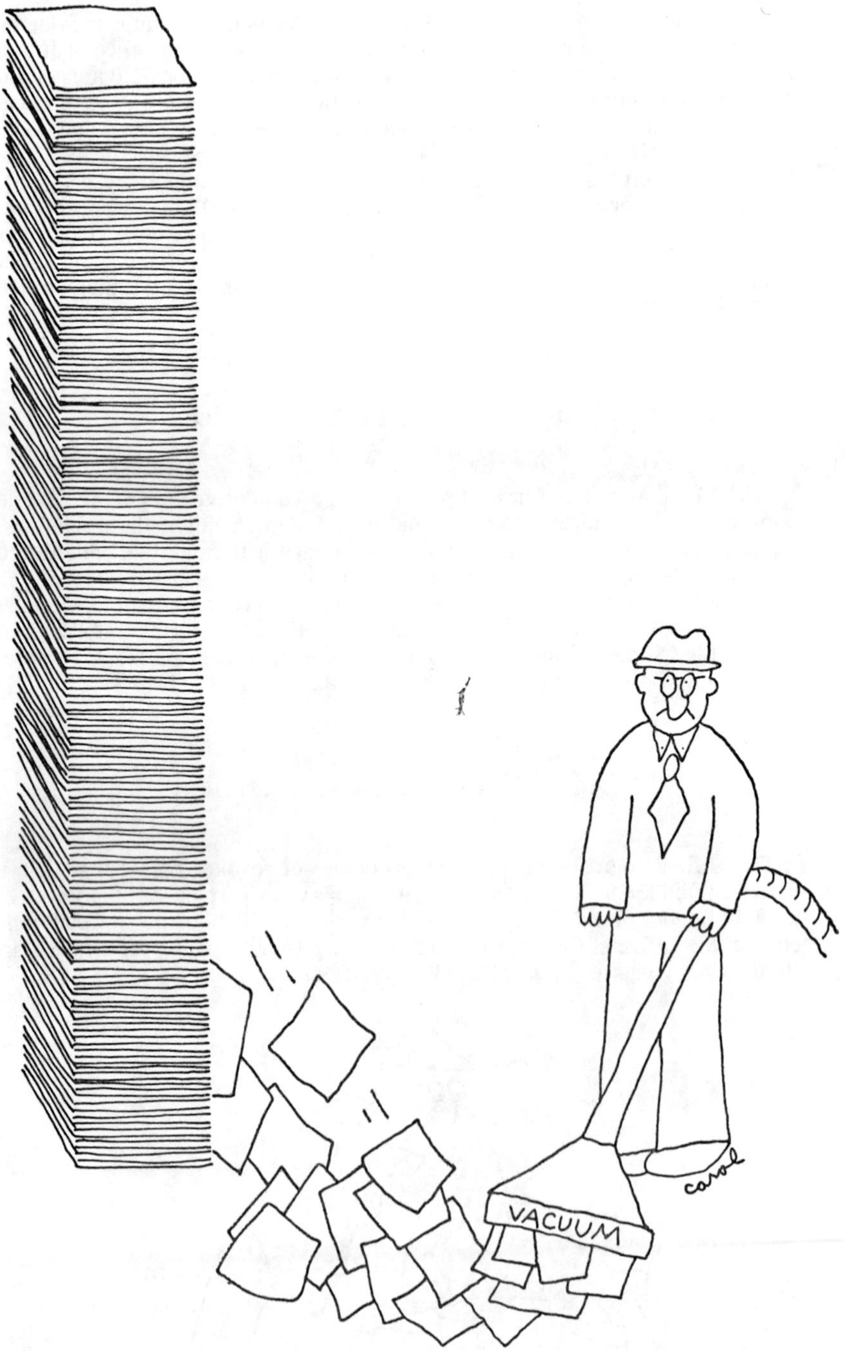
VACUUM
carol

Department of Labor

The Department of Labor (DOL) fosters and promotes the welfare of the Nation's wage earners. This includes improving their working conditions and opportunities for employment. To carry out its mission, DOL administers Federal labor laws guaranteeing workers' rights to safe and healthful working conditions, a minimum hourly wage and overtime pay, freedom from employment discrimination, unemployment insurance and workers' compensation. It also protects workers' pension rights; provides for job training programs; works to strengthen free collective bargaining; and keeps track of changes in employment, prices and other national economic measurements. Fiscal year 1985 budget of $23,893 million, or 2.55% of the total Federal budget; 19,137 paid employees, or 0.65% of the total civilian work force. (CFR reference: Title 29) For information on individual components of the Department of Labor, see the component descriptions below.

Key Offices and Telephone Numbers

Address: 200 Constitution Avenue NW, Washington, DC 20210

General Information	(202) 523-8165
Personnel Locator	(202) 523-6666
Public/Consumer Information	
Coordinator of Consumer Affairs	(202) 523-6060
Office of Information and Public Affairs	(202) 523-7316
Procurement Information	
Office of Procurement and Grants Management	(202) 523-6445
Office of Small and Disadvantaged Business Utilization	(202) 523-9148
Competition Advocate	(202) 523-9174
Press Inquiries	
Division of Media and Editorial Services	(202) 523-7316
Press release information recording	(202) 523-6899
Other Key Offices	
Agency Committee Management	(202) 523-6019
Congressional Liaison/Legislative Affairs	(202) 523-6141
Ethics in Government Act	(202) 523-7675
Fraud, Waste and Mismanagement Hotline	(800) 424-5409
In the Washington, DC area	(202) 357-0227
Freedom of Information/Privacy Act	(202) 523-8188
General Counsel	(202) 523-7675
Library	(202) 523-6992
Paperwork Reduction Act (ADP/IRM)	(202) 523-6073
Personnel	(202) 523-6551
Statistical Information, see the Bureau of Labor Statistics below	
Current economic statistics recording	(202) 523-9658

Key Information Resources

Available **FREE** from the Office of Information and Public Affairs are a fact sheet entitled *Department of Labor*, which describes the activities of the major agencies of the Department, and *Publications of the U.S. Department of Labor*, a subject listing of documents published by the Department.

Department of Labor Telephone Directory

Contact the Government Printing Office (GPO) for information on the most current edition.

Labor Department Subscription Services

The following is a list of Labor Department subscription services available from the GPO. For further information, including order forms, consult the *Government Subscription Services* (Price List 36), available **FREE** from the GPO. See the GPO subscription order form.

Area Trends in Employment and Unemployment
Area Wage Surveys
Coal Mine Inspection Manual
Comparison of State Unemployment Insurance Laws
CPI Detailed Report
Current Wage Developments
Employment and Earnings
Mine Safety and Health
Monthly Labor Review
Occupational Outlook Quarterly
OSHA Standards and Regulations
Producer Price Indexes
Producer Prices and Price Indexes (see *Producer Price Indexes*)
Unemployment in States and Local Areas
United States Department of State Indexes of Living Costs Abroad and
    Quarters Allowances, and Hardship Differentials

Bureau of Labor-Management Relations and Cooperative Programs

The Bureau of Labor-Management Relations and Cooperative Programs (BLMRCP) provides information and assistance in the development and implementation of cooperative labor-management programs; assists employers and unions in handling problems caused by major economic and technological change; reports on current and potentially critical dispute situations; and provides staff assistance to Presidential energy boards and other ad hoc boards and commissions dealing with major disputes. (CFR reference: Title 29, Chapter II) For further information, contact the BLMRCP, 200 Constitution Avenue NW, Washington, DC 20210; (202) 523-6045.

Bureau of Labor Statistics

The Bureau of Labor Statistics (BLS) is the Government's principal fact-finding agency in the area of labor economics. It collects, processes, analyzes and disseminates data relating to employment, unemployment and other characteristics of the labor force; prices and family expenditures; wages, other worker compensation and industrial relations; productivity and technological change in the work place; and occupational safety and health. Available **FREE** from this office are *How to Get Information from the Bureau of Labor Statistics, Telephone Contacts for Data Users, BLS Information in Print, BLS Information Online, BLS Data Files on Tape,* and *Mailing Lists for News Releases and Announcements.* For further information, contact the Information Office, BLS, 441 G Street NW, Washington, DC 20212; (202) 523-1221.

Employment and Training Administration

The Employment and Training Administration (ETA) administers programs that relate to employment services, job training and unemployment insurance. Component offices and services of ETA administer a Federal-State employment security system; fund and oversee programs to provide work experience and training for groups having difficulty entering or returning to the work force; formulate and promote apprenticeship standards and programs; and conduct research, development and evaluation programs. (CFR reference: Title 20, Chapter V) For further information, contact the Public Affairs Office, ETA, 200 Constitution Avenue NW, Washington, DC 20210; (202) 523-6871.

Employment Standards Administration

The Employment Standards Administration (ESA) administers and enforces such Federal standards as statutory minimum wages, overtime pay and wage rates to be paid on Government-assisted construction programs. ESA also enforces laws prohibiting job discrimination against women, minorities, handicapped persons and veterans employed by Federal contractors, and administers workers' compensation programs for Federal employees and certain categories of private sector employees. (CFR reference: Title 20, Chapter VI) For further information, contact the Public Affairs Office, ESA, 200 Constitution Avenue NW, Washington, DC 20210; (202) 523-8743.

Mine Safety and Health Administration

The Mine Safety and Health Administration (MSHA) helps protect the safety and health of U.S. miners. It develops and enforces mandatory safety and health standards for mines and the minerals industry and investigates accidents. MSHA provides assistance to the States in development of State mine safety and health programs. (CFR reference: Title 30, Chapter I) For further information, contact the Office of Information and Public Affairs, MSHA, 4015 Wilson Boulevard, Room 601, Arlington, VA 22203; (703) 235-1452.

Occupational Safety and Health Administration

The Occupational Safety and Health Administration (OSHA) develops and enforces worker safety and health regulations. OSHA sets standards to protect workers against safety and health hazards, conducts workplace inspections to enforce these regulations and issues citations and proposes penalties for violations to the standards. (CFR reference: Title 29, Chapter XVII) For further information, contact the Office of Information and Consumer Affairs, OSHA, 200 Constitution Avenue NW, Washington, DC 20210; (202) 523-8151.

Office of Labor-Management Standards

The Office of Labor-Management Standards (OLMS) administers several laws that regulate certain internal union procedures and protect the rights of members in approximately 50,000 unions. These laws govern the handling of union funds; the reporting and disclosure of certain financial transactions and administrative practices of unions, union officers and employees, surety companies, employers, and labor relations consultants; the election of union officers; and the imposition and administration of trusteeships. (CFR reference: Title 29, Chapter IV) For further information, contact the Public Affairs Office, OLMS, 200 Constitution Avenue NW, Washington, DC 20210; (202) 523-7344.

Pension and Welfare Benefits Administration

The Pension and Welfare Benefits Administration (PWBA), along with the Internal Revenue Service, administers *the Employee Retirement Income Security Act of 1974* (ERISA). This Act requires administrators of private pension and welfare plans to provide plan participants with easily understandable summaries of plans; to file those summaries with the PWBA; and to report annually on the financial operation of the plans and bonding of persons charged with handling plan funds and assets. (CFR reference: Title 29, Chapter XXV) For further information, contact the Division of Public Information, PWBA, 200 Constitution Avenue NW, Washington, DC 20210; (202) 523-8921.

Veterans' Employment and Training Service

The Veterans' Employment and Training Service (VETS) is responsible for seeing that the policies of the Labor Department regarding national employment and training programs for veterans are carried out by local public employment services and private sector contractors. VETS also promulgates policies, procedures and regulations related to employment and training opportunities mandated by legislation for veterans and other eligible persons with priority services given to disabled and Vietnam-era veterans. For further information, contact the Assistant Secretary for Veterans' Employment and Training Service, 200 Constitution Avenue NW, Washington, DC 20210; (202) 523-9116.

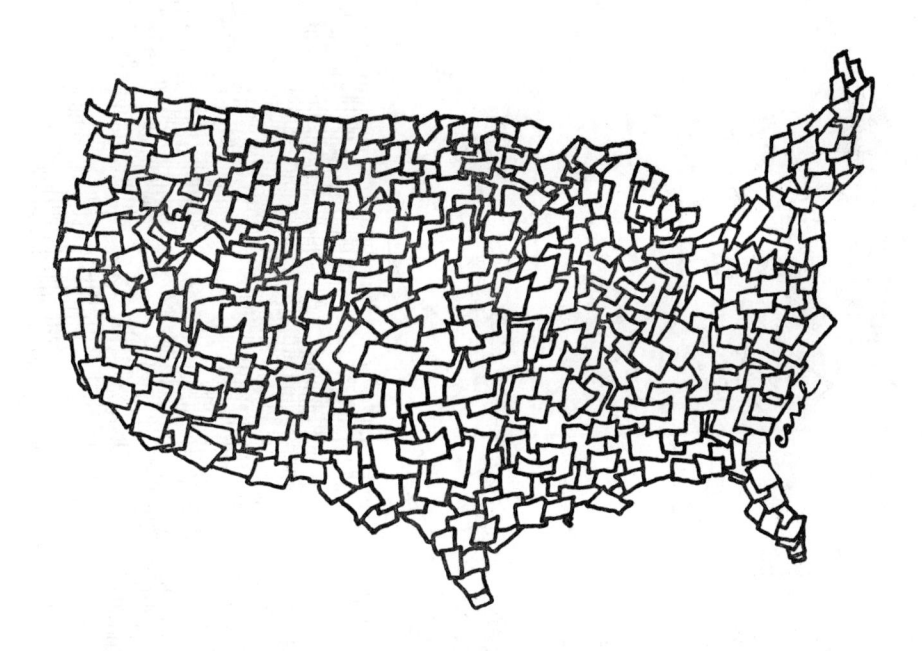

210 **FEDfind**

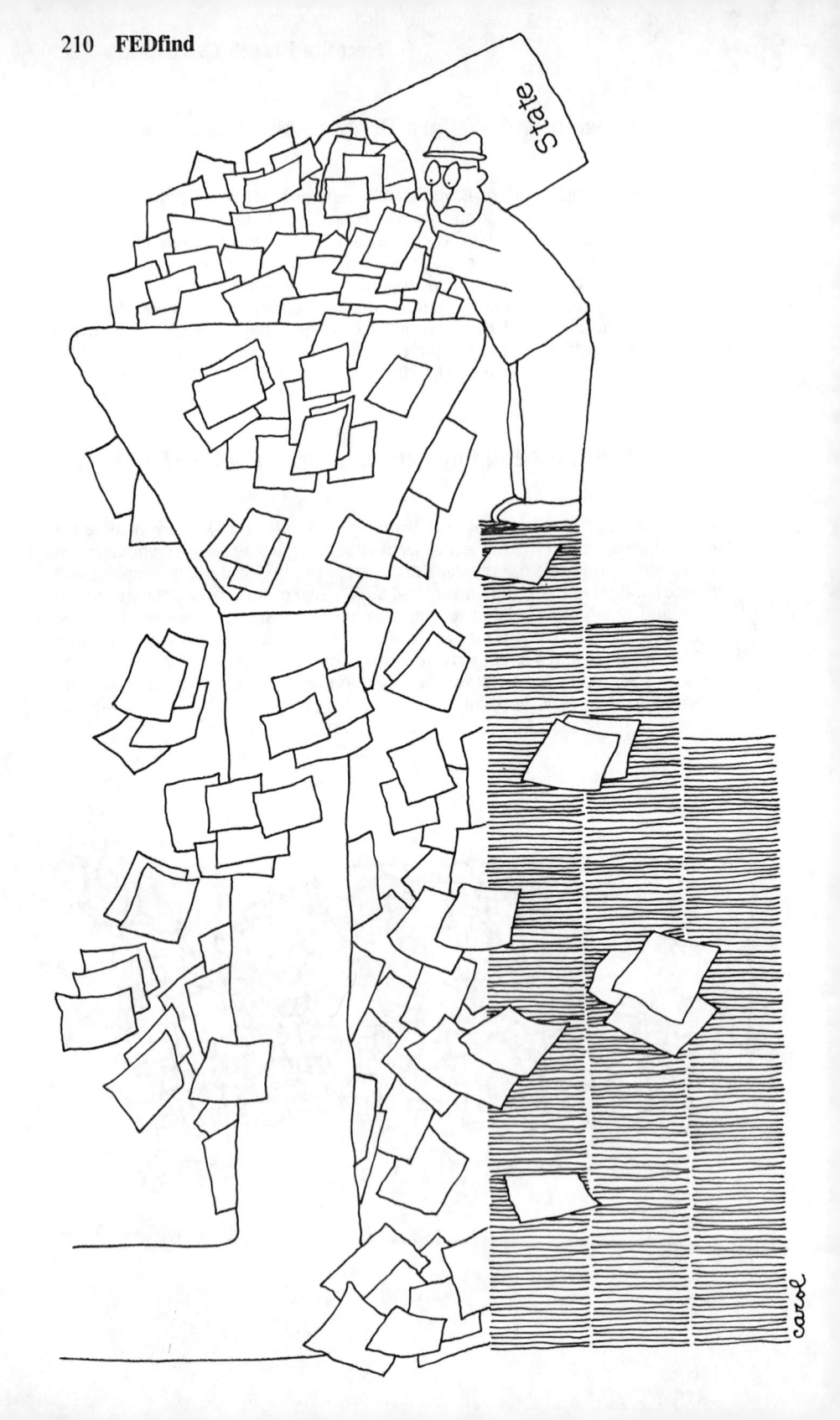

Department of State

The Department of State formulates and executes the foreign policy of the United States under the direction of the President. It determines and analyzes the facts relating to U.S. overseas interests, makes recommendations on policy and future action and takes the necessary steps to carry out established policy. In so doing, the Department consults with foreign governments, speaks for the United States in the United Nations and in more than 50 major international organizations in which the U.S. participates. Fiscal year 1985 budget of $2,645 million, or 0.28% of the total Federal budget; 24,837 paid employees, or 0.84% of the total civilian work force. (CFR reference: Title 22, Chapter I)

Key Offices and Telephone Numbers

Address: 2201 C Street NW, Washington, DC 20520

General Information	(202) 647-4000
Personnel Locator	(202) 647-3686
Public/Consumer Information	
Public Information Service	(202) 647-6575
Overseas Citizens Services	(202) 647-5225
Passport Services	(202) 523-1355
Visa Services	(202) 663-1972
Procurement Information	
Procurement Division	(703) 235-9531
Office of Small and Disadvantaged Business Utilization	(703) 235-9579
Competition Advocate	(703) 235-2352
Press Inquiries	
Office of Press Relations	(202) 647-2492
Other Key Offices	
Agency Committee Management	(202) 647-7645
Congressional Liaison/Legislative Affairs	(202) 647-8774
Ethics in Government Act	(202) 647-5036
Fraud, Waste and Mismanagement Hotline	(202) 647-3320
Toll Free, call GAO	(800) 424-5454
Freedom of Information/Privacy Act	(202) 647-8484
General Counsel	(202) 647-9598
Library	(202) 647-1099
Paperwork Reduction Act (ADP/IRM)	(202) 647-1492
Personnel	(202) 647-6131

Key Information Resources

Available **FREE** from the Public Information Service is *Selected State Department Publications*. It provides descriptions and ordering information for most of the major publications and series of the State Department.

Department of State Telephone Directory

Contact the Government Printing Office (GPO) for information on the most current edition.

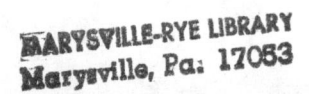

Subject Bibliographies

The GPO publishes a variety of documents that are compiled by the State Department or that relate to foreign affairs. The following subject bibliographies (SB) are available **FREE** from the GPO. See the GPO SB order form.

Africa (SB-284)
Asia and Oceania (SB-288)
Canada (SB-278)
China (SB-299)
Foreign Area Studies (SB-166)
Foreign Investment (SB-275)
Foreign Trade and Tariffs (SB-123)
Latin America and the Caribbean (SB-287)
Maps, United States and Foreign (SB-102)
Middle East (SB-286)
Soviet Union (SB-279)

State Department Subscription Services

The following is a list of State Department subscription services available from the GPO. For further information, including order forms, consult the *Government Subscription Services* (Price List 36), available **FREE** from the GPO. See the GPO subscription order form.

Background Notes on the Countries of the World
Department of State Bulletin
Diplomatic List
Employees of Diplomatic Missions
Key Officers of Foreign Service Posts
Maximum Travel Per Diem Allowances for Foreign Areas
Standardized Regulations (Government Civilians, Foreign Areas)
State
Treaties and Other International Acts Series

Treaties in Force

An annual list of treaties and other international agreements—of which the United States is a party—in force as of January 1, 1985. The original text source is cited for each treaty. May 1985. 348pp. $9.00. GPO S/N 044-000-02048-3. (S 9.14:985) See the GPO order form.

Atlas of United States Foreign Relations

A compendium of more than 90 maps and charts that provides basic information about U.S. foreign relations. Its six sections deal with U.S. national security, trade and investment, international organizations, elements of the world economy, development assistance and foreign relations machinery. A 1986 edition is planned. 1983. 96pp. $5.00. GPO S/N 044-000-01973-6. (S 1.3/a:At 6/comp) See the GPO order form.

International Relations Dictionary

Identifies and provides information about terms, phrases, acronyms, catch words and abbreviations used in the conduct of foreign affairs. Each entry in the dictionary consists of the term itself with its definition; a section that includes documentation for the term; and a section that provides cross-references to other dictionary entries. 1980, 2nd ed. 84pp. $5.00. GPO S/N 044-000-01853-5. (S 1.69:221-2) See the GPO order form.

American Foreign Policy: Current Documents Series

Prepared by the Office of the Historian of the Department of State, the volumes in this series present the principal public foreign policy messages, addresses, statements, interviews, press briefings and conferences, and congressional testimony of the U.S. Government. Recent volumes may be purchased from the GPO. For further information about the series, contact the Office of the Historian, Department of State, Washington, DC 20520; (202) 633-1129.

Foreign Relations of the United States

A Department of State series, totaling more than 300 volumes, that presents the official documentary record of foreign policy and diplomacy of the United States. For further information about this series, contact the Office of the Historian, see entry above. A **FREE** subject bibliography (SB) on this subject— SB-210—is available. It provides information on volumes in this series that are for sale by GPO. See the GPO SB order form.

United States Foreign Service

The U.S. Foreign Service (FS) is the component of the State Department that is principally responsible for conducting relations with other countries. An Ambassador is the personal representative of the President and reports to the President through the Secretary of State. Ambassadors have full responsibility for implementing the U.S. foreign policy by U.S. Government personnel within their country of assignment, except those under military commands. Their responsibilities include negotiating agreements between the United States and the host country, explaining and disseminating official U.S. policy and maintaining cordial relations with the country's government and people. As of September 1, 1985, FS representatives at 141 embassies, 11 missions, 73 consulates general, 34 consulates, 3 branch offices and 30 consular agencies throughout the world reported to the State Department. For further information, contact the Public Information Service, Bureau of Public Affairs, Department of State, 2201 C Street NW, Washington, DC 20520; (202) 647-6575.

United States Mission to the United Nations

The United Nations (U.N.) is an international organization whose purposes are: to maintain international peace and security; to develop friendly relations among nations; to achieve international cooperation in solving international problems of an economic, social, cultural, or humanitarian character and in promoting respect for human rights; and to be a center for harmonizing the actions of nations in the attainment of these common ends. For further information, contact the United Nations, New York, NY 10017; (212) 754-1234. In Washington, DC, contact the U.N. Information Centre, 1889 F Street NW, Washington, DC 20006; (202) 289-8670.

Department of Transportation

The Department of Transportation (DOT) develops and administers national transportation policies and associated programs. DOT accomplishes this through nine operating administrations whose jurisdictions include highway planning, development and construction; urban mass transit; railroads; aviation; and the safety of waterways, ports, highways, and oil and gas pipelines. Fiscal year 1985 budget of $25,087 million, or 2.68% of the total Federal budget; 63,236 paid employees, or 2.14% of the total civilian work force. (CFR reference: Title 49) For information on individual components of the Department of Transportation, see the component descriptions below.

Key Offices and Telephone Numbers

Address: 400 7th Street SW, Washington, DC 20590

General Information and Personnel Locator	(202) 426-4000
Public/Consumer Information	
Office of Public Affairs	(202) 426-4321
Consumer Affairs—Automobiles	(202) 426-9550
Consumer Affairs—Airlines	(202) 755-2220
National Response Center for reporting oil and chemical spills	(800) 424-8802
In the Washington, DC area	(202) 426-2675
Air Safety Hotline	(800) 255-1111
In the Washington, DC area	(202) 426-9365
Auto Safety Hotline	(800) 424-9393
In the Washington, DC area	(202) 426-0123
Technology Sharing Office	(800) 225-1612
Procurement Information	
Office of Installations and Logistics	(202) 426-4237
Office of Small and Disadvantaged Business Utilization	(202) 426-1930
Competition Advocate	(202) 426-8553
Press Inquiries	
News Division	(202) 426-4321
Broadcast News Service recording	(800) 424-8807
In the Washington, DC area	(202) 426-1921
Other Key Offices	
Agency Committee Management	(202) 426-4277
Congressional Liaison/Legislative Affairs	(202) 472-9705
Ethics in Government Act	(202) 426-4713
Fraud, Waste and Mismanagement Hotline	(800) 424-9071
In the Washington, DC area	(202) 755-1855
Freedom of Information Act	(202) 426-4542
Privacy Act	(202) 426-1887
General Counsel	(202) 426-4702
Library	(202) 426-1792
Paperwork Reduction Act (ADP/IRM)	(202) 426-1887
Personnel	(202) 426-2551
Statistical Information, Transportation Systems Center, Cambridge, MA	(617) 494-2429

Key Information Resources

Department of Transportation Telephone Directory

Contact the Government Printing Office (GPO) for information on the most current edition.

Transportation Department Subscription Services

The following is a list of Transportation Department subscription services available from the GPO. For further information, including order forms, consult *Government Subscription Services* (Price List 36), available **FREE** from the GPO. See the GPO subscription order form.

Aeronautical Information Publication
Air Traffic Control, Handbook 7110.65
Airman's Information Manual: Basic Flight Information and ATC
  Procedures
Contractions, Handbook 7340.11
Data Communications, Handbook 7110.80
FAA General Aviation News
Federal Aviation Regulations
Federal Motor Vehicle Safety Standards and Regulations With
  Amendments and Interpretations
Flight Services, Handbook 7110.10
IFR and VFR Pilot Exam-O-Grams
International Flight Information Manual
International Notices to Airmen
Location Identifiers, Handbook 7350
Manual on Uniform Traffic Control Devices, etc.
Marine Safety Manuals
Navigation and Vessel Inspection Circulars
Notices to Airmen
Private Pilot Practical Test Standards, FAA-S-8081-1
Public Roads, A Journal of Highway Research
Standard Highway Signs
Summary of Airworthiness Directives
Summary of Supplemental Type Certificates
Transportation Department Telephone Directory
Type Certificate Data Sheets and Specifications

Federal Aviation Administration

The Federal Aviation Administration (FAA) regulates the Nation's aviation system for safety and effectiveness. The FAA issues and enforces regulations relating to the manufacture, operation and maintenance of aircraft; certifies the competence of aviators; certifies airports and inspects air navigation facilities; operates and maintains air traffic control towers and centers; develops air traffic regulations, including those for civil aircraft safety; and allocates the use of airspace. (CFR reference: Title 14, Chapter I) Available **FREE** is the *Guide to Federal Aviation Administration Publications*. For this publication or further information, contact the FAA Public Inquiry Center, APA-430, 800 Independence Avenue SW, Washington, DC 20591; (202) 426-8058.

Federal Highway Administration

The Federal Highway Administration (FHWA) sets highway safety standards and administers the Federal aid highway program. It regulates the safety performance of commercial motor carriers engaged in interstate commerce; conducts safety inspections of motor carrier vehicles and operations; regulates the movement of dangerous cargoes on the highways; enforces applicable laws; and controls outdoor advertising along Federal-aid highways. (CFR references, Titles and Chapters: 23, I, II; 49, III) For further information, contact the Office of Management Systems, FHWA, 400 7th Street SW, Washington, DC 20590; (202) 426-0630.

Federal Railroad Administration

The Federal Railroad Administration (FRA) administers and enforces rail safety laws and regulations. This includes activities relating to the following: track maintenance; equipment standards and safety appliances; locomotives, signals and power brakes; hours of service; transport of dangerous materials; reporting of accidents; and the inspection of rail facilities and records. The FRA also administers railroad financial assistance programs and conducts research and development in support of improved rail safety. (CFR reference: Title 49, Chapter II) For further information, contact the Office of Public Affairs, FRA, 400 7th Street SW, Washington, DC 20590; (202) 426-0881.

Maritime Administration

The Maritime Administration conducts programs to aid in the development, promotion and operation of the U.S. merchant marine. It assists the maritime community in the areas of ship design and construction; promotion of U.S. flag vessels; guarantees financing as an aid to ship owners in the construction and reconstruction of commercial vessels; provides financial support to help U.S.-flag ship operators narrow the cost advantages of their foreign counterparts; and operates the U.S. Merchant Marine Academy. (CFR reference: Title 46, Chapter II) For further information, contact the Office of External Affairs, Maritime Administration, 400 7th Street SW, Washington, DC 20590; (202) 426-5807.

National Highway Traffic Safety Administration

The National Highway Traffic Safety Administration (NHTSA) runs programs that relate to safe performance of motor vehicles, drivers and pedestrians. It regulates safety performance for new and used vehicles and their equipment, investigates safety defects in motor vehicles, sets and enforces fuel economy standards, administers the Federal odometer law, enforces the uniform national maximum speed limit, and provides consumer information on motor vehicle crashworthiness, ease of maintenance and repair. (CFR references, Titles and Chapters: 23, II, III; 49, V) For further information, contact the Office of Public and Consumer Affairs, NHTSA, 400 7th Street SW, Washington, DC 20590; (202) 426-9550.

Research and Special Programs Administration

The Research and Special Programs Administration (RSPA) is the research, analysis and technical development arm of the Department of Transportation. Its work focuses on pipeline safety, hazardous cargo transportation, transportation emergency preparedness, safety training, and multimodal transportation research and development activities, including programs involving the academic community. (CFR reference: Title 49, Chapter I) For further information, contact the Office of Administration, RSPA, 400 7th Street SW, Washington, DC 20590; (202) 426-4934.

Saint Lawrence Seaway Development Corporation

The Saint Lawrence Seaway Development Corporation is a wholly Government-owned enterprise responsible for the development, operation and maintenance of that part of the Seaway between Montreal and Lake Erie that lies within the territorial limits of the United States. The Seaway Corporation charges tolls in accordance with rates for users of the Seaway that it negotiates with the St. Lawrence Seaway Authority of Canada. The Corporation coordinates its activities with its Canadian counterpart, particularly with respect to overall operations, traffic control, navigation aids, safety and season extension. (CFR reference: Title 33, Chapter IV) For further information, contact the Director of Communications, St. Lawrence Seaway Development Corporation, 400 7th Street SW, Washington, DC 20590; (202) 426-3346.

United States Coast Guard

The U.S. Coast Guard (USCG) is the primary Federal maritime law enforcement agency. The Coast Guard enforces safety standards for U.S. merchant marine vessels and for offshore structures on the Outer Continental Shelf; regulates ports and vessels for security purposes, including supervision of the movements of dangerous cargoes; investigates accidents and violations of laws involving commercial vessels; regulates pilot services on the Great Lakes; regulates the construction, maintenance and operation of bridges over U.S. navigable waters; licenses the construction, ownership and operation of deepwater ports; and sets and enforces safety standards for recreational and small boats. The USCG operates as a part of the U.S. Navy in time of war or when the President so directs. (CFR references, Titles and Chapters: 33, I; 46, I, III; 49, IV) For further information, contact the Information Office, U.S. Coast Guard, 2100 2nd Street SW, Washington, DC 20593; (202) 426-2158.

Urban Mass Transportation Administration

The missions of the Urban Mass Transportation Administration (UMTA) are to assist in the development of improved mass transportation facilities, equipment and methods in cooperation with State and local transportation authorities; to encourage the planning and establishment of area-wide urban mass transportation systems; to provide technical and financial assistance to State and local governments; and to encourage private sector involvement in local mass transportation systems. (CFR reference: Title 49, Chapter VI) For further information, contact the Office of Public Affairs, UMTA, 400 7th Street SW, Washington, DC 20590; (202) 426-4043. Technical information may be obtained by contacting the Transit Research Information Center at (202) 426-9157.

220 **FEDfind**

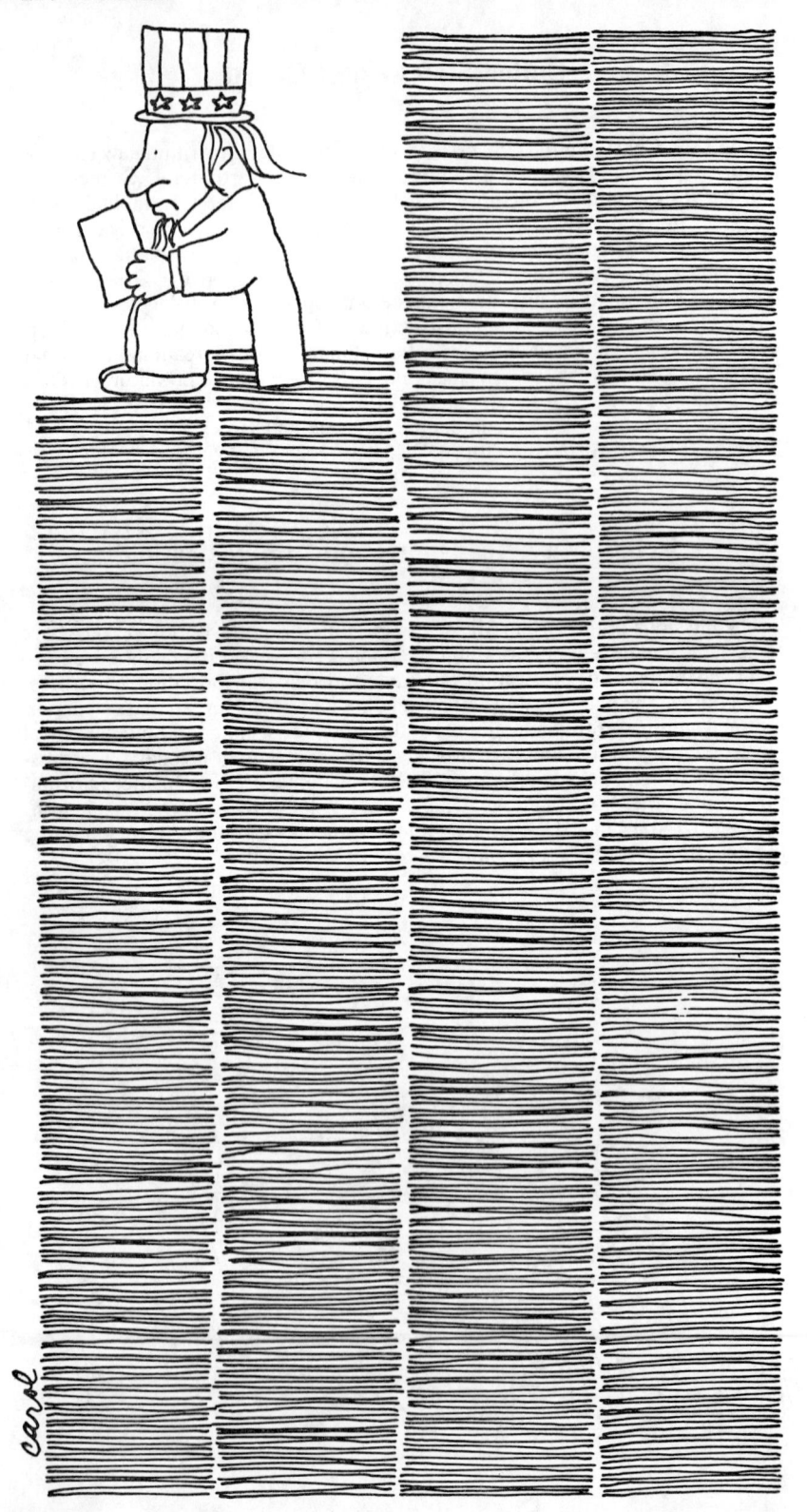

Department of the Treasury

The Department of the Treasury develops and recommends economic, monetary, fiscal and tax policies; manufactures coins and currency; enforces laws relating to alcohol, tobacco and firearms; administers the tax system; and issues Government checks. In addition, numerous other functions are carried out by the bureaus and divisions that comprise the Department. below. Fiscal year budget of $165,043 million, or 17.62% of the total Federal budget; 131,643 paid employees, which is 4.46% of the total civilian work force. (CFR reference: Title 31) For information on individual components of the Department of the Treasury, see the component descriptions below.

Key Offices and Telephone Numbers

Address: 15th Street and Pennsylvania Avenue NW, Washington, DC 20220

General Information	(202) 566-2000
Personnel Locator	(202) 566-2111

Public/Consumer Information

Public Affairs Office	(202) 566-2041
Thefts, losses or discoveries of explosive materials hotline	(800) 424-9555
In the Washington, DC area	(202) 566-7777

Public Debt Investor's Telephone Information

Treasury notes and bonds recording	(202) 287-4088
Treasury bills recording	(202) 287-4091
Treasury securities recording	(202) 287-4100
Treasury checks mailed recording	(202) 287-4113
Treasury securities sales recording	(202) 287-4217
U.S. Savings Bonds information	(202) 447-1775
Telephone number for the deaf	(202) 287-4097

Procurement Information

Office of Procurement	(202) 566-2586
Office of Small and Disadvantaged Business Utilization	(202) 566-9616
Competition Advocate	(202) 566-9864

Press Inquiries

Public Affairs Office	(202) 566-2041

Other Key Offices

Agency Committee Management	(202) 566-2463
Congressional Liaison/Legislative Affairs	(202) 566-2037
Ethics in Government Act	(202) 566-2977
Fraud, Waste and Mismanagement Hotline	(800) 826-0407
In the Washington, DC area	(202) 566-7901
Freedom of Information/Privacy Act	(202) 566-2789
General Counsel	(202) 566-2093
Library	(202) 566-2777
Paperwork Reduction Act (ADP/IRM)	(202) 566-5847
Personnel	(202) 447-1460

Statistical Information, see the Internal Revenue Service's Statistics of Income Division below

Key Information Resources

Department of the Treasury Telephone Directory

Contact the Government Printing Office (GPO) for information on the most current edition.

Treasury Department Subscription Services

The following is a list of Treasury Department subscription services available from the GPO. For further information, including order forms, consult *Government Subscription Services* (Price List 36), available **FREE** from the GPO. See the GPO subscription order form.

- Alcohol, Tobacco, and Firearms
- Bulletin Index-Digest System
- Cumulative List of Organizations, Described in Section 170(c) of the Internal Revenue Code of 1954, Revised to Oct. 31, 1984, Publication No. 78
- Customs Bulletin
- Customs Regulations of the United States
- Daily Treasury Statement
- Internal Revenue Bulletin
- Monthly Statement of the Public Debt of the United States
- Monthly Treasury Statement of Receipts and Outlays of the United States Government
- Statistics of Income Bulletin
- Tables of Redemption Values for U.S. Savings Bonds, Series E and Series EE
- Treasury Bulletin

Executive Branch Departments

Bureau of Alcohol, Tobacco and Firearms

The Bureau of Alcohol, Tobacco and Firearms (BATF) enforces laws and regulations governing the legal flow of firearms, explosives, and alcoholic and tobacco products. As part of its tax collection function, BATF regulates the tobacco, alcohol, firearms and explosives industries. It specifically licenses manufacturers, dealers and users of explosives. (CFR reference: Title 27, Chapter I) For further information, contact the Director, BATF, 1200 Pennsylvania Avenue NW, Washington, DC 20226; (202) 566-7777.

Bureau of Engraving and Printing

The Bureau of Engraving and Printing designs, engraves and prints United States currency, postage stamps, Treasury obligations (bills, bonds, certificates, notes, revenue and customs stamps) and other Government securities. The Bureau also advises and assists Federal agencies in the design and production of other Government documents that, because of their value, require security or counterfeit deterrence characteristics. (CFR reference: Title 31, Chapter VI) For further information, contact the Public Affairs Section, Bureau of Engraving and Printing, 14th and C Streets SW, Washington, DC 20228; (202) 447-0193.

Bureau of the Public Debt

The Bureau of Public Debt supports the management of the public debt, prepares Department of the Treasury circulars offering public debt securities; develops security issues regulations; and oversees the transactions in outstanding securities. It also maintains control over public debt receipts and expenditures, securities and interest costs; keeps accounts of owners of securities and authorizes the payment of principal and interest; and makes decisions on claims concerning lost, stolen, destroyed or mutilated securities. For further information, contact the Office of the Commissioner, Bureau of the Public Debt, Washington, DC 20239; (202) 376-4300. Requests for information relating to holdings of all series of savings bonds, savings notes, and retirement plan and individual retirement bonds should be addressed to the Bureau of the Public Debt, 200 3rd Street, Parkersburg, WV 26106; (304) 420-6516.

Federal Law Enforcement Training Center

The Federal Law Enforcement Training Center (FLETC) is an interagency training facility that serves more than 50 Federal law enforcement organizations. Its major program is to teach law enforcement skills to police and investigative personnel. The FLETC also conducts advanced and specialized training in areas such as white collar crime, procurement/contract fraud, law enforcement photography and marine law enforcement. (CFR reference: Title 31, Chapter VII) For further information, contact the Public Affairs Office, Federal Law Enforcement Training Center, Glynco, GA 31524, (912) 267-2447; Washington office: 1200 Pennsylvania Avenue NW, Washington, DC 20226; (202) 566-2951.

Financial Management Service

The Financial Management Service (FMS) performs functions that relate to money management. It is responsible for the Government's cash management program, payments and collections, the investment of social security and other trust funds, and the operation of a central accounting and reporting system. For further information, contact the Office of External Affairs, Financial Management Service, Treasury Annex, Pennsylvania Avenue and Madison Place NW, Washington, DC 20226; (202) 566-6576.

Internal Revenue Service

The Internal Revenue Service (IRS) administers and enforces the internal revenue laws. Basic IRS activities include determination, assessment and collection of taxes; providing taxpayer service and education; ensuring resolution of taxpayer complaints; determination of pension plan qualifications; and preparation and issuance of rulings and regulations to supplement the provisions of the Internal Revenue Code. (CFR reference: Title 26, Chapter I) For further information, contact any District Office or the Public Affairs Division, IRS Headquarters, 1111 Constitution Avenue NW, Washington, DC 20224; (202) 566-4743.

Internal Revenue Service
Statistics of Income Division

The Statistics of Income (SOI) Division develops and evaluates data on individual and corporate taxpayers' filing characteristics, and provides statistical and economic analyses as requested. As the tabulator of income tax and information returns, the Division plays a statistical role for other offices within the Treasury Department and the Congressional Joint Committee on Taxation, which are concerned with analysis and forecasting of tax receipts and development of tax policy. The principal products of the SOI Division include four annual core data series on individuals, corporations, partnerships and sole proprietorships. Available **FREE** is the brochure *SOI Publications and Other Information Available*. Statistics of Income Division D:R:S, Internal Revenue Service, 1111 Constitution Avenue NW, Washington, DC 20224; (202) 376-0218.

Office of the Comptroller of the Currency

The Office of the Comptroller of the Currency licenses and regulates national banks. Specifically, the Office charters new national banks; approves bank mergers and conversions when the resulting institution is a national bank, and the establishment of branches by national banks; regulates the operation of national banks, including trust activities and overseas operations; and examines national banks for their financial and operational soundness, quality of their management, and their compliance with laws, rules and regulations. (CFR reference: Title 12, Chapter I) For further information, contact the Communications Division, Office of the Comptroller of the Currency, 490 L'Enfant Plaza East SW, Washington, DC 20219; (202) 447-1800.

United States Customs Service

The U.S. Customs Service collects the revenue from imports and enforces customs and related laws. It is responsible for such activities as assessing and collecting customs duties and excise taxes; interdicting and seizing contraband, including narcotics and illegal drugs; processing persons, carriers, cargo and mail into and out of the United States; and detecting and apprehending persons engaged in fraudulent practices related to customs laws. The Service also administers and enforces pollution regulations and import quotas. (CFR reference: Title 19, Chapter I) For further information, contact the Public Affairs Office, U.S. Customs Service, 1301 Constitution Avenue NW, Washington, DC 20229; (202) 566-8195.

United States Mint

The U.S. Mint is responsible for manufacturing enough coins for the Nation's commerce. The Mint distributes the coins for general circulation through the facilities of the Federal Reserve Banks. Other operations include the custody, processing and movement of Treasury gold and silver bullion and the disbursing of these metals for authorized purposes; and the manufacture of national medals and proof coin sets for sale to the public. (CFR reference: Title 31, Chapter I) For further information, contact the U.S. Mint, 633 3rd Street NW, Washington, DC 20220; (202) 376-0837.

United States Savings Bonds Division

The U.S. Savings Bonds Division promotes the sale and retention of U.S. savings bonds. Through its 18 district offices, personal contact is made with financial institutions, business, labor, farm, school, the media and community leaders to gain awareness and understanding of the savings bonds program. For further information, contact the Office of Public Affairs, U.S. Savings Bonds Division, 1111 20th Street NW, Washington, DC 20226; (202) 634-5377.

United States Secret Service

The U.S. Secret Service is responsible for detecting and arresting any person who violates laws relating to coins, currency and securities of the United States and of foreign governments. In addition, the Secret Service protects the President of the United States and members of his immediate family; the President-elect, and other select officials and major Presidential and Vice Presidential candidates. (CFR reference: Title 31, Chapter IV) For further information, contact any District Office or the Office of Public Affairs, U.S. Secret Service, 1800 G Street NW, Washington, DC 20223; (202) 535-5708.

226 **FEDfind**

Chapter 9
Executive Branch Agencies

In addition to the thirteen executive branch departments (described in Chapter 8) and their respective agencies, the U.S. Government relies on other organizational entities such as commissions, independent and quasi-official agencies to administer the laws of the Nation. A brief description of the mission and selected activities of each organization is included.

Also provided are the organizations' budgets for fiscal year 1985 (ended September 30, 1985) and the number of civilian personnel assigned as of January 1985. Percentages for each figure are provided to help you better appreciate the relative resources (dollars and people) used by each organization to accomplish its mission.

The "CFR *(Code of Federal Regulations)* reference" cites where detailed information on the organization may be found. (The *United States Government Manual* may be consulted for more detailed information concerning the programs and activities of each organization.)

Provided also are the sections "Key Offices and Telephone Numbers" and "Key Information Resources." These are designed to help you find the information you need quickly and are described in the Introduction—"How to Use *FEDfind*.

The address and telephone numbers are for the headquarters office. Check your local telephone directory under "United States Government" to see if a local office is located near you.

Listed below are the organizations described in this chapter. Those marked by an asterisk (*) are quasi-official agencies (not agencies as defined in Title 5, U.S. Code 105, but nevertheless required by statute to publish certain information on their programs and activities in the *Federal Register*).

ACTION
Administrative Conference of the United States
Advisory Commission on Intergovernmental Relations
Agency for International Development
American Battle Monuments Commission
Appalachian Regional Commission
Board for International Broadcasting
Central Intelligence Agency
Commission on Civil Rights
Commission on Fine Arts
Commodity Futures Trading Commission
Consumer Product Safety Commission

Environmental Protection Agency
Equal Employment Opportunity Commission
Export-Import Bank of the United States
Farm Credit Administration
Federal Communications Commission
Federal Deposit Insurance Corporation
Federal Election Commission
Federal Emergency Management Agency
Federal Energy Regulatory Commission
Federal Home Loan Bank Board
Federal Labor Relations Authority
Federal Maritime Commission
Federal Mediation and Conciliation Service
Federal Reserve System
Federal Trade Commission
General Service Administration
Inter-American Foundation
Interstate Commerce Commission
Legal Services Corporation*
National Aeronautics and Space Administration
National Archives and Records Administration
National Capital Planning Commission
National Commission on Libraries and Information Science
National Credit Union Administration
National Foundation on the Arts and the Humanities
National Labor Relations Board
National Mediation Board
National Railroad Passenger Corporation*
National Science Foundation
National Transportation Safety Board
Nuclear Regulatory Commission
Occupational Safety and Health Review Commission
Office of Personnel Management
Overseas Private Investment Corporation
Panama Canal Commission
Peace Corps
Pennsylvania Avenue Development Corporation
Pension Benefit Guaranty Corporation
Postal Rate Commission
President's Council on Physical Fitness and Sports
Railroad Retirement Board
Securities and Exchange Commission
Selective Service System
Small Business Administration
Smithsonian Institution*
Tennessee Valley Authority
United States Arms Control and Disarmament Agency
United States Information Agency
United States International Development Cooperation Agency
United States International Trade Commission
United States Merit Systems Protection Board
United States Postal Service
United States Railway Association*
Veterans Administration

ACTION

ACTION is the national volunteer agency. It supports programs that enable Americans to volunteer their services to help meet basic human needs and self-help efforts of low-income individuals and communities in the United States. ACTION administers and coordinates the following domestic volunteer activities: Volunteers In Service To America (VISTA); Foster Grandparent Program (FGP), Retired Senior Volunteer Program (RSVP), Senior Companion Program (SCP), National Center for Service Learning, Young Volunteers in ACTION, Vietnam Veterans Leadership Program, and the ACTION Drug Prevention Program. Fiscal year 1985 budget $129 million, or 0.014% of the total Federal budget; 507 paid employees, or 0.011% of the total civilian work force. (CFR reference: Title 45, Chapter XII)

Key Offices and Telephone Numbers

Address: 806 Connecticut Avenue NW, Washington, DC 20525

General Information	(202) 634-9108
Personnel Locator	(202) 634-9135
Public/Consumer Information	
Office of Legislative, Public and Intergovernmental Affairs	(202) 634-9108
Volunteer Demonstration Programs Information	(800) 424-8867
In the Washington, DC area	(202) 634-9406
Procurement Information	
Office of Contracts and Grants Management	(202) 634-9148
Competition Advocate	(202) 634-9382
Press Inquiries	
Office of Legislative, Public and Intergovernmental Affairs	(202) 634-9131
Other Key Offices	
Agency Committee Management	(202) 634-9380
Congressional Liaison/Legislative Affairs	(202) 634-9108
Ethics in Government Act	(202) 634-9333
Fraud, Waste and Mismanagement Hotline	(800) 424-5454
In the Washington, DC area	(202) 633-6987
Freedom of Information/Privacy Act	(202) 634-9242
General Counsel	(202) 634-9333
Library	(202) 634-9772
Paperwork Reduction Act (ADP/IRM)	(202) 634-9242
Personnel	(202) 634-9262

Key Information Resources

General literature, recruitment material and program-specific publications (e.g., VISTA, RSVP, FGP, etc.) are available **FREE** upon request from the Office of Legislative, Public and Intergovernmental Affairs.

Administrative Conference of the United States

The Administrative Conference of the United States oversees administrative procedures for all Federal agencies. It studies the efficiency and fairness of administrative processes in the Federal Government and makes recommendations for improvements to the President, the Congress, the agencies concerned and the Judicial Conference. Recommendations adopted by the Conference may call for new legislation or for action on the part of affected agencies. Fiscal year 1985 budget $1,478,000, or 0.00016% of the total Federal budget; 21 paid employees, or 0.00071% of the total civilian work force. (CFR reference: Title 1, Chapter III)

Key Offices and Telephone Numbers

Address: 2120 L Street NW, Suite 500, Washington, DC 20037

General Information and Personnel Locator	(202) 254-7020
Public/Consumer Information	
Administrative Officer	(202) 254-7065
Procurement Information	
Administrative Officer	(202) 254-7065
Press Inquiries	
Administrative Officer	(202) 254-7065
Other Key Offices	
Agency Committee Management	(202) 254-7020
Congressional Liaison/Legislative Affairs	(202) 254-7020
Ethics in Government Act	(202) 254-7020
Fraud, Waste and Mismanagement Hotline	(800) 424-5454
In the Washington, DC area	(202) 633-6987
Freedom of Information/Privacy Act	(202) 254-7020
General Counsel	(202) 254-7020
Library	(202) 254-7065
Paperwork Reduction Act (ADP/IRM)	(202) 254-7065
Personnel	(202) 254-7020

Key Information Resources

The Administrative Conference furnishes copies of its recent recommendations and reports upon request. A bibliography, reprinted from the *Administrative Law Review*, is available **FREE** from the Information Officer. The bibliography serves as a publications list for the period 1968-1983. The Conference library maintains copies of all official Conference documents for public inspection.

Federal Administrative Procedure Sourcebook

Compiled by the Administrative Conference of the United States, this sourcebook is a basic introduction and reference book on the major Federal procedural statutes. The text of each statute is provided, along with explanatory material, legislative history, related documents, sources of additional relevant materials and a bibliography. Statutes included are the *Administrative Procedure Act, Agency Practice Act, Claims and Debt Collections Acts, Contract Disputes Act, Equal Access to Justice Act, Ethics in Government Act, Federal Advisory Committee Act, Federal Tort Claims Act, Freedom of Information Act, Government in the Sunshine Act, National Environmental Policy Act, Paperwork Reduction Act, Privacy Act* and *Regulatory Flexibility Act*. 1985. 984pp. $21.00. GPO S/N 052-003-00989-7. (Y 3.Ad 6:2 P94) See the GPO order form.

Executive Branch Agencies 231

Advisory Commission on Intergovernmental Relations

The Advisory Commission on Intergovernmental Relations (ACIR) monitors the operation of the American Federal system of government and makes recommendations for its improvement. The Commission is a permanent national bipartisan body of 26 members that represents the executive and legislative branches of the Federal Government (nine members), State and local government (14 members), and the public (three members). A long-range effort of the Commission has been to seek ways to improve Federal, State, and local governmental taxing practices and policies to achieve equitable allocation of resources, increased efficiency in collection and administration, and reduced compliance burdens upon the taxpayers. Fiscal year 1985 budget $1,982,000, or 0.000215 of the total Federal budget; 38 paid employees, or 0.0013% of the total civilian work force. (CFR reference: Title 5, Chapter VII)

Key Offices and Telephone Numbers

Address: 1111 20th Street NW, Suite 2000, Washington, DC 20575

General Information and Personnel Locator	(202) 653-5540
Public/Consumer Information	
Communications and Publications Office	(202) 653-5536
Procurement Information	
Budget and Management Officer	(202) 653-5640
Press Inquiries	
Communications and Publications Office	(202) 653-5536
Other Key Offices	
Ethics in Government Act	(202) 653-5640
Fraud, Waste and Mismanagement Hotline	(800) 424-5454
In the Washington, DC area	(202) 633-6987
Freedom of Information/Privacy Act	(202) 653-5540
Paperwork Reduction Act (ADP/IRM)	(202) 653-5640
Personnel	(202) 653-5640

Key Information Resources

Available **FREE** from the Communications and Publications Office is a brochure entitled *ACIR* and an annotated publications list.

Agency for International Development

The Agency for International Development (AID) carries out economic assistance programs to help people of developing countries help themselves to develop their human and economic resources, increase their productive capacities, and improve the quality of human life as well as promote economic and political stability in friendly countries. AID also conducts humanitarian relief activities in support of those who suffer from natural calamities such as earthquakes, famine, floods and drought. Fiscal year 1985 budget $1,207 million, or 0.13% of the total Federal budget; 5,130 paid employees, or 0.17% of the total civilian work force. Note: AID was legally transferred in 1979 to the U.S. International Development Cooperation Agency (IDCA), but its internal structure remains the same and it continues to operate independently of the IDCA. (CFR references, Titles and Chapters: 22, II; 41, 7; 48, 7)

Key Offices and Telephone Numbers

Address: 320 21st Street NW, Washington, DC 20523

General Information	(202) 647-1850
Personnel Locator	(202) 663-1450
Public/Consumer Information	
Office of Public Inquiries	(202) 647-1850
Procurement Information	
Office of Acquisition	(703) 235-8846
Office of Small and Disadvantaged Business Utilization	(703) 235-2333
Competition Advocate	(703) 235-9159
Press Inquiries	
Office of Press Relations	(202) 647-4274
Other Key Offices	
Agency Committee Management	(202) 647-3378
Congressional Liaison/Legislative Affairs	(202) 647-3652
Ethics in Government Act	(202) 632-8556
Fraud, Waste and Mismanagement Hotline	(800) 424-5454
In the Washington, DC area	(202) 633-6987
Freedom of Information/Privacy Act	(202) 647-1850
General Counsel	(202) 647-8556
Library	(703) 235-8936
Paperwork Reduction Act (ADP/IRM)	(202) 632-7962
Personnel	(202) 663-1400

Key Information Resources

Available **FREE** from the Office of Public Inquiries are the annual report, *Development Issues: U.S. Actions Affecting Developing Countries* and the *U.S. Annual AID Review*.

AID Research and Development Abstracts

A quarterly publication that includes abstracts of AID-supported publications. Reports described may be ordered in paper or microfiche format from the address below. Subscription price: $10.00 a year. AID Document Information Handling Facility, 7222 47th Street, Chevy Chase, MD 20815; (301) 951-7191.

Horizons

A quarterly publication for professionals working in the field of international development. **FREE** to professionals. Office of Publications, AID, Washington, DC 20523; (202) 647-4330.

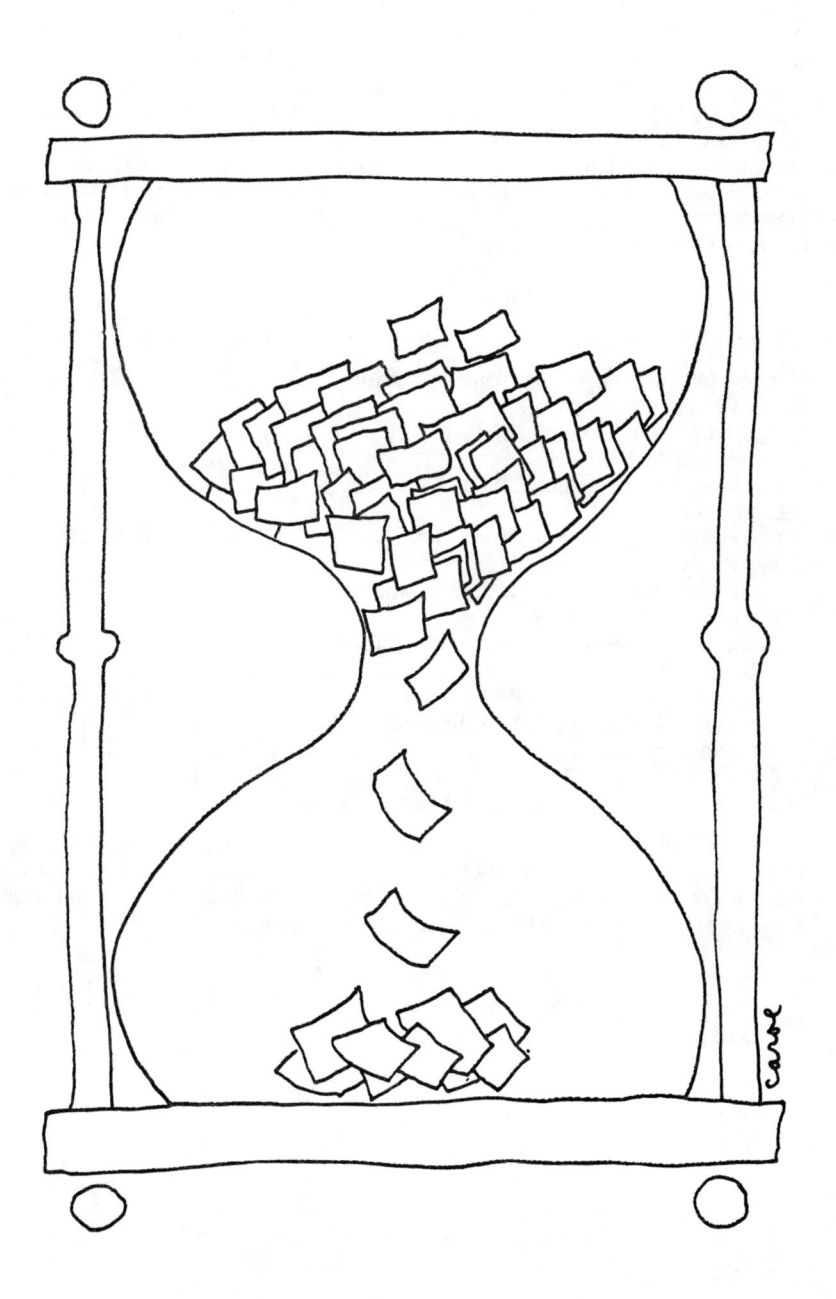

American Battle Monuments Commission

The American Battle Monuments Commission (ABMC) designs, constructs and maintains military cemeteries and memorials on foreign soil, in addition to certain memorials on American soil. The Commission provides to the general public (upon request) the exact location and other information concerning place of interment or memorialization of the dead; best routes and modes of travel in country to cemeteries and memorials; and arranges for the placement of floral decorations at gravesites or the Tablets of the Missing. For next of kin and members of the immediate family, the Commission also provides letters authorizing "non-fee" passports; escort service within the cemetery; color lithographs of cemeteries together with photographs of the appropriate gravesite or section of the Tablets of the Missing. Fiscal year 1985 budget $11 million, or 0.0012% of the total Federal budget; 404 paid employees, or 0.014% of the total civilian work force. (CFR reference: Title 36, Chapter IV)

Key Offices and Telephone Numbers

Address: 20 Massachusetts Avenue NW, Washington, DC 20314

General Information and Personnel Locator	(202) 272-0533
Public/Consumer Information	
Operations and Finance Office	(202) 272-0536
Procurement Information	
Operations and Finance Office	(202) 272-0536
Press Inquiries	
Operations and Finance Office	(202) 272-0536
Other Key Offices	
Congressional Liaison/Legislative Affairs	(202) 272-0536
Ethics in Government Act	(202) 272-0537
Fraud, Waste and Mismanagement Hotline	(800) 424-5454
In the Washington, DC area	(202) 633-6987
Freedom of Information/Privacy Act	(202) 272-0536
Paperwork Reduction Act (ADP/IRM)	(202) 272-0536
Personnel	(202) 272-0534

Key Information Resources

Available **FREE** is the booklet *American Memorials and Overseas Military Cemeteries* that describes the ABMC, the sites it oversees and the services it provides to the general public concerning friends and relatives of those interred in or memorialized at ABMC cemeteries and memorials.

Executive Branch Agencies 235

Appalachian Regional Commission

The Appalachian Regional Commission (ARC) is a Federal-State governmental agency that supports economic, physical, and social development of the 13 Appalachian States. Areas served include all of West Virginia and parts of Alabama, Georgia, Kentucky, Maryland, Mississippi, New York, North Carolina, Ohio, Pennsylvania, South Carolina, Tennessee and Virginia. Because of the State-Federal nature of the Commission, its staff members are not Federal employees. Commission expenses are shared equally by the Federal Government and the Appalachian States. Fiscal year 1985 budget $201 million, or 0.021% of the total Federal budget; 7 paid employees, or 0.00024% of the total civilian work force. (CFR reference: Title 5, Chapter IX)

Key Offices and Telephone Numbers

Address: 1666 Connecticut Avenue NW, Washington, DC 20235

General Information and Personnel Locator	(202) 673-7968
Public/Consumer Information	
Public Affairs Office	(202) 673-7968
Procurement Information	
Office of Administration	(202) 673-7886
Press Inquiries	
Public Affairs Office	(202) 673-7968
Other Key Offices	
Congressional Liaison/Legislative Affairs	(202) 673-7822
Ethics in Government Act	(202) 673-7822
Fraud, Waste and Mismanagement Hotline	(800) 424-5454
In the Washington, DC area	(202) 633-6987
Freedom of Information/Privacy Act	(202) 673-7874
General Counsel	(202) 673-7874
Personnel	(202) 673-7896

Key Information Resources

Available **FREE** from the Public Affairs Office are their annual report and the journal *Appalachia*. The March 1985 journal is a special issue on the 20th anniversary of the ARC. This special edition provides an overview of the changes in Appalachia during the past two decades.

Board for International Broadcasting

The Board for International Broadcasting oversees the operations of Radio Liberty (RL), which broadcasts to the Soviet Union, and Radio Free Europe (RFE), which broadcasts to Poland, Romania, Czechoslovakia, Hungary and Bulgaria. The Radios are operated as a merged, nonprofit radio corporation, RFE/RL, Inc. The Board makes Federal grants to the Radios and reviews their operations to ensure the quality, effectiveness and professional integrity of their broadcasting within the context of the foreign policy objectives of the United States. Fiscal year 1985 budget $97 million, or 0.010% of the total Federal budget; 18 paid employees, or 0.00061% of the total civilian work force. (CFR reference: Title 22, Chapter XIII)

Key Offices and Telephone Numbers

Address: 1201 Connecticut Avenue NW, Suite 400, Washington, DC 20036

General Information and Personnel Locator	(202) 254-8040
Public/Consumer Information	
Program Officer	(202) 254-8040
Procurement Information	
Program Officer	(202) 254-8040
Press Inquiries	
Program Officer	(202) 254-8040
Other Key Offices	
Congressional Liaison/Legislative Affairs	(202) 254-8040
Ethics in Government Act	(202) 254-8040
Fraud, Waste and Mismanagement Hotline	(800) 424-5454
In the Washington, DC area	(202) 633-6987
Freedom of Information/Privacy Act	(202) 724-7400
Paperwork Reduction Act (ADP/IRM)	(202) 254-8040
Personnel	(202) 254-8040

Key Information Resources

The Board's annual report, plus previous editions, are available **FREE** from the Program Officer.

Central Intelligence Agency

The Central Intelligence Agency (CIA) collects, produces and disseminates foreign intelligence related to national security. This includes intelligence on foreign aspects of narcotics production and trafficking. Established under the National Security Council (NSC), the CIA makes recommendations to the NSC for the coordination of such intelligence activities of the departments and agencies of the Government. The CIA also conducts counterintelligence activities outside the United States. The collection of foreign intelligence or counterintelligence within the United States is coordinated with the Federal Bureau of Investigation, as required by procedures agreed upon by the Director of Central Intelligence and the Attorney General. The budget and number of employees of the CIA are classified. (CFR reference: Title 32, Chapter XIX)

Key Offices and Telephone Numbers

Address: Washington, DC 20505

General Information and Personnel Locator	(703) 351-1100
Public/Consumer Information	
Public Affairs Office	(703) 351-7676
Procurement Information	
Procurement Management Staff	(703) 281-8167
Press Inquiries	
Public Affairs Office	(703) 351-7676
Other Key Offices	
Congressional Liaison/Legislative Affairs	(703) 351-6121
Ethics in Government Act	(703) 351-6378
Fraud, Waste and Mismanagement Hotline	(800) 424-5454
In the Washington, DC area	(202) 633-6987
Freedom of Information/Privacy Act	(703) 351-2083
General Counsel	(703) 351-6111
Personnel	(703) 351-2141

Key Information Resources

Information on CIA publications may be obtained from the Public Affairs Office by requesting a copy of the **FREE** catalog, *CIA Publications Released to the Public*. Also available **FREE** from this office are their publications *Fact Book on Intelligence* and *Intelligence: The Acme of Skill*.

The World Factbook 1985

An annual reference book that provides a brief resume of each country of the world with vital information. It includes statistics on the land, nationality, religion, language, literacy, political parties, economy, exports and imports and more. July 1985. 284pp. $14.00. GPO S/N 041-015-00159-1. (PrEx 3.15:985) See the GPO order form.

Commission on Civil Rights

The Commission on Civil Rights (CCR) makes findings of fact on discrimination or denials of equal protection of the laws because of race, color, religion, sex, age, handicap, national origin, or in the administration of justice. Included among specific fact-finding efforts are voting rights, enforcement of Federal civil rights laws, and equality of opportunity in education, employment, and housing. Findings and recommendations of the Commission are submitted to the President and Congress; the Commission has no enforcement authority. Its recommendations may be implemented by statute, executive order or regulation. Fiscal year 1985 budget $12,869,000, or 0.0014% of the total Federal budget; 254 paid employees, or 0.0086% of the total civilian work force. (CFR reference: Title 45, Chapter VII)

Key Offices and Telephone Numbers

Address: 1121 Vermont Avenue NW, Washington, DC 20425

General Information and Personnel Locator	(202) 376-8177
Public/Consumer Information	
Office of Congressional and Public Affairs	(202) 376-8307
For deaf and hearing-impaired persons, TTY	(202) 376-8449
Complaints alleging denials of civil rights	
Office of Federal Civil Rights Evaluation	(202) 376-8518
Procurement Information	
Office of Management	(202) 376-8129
Press Inquiries	
Press and Communications Division	(202) 376-8312
Other Key Offices	
Agency Committee Management	(202) 376-8582
Congressional Liaison/Legislative Affairs	(202) 376-8303
Ethics in Government Act	(202) 376-8339
Fraud, Waste and Mismanagement Hotline	(800) 424-5454
In the Washington, DC area	(202) 633-6987
Freedom of Information/Privacy Act	(202) 376-8355
General Counsel	(202) 376-8355
Library	(202) 376-8110
Paperwork Reduction Act (ADP/IRM)	(202) 376-8129
Personnel	(202) 376-8330

Key Information Resources

A catalog of CCR publications and handbook are available **FREE** from the Office of Congressional and Public Affairs.

Commission of Fine Arts

The Commission of Fine Arts (CFA) provides expert artistic advice on matters relating to the appearance of Washington, DC's public buildings, parks and other architectural elements of the Capital. In particular, the Commission develops architectural designs that complement Washington's historic structures and districts, oversees building-height limits and preserves the Capital's tree-lined avenues and riverscapes. Fiscal year 1985 budget $374,000, or 0.00004% of the total Federal budget; 7 paid employees, or 0.00024% of the total civilian work force. (CFR references, Titles and Chapters: 36, X; 45, XXI)

Key Offices and Telephone Numbers

Address: 708 Jackson Place NW, Washington, DC 20006

General Information and Personnel Locator	(202) 566-1066
Public/Consumer Information	
Secretary and Administrative Officer	(202) 566-1066
Procurement Information	
Administrative Officer	(202) 566-1066
Press Inquiries	
Secretary and Administrative Officer	(202) 566-1066
Other Key Offices	
Agency Committee Management	(202) 566-1066
Congressional Liaison/Legislative Affairs	(202) 566-1066
Ethics in Government Act	(202) 566-1066
Fraud, Waste and Mismanagement Hotline	(800) 424-5454
In the Washington, DC area	(202) 633-6987
Freedom of Information/Privacy Act	(202) 566-1066
Paperwork Reduction Act (ADP/IRM)	(202) 566-1066
Personnel	(202) 566-1066

Key Information Resources

Available **FREE** from the Secretary and Administrative Officer is the publication *The Commission of Fine Arts: A Brief History 1910–1980* that includes a list of CFA publications.

Commodity Futures Trading Commission

The Commodity Futures Trading Commission (CFTC) regulates transactions involving futures delivery, options and leverage contracts in commodities. It ensures that the futures trading process is fair and that it protects both the rights of customers and the financial integrity of the marketplace. The Commission approves the rules under which the 11 exchanges in the United States operate and monitors exchange enforcement of those rules. This includes setting minimum financial requirements for futures brokers and options dealers. The CFTC reviews the terms of proposed futures contracts, and registers companies and individuals who handle customer funds or give trading advice. Fiscal year 1985 budget $27,878,000, or 0.0030% of the total Federal budget; 538 paid employees, or 0.018% of the total civilian work force. (CFR reference: Title 17, Chapter I)

Key Offices and Telephone Numbers

Address: 2033 K Street NW, Washington, DC 20581

General Information and Personnel Locator	(202) 254-6387
Public/Consumer Information	
Office of Communications and Educational Services	(202) 254-8630
(information on complaints against commodity brokers)	
Procurement Information	
Administrative Services Division	(202) 254-9735
Press Inquiries	
Office of Communications and Educational Services	(202) 254-8630
Other Key Offices	
Agency Committee Management	(202) 254-9880
Congressional Liaison/Legislative Affairs	(202) 254-3596
Ethics in Government Act	(202) 254-8058
Fraud, Waste and Mismanagement Hotline	(800) 424-5454
In the Washington, DC area	(202) 633-6987
Freedom of Information/Privacy Act	(202) 254-3382
General Counsel	(202) 254-9880
Library	(202) 254-5901
Paperwork Reduction Act (ADP/IRM)	(202) 254-7556
Personnel	(202) 254-3275

Key Information Resources

Available **FREE** from the Office of Communications and Educational Services is the introductory brochure *Commodity Futures Trading Commission*, which includes a list of CFTC publications.

Consumer Product Safety Commission

The Consumer Product Safety Commission (CPSC) is responsible for protecting the public against unreasonable risks of injury associated with consumer products. To fulfill this mission, the Commission has the authority to develop, issue and enforce safety standards governing the design, construction, contents, performance and labeling of consumer products. The CPSC has the authority to ban hazardous consumer products where appropriate. Fiscal year 1985 budget $35 million, or 0.0037% of the total Federal budget; 567 paid employees, or 0.019% of the total civilian work force. (CFR reference: Title 16, Chapter II)

Key Offices and Telephone Numbers

Address: 1111 18th Street NW, Washington, DC 20207

General Information and Personnel Locator	(301) 492-6600
Public/Consumer Information	
Office of Information and Public Affairs	(301) 492-6580
Consumer Product Safety Hotline	(800) 638-2772
For deaf and hearing impaired persons, TTY	(800) 638-8270
In Maryland only	(800) 492-8104
Procurement Information	
Contracts Branch and Competition Advocate	(301) 492-6444
Press Inquiries	
Media Relations Division	(202) 634-7780
Other Key Offices	
Agency Committee Management	(301) 492-6957
Congressional Liaison/Legislative Affairs	(202) 634-6606
Ethics in Government Act	(301) 492-6980
Fraud, Waste and Mismanagement Hotline	(800) 424-5454
In the Washington, DC area	(202) 633-6987
Freedom of Information/Privacy Act	(301) 492-6800
General Counsel	(301) 492-6980
Library	(301) 492-6544
Paperwork Reduction Act (ADP/IRM)	(301) 492-6529
Personnel	(301) 492-6660

Key Information Resources

Available **FREE** from the Office of the Secretary or CPS Hotline are three leaflets, *The National Injury Information Clearinghouse*, *Accident Investigations* and *The National Electronic Injury Surveillance System (NEISS)*.

help keep
environmentclean

Environmental Protection Agency

The Environmental Protection Agency (EPA) fosters the protection and enhancement of the environment—to control and abate pollution in the areas of air, water, solid waste, pesticides, radiation and toxic substances. EPA accomplishes its work in cooperation with State and local governments. Its activities in each area of pollution include the development of national programs and technical policies; national emission standards and effluent guidelines; rules and procedures for industry reporting, registration and certification programs; and ambient air standards. EPA issues permits for industrial discharges of pollutants and for disposal of industrial waste, sets standards that limit the amount of radioactivity in the environment, reviews proposals for new nuclear facilities, evaluates and regulates new chemicals and chemicals with new uses and establishes and monitors tolerance levels for pesticides occurring in or on foods. Fiscal year 1985 budget $4,511 million, or 0.48% of the total Federal budget; 12,650 paid employees, or 0.43% of the total civilian work force. (CFR references, Titles and Chapters: 40, I; 41, 115; 48, 15)

Key Offices and Telephone Numbers

Address: 401 M Street SW, Washington, DC 20460

General Information and Personnel Locator	(202) 382-2090
Public/Consumer Information	
Office of Public Affairs	(202) 382-4355
Public Information Center	(800) 828-4445
In the Washington, DC area	(202) 829-3535
Toxic Substances Control Act Information	(800) 424-9065
In the Washington, DC area	(202) 554-1404
Hazardous Waste and Superfund Information	(800) 424-9346
In the Washington, DC area	(202) 382-3000
Pesticide Information Clearinghouse	(800) 858-7378
Pesticide Registration and Emergency Response	(703) 557-7700
Procurement Information	
Procurement and Contracts Management Division	(202) 382-5020
Office of Small and Disadvantaged Business Utilization	(703) 557-7777
Competition Advocate	(202) 475-9428
Press Inquiries	
Press Division	(202) 382-4355
Other Key Offices	
Agency Committee Management	(202) 382-5036
Congressional Liaison/Legislative Affairs	(202) 382-5200
Ethics in Government Act	(202) 475-8064
Fraud, Waste and Mismanagement Hotline	(800) 424-4000
In the Washington, DC area	(202) 382-4977
Freedom of Information/Privacy Act	(202) 382-4048
General Counsel	(202) 475-8040
Library	(202) 382-5921
Paperwork Reduction Act (ADP/IRM)	(202) 382-4465
Personnel	(202) 382-3144
Recording	(202) 755-5055

Key Information Resources

EPA does not issue a publications list. By calling the hotlines listed above, you ought to be able to access the information you need. Furthermore, GPO makes available a semiannual EPA telephone directory (see GPO order form). Also, Government Institutes, Inc. publishes a variety of reference materials related to EPA. For more information, contact them at 966 Hungerford Drive, Suite 24, Rockville, MD 20850; (301) 251-9250. The newsletter *Inside E.P.A. Weekly Report* is available from Inside Washington Publishers, Inc. for $565.00 a year; P.O. Box 7167, Washington, DC 20044; (800) 424-9068 or (202) 347-7618. Also available from Inside Washington Publishers is *Inside E.P.A.'s Environmental Policy Alert*, a biweekly, subscription price: $295.00 a year.

EPA Journal

A monthly magazine (except for January/February and July/August) that deals with the protection of the Nation's land, air and water systems. Subscription price: $20.00 a year. GPO List ID EPAJ. (EP 1.67:) See the GPO subscription order form.

Monthly Awards for Construction Grants for Wastewater Treatment Works

The annual companion issue, "State Priority List for Construction Grants for Wastewater Treatment Works," is incorporated in an issue near the end of each calendar year. Subscription price: $51.00 a year. GPO List ID MCGWT. (EP 1.56:) See the GPO subscription order form.

Test Methods for Evaluating Solid Waste, Physical/Chemical Methods, EPA Publication SW-846

A subscription service that consists of a basic manual and supplementary material for an indeterminate period. The manual covers the procedures that may be used by a regulated community or others to determine whether a specific waste is a hazardous waste as defined by regulations promulgated under Section 3001 of the *Resource Conservation and Recovery Act*. Issued in looseleaf form, punched for 3-ring binder. Subscription price: $55.00. GPO List ID TMESW. (EP 1.17:) See the GPO subscription order form.

Equal Employment Opportunity Commission

The Equal Employment Opportunity Commission (EEOC) enforces the anti-discrimination provisions of the 1964 *Civil Rights Act* and other laws, as regards discrimination based on race, color, religion, sex, national origin, age or handicap in hiring, promoting, firing, wages, testing, training, apprenticeships and all other conditions of employment. To accomplish this end, the EEOC issues guidelines on employment discrimination, investigates charges of discrimination and makes public its decisions and litigates non-compliance cases. The Commission has jurisdiction over all employers with 15 or more employees, including States, localities, private educational institutions and the Federal Government. Fiscal year 1985 budget $158 million, or 0.017% of the total Federal budget; 3,231 paid employees, or 0.11% of the total civilian work force. (CFR reference: Title 29, Chapter XIV)

Key Offices and Telephone Numbers

Address: 2401 E Street NW, Washington, DC 20507

General Information	(800) USA-EEOC
Personnel Locator	(202) 634-1947
Public/Consumer Information	
Office of Public Information	(800) USA-EEOC
Procurement Information	
Procurement Management Division	(202) 634-7070
Competition Advocate	(202) 634-7048
Press Inquiries	
Office of Communications	(202) 634-6036
Other Key Offices	
Congressional Liaison/Legislative Affairs	(202) 634-6930
Ethics in Government Act	(202) 634-6460
Fraud, Waste and Mismanagement Hotline	(800) 424-5454
In the Washington, DC area	(202) 633-6987
Freedom of Information/Privacy Act	(202) 634-6592
General Counsel	(202) 634-6400
Library	(202) 634-6991
Paperwork Reduction Act (ADP/IRM)	(202) 634-6814
Personnel	(202) 634-7002

Key Information Resources

Available **FREE** from the Office of Public Information are pamphlets, fact sheets, posters, guidelines and regulations. Some material is available in Spanish.

Export-Import Bank of the United States

The Export-Import Bank of the United States (Eximbank) aids in financing and facilitating the export of U.S. goods and services. The bank offers financing for U.S. exporters competitive with financing provided by foreign export credit agencies to assist sales by their own nations' exporters. The programs take the form of loans or the issuance of guarantees and insurance, so that U.S. exporters and private banks may extend appropriate financing while providing a reasonable assurance of repayment. Direct lending by Eximbank is limited to larger sales of U.S. products and services. Fiscal year 1985 net budget outlay -$384 million, or -0.041% of the total Federal budget; 367 paid employees, or 0.012% of the total civilian work force. (CFR reference: Title 12, Chapter IV)

Key Offices and Telephone Numbers

Address: 811 Vermont Avenue NW, Washington, DC 20571

General Information	(202) 566-8990
Personnel Locator	(202) 566-2117
Public/Consumer Information	
Office of Public Affairs and Publications	(800) 424-5201
In the Washington, DC area	(202) 566-8990
Procurement Information	
Small Business Advisory Service	(800) 424-5201
In the Washington, DC area	(202) 566-8860
Office of Small and Disadvantaged Business Utilization	(202) 566-8951
Press Inquiries	
Office of Public Affairs and Publications	(800) 424-5201
In the Washington, DC area	(202) 566-8990
Other Key Offices	
Agency Committee Management	(202) 566-8871
Congressional Liaison/Legislative Affairs	(202) 566-8967
Ethics in Government Act	(202) 566-8334
Fraud, Waste and Mismanagement Hotline	(800) 424-5454
In the Washington, DC area	(202) 633-6987
Freedom of Information/Privacy Act	(202) 566-8812
General Counsel	(202) 566-8334
Library	(202) 566-8320
Paperwork Reduction Act (ADP/IRM)	(202) 566-8111
Personnel	(202) 566-8834

Key Information Resources

A *Program Selection Chart* is available **FREE** from the Office of Public Affairs and Publications that describes the Eximbank and its activities. **FREE** from the Small Business Advisory Service is the publication *Programs for Small Business* that provides export markets information.

Farm Credit Administration

The Farm Credit Administration (FCA) supervises, examines and coordinates the borrower-owned banks and associations that comprise the cooperative Farm Credit System. The system consists of Federal land banks and associations, Federal intermediate credit banks, production credit associates and banks for cooperatives. These institutions provide credit and related services to farmers, ranchers, producers or harvesters of aquatic products; persons engaged in providing on-the-farm services; rural homeowners; and associations of farmers, ranchers, or producers or harvesters of aquatic products. Fiscal year 1985 budget $20,452,000, or 0.0022% of the total Federal budget; 311 paid employees, or 0.011% of the total civilian work force. (CFR reference: Title 12, Chapter VI)

Key Offices and Telephone Numbers

Address: 1501 Farm Credit Drive, McLean, VA 22102

General Information and Personnel Locator	(703) 883-4000
Public/Consumer Information	
Congressional and Public Affairs Division	(202) 883-4056
Procurement Information	
Administrative Division	(703) 833-4147
Press Inquiries	
Congressional and Public Affairs Division	(703) 883-4056
Other Key Offices	
Congressional Liaison/Legislative Affairs	(703) 883-4056
Ethics in Government Act	(703) 883-4135
Fraud, Waste and Mismanagement Hotline	(800) 424-5454
In the Washington, DC area	(202) 633-6987
Freedom of Information/Privacy Act	(703) 883-4056
General Counsel	(703) 883-4020
Library	(703) 883-4296
Paperwork Reduction Act (ADP/IRM)	(703) 883-4117
Personnel	(703) 883-4135

Key Information Resources

Publications issued by the FCA and the Farm Credit System may be obtained from the Congressional and Public Affairs Division. No catalog or list of publications is available.

Federal Communications Commission

The Federal Communications Commission (FCC) regulates domestic interstate and foreign communications by radio, television, wire, cable and telephone. To accomplish its mission, the Commission issues licenses and approves renewals and ownership transfers for broadcast stations (AM/FM radio and television) and oversees compliance by broadcasters with laws and FCC policies. The Commission controls the service offerings, rates and practices of telephone, telegraph, radio and satellite communications. The Commission also regulates cable television systems and business, safety and personal radio services. Fiscal year 1985 budget $94 million, or 0.010% of the total Federal budget; 1,999 paid employees, or 0.068% of the total civilian work force. (CFR reference: Title 47, Chapter I)

Key Offices and Telephone Numbers

Address: 1919 M Street NW, Washington, DC 20554

General Information	(202) 632-7000
Personnel Locator	(202) 632-7106
Public/Consumer Information	
Office of Consumer Assistance	(202) 632-7000
Procurement Information	
Procurement Branch	(202) 634-1528
Small Business Division	(202) 632-7260
Competition Advocate	(202) 634-1530
Press Inquiries	
News Media Division	(202) 254-7674
News highlights recording of releases and texts	(202) 632-0002
Other Key Offices	
Agency Committee Management	(202) 632-6390
Congressional Liaison/Legislative Affairs	(202) 632-6405
Ethics in Government Act	(202) 632-7143
Fraud, Waste and Mismanagement Hotline	(800) 424-5454
In the Washington, DC area	(202) 633-6987
Freedom of Information/Privacy Act	(202) 632-7143
General Counsel	(202) 632-7020
Library	(202) 632-7100
Paperwork Reduction Act (ADP/IRM)	(202) 632-6390
Personnel	(202) 632-7106

Key Information Resources

Available **FREE** from the Office of Consumer Assistance is *Information Seeker's Guide: How to Find Information at the Federal Communications Commission.*

Federal Communications Commission Reports

A monthly publication that includes all decisions, reports, memorandum opinions, orders, statements of policy, public notices and all other official utterances and acts that are or may be of precedential value or public interest. Subscription price: $45.00 a year. GPO List ID FCCR. (CC 1.12/2a:) See the GPO subscription order form.

F.C.C. Week

A weekly that covers activities at the FCC, Congress and other Federal Government agencies involved in telecommunications. Subscription price: $427.00 a year. ISSN 0738-5714. Capitol Publications, Inc., 1300 N. 17th Street, Arlington, VA 22209; (703) 528-5400.

Federal Deposit Insurance Corporation

The Federal Deposit Insurance Corporation (FDIC) insures deposits, up to the legal limit, in national banks, in State banks that are members of the Federal Reserve System, and in State banks that apply for Federal Deposit Insurance and meet prescribed qualifications. The FDIC regulates member banks with regard to reports and examinations of bank conditions; deposit interest payments; relocation of bank offices or branches; reduction or retirement of bank capital; bank mergers that result in an FDIC-regulated bank; cease-and-desist orders to banks or their officials engaging in unsound or illegal practices; receivership for failed insured national banks and, when appointed, failed State banks; enforcement of fair credit, consumer and truth-in-lending laws affecting banks; regulations and reporting requirements of the Securities Exchange Act affecting bank-issued securities; reports of bank stock ownership changes and acquisitions of controlling interest in a bank; adequate bank security systems. The FDIC has authority to terminate insurance coverage of banks that violate laws and regulations. Fiscal year 1985 net budget outlay -$1,942 million, or -0.21% of the total Federal budget; 5,076 paid employees, or 0.017% of the total civilian work force. (CFR reference: Title 12, Chapter III)

Key Offices and Telephone Numbers

Address: 550 17th Street NW, Washington, DC 20429

General Information and Personnel Locator	(202) 393-8400
Public/Consumer Information	
Corporate Communications Office	(202) 389-4221
Banking Consumer Hotline	(800) 424-5488
In the Washington, DC area	(202) 898-3536
Procurement Information	
Contracts and Acquisitions Unit	(202) 898-3661
Press Inquiries	
Corporate Communications Office	(202) 389-4221
Other Key Offices	
Congressional Liaison/Legislative Affairs	(202) 389-4496
Ethics in Government Act	(202) 898-7272
Fraud, Waste and MismanagementHotline	(800) 424-5454
In the Washington, DC area	(202) 633-6987
Freedom of Information/Privacy Act	(202) 898-3812
General Counsel	(202) 898-3743
Library	(202) 898-7435
Paperwork Reduction Act (ADP/IRM)	(202) 898-3810
Personnel	(202) 898-3878

Key Information Resources

A *FDIC Publications* list is available **FREE** from the Corporate Communications Office. The list includes FDIC's various statistical publications.

Federal Election Commission

The Federal Election Commission (FEC) is an independent agency that regulates the financing of political campaigns for Federal office. Its primary responsibility is to monitor and enforce laws that provide for disclosure of financial activities of Federal candidates and political action committees (PACs) supporting such candidates, limitations on contributions and expenditures regarding such Federal candidates and PACs, the organization and registration of PACs, and the public financing of Presidential elections. Fiscal year 1985 budget $13,016,000, or 0.0014% of the total Federal budget; 251 paid employees, or 0.0085% of the total civilian work force. (CFR reference: Title 11, Chapter I)

Key Offices and Telephone Numbers

Address: 999 E Street NW, Washington, DC 20463

General Information and Personnel Locator	(202) 376-5134
Public/Consumer Information	
Office of Public Communications	(800) 424-9530
In the Washington, DC area	(202) 376-3140
Clearinghouse on Election Administration	(800) 424-9530
In the Washington, DC area	(202) 376-5670
Procurement Information	
Administration Division	(202) 376-5270
Press Inquiries	
Press Office	(800) 424-9530
In the Washington, DC area	(202) 376-3155
Other Key Offices	
Agency Committee Management	(202) 376-5270
Congressional Liaison/Legislative Affairs	(202) 376-5136
Ethics in Government Act	(202) 376-5690
Fraud, Waste and Mismanagement Hotline	(800) 424-5454
In the Washington, DC area	(202) 633-6987
Freedom of Information/Privacy Act	(202) 376-3155
General Counsel	(202) 376-5690
Library	(202) 376-5312
Personnel	(202) 376-5290

Key Information Resources

Available **FREE** from the Office of Public Communications are the booklets *The FEC and The Federal Campaign Finance Law* and *Free Publications*.

The Campaign Contribution Tracking System

A computerized online database system of FEC PAC-related contributions information. Washington On-Line, 507 8th Street SE, Washington, DC 20003; (202) 543-9101.

Federal Emergency Management Agency

The Federal Emergency Management Agency (FEMA) is the single point for national emergency preparedness, relief operations and recovery assistance. Emergencies under the jurisdiction of this agency include natural, manmade, and nuclear emergencies. FEMA coordinates emergency preparedness and response resources at the Federal, State and local levels of government in preparing for and responding to these emergencies. Fiscal year 1985 budget $469 million, or 0.050% of the total Federal budget; 2,766 paid employees, or 0.094% of the total civilian work force. (CFR reference, Titles and Chapters: 41, 44; 44, I; 48, 44)

Key Offices and Telephone Numbers

Address: 500 C Street SW, Washington, DC 20472

General Information and Personnel Locator	(202) 646-4600
Public/Consumer Information	
Office of Public Affairs	(202) 646-4600
Federal Insurance Administration	(800) 638-6620
In the Washington, DC area	(202) 646-2781
Federal Crime Insurance Program	(800) 638-8780
In the Washington, DC area	(301) 251-1660
Procurement Information	
Office of Acquisition Management	(202) 646-3744
Small Business and Competition Advocate	(202) 646-3743
Press Inquiries	
News and Information Division	(202) 646-4600
Other Key Offices	
Agency Committee Management	(202) 646-2644
Congressional Liaison/Legislative Affairs	(202) 646-4500
Ethics in Government Act	(202) 646-4105
Fraud, Waste and Mismanagement Hotline	(800) 424-5454
In the Washington, DC area	(202) 633-6987
Freedom of Information/Privacy Act	(202) 646-3981
General Counsel	(202) 646-4106
Library	(202) 646-3771
Paperwork Reduction Act (ADP/IRM)	(202) 646-2965
Personnel	(202) 646-3962

Key Information Resources

Available **FREE** from the Office of Public Affairs are the *FEMA Publications Catalog* and *FEMA Motion Picture Catalog*.

Federal Energy Regulatory Commission

The Federal Energy Regulatory Commission (FERC) regulates the interstate aspects of the electric power and natural gas industries. The Commission has the power to license private hydroelectric facilities, regulate the service rates of public utilities selling electricity in interstate commerce at wholesale, regulate the services and rates of natural gas pipeline companies selling at wholesale and independent producers of natural gas selling interstate, regulate accounting and reporting procedures for public utilities and regulate transportation tariffs on oil and natural gas pipelines. Fiscal year 1985 budget $97,530,000, or 0.010% of the total Federal budget; 1,486 paid employees, or 0.050% of the total civilian work force. (CFR reference: Title 18, Chapter I)

Key Offices and Telephone Numbers

Address: 825 N. Capitol Street NE, Washington, DC 20426

General Information and Personnel Locator	(202) 357-5200
Public/Consumer Information	
Public Inquiries Branch	(202) 357-8055
Public Reference Section	(202) 357-8118
Procurement Information	
Procurement Branch	(202) 357-5612
Press Inquiries	
Media Relations Branch	(202) 357-8380
Commission actions recording	(202) 357-8555
Other Key Offices	
Agency Committee Management	(202) 357-8300
Congressional Liaison/Legislative Affairs	(202) 357-8373
Ethics in Government Act	(202) 357-8002
Fraud, Waste and Mismanagement Hotline	(800) 424-5454
In the Washington, DC area	(202) 633-6987
Freedom of Information/Privacy Act	(202) 357-8055
General Counsel	(202) 357-8000
Library	(202) 357-5479
Paperwork Reduction Act (ADP/IRM)	(202) 357-5565
Personnel	(202) 357-8071

Key Information Resources

Available **FREE** from the Public Inquiries Branch is a *Guide to Public Information at the Federal Energy Regulatory Commission*.

Inside F.E.R.C.

A weekly that covers the activities of FERC. Subscription price: $675.00 a year. ISSN 0163-948X. *Inside F.E.R.C.*, McGraw-Hill, Inc., 1221 Avenue of the Americas, New York, NY 10020; (800) 223-6180 or (212) 512-6410.

Federal Home Loan Bank Board

The Federal Home Loan Bank Board (FHLBB) is an independent agency that regulates federally-chartered savings and loan associations that specialize in the financing of residential real estate. The Board is the country's major private source of financing for the construction and purchase of homes. The FHLBB operates the Federal Savings and Loan Insurance Corporation (FSLIC), which insures deposits in savings accounts in FSLIC-insured savings and loan associations. Fiscal year 1985 budget $414 million, or 0.044% of the total Federal budget; 1,533 paid employees, or 0.052% of the total civilian work force. (CFR reference: Title 12, Chapter V)

Key Offices and Telephone Numbers

Address: 1700 G Street NW, Washington, DC 20552

General Information and Personnel Locator	(202) 377-6000
Public/Consumer Information	
Communications Office	(202) 377-6678
Mortgage rates recording	(800) 424-5405
In the Washington, DC area	(202) 377-6988
Procurement Information	
Procurement Management Branch	(202) 377-6030
Office of Small and Disadvantaged Business Utilization	(202) 377-6666
Competition Advocate	(202) 377-6173
Press Inquiries	
Communications Office	(202) 377-6677
Other Key Offices	
Agency Committee Management	(202) 377-6577
Congressional Liaison/Legislative Affairs	(202) 377-6288
Ethics in Government Act	(202) 377-6404
Fraud, Waste and Mismanagement Hotline	(800) 424-5454
In the Washington, DC area	(202) 633-6987
Freedom of Information/Privacy Act	(202) 377-6933
General Counsel	(202) 377-6404
Law Library	(202) 377-6470
Research Library	(202) 377-6296
Paperwork Reduction Act (ADP/IRM)	(202) 377-6072
Personnel	(202) 377-6060

Key Information Resources

Available **FREE** from the Communications Office are the *FHLBB Publications List*, *Questions and Answers Concerning Your INSURED Savings*, *How FSLIC Insurance Works* and *Deposit Insurance Coverage for Family Savings*.

Federal Labor Relations Authority

The Federal Labor Relations Authority (FLRA) oversees the Federal employees labor relations program. The Authority administers the law that protects the right of Federal Government employees to organize, bargain collectively and participate through labor organizations of their own choosing in decisions that affect them. Specifically, the FLRA determines the appropriateness of bargaining units; supervises and conducts representation elections; prescribes criteria and resolves issues relating to the granting of consultation rights to labor organizations with respect to internal agency policies and Government-wide rules and regulations; and resolves negotiability disputes, unfair labor practice complaints and exceptions to arbitration awards. Fiscal year 1985 budget $17,300,000, or 0.0018% of the total Federal budget; 321 paid employees, or 0.011% of the total civilian work force. (CFR references, Titles and Chapters: 5, XIV; 22, XIV)

Key Offices and Telephone Numbers

Address: 500 C Street SW, Washington, DC 20424

General Information and Personnel Locator	(202) 382-0711
Public/Consumer Information	
Congressional Affairs and Public Information Office	(202) 382-0731
Procurement Information	
Office of the Comptroller	(202) 382-0724
Competition Advocate	(202) 382-0711
Press Inquiries	
Congressional Affairs and Public Information Office	(202) 382-0731
Other Key Offices	
Congressional Liaison/Legislative Affairs	(202) 382-0731
Ethics in Government Act	(202) 382-0715
Fraud, Waste and Mismanagement Hotline	(800) 424-5454
In the Washington, DC area	(202) 633-6987
Freedom of Information/Privacy Act	(202) 382-0834
General Counsel	(202) 382-0742
Library	(202) 382-0765
Paperwork Reduction Act (ADP/IRM)	(202) 382-0711
Personnel	(202) 382-0751

Key Information Resources

It is possible for anyone to inspect formal case documents or read FLRA publications at the Authority's headquarters office or its eight regional offices. The Authority assists in arranging for reproduction of documents and ordering of hearings. Requests for publications should be submitted to the Director of Administration.

FLRA Publications

A subscription service that includes material issued irregularly by the FLRA during a 12-month period beginning at the time of subscription. Subscription price: $33.00 a year. Single copy price: Subject Matter Indexes, $4.50; Digest and Tables of Cases, $5.00; Subject Matter Index and Tables of Cases (Federal Service Impasses Panel), $4.00; Report of Case Handling Developments of the Office of the General Counsel, $3.75. GPO List ID PFLRA. See the GPO subscription order form.

Federal Maritime Commission

The Federal Maritime Commission (FMC) regulates the waterborne foreign and domestic offshore commerce of the United States. This is accomplished by regulating issuance of licenses to independent ocean freight forwarders, carrier rates and agreements, and the activities of terminal operators. FMC maintains surveillance over steamship conferences and common carriers by water; assures that only the rates on file with the Commission are charged; guarantees equal treatment to shippers, carriers and others subject to shipping statutes; and ensures that adequate levels of financial responsibility are maintained for indemnification of passengers. Fiscal year 1985 budget $11,606,000, or 0.0012% of the total Federal budget; 231 paid employees, or 0.0078% of the total civilian work force. (CFR reference: Title 46, Chapter IV)

Key Offices and Telephone Numbers

Address: 1100 L Street NW, Washington, DC 20573

General Information and Personnel Locator	(202) 523-5773
Public/Consumer Information	
Office of the Secretary	(202) 523-5725
Procurement Information	
Office of Management Services	(202) 523-5900
Press Inquiries	
Office of the Secretary	(202) 523-5725
Other Key Offices	
Agency Committee Management	(202) 523-5866
Congressional Liaison/Legislative Affairs	(202) 523-5740
Ethics in Government Act	(202) 523-5740
Fraud, Waste and Mismanagement Hotline	(800) 424-5454
In the Washington, DC area	(202) 633-6987
Freedom of Information/Privacy Act	(202) 523-5725
General Counsel	(202) 523-5740
Library	(202) 523-5762
Paperwork Reduction Act (ADP/IRM)	(202) 523-5725
Personnel	(202) 523-5773

Key Information Resources

Available **FREE** from the Office of the Secretary is the annual report. No catalog or list of publications is available.

Automobile Manufacturers' Measurements

A subscription service that shows weights and measurements described by automobile manufacturers for each make and model of domestic and foreign automobiles. The publication is intended to help shippers determine the appropriate measurement of automobiles in domestic offshore trade. Subscription price: $15.00 for the basic manual and one change. GPO List ID AMM. See the GPO subscription order form.

Federal Mediation and Conciliation Service

The Federal Mediation and Conciliation Service (FMCS) promotes sound labor-management practices and prevents or minimizes work stoppages that disrupt the flow of interstate commerce by providing mediation services to disputing parties. The FMCS advocates collective bargaining, mediation and voluntary arbitration as the preferred ways for settling issues between employers and representatives of employees and helps in the development of the art, science and practice of dispute resolution. Fiscal year 1985 budget $23,705,000, or 0.0025% of the total Federal budget; 356 paid employees, or 0.012% of the total civilian work force. (CFR reference: Title 29, Chapter XII)

Key Offices and Telephone Numbers

Address: 2100 K Street NW, Washington, DC 20427

General Information and Personnel Locator	(202) 653-5290
Public/Consumer Information	
Office of Information/Public Affairs	(202) 653-5290
Procurement Information	
Office of Administrative Services	(202) 653-5310
Press Inquiries	
Office of Information/Public Affairs	(202) 653-5290
Other Key Offices	
Agency Committee Management	(202) 653-5290
Congressional Liaison/Legislative Affairs	(202) 523-5290
Ethics in Government Act	(202) 653-5305
Fraud, Waste and Mismanagement Hotline	(800) 424-5454
In the Washington, DC area	(202) 633-6987
Freedom of Information/Privacy Act	(202) 653-5305
General Counsel	(202) 653-5305
Library	(202) 653-5305
Paperwork Reduction Act (ADP/IRM)	(202) 653-5310
Personnel	(202) 653-5260

Key Information Resources

Available **FREE** from the Office of Information/Public Affairs is the brochure *Securing Labor-Management Peace Through Mediation* that describes the functions of the FMCS. Other brochures, as well as the annual report, are available from this office.

Federal Reserve System

The Board of Governors of the Federal Reserve System (Fed) determines general monetary and credit policies and formulates the rules and regulations for carrying out those policies. The Fed supervises and examines Federal Reserve banks and the system's member banks, issues regulations under consumer credit protection laws and regulates the growth of bank holding companies. The Fed's policy activities include fixing reserve requirements maintained by member banks against deposits, setting the maximum rate of interest that may be paid by member banks on time and savings deposits, determining the discount rate charged by Federal Reserve banks and influencing credit conditions through open market operations. Fiscal year 1985 budget $1,200 million, or 0.13% of the total Federal budget; 1,591 paid employees, or 0.054% of the total civilian work force. (CFR reference: Title 12, Chapter II)

Key Offices and Telephone Numbers

Address: 20th Street and Constitution Avenue NW, Washington, DC 20551

General Information and Personnel Locator	(202) 452-3000
Public/Consumer Information	
Office of Public Affairs	(202) 452-3215
Publications Services	(202) 452-3244
Procurement Information	
Division of Support Services	(202) 452-3575
Press Inquiries	
Office of Public Affairs	(202) 452-3204
Other Key Offices	
Congressional Liaison/Legislative Affairs	(202) 452-3263
Ethics in Government Act	(202) 452-3608
Fraud, Waste and Mismanagement Hotline	(800) 424-5454
In the Washington, DC area	(202) 633-6987
Freedom of Information/Privacy Act	(202) 452-3684
General Counsel	(202) 452-3293
Library (Research)	(202) 452-3332
Law Library	(202) 452-3284
Paperwork Reduction Act (ADP/IRM)	(202) 452-3217
Personnel	(202) 452-3433

Key Information Resources

Available **FREE** from Publications Services are *Public Information Materials* and *Federal Reserve Board Publications* list.

Federal Trade Commission

The Federal Trade Commission (FTC) helps maintain free and fair competition in the American economic system. The Commission has authority to act against and prevent general restraint of trade in interstate commerce; false or deceptive advertising of consumer goods and other unfair or deceptive practices; activities that tend to lessen competition or create a monopoly, such as price discrimination and certain mergers and acquisitions. The FTC also formulates its own "trade regulation rules" that have the force of law. When laws are violated, the FTC may issue a cease-and-desist order, conduct formal litigation or seek civil penalties. Fiscal year 1985 budget $65 million, or 0.0069% of the total Federal budget; 1,433 paid employees, or 0.049% of the total civilian work force. (CFR reference: Title 16, Chapter I)

Key Offices and Telephone Numbers

Address: Pennsylvania Avenue at 6th Street NW, Washington; DC 20580

General Information and Personnel Locator	(202) 523-3598
Public/Consumer Information	
Public Reference Branch	(202) 523-3598
Office of Public Affairs	(202) 523-3830
Meetings announcements recording	(202) 523-3806
Procurement Information	
Procurement and Contracting Branch, Office of Small and Disadvantaged Business Utilization and Competition Advocate	(202) 523-5552
Press Inquiries	
News Division	(202) 523-1585
News recording	(202) 523-3540
Other Key Offices	
Congressional Liaison/Legislative Affairs	(202) 523-3504
Ethics in Government Act	(202) 523-3776
Fraud, Waste and Mismanagement Hotline	(800) 424-5454
In the Washington, DC area	(202) 633-6987
Freedom of Information/Privacy Act	(202) 523-3640
General Counsel	(202) 523-3613
Library	(202) 523-3871
Paperwork Reduction Act (ADP/IRM)	(202) 523-3776
Personnel	(202) 523-5040

Key Information Resources

Available **FREE** from the Public Reference Branch are *A Guide to the Federal Trade Commission*, *What's Going on at the FTC?*, *Consumer Quiz* and the publications list, *FTC "Best-sellers"*.

General Services Administration

The General Services Administration (GSA) manages the Federal Government's property and records, including construction and operation of buildings, procurement and distribution of supplies, utilization and disposal of property, transportation, traffic and communications management. GSA also stockpiles strategic materials and manages the Government-wide automatic data processing (ADP) resources and information resources management (IRM) program. Fiscal year 1985 net budget outlay -$214 million, or -0.023% of the total Federal budget; 29,678 paid employees, or 1.01% of the total civilian work force. (CFR references, Titles and Chapters: GSA overall, 41, 5; Office of Acquisition Policy, 41, 5A; Contract Appeals Board, 48, 61; Federal Acquisition Regulation, 48, 5; Federal Information Resources Management Regulations, 41, Subtitle E, Ch. 201; Federal Procurement Regulations System, 41, 1 and 5A; Federal Property Management Regulations System, 41, 101 and 105)

Key Offices and Telephone Numbers

Address: 18th and F Streets NW, Washington, DC 20405

General Information	(202) 523-1250
Personnel Locator	(202) 472-1082
Public/Consumer Information	
Office of Media Relations	(202) 566-1231
Publications Division	(202) 566-1235
Procurement Information	
Office of Acquisition Management and Contract Clearance and Competition Advocate	(202) 566-1867
Office of Small and Disadvantaged Business Utilization	(202) 566-1021
Press Inquiries	
Office of Media Relations	(202) 523-1231
Other Key Offices	
Agency Committee Management	(202) 566-0945
Congressional Liaison/Legislative Affairs	(202) 566-1250
Ethics in Government Act	(202) 566-0765
Fraud, Waste and Mismanagement Hotline	(800) 424-5210
In the Washington, DC area	(202) 566-1780
Freedom of Information/Privacy Act	(202) 535-7691
General Counsel	(202) 566-1200
Library	(202) 535-7788
Paperwork Reduction Act (ADP/IRM)	(202) 566-1000
Personnel	(202) 566-0398

Key Information Resources

Available **FREE** from the Publications Division is *GSA Publications That Could Benefit You*.

Consumer Information Center

GSA's Consumer Information Center (CIC) assists Federal agencies promote and distribute consumer information to the general public. The CIC publishes a quarterly *Consumer Information Catalog* that lists more than 200 free or moderately priced Federal Government publications of interest to consumers. Topics covered include careers and education, children, Federal benefits, financial planning, food and nutrition, gardening, health, housing, small business, and travel and hobbies. For a **FREE** copy of the *Catalog*, write to the CIC, Pueblo, CO 81009.

Consumer's Resource Handbook

A directory, compiled by the U.S. Office of Consumer Affairs, that lists more than 2,000 names and addresses of Federal, State and local consumer protection offices, corporate consumer offices, trade associations, consumer-mediation groups and Better Business Bureaus, 1986. 91pp. **FREE**. Consumer Information Center, Pueblo, CO 81009.

Federal Information Centers

GSA's Federal Information Centers (FIC) provide assistance to people who have a question or problem related to Federal Government services, programs or regulations, but who do not know where to turn for an answer. The approximately 12,000 inquiries received each day routinely concern veterans' benefits, social security, immigration and naturalization, patents, copyrights, tax assistance, wage and hour laws, Medicare and Federal job information. FIC information specialists either answer a question directly or refer the questioner to a source of assistance. Citizens in more than 70 cities across the Nation have direct access to an FIC via local or toll-free "800" telephone service. (see your local telephone directory under "United States Government.")

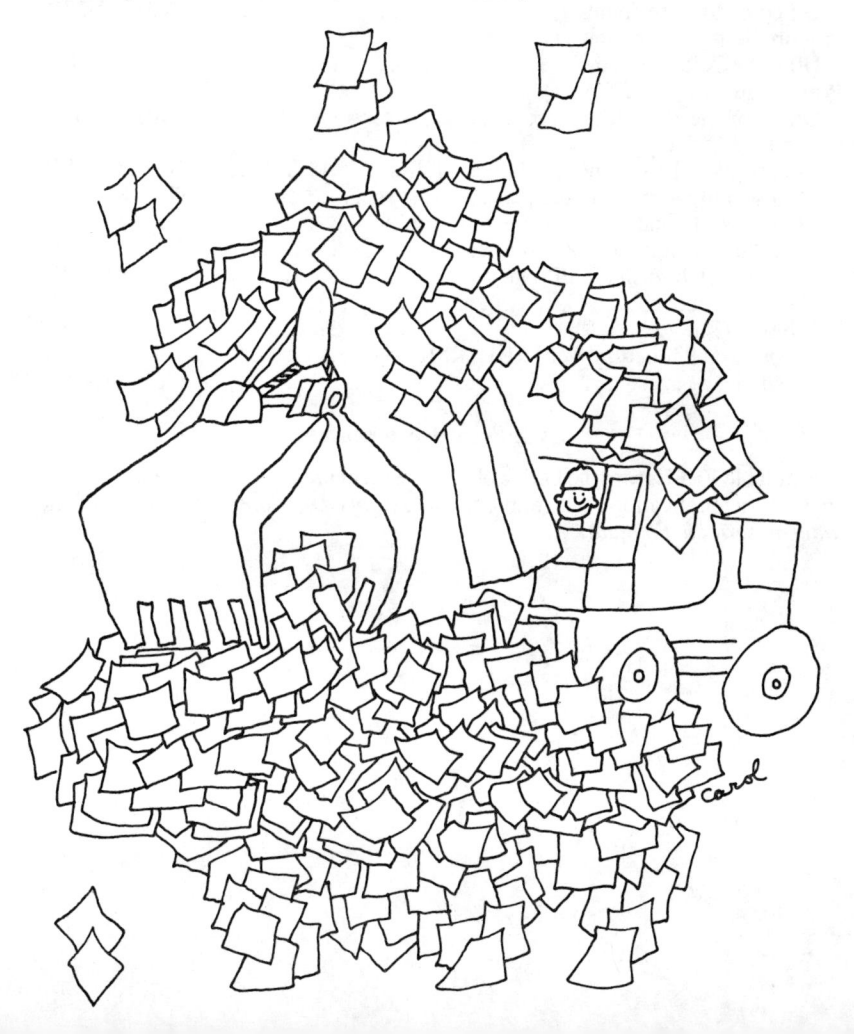

Inter-American Foundation

The Inter-American Foundation (IAF) is an independent Government corporation that supports economic and social development in Latin America and the Caribbean. The IAF makes grants primarily to private, indigenous groups that carry out self-help projects to benefit the poor. Most grants are made to grassroots organizations, including community associations and small urban enterprises, or to larger organizations that work with local groups and provide them with credit, technical assistance, training and marketing services. Fiscal year 1985 budget $6 million, or 0.00064% of the total Federal budget; 67 paid employees, or 0.0023% of the total civilian work force. (CFR reference: Title 22, Chapter X)

Key Offices and Telephone Numbers

Address: 1515 Wilson Boulevard, Rosslyn, VA 22209

General Information and Personnel Locator	(703) 841-3800
Public/Consumer Information	
Office of the President	(703) 841-3810
Procurement Information	
Office of Administration	(703) 841-3869
Press Inquiries	
Office of the President	(703) 841-3810
Other Key Offices	
Congressional Liaison/Legislative Affairs	(703) 841-3810
Ethics in Government Act	(703) 841-3812
Fraud, Waste and Mismanagement Hotline	(800) 424-5454
In the Washington, DC area	(202) 633-6987
Freedom of Information/Privacy Act	(703) 841-3813
General Counsel	(703) 841-3813
Library (Law)	(703) 841-3813
Paperwork Reduction Act (ADP/IRM)	(703) 841-3870
Personnel	(703) 841-3866

Key Information Resources

Available **FREE** from the Office of the President are their annual report, which includes a publications list, and the *Grassroots Development Journal of the Inter-American Foundation*.

Interstate Commerce Commission

The Interstate Commerce Commission (ICC) regulates interstate surface transportation, including trains, trucks, buses, water carriers, freight forwarders, transportation brokers and a coal slurry pipeline. The activities of the Commission include granting operating authority to carriers; regulating carrier rates; approving the construction or abandonment of railroads; investigating carrier operations, adequacy of service, purchases and mergers; and formulating and enforcing uniform systems of accounts for carriers. Fiscal year 1985 budget $50 million, or 0.0053% of the total Federal budget; 1,025 paid employees, or 0.035% of the total civilian work force. (CFR reference: Title 49, Chapter X)

Key Offices and Telephone Numbers

Address: 12th Street and Constitution Avenue NW, Washington, DC 20423

General Information	(202) 275-7119
Personnel Locator	(202) 275-0885
Public/Consumer Information	
Office of Compliance and Consumer Assistance	(202) 275-7849
Office of Public Affairs	(202) 275-7252
Procurement Information	
Procurement and Contracts Branch	(202) 275-0893
Small Business Assistance Office	(202) 275-7597
Competition Advocate	(202) 275-0890
Press Inquiries	
Office of Public Affairs	(202) 275-7252
Other Key Offices	
Congressional Liaison/Legislative Affairs	(202) 275-7524
Ethics in Government Act	(202) 275-7288
Fraud, Waste and Mismanagement Hotline	(800) 424-5454
In the Washington, DC area	(202) 633-6987
Freedom of Information/Privacy Act	(202) 275-7076
General Counsel	(202) 275-7312
Library	(202) 275-7299
Paperwork Reduction Act (ADP/IRM)	(202) 275-7480
Personnel	(202) 275-7288

Key Information Resources

Available **FREE** from the Office of Public Affairs is the *ICC Annual Report*, which includes a publications list as an appendix.

ICC Register

A daily summary of motor carrier applications and of decisions and notices issued by the ICC. Subscription price: $255.00 a year. Single copy price: $1.75. GPO List ID ICREG. (IC 1.35:) See the GPO subscription order form.

Legal Services Corporation

The Legal Services Corporation (LSC) is a private, nonprofit organization that provides financial support for legal assistance in noncriminal proceedings to persons financially unable to afford legal services. The Corporation also makes grants to and contracts with individuals, firms, corporations and organizations for the purpose of providing legal assistance to these clients. The LSC also conducts research and technical assistance activities. Fiscal year 1985 budget $300 million, or 0.032% of the total Federal budget; 11,570 paid employees, or 0.39% of the total civilian work force. (CFR reference: Title 45, Chapter XVI)

Key Offices and Telephone Numbers

Address: 400 Virginia Avenue SW, Washington, DC 20024

General Information and Personnel Locator	(202) 863-1820
Public/Consumer Information	
Office of Public Affairs	(202) 863-1843
Procurement Information	
Office of Management Services	(202) 863-1820
Press Inquiries	
Office of Public Affairs	(202) 863-1843
Other Key Offices	
Congressional Liaison/Legislative Affairs	(202) 863-1842
Ethics in Government Act	(202) 632-7642
Fraud, Waste and Mismanagement Hotline	(800) 424-5454
In the Washington, DC area	(202) 633-6987
Freedom of Information/Privacy Act	(202) 863-1839
General Counsel	(202) 863-1839
Library	(202) 863-1414
Personnel	(202) 863-1847

Key Information Resources

Available **FREE** from the Office of Public Affairs are an annual report and a *Fact Book*.

National Aeronautics and Space Administration

The National Aeronautics and Space Administration (NASA) conducts research and development for the solution of problems of flight within and outside the Earth's atmosphere. It develops, constructs, tests and operates aeronautical and space vehicles, conducts activities required for the exploration of space with manned and unmanned vehicles, arranges for the peaceful use of NASA's scientific and engineering resources with other nations and provides for the dissemination of information about NASA's activities and accomplishments developed as a result of its programs. Fiscal year 1985 budget $7,318 million, or 0.78% of the total Federal budget; 21,876 paid employees, or 0.74% of the total civilian work force. (CFR references, Titles and Chapters: 14, V; 41, 18; 48, 18)

Key Offices and Telephone Numbers

Address: 400 Maryland Avenue SW, Washington, DC 20546

General Information and Personnel Locator	(202) 453-1000
Public/Consumer Information	
Information Center	(202) 453-1000
Educational Affairs Office	(202) 453-8320
Procurement Information	
Procurement Management Division	(202) 453-2130
Office of Small and Disadvantaged Business Utilization	(202) 453-2088
Competition Advocate	(202) 453-2406
Press Inquiries	
News Room	(202) 453-8400
Other Key Offices	
Agency Committee Management	(202) 453-2975
Congressional Liaison/Legislative Affairs	(202) 453-1055
Ethics in Government Act	(202) 453-2450
Fraud, Waste and Mismanagement Hotline	(800) 424-9183
In the Washington, DC area	(202) 755-3402
Freedom of Information/Privacy Act	(202) 453-8342
General Counsel	(202) 453-2450
Library Headquarters	(202) 453-8545
Goddard Space Flight Center Library	(301) 344-7218
Paperwork Reduction Act (ADP/IRM)	(202) 453-2800
Personnel	(202) 453-8478

Key Information Resources

Available **FREE** is *NASA Publications* from the Information Center.

NASA Headquarters Telephone Directory

A quarterly publication that provides organizational and alphabetical listings with telephone, code, room numbers and listings of official addresses. Subscription price: $14.00 a year. Single copy price: $3.75. GPO List ID NHTD. (NAS 1.24:) See the GPO subscription order form.

NASA Activities

A monthly publication that provides general information and scheduled activities of NASA. Subscription price: $23.00 a year. Single copy price: $2.00. GPO List ID NACT. (NAS 1.46:) See the GPO subscription order form.

NASA Grant and Cooperative Agreement Handbook

A subscription service that prescribes policies and regulations relating to the award and administration of NASA research grants. Issued as a basic manual and changes for an indeterminate period. Subscription price: $23.00. GPO List ID NGH. (NAS 1.18:G 76/2/983) See the GPO subscription order form.

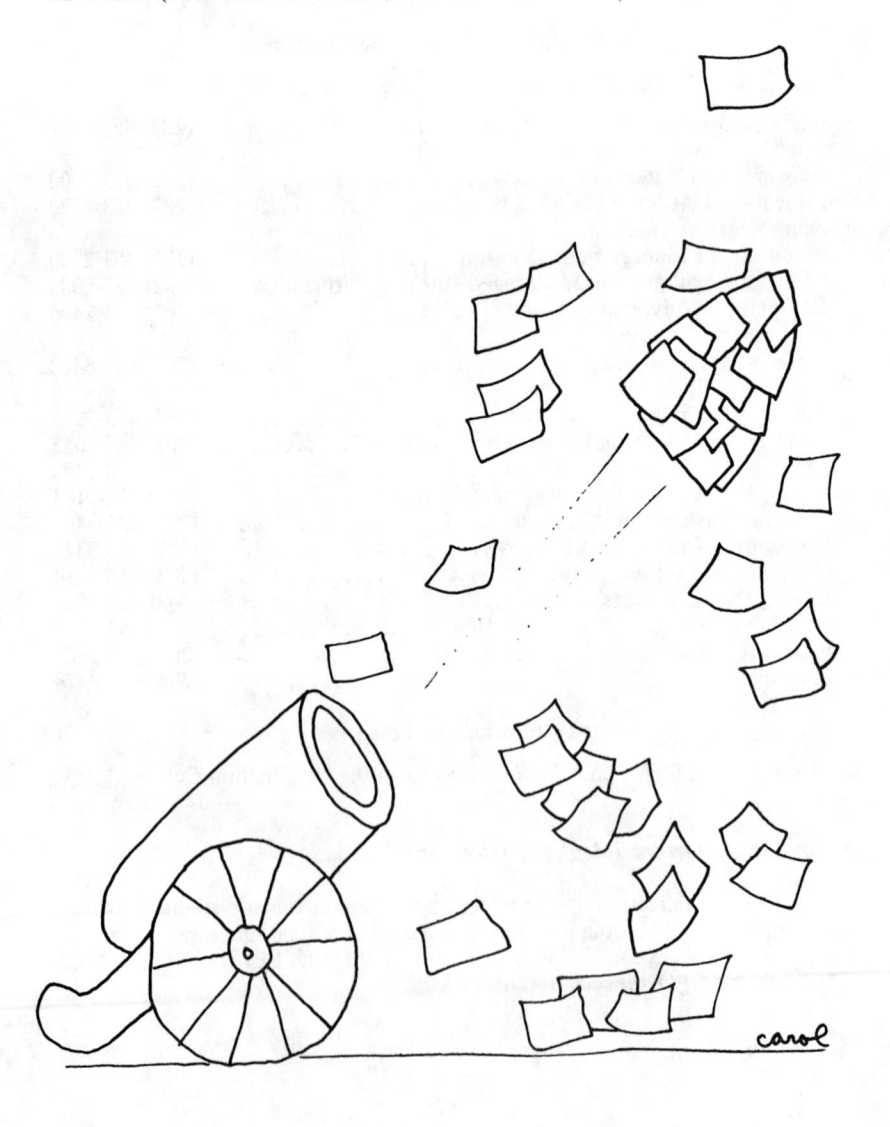

Executive Branch Agencies 267

National Archives and Records Administration

The National Archives and Records Administration (NARA) provides for the preservation, display, use, appraisal and disposition of the records of the United States Government. In the National Archives Building and regional branches, NARA preserves and makes available for further Government use and for private research the Nation's records of enduring value. Other NARA activities include the operation of the Presidential library system, custody and control of the Nixon and Carter Presidential historical materials, administration of a regional network of storage facilities for Federal agencies' records and publication of legislative, regulatory, Presidential and other widely used Government materials. Fiscal year 1985 budget $100 million, or 0.011% of the total Federal budget; 3,000 paid employees, or 0.10% of the total civilian work force. (CFR reference: Title 36, Chapter XII)

Key Offices and Telephone Numbers

Address: 8th Street and Pennsylvania Avenue NW, Washington, DC 20408

General Information and Personnel Locator	(202) 523-3218
Public/Consumer Information	
Education and Exhibits Branch	(202) 523-3097
Office of Records Administration	(202) 724-1457
Reference Service Branch	(202) 523-3218
Technical Services Branch	(202) 523-3164
Procurement Information	
Property and Procurement Branch	(202) 523-3085
Competition Advocate	(202) 523-3214
Press Inquiries	
Office of Public Affairs	(202) 523-3099
Other Key Offices	
Agency Committee Management	(202) 523-3214
Congressional Liaison/Legislative Affairs	(202) 523-3616
Ethics in Government Act	(202) 523-3618
Fraud, Waste and Mismanagement Hotline	(800) 424-5454
In the Washington, DC area	(202) 633-6987
Freedom of Information/Privacy Act	(202) 523-3130
General Counsel	(202) 523-3618
Library—Research Services	(202) 523-3286
Paperwork Reduction Act (ADP/IRM)	(202) 523-3170
Personnel	(202) 724-1513

Key Information Resources

Information on NARA publications, including facsimiles of certain documents, finding aids to collections, microfilm copies of many important records, and *Prologue*, a scholarly journal published quarterly, are available from the Technical Services Branch. Records management publications produced by NARA are available from the Office of Records Administration.

National Historical Publications and Records Commission

The National Historical Publications and Records Commission (NHPRC) plans and makes recommendations for the publication of important historical documents. It works with various public and private institutions in gathering, annotating and publishing papers and records of national historical significance.

268   FEDfind

The NHPRC also provides subvention grants to nonprofit presses to help support publication costs of sponsored editions. In addition, the Commission conducts an educational program to help train persons in the fields of documentary editing and archival administration. For further information contact NHPRC, National Archives, Washington, DC 20408; (202) 523-5384.

National Audiovisual Center

The Center is the central distribution and information source for audiovisual materials produced by the U.S. Government. Included in its collection are more than 8,000 video cassettes, films, slide/tape kits, film strips and audio cassette programs. For further information on collection directories, contact the National Audiovisual Center, Information Services PB, 8700 Edgeworth Drive, Capitol Heights, MD 20743; (800) 638-1300 or (301) 763-1896 in Maryland.

National Capital Planning Commission

The National Capital Planning Commission (NCPC) is the central planning agency for the Federal Government in the National Capital region. It provides overall coordination for planning and development in the region, which includes the District of Columbia, all land areas within the boundaries of Montgomery and Prince Georges Counties in Maryland, and Arlington, Fairfax, Loudon and Prince William Counties in Virginia. The three primary functions performed by the NCPC are comprehensive planning to ensure the orderly development of the Federal Establishment and protection of Federal interests in the National Capital region, plan and program review, and preparation of the Federal Capital Improvements Program. Fiscal year 1985 budget $2,556,000, or 0.00027% of the total Federal budget; 50 paid employees, or 0.0017% of the total civilian work force. (CFR reference: Title 1, Chapter IV)

Key Offices and Telephone Numbers

Address: 1325 G Street NW, Washington, DC 20576

General Information and Personnel Locator	(202) 724-0174
Public/Consumer Information	
Public Affairs Office	(202) 724-0174
Procurement Information	
Management Services Section	(202) 724-0206
Press Inquiries	
Public Affairs Office	(202) 724-0174
Other Key Offices	
Congressional Liaison/Legislative Affairs	(202) 724-0174
Ethics in Government Act	(202) 724-0170
Fraud, Waste and Mismanagement Hotline	(800) 424-5454
In the Washington, DC area	(202) 633-6987
Freedom of Information/Privacy Act	(202) 724-0170
General Counsel	(202) 724-0170
Paperwork Reduction Act (ADP/IRM)	(202) 724-0206
Personnel	(202) 724-0206

Key Information Resources

Available **FREE** from the Public Affairs Office is a publications list.

National Commission on Libraries and Information Science

The National Commission on Libraries and Information Science (NCLIS) is an independent agency that serves as an objective advisor on the Nation's library and information policies to the President and the Congress, as well as to organizations and agencies in both the public and private sectors nationwide. The Commission's primary objective is to foster Federal Government policies and plans for library and information services that will provide for the informational needs of the Nation, including the special library and the rural areas, of economically, socially or culturally deprived persons, and of elderly persons. The Commission supports programs and projects that identify the needs of users of library and information services in the U.S.; the NCLIS works to improve the services, products and mechanisms that help to meet these needs for all the Nation's citizens. Fiscal year 1985 budget $720,000, or 0.000077% of the total Federal budget; 9 paid employees or 0.00031% of the total civilian work force. (CFR reference: Title 45, Chapter XVII)

Key Offices and Telephone Numbers

Address: 3122 GSA Building, 7th and D Streets SW, Washington, DC 20202

General Information and Personnel Locator	(202) 382-0840
Other Key Offices	
Ethics in Government Act	(202) 382-0840
Fraud, Waste and Mismanagement Hotline	(800) 424-5454
In the Washington, DC area	(202) 633-6987
Freedom of Information/Privacy Act	(202) 653-0840
Library	(202) 653-0840
Paperwork Reduction Act (ADP/IRM)	(202) 653-0840
Personnel	(202) 653-0840

Key Information Resources

Available **FREE** is an annual report that includes, among other things, an NCLIS publications list.

National Credit Union Administration

The National Credit Union Administration (NCUA) regulates all Federally chartered credit unions. Federal credit union (FCU) charters are granted by the NCUA to groups sharing a common bond of occupation or association, or to groups within a well-defined neighborhood, community or rural district. In addition to the granting of charters, the NCUA examines the FCUs and administers the National Credit Union Share Insurance Fund and the NCU Central Liquidity Facility. The Central Liquidity Facility is a mixed-ownership Government corporation whose purpose is to supply emergency loans to member credit unions. Fiscal year 1985 net budget outlays -$855 million, or -0.091% of the total Federal budget; 600 paid employees, or 0.020% of the total civilian work force. (CFR reference: Title 12, Chapter VII)

Key Offices and Telephone Numbers

Address: 1776 G Street NW, Washington, DC 20456

General Information and Personnel Locator	(202) 357-1100
Public/Consumer Information	
Public and Congressional Affairs Office	(202) 357-1050
Investment Hotline	(800) 424-3205
Procurement Information	
Administrative Office	(202) 357-1055
Press Inquiries	
Public and Congressional Affairs Office	(202) 357-1050
News Service	(800) 424-5531
Other Key Offices	
Congressional Liaison/Legislative Affairs	(202) 357-1050
Ethics in Government Act	(202) 357-1030
Fraud, Waste and Mismanagement Hotline	(800) 424-5454
In the Washington, DC area	(202) 633-6987
Freedom of Information/Privacy Act	(202) 357-1055
General Counsel	(202) 357-1030
Paperwork Reduction Act (ADP/IRM)	(202) 357-1055
Personnel	(202) 357-1156

Key Information Resources

A list of publications is available **FREE** from the Public and Congressional Affairs Office.

Accounting Manual for Federal Credit Unions

A subscription service of a basic manual and supplementary material for an indeterminate period. Subscription price: $25.00. GPO List ID AMFCU. See the GPO subscription order form.

National Credit Union Administration Rules and Regulations

A subscription service of a basic manual and changes for an indeterminate period. Subscription price: $20.00. GPO List ID NCRR. (NCU 1.6:R 86/985) See the GPO subscription order form.

National Foundation on the Arts and the Humanities

The National Foundation on the Arts and the Humanities encourages and supports national progress in the humanities and the arts. The National Endowment for the Arts (NEA), one component of the Foundation, awards grants to individuals, State and regional arts agencies, and nonprofit organizations representing the highest quality in the fields of design arts, dance, expansion arts, folk arts, literature, media arts (film, radio and television), museums, music, opera, musical theater and the visual arts. The other major component of the Foundation is the National Endowment for the Humanities (NEH). The Endowment makes grants to individuals, groups or institutions to increase understanding and appreciation of the humanities. The "humanities" include (but are not limited to) the study of the following: language, both modern and classical; linguistics; literature; history; jurisprudence; philosophy; archaeology; comparative religion; ethics; and the history, criticism and theory of the arts. Fiscal year 1985 budget $317 million, or 0.034% of the total Federal budget; 587 paid employees, or 0.020% of the total civilian work force. (CFR reference: Title 45, Chapter XI)

Key Offices and Telephone Numbers

Address: 1100 Pennsylvania Avenue NW, Washington, DC 20506

NEA—General Information and Personnel Locator	(202) 682-5400
NEH—General Information and Personnel Locator	(202) 786-0438
Public/Consumer Information	
NEA—Public Information Office	(202) 682-5400
NEH—Public Information Office	(202) 786-0438
Procurement Information	
NEA—Contracts and Procurement Office	(202) 682-5417
NEH—Administrative Services Office	(202) 786-0233
Press Inquiries	
NEA—Press Office	(202) 682-5440
NEH—Media Relations Office	(202) 786-0449
Other Key Offices	
Agency Committee Management—NEA	(202) 682-5433
Agency Committee Management—NEH	(202) 786-0322
Congressional Liaison/Legislative Affairs—NEA	(202) 682-5434
Congressional Liaison/Legislative Affairs—NEH	(202) 786-0328
Ethics in Government Act—NEA	(202) 682-5418
Ethics in Government Act—NEH	(202) 786-0322
Fraud, Waste and Mismanagement Hotline	(800) 424-5454
In the Washington, DC area	(202) 633-6987
Freedom of Information/Privacy Act—NEA	(202) 682-5418
Freedom of Information/Privacy Act—NEH	(202) 786-0322
General Counsel—NEA	(202) 682-5418
General Counsel—NEH	(202) 786-0322
Library—NEA	(202) 682-5485
Library—NEH	(202) 682-5485
Personnel—NEA	(202) 682-5405
Personnel—NEH	(202) 786-0415

Key Information Resources

Available **FREE** from the NEA Public Information Office is a *Guide to the NEA*. The brochure *NEH Program Announcement* is available **FREE** from the NEH Public Information Office.

Arts Review

A quarterly publication that covers NEA programs and policies, funding categories, activities of grantees and issues in the arts. Subscription price: $10.00 a year. Single copy price: $3.50. GPO List ID TCP. (NF 2.11:) See the GPO subscription order form.

Humanities

A bimonthly publication that describes the NEH programs, projects and issues in the humanities. It includes recent grants, deadlines and information for applicants seeking funds. Subscription price: $14.00 a year. Single copy price: $2.50. GPO List ID NR. (NF 3.11:) See the GPO subscription order form.

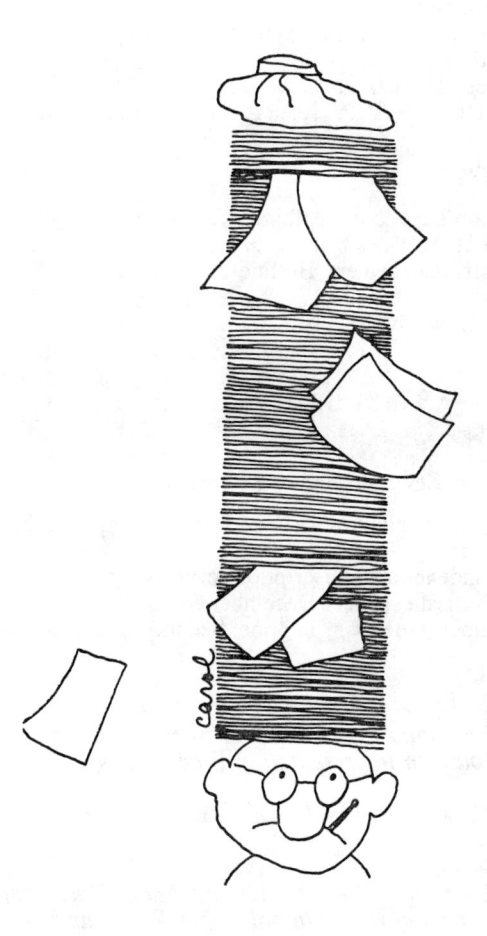

National Labor Relations Board

The National Labor Relations Board (NLRB) administers laws that relate to collective bargaining between employers and labor organizations. The Board deals with unfair labor practices by employers and labor organizations, and conducts secret ballot elections to determine whether or not employees want to be represented by a labor union. The NLRB may act only when it is formally requested to do so by individuals, employers or unions. Hearings are held by NLRB field offices in unfair labor practice cases; when violations are found, recommendations for remedies are made. Fiscal year 1985 budget $134 million, or 0.014% of the total Federal budget; 2,646 paid employees, or 0.090% of the total civilian work force. (CFR reference: Title 29, Chapter I)

Key Offices and Telephone Numbers

Address: 1717 Pennsylvania Avenue NW, Washington, DC 20570

General Information and Personnel Locator	(202) 254-8064
Public/Consumer Information	
Information Division	(202) 632-4950
Procurement Information	
Facilities and Services Branch	(202) 633-0623
Competition Advocate	(202) 633-0623
Press Inquiries	
Information Division	(202) 632-4950
Other Key Offices	
Congressional Liaison/Legislative Affairs	(202) 632-4950
Ethics in Government Act	(202) 254-9200
Fraud, Waste and Mismanagement Hotline	(800) 424-5454
In the Washington, DC area	(202) 633-6987
Freedom of Information/Privacy Act	(202) 254-9350
General Counsel	(202) 254-9150
Library	(202) 254-9056
Paperwork Reduction Act (ADP/IRM)	(202) 254-9480
Personnel	(202) 254-9106

Key Information Resources

A list of publications is available **FREE** from the Information Division.

The following three indexes are subscription services consisting of four irregularly-issued cumulative issues, plus a December edition that may be purchased separately. The December issues vary in price. See the GPO subscription order form.

Classified Index of Decisions of the Regional Directors of the National Labor Relations Board in Representation Proceedings

Subscription price: $17.00. GPO List ID CDLRB. (LR 1.8/6-2:)

Classified Index of Dispositions of ULP (Unfair Labor Practices) Charges by the General Counsel of the National Labor Relations Board

Subscription price: $22.00. GPO List ID CIDUL. (LR 1.8/8:)

Classified Index of National Labor Relations Board Decisions and Related Court Decisions

Subscription price: $26.00. GPO List ID CINLR. (LR 1.8/6:)

National Labor Relations Board Case Handling Manual

A subscription service in the form of a basic manual in three parts and occasional supplements, issued for an indeterminate period. Part One relates to unfair labor practice proceedings, Part Two relates to representation proceedings and Part Three relates to compliance proceedings. Subscription price: $50.00. GPO List ID NLRBC. (LR 1.6/2:C 26) See the GPO subscription order form.

National Labor Relations Board Election Report

A monthly publication that lists the outcome of secret-ballot voting by employees in NLRB-conducted representation elections as officially certified following resolution of post-election objections and/or challenges. Subscription price: $27.00 a year. Single copy price: $2.50. GPO List ID NLRER. (LR 1.16:) See the GPO subscription order form.

Rules and Regulations and Statements of Procedure

A subscription service of a basic manual and supplementary material for an indeterminate period. It includes NLRB statements of procedure, rules and regulations; a topic index; NLRB organization and functions; and the text of the *Labor Management Relations Act* of 1947, as amended. Subscription price: $22.00. GPO List ID NLRR. (LR 1.6:R 86/ser.8/) See the GPO subscription order form.

Weekly Summary of the National Labor Relations Board Cases

A weekly synopsis of each published decision of the NLRB in unfair labor practices and representative election cases; lists decisions of the NLRB administrative law judges and directions of elections by NLRB regional directors; carries guideline memoranda of the NLRB general counsel to field offices on important case-handling subjects; and carries notices of publication of volumes of NLRB decisions and orders, the *NLRB Annual Report*, and other agency informational literature. Subscription price: $84.00 a year. Single copy price: $1.75. GPO List ID NLRBW. (LR 1.15/2:) See the GPO subscription order form.

National Mediation Board

The National Mediation Board (NMB) assists in maintaining a free flow of commerce in the railroad and airline industries by resolving disputes that could otherwise disrupt travel or imperil the economy. The Board also handles railroad and airline employee representation disputes. The Board's major responsibilities include the mediation of disputes over wages, hours and working conditions that arise between rail or air carriers and organizations representing their employees and the investigation of representation disputes and certification of employee organizations as representatives of crafts or classes of carrier employees. Fiscal year 1985 budget $5,502,000, or 0.00059% of the total Federal budget; 55 paid employees, or 0.0019% of the total civilian work force. (CFR reference: Title 29, Chapter X)

Key Offices and Telephone Numbers

Address: 1425 K Street NW, Washington, DC 20572

General Information and Personnel Locator	(202) 523-5920
Public/Consumer Information	
Special Assistant to the Chairman	(202) 523-5335
Procurement Information	
Administrative Officer	(202) 523-5950
Press Inquiries	
Special Assistant to the Chairman	(202) 523-5335
Other Key Offices	
Ethics in Government Act	(202) 523-5944
Fraud, Waste and Mismanagement Hotline	(800) 424-5454
In the Washington, DC area	(202) 633-6987
Freedom of Information/Privacy	(202) 523-5944
General Counsel	(202) 523-5944
Paperwork Reduction Act (ADP/IRM)	(202) 523-5920
Personnel	(202) 523-5950

Key Information Resources

Available **FREE** from the Office of the Special Assistant to the Chairman are NMB's annual report, *The Railway Labor Act*, *The Railway Labor Act at 50* and *The NMB at 50*.

Executive Branch Agencies 277

National Railroad Passenger Corporation

The National Railroad Passenger Corporation (Amtrak) operates a national transportation system of approximately 24,000 route miles. Amtrak owns or leases the stations and owns its own repair and maintenance facilities. It provides all reservation, station, and on-board service staffs, and train and engine operating crews in the Northeast Corridor. Outside the Northeast Corridor, Amtrak contracts with 21 privately owned railroads for the right to operate over their track. Amtrak compensates each railroad for its services. Fiscal year 1985 budget $684 million, or 0.073% of the total Federal budget. (CFR reference: Title 49, Chapter VII)

Key Offices and Telephone Numbers

Address: 400 N. Capitol Street NW, Washington, DC 20001

General Information and Personnel Locator	(202) 383-3000
Public/Consumer Information	
Office of Customer Relations	(202) 383-2121
Procurement Information	
Purchasing Department	(202) 383-2178
Press Inquiries	
Corporate Communications Department	(202) 383-3860
Other Key Offices	
Congressional Liaison/Legislative Affairs	(202) 383-3937
Fraud, Waste and Mismanagement Hotline	(800) 424-5454
In the Washington, DC area	(202) 633-6987
Freedom of Information/Privacy Act	(202) 383-2727
General Counsel	(202) 383-2826
Personnel	(202) 383-2000

Key Information Resources

Available **FREE** from the Corporate Communications Department is the annual report.

National Science Foundation

The National Science Foundation (NSF) promotes the progress of science and engineering through the support of research and education programs. The Foundation initiates and supports fundamental and long-term research in all the scientific and engineering disciplines. This support is made through grants, contracts and other agreements awarded to universities, university consortia, and nonprofit and other research organizations. Most of the research is intended to resolve scientific questions concerning fundamental life processes, natural laws and phenomena, fundamental processes influencing the human environment and the forces affecting people as members of society as well as the behavior of society. Fiscal year 1985 budget $1,313 million, or 0.14% of the total Federal budget; 1,890 paid employees, or 0.064% of the total civilian work force. (CFR references, Titles and Chapters: 41, 25; 45, VI; 48, 25)

Key Offices and Telephone Numbers

Address: 1800 G Street NW, Washington, DC 20550

General Information	(202) 357-9498
Personnel Locator	(202) 357-9859
Public/Consumer Information	
Office of Legislative and Public Affairs	(202) 357-9498
Procurement Information	
Division of Grants and Contracts	(202) 357-7880
Office of Small and Disadvantaged Business Utilization	(202) 357-7464
Competition Advocate	(202) 357-7880
Press Inquiries	
Office of Legislative and Public Affairs	(202) 357-9498
Other Key Offices	
Agency Committee Management	(202) 357-9520
Congressional Liaison/Legislative Affairs	(202) 357-9730
Ethics in Government Act	(202) 357-7439
Fraud, Waste and Mismanagement Hotline	(800) 424-5454
In the Washington, DC area	(202) 633-6987
Freedom of Information/Privacy Act	(202) 357-9498
General Counsel	(202) 357-9435
Library	(202) 357-7811
Paperwork Reduction Act (ADP/IRM)	(202) 357-9482
Personnel	(202) 357-9859
Telephonic device for the deaf (TDD)	(202) 357-7492

Key Information Resources

Available from the Office of Legislative and Public Affairs is a **FREE** list of NSF reports and other brochures currently in print.

NSF Bulletin

A monthly newsletter of information about programs and the availability of new publications. Available **FREE** upon written request from the Office of Legislative and Public Affairs.

Antarctic Journal of the United States

A quarterly magazine, plus an October Annual Review Issue, that includes scientific and logistic reports on the United States' Antarctic program accounts of collaborative activities undertaken in the United States, authoritative discussions of antarctic matters, and other material of current and historical significance. Subscription price: $16.00 a year. Single copy price: $1.50; Annual Review Issue: $10.00. GPO List ID AJUS. (NS 1.26:) See the GPO subscription order form.

Mosaic

A bimonthly magazine that includes non-technical articles about NSF-supported research. Subscription price: $15.00 a year. Single copy price: $2.75. GPO List ID MOS. (NS 1.29:) See the GPO subscription order form.

NSF Grant Policy Manual

A subscription service that consists of a compendium of basic NSF grant policies and procedures for use by the grantee community and by NSF staff. Subscription price: $13.00 for an indeterminate period. GPO List ID NSFGP. (NS 1.20:G 76) See the GPO subscription order form.

National Transportation Safety Board

The National Transportation Safety Board (NTSB) promotes transportation safety by conducting independent investigations of accidents and by formulating safety improvement recommendations. The Board is responsible for investigating all major accidents in civil aviation and in surface transportation, including pipelines. In addition, the Board conducts safety studies, publishes recommended procedures for accident investigations and establishes regulatory requirements for reporting accidents. Fiscal year 1985 budget $22 million, or 0.0023% of the total Federal budget; 336 paid employees, or 0.011% of the total civilian work force. (CFR reference: Title 49, Chapter VIII)

Key Offices and Telephone Numbers

Address: 800 Independence Avenue SW, Washington, DC 20594

General Information and Personnel Locator	(202) 382-6700
Public/Consumer Information	
Public Inquiries Section	(202) 382-6735
Procurement Information	
Operations and Facilities Division	(202) 382-6731
Press Inquiries	
Office of Government and Public Affairs	(202) 382-6600
Other Key Offices	
Congressional Liaison/Legislative Affairs	(202) 382-6600
Ethics in Government Act	(202) 382-6540
Fraud, Waste and Mismanagement Hotline	(800) 424-5454
In the Washington, DC area	(202) 633-6987
Freedom of Information/Privacy Act	(202) 382-6700
General Counsel	(202) 382-6540
Paperwork Reduction Act (ADP/IRM)	(202) 382-6700
Personnel	(202) 382-6717

Key Information Resources

Available **FREE** from the Public Inquiries Section is the brochure *NTSB Documents and Information*.

Nuclear Regulatory Commission

The Nuclear Regulatory Commission (NRC) regulates the civilian uses of nuclear materials and facilities to protect the public health and safety and the environment. The Commission fulfills its responsibilities through a system of licensing and regulation that includes—among other concerns—the siting, construction, operation, and security of all civilian reactors, nuclear fuel storage facilities, and radioactive waste disposal, as well as the commercial uses of nuclear materials. The Commission inspects licensed facilities and enforces regulations through civil penalties, issuance of orders and other types of actions. Fiscal year 1985 budget $468 million, or 0.050% of the total Federal budget; 3,578 paid employees, or 0.12% of the total civilian work force. (CFR references, Titles and Chapters: 10, I; 41, 20)

Key Offices and Telephone Numbers

Address: 1717 H Street NW, Washington, DC 20555

General Information and Personnel Locator	(301) 492-7000
Public/Consumer Information	
Office of Public Affairs	(301) 492-7715
Regulation or petition for rulemaking status	(800) 368-5642
NRC principal Public Document Room	(202) 634-3273
Local Public Document Room information	(800) 638-8081
Procurement Information	
Division of Contracts	(301) 492-4347
Office of Small and Disadvantaged Business Utilization	(301) 492-4665
Competition Advocate	(301) 492-4347
Press Inquiries	
Office of Public Affairs	(301) 492-7715
Other Key Offices	
Agency Committee Management	(202) 634-3255
Congressional Liaison/Legislative Affairs	(202) 634-1443
Ethics in Government Act	(202) 634-3288
Fraud, Waste and Mismanagement Hotline	(800) 424-5454
In the Washington, DC area	(202) 633-6987
Freedom of Information/Privacy Act	(301) 492-7211
General Counsel	(202) 634-3288
Library	(301) 492-7748
Paperwork Reduction Act (ADP/IRM)	(301) 492-7335
Personnel	(301) 492-8238

Key Information Resources

Available **FREE** from the Office of Public Affairs are the *NRC Fact Sheet*, *Citizen's Guide to U.S. Nuclear Regulatory Commission Information* and the *Public Document Room User's Guide*.

Inside N.R.C.

A biweekly newsletter covering the activities and analysis of NRC-related issues. Subscription price: $940.00 a year. ISSN 0149-0252. *Inside N.R.C.*, McGraw-Hill, Inc., 1221 Avenue of the Americas, New York, NY 10020; (800) 223-6180 or (212) 512-6410.

Occupational Safety and Health Review Commission

The Occupational Safety and Health Review Commission (OSHRC) rules on cases forwarded by the Department of Labor when disagreements arise over the results of safety and health inspections performed by Labor's Occupational Safety and Health Administration (OSHA). The Commission acts as a court to rule on alleged job safety and health violations cited by OSHA that are contested by employers, employees or their representatives after a workplace inspection has taken place. Fiscal year 1985 budget $5,728,000, or 0.00061% of the total Federal budget; 86 paid employees, or 0.0029% of the total civilian work force. (CFR reference: Title 29, Chapter XX)

Key Offices and Telephone Numbers

Address: 1825 K Street NW, Washington, DC 20006

General Information and Personnel Locator	(202) 634-7943
Public/Consumer Information	
Public Information Office	(202) 634-7943
Procurement Information	
Administrative Services Office	(202) 634-6621
Press Inquiries	
Public Information Office	(202) 634-7943
Other Key Offices	
Congressional Liaison/Legislative Affairs	(202) 634-4015
Ethics in Government Act	(202) 634-4015
Fraud, Waste and Mismanagement Hotline	(800) 424-5454
In the Washington, DC area	(202) 633-6987
Freedom of Information/Privacy Act	(202) 634-7943
General Counsel	(202) 634-4015
Library	(202) 634-7933
Personnel	(202) 634-7991

Key Information Resources

The Public Information Office makes available **FREE** *OSHRC: An Introduction*, *OSHRC Act* and *The Rules of Procedure of the OSHRC*.

Office of Personnel Management

The Office of Personnel Management (OPM) administers the Federal Government merit employment system. This includes recruiting, examining, training and promoting workers. OPM conducts nationwide recruiting and examination of applicants for positions in the Federal civil service at General Schedule (GS) grades 1 through 15 and Wage Grade (blue collar) positions. OPM provides technical assistance to Federal trainers and managers on training matters and offers a broad range of courses through a nationwide network of training centers. Other programs managed by OPM cover incentive awards, personnel management, employee benefits and ethics in government. Fiscal year 1985 budget $23,727 million, or 2.53% of the total Federal budget; 6,588 paid employees, or 0.22% of the total civilian work force. (CFR references, Titles and Chapters: 5, I; 41, 16; 45, VIII)

Key Offices and Telephone Numbers

Address: 1900 E Street NW, Washington, DC 20415

General Information	(202) 632-5491
Personnel Locator	(202) 632-9594
Public/Consumer Information	
Office of Public Affairs	(202) 632-5491
Procurement Information	
Acquisition Branch	(202) 632-5476
Competition Advocate	(202) 632-4437
Press Inquiries	
Office of Public Affairs	(202) 632-7433
Other Key Offices	
Agency Committee Management	(202) 632-6161
Congressional Liaison/Legislative Affairs	(202) 632-6514
Ethics in Government Act	(202) 632-4632
Fraud, Waste and Mismanagement Hotline	(202) 632-4423
Toll Free, call GAO	(800) 424-5454
Freedom of Information/Privacy Act	(202) 632-7714
General Counsel	(202) 632-4632
Library	(202) 632-7640
Paperwork Reduction Act (ADP/IRM)	(202) 632-4437
Personnel	(202) 632-5400

Key Information Resources

See Chapter 3, "Civilian Personnel Management," and the Index for information on publications by OPM plus other sources of information in the civilian personnel field.

U.S. Office of Personnel Management Telephone Directory

Contact the Government Printing Office (GPO) for information on the most current edition.

Overseas Private Investment Corporation

The Overseas Private Investment Corporation (OPIC) assists United States investors to make profitable investments in more than 90 developing countries. OPIC offers U.S. investors help in finding investment opportunities, insurance to protect their investments, loans and loan guarantees to help finance their projects, and partial funding for feasibility studies. It encourages investment projects that will help the social and economic development of these countries by reducing or eliminating certain perceived political risks for investors and providing financing and assistance not otherwise available. OPIC helps to reduce the usual risks and problems that can make investment opportunities in developing areas less attractive than in advanced countries. At the same time, OPIC helps U.S. balance of trade payments through the profits returned to American businesses, as well as by the U.S. jobs and exports created. Fiscal year 1985 net budget outlay -$100.5 million, or -0.011% of the total Federal budget; 156 paid employees, or 0.0052% of the total civilian work force. Note: OPIC was legally transferred in 1979 to the U.S. International Development Cooperation Agency (IDCA), but its internal structure remains the same and it continues to operate independently of IDCA. (CFR reference: Title 22, Chapter VII)

Key Offices and Telephone Numbers

Address: 1615 M Street NW, Washington, DC 20527

General Information and Personnel Locator	(202) 457-7200
Public/Consumer Information	
Office of Public Affairs	(202) 457-7093
Procurement Information	
Contracting and Administrative Services	(202) 457-7150
Press Inquiries	
Press Office	(202) 457-7093
Other Key Offices	
Congressional Liaison/Legislative Affairs	(202) 457-7090
Ethics in Government Act	(202) 457-7025
Fraud, Waste and Mismanagement Hotline	(800) 424-5454
In the Washington, DC area	(202) 633-6987
Freedom of Information/Privacy Act	(202) 457-7020
General Counsel	(202) 457-7020
Library	(202) 457-7123
Paperwork Reduction Act (ADP/IRM)	(202) 457-7091
Personnel	(202) 457-7082

Key Information Resources

Available **FREE** from the Office of Public Affairs are an annual report, *Corporate Brochure*, a series of program-specific publications, and *TOPICS*, the corporation's quarterly newsletter.

Panama Canal Commission

The Panama Canal Commission (PCC) manages, operates and maintains the Panama Canal and its complementary facilities and equipment. The Commission coordinates the operation of the Canal with the Republic of Panama, including some civil protection functions. The Commission will perform these functions until December 31, 1999, when the Republic of Panama will assume full responsibility for the Canal. Fiscal year 1985 net budget outlay -$3 million, or -0.00032% of the total Federal budget; 8,056 paid employees, or 0.27% of the total civilian work force. (CFR reference: Title 35, Chapter I)

Key Offices and Telephone Numbers

Address: 2000 L Street NW, Washington, DC 20036

General Information and Personnel Locator	(202) 634-6441
Public/Consumer Information	
Office of the Secretary	(202) 634-6441
Procurement Information	
Procurement Office, 4400 Dauphine Street, New Orleans, LA 70140	(504) 948-5299
Competition Advocate, Washington, DC Office	(202) 634-6441
Press Inquiries	
Office of the Secretary	(202) 634-6441
Other Key Offices	
Congressional Liaison/Legislative Affairs	(202) 634-6441
Ethics in Government Act	(202) 634-6441
Fraud, Waste and Mismanagement Hotline	(800) 424-5454
In the Washington, DC area	(202) 633-6987

Key Information Resources

Information concerning contracts and other matters may be obtained from the PCC, APO Miami, 34011; telephone 011507-52-7723.

Fiscal year 1984 and 1985 annual reports are available from the Office of the Secretary for $2.00 each. Make check payable to the "Panama Canal Commission."

Peace Corps

The Peace Corps promotes world peace and friendship by providing trained volunteers to the peoples of Latin America, Africa, the Near East, Asia and the Pacific to help them meet their basic needs. Volunteers work primarily in the areas of agriculture/rural development, small business assistance, health and education. An auxiliary effort is the Peace Corps Partnership Program. This program provides opportunities for school, civil, neighborhood and youth organizations in the United States to financially sponsor construction of facilities recommended by Peace Corps volunteers. Fiscal year 1985 budget $118 million, or 0.013% of the total Federal budget; 1,129 paid employees, or 0.038% of the total civilian work force. (CFR reference: Title 22, Chapter III)

Key Offices and Telephone Numbers

Address: 806 Connecticut Avenue NW, Washington, DC 20526

General Information	(202) 254-5010
Personnel Locator	(202) 254-6886
Public/Consumer Information	
Office of Public Affairs	(202) 254-5010
Peace Corps Information Collection and Exchange	(800) 424-8580 Ext. 228 or 229
Office of Recruitment	(800) 424-8580 Ext. 293
Peace Corps Partnership projects	(800) 424-8580 Ext. 227
Procurement Information	
Office of Contracts	(202) 254-3513
Competition Advocate	(202) 254-7280
Press Inquiries	
Office of Public Affairs	(202) 254-5010
Other Key Offices	
Agency Committee Management	(202) 254-6360
Congressional Liaison/Legislative Affairs	(202) 254-7210
Ethics in Government Act	(202) 254-3114
Fraud, Waste and Mismanagement Hotline	(800) 424-5454
In the Washington, DC area	(202) 633-6987
Freedom of Information/Privacy Act	(202) 254-6020
General Counsel	(202) 254-3114
Library	(202) 254-3307
Paperwork Reduction Act (ADP/IRM)	(202) 254-7394
Personnel	(800) 424-8580 Ext. 214
Recorded employment opportunities	(202) 254-3400

Key Information Resources

For recruitment literature, contact the Office of Recruitment. For technical publications relating to training, programming and technical developments in the field, contact the Peace Corps Information Collection and Exchange, Office of Training and Program Support.

Pennsylvania Avenue Development Corporation

The Pennsylvania Avenue Development Corporation (PADC) is responsible for the improvement of the District of Columbia's Pennsylvania Avenue and adjacent blocks on the north side of the Avenue between the Capitol and the White House. Improvements are made consistent with a comprehensive development plan approved by Congress in 1975. The PADC carries out the plan through a combination of public improvements with support of private investment, and ensures development, maintenance and use of the area compatible with its historic and ceremonial significance. Fiscal year 1985 budget $9,918,000, or 0.0011% of the total Federal budget; 35 paid employees, or 0.0012% of the total civilian work force. (CFR reference: Title 36, Chapter IX)

Key Offices and Telephone Numbers

Address: 1331 Pennsylvania Avenue NW, Suite 1220 North, Washington, DC 20004

General Information and Personnel Locator	(202) 724-9091
Public/Consumer Information	
Administrative Office	(202) 724-9067
Procurement Information	
Administrative Office	(202) 724-9067
Press Inquiries	
Administrative Office	(202) 724-9067
Other Key Offices	
Congressional Liaison/Legislative Affairs	(202) 724-9067
Ethics in Government Act	(202) 724-9088
Fraud, Waste and Mismanagement Hotline	(800) 424-5454
In the Washington, DC area	(202) 633-6987
Freedom of Information/Privacy Act	(202) 724-9088
General Counsel	(202) 724-9088
Personnel	(202) 724-9067

Key Information Resources

The *Pennsylvania Avenue Plan—1974* is available for $4.00, payable to the PADC, from the Administrative Office. Available **FREE** from this office is the PADC annual report.

Pension Benefit Guaranty Corporation

The Pension Benefit Guaranty Corporation (PBGC) provides for coverage of basic pension benefits of most private benefit plans if they terminate with insufficient funds. PBGC administers two benefit insurance programs—single-employer and multi-employer insurance plans. Some 100,000 plans cover more than 37 million workers. In accordance with the *Employee Retirement Income Security Act* (ERISA), the PBGC provides free advice and assistance to individuals on the economic desirability of establishing tax-qualified Individual Retirement Accounts (IRAs) or certain other individual retirement programs, and on transferring amounts to such IRAs or other programs from qualified pension plans when an employee receives a total pension payout. Fiscal year 1985 net budget outlay -$19,114,000, or -0.0020% of the total Federal budget; 475 paid employees, or 0.016% of the total civilian work force. (CFR reference: Title 29, Chapter XXVI)

Key Offices and Telephone Numbers

Address: 2020 K Street NW, Washington, DC 20006

General Information and Personnel Locator	(202) 956-5000
Public/Consumer Information	
Communications and Public Affairs Department	(202) 956-5040
Benefit Payments Department	(202) 956-5052
Copies of premium forms	(202) 956-5025
Procurement Information	
Procurement Division	(202) 956-5006
Press Inquiries	
Communications and Public Affairs Department	(202) 956-5040
Other Key Offices	
Congressional Liaison/Legislative Affairs	(202) 956-5010
Ethics in Government Act	(202) 956-5020
Fraud, Waste and Mismanagement Hotline	(800) 424-5454
In the Washington, DC area	(202) 633-6987
Freedom of Information/Privacy Act	(202) 956-5039
General Counsel	(202) 956-5020
Library (Law)	(202) 956-5021
Personnel	(202) 956-5008

Key Information Resources

Available **FREE** from the Communications and Public Affairs Department is the brochure *Your Guaranteed Benefits*.

Postal Rate Commission

The Postal Rate Commission (PRC) submits recommended decisions to the United States Postal Service (USPS) on postage rates, fees and mail classifications. In addition, the Commission may receive, study and issue recommended decisions or public reports to the USPS on complaints received from the mailing public as to postage rates, postal classifications, postal services of a nationwide scope, and the closing or consolidation of small post offices. Fiscal year 1985 budget $4,395,000, or 0.00047% of the total Federal budget; 64 paid employees, or 0.0022% of the total civilian work force. (CFR reference: Title 39, Chapter III)

Key Offices and Telephone Numbers

Address: 1333 H Street NW, Suite 300, Washington, DC 20268

General Information and Personnel Locator	(202) 789-6800
Public/Consumer Information	
Consumer Advocate	(202) 789-6830
Public Information Office	(202) 789-6800
Procurement Information	
Administrative Office	(202) 789-6840
Press Inquiries	
Public Information Office	(202) 789-6800
Other Key Offices	
Ethics in Government Act	(202) 789-6820
Fraud, Waste and Mismanagement Hotline	(800) 424-5454
In the Washington, DC area	(202) 633-6987
Freedom of Information/Privacy Act	(202) 789-6820
General Counsel	(202) 789-6820
Library	(202) 789-6877
Personnel	(202) 789-6840

Key Information Resources

The Public Information Office does not have a publications list, but makes available its recommended decisions, advisory opinions and public reports.

President's Council on Physical Fitness and Sports

The President's Council on Physical Fitness and Sports (PCPFS) serves as a catalyst to promote, encourage and motivate physical fitness and sports programs for all Americans. The Council is charged by Executive Order Number 12489 to advise the President of the United States and the Secretary of the Department of Health and Human Services on ways to maintain an effective national physical fitness program. This includes, among other things, advising the President and Secretary on ways and means of enhancing opportunities for participation in physical fitness and sports and on actions at all levels of government and in the private sector to improve physical activity programs and services. Fiscal year 1985 budget $1,300,000, or 0.00014% of the total Federal budget; 15 paid employees, or 0.00051% of the total civilian work force.

Key Offices and Telephone Numbers

Address: 450 5th Street NW, Suite 7103, Washington, DC 20001

General Information and Personnel Locator	(202) 272-3421
Public/Consumer Information	
Director of Information	(202) 272-3430
Procurement Information	
Administrative Office	(202) 272-3421
Press Inquiries	
Director of Information	(202) 272-3430
Other Key Offices	
Ethics in Government Act	(202) 632-7642
Fraud, Waste and Mismanagement Hotline	(800) 424-5454
In the Washington, DC area	(202) 633-6987
Freedom of Information/Privacy Act	(202) 272-3421

Key Information Resources

Available **FREE** from the Director of Information is the *PCPFS Information Guide* and *Publications List*. The Council also publishes the bimonthly *PCPFS Newsletter* that is the main vehicle for disseminating information to physical fitness educators and other professionals about the organization, upcoming national events and special interest features.

Railroad Retirement Board

The Railroad Retirement Board (RRB) administers retirement/survivor and unemployment/sickness benefit programs for the Nation's railroad workers and their families. This includes payment of annuities to individuals who have completed at least 10 years creditable service upon attainment of specified ages, or at any age if permanently disabled. The Board also provides medical benefits and unemployment compensation to qualified persons. It maintains a placement service for unemployed railroad personnel through its field offices. Fiscal year 1985 budget $4,129 million, or 0.44% of the total Federal budget; 1,577 paid employees, or 0.053% of the total civilian work force. (CFR reference: Title 20, Chapter II)

Key Offices and Telephone Numbers

Address: 844 Rush Street, Chicago, IL 60611
Washington Office: 2000 L Street NW, Washington, DC 20036

General Information and Personnel Locator	(312) 751-4500
Washington Legislative Liaison Office	(202) 653-9540
Public/Consumer Information	
Executive Director	(312) 751-4930
Procurement Information	
Procurement Executive	(312) 751-4970
Competition Advocate	(312) 751-4567
Press Inquiries	
Executive Director	(312) 751-4930
Other Key Offices	
Agency Committee Management	(312) 751-4915
Congressional Liaison/Legislative Affairs	(202) 653-9536
Ethics in Government Act	(312) 751-4500
Fraud, Waste and Mismanagement Hotline	(800) 424-5454
In the Washington, DC area	(202) 633-6987
Freedom of Information/Privacy Act	(312) 751-4692
General Counsel	(312) 751-4970
Library	(312) 751-4916
Paperwork Reduction Act (ADP/IRM)	(312) 751-4850
Personnel	(312) 751-4570

Key Information Resources

Available **FREE** from the Washington Legislative Liaison Office are the Board's annual report and statistical supplement.

Securities and Exchange Commission

The Securities and Exchange Commission (SEC) provides for financial information disclosure to the investing public and protects the interests of the investing public against malpractice in the securities and financial markets. Responsibilities of the SEC include supervision and regulation of securities markets, mutual funds and other investment companies, and public utility holding companies; regulation of brokers, dealers, investment counselors and advisors; full disclosure by securities issuers through SEC registration statements and asset reports; and prevention and suppression of fraud through investigations. Fiscal year 1985 budget $103 million, or 0.011% of the total Federal budget; 2,040 paid employees, or 0.070% of the total civilian work force. (CFR reference: Title 17, Chapter II)

Key Offices and Telephone Numbers

Address: 450 5th Street NW, Washington, DC 20549

General Information and Personnel Locator	(202) 272-3100
Public/Consumer Information	
Office of Public Affairs	(202) 272-2650
Office of Consumer Affairs and Information Services	(202) 272-7440
Public Reference Room	(202) 272-7450
Procurement Information	
Procurement and Contracts Branch	(202) 272-7010
Press Inquiries	
Office of Public Affairs	(202) 272-2650
Other Key Offices	
Agency Committee Management	(202) 272-2600
Congressional Liaison/Legislative Affairs	(202) 272-2500
Ethics in Government Act	(202) 272-3171
Fraud, Waste and Mismanagement Hotline	(800) 424-5454
In the Washington, DC area	(202) 633-6987
Freedom of Information/Privacy Act	(202) 272-7422
General Counsel	(202) 272-3171
Library	(202) 272-2618
Paperwork Reduction Act (ADP/IRM)	(202) 272-2700
Personnel	(202) 272-2519

Key Information Resources

Available **FREE** from the Office of Public Affairs are the brochure *SEC Publications* and *Index of Public Use Forms*.

Directory of Companies Required to File Annual Reports With the Securities and Exchange Commission

This publication includes listings of companies required to file annual reports under the *Securities Exchange Act of 1934* as of April 30, 1985. The companies are presented alphabetically and by industry classification. 1985. 492pp. $17.00. GPO S/N 046-000-00135-4. (SE 1.27:985) See the GPO order form.

Official Summary of Security Transactions and Holdings

A monthly publication comprised of securities holdings figures showing owners, relationships to issues, amounts of securities bought or sold by each owner, their individual holdings at the end of the reported month, and types of securities. Subscription price: $59.00 a year. Single copy price: $6.00. GPO List ID OSST. (SE 1.9:) See the GPO subscription order form.

SEC Monthly Statistical Review

A monthly publication that includes statistical summaries of new securities, security sales, common stock prices, stock transactions and other phases of securities exchange. Subscription price: $22.00 a year. Single copy price: $3.75. GPO List ID STBU. (SE 1.20:) See the GPO subscription order form.

Selective Service System

The Selective Service System is responsible for supplying to the Armed Forces manpower adequate to ensure the security of the United States. It oversees the registration of male citizens of the United States and all other male persons who are in the United States and who are between the ages of 18 and 26 years. Exempt are members of the active Armed Forces, foreign diplomatic and consular personnel and nonimmigrant aliens. Fiscal year 1985 budget $26,519,000, or 0.0028% of the total Federal budget; 308 paid employees, or 0.010% of the total civilian work force. (CFR reference: Title 32, Chapter XVI)

Key Offices and Telephone Numbers

Address: 1023 31st Street NW, Washington, DC 20435

General Information and Personnel Locator	(202) 724-0424
Public/Consumer Information	
Office of Public Affairs	(202) 724-0790
Registrant Information Office	(800) 621-5388
Procurement Information	
Procurement Office	(202) 724-0795
Competition Advocate	(202) 724-1058
Press Inquiries	
Office of Public Affairs	(202) 724-0790
Other Key Offices	
Congressional Liaison/Legislative Affairs	(202) 724-0413
Ethics in Government Act	(202) 724-8095
Fraud, Waste and Mismanagement Hotline	(800) 424-5454
In the Washington, DC area	(202) 633-6987
Freedom of Information/Privacy Act	(202) 724-1167
General Counsel	(202) 724-1167
Paperwork Reduction Act (ADP/IRM)	(703) 724-0872
Personnel	(202) 724-0435

Key Information Resources

Available **FREE** from the Office of Public Affairs are a series of fact sheets and information brochures.

Small Business Administration

The Small Business Administration (SBA) promotes American small businesses' activity through financial assistance and counseling. It provides management and technical assistance to firms receiving SBA financial assistance and to other small concerns, licenses and regulates small business investment companies, serves as a source of equity and venture capital assistance for small concerns; and provides procurement assistance to help small concerns in buying from and selling to the Federal Government. Fiscal year 1985 budget $1,631 million, or 0.17% of the total Federal budget; 5,083 paid employees, or 0.17% of the total civilian work force. (CFR references, Titles and Chapters: 13, I; 48, 22)

Key Offices and Telephone Numbers

Address: 1441 L Street NW, Washington, DC 20416

General Information and Personnel Locator	(202) 653-6600
Public/Consumer Information	
Office of Public Communications	(202) 653-6822
Office of Advocacy, Answer Desk	(800) 368-5855
In the Washington, DC area	(202) 653-7561
Procurement Information	
Office of Procurement and Grants Management	(202) 653-6639
Office of Small and Disadvantaged Business Utilization	(202) 653-6639
Press Inquiries	
Office of Public Communications	(202) 653-6822
Other Key Offices	
Agency Committee Management	(202) 653-6748
Congressional Liaison/Legislative Affairs	(202) 653-6545
Ethics in Government Act	(202) 653-6715
Fraud, Waste and Mismanagement Hotline	(202) 653-7557
Toll Free, call GAO	(800) 424-5454
Freedom of Information/Privacy Act	(202) 653-6460
General Counsel	(202) 653-6642
Library	(202) 653-6914
Paperwork Reduction Act (ADP/IRM)	(202) 653-6857
Personnel	(202) 653-6567

Key Information Resources

Available **FREE** from the Office of Advocacy are lists of SBA publications for sale.

Smithsonian Institution

The purpose of the Smithsonian Institution is to carry out the terms of the will of James Smithson of England, who in 1829 bequeathed his entire estate to the United States "to found at Washington, under the name the Smithsonian Institution, an establishment for the increase and diffusion of knowledge among men." To carry out Smithson's mandate, the Institution, as an independent trust establishment, performs fundamental research; publishes the results of studies, explorations and investigations; preserves for study and reference more than 100 million items of scientific, cultural and historical interest; and maintains exhibits representative of the arts, American history, technology, aeronautics and space exploration, and natural history. The Institution also participates in international exchange of learned publications and engages in programs of education and national and international cooperative research and training, supported by its trust endowments and gifts, grants and contracts, and funds appropriated to it by Congress. Fiscal year 1985 budget $226 million, or 0.024% of the total Federal budget; 5,500 paid employees, or 0.19% of the total civilian work force. (CFR reference: Title 36, Chapter V)

Key Offices and Telephone Numbers

Address: 1000 Jefferson Drive SW, Washington, DC 20560

General Information and Personnel Locator	(202) 357-1300
Public/Consumer Information	
Office of Public Affairs	(202) 357-2627
Smithsonian Visitor Information Center	(202) 357-2700
Dial-A-Museum recording	(202) 357-2020
Dial-A-Phenomenon recording	(202) 357-2000
Procurement Information	
Office of Supply Services	(202) 287-3343
Press Inquiries	
Office of Public Affairs	(202) 357-2627
Other Key Offices	
Congressional Liaison/Legislative Affairs	(202) 357-2962
Ethics in Government Act	(202) 632-7642
Fraud, Waste and Mismanagement Hotline	(800) 424-5454
In the Washington, DC area	(202) 633-6987
Freedom of Information/Privacy Act	(202) 357-2583
General Counsel	(202) 357-2583
Library	(202) 357-2139
Paperwork Reduction Act (ADP/IRM)	(202) 357-1360
Personnel	(202) 357-2465
Recording	(202) 357-1452

Key Information Resources

Available **FREE** from the Smithsonian Institution Press is an annual catalog of trade books. Contact them at 955 L'Enfant Plaza SW, Room 2100, Washington, DC 20002; (202) 287-3738.

Tennessee Valley Authority

The Tennessee Valley Authority (TVA) is a Government-owned corporation that conducts programs for the advancement of economic growth in the Tennessee Valley region. The TVA's activities include flood control, electric power production, navigation development, recreation improvement, fertilizer development, and forestry and wildlife development. Its power program is financially self-supporting; other programs are financed primarily by appropriations from Congress. Fiscal year 1985 budget $914 million, or 0.098% of the total Federal budget; 32,824 paid employees, or 1.11% of the total civilian work force. (CFR reference: Title 18, Chapter XIII)

Key Offices and Telephone Numbers

Address: 400 W. Summit Hill Drive, Knoxville, TN 37902
Washington Liaison Office: 412 1st Street SE, Washington, DC 20444

General Information and Personnel Locator	(615) 632-2101
Washington Liaison Office	(202) 245-0101
Public/Consumer Information	
Information Office	(615) 632-8000
Citizen Action Office (Tennessee)	(800) 362-9250
Citizen Action Office (Alabama, Arkansas, Georgia, Kentucky, Mississippi, North Carolina, Virginia)	(800) 251-9242
Procurement Information	
Division of Purchasing	(615) 751-2624
Office of Small and Disadvantaged Business Utilization	(615) 751-2623
Press Inquiries	
Information Office	(615) 632-8000
Other Key Offices	
Congressional Liaison/Legislative Affairs	(202) 245-0101
Ethics in Government Act	(615) 632-2241
Fraud, Waste and Mismanagement Hotline	(800) 424-5454
In the Washington, DC area	(202) 633-6987
Freedom of Information Act/Privacy Act	(615) 632-4131
General Counsel	(615) 632-2241
Library	(615) 632-3466
Paperwork Reduction Act (ADP/IRM)	(615) 632-7885
Personnel	(615) 632-3264

Key Information Resources

The TVA publishes no publications catalog or listing. Enquiries about TVA documents should be made to the Information Office or Citizen Action Office.

United States Arms Control and Disarmament Agency

The United States Arms Control and Disarmament Agency (ACDA) formulates and implements arms control and disarmament policies that promote the national security of the United States and its relations with other countries. The ACDA conducts studies and provides advice relating to arms control and disarmament policy formulation; prepares for and manages United States participation in international negotiations in the arms control and disarmament field; and prepares for, operates, or—as needed—directs U.S. participation in international control systems that may result from U.S. arms control or disarmament activities. The ACDA director functions as the principal advisor to the President, the National Security Council and the Secretary of State in arms control and disarmament matters. Fiscal year 1985 budget $16,462,000, or 0.0018% of the total Federal budget; 241 paid employees, or 0.0082% of the total civilian work force. (CFR references, Titles and Chapters: 22, VI; 41, 23)

Key Offices and Telephone Numbers

Address: 320 21st Street NW, Washington, DC 20451

General Information	(202) 647-8714
Personnel Locator	(202) 647-2035
Public/Consumer Information	
Office of Public Affairs	(202) 647-8714
Procurement Information	
Contracting Office	(703) 235-8248
Press Inquiries	
Office of Public Affairs	(202) 647-8714
Other Key Offices	
Agency Committee Management	(202) 647-3442
Congressional Liaison/Legislative Affairs	(202) 647-8198
Ethics in Government Act	(202) 647-3530
Fraud, Waste and Mismanagement Hotline	(800) 424-5454
In the Washington, DC area	(202) 633-6987
Freedom of Information/Privacy Act	(202) 647-3442
General Counsel	(202) 647-3582
Library	(202) 647-1592
Paperwork Reduction Act (ADP/IRM)	(202) 647-3708
Personnel	(202) 647-2035

Key Information Resources

Available **FREE** from the Office of Public Affairs are single copies of the ACDA annual report, *World Military Expenditures and Arms Transfers*, *Documents on Disarmament* and *Arms Control and Disarmament Agreements: Texts and Histories of Negotiations*.

Arms Control Fact Book

This guide is divided into three sections: Part I gives brief descriptions of arms control agreements and treaties, negotiations and other terms; Part II profiles organizations worldwide that are involved in arms control or disarmament; and Part III features a guide to acronyms, a chronology of events, recent U.S. legislation and data on foreign nations. 1985. 140pp. $15.95. ISBN 0-89950-180-X. (84-43243) McFarland & Co., P.O. Box 611, Jefferson, NC 28640; (919) 246-4460.

United States Information Agency

The United States Information Agency (USIA) conducts the U.S. Government's overseas information and cultural programs. The USIA is known overseas as the U.S. Information Service (USIS). Its goals are to strengthen foreign understanding of American society and to support United States policies. Approaches and methods to accomplish its goals include international radio broadcasting, motion pictures, television, exhibits, personal contacts, lectures and seminars, American Centers, libraries, English-language instruction, press placement, magazines and other publications, book translation and distribution, and assistance to foreign press and television journalists working in the United States. USIA also develops and administers international academic and cultural exchange programs. The Agency advises the President and various departments and agencies on worldwide public opinion and its relevance to the formulation and conduct of U.S. foreign policy. Fiscal year 1985 budget $694 million, or 0.074% of the total Federal budget; 8,369 paid employees, or 0.28% of the total civilian work force. (CFR references, Titles and Chapters: 22, V; 41, 19; 48, 19)

Key Offices and Telephone Numbers

Address: 400 C Street SW, Washington, DC 20547

General Information	(202) 647-8714
Personnel Locator	(202) 485-7700
Public/Consumer Information	
Office of Public Liaison	(202) 485-2355
Procurement Information	
Office of Contracts	(202) 485-6398
Competition Advocate	(202) 485-6058
Press Inquiries	
Office of Public Liaison	(202) 485-2355
Other Key Offices	
Agency Committee Management	(202) 485-8676
Congressional Liaison/Legislative Affairs	(202) 485-7976
Ethics in Government Act	(202) 485-7976
Fraud, Waste and Mismanagement Hotline	(800) 424-5454
In the Washington, DC area	(202) 633-6987
Freedom of Information/Privacy Act	(202) 485-7499
General Counsel	(202) 485-7976
Library	(202) 485-8922
Paperwork Reduction Act (ADP/IRM)	(202) 485-8676
Personnel	(202) 485-2618

Key Information Resources

The USIA is prohibited from distributing its program materials, except those exempted by congressional action, within the United States. On request, such materials are made available at the Agency for information purposes only. Lists of USIA research reports are available to various Federal depository libraries. Contact the USIA library for further information.

Available **FREE** from the Office of Public Liaison are the brochure *USIA in Brief* and various leaflets and fact sheets.

English Teaching Forum

A quarterly journal for the teacher of English outside the United States. Subscription price: $14.00 a year. Single copy price: $4.75. October issue: $7.50. GPO List ID ETF. (ICA 1.11:) See the GPO subscription order form.

Problems of Communism

A bimonthly magazine that provides analyses and significant background information on various aspects of world communism today. Subscription price: $16.00 a year. Single copy price: $2.75. GPO List ID PROC. (ICA 1.9:) See the GPO subscription order form.

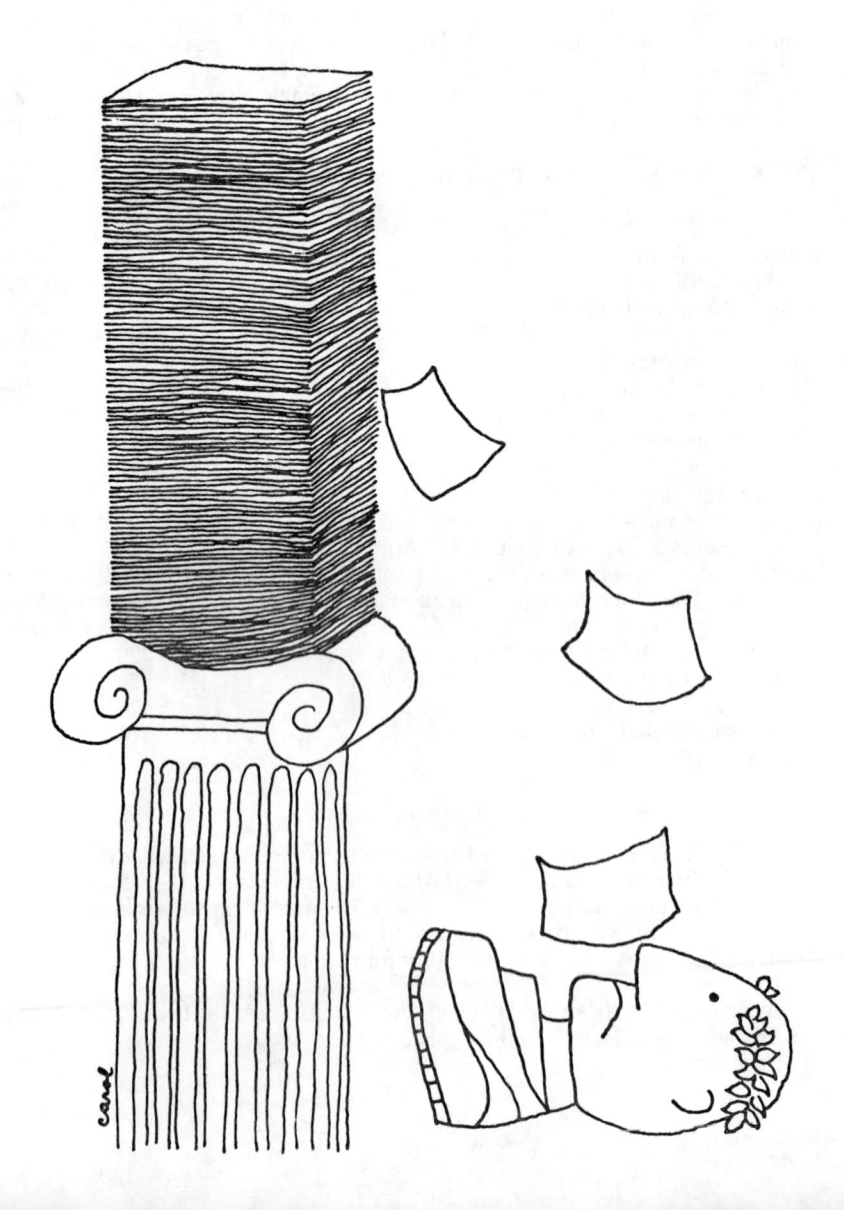

United States International Development Cooperation Agency

The U.S. International Development Cooperation Agency (IDCA) is the focal point within the Government for international economic matters affecting U.S. relations with developing countries. The agency helps ensure that development goals are taken into account in executive branch decision making on trade, financing and monetary affairs, technology and other economic policy issues affecting less developed nations. IDCA provides direction for U.S. bilateral development assistance programs and U.S. participation in multilateral development organizations. Three organizational components of IDCA that assist in carrying out its responsibilities are the Agency for International Development (AID), the Trade and Development Program (TDP), and the Overseas Private Investment Corporation (OPIC). Fiscal year 1985 budget $1,121 million, or 0.12% of the total Federal budget; 5,141 paid employees, or 0.11% of the total civilian work force. (CFR reference: Title 22, Chapter XII)

ICDA was established on October 1, 1979, through a reorganization plan. AID, OPIC and the TDP were legally transferred to the IDCA in 1979, but both the internal structure and operations of these agencies remained the same and operate independently of IDCA. For further information on AID or OPIC, see their respective entries in this chapter. Further information on the TDP may be obtained from the Assistant Director/Operations, Trade and Development Program, Room 309, State Annex 16, Washington, DC 20523; (703) 235-3663.

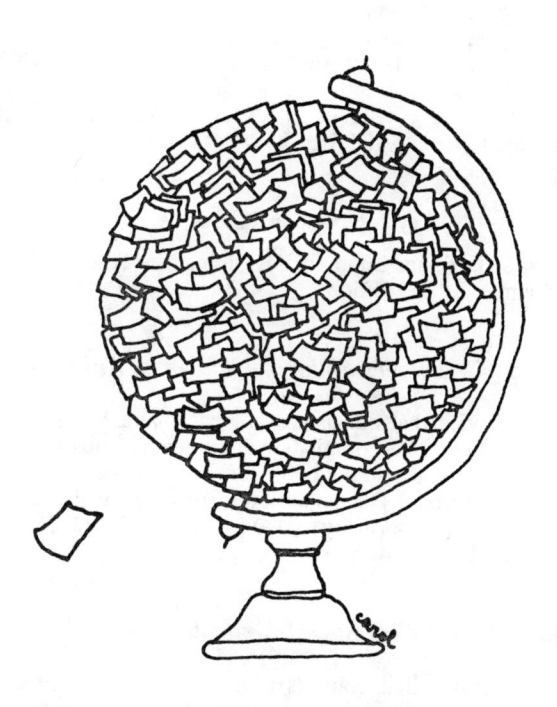

United States International Trade Commission

The U.S. International Trade Commission (ITC) investigates and reports to the President and Congress on matters involving international trade and tariffs. This includes advising them on the potential effect on American industry of proposed modification of import duties and other trade barriers, assessing the economic impact of changes in tariff preferences under the Generalized System of Preferences, and investigating possible injury to U.S. domestic industries of unfair trade practices by foreign countries. Fiscal year 1985 budget $20,970,000, or 0.0022% of the total Federal budget; 444 paid employees, or 0.015% of the total civilian work force. (CFR reference: Title 19, Chapter II)

Key Offices and Telephone Numbers

Address: 701 E Street NW, Washington, DC 20436

General Information and Personnel Locator	(202) 523-0161

Public/Consumer Information

Public and Consumer Affairs Office	(202) 523-0235
Trade Remedy Assistance Center	(202) 523-0488

Procurement Information

Office of Management Services	(202) 724-2741
Competition Advocate	(202) 523-0463

Press Inquiries

Public and Consumer Affairs Office	(202) 523-0235

Other Key Offices

Congressional Liaison/Legislative Affairs	(202) 523-0287
Ethics in Government Act	(202) 632-7642
Fraud, Waste and Mismanagement Hotline	(800) 424-5454
In the Washington, DC area	(202) 633-6987
Freedom of Information/Privacy Act	(202) 523-0161
General Counsel	(202) 523-0350
Library	(202) 523-0013
Paperwork Reduction Act (ADP/IRM)	(202) 523-4463
Personnel	(202) 523-0182

Key Information Resources

A **FREE** *Citizen's Guide* and brochure describing the ITC is available from the Public and Consumer Affairs Office.

History of the Tariff Schedules of the United States, Annotated

A subscription service that consists of a basic manual and supplementary material issued for a year. This compilation documents changes in the legal text of United States tariff schedules, including prospective changes and changes in statistical annotations through December 1980. Subscription price: $55.00 a year (priority), $43.00 a year (non-priority). GPO List ID HIST. (ITC 1.10/2:981) See the GPO subscription order form.

Tariff Schedules of the United States, Annotated

A subscription service that consists of a basic manual and supplemental material for an indeterminate period. The manual is for use in classification of

Executive Branch Agencies 303

imported merchandise for rate of duty and statistical purposes. It includes the legal text of the Tariff Schedules of the U.S., as amended and modified, together with annotations prescribing statistical information to be supplied on customs forms. In looseleaf form, punched for 3-ring binder. Subscription price: $56.00 (priority). GPO List ID TSA86. (ITC 1.10:986) See the GPO subscription order form.

United States Merit Systems Protection Board

The U.S. Merit Systems Protection Board (MSPB) is an independent, quasi-judicial agency set up to protect the integrity of Federal merit systems and the rights of Federal employees working in the systems. This includes protection against partisan political and other abuse and to ensure adequate protection for employees against unlawful abuses by agency management. In overseeing the personnel practices of the Federal Government, the Board conducts special studies of the merit system; hears and decides charges of wrongdoing and employee appeals of adverse actions; and orders corrective and disciplinary actions against an executive agency or employee when appropriate. The Office of the Special Counsel is an independent investigative and prosecutorial component of the MSPB. It investigates allegations of prohibited personnel practices, prohibited political activities by Federal and certain State and local employees, arbitrary or capricious withholding of information in violation of the *Freedom of Information Act*, and other activities prohibited by civil service laws, rules or regulations. The Special Counsel initiates disciplinary and corrective actions before the MSPB when warranted. Fiscal year 1985 budget $23 million, or 0.0025% of the total Federal budget; 450 paid employees, or 0.015% of the total civilian work force. (CFR reference: Title 5, Chapter II)

Key Offices and Telephone Numbers

Address: 1120 Vermont Avenue NW, Washington, DC 20419

General Information and Personnel Locator	(202) 653-7124
Public/Consumer Information	
Information Office	(202) 653-7125
Office of the Special Counsel	(800) 872-9855
In the Washington, DC area	(202) 653-7188
Procurement Information	
Contracts and Material Management Division	(202) 653-7654
Press Inquiries	
Information Office	(202) 653-7125
Other Key Offices	
Congressional Liaison/Legislative Affairs	(202) 653-7125
Ethics in Government Act	(202) 653-7168
Fraud, Waste and Mismanagement Hotline	(800) 872-9855
In the Washington, DC area	(202) 653-7188
Freedom of Information/Privacy Act	(202) 653-7168
General Counsel	(202) 653-7168
Paperwork Reduction Act (ADP/IRM)	(202) 653-8900
Personnel	(202) 653-7120

Key Information Resources

Available **FREE** from the MSPB Information Office are *Questions and Answers on the MSPB*, *How to File an Appeal with the MSPB* (also available in Spanish) and *Appeal Rights and Procedures*.

Executive Branch Agencies 305

United States Postal Service

The U.S. Postal Service (USPS) provides mail processing and delivery services to individuals and businesses within the United States. It is also responsible for the protection of the mails from loss or theft and for the apprehension of those who violate postal laws. The USPS operates nearly 40,000 post office branches, stations and community post offices. Fiscal year 1985 budget $1,210 million, or 0.13% of the total Federal budget; 714,054 paid employees, or 24.2% of the total civilian work force. (CFR reference: Title 39, Chapter I)

Key Offices and Telephone Numbers

Address: 475 L'Enfant Plaza SW, Washington, DC 20260-0010

General Information	(202) 268-2020
Personnel Locator	(202) 268-2000
Public/Consumer Information	
Public and Employee Communications Department	(202) 268-2164
Consumer Advocate	(202) 268-2281
Telephonic device for the deaf (TDD)	(202) 268-2310
Customer Services Department	(202) 268-2200
Chief Postal Inspector	(202) 268-4267
Office of Stamps and Customer Programs	(202) 268-2314
Philatelic Sales Branch	(703) 573-5416
Procurement Information	
Procurement and Supply Department	(202) 268-4040
Small Business Liaison Office	(202) 268-4632
Press Inquiries	
News Division	(202) 268-2164
Other Key Offices	
Congressional Liaison/Legislative Affairs	(202) 268-3733
Ethics in Government Act	(202) 268-2951
Fraud, Waste and Mismanagement Hotline	(800) 424-5454
In the Washington, DC area	(202) 633-6987
Freedom of Information/Privacy Act	(202) 268-2970
General Counsel	(202) 268-2951
Library	(202) 268-2904
Paperwork Reduction Act (ADP/IRM)	(202) 268-5256
Personnel	(202) 268-3466

Key Information Resources

Available **FREE** at your local post office is *A Consumer's Directory of Postal Services and Products* and other pamphlets on mailability, philatelic products, postage rates and fees, and access to the *National ZIP Code and Post Office Directory* (Publication 65).

Memo to Mailers

A monthly U.S. Postal Service (USPS) publication for customers originating significant quantities of mail. It contains information on USPS programs, automation topics and cost reduction benefits. **FREE.** Memo to Mailers, P.O. Box 1, Linwood, NJ 08221-0001.

The Postal Service Guide to U.S. Stamps

A guide to current pricing for single used and unused stamps, plate blocks and first day covers for most U.S. stamp issues. 1985, 12th ed. 312pp. $3.50. ISBN 0-9604756-5-6. Available at many post offices, philatelic centers and by mail from the Philatelic Sales Division, USPS, Washington, DC 20265-9997. Make check payable to the "U.S. Postal Service." For information about stamp collecting and a **FREE** catalog, write: U.S. Stamp Information Service, Philatelic Sales Division, USPS, Washington, DC 20265-9992.

USPS Subscription Services

The following is a list of USPS subscription services available from the Government Printing Office (GPO). For more detailed information, including order forms, consult *Government Subscription Services* (Price List 36), available **FREE** from the GPO. See the GPO subscription order form.

Administrative Support Manual
Domestic Mail Manual
Employee and Labor Relations Manual
Financial Management Manual
International Mail
Postal Bulletin
Postal Contracting Manual
Postal Life
Postal Operations Manual

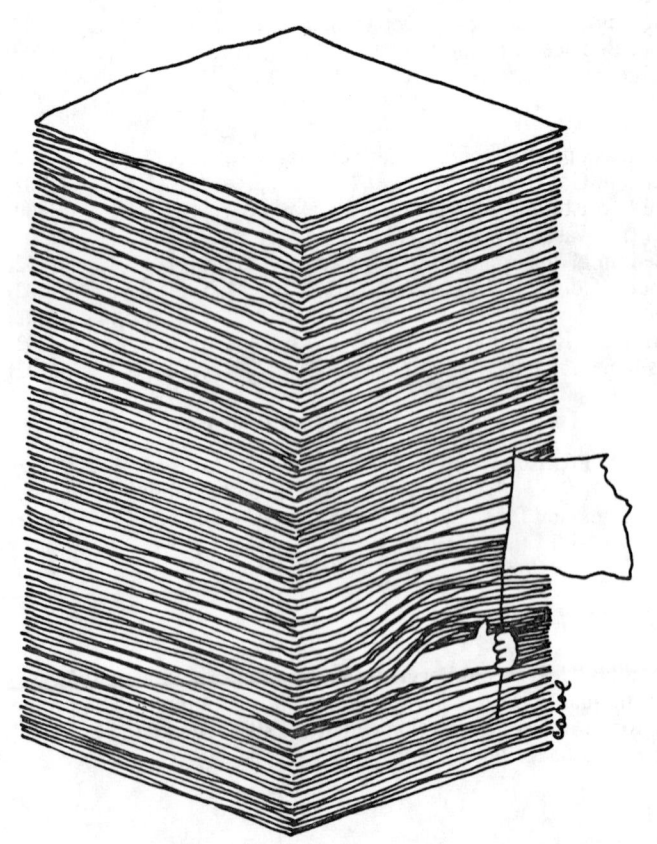

United States Railway Association

The U.S. Railway Association (USRA) authorizes and directs the maintenance of rail service in the Midwest and Northeast regions of the United States. The Railway Association developed and now implements a system plan that covers these two regions, whose goal is a financially self-sustaining, competitive, efficient, safe and environmentally sound rail service system. The system plan provided for the creation of the Consolidated Rail Corporation (Conrail). Fiscal year 1985 budget $3 million, or 0.00032% of the total Federal budget; 25 paid employees, or 0.00085% of the total civilian work force. (CFR reference: Title 49, Chapter IX)

Key Offices and Telephone Numbers

Address: 955 L'Enfant Plaza North SW, Washington, DC 20595

General Information and Personnel Locator	(202) 488-8777
Public/Consumer Information	
Public Affairs Office	(202) 488-8777
Procurement Information	
Facilities and Equipment	(202) 488-8777
Press Inquiries	
Public Affairs Office	(202) 488-8777
Other Key Offices	
Congressional Liaison/Legislative Affairs	(202) 488-8777
Ethics in Government Act	(202) 488-8777 Ext. 502
Fraud, Waste and Mismanagement Hotline	(800) 424-5454
In the Washington, DC area	(202) 633-6987
Freedom of Information/Privacy Act	(202) 488-8777
General Counsel	(202) 488-8777
Library	(202) 488-8777
Personnel	(202) 488-8777

Key Information Resources

Available **FREE** from the Public Affairs Office is a fact sheet on the USRA.

Veterans Administration

The Veterans Administration (VA) administers a system of benefits for military service veterans and their dependents. These benefits include compensation payments for disabilities or death related to military service, pension based on financial need for totally disabled veterans, education and rehabilitation, home loan guaranty, burial, and a medical program involving a widespread system of nursing homes, clinics and 172 medical centers. Fiscal year 1985 budget $26,333 million, or 2.31% of the total Federal budget; 241,929 paid employees, or 5.2% of the total civilian work force. (CFR references, Titles and Chapters: 38, I: 41, 8: 48, 8)

Key Offices and Telephone Numbers

Address: 810 Vermont Avenue NW, Washington, DC 20420

General Information	(202) 393-4120
Personnel Locator	(202) 389-3022
Public/Consumer Information	
Office of Public and Consumer Affairs	(202) 389-2741
Procurement Information	
Building and Supply Service	(202) 389-2798
Procurement Service	(202) 389-3054
Office of Small and Disadvantaged Business Utilization	(202) 376-6996
Competition Advocate	(202) 389-2247
Press Inquiries	
Office of Public and Consumer Affairs	(202) 385-2741
Other Key Offices	
Agency Committee Management	(202) 389-3113
Congressional Liaison/Legislative Affairs	(202) 389-2239
Ethics in Government Act	(202) 389-3671
Fraud, Waste and Mismanagement Hotline	(800) 368-5899
In the Washington, DC area	(202) 389-5394
Freedom of Information/Privacy Act	(202) 389-3616
General Counsel	(202) 389-3831
Library	(202) 389-3085
Paperwork Reduction Act (ADP/IRM)	(202) 389-5458
Personnel	(202) 389-2381

Key Information Resources

Available **FREE** from any VA regional office (see your telephone directory under "United States Government") is *A Summary of Veterans Administration Benefits*.

Federal Benefits for Veterans and Dependents

A handbook of the various benefits available to veterans and their dependents, including medical care, disability payments, education, home-loan guarantees, job training and burial assistance. Also includes a list of VA facilities—where to go for help and a list of medical centers for alcohol or drug dependence treatment. A 1986 edition is planned. 1985. 85pp. $2.50. GPO S/N 051-000-00170-2. (VA 1.34:Is 1/28) See the GPO order form.

Chapter 10
The Budget Process

The Federal budget is the principal policy statement by which an administration proposes to spend monies based on anticipated revenues. It is a statement of priorities as to which programs, organizations and functions will receive funding, and at what levels. When passed by the Congress and signed by the President, the budget becomes law. The amount of funds specified in the legislation is then legally binding for all Federal agencies for a given fiscal year (FY) (October 1 through September 30). Agencies may not spend more than is specified unless they are able to secure supplemental appropriations through the same legal channels as the original budget.

While Federal budgeting is a continuous process, it may be examined in four phases: (1) executive branch preparation and submission, (2) congressional action or the congressional budget process, (3) implementation and control of the enacted budget, and (4) review and audit. The Federal budget-making process is depicted in Figure 10-1, which summarizes the major steps in the process. Figure 10-2 presents a timetable for various phases of the congressional budget process, along with the actions that take place at each point. Figure 10-3 provides a summary of the FY85 Federal budget receipts and outlays, including relative percentages for each respective entry.

The information resources described in this chapter are organized under the following headings.

- General Information
- Executive Preparation and Submission
    Policy Directives
    OMB Technical Staff Papers
    Budget Documents, Fiscal Year 1987
- Congressional Budget Process
- Implementation and Control
- Review and Audit

General Information

A Glossary of Terms Used in the Federal Budget Process

A product of the General Accounting Office (GAO), with assistance from the Department of the Treasury, the Office of Management and Budget, and the Congressional Budget Office, this glossary provides a basic reference document of definitions for use by Congress, Federal agencies and all others interested in

310 FEDfind

SUMMARY OF MAJOR STEPS IN THE BUDGET PROCESS

Phase 1—Executive Preparation & Submission. (Beginning 19 months before fiscal year.)[1]

Phase 2—Congressional Budget Process. Includes action on appropriations and revenue measures. (Beginning 10-1/2 months before fiscal year.)[2]

Phase 3—Implementation & Control of Enacted Budget. (During fiscal year.)

Phase 4—Review & Audit

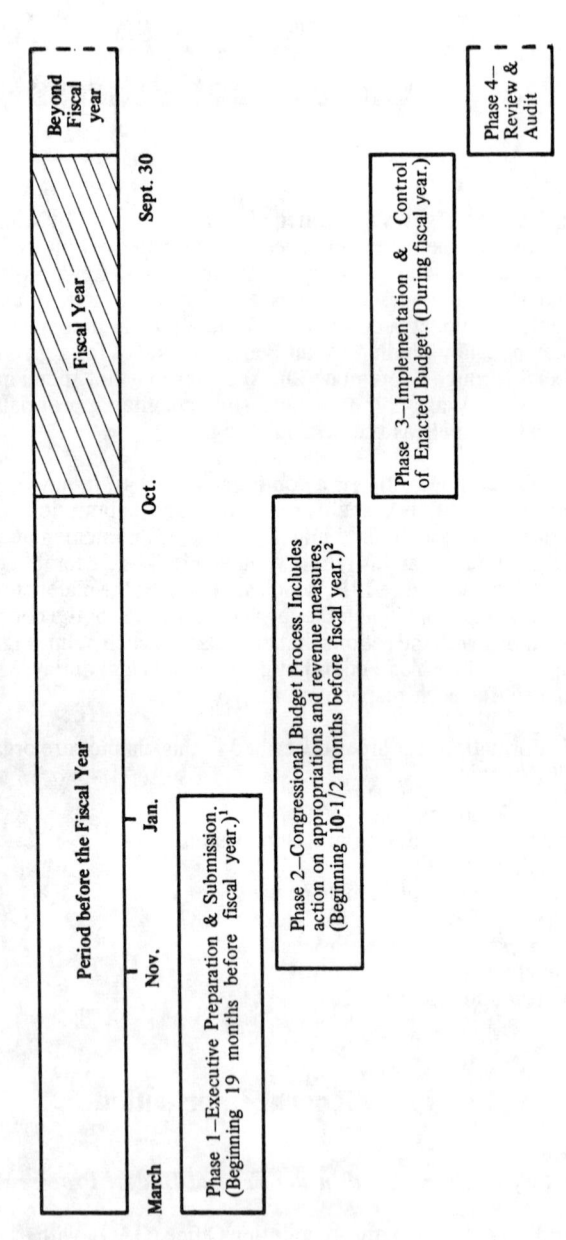

(Source: A Glossary of Terms Used in the Federal Budget Process, 3rd ed., 1981)

Figure 10-1. The Federal Budget-Making Process

First Monday after January 3 (FY 1987 President submits budget to Congress.
  budget only: February 5).

February 15	Congressional Budget Office (CBO) issues annual report to Budget Committees.
February 25	Committees submit views and estimates to Budget Committees.
April 1	Senate Budget Committee reports budget resolution.
April 15	Congress completes budget resolution.
June 10	House Appropriations Committee reports last annual appropriation bill.
June 15	Congress completes reconciliation.
June 30	House completes action on annual appropriation bills.
August 15	Office of Management and Budget (OMB) and CBO estimate deficit for upcoming fiscal year.
August 20	OMB and CBO submit report to Comptroller General.
August 25	Comptroller General submits report to President.
September 1	Initial Presidential reduction order issued (if required).
September 5	Deadline for President to propose reductions in defense contracts.
September 30	General Accounting Office (GAO) certification of outlay savings with respect to proposed defense contract reductions.
October 1	Initial Presidential reduction order effective; fiscal year begins.
October 5	OMB and CBO submit revised report to Comptroller General.
October 10	Comptroller General submits revised report to President.
October 15	Fiscal presidential reduction order issued (if required) and becomes effective.
September-October	Congressional alternative to Presidential order, if any, developed and adopted.
November 15	Comptroller General compliance report issued.

Figure 10-2. Congressional Budget Timetable

BUDGET RECEIPTS	Actual	Percent
Individual income taxes	$ 330,918	45.08%
Corporation income taxes	61,331	8.36
Social insurance taxes and contributions:		
Employment taxes and contributions	238,288	32.46
Unemployment insurance	25,758	3.51
Other retirement contributions	4,759	0.65
Excise taxes	35,865	4.89
Estate and gift taxes	6,422	0.87
Customs duties	12,079	1.65
Miscellaneous receipts	18,576	2.53
Total	733,996	100.00

BUDGET OUTLAYS		
Legislative Branch	1,610	0.17
The Judiciary	966	0.10
Executive Office of the President	111	0.02
Funds Appropriated to the President	11,277	1.20
Department of Agriculture	49,596	5.29
Department of Commerce	2,140	0.23
Department of Defense—Military	244,054	26.05
Department of Defense—Civil	18,844	2.01
Department of Education	16,682	1.78
Department of Energy	10,186	1.09
Department of Health and Human Services	315,553	33.68
Department of Housing and Urban Development	28,671	3.06
Department of the Interior	4,828	0.52
Department of Justice	3,518	0.38
Department of Labor	23,893	2.55
Department of State	2,645	0.28
Department of Transportation	25,087	2.68
Department of the Treasury:		
General revenue sharing	4,584	0.49
Interest on the public debt	178,945	19.10
Other	−18,486	−1.97
Environmental Protection Agency	4,511	0.48
General Services Administration	−214	−0.02
National Aeronautics and Space Administration	7,318	0.78
Office of Personnel Administration	23,727	2.53
Small Business Administration	283	0.03
Veterans Administration	26,333	2.81
Other independent agencies	9,121	0.97
Allowances, undistributed	—	—
Undistributed offsetting receipts:		
Other interest	−2	−0.0002
Employer share, employee retirement	−27,359	−2.92
Interest received by trust funds	−26,070	−2.78
Rents and royalties on the Outer Continental Shelf lands	−5,542	−0.59
Total	936,809	100.0
Budget surplus (+) or deficit (−)	−202,813	
Off-budget surplus (+) or deficit (−)	−9,118	
Total surplus (+) or deficit (−)	−211,931	

Figure 10-3. Summary of Receipts and Outlays of the U.S. Government, Fiscal Year 1985 (in millions)

the process of Federal budget making. Frequent changes in the definitions of terms requires caution in the use of the glossary. Definitions provided in official documents take precedence over those in the glossary. Relevant accounting, economic and tax terms are also defined to help the user appreciate the dynamics of the process. The document presents an overview of the Federal budget process and diagrams the roles of the key organizational elements relative to the time frame in which the process takes place. Included as appendices are the budget functional classification system used for analyzing and understanding the budget, an explanation of the budget account identification code and program and financing schedule, and a bibliography. 1981, 3rd ed. 136pp. **FREE**. GAO report number PAD-81-27. See the GAO order form.

Financial Management Functions in the Federal Government

This publication describes the functions of the key agencies in the Federal Government responsible for providing financial and management guidance to operating agencies involved in the Federal budgeting process. The material on Federal budgeting summarizes the procedures followed in the annual preparation and execution of the Federal budget; provides an awareness of the checks and balances built into the process, including the respective roles of the key agencies and offices of the executive and legislative branches; and promotes an understanding of the forms and terminology associated with the Federal budget process. A chapter is dedicated to each of the following agencies and offices: Office of Management and Budget, Department of the Treasury, Office of Personnel Management, General Services Administration, General Accounting Office, Congressional Budget Office, Cost Accounting Standards Board and Joint Financial Management Improvement Program (JFMIP). 1986. **FREE**. approx. 120pp. JFMIP, 666 11th Street NW, Suite 705, Washington, DC 20001; (202) 376-5415.

Financial Handbook for Federal Executives and Managers

A handbook written to help the nonfinancial manager understand financial management, it was designed to promote a closer working relationship among financial and nonfinancial managers. In nontechnical terms, the handbook provides information on the functions of the "central agencies," budget preparation, administrative control of funds, accounting systems, financial reporting, internal controls, cash management/debt collection, assuring proper payments, productivity and performance measurement, special cost studies, property and inventory, Federal assistance programs, procurement, auditing, and training and development of financial staff. A "Suggested References" list is provided with most of the subjects cited above. 1984. 64pp. **FREE**. JFMIP, see entry above.

Financial Management Directory

An annual personnel directory published to foster improved communications among financial managers in the Federal Government. Former Joint Financial Management Improvement Project executive director Susumu Uyeda recommends in the foreword that "the Directory be used in establishing a financial manager's network on a continuous basis to learn from other's experience and knowledge, thereby eliminating the need to reinvent the wheel over and over again." The directory is organized alphabetically by department/agency. For each management position, it includes organizational affiliation and address, a general telephone number for the agency, and the individual's name, job title and telephone number. September 1985. 151pp. **FREE**. JFMIP, see entry above, *Financial Handbook*. . . .

Executive Preparation and Submission

Managing the Cost of Government: Building an Effective Financial Management Structure

A two-volume report prepared by the General Accounting Office (GAO), this document explains the Comptroller General of the United States' view that a major overhaul of the Federal Government's financial management structure is needed, and discusses the elements of a new system. *Volume I: Major Issues* highlights selected major problem areas in the current Federal Government financial management process, the direction reform might take, and steps needed to initiate reform. *Volume II: Conceptual Framework* discusses further the issues raised in the first volume. 1985. Volume I, 23pp., **FREE**, GAO report number AFMD-85-35. Volume II, 65pp., **FREE**, GAO report number AFMD-85-35-A. See the GAO order form.

Public Budgeting and Finance

A quarterly publication cosponsored by the American Association for Budget and Program Analysis (AABPA) and the Section on Budgeting and Financial Management of the American Society for Public Administration, this journal includes articles on public sector budgeting, program analysis, finance and related fields. The journal covers Federal, State and local government issues. Members of the AABPA receive the journal **FREE**. Subscription price: $25.00 a year for institutes, $15.00 a year for individuals. AABPA, P.O. Box 1157, Falls Church, VA 22041; (703) 941-4300.

Policy Directives

The following Executive Office of the President (EOP) directives, arranged in numerical order, are available **FREE** from EOP Publications, 726 Jackson Place NW, Room 2200, Washington, DC 20503; (202) 395-7332.

Responsibilities for Disclosure with Respect to the Budget

This Office of Management and Budget (OMB) Circular No. A-10 provides guidance on responsibilities for disclosure of information with respect to the preparation of the President's budget. The circular is applicable to those budget documents transmitted annually by the President to Congress and to communications concerning the formulation of the budget and related documents, as well as to budget amendments, supplemental estimates, and other proposals for the granting of new obligational authority that are transmitted after the transmission of the original budget. It does not apply to the budget requests of the legislative and judicial branches of Government. 1976, with change transmittals. 5+pp. **FREE**. EOP Publications, see the introduction to this section.

Preparation and Submission of Budget Estimates

This annually issued Office of Management and Budget (OMB) Circular No. A-11 provides instructions for the preparation of annual budgets for all agencies of the Government and privately owned (Government sponsored) enterprises. These include the legislative branch and the judiciary. Issued in June or July. **FREE**. EOP Publications, see the introduction to this section.

Object Classification

This Office of Management and Budget (OMB) Circular No. A-12 prescribes the classification system used in recording the Federal Government's financial transactions by objects. The object classification provides a method of recording the financial transactions in terms of the nature of the services or articles for which obligations are first incurred, rather than in terms of the purpose or program served. This classification is used in the preparation of the object classification schedule for submission of budget estimates to OMB. 1977, with change transmittals. 60pp. FREE. EOP Publications, see the introduction to this section.

Distribution of Appropriations and Other Budget Authority Made to the President

This Office of Management and Budget (OMB) Circular No. A-31 sets forth procedures for the distribution of appropriations and other budget authority made to the President. It also lists the agencies that coordinate or make allocations from these appropriations and other budget authority. 1972, with change transmittals. 4+pp. FREE. EOP Publications, see the introduction to this section.

Instructions on Budget Execution

This Office of Management and Budget (OMB) Circular No. A-34 provides instructions on budget execution, i.e., financial plans, apportionments, reapportionments, deferrals, proposed and enacted recissions, systems for administrative control of funds, allotments, operating budgets, and reports on budget execution. All appropriations, funds, and other authorizations, except deposit funds, are subject to the circular. The Director of OMB may substitute alternative requirements for those included in the circular upon written notification to the agency or agencies involved. 1976, with change transmittals. 89pp. FREE. EOP Publications, see the introduction to this section.

Position Management Systems and Employment Ceilings

This Office of Management and Budget (OMB) Circular No. A-64 establishes guidelines for the uniform development, implementation and administration of position management programs. It also sets forth information on the concepts and procedures to be followed with regard to employment ceilings, their observance and related reporting to the OMB. Beginning with the fiscal year 1982 budget, all non-defense agencies have prepared estimates relating to personnel requirements in terms of full-time equivalent (FTE) employment as specified in OMB Circular No. A-11, *Preparation and Submission of Budget Estimates*. 1980. 12pp. FREE. EOP Publications, see the introduction to this section.

Federal Credit Policy

This Office of Management and Budget (OMB) Circular No. A-70 establishes Federal Government policies and guidelines that agencies are to follow in proposing or reviewing legislation to establish credit programs; in reviewing existing credit program legislation and proposing changes in such legislation; in evaluating congressional and other proposals on credit; and in reviewing existing credit programs and establishing or changing policies for managing those programs. 1984. 16pp. FREE. EOP Publications, see the introduction to this section.

Discount Rates to be Used in Evaluating Time-Distributed Costs and Benefits

This Office of Management and Budget (OMB) Circular No. A-94 prescribes a standard discount rate to be used in evaluating the measurable costs and/or benefits of programs or projects when they are distributed over time. The circular applies to all agencies of the executive branch of the Federal Government except the U.S. Postal Service. The discount rates prescribed are required for use in program analyses submitted to OMB in support of legislative and budget programs. 1972. 6pp. FREE. EOP Publications, see the introduction to this section.

Monitoring Federal Outlays

This Office of Management and Budget (OMB) Circular No. A-112 provides instructions for the preparation and submission of reports designed to assist in the continuing effort to monitor Federal spending. Each executive department or agency is required to prepare a monthly outlay plan for each new fiscal year along with periodic reports on the progress relative to that plan. The reports are identical to the coverage in the annual budget documents and include outlay information for all appropriations and funds, except deposit funds, administered by the department or agency. 1976. 9pp. FREE. EOP Publications, see the introduction to this section.

Financial Management Systems

This Office of Management and Budget (OMB) Circular No. A-127 prescribes policies and procedures to be followed by executive branch agencies in developing, operating, evaluating and reporting on financial management systems. It requires each agency to establish and maintain a single, integrated financial management system, which may be supplemented by subsidiary systems, that meets a series of basic objectives. The objectives include systems operations, system integrity, support for budgets, support for management and full financial disclosure. 1984. 11pp. FREE. EOP Publications, see the introduction to this section.

Managing Federal Credit Programs

This Office of Management and Budget (OMB) Circular No. A-129 prescribes policies and procedures for managing Federal credit programs and for collecting loans and other receivables. It sets standards for extending credit, servicing accounts, collecting delinquent receivables and writing off uncollectible accounts. The circular builds upon the policies in OMB Circular No. A-70, *Policies and Guidelines for Federal Credit Programs,* that establish standards for proposing, reviewing and evaluating credit programs. 1985. 25pp. FREE. EOP Publications, see the introduction to this section.

OMB Technical Staff Papers

The Office of Management and Budget (OMB) has produced a series of technical staff papers that explain treatment of various fiscal transactions in the budget, methods for deriving budget estimates and similar topics. The documents are intended to aid budget technicians and other users by increasing their understanding of how the budget is assembled. The papers are the responsibility of the authors and do not imply endorsement or review by OMB. Copies of the following papers may be obtained from the OMB, Fiscal Analysis Branch, 726 Jackson Place NW, Room 6025, Washington, DC 20503; (202) 395-3945.

Title	Date	Number
The Budget in Constant Dollars	7/01/75	BRD/FAB 75-1
Automatic Cost-of-Living Increases in Federal Programs	7/30/75	BRD/FAB 75-2
Federal Pay Raise Projections	7/30/75	BRD/FAB 75-3
The Catalog of Federal Domestic Assistance	7/30/75	BRD/FAB 75-4
The OMB Model to Project Interest on the Public Debt	8/11/75	BRD/FAB 75-5
Method of Projecting Outlays for Unemployment Assistance	10/01/75	BRD/FAB 75-6
The OMB Long Range Projection System	12/12/75	BRD/FAB 75-8
The Federal Financing Bank and the Budget	1/26/76	BRD/FAB 76-1
Overview of the Current "State-of-the-Art" of Federal Outlay Estimating	12/15/77	BRD/BPB 77-1
The Functional Classification in the Budget (1979 Revision)	2/22/79	BRD/FAB 79-1
Payment for Individuals	11/26/79	BRD/FAB 79-2
Sensitivity of Federal Expenditures to Unemployment	4/18/80	BRD/FAB 80-1
Impact of Changing Demographic Patterns on Future Housing Needs: 1980–2000	7/23/80	SS/EG 80-1
The Effects of Population Change on the Budget: Demographic Background	7/31/80	BRD/FAB 80-2

Budget Documents, Fiscal Year 1987

Budget of the United States Government, Fiscal Year 1987

This document is President Ronald Reagan's fiscal year 1987 budget proposal. It contains the President's budget message; an overview of his budget proposals; explanations of national needs, agency missions and basic programs; an analysis of estimated receipts, including the President's tax program; a description of the budget system; and summary tables on the budget as a whole. February 1986. Enquire of GPO for price, etc. (PrEx 2.8/987) See the GPO order form.

United States Budget in Brief, Fiscal Year 1987

An abridged version of the above proposal, this document provides a concise, non-technical overview of President Ronald Reagan's budget proposals. It includes summary and historical tables on the Federal budget. A chapter on the budget process and a glossary of terms are also included. February 1986. Enquire of GPO for price, etc. (PrEx 2.8/987/brief) See the GPO order form.

Budget of the United States Government, Fiscal Year 1987, Appendix

This document provides detailed information on the various appropriations and funds that comprise the budget. This includes the following for each agency: the proposed text of appropriation language, budget schedules for each account, new legislative proposals, explanations of the work to be performed and the funds needed and proposed general provisions applicable to the schedules of permanent positions. February 1986. Enquire of GPO for price, etc. (PrEx 2.8/987/app.) See the GPO order form.

Special Analyses, Budget of the United States Government, Fiscal Year 1987

An 11-part series that provides analyses of alternative views of the budget, i.e., current services and national income accounts; economic and financial analyses of the budget as a whole; and Government-wide information on selected programs financed by the Federal budget. February 1986. Enquire of GPO for price, etc. (PrEx 2.8/5:987) See the GPO order form.

Historical Tables, Budget of the United States Government, Fiscal Year 1987

A new annual budget document that provides data on budget receipts, outlays, surpluses or deficits, and Federal debt covering extended time periods. The tables include various combinations of budget components in current prices, constant prices, and as percentages of the budget totals and of the gross national product. Most data cover the time period 1940 through 1990. February 1986. Enquire of GPO for price, etc. (PrEx 2.8/8:987) See the GPO order form.

Management of the United States Government, Fiscal Year 1987

This new annual budget document describes the Administration's program to improve the management of the Federal Government. Part 1 of the report, The

President's Management Improvement Program: Reform '88, includes sections on eliminating fraud, waste and abuse; controlling the cost of administering Federal programs; financial management; productivity initiatives; Federal information technology; and program delivery improvements. Part 2 discusses the role that the Congress plays—and the initiatives it takes—in improving Government operations. Appendices include management improvements and savings targeted by Congress and a status report on the recommendations of the President's Private Sector Survey on Cost Control, i.e., the Grace Commission. February 1986. Enquire of GPO for price, etc. (PrEx 2.8/9:987) See the GPO order form.

Budget Tapes, Fiscal Year 1987

The Budget of the United States—Fiscal Year 1987, as submitted by President Ronald Reagan in February 1986, includes three magnetic tape files. The Master Account Title File contains the identification codes for all appropriation accounts; the agency, bureau, and appropriation account titles; and a complete cross-reference of all Office of Management and Budget appropriation accounts to the Treasury identification codes. The Receipt Account Title File contains titles and codes related to the receipt accounts in the budget. The Budget Preparation System Master File contains approximately 48,000 records that provide the financial input to the production of the tables and analyses of the budget. Annual. February 1986. $140.00, includes the publication *Budget Preparation System—1987 Budget Tape Documentation*. Enquire of NTIS for price, etc. See the NTIS order form.

Economic Report to the President

An annual report prepared for the President by the Council of Economic Advisors, this volume presents the full text of President Ronald Reagan's report to the Congress on the economic condition of the Nation. The report also covers economic topics such as inflation, unemployment, economic growth, international currency activities, wage and price stability, Government spending and more. An appendix of more than 100 statistical tables relating to income, employment and production is included. February 1986. Enquire of GPO for price, etc. (Pr 40.9:986) See the GPO order form.

An Analysis of the President's Budgetary Proposals for Fiscal Year 1987

An annual analysis by the Congressional Budget Office (CBO) prepared at the request of the Senate Committee on Appropriations, this document provides Members with an overview of President Ronald Reagan's budgetary proposals for fiscal year 1987. The report describes the problem of chronic budget deficits faced by the Federal Government under existing tax laws and current spending programs, and describes the Administration's proposals for dealing with the problem. It discusses the economic outlook and the assumptions used for the 1987 budget. The report also presents the CBO's re-estimates of the budgetary impact of the Administration's proposals based on alternative economic assumptions and on CBO's technical estimating methods and programmatic assumptions. An analysis of major budget increases proposed for national defense programs is included. February 1986. approx. 152pp. **FREE**. CBO Publications, Room 413, House Annex No. 2, Second and D Streets SW, Washington, DC 20515; (202) 226-2809.

Guide to the Federal Budget, Fiscal 1987 Edition

An annual guide to the current fiscal year 1987 budget proposal and the steps that will determine it, this book describes those steps, explains their significance, details the procedures under which they will probably take place, identifies steps that may fall by the wayside, and lists the important decision makers involved at each stage. The guide also explains how to read and use the FY 1987 budget and includes descriptions of each of the five major budget documents submitted by the President to Congress. March 1986. 171pp. $10.00. ISBN 0-87766-331-9. ISSN 0730-9511. (82-643840) The Urban Institute, P.O. Box 19958, Baltimore, MD 21211; (301) 388-6951.

Federal Budget Report

This biweekly newsletter provides an objective, nonpartisan view of congressional and Presidential budget activities. Included are special reports on selected budget topics and controversies, e.g., a guide to supplemental appropriations, an explanation of the various "alternative" tax systems (flat tax, consumption tax, value-added tax, etc.) that are under consideration in Washington, and an analysis of the relationship between the deficit and monetary policy. Edited by Stanley E. Collender. Subscription price: $245.00 a year. Federal Budget Report, 1900 M Street NW, Suite 200, Washington, DC 20036; (202) 955-4278.

Congressional Budget Process

Congressional Budget and Impoundment Control Act of 1974

This Act (Public Law 93-344) amended the *Budget and Accounting Act of 1921*, created new procedures for the reporting and treatment of impounded funds, established a new budgetary timetable and created the Congressional Budget Office (CBO). The Act is intended: (1) to assume effective congressional control over the budgetary process; (2) to provide for the congressional determination each year of the appropriate level of Federal revenues and expenditures; (3) to provide a system of impoundment control; (4) to establish national budget priorities; and (5) to provide for the furnishing of information by the executive branch in a manner that will assist the Congress in discharging its duties. 1974. Superintendent of Documents. Out-of-print. See the next entry.

Balanced Budget and Emergency Deficit Control Act of 1985

This Act (Public Law 99-177), known as the Gramm-Rudman-Hollings amendment after its chief Senate sponsors, amends the *Congressional Budget and Impoundment Control Act of 1974*, described above. It sets a strict timetable for achieving a balanced Federal budget by fiscal year 1991. Deficit targets are established for each fiscal year, starting with 1986. In the event that the deficit is anticipated to exceed the required levels for any fiscal year, an automatic deficit reduction procedure would be used to achieve across-the-board reductions in the Federal budget of non-exempt programs. The *Congressional Budget and Impoundment Control Act of 1974*, as amended by Public Law 99-177, is available from the House or Senate Budget Committees, see entries below.

The Congressional Budget Process: A General Explanation

A committee print of the House Committee on the Budget, this document provides an introduction to and overview of the congressional budget process. It includes chapters entitled: Why a Budget?; Need for Budget Reform; Background of Budget Reform; House and Senate Budget Committees; Congressional Budget Office; Congressional Budget Process; Budget Information, Program Evaluation, and Effective Dates; Impoundment Control; Economics and the Budget Process; and the *Congressional Budget and Impoundment Control Act of 1974* (Public Law 93-344, as amended. Attachments to the booklet include: Congressional Budget Process Timetable, Functional Classification Codes and Program Categories, First Concurrent Resolution on the Budget for Fiscal Year 1985 (Conference Report), Terms Used in the Federal Budget Process, House Rules Relating to the Budget Act, and House Precedents Interpreting the Congressional Budget Act. 1985. A revision is planned for 1986 that reflects Public Law 99-177, see entry above. 199pp. FREE. House Budget Committee, 214 House Annex No. 1, Washington, DC 20515; (202) 226-7217.

The Congressional Budget Process: How It Works

A Committee print that provides a general explanation of the budget process as established with the enactment of the *Congressional Budget and Impoundment Control Act of 1974* (Public Law 93-344), as amended by the *Balanced Budget and Emergency Deficit Control Act of 1985* (Public Law 99-177). The document includes, among other things, a historical table of action on budget resolutions, examples of budget resolution language and a glossary of budget terms. 1986. 24pp. FREE. Senate Budget Committee, 820 Hart Building, Washington, DC 20510; (202) 224-3024.

Implementation and Control

Principles of Federal Appropriations Law

Federal funds are made available for obligation and expenditure by means of appropriations acts (or occasionally by other legislation) and subsequent administrative actions that release appropriations to the spending agencies. This manual presents the basic principles of appropriations law, as well as a discussion of the statutes and regulations and significant decisions rendered by the Comptroller General, head of the General Accounting Office (GAO), and the courts. Prepared by the staff of the Office of General Counsel, GAO, it is intended for use by GAO staff, other Government agencies, congressional staff and the public. 1982. 1,011pp. $22.00. GPO S/N 020-000-00211-5. (GA 1.14:F 31) See the GPO order form.

Daily Treasury Statement, Cash and Debt Operations of the United States Treasury

A subscription service, this source provides current information on the outlays/expenditures and receipts of funds relative to the current budget year, as well as the debt position of the U.S. Government. The components of this periodical are each sold separately as monthly subscriptions, as described below. Published daily except Saturdays, Sundays and holidays. Subscription price: $110.00 a year; no single copies sold. GPO List ID DTS. (T 1.5:) See the GPO subscription order form.

Monthly Statement of the Public Debt of the United States

This subscription service provides current figures on the debt position of the U.S. Government. Subscription price: $25.00 a year; no single copies sold. GPO List ID MSPD. (T 1.5:) See the GPO subscription order form.

Monthly Treasury Statement of Receipts and Outlays of the United States Government

This subscription service provides current information on the outlays/expenditures and receipts of funds relative to the current budget year. Subscription price: $27.00 a year; no single copies sold. GPO List ID MTSRO. (T 1.5:) See the GPO subscription order form.

Federal Expenditures by State for Fiscal Year 1985

An annual publication that reports on Federal expenditures for State and territories shown by program and agency outlays, whenever possible. Coverage includes Federal Government expenditures for grants to State and local governments, salaries and wages, procurement, direct payments for individuals and other programs for which data were available by State and territory. Expenditure amounts not provided in this report include such data as net interest on the Federal Government debt, international payments and foreign aid, current operational expenses not included under salaries or procurement, and expenditures for selected Federal agencies (such as the Central Intelligence Agency

[CIA] and National Security Agency [NSA]). This publication is part of the *Consolidated Federal Funds Report* (CFFR) series. March 1986. approx. 63pp. **FREE**. Governments Division, Bureau of the Census, Washington, DC 20233; (301) 763-7366.

Consolidated Federal Funds Report, Fiscal Year 1984

The *Consolidated Federal Funds Report* (CFFR) is an annual compilation of Federal Government expenditures or obligations in State, county and subcounty areas of the United States, including U.S. territories and the District of Columbia. This report replaces the discontinued *Geographic Distribution of Federal Funds* reports compiled by the Community Services Administration (dismantled in 1981). Volume I of the CFFR presents data by State and county area. Coverage includes all Federal Government finance object categories: grants, salaries and wages, procurement, direct payments for individuals, other direct payments, direct loans, guaranteed or insured loans and insurance. Amounts reported were $731.2 billion for fiscal year 1984. Excluded from CFFR coverage are such items as interest on the Federal Government debt, travel expenses when not provided under contract, and international payments and foreign aid. Volume II presents data by State, county area and municipal or township government. Coverage is limited to the object categories of grants, procurement, direct loans, guaranteed loans and insurance. Statistics for other categories were not available at the subcounty level of detail. All data in Volumes I and II of the CFFR are presented by object category, with some detail for defense/nondefense breakdowns. Geographic detail of Federal expenditures on a program basis is provided in *Federal Expenditures by State for Fiscal Year 1985* described above. The entire CFFR data file is available on magnetic computer tape from the Data User Services Division, Bureau of the Census, Washington, DC 20233; (301) 763-4100. Volume I, March 1985, 97pp., is available **FREE** from the Governments Division, Bureau of the Census, Washington, DC 20233; (301) 763-7366. Volume II, March 1985, 559pp., $18.00. GPO S/N 003-024-06201-1, (C 3.266/2:984/v.2) See the GPO order form.

United States Government Annual Report and Appendix

These Treasury Department documents are the official publication of the details of receipts and outlays with which all other reports containing similar data must be in agreement. The annual report presents budgetary results at the summary level. The appendix presents the individual receipt and appropriation accounts at the detail level. It is used by the Congressional Budget Office in serving the needs of Congress; the Office of Management and Budget in reviewing the President's Budget programs; the General Accounting Office in performing its audit activities; the various departments and agencies of the Government in reconciling their accounts; and the general public in reviewing the operations of their Government. Published annually in December for the period covering the prior fiscal year. **FREE**. Financial Management Service, Department of the Treasury, Washington, DC 20226.

Facts and Figures on Government Finance

This subscription service, updated quarterly, presents current and historical data on revenue, expenditures, debt and tax rates of Federal, State and local government, and related economic factors. Also included is a topical index and glossary. March 1986, 23rd edition. 364pp. ISBN 0-9606762-8-7. (44-7109) $75.00, includes four quarterly updates. Tax Foundation, Inc., One Thomas Circle NW, Suite 500, Washington, DC 20005; (202) 822-9050.

Review and Audit

See Chapter 11, "Program Administration and Evaluation," for materials related to this aspect of the budget process.

Chapter 11
Program Administration and Evaluation

The term "program"—as used with respect to U.S. Government operations—is defined generally as an organized set of activities directed toward a common purpose or goal, undertaken or proposed by an agency to carry out its responsibilities. Federal programs are increasing in complexity—both in relation to world and national affairs and State and local interests—and the requirement for accountability has heightened demand for information about the programs. Public officials, legislators and private citizens want to understand more about the operations of their Government. There is a growing need to know if Government funds are being handled properly and in compliance with laws and regulations, whether agencies are achieving the purposes for which their programs were authorized and funded, and whether they are doing so economically and efficiently.

For administrative purposes, the Government has classified its programs that address national needs using 16 budget categories. Three additional categories are included to round out the complete budget. This budget functional classification system, including subfunctions, is outlined in Figure 11-1. For budgetary purposes, each Federal activity is included in one primary category, although many activities serve more than one purpose. *A Glossary of Terms Used in the Federal Budget Process*, described in the first section of Chapter 10, provides definitions of the terms.

The Government Printing Office (GPO) makes available **FREE** the subject bibliography (SB) *Accounting and Auditing* (SB-42) that lists the publications for sale by GPO in this area. See the GPO SB order form.

The information resources described in this chapter are organized under the following headings.

- Policy Directives
- Congressional Sourcebook Series
- Program Catalogs
- Program Operations
- Program Evaluation

Administration of Justice
  Federal Law Enforcement Activities
  Federal Litigative and Judicial Activities
  Federal Correctional Activities
  Criminal Justice Assistance

Allowances
  Civilian Agency Pay Raises
  Contingencies for Specific Requirements
  Contingencies for Relatively Uncontrollable Programs
  Contingencies for Other Requirements

Agriculture
  Farm Income Stabilization
  Agricultural Research and Services

Commerce and Housing Credit
  Mortgage Credit and Thrift Insurance
  Postal Service
  Other Advancement and Regulation of Commerce

Community and Regional Development
  Community Development
  Area and Regional Development
  Disaster Relief and Insurance

Education, Training, Employment, & Social Services
  Elementary, Secondary and Vocational Education
  Higher Education
  Research and General Education Aids
  Training and Employment
  Other Labor Services
  Social Services

Energy
  Energy Supply
  Energy Conservation
  Emergency Energy Preparedness
  Energy Information, Policy and Regulation

General Government
  Legislative Functions
  Executive Direction and Management
  Central Fiscal Operations
  Central Property and Records Management
  Central Personnel Management
  Other General Government

General Purpose Fiscal Assistance
  General Revenue Sharing
  Other General Purpose Fiscal Assistance

General Science, Space and Technology
  General Science and Basic Research
  Space Flight
  Space Science, Applications and Technology
  Supporting Space Activity

Figure 11-1. Budget Functional Categories

Health
  Health Care Services
  Health Research
  Education and Training of the Health Care Workforce
  Consumer and Occupational Health and Safety

Income Security
  General Retirement and Disability Insurance
  Federal Employee Retirement and Disability
  Unemployment Compensation
  Housing Assistance
  Food and Nutrition Assistance
  Other Income Security

Interest
  Interest on the Public Debt
  Other Interest

International Affairs
  Foreign Economic and Financial Assistance
  Military Assistance
  Conduct of Foreign Affairs
  Foreign Information and Exchange Activities
  International Financial Programs

National Defense
  Department of Defense—Military
  Atomic Energy Defense Activities
  Defense-Related Activities

Natural Resources and Environment
  Water Resources
  Conservation and Land Management
  Recreational Resources
  Pollution Control and Abatement
  Other Natural Resources

Transportation
  Ground Transportation
  Air Transportation
  Water Transportation
  Other Transportation

Undistributed Offsetting Receipts
  Employer Share, Employee Retirement
  Interest Received by Trust Funds
  Rents and Royalties on the Outer Continental Shelf

Veterans Benefits and Services
  Income Security for Veterans
  Veterans Education, Training and Rehabilitation
  Hospital and Medical Care for Veterans
  Veterans Housing
  Other Veterans Benefits and Services

Figure 11-1. Budget Functional Categories—Continued

Policy Directives

The following Executive Office of the President (EOP) directives, arranged in numerical order, are available **FREE** from EOP Publications, 726 Jackson Place NW, Room 2200, Washington, DC 20503; (202) 395-7332.

Audit Followup

This Office of Management and Budget (OMB) Circular No. A-50 provides the policies and procedures for use by executive branch agencies when considering reports issued by the Inspectors General (IG), other executive branch audit organizations, the General Accounting Office (GAO) and non-Federal auditors where followup is necessary. The circular requires that each agency establish systems to assure the prompt and proper resolution and implementation of audit recommendations. 1982. 8pp. **FREE.** EOP Publications, see the introduction to this section.

Audit of Federal Operations and Programs

This Office of Management and Budget (OMB) Circular No. A-73 sets forth policies to be followed in the audit of Federal operations and programs. The primary objectives of the circular are to promote improved audit practices, achieve more efficient use of audit staff, improve coordination of audits, and require application of audit standards issued by the Comptroller General, the head of the General Accounting Office (GAO). 1983. 5pp. **FREE.** EOP Publications, see the introduction to this section.

Federal Domestic Assistance Program Information

This Office of Management and Budget (OMB) Circular No. A-89 provides the basis for a systematic and periodic collection and uniform submission of information on all federally financed domestic assistance programs to the OMB by Federal agencies. It also establishes Federal policies related to the delivery of this information to the public, including through the use of electronic media. 1984. 7pp. **FREE.** EOP Publications, see the introduction to this section.

Internal Control Systems

This Office of Management and Budget (OMB) Circular No. A-123 prescribes policies and standards to be followed by executive branch agencies in establishing, maintaining, evaluating, improving and reporting on internal controls in their program and administrative activities. Internal controls is the plan of organization and methods and procedures adopted by management to provide reasonable assurance that obligations and costs are in compliance with applicable law; funds, property and other assets are safeguarded against waste, loss, unauthorized use or misappropriation; and revenues and expenditures applicable to agency operations are properly recorded and accounted for to permit the preparation of accounts and reliable financial and statistical reports and to maintain accountability over the assets. 1983. 10pp. **FREE.** EOP Publications, see the introduction to this section.

Audit Requirements for State and Local Governments

Pursuant to the *Single Audit Act of 1984* (Public Law 98-502), this Office of Management and Budget (OMB) Circular No. A-128 establishes audit requirements for State and local governments that receive Federal aid and defines Federal responsibilities for implementing and monitoring those requirements. The circular supersedes Attachment P, "Audit Requirements," of OMB Circular No. A-102, "Uniform Requirements for Grants to State and Local Governments." 1985. 13pp. FREE. EOP Publications, see the introduction to this section.

Congressional Sourcebook Series.

The General Accounting Office (GAO) produces the *Congressional Sourcebook Series* to assist congressional analysts identify sources of Federal Government information. Publication of the source information in this series is required by the *Congressional Budget Act of 1974* (Public Law 93-344). The series consists of the following directories: (1) *Requirements for Recurring Reports to the Congress*, (2) *Federal Evaluations*, and (3) *Federal Information Sources and Systems*. Each volume includes information compiled through Government-wide inventories, and is divided into two sections, citations and index. For each entry in the citation section, there is a range of information that includes issuing agency, standard bibliographic information, a descriptive abstract, budget and program data, authorizing legislation, congressional recipients, geographic coverage and public availability. Indexes include subject, title (just for *Federal Information Sources and Systems*), agency, Congressional committee, legal reference, Federal budget functional category and program (except for *Requirements for Recurring Reports to the Congress*).

Requirements for Recurring Reports to the Congress

Part of the GAO's *Congressional Sourcebook Series*, this directory cites reports required of Federal departments and agencies on a recurring basis in addition to voluntary reports. It describes approximately 2,300 statutory and non-statutory reporting requirements, and enables Congress to determine if a reporting requirement exists before legislating a new one. 1985. 790pp. $20.00. GAO report number AFMD-85-4. Copies of this directory are available **FREE** to the Congress; Federal, State and local government agencies; members of the press; and academic libraries. Others must prepay by check made payable to the "Superintendent of Documents." See the GAO order form.

Federal Evaluations

Part of the GAO's *Congressional Sourcebook Series*, this directory identifies evaluative studies of Federal programs and activities conducted by or for executive agencies and the GAO. The most recent directory describes approximately 2,200 program and management evaluations prepared Government-wide between April 1, 1983, and March 31, 1984. 1985. 752pp. $19.00. GAO report number AFMD-85-2. Copies of this directory are available **FREE** to the Congress; Federal, State and local government agencies; members of the press; and academic libraries. Others must prepay by check made payable to the "Superintendent of Documents." See the GAO order form.

Federal Information Sources and Systems

Part of the GAO's *Congressional Sourcebook Series*, this directory provides descriptions of major information sources (facilities and publications) and systems containing fiscal, budgetary and program-related information on the Federal agency programs they support. It includes approximately 2,500 such sources and systems and is designed to aid in accessing data on programs or policies. 1985. 1,041pp. $24.00. GAO report number AFMD-85-3. Copies of this directory are available **FREE** to the Congress; Federal, State and local government agencies; members of the press; and academic libraries. Others must prepay by check made payable to the "Superintendent of Documents." See the GAO order form.

Congressional Information Sources Inventories and Directories Data Base

The CISID Data Base is comprised of computer files from which the *Congressional Sourcebook Series* is derived. The database may be accessed online at two locations. At the General Accounting Office (GAO), outputs may be generated for GAO personnel based on various selection criteria from the CISID files. SCORPIO (Subject-Content-Oriented-Retriever-for-Processing-Information-Online) terminals of the Library of Congress' Congressional Research Service are available to congressional staff who may browse, search and display all citations.

Program Catalogs

Catalog of Federal Domestic Assistance

The CFDA is a compendium of Federal Government programs, projects, services and activities that provide assistance or benefits to individuals, corporations, nonprofit organizations, and State and local governments. It covers financial and nonfinancial assistance programs administered by departments and establishments of the Federal Government. As the basic reference source of Federal programs, the primary purpose of the CFDA is to assist users in identifying programs that meet objectives of the potential applicant, and to obtain general information on Federal assistance programs. In addition, the intent of the CFDA is to improve coordination and communication between the Federal Government and State and local governments. The General Services Administration (GSA) maintains a Federal assistance information database (see next entry) from which program information for this catalog is obtained. Subscription service consists of a basic manual and supplementary material for one year. In looseleaf form, punched for 3-ring binder. June 1985, 19th ed. Subscription price: $36.00. GPO List ID COFA. (PrEx 2.2:F31/2/984) (73-600118) See the GPO subscription order form.

Federal Assistance Programs Retrieval System

A computerized question/answer information retrieval system, FAPRS provides information on Federal loan, grant and other assistance programs intended to help individuals or communities meet their needs. Based on the input supplied, the FAPRS output consists of the titles and identifying numbers of the applicable Federal programs from the *Catalog of Federal Domestic Assistance* (see entry above). After a review of this list of programs, additional information may be retrieved by (1) referring directly to the *Catalog* for specific information on a program, (2) obtaining from the system a complete program description by program number(s), (3) requesting the system to print desired sections of program descriptions, or (4) obtaining a list of applicable Office of Management and Budget circular coordination requirements for each program. For further information on FAPRS, the location of the nearest State access point, or a list of the timesharing companies from which one may arrange for direct access to the system, contact the Federal Program Information Branch, General Services Administration (KHED), Washington, DC 20405; (202) 453-4126.

Federal Benefit Programs: A Profile

A General Accounting Office (GAO) staff study that profiles 150 Federal benefit programs that provide cash or noncash assistance to persons demonstrating need or who qualify for benefits as a result of either contributions made by them or on their behalf or military service. These programs spent more than $400 billion in Federal tax dollars in fiscal year 1983, excluding administrative costs, or about 49 percent of the United States Budget. For 91 selected programs, the study provides financial and other related data; describes their purposes, who is eligible for them and the benefits available; and identifies the Federal agencies that administer them and the congressional committees that oversee them. October 17, 1985. 102pp. FREE. GAO report number HRD 86-14. See the GAO order form.

Government Assistance Almanac 1985–86

A guide to Federal programs available to the American public. The 1,013 programs include grants, loans, insurance and other forms of financial assistance, as well as technical assistance, advisory services, investigation of complaints, training, and the sale, donation, exchange, or use of Federal property, facilities and equipment. Included for each program is a brief description of its purpose and allowable uses; basic information about who's eligible to apply for or benefit from the program; and, for financial assistance, the range and average amounts of aid in recent years. Tables list funding levels for each program during the last four fiscal years (FY) (October 1 through September 30), both by program and by Federal department or agency, and the 50 largest and 50 smallest programs in FY 85. Included is a section that offers advice on seeking Federal assistance and an extensive 100-page index. By J. Robert Dumouchel. 1985. 597pp. $19.95 plus $3.50 shipping and handling. ISBN 0-934891-00-1. ISSN 0883-8690. (85-16253) Foggy Bottom Publications, P.O. Box 57150, Washington, DC 20037; (202) 337-4352.

Federal Assistance Award Data System Users Guide

The Federal Assistance Award Data System (FAADS) is a computer-based collection of information on Federal financial assistance award transactions. All major departments and agencies with grant-making authority report information for incorporation in the FAADS. This guide describes the nature and scope of the system. Detailed descriptions of the data elements, output record and computer tape format are provided. Typical information includes the name and location of the recipient, amount of Federal funding (generally on an obligations basis), project description, and the Federal program under which funding has been awarded. It is the objective of the FAADS to expand coverage to include all Federal Government financial assistance awards included in the *Catalog of Federal Domestic Assistance* (CFDA), as well as financial assistance awards made by Federal agencies but not included in the CFDA. The Bureau of the Census serves as the executive agent responsible for operating the FAADS. Policy oversight is provided by the Management Reform Division of the Office of Management and Budget. For a copy of this guide or the location of the nearest State access point, contact the Governments Division, Bureau of the Census, Washington, DC 20233; (301) 763-5276.

A Catalog of Federal Grant-in-Aid Programs to State and Local Governments: Grants Funded FY 1984

This volume is the third update of an original inventory that covered congressional action from January 1, 1978, through December 31, 1980. The current update provides a snapshot of the scope and major features of Federal grant programs as of the end of fiscal year 1984 (September 30, 1984). Included for each of the 534 grant-in-aid programs in the catalog are budget subfunction and title, U.S. Code reference, grant type, recipient's maximum allotment formula factor(s), Federal share, responsible agency, *Catalog of Federal Domestic Assistance* number. December 1985. 48pp. $4.75. Report number M-139. Advisory Commission on Intergovernment Relations, 1111 20th Street NW, Suite 2000, Washington, DC 20575; (202) 653-5536.

Encyclopedia of U.S. Government Benefits

A reference work that describes services and benefits available from the Federal Government intended to help individuals, this encyclopedia is organized alphabetically, primarily by benefit classification rather than by department, agency or act of legislation initiating the benefit. Cross-references are used to assist the user in locating benefits easily. 1985, 3rd ed. 476pp. $22.45. ISBN 0-396-08438-9. Dodd Mead, P.O. Box 141000, Nashville, TN 37214; (800) 251-4000 or (800) 821-4370.

Getting Yours: The Complete Guide to Government Money

This guide contains descriptions of grant, loan and other money programs available from the Federal Government. Prepared by Matthew Lesko, the book provides information on how businesses, individuals and organizations may use these programs. For each program, the book provides information on type of assistance, applicant eligibility, objective and contact (name, address and telephone number). 1984, 2nd ed. 292pp. $7.95. ISBN 0-14-046652-5. (84-60953) Viking Penguin Inc., Attn: Direct Mail Order Dept., 299 Murray Hill Parkway, E. Rutherford, NJ 07073; (800) 631-3577 or (212) 337-5200.

Program Operations

Budget and Program Newsletter

A weekly newsletter that concentrates on Federal Government program and budget issues, this publication addresses such questions as what is happening in the world of program evaluation, how budget-cutting will affect specific programs, how program managers can have maximum impact, what new program changes are in the mill, etc. Also, several information-related issues are addressed, such as what reorganization plans are underway, how the merit pay system can affect you, and various other concerns of individuals interested in following these types of issues. Subscription price: $125.00 a year. Budget and Program Newsletter, P.O. Box 6269, Washington, DC 20015; (202) 881-1777.

Program Evaluation

Standards for Audit of Governmental Organizations, Programs, Activities & Functions

This General Accounting Office (GAO) document provides audit standards that must be followed by Federal auditors when auditing Federal organizations, programs, activities, functions and funds received by contractors, nonprofit organizations and other external organizations. These standards relate to the scope and quality of the audit effort and to the characteristics of professional and meaningful audit reports. The three elements of expanded scope auditing covered in the standards are financial and compliance, economy and efficiency, and program results. The Office of Management and Budget (OMB) has cited the standards, commonly known as the "Yellow Book," in OMB circulars as basic audit criteria for Federal executive departments and agencies to follow. Federal legislation requires that Inspectors General follow these standards. A third edition is to be published in 1986. 1981, 2nd ed. 89pp. $4.75. GPO S/N 020-000-00205-1. (GA 1.14:Au 2/981) Since issuing the standards in 1972, GAO has issued publications explaining and supplementing the standards, demonstrating how auditing can improve the efficiency and effectiveness of Government operations and programs. These publications, with their respective publication year, pagination and GPO S/N, are listed below. See the GPO order form.

Audit Standards Supplement Series

Auditors: Agents for Good Government, 1973, 6pp., $3.00, 020-000-00109-7.

Benefits of Expanded Scope Auditing at the Local Level, 1979, 10pp., $2.75, 020-000-00179-8.

Case Study—How Auditors Develop Findings—Increasing the Productivity of City Water Meter Readers, 1976, 17pp., $3.25, 020-000-00134-8.

Examples of Findings from Governmental Audits, 1973, 33pp., $4.25, 020-000-00115-1.

Illustrative Report Prepared in Accordance with GAO Audit Standards—Air Pollution Control Program, Sassafras County, Maryland, 1975, 50pp., $4.50, 020-000-00128-3.

Joint Audit: Lessons Learned, 1980, 17pp., $3.25, 020-000-00182-8.

The Audit Survey—A Key Step in Auditing Government Programs, 1978, 15pp., $3.00, 020-000-00158-2.

Using Auditing to Improve Efficiency and Economy, 1976, 40pp., $3.00, 020-000-00133-0.

Using Broad Scope Auditing to Serve Management (Out-of-print).

What GAO is Doing to Improve Government Auditing Standards (Out-of-print).

CARE Audit Methodology

A General Accounting Office (GAO) manual describing its Controls and Risk Evaluation (CARE) audit methodology. CARE is an audit approach to identify and evaluate the adequacy of controls in the accounting systems of an agency and determine the degree of conformance of these systems with the Comptroller General's accounting principles, standards and other requirements. The publication is comprised of an executive summary, a work program and a series of eight appendices. The work program is for operational financial management and audit staffs who manage the reviews and evaluations of systems. The appendices provide detailed guidance to financial management and audit staff who review and evaluate systems. July 1985. 600pp. **FREE**. GAO accession number 127570. See the GAO order form.

Evaluating Federal Programs: An Overview for the Congressional User

This pamphlet was written by the General Accounting Office (GAO) to aid the congressional user who is somewhat familiar with approaches for evaluating current and proposed programs, but who needs general guidelines or helpful hints for improving the usefulness of evaluative information. Though originally designed for the congressional user, others may find it helpful. 1976. 16pp. **FREE**. GAO report number PAD-76-30. See the GAO order form.

Standards for Internal Controls in the Federal Government

Developed by the General Accounting Office (GAO), these standards are to be followed by executive agencies in establishing and maintaining systems of internal control as required by the *Federal Managers' Financial Integrity Act of 1982* (31 U.S. Code 3512[b]). Internal control systems are intended to provide reasonable assurance that the following objectives are achieved: obligations and costs comply with applicable law; all assets are safeguarded against waste, loss, unauthorized use and misappropriation; revenues and expenditures applicable to agency operations are recorded and accounted for properly so that accounts and reliable financial and statistical reports may be prepared and accountability of the assets may be maintained. 1983. 12pp. **FREE**. GAO accession number 122341. See the GAO order form.

Program Administration and Evaluation 333

Efforts to Prevent Fraud, Waste and Mismanagement

A semiannual progress report to the President, by the President's Council on Integrity and Efficiency (PCIE), that describes the continuing effort of the Inspectors General to reduce waste, fraud and abuse and improve the management of the Federal Government. Second six months, fiscal year 1985, January 1986. approx. 24pp. $1.75. GPO S/N 040-000-00480-7. (Pr 40.8:In 8/M 68) See the GPO order form. Available **FREE,** as long as supply lasts, from the Office of Communications and Public Liaison, Executive Office of the President, 726 Jackson Place NW, Room 6235, Washington, DC 20503; (202) 395-7381.

We Can Blow the Whistle on Government Waste

A report that summarizes a few of the 2,478 recommendations made by the President's Private Sector Survey on Cost Control (Grace Commission) for reducing Federal Government waste, inefficiency and fiscal excess. 1985. 20pp. Single copy **FREE**. Citizens Against Government Waste, P.O. Box 1000, Washington, DC 20044; (800) USA-DEBT.

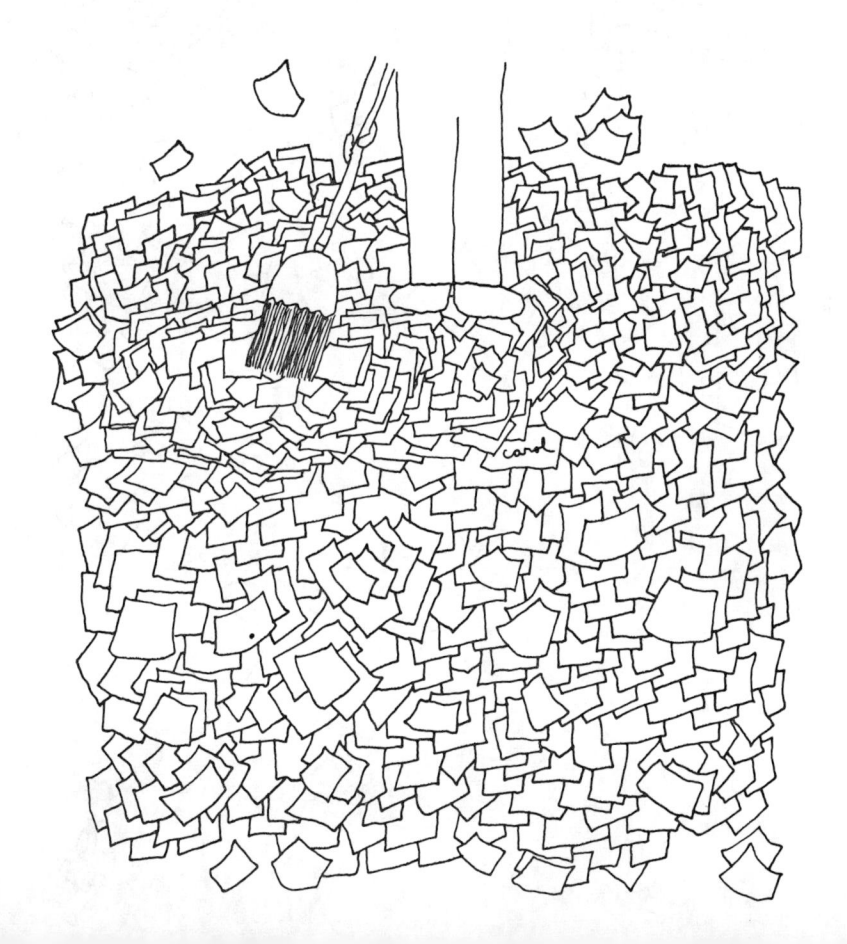

334 **FEDfind**

Chapter 12
Statistical Programs

The United States Government collects and publishes a wide array of statistics that cover a broad range of subjects. A total of some $1.5 billion is spent annually on activities related to gathering, compiling, analyzing and disseminating Federal statistics. Among the topics for which statistical information is available are manufacturing, trade, agriculture, demographics, energy, health care, education, law enforcement and criminal justice. Information is made available regularly on general economic activities and trends, the supply of raw materials, the production of market products, prices and markets, and many other subjects of more specialized interest. This information is used by the public, academia and the professions, as well as by the Federal Government for decision-making purposes.

The many functions of the Federal Government are divided among various agencies and the statistics necessary for the performance of these functions generally are developed within those agencies. In addition, many different acts of Congress direct certain agencies to collect specific kinds of statistical information. In fact, the origin of Federal data collection activity may be traced back to the Constitution of the United States, which required an enumeration of the population within three years after the first meeting of the Congress and every 10 years thereafter.

The information resources described in this chapter are organized under the following headings.
- Central Coordinating Office
- Statistics—Future, Present and Past
- Selected Information Sources
- Subject Bibliographies
- Independent Organizations

The ten most prolific statistics-producing agencies are listed below. Each is described in detail in Chapter 8, "Executive Branch Departments," under its respective department.

Agriculture
  Statistical Reporting Service (SRS)

Commerce
  Bureau of the Census
  Bureau of Economic Analysis (BEA)

Education
  Center for Statistics (CS)

Energy
  Energy Information Administration (EIA)

Health and Human Services
  National Center for Health Statistics (NCHS)
  Office of Research, Statistics and International Policy, Social Security Administration

Justice
  Bureau of Justice Statistics (BJS)

Labor
  Bureau of Labor Statistics (BLS)

Treasury
  Statistics of Income Division, Internal Revenue Service

Although Federal Government statistics are produced in a decentralized system, a central coordinating organization exists to provide general policy guidance on the development of an integrated statistical system to meet Federal data needs. This coordinating function is managed by the Statistical Policy Office, Office of Information and Regulatory Affairs (OIRA), in the Office of Management and Budget (OMB).

Central Coordinating Office

The Office of Management and Budget's (OMB) Statistical Policy Office is responsible for: (1) ensuring the uniformity of statistics across agencies, through common definitions and standards such as the Standard Industrial Classification (SIC) and the Metropolitan Statistical Area (MSA); (2) overseeing the quality of statistical data through periodic revision or updating of major surveys such as the Consumer Price Index and Current Population Survey; (3) improving the efficiency of data collection and analysis through greater interchange of data among agencies, elimination of duplicative surveys, and introduction of innovative survey techniques; and (4) improving the accessibility of Federal statistics to the public.

The Statistical Policy Office was established within OMB's Office of Information and Regulatory Affairs (OIRA) in August 1981, following passage of the *Paperwork Reduction Act of 1980* (Public Law 96-511). OMB's Statistical Policy Office is the successor to the Office of Federal Statistical Policy and Standards, Department of Commerce, and to predecessor organizations in OMB concerned with statistical policy. OIRA issues an annual report on Federal statistics, described below.

Federal Statistics: A Special Report on the Statistical Programs and Activities of the United States Government—Fiscal Year 1986

Prepared by the Statistical Policy Office of the Office of Management and Budget's (OMB) Office of Information and Regulatory Affairs (OIRA), this annual report covers the major statistical agencies whose sole mission is to compile and publish statistics, as well as the components of other Federal agencies whose statistical work is conducted to support program missions. The report provides information on dollar obligations for statistical activities in 1984, 1985 and 1986 for each of the Federal agencies, and describes major programs and activities, highlighting changes under way or planned for 1986. Major developments during the period 1982-1986 are discussed under three broad areas of statistics: natural resources and environment, economic, and social and demographic. Other material provided includes information on funding of Government statistical programs through interagency agreements and highlights of two initiatives in the Treasury and Labor Departments to reform the management of statistical resources. June 1985. 52pp. FREE, while supplies last. Statistical Policy Office, OIRA, OMB, 726 Jackson Place NW, Room 3001, Washington, DC 20503; (202) 395-3093. Also from the National Technical Information Service (NTIS) for $11.95 in paper or $5.95 for microfiche, NTIS order number PB85-232049/GBD. See the NTIS order form.

Statistics—Future, Present and Past

The Federal Statistical System 1980 to 1985

A Congressional Research Service (CRS) report, prepared by Baseline Data Corporation, Inc. under contract to CRS, that provides a review of the status of the Federal statistical system, highlighting major developments in recent years. The study examines the activities of the Office of Management and Budget (OMB) in executing the statistical policy and coordination provisions of the *Paperwork Reduction Act of 1980* (Public Law 96-511, Section 3504), as well as major statistical activities in 26 agencies. Provided also are details with respect to budgets, personnel resources and policies in various Federal agencies responsible for the collection and analysis of statistical information. November 1984. 284pp. FREE. A companion CRS report, also prepared for the House Committee on Government Operations, is *An Update on the Status of Major Statistical Agencies: Fiscal Year 1986*, May 1985, 88pp. Contact your Member of Congress by mail at U.S. House of Representatives, Washington, DC 20515 or U.S. Senate, Washington, DC 20510, or through the U.S. Capitol switchboard, (202) 224-3121.

Status of the Statistical Community After Sustaining Budget Reductions

A General Accounting Office (GAO) staff study that reviews the changes that nine of the more prominent Federal statistical agencies made to accommodate the Reagan Administration's first term budget reductions. The study discusses the rationale used by the agencies in deciding on the changes and provides information on users' reactions to the changes. July 18, 1984. 61pp. FREE. GAO report number IMTEC-84-17. See the GAO order form.

Developments in United States Federal Statistics, 1979–1981

Prepared by the Office of Information and Regulatory Affairs (OIRA) for the 15th session of the Committee on Improvement of National Statistics (held

November 1981 in Santiago, Chile), this report reviews important developments in the statistical programs of the major Federal statistical agencies and briefly describes their activities and some data products. 1981. 36pp. FREE. A companion publication covering 1981-1983 is also available from OIRA, Office of Management and Budget, 726 Jackson Place NW, Room 3001, Washington, DC 20503; (202) 395-3093.

A Framework for Planning U.S. Federal Statistics for the 1980's

This study reviews the organization and operations of the Federal statistical agencies, individual statistical programs and crosscutting issues, and makes recommendations for their improvement. Information is included on the agencies that produce data on particular subjects, and the data series and products that result. These statistical subject areas include agriculture; construction; criminal justice; economic accounts; education; energy; finance; health; housing; income maintenance and welfare; income, wealth, and consumption; labor; population; price; production and distribution; science and technology; environment and occupational safety and health; and transportation. The following crosscutting issues in statistics are covered: standards development; civil rights data; confidentiality; Federal-State-local cooperative systems of data collection; industrial directory, interagency funding, international statistics; longitudinal surveys; long-term economic growth models; reporting burden; multipurpose sample vehicles; professional staffing; statistical methodology; social indicators; and user access to Federal data. 1978. 440pp. $11.00. GPO S/N 003-005-00183-2. (C 1.2:F 84/2) See the GPO order form.

Revolution in United States Government Statistics, 1926-1976

Developments in important areas such as sampling applications, national income accounts, use of computers, and coordinating mechanisms during the 50-year period covered are traced in this document. The final chapter considers major issues unresolved as of 1976, leading to the topics addressed in *A Framework for Planning U.S. Federal Statistics for the 1980's*, discussed above. 1978. 257pp. Out-of-print. GPO S/N 003-005-00181-6. (C 1.2:St 2/10/926-76)

Selected Information Sources

Statistical Policy Handbook

A document of directives for the conduct of Federal statistical activities, information about interagency committees that have a significant role in Federal statistics and selected statistical publications. Directives provide standards and guidelines for such activities as statistical surveys and publications, release of statistical information, industrial and occupational classifications race and ethnic categories for Federal statistics, metropolitan statistical area classifications and definition of poverty for statistical purposes. 1978. 85pp. $5.50. Out-of-print. GPO S/N 003-005-00179-4. (C 1.8/3:St 2/2)

State Data Center Program

In cooperation with State governments, the Census Bureau administers a network of 44 State Data Centers that offer facts and figures from the Bureau, other Federal agencies and State sources. Each State Data Center is designed to serve the information needs of community leaders, local government officials, the business community, the news media—anyone who needs to know more about the social and economic characteristics of a State, county, city or neighborhood. Copies of each census publication, microfiche, map and summary computer tape produced for a State are provided free to the appropriate State Data Center. The materials include the Bureau's population and housing census reports as well as extensive reports from its economic censuses in such areas as retail and wholesale trade, manufacturing, construction, agriculture, services and transportation. A listing of the centers appears in *State Data Center Program State Coordinating Organizations*, available **FREE** from Customer Services, Data User Services Division, Bureau of the Census, Washington, DC 20233; (301) 763-4100.

Statistical Abstract of the United States 1985

Compiled annually by the Census Bureau, this basic reference document contains summary statistics from governmental and nongovernmental sources on the industrial, social, political and economic organizations of the United States. It is designed to serve as a convenient volume for statistical reference and as a guide to other statistical publications and sources. March 1985. 1,019pp. Paper cover, $19.00, GPO S/N 003-024-06136-8; cloth cover, $23.00, GPO S/N 003-024-06135-0. (C 3.134:985) See the GPO order form.

Reflections of America

This publication commemorates the 100th edition (1879–1979) of the *Statistical Abstract of the United States*, an annual that over the years has provided a measurable description of the Nation's growth. It is a volume of essays that go behind the figures to an assessment of some of the principal changes that have taken place in American society since the first *Abstract* appeared in 1879. Each author has interpreted the *Abstract* and commented on the particular relevance of statistical change in his or her special field. The fields, a chapter on each, include agriculture, arts, attitudes, business, cities, classes, communications, conservation, crime, economy, education, employment and income, health, housing, international relations and trade, minorities, population, poverty, quality of life, transportation, voting and women. 1980. 212pp. $10.00. GPO S/N 003-024-02921-9. (C 3.2:Am 3/5) See the GPO order form.

American Statistics Index

A guide and index to more than 500 statistical publications of the Federal Government. The ASI is published in two parts: index and abstracts. The index section contains a number of separate indexes that include subjects and names, categories, publication titles and agency report numbers. The publications abstracts provide bibliographic data, a description of the publication's subject matter and purpose, and an outline of specific contents (e.g., tables, articles, etc.) with references to specific page numbers in the original sources. A "base edition" provides selective coverage of publications from the early 1960s through January 1974. ASI annuals provide cumulative coverage of each subsequent year. Monthly updates, to be used with the most recent annual, index and abstract each entirely new periodical, and only new articles, special tables, and format changes of established periodicals. Every third monthly index is also a quarterly cumulation. Enquire for price information. Congressional Information Service, Inc., 4520 East-West Highway, Suite 800, Bethesda, MD 20814; (800) 638-8380 or (301) 654-1550.

Data Map: Index of Published Tables of Statistical Data

An index to statistics in more than 10,000 tables in 29 standard reference sources, 17 of which are Federal Government sources. Using its subject index, the user may identify the title of the table and the publication and page number where it may be found. Revised annually to include current editions of annual statistical publications. June 1986, 3rd ed. approx. 912pp. $150.00. ISBN 0-89774-293-1. (85-43552) Oryx Press, 2214 North Central at Encanto, Phoenix, AZ 85004; (800) 457-ORYX or (602) 254-6156.

Schedule of Release Dates for Principal Federal Economic Indicators for 1986

An annual news release of the Office of Management and Budget (OMB), this schedule provides a calendar of target dates for the release of principal economic indicators such as the producer price index, consumer price index, employment situation, leading indicators, etc. Telephone numbers of issuing agencies are included to aid in making direct inquiries. December 1985. 25pp. $9.95 for paper copy or $5.95 for microfiche. NTIS order number PB86-130705/GBD. See the NTIS order form.

Compilation, Release and Evaluation of Principal Federal Economic Indicators

The revised Statistical Policy Directive No. 3 clarifies and strengthens Office of Management and Budget (OMB) guidance to Federal agencies on the compilation and release of principal economic indicators. It includes more stringent procedures for announcing changes in data collection, analysis and estimation methods, and it adds a new requirement for periodic evaluation of the performance of each economic indicator. *Federal Register*, September 25, 1985, Vol. 50, No. 186, pp. 38932-38934.

Economic Indicators

Prepared monthly by the Joint Economic Committee, this publication provides economic information on prices, wages, production, business, activity, purchasing power, credit, money and Federal finance. Subscription price: $27.00 a year. Single copy price: $2.50. GPO List ID ECIN. (Y 4.Ec 7:) See the GPO subscription order form.

Supplement to Economic Indicators: Historical and Descriptive Background

An explanatory text and historical data for each series that appears in the monthly *Economic Indicators*. The supplement is prepared for the Joint Economic Committee of Congress by the Council of Economic Advisers. 1980. 148pp. Out-of-print. (Y 4.Ec 7:Ec 7/980/supp.)

Congressional Research Service—CRS Stats Line

The Library of Congress Congressional Research Service (CRS) Stats Line is a recorded message that gives current figures for selected economic indicators. The indicators listed are Consumer Price Index (CPI), Federal Deficit, Gross National Product (GNP), Housing Starts, Prime Rate, Public Debt, Unemployment, and U.S. Merchandise Trade Balance. The recording is updated weekly. CRS Stats Line—(202) 287-7034.

Economic Statistics

A nontechnical Congressional Research Service (CRS) guide to selected economic statistics, those relating to economic growth, employment and income, monetary conditions, inflation and Federal finance. For each topic, CRS provides a definition, the issuing agency, frequency of release, names of relevant press releases and other publications, and citations to related CRS issue briefs and reports. Tables of historical data are included for each, with many going back to 1929. 1984. 67pp. **FREE**. CRS Report No. 84-81C. Contact your Member of Congress by mail at U.S. House of Representatives, Washington, DC 20515 or U.S. Senate, Washington, DC 20510, or through the U.S. Capitol switchboard, (202) 224-3121.

Economics Sourcebook of Government Statistics

This is a guide to more than 50 sources of economic statistics compiled and issued by Federal Government agencies. These economic indicators of business and financial conditions encompass measures of inflation, profits, interest rates, unemployment, employment, earnings, international trade and finance, deficits and other statistical series. For each series, the book indicates how the data were obtained, what is covered, when the report is released, and where current and historical data are published. In addition, the limitations and potential misuses of the indicators are described in nontechnical terms. Addresses and telephone numbers of agencies' public information offices are also included. An appendix lists additional sources of business and financial information, including periodicals, handbooks, corporate reports and other publications available from the private sector. The authors are Arline Alchian Hoel, Kenneth W. Clarkson, and Roger LeRoy Miller. 1983. 228pp. $29.00. ISBN 0-669-06579-X. (82-49324) Lexington Books, D.C. Heath and Co., 2700 N. Richardt Avenue, Indianapolis, IN 46219; (800) 428-8071 or (800) 334-3284.

Handbook of United States Economic and Financial Indicators

A handbook that defines more than 200 major standard measures of economic activity in the United States. It is arranged alphabetically by indicator. Because some indicators are known by more than one name, cross references are included in the text, and a subject index covers the various terms and concepts implied by the indicators. Each entry includes a brief description and definition; an explanation of how the indicator is derived, used and compiled; where it is published; and where the reader may obtain more information on the subject. Written by Frederick M. O'Hara, Jr. and Robert Sicignano. 1985. 231pp. $35.00. ISBN 0-313-23954-1. (84-22469) Greenwood Press, P.O. Box 5007, Westport, CT 06881; (203) 226-3571.

Statistical Policy Working Papers

A series of technical documents prepared by working groups or task forces of the Federal Committee on Statistical Methodology, operated under the auspices of the Office of Management and Budget's (OMB) Office of Information and Regulatory Affairs (OIRA) and its predecessor organizations. There are 11 papers in the series. Statistical Policy Office, OIRA, 726 Jackson Place NW, Room 3001, Washington, DC 20503; (202) 395-3093.

1. Report on Statistics for Allocation of Funds; GPO S/N 003-005-00178-6, $5.00. Out-of-print.

2. Report on Statistical Disclosure and Disclosure-Avoidance Techniques; GPO S/N 003-005-00177-8, $5.00. Out-of-print.

3. An Error Profile: Employment as Measured by the Current Population Survey. Out-of-print.

4. Glossary of Nonsampling Error Terms: An Illustration of a Semantic Problem in Statistics (A limited number of copies are available from OIRA).

5. Report on Exact and Statistical Matching Techniques. Out-of-print.

6. Report on Statistical Uses of Administrative Records; GPO S/N 003-005-00185-9, $5.00. Out-of-print.

7. An Interagency Review of Time-Series Revision Policies (A limited number of copies are available from OIRA.)

8. Statistical Interagency Agreements. (A limited number of copies are available from OIRA.)

9. Contracting for Surveys; 64pp., NTIS order number PB83-233148/GBD; $11.95 paper; $5.95 microfiche. See the NTIS order form.

10. Approaches to Developing Questionnaires; 164p., NTIS order number PB84-105055/GBD; $16.95 paper; $5.95 microfiche. See the NTIS order form.

11. A Review of Industry Coding Systems; 120pp., NTIS order number PB84-135276/GBD; $16.95 paper; $5.95 microfiche. See the NTIS order form.

The Metropolitan Statistical Area Classification 1980

A pamphlet that provides information on the standards for establishing Standard Metropolitan Statistical Areas (SMSA) and the Standard Consolidated

Statistical Areas (SCSA). This document contains the official SMSA standards; a nontechnical summary of the standards; a background statement on the development of the metropolitan concept in Federal statistics; and the procedures followed and data sources used in implementing the standards. 1980. **FREE**. Statistical Policy Office, see entry above.

Standard Occupational Classification Manual

This reference book provides definitions for more than 600 occupational groups to be used in the collection, tabulation and analysis of data about occupations. This revision of the original 1977 edition includes specific references to the *Dictionary of Occupational Titles*, and is to be used in the Census Bureau's classification of occupations. 1980. 547pp. $17.00. GPO S/N 003-005-00187-5. (C 1.8/3:Oc 1/980) See the GPO order form.

Enterprise Standard Industrial Classification Manual

This manual contains information on classification by enterprises (business organizations). These classifications are used with the Standard Industrial Classifications (SIC) to provide a means for linking establishment (plants and facilities) statistics and enterprise statistics. The classifications promote the comparability of statistics describing various facets of the Nation's economy. 1975. Out-of-print.

Standard Industrial Classification Manual

A reference document containing titles and descriptions of industries and alphabetical indexes for both manufacturing and nonmanufacturing industrial establishments (e.g., factories, mills, stores, hotels, mines, farms, banks, depots, warehouses). The Standard Industrial Classification (SIC) was developed for use in the classification of establishments by type of activity in which they are engaged; for purposes of facilitating the collection, tabulation, presentation, and analysis of data relating to establishments; and for promoting uniformity and comparability in the presentation of statistical data collected. GPO S/N for the basic 1972 manual 041-001-00066-6 (PrEx 2.6/2:In 27/972), 649pp., $15.00. GPO S/N for the 1977 supplement 003-005-00176-0 (PrEx 2.6/2:In 27/977/supp.), 15pp., $2.75. See the GPO order form. The SIC codes as of 1977 are also available on tape from the National Technical Information Service. NTIS order number PB296331/GBD, $140.00. See the NTIS order form.

A Directory of Computerized Data Files

A directory that provides information on more than 800 statistical, numeric, and textual Federal data files available from the National Technical Information Service (NTIS). The inventory includes collections from the Bureau of Labor Statistics, National Center for Health Statistics, Department of Energy, Department of Agriculture, Federal Communications Commission, and others—more than 50 Federal sources in all. Each file is described in the abstracts section. It is subdivided into 27 subject categories in three principal areas: economics, social sciences, and science and technology. Subject categories range from agricultural economics to vital statistics, from demography to transportation. The directory has three indexes: originating agency (or its contractor), subject matter arranged in alphabetical order by key word or key phrase; and NTIS accession number. 1984. 387pp. $48.00 paper or $40.00 microfiche. NTIS order number PB85-155174/GBD. See the NTIS order form.

Subject Bibliographies

Most of the statistical publications produced by the Federal Government are for sale by the Government Printing Office (GPO). They may be identified using the following **FREE** subject bibliographies (SB). See the GPO SB order form.

- Agricultural Research, Statistics, and Economic Reports (SB-162)
- Census of Agriculture (SB-277)
- Census of Business (SB-152)
- Census of Construction (SB-157)
- Census of Governments (SB-156)
- Census of Manufactures (SB-146)
- Census of Mineral Industries (SB-310)
- Census of Population (SB-181)
- Census of Transportation (SB-149)
- Educational Statistics (SB-83)
- Statistical Publications (SB-273)
- Vital and Health Statistics (SB-121)

Independent Organizations

No less than five independent organizations pursue and promote the development of a Federal statistical program responsive to the needs of the country's citizens, business people, professionals and government employees—Federal, State and local. The five organizations described here.

- Association of Public Data Users
- Committee on National Statistics
- Consortium of Social Science Associations
- Council of Professional Associations on Federal Statistics
- Interagency Committee on Dissemination of Statistics

Association of Public Data Users

The Association of Public Data Users (APDU) was founded in 1976 to facilitate the use of machine-readable public data files of the Federal Government. APDU is a network of data users, producers and distributors concerned with information about data files, software and data user problems. Its goal is to increase the knowledge base of its members about new sources of information and to increase the awareness of Federal agencies about the requirements of data users. Some areas of interest of the association include population data, demographic and economic characteristics, income and expenditures, energy, health, housing, criminal justice and manpower. Membership is open to institutions and individuals. For further information, contact APDU at Princeton University Computer Center, 87 Prospect Avenue, Princeton, NJ 08544; (609) 452-6025/6052.

Committee on National Statistics

The Committee on National Statistics was established in 1972 by the National Research Council of the National Academy of Sciences. It provides for the continuous review of Federal statistical activities by a group of professionals with no direct relationship with the Federal Government. The Committee and its staff are associated with the Academy's Commission on Behavioral and Social Sciences and Education. Its interests cover all fields, but concentrate on statistical issues important to the public—important in the sense that public decisions or understanding may be affected by the need for relevant and accurate information or by the need for good statistical methodology. Thus the Committee is concerned not only with statistical activities of the Government, but also with the application of statistics in public affairs, in science and in private decision making. The Committee holds conferences and, on request of Federal agencies and commissions, conducts special studies and reviews draft reports on statistical matters. For further information, contact the Committee at the National Academy of Sciences, 2101 Constitution Avenue NW, Washington, DC 20418; (202) 334-3096.

Consortium of Social Science Associations

The Consortium of Social Science Associations (COSSA), established in 1981, represents more than 185,000 professionals in the social and behavioral science disciplines. The Consortium functions as a bridge between the academic research community and the Federal Government. One of the primary missions of COSSA is to inform and educate officials of the legislative and executive branches about the importance of social and behavioral science research and the need to maintain adequate statistical program support for such research. To keep members informed about legislative actions and Federal policies that bear on the conduct of social and behavioral science research, COSSA issues the biweekly newsletter *COSSA Washington Update*.

The member societies of COSSA are listed below.

- American Anthropological Association
- American Economic Association
- American Historical Association
- American Political Science Association
- American Psychological Association
- American Sociological Association
- American Statistical Association
- Association of American Geographers
- Association of American Law Schools
- Linguistic Society of America

For further information, contact COSSA at 1200 17th Street NW, Suite 520, Washington, DC 20036; (202) 887-6166.

Council of Professional Associations on Federal Statistics

The Council, known as COPAFS, is a coalition of 16 professional associations that share a common concern about Federal statistical policy and programs. Established in 1980, COPAFS is concerned with the scope, economy and compatibility of data collection efforts; quality of data; access to information; and adequacy of data dissemination. In these areas, COPAFS observes and informs member associations of important developments, analyzes key issues, serves as a forum for the exchange of views and concerns, facilitates member associations' action on critical issues, proposes improvements or remedies, and advises decision makers in the Federal executive and legislative branches of the professions' views. The Council's monthly newsletter, *News from COPAFS*, keeps its members informed about these matters. It is available to non-members for $30.00 a year.

The members of the Council are listed below.

- American Agricultural Economics Association
- American Association for Public Opinion Research
- American Economic Association
- American Marketing Association
- American Political Science Association
- American Psychological Association
- American Public Health Association
- American Sociological Association
- American Statistical Association
- Association for University Business and Economic Research
- Association for Vital Records and Health Statistics
- Association of Public Data Users
- Gerontological Society of America
- Industrial Relations Research Association

Statistical Programs 347

- Population Association of America
- Society of Actuaries

Together, the membership of COPAFS' constituent associations include more than 200,000 members. For further information, contact COPAFS at 806 15th Street NW, Suite 440, Washington, DC 20005; (202) 783-5808.

Interagency Committee on Dissemination of Statistics

The newest of the independent committees was formed in 1984 when the OMB-chaired Interagency Committee on Data Access and Use was dismantled. As with its predecessor committee, this group's goal is to enhance Federal statistical agencies' efforts in making their data more available to the public and in providing improved services to data users. Using both individual and cooperative activities of its members, the Committee develops ideas to expand the dissemination of Federal statistical information. For further information contact the committee's chairman, John H. Weiner, c/o Department of Energy, Office of Planning and Resources, EI-33, Room 2H-087, Washington, DC 20585; (202) 252-6537.

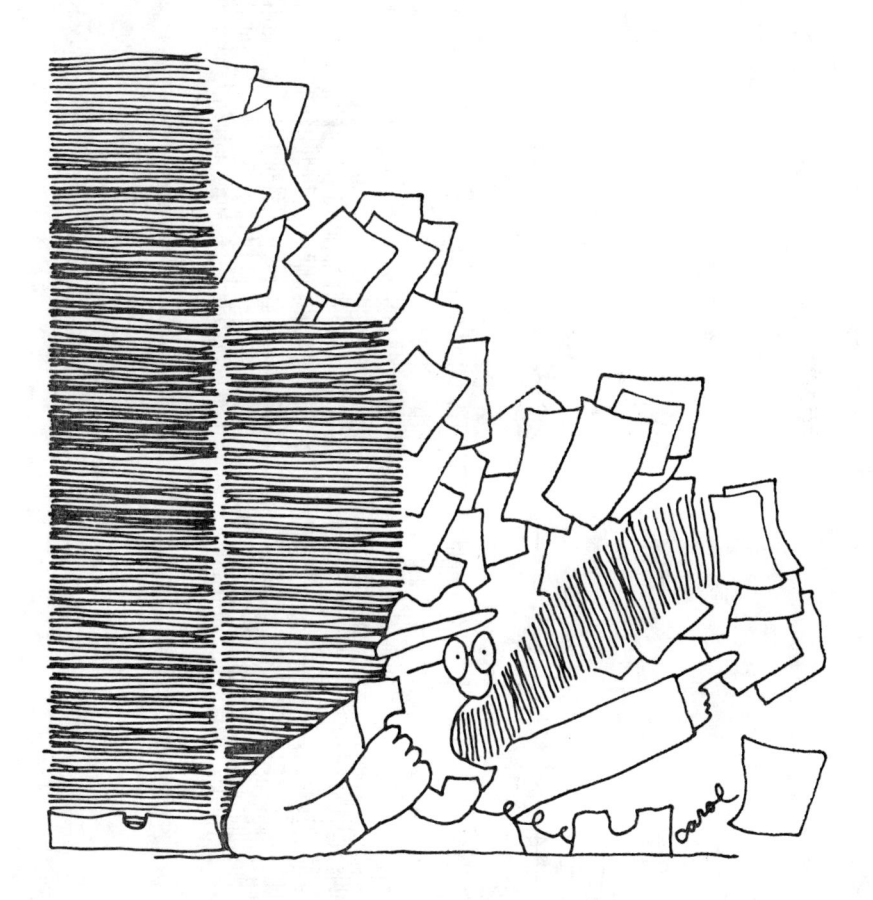

348 **FEDfind**

Chapter 13
Science and Technology

The United States Government is one of the world's largest producers of scientific and technical (S&T) information. Organizations that engage in Government-supported scientific research and development (R&D) include Federal Government laboratories, universities and colleges, industrial firms under Federal contract, nonprofit organizations and federally funded R&D centers. The keys to identifying and accessing this S&T information are a variety of products and services that facilitate the use of Government technology. This chapter provides descriptions and contact information to tap this vast S&T resource.

The information resources described in this chapter are organized under the following headings.

- General Guides
- Resource Guides and Catalogs
- Current Awareness Products
- Foreign Technology Developments
- Computerized Information Resources
- Small Business Innovation Research Program
- Subject Bibliographies

The five most prolific science and technology information-producing agencies of the U.S. Government are listed below. Each is described in either Chapter 8 or Chapter 9 under its respective department or agency, as well as Chapter 17 solely on NTIS.

- Commerce—National Bureau of Standards (NBS)
- Commerce—National Technical Information Service (NTIS)
- Defense—Defense Technical Information Center (DTIC)
- Energy—Office of Scientific and Technical Information
- National Aeronautics and Space Administration (NASA)—Scientific and Technical Information Facility

General Guides

A Guide to U.S. Government Scientific and Technical Resources

This reference work provides a logical progression through the various stages of scientific and technical (S&T) literature production—from the initial search for research funds and examination of research in progress, through publication of data in various formats. It culminates with an examination of indexes, abstracts and machine-readable databases. Each chapter focuses on a specific category of information such as patents and trademarks, discusses its place in the flow of S&T information communication, and describes the major sources of information on the subject, including non-bibliographic sources where appropriate. Other chapters include grants, awards, fellowships and scholarships; research in progress; technical reports; periodicals; scientific translations; standards and specifications; audiovisual and non-book resources; indexes and abstracts; databases; information analysis centers and reference sources. Written by Rao Aluri and Judith Schiek Robinson. 1983. 259pp. $23.50. ISBN 0-87287-377-3. (83-14991) Libraries Unlimited, Inc., P.O. Box 263, Littleton, CO 80160; (303) 770-1220.

LC Science Tracer Bullet Series

Designed to help a reader begin to locate published materials on a given topic, this Library of Congress (LC) series of reference guides provides information on such topics as alcohol fuels, edible wild plants, genetic engineering, solar energy, etc. Each *Tracer Bullet* gives the reader information on basic texts, bibliographies, state-of-the-art reports, conference proceedings, and government publications, as well as abstracting and indexing services useful in finding journal articles and technical reports. Because these compilations are intended to put a reader "on target," they are called "tracer bullets." Fast-changing subjects are covered by supplements and occasional updates. A master list of the *Tracer Bullet* series plus a sample copy is **FREE**. Single copies of the *Tracer Bullet* are also available **FREE**. Science Reference Section, Science and Technology Division, Library of Congress, Washington, DC 20540; (202) 287-5580.

Resource Guides and Catalogs

Directory of Federal Laboratory & Technology Resources 1986–87

A biennial directory of scientific and technical (S&T) resources provided by U.S. Government agencies, their laboratories and engineering centers. The resources identified include experts at Federal laboratories, equipment available for sharing, special services that provide materials to the research and development and engineering communities, descriptions of more than 70 Federal technical information centers and software sources. More than 900 resource summaries are arranged into 31 subject categories. Subject term, State, resource name and agency indexes are also provided. For further information, contact NTIS and request brochure PR-746/GBD. January 1986. 280pp. $29.00. NTIS order number PB86-100013/GBD. See the NTIS order form.

Federal Laboratory Directory 1982

This directory provides information about some 388 U.S. Government laboratories with ten or more full-time professionals engaged in research and development. Also included is summary data, arranged by Federal agency and by State, that provides an overview of the Federal laboratory system and laboratory lists by staff size, by State and by supporting agency. Laboratory lists provide cross references to the main entries. For each laboratory, a contact for obtaining technical information is provided by name, address and telephone number. Also given for each laboratory is a mission statement and listing of major scientific or testing equipment. Prepared by the Office of Research and Technology Applications (ORTA), National Bureau of Standards (NBS) in cooperation with the Federal Laboratory Consortium for Technology Transfer. A new edition is planned for 1986. Copies of the current edition are available **FREE**—while supply lasts—from its editor, James M. Wyckoff at NBS, ORTA, Washington, DC 20234; (301) 921-3814. 1983. 263pp. $8.00. NBS Special Publication 646. (82-600663)

DTIC Referral Data Bank Directory

A Defense Technical Information Center (DTIC) directory that describes more than 400 sources of specialized scientific and technical information operated or supported by the Department of Defense or other Federal agencies. These sources include information centers, specialized libraries, laboratories, testing facilities and other research activities. Each entry includes the agency name, address, telephone number, point-of-contact, special subject areas, services, charges and mission information. The directory is arranged numerically by referral number and includes three indexes: referral, point-of-contact and subject. Compiled by Margaret W. Mullen. 1984, 9th ed. 464pp. $25.00. NTIS report number AD-A138400/GBD. See the NTIS order form.

Information Analysis Centers Directory

Information Analysis Centers (IAC) collect, review, analyze, appraise, summarize and store information on highly specialized technical subjects. This directory describes the capabilities, products and services offered by 21 IACs supported by the Department of Defense (DOD). 1985. 32pp. **FREE**. Defense Technical Information Center, Program Manager for IACs (DTIC-DF), Cameron Station, Alexandria, VA 22304; (202) 274-6260.

Basic Research Program: Department of Defense

This Department of Defense (DOD) publication is intended to assist private-sector researchers find possible sponsors within the DOD. It shows the divisions with DOD service research offices that correspond to the various disciplines and highlights representative programs within each area. 1985. 96pp. $3.50. GPO S/N 008-040-00189-0. (D 1.2:R 31/9/985) See the GPO order form.

Research and Technology Objectives and Plans Summary

An annual compilation of National Aeronautics and Space Administration (NASA) funded research and technology programs, this summary is designed to facilitate communications and coordination among concerned technical personnel in the Federal Government, industry and the academic community. The publication briefly describes NASA's research and development (R&D) objectives, identifies the installation of primary interest to that R&D and provides a point of contact for technical information. October 1985. 186pp. **FREE**. NASA Scientific and Technical Information Facility, P.O. Box 8757, Baltimore/Washington International Airport, MD 21240; (301) 621-0147.

Industrial Applications Centers

The National Aeronautics and Space Administration (NASA) administers seven Industrial Applications Centers (IAC) to assist small business and the nonaerospace industrial sector to gain access to—and apply technical information resulting from— aerospace research and development. Each IAC is based at a university or a not-for-profit research institute, and is staffed with specialists skilled in the use of computer search and retrieval techniques. For more information about these centers and NASA's Technology Utilization Program, contact the Director, Technology Utilization and Industry Affairs Division, NASA Scientific and Technical Information Facility, P.O. Box 8757, Baltimore/Washington International Airport, MD 21240; (301) 621-0242.

COSMIC Software Catalog

Abstracts, indexes and ordering information for more than 1,300 computer programs developed by the National Aeronautics and Space Administration (NASA) and distributed by NASA's Computer Software Management and Information Center (COSMIC) are listed in this annual directory. Each program is assigned to one of 75 subject categories. The accompanying abstract explains the program's capabilities, provides information to assist in the determination of potential application areas, notes the programming language, machine environment, size, and prices of the source code and supporting documentation. Keyword and author indexes are included. 1985. 600pp. Printed hardcopy, $25.00; microfiche 24X or 48X, $10.00; magnetic tape, ASCII or EBCDIC, $50.00. COSMIC, 112 Barrow Hall, The University of Georgia, Athens, GA 30602; (404) 542-3265. For further information on COSMIC, request the **FREE** brochure, *Discovering New Worlds With NASA Software from COSMIC.*

Catalogs of Government Patents

An annual catalog that describes Federal Government inventions available for commercial licensing, both exclusively and non-exclusively. Each catalog includes more than 1,200 summaries of both patents and patent applications arranged in 43 subject-oriented categories. Within each category, all patent applications are listed chronologically by filing date followed by patents. Subject term and inventor indexes are also included. The catalogs provide forms for ordering patents and patent applications. For additional information, contact NTIS and request brochure PR-735/GBD. Published around April for the previous year. The respective catalog coverage year and NTIS order number for available catalogs follow. The price for the 1985 edition is $29.00, while all others are $25.00 each. See the NTIS order form.

- 1985, PB86-116175/GBD
- 1984, PB85-106979/GBD
- 1983, PB84-117589/GBD
- 1982, PB83-159046/GBD
- 1981, PB83-179192/GBD

Current Awareness Products

Abstract Newsletter

The National Technical Information Service (NTIS) *Abstract Newsletter* service provides 27 weekly specialty newsletters. The newsletters cover the most recent published reports on research projects conducted or sponsored by the Federal Government. The specific newsletters and respective costs in the U.S., Canada and Mexico are listed below (in U.S. dollars). For further information, contact NTIS and request brochure PR-205/GBD. See the NTIS order form.

Administration and Management	$ 89
Agriculture & Food	89
Behavior & Society	79
Biomedical Technology & Human Engineering	79
Building Industry Technology	79
Business & Economics	79
Chemistry	89
Civil Engineering	89
Communication	89
Computers, Control & Information Theory	109
Electrotechnology	79
Energy	109
Environmental Pollution & Control	109
Foreign Technology	109
Government Inventions for Licensing	205
Health Planning & Health Services Research	89
Library & Information Science	79
Manufacturing Technology	125
Materials Sciences	89
Medicine & Biology	89
NASA Earth Resources Survey Program (bimonthly)	79
Natural Resources & Earth Sciences	89
Ocean Technology & Engineering	79
Physics	79
Problem-Solving Information for State & Local Governments	79
Transportation	89
Urban & Regional Technology & Development	79

Technical Abstract Bulletin

The *Technical Abstract Bulletin* (TAB) is a biweekly listing (classified Confidential) of all classified and unclassified/ limited access scientific and technical reports received by the Department of Defense (DOD) Defense Technical Information Center (DTIC) within the processing period. (Unclassified/unlimited reports are listed in the National Technical Information Service [NTIS] newsletters, see above.) It is divided into two sections—bibliographic records and indexes. The bibliographic section lists reports by subject fields. The index lists all new documents—including those announced only by NTIS. It is distributed **FREE** to authorized DTIC users who have requested it and who possess facility clearances. DTIC, Cameron Station, Building 5, Alexandria, VA 22314; (202) 274-7633.

NASA Tech Briefs

A quarterly journal of articles on innovations and improved products or processes developed for the National Aeronautics and Space Administration (NASA) thought to have commercial potential. Special sections are included for books and reports, computer programs and new product ideas. Information on NASA's patent licensing program and additional services of their Technology Utilization Program are also described. **FREE** to qualified companies. Contact the Director, Technology Utilization and Industry Affairs Division, NASA Headquarters, Washington, DC 20546.

Government Inventions for Licensing

This weekly newsletter summarizes annually some 2,000 U.S. Government held patents or patent applications. These inventions are available to U.S. companies for licensing, often exclusively. Each issue divides inventions into eleven subject disciplines. Along with the invention title, a summary (abstract) of the patent, the inventor's name and the main drawing (when appropriate) are listed. For additional information, contact NTIS and request brochure PR-750/GBD. Subscription price: $205.00 a year. See the NTIS order form.

Tech Notes

A monthly subscription service that provides "fact sheets" describing the latest technological advances developed by U.S. Government agencies and their contractors. Each "fact sheet" (usually illustrated) describes a specific process, invention, computer software package, technique or equipment chosen to have potential commercial or practical application. The "fact sheets" are available in 10 subject categories: computers, electrotechnology, energy, engineering, life sciences, machinery and tools, manufacturing, materials, physical sciences, and testing and instrumentation. Users may subscribe to any one category or combination of categories. The annual subscription rates per number of copies or categories are: 1, $68.00; 2, $127.00; 3, $178.00; 4, $224.00; 5, $264.00; 6 or more, $287.00. The annual *Federal Technology Catalog*, described below, is provided **FREE** to subscribers. For further information, contact the National Technical Information Service (NTIS) and request brochure PR-365/GBD. See the NTIS order form.

Federal Technology Catalogs

Each annual catalog describes more than 1,000 new applications, processes and equipment developed by the U.S. Government chosen as having potential commercial or practical application. Brief summaries of technologies are arranged into 24 subject categories, including computers, engineering, life sciences, machinery and tools, manufacturing, materials, physical sciences, and testing and instrumentation. For each summary a source is given for further information that includes an individual to contact, with address and telephone number. A subject index is also included. Published around April for the previous year. For further information, contact NTIS and request brochure PR-732/GBD. The respective catalog coverage year, price and NTIS order number for available catalogs are: 1985, $25.00, PB86-116167/GBD; 1984, $23.50, PB85-106987/GBD; 1983, $23.50, PB84-105634/GBD; 1982, $19.50, PB83-121533/GBD. See the NTIS order form.

Foreign Technology Developments

Foreign Technology

A weekly newsletter that provides some eighty abstracts of foreign technology and research. Based on the abstracts, one may order the full texts using an order form provided in each newsletter. The reports cover the following disciplines: biomedical technology; civil, construction, structural and building engineering; communications; computer technology; electro/optical technology; energy; manufacturing and industrial engineering; materials sciences; physical sciences (applied); transportation technology, mining and mineral industries; and foreign government-owned inventions for licensing. Subscription price: $109.00 a year. For further information, contact the National Technical Information Service (NTIS) and ask for brochure PR-731/GBD. See the NTIS order form.

Computerized Information Resources

The following are computer-based information systems that relate to this chapter. For more information on this and other online services, see Appendix D, "Computerized Information Resources."

Federal Technology Transfer—Online

A reference guide for online computer searching of U.S. Government inventions and National Technical Information Service (NTIS) *Tech Notes*. The booklet describes both the *Tech Notes* and Federal inventions and explains the value of these two collections and the methods for searching them. It also provides an introduction to the subject of Federal technology transfer and a listing of the NTIS subject categories used to classify the information in the databases. 1984. 36pp. **FREE**. NTIS order number PR-725/GBD. See the NTIS order form.

Federal Research in Progress

The Federal Research in Progress (FEDRIP) Database is a computer-based online information system that provides summaries describing current research performed by, or under the sponsorship of, U.S. Government agencies. All FEDRIP summaries include title, principal investigator, performing organization and sponsoring organization. Most summaries also include a description of the research, the objective, approach, progress report and other information. Subject descriptions are also available in most summaries. Updated semiannually. FEDRIP is available online through DIALOG Information Services, (800) 227-1960 and Mead Data Central, (800) 227-4908. The database is also available as a batch subscription service through NERAC, Inc., Mansfield Professional Park, Storrs, CT 06268; (203) 429-3000. For more information, contact the Office of Product Management, National Technical Information Service, 5285 Port Royal Road, Springfield, VA 22161; (703) 487-4929.

Defense RDT&E Online System

The Defense Research, Development, Test and Evaluation (RDT&E) Online System (DROLS) provides online access to authorized users to the Defense Technical Information Center (DTIC) collection. DROLS provides access to four separate databases. The Research and Development Program Planning Database contains planned R&D project and task level summaries. The Research and Technology Work Unit Information System Database is comprised of ongoing Department of Defense (DOD) research and technology efforts at the work unit level. The Technical Reports Database consists of bibliographic records of technical reports submitted to DTIC. The Independent Research and Development Database contains information on contractors' independent R&D efforts shared with DOD. This database is proprietary and made available to classified DOD terminals only. DTIC, Online Support Office (DTIC-ZM), Cameron Station, Building 5, Alexandria, VA 22304; (202) 274-7709.

Small Business Innovation Research Program

The Small Business Innovation Development Act of 1982 authorized the Small Business Innovation Research (SBIR) Program. The Act calls for agencies with research and research and development (R&D) budgets in excess of $100 million to establish SBIR programs. The program requires that qualified small firms receive a fixed annual percentage of R&D dollars of the participating Federal agencies. The Small Business Administration (SBA) coordinates and monitors the overall activity of the program. The SBA publishes a *Pre-Solicitation Announcement* (PSA) in September, December, March and June each year. These PSAs provide information on SBIR Program Solicitations scheduled to be released during the following three-month period. Copies of the actual solicitation are available from the participating agencies in accordance with procedures provided in the PSA. For further information on the SBIR Program and the current PSA, contact the Office of Innovation, Research and Technology, SBA, 1441 L Street NW, Room 500, Washington, DC 20416; (202) 653-6458.

SBIR Technology Assistance

The Small Business Administration (SBA) Office of Innovation, Research and Technology, in cooperation with the University of Connecticut and the University of Southern California, provides a fast-reaction technology information service for small businesses interested in participating in the Small Business Innovation Research (SBIR) program. The service provides, within five days, state-of-the-art information useful in preparing SBIR proposals or in guiding SBIR research efforts. The output is a comprehensive bibliography (often with abstracts) derived from a computerized search of a wide variety of databases. The cost of this service to small businesses is $125.00 per inquiry. SBA provides supplemental funding to offset actual costs, which are significantly higher. Documents may also be ordered for an additional fee and are typically delivered within three weeks. To obtain this service or additional information, contact one of the following university-based centers. For small firms in the States of Alaska, Arizona, California, Colorado, Hawaii, Idaho, Montana, Nevada, North Dakota, Oregon, South Dakota, Utah, Washington and Wyoming, contact University of Southern California, Western Research Application Center (WESRAC), 3716 S. Hope Street, #200, Los Angeles, CA 90007; (213) 743-6132. For firms in all other States, contact University of Connecticut, New England Research Application Center (NERAC), Mansfield Professional Park, Storrs, CT 06268; (203) 486-4586.

Proposal Preparation for Small Business Innovation Research (SBIR)

Prepared by the Small Business Administration (SBA) Office of Innovation, Research and Technology, this publication is a guide to SBIR programs proposal preparation. The pamphlet contains three chapters corresponding to a process through which a firm determines the suitability of SBIR participation, selects projects and finally prepares proposals. 1984. 18pp. **FREE**. SBA, SBIR T1, P.O. Box 15434, Ft. Worth, TX 76119.

Subject Bibliographies

Most of the science and technology publications for sale by the Government Printing Office (GPO) may be identified using the following subject bibliographies (SB) available **FREE** from GPO. See the GPO SB order form.

- Earth Sciences (SB-160)
- NASA Scientific and Technical Publications (SB-257)
- Science Experiments and Projects (SB-243)

Chapter 14
Government Procurement and Business Information

The U.S. Government is the largest buyer of goods and services in the free world. Any firm seeking to expand its scope of operations should consider the possibilities of doing business with the Federal Government—but it takes information to make successful use of these opportunities. In general, a firm must know where in the Federal structure to market its products or services, how to make them known, where and how to obtain and complete the necessary paperwork, and how to bid on Government procurements. The first part of this chapter describes key information resources on U.S. Government procurement procedures.

The Federal Government also publishes a wealth of information on domestic and international business. To help find and use this information, the second part of this chapter provides descriptions of key resources that the Government makes available—at little or no cost.

The information resources described in this chapter are organized under the following headings.
- Policy Directives
- Government Procurement
- Government Procurement References
- Government Procurement Periodicals
- Business Information Resources
- Exporting Information References
- Exporting Information Periodicals
- Computerized Information Resources
- Subject Bibliographies

Policy Directives

The following directives, arranged in numerical order, relate to Federal procurement policy and are administered by the Executive Office of the President (EOP) Office of Federal Procurement Policy. Copies of the directives are available **FREE** from EOP Publications, 726 Jackson Place NW, Room 2200, Washington, DC 20503; (202) 395-7332.

Cost Principles for Educational Institutions

Office of Management and Budget (OMB) Circular No. A-21 establishes principles for determining costs applicable to grants, contracts and other agreements with educational institutions. The principles are designed to ensure that the Federal Government bear its fair share of total costs, determined in accordance with generally accepted accounting principles. Provision for profit or other increment above cost is not addressed in this circular. 1979. 53pp. **FREE**. A revision, Transmittal Memorandum No. 1, *Cost Principles for Universities*, changes the procedures covering allocation of personal services costs and recognizes interest costs in certain circumstances. 1982. 15pp. **FREE**. EOP Publications, see entry above.

Use of Management and Operating Contracts

Office of Management and Budget (OMB) Circular No. A-49 establishes general criteria to assist Federal agencies in developing policies concerning the use of management and operating contracts. As used in this circular, the term "management and operating contract" applies to cost-reimbursement contracts under which the Government contracts with nonprofit institutions, private businesses or universities to (a) administer, on behalf of the Government, research or development establishments wholly devoted to Government work or Government research or development programs; (b) administer and operate Government-owned or -leased industrial facilities; or (c) provide such personal or professional services as are authorized by law. 1959. 6pp. **FREE**. EOP Publications, see introduction to this section.

Performance of Commercial Activities

Office of Management and Budget (OMB) Circular No. A-76 establishes Federal policy regarding the performance of commercial activities. The Supplement to the circular sets forth procedures for determining whether commercial activities should be performed under contract with commercial sources or in-house using Federal Government facilities and personnel. 1983, 10pp., **FREE**; Supplement, 1983, 124pp., **FREE**. EOP Publications, see introduction to this section.

Uniform Administrative Requirements for Grant-in-Aid to State and Local Governments

Office of Management and Budget (OMB) Circular No. A-102 promulgates standards for establishing consistency and uniformity among Federal agencies in the administration of grants to State, local and federally recognized Indian tribal governments. Also included in the circular are standards to ensure the consistent implementation of sections of the *Intergovernmental Cooperation Act of 1968*. 1981. 124pp. **FREE**. EOP Publications, see introduction to this section.

Major System Acquisitions

Office of Management and Budget (OMB) Circular No. A-109 establishes policies to be followed by executive branch agencies in the acquisition of major systems. Major system acquisition programs are those programs that (a) are directed at and critical to fulfilling an agency mission, (b) entail the allocation of relatively large resources, and (c) warrant special management attention. 1976. 12pp. **FREE**. EOP Publications, see introduction to this section.

Uniform Administrative Requirements for Grants and Other Agreements with Institutions of Higher Education, Hospitals and Other Nonprofit Organizations

Office of Management and Budget (OMB) Circular No. A-110 promulgates standards for obtaining consistency and uniformity among Federal agencies in the administration of grants to, and other agreements with, public and private institutions of higher education, public and private hospitals, and other quasi-public and private nonprofit organizations. This circular replaces the varying and often conflicting requirements previously imposed by Federal agencies as conditions of grants and other agreements with recipients. 1976. 28pp. **FREE**. EOP Publications, see introduction to this section.

Management of Federal Audiovisual Activities

Office of Management and Budget (OMB) Circular No. A-114 prescribes policies and procedures to improve Federal audiovisual management. The circular provides policies governing the consolidation, use and management of Federal audiovisual resources, and prescribes a Government-wide contracting system for the procurement of motion picture film productions. 1985. 20pp. **FREE**. EOP Publications, see introduction to this section.

Federal Participation in the Development and Use of Voluntary Standards

Office of Management and Budget (OMB) Circular No. A-119 establishes policy to be followed by executive branch agencies in working with voluntary standards bodies. It also establishes policy to be followed by executive branch agencies in adopting and using voluntary standards. 1982. 16pp. **FREE**. EOP Publications, see introduction to this section.

Guidelines for the Use of Consulting Services

Office of Management and Budget (OMB) Circular No. A-120 establishes policy and guidelines to be followed by executive branch agencies in determining and controlling the appropriate use of consulting services obtained from individuals and organizations. The provisions of the circular apply to consulting services obtained by personnel appointment, procurement contract and advisory committee membership. 1980. 5pp. **FREE**. EOP Publications, see introduction to this section.

Patents—Small Business Firms and Nonprofit Organizations

Office of Management and Budget (OMB) Circular No. A-124 provides policies, procedures and guidelines with respect to inventions made by small business firms and nonprofit organizations, including universities, under funding agreements with Federal agencies where a purpose is to perform experimental, developmental or research work. The circular also includes a standard patent rights clause. 1982. 22pp. **FREE**. EOP Publications, see introduction to this section.

Prompt Payment

Office of Management and Budget (OMB) Circular No. A-125 prescribes policies and procedures to be followed by executive branch agencies in paying for property and services acquired under Federal contract. The *Prompt Payment Act*, Public Law 97-177, requires Federal agencies to pay their bills on time, to pay interest penalties when payments are made late, and to take discounts only when payments are made within the discount period. Inquiries concerning the applicable interest rate may be directed to the Department of the Treasury, Appropriation and Investment Branch at (202) 566-5651. 1982. 7pp. **FREE**. EOP Publications, see introduction to this section.

Government Procurement

Business Service Centers

Through Business Service Centers (BSC) operated by the General Services Administration (GSA), one may obtain information on and assistance in doing business with the Federal Government. BSCs have permanent staffs in 13 major cities (see Figure 14-1) plus business information specialists at 100 more locations. Occasionally BSCs hold special conferences to explain particular business opportunities or to help potential local Federal suppliers. BSCs also distribute Federal directories, publications lists, references and regulations, and a variety of technical publications concerning contracts, contracting procedures, contract and bidding forms, specifications and standards, and specialized purchasing programs.

Government Procurement References

Doing Business With the Federal Government

Prepared by the General Services Administration (GSA), this publication explains the general principles and procedures of Federal business operations. The booklet covers what paperwork is needed and why, whom to contact for news of opportunities or help in utilizing them, and exactly what products and services are needed by each Federal agency with separate procurement capabilities. The publication also gives detailed, nationwide address lists for procurement offices, by agency. Copies of the booklet are available **FREE** from the nearest Business Service Center or from the Government Printing Office. 1981. 44pp. $4.50. GPO S/N 022-000-00186-8. (GS 1.2:B 96/2/981) See the GPO order form.

Government Procurement and Business Information

Region 1
(CT, ME, MA, NH, RI, VT)
John W McCormack PO & Cthse
Boston, MA 02109
(617) 223-2868

Region 2
(NY, NJ, PR, VI)
26 Federal Plaza
New York, NY 10278
(212) 264-1234

National Capitol Region
(DC, Surrounding Counties of
MD-VA Metro Area)
7th & D Sts SW, Rm 1050
Washington, DC 20407
(202) 472-1804

Region 3
(PA, DE, MD, VA, WV)
9th & Market Sts, Rm 1143
Philadelphia, PA 19107
(215) 597-9613

Region 4
(NC, SC, TN, MS, AL, GA, FL, KY)
75 Spring Street, SW
Atlanta, GA 30303
(404) 221-5103

Region 5
(IL, WI, MI, IN, OH, MN)
230 S. Dearborn St
Chicago, IL 60604
(312) 353-5383

Region 6
(KS, IA, MO, NE)
1500 E Bannister Rd
Kansas City, MO 64131
(816) 926-7203

Region 7
(AR, LA, NM, OK, TX)
819 Taylor St, Rm 6A04
Fort Worth, TX 76102
(817) 334-3284

Region 8
(CO, WY, MT, UT, ND, SD)
Building 41
Denver Federal Ctr
Denver, CO 80225
(303) 236-7401

Region 9
(No CA, HI, NV—except
Clark County)
525 Market St
San Francisco, CA 94105
(415) 974-9000

(AZ, So CA, Clark County NV)
300 N Los Angeles St, Rm 3259
Los Angeles, CA 90012
(213) 688-3210

Region 10
(WA, OR, ID, AK)
440 Federal Bldg
915 Second Ave
Seattle, WA 98174
(206) 442-5556

U.S. Government Purchasing and Sales Directory

An aid for the small business that wants to sell to the Federal Government, this directory provides an alphabetical listing of the products and services purchased by both military and civilian departments, with addresses of the offices that have bought them. It also includes an explanation of the ways in which the Small Business Administration (SBA) helps businesses obtain Government prime contracts and subcontracts, data on Government sales of surplus property, and a description of the scope of the Government market for research and development. The publication is prepared by SBA Office of Procurement and Technical Assistance. 1984, 10th ed. 199pp. $5.50. GPO S/N 045-000-00226-8. (SBA 1.13/3:984) See the GPO order form.

Federal Procurement Data Center Reports

The Federal Procurement Data Center (FPDC), part of the General Services Administration (GSA), collects and makes available information on most products and services—including research and development (R&D)—bought by the Federal Government. Federal law requires executive branch departments and agencies to report specific data on all contracts of more than $10,000 for goods or services awarded with appropriated funds. These reports form the basis of an automated information system available to both public and private sectors. The system provides information on how much the Government has spent on clothing, food, furniture, fuel, building materials, automated data processing (ADP) services, weapons, or other items, and who the seller was.

The FPDC provides two types of reports that include information based on individual contracts of more than $10,000 ($25,000 for the Department of Defense). The quarterly *FPDC Standard Report* contains statistical procurement information in "snapshot" form for more than 60 Federal agencies, as well as several charts, graphs and tables that compare procurement activities by State, major product and service codes, method of procurement and contractors. The report also includes quarterly and year-to-date breakdowns of amounts and percentages spent on small, women-owned and minority business. It also may serve as a guide to define the need for an *FPDC Special Report* to satisfy more specific procurement information needs. The *Standard Report* is available **FREE** from the FPDC. (PrEx 2.24/13:)

An *FPDC Special Report* is prepared upon request for a fee based on computer and labor costs. Special reports are tailored to the specific procurement information needs of the customer and are based on 25 data elements or categories that may be searched and cross-tabulated in hundreds of ways. A special report may provide information to analyze Government procurement data and trends, identify competitors and locate Federal markets for individual products or services. It typically costs $250 to $400, depending on the number of fiscal years (October 1–September 30) involved and the complexity of the report.

FPDC also provides, on a reimbursable basis, other information such as computer tapes of the entire contents of the FPDC database by fiscal year; mailing lists of contractors who sell to the Government sorted by region, product and service code, etc.; and mailing lists of Government purchasing offices and their addresses. FPDC, 4040 N. Fairfax Drive, Suite 900, Arlington, VA 22203; (703) 235-1326.

Government Procurement and Business Information 365

Selling to the Military

A guide and directory that provides information on selling products and services to the Department of Defense (DOD). It includes general information on how to get started, including sample forms and where to find information for locating sales opportunities. It includes a directory of the major buying offices of the Army, Air Force, Navy and Defense Logistics Agency (DLA). Also provided is a listing that designates which common items used by the military services are procured through DLA or the General Services Administration (GSA), i.e., coordinated procurement commodity assignments. Other chapters cover research and development procurement, Government system of specifications, buying property from the U.S. Government, military exchange services and Small Business Administration and GSA regional offices. 1983. 141pp. $6.00. GPO S/N 008-000-00392-1. (D 1.2:Se 4/983) See the GPO order form.

Guide to the Defense Contracting Regulation for Small Business, Small Disadvantaged Business, Women-Owned Small Business

This guide explains the basic purchasing rules and regulations of the Department of Defense (DOD). It is intended to provide assistance in locating sales opportunities in the DOD. Every DOD purchasing office has at least one person designated as an Office of Small and Disadvantaged Business Utilization (OSDBU) specialist. These individuals provide information about contracting and subcontracting opportunities with DOD contracting offices. They also provide assistance when problems arise during the performance of a contract. 1985. 57pp. **FREE**. Your nearest OSDBU or Directorate of OSDBU, Office of the Secretary of Defense, Washington, DC 20301. GPO S/N 008-000-00411-1. $2.25. (D 1.6/2:C 76) See the GPO order form.

Selling to NASA

Prepared by the Office of Small and Disadvantaged Business Utilization (OSDBU), this handbook is intended to assist prospective contractors in doing business with the National Aeronautics and Space Administration (NASA). It includes information on NASA, its procurement process, marketing one's capabilities, special assistance programs, NASA field installations and sources of additional help. Single copies are available **FREE** from the OSDBU, NASA Headquarters, Washington, DC 20546; (202) 453-2088. 1984. 44pp. $2.50. GPO S/N 033-000-00925-9. (NAS 1.2:Se 4/984) See the GPO order form.

A Guide to Doing Business With the Department of State

This publication is designed to assist small, minority and female-owned firms seeking to do business with the Department of State in identifying procurement opportunities. It provides names and telephone numbers of contacts within the Department, other agencies within the Washington, DC area, contacts at overseas embassies, and information on procurement contracts. It is issued by the Office of Small and Disadvantaged Business Utilization (OSDBU), which is responsible for the implementation of the Department's activities on behalf of small and disadvantaged businesses and female-owned businesses. Single copies are available **FREE** from the OSDBU, Department of State, Room 513 (5A-6), Washington, DC 20520; (703) 235-9579. 1985. 52pp. $1.25. GPO S/N 044-000-02071-8. (S 1.69:351/6) See the GPO order form.

How to Sell to the United States Department of Commerce

This booklet provides an introduction to the Department of Commerce's procurement process and directs one to sources of detailed information and guidance. The publication was prepared by the Department's Office of Small and Disadvantaged Business Utilization (OSDBU) and offers information on the mission and functions of the various components of the Department, what the Department buys, how it buys, procurement offices, unsolicited proposals, special procurement programs and more. Single copies are available **FREE** from the OSDBU, Department of Commerce, Room H6411, Washington, DC 20230; (202) 377-5614. 1984. 20pp. $1.50. GPO S/N 003-000-00634-4. (C 1.2:Se 4/2) See the GPO order form.

Guide to Specifications, Standards and Commercial Item Descriptions of the Federal Government

Intended for current and prospective contractors to understand better the problems involved in their development and use, this booklet answers the questions most frequently asked by businesses about Federal Government specifications, standards and commercial item descriptions (CID). The booklet also explains the importance and advantages of knowing exactly what the Government proposes to buy—and exactly what is expected of the contractor concerning quality, performance and delivery. The publication defines and describes the various types of specifications, standards and CIDs, how they are developed and used in the procurement process, and how to obtain them. One chapter is also included on how industry participates in the development of Government specifications and standards. 1984. 24pp. **FREE** from Business Service Centers, see Figure 14-1.

List of Commodities and Services

This listing is of services and articles used in connection with the filing of mailing list applications. Persons or concerns who wish to be added to a particular agency's bidder's mailing list for supplies or services must file a Bidder's Mailing List Application (SF-129), along with the Bidder's Mailing List Application Code Sheet (GSA Form 3038), with each procurement office of the Federal agency with which they wish to do business. This is done in accordance with the Bidder's Mailing List Instructions (GSA Form 2459). The listing is prepared by the General Services Administration (GSA) Federal Supply and Services Office and is identified as GSA Form 1382. Available **FREE** from any GSA Business Service Center or from GSA (BRC), Centralized Mailing Lists Services, Building 41, Denver Federal Center, Denver, CO 80225.

A Guide for Private Industry

A pamphlet that tells how to obtain specifications and standards required for doing business with the Department of Defense (DOD). 1983. 8pp. **FREE**. Naval Publications and Forms Center, 5801 Tabor Avenue, Philadelphia, PA 19120.

Small Business Subcontracting Directory

An annual Small Business Administration (SBA) publication that lists major prime contractors to the Federal Government with high potential for subcontracting to small business concerns. The companies were selected from the SBA portfolio of prime contractors whose subcontracting activities under Federal contracts will be monitored for compliance under the SBA Subcontracting Assistance Program. Companies are listed alphabetically by name within each of the ten SBA regions. Each listing includes company name, address, small business representative name and telephone number, and type of business. Spring 1986. approx. 86pp. **FREE**. Available from Small and Disadvantaged Business Utilization offices or from the Office of Procurement Assistance, SBA, 1441 L Street NW, Room 600, Washington, DC 20416; (202) 653-6826.

Small Business Subcontracting Directory

This directory is an aid to small and small disadvantaged business concerns seeking subcontracting opportunities with Department of Defense (DOD) contractors. The directory is arranged alphabetically, by State, and includes the name and address of the DOD prime contractor, the name and telephone number of the Small Business Liaison Officer, and the product or service being provided to the DOD. 1985. 140pp. $5.00. GPO S/N 008-040-00188-1. (D 1.2:B 96/2/985) See the GPO order form.

Small and Disadvantaged Business Utilization Specialists

A directory of locations of various Department of Defense (DOD) procurement offices, this publication provides the names and addresses for their small and disadvantaged business specialists. These specialists assist small businesses, small disadvantaged businesses and women-owned businesses, and firms in labor surplus areas to market their products and services to the DOD. 1983. 57pp. $4.50. GPO S/N 008-000-00390-4. (D 1.2:B 96/983) See the GPO order form.

Government Contract Principles

As an introduction to Government procurement, this manual presents the general statutory and regulatory authorities affecting the award and performance of Federal Government contracts, together with significant legal decisions rendered by the Comptroller General, the courts and agency boards of contract appeals. The document was prepared by the Office of the General Counsel of the General Accounting Office. 1980, 3rd ed. 142pp. $6.50. Out-of-print. GPO S/N 020-000-00200-0. (GA 1.14:C 76/980)

Desk Guide to Price and Cost Analysis

This guide contains advice intended to help the Federal Government buyer determine what steps should be taken to arrive at fair and reasonable contract prices. It was prepared by the Office of Federal Procurement Policy of the Office of Management and Budget (OMB). 1980. 21pp. $1.75. Out-of-print. GPO S/N 041-001-00230-8. (PrEx 2.22:5)

Procurement and Technology Assistance

A booklet that explains how Federal purchases are made by soliciting bids from and negotiating contracts with owners of small businesses. It gives sources of information to help keep sellers up-to-date on Federal purchasing programs. Also provided is information about technical aid and other assistance offered by the Small Business Administration (SBA) to help firms secure Government contracts. 1983. 23pp. **FREE**. SBA, Office of Publications, 1441 L Street NW, Washington, DC 20416; (202) 653- 6365.

Federal Contract Compliance Manual

This document details the policies and procedures to be followed by personnel of the Department of Labor's Office of Federal Contract Compliance Program in enforcing the rules and regulations of the *Code of Federal Regulations,* Title 41, Chapter 60. 1979. 504pp. $16.00. GPO S/N 029-016-00074-7. (L 36.8:C 76) See the GPO order form.

Procurement Law

Intended for use by military lawyers, this manual provides information on the basic principles of Federal Government contract law, contract formation, contract performance, claims and litigation and other related matters. Punched for 3-ring looseleaf binder. 1983. 110pp. $8.00. GPO S/N 008-020-00935-1. (D 101.22:27-153/4) See the GPO order form.

Bid Protests at GAO—A Descriptive Guide

A booklet that provides information on the General Accounting Office's (GAO) procedures for deciding legal questions arising from the award of Federal Government contracts. The booklet describes the where, when and how to file a bid protest, as well as how GAO handles them and what to expect in the way of remedies. An appendix includes the "Bid Protest Regulations" that incorporate changes required by the *Competition in Contracting Act of 1984.* 1985, 2nd ed. 21pp. **FREE**. See the GAO order form.

Procurement Planning Service Directories

An annual series of three Dun and Bradstreet (D&B) procurement directories designed to link the buyers and sellers of services in the Federal Government marketplace. The three directories are: *Information Services*, *Management Services* and *Facilities Services*. Each includes information on companies, their capabilities and previous Government experience to help Federal program managers in their planning of purchases. These "yellow pages" have a special designation code for small businesses. Also included is a collection of successful request for proposal (RFP) abstracts, by subject matter, that are available by order for reference purposes. **FREE** to Federal offices, others enquire for price information. D&B, P.O. Box 6034, Rockville, MD 20852; (800) 447-4454 or (301) 468-7210.

Government Sales Consultants Monograph Series

A series of publications that focus on various aspects of Federal Government procurement. Current titles include *Federal Government Sole Source Procurements, The Government as a Customer, Selling from a GSA Schedule, Bid*

Protests, Overview of the Federal Procurement Process, Procurement Techniques, Negotiated Procurement Techniques and *Life Cycle Cost Evaluation*. For further information, contact GSC, 4407 Carrico Drive, Annandale, VA 22003; (703) 354-4050.

Government Procurement Periodicals

Commerce Business Daily

The *Commerce Business Daily* (CBD) is a daily publication from the Department of Commerce that lists new business proposals for products and services wanted or offered by the U.S. Government. These include unclassified requests for bids and proposals, procurements reserved for small business, prime contracts awarded, Federal contractors seeking subcontractor assistance, and upcoming sales of Government property. There is also Government research and development (R&D) leads and information on current foreign government procurement offers in the United States. A **FREE** information kit, including a sample copy, is available from the CBD, Room 1515, Department of Commerce, Washington, DC 20230. Subscription price: $160.00 a year (priority), $81.00 (non-priority). A special six-month introductory subscription is available at $88.00 (priority), $45.00 (non-priority). GPO List ID COBD. (C 1.76:) See the GPO subscription order form.

Federal Acquisition Regulation

The *Federal Acquisition Regulation* (FAR) is the primary regulation for use by all Federal executive agencies in their acquisition of supplies and services with appropriated funds. It is used together with agency supplemental regulations. It provides for uniformity in the Federal acquisition process. The DOD FAR Supplement must be used in conjunction with the FAR for DOD acquisitions, and the NASA FAR Supplement must be used in conjunction with the FAR for NASA acquisitions. Subscription service consists of a basic manual and changes, Federal Acquisition Circulars issued for an indeterminate period. Punched for 3-ring looseleaf binder. Subscription price: $90.00. GPO List ID FEACR. (D 1.6/11:984/) See the GPO subscription order form.

DOD FAR Supplement

The Department of Defense (DOD) Supplement to the Federal Acquisition Regulation (FAR) implements the FAR in DOD, as well as provides supplementary material that is unique to DOD. It must be used in conjunction with the FAR. Subscription service consists of a basic manual and changes for an indeterminate period. Punched for 3-ring looseleaf binder. Subscription price: $66.00. GPO List ID DFARS. (D 1.6/11:) See the GPO subscription order form.

NASA FAR Supplement

The National Aeronautics and Space Administration (NASA) Supplement to the Federal Acquisition Regulation (FAR) implements the FAR in NASA, as well as provides supplementary material that is unique to NASA. It must be used in conjunction with the FAR. Subscription service consists of a basic manual and changes for an indeterminate period. Punched for 3-ring looseleaf binder. Subscription price: $51.00. GPO List ID NFARS. (NAS 1.6/2:981) See the GPO subscription order form.

Small Business Preferential Subcontract Opportunities Monthly

This periodical identifies Federal Government contracts whose individual values exceed $500,000 and construction contracts of more than $1,000,000. The listings are organized alphabetically by prime contractor within each of the ten Small Business Administration (SBA) regions. Each listing includes company name and address, as does a complete list of agencies cited that is included in each issue. Subscription price: $72.00 a year. Government Data Publications, 1120 Connecticut Avenue NW, Washington, DC 20036; (718) 627-0819.

Federal Grants and Contracts Weekly

A periodical describing newly announced Federal grants and most nondefense contracts that involve project opportunities in research, training and services. Also included are news analysis, agency profiles and updates on new legislation, regulations, budget developments and publications. ISSN 0194-2247. Subscription price: $191.00 a year. Capitol Publications, Inc., 1300 N. 17th Street, Arlington, VA 22209; (703) 528-5400.

Postal Contracting Manual

This manual contains the policies and procedures relating to U.S. Postal Service (USPS) contracts for mail transportation, construction, leasing, repairs, alterations, equipment, supplies and services. The book explains USPS procurement policies and contract clauses and lists forms required for bidding. Subscription service consists of a basic manual and supplemental material for an indeterminate period. Punched for 3-ring looseleaf binder. Subscription price: $75.00. GPO List ID POCM. (P 1.2/6:971/rep.-3) See the GPO subscription order form.

Business Information Resources

Roadmap

Roadmap is an information service program established to assist small and medium-sized firms obtain business information from the Federal Government. It is operated by the Office of Business Liaison of the Department of Commerce. Information is available on trade, taxes, Federal Government procurement, funding sources, product standards, business licenses, franchising, exporting, marketing, statistical information sources and regulatory matters. The program assists in identifying sources of business information, a Government report, commodity information or information about a Government program. The office either finds an answer to a question or puts one in contact with an individual who can. The Roadmap program does not serve as an advocate for an individual business, nor does it intervene on behalf of a business. Department of Commerce, Office of Business Liaison, Room 5898-C, Washington, DC 20230; (202) 377-3176.

Handbook for Small Business: A Survey of Small Business Programs of the Federal Government

This guide contains descriptions of selected Government programs designed specifically to assist small businesses, and how and where further information may be obtained about these programs. Information includes—but is not limited to— financial, management and technical assistance, and economic development programs. Federal agencies also help small firms obtain a fair share of Government procurement, apply for Government grants and enter local, national and international markets. The handbook is organized alphabetically by the departments and agencies that have small business programs. Under each heading, a listing is provided of separate offices that offer small business assistance programs, publications of interest to small firm owners and operators, telephone numbers, addresses and related information. The handbook was compiled by the Committee on Small Business of the U.S. Senate. 1984, 5th ed. 248pp. $7.00. GPO S/N 052-071-00680-0. (Y 1.1/3:98-33) See the GPO order form.

Directory of Federal and State Business Assistance

Prepared specifically for U.S. businesses, the goal of this directory is to provide quick access to the specific Federal or State resource a business requires. The first section includes thorough summaries detailing specific services provided by U.S. Government agencies. More than 170 such offices are included, covering assistance in procurement, exporting, financing, marketing, management, information, and many other areas. A detailed subject index offers quick access to the appropriate resource. The second section of the directory describes more than 300 State programs specifically designed to assist businesses. Such assistance may involve loans, information, technical help, and management. Prepared by the Center for the Utilization of Federal Technology, National Technical Information Service (NTIS). 1986. approx. 300pp. $19.00. NTIS order number PB86-100344/GBD. See the NTIS order form.

Small Business Guide to Federal R&D Funding Opportunities

A source of information about opportunities for obtaining Federal funding for research and development (R&D) activities, this publication provides information as to how Federal grants and contracts are awarded, including criteria that companies must meet in order to do business with the Federal Government; procedures used by Federal R&D programs to publicize funding opportunities and to solicit ideas from the private sector; and certain Federal laws, regulations and policies that affect small business participation in federally funded R&D activities. The major portion of the guide provides brief descriptions of the R&D program priorities of a number of Federal departments and agencies that offer funding opportunities for small, technically and managerially competent R&D firms. For each agency or program element, the name, address and telephone number of a small business specialist is provided; in many instances, the same information is provided for technical representatives as well. The guide was prepared for the National Science Foundation's Office of Small Business R&D by Human Sciences Research, Inc., McLean, VA. 1983, 4th edition. 136pp. $11.00. NTIS order number PB83-192401/GBD. (NS 1.20:Sm 1) See the NTIS order form.

Information and Steps Necessary to Form Research and Development Limited Partnerships

An overview of the structure, formation and operation of Research and Development Limited Partnerships (RDLP) and the steps required to implement an RDLP. It guides the potential general partner through understanding the nature and purpose of an RDLP; the antitrust implications of RDLPs and the Internal Revenue Service regulations regarding structuring to receive favorable tax treatment; and creating a business plan, executing the "Partnership Agreement," establishing agreements between the partnership and other parties, and preparing the RDLP prospectus. 1983. 105pp. $16.95. NTIS report number PB84-156058/GBD. See the NTIS order form. For further information on RDLPs and the Industrial Technology Partnerships Program, contact the Office of Productivity, Technology and Innovation, Department of Commerce, 14th and Constitution Avenue NW, Room 4828, Washington, DC 20230; (202) 377-8080.

Guide to Innovation Resources and Planning for Small Business

A guide to assist smaller technology-based companies translate ideas into new products and processes. The guide is also intended for State and local governments looking at innovation as a tool for economic development, or associations with constituents involved in innovation. The first section of the guide describes the innovation process. The second section identifies resources available to those involved in innovation. This includes many different types of programs, organizations and techniques to promote innovation. The capabilities of some 135 Federal and State units providing assistance are summarized and addresses and telephone numbers are provided. Prepared by the Office of Productivity, Technology and Innovation in the Department of Commerce. 1984. A 1986 edition is planned. 90pp. $13.50. NTIS order number PB84-176304/GBD. See the NTIS order form.

Franchise Opportunities Handbook

A Department of Commerce guide that lists some 1,300 franchisors, including automobile products, photocopy and quick printer services, fast-food operations, security services, donut shops, motels, lawn services, rental services and campgrounds. It summarizes how they operate, their sizes, years in business, equity-capital requirements and aid they provide for financing, training and management support. Included also are company officials' names and addresses. 1985. 458pp. $15.00. GPO S/N 003-008-00198-0. (C 61.31:985) See the GPO order form.

Franchising in the Economy 1984–1986

A report on a survey of franchisors of business franchising establishments in the United States that provides information on product and trademark franchising, business format, trends and outlook international markets, minority franchises, restaurants, convenience stores, and other areas of interest to the prospective entrepreneur. 1985. 99pp. $3.50. GPO S/N 003-008-00199-8. (C 62.16:984-86) See the GPO order form.

U.S. Industrial Outlook

Published at the beginning of each year, this publication provides objective industry-by-industry analyses and forecasts for 350 industries, with projections to 1990. It is produced by Department of Commerce industry analysts using the latest Census of Manufacturers and other Federal data. The service sector and emerging growth industries are covered. January 1986. 693pp. $15.00. GPO S/N 003-008-00197-1. (C 62.17:985) See the GPO order form.

Guide to Service Industry Statistics and Related Data

A Bureau of the Census publication that identifies information available on service industries, this guide provides background on how the data are collected and how the information may be used. Included are sections on the classification system used to collect and summarize data, the types of geographic areas (political and statistical) for which industry or kind-of-business data are available from major economic statistics programs, and the kinds of data available on various establishments engaged in service and service-type activities. References are included on service industry data programs of other agencies. 1984. 58pp. Single copy **FREE**. Customer Services, Data Users Services Division, Bureau of the Census, Washington, DC 20233; (301) 763-4100.

Exporting Information References

Is Exporting for You?

This booklet suggests questions that should be asked before one considers entering the export business. It includes brief descriptions of the benefits of exporting, understanding the export process, how to identify overseas markets, evaluating one's competition, and a reference matrix for matching international trade business needs with the assistance offered by public and private sector organizations. 1984. 8pp. FREE. Any Small Business Administration office or direct from SBA, P.O. Box 15434, Ft. Worth, TX 76119.

Market Overseas with U.S. Government Help

This publication describes Federal Government international trade and investment programs that may benefit small businesses. 1984. 12pp. FREE. Small Business Administration, P.O. Box 15434, Ft. Worth, TX 76119.

Foreign Business Practices

The material in this publication provides information about practical aspects of exporting, international licensing and investing. This includes information on foreign laws that regulate the use of foreign agents and distributors, focusing on the conditions that govern the conduct and termination of trading transactions involving them, as well as the resolution of international trade and investment disputes through commercial arbitration. Patent, trademark and other industrial property rights are discussed on a country-by-country basis. There is also a section on foreign licensing and joint ventures, as well as information about the increasing impact of product liability on international commerce. Prepared by the Office of Trade Finance, International Trade Administration, Department of Commerce. 1985. 92pp. $3.50. GPO S/N 003-009-00460-8. (C 61.2:P 88/985) See the GPO order form.

A Basic Guide to Exporting

A description of the overall export process and a step-by-step guide to establishing an international trade business. 1981. 141pp. $6.50. GPO S/N 003-009-00349-1. (C 61.8:Ex 7/3) See the GPO order form.

The Export Trading Company Guidebook: Export Trading Companies

Export trading companies (ETC) assume the risks associated with international trade by taking title to goods domestically and handling subsequent export operations for the small business owner. This guidebook provides information on the functions and advantages of establishing or using an ETC. 1984. 144pp. $4.75. GPO S/N 003-009-00364-4. (C 61.8:Ex 7/4) See the GPO order form.

Services for Exporters from the U.S. Government

A catalog of Federal department and agency services, programs and publications available to exporters. It was prepared by the Congressional Research Service for use by the Subcommittee on Oversight and Investigations, Committee on Energy and Commerce, in their review of Federal assistance to U.S. exporters. The report contains the principal features of each program, service and publication; prices and eligibility criteria, if any; name, address and telephone number of a person or office in each agency whom one may contact for assistance; and an appendix in which the various programs and services are keyed to specific users and purposes to help exporters locate the assistance appropriate to their needs. The eight specific user categories or "keys" are listed below.

- Key to Federal Programs for Exporters of Agricultural and Food Products
- Key to Federal Programs for Exporters of Manufactured Goods
- Key to Federal Programs to Aid Export Market Research
- Key to Federal Programs to Aid New Exporters
- Key to Federal Programs for Exhibiting Products Overseas
- Key to Federal Programs Designed for Small Businesses and Minority-Owned Firms That Export
- Key to Federal Programs for Financing Exports
- Key to Programs for Investing Overseas

The report is a description, not an evaluation, of the assistance offered by the Federal Government. 1984. 176pp. $4.25. GPO S/N 052-070-05977-0. (Y 4.En 2/3:98-GG) See the GPO order form.

Key Officers of Foreign Service Posts: Guide for Business Representatives

A directory of key officers at United States Foreign Service posts with whom American business representatives would most likely have contact, this guide also lists Department of Commerce District Offices that provide information and assistance on international trade matters. All embassies, missions, consulates general and consulates are listed. At larger posts, Commercial Officers represent U.S. commercial interests within their country of assignment. Specializing in U.S. export promotion, Commercial Officers assist American business by arranging appointments with local business and government officials; providing counsel on local trade regulations, laws and customs; identifying importers, buyers, agents, distributors and joint venture partners for U.S. firms; and other business assistance. At smaller posts, U.S. commercial interests are represented by Economic/Commercial Officers who also have economic responsibilities. Also listed, as appropriate, are the Chief and Deputy Chief of Mission, Financial Attaches, Political Officers, Labor Officers, Consular Officers, Administrative Officers, Regional Security Officers, Scientific Attaches, Agricultural Officers, AID (Agency for International Development) Mission Directors and Public Affairs Officers. Issued three times a year. Subscription price: $10.00 a year. Single copy price: $3.75. GPO List ID KOFS. (S 1.40/2:Of2/) See the GPO subscription order form.

Washington Embassies: A Guide for the Private Sector

A guide to 130 Washington, DC embassies to assist corporate and association executives in dealing with the international marketplace. The book includes: whom to contact when travelling abroad; which ambassadors entertain groups planning trips to their countries; which countries participate in U.S. trade shows, provide trade briefings and publish trade newsletters; and how to estimate the economic value of the diplomatic presence in Washington. Written by Dr. Carl Bartz. 1985. 213pp. $15.00. Greater Washington Society of Association Executives, 1426 21st Street NW, Suite 200, Washington, DC 20036; (202) 429-9370.

U.S. Export Management Companies Directory

A directory listing export management firms that assist companies with a single product or a whole range of activities involved in getting into foreign markets. More than 1,100 companies are listed by geographic location and indexed by 36 basic product/service categories. 1981. 192pp. $7.00. GPO S/N 003-009-00342-3. (C 61.2:Ex 7/5) See the GPO order form.

European Trade Fairs: A Guide for Exporters

This guide describes how to choose a market in Europe, how to identify the right fairs in which to participate and how to make fairs as productive as possible. 1981. 81pp. $5.00. GPO S/N 003-009-00341-5. (C 61.8:Eu 7/2) See the GPO order form.

Official U.S. and International Financing Institutions

A guide for exporters and investors that provides information on sources of financing, insurance and procurement for U.S. exports and investments. It describes programs of various agencies and institutions, guides for exporters, contact points and current interest rates and fees. 1985. 20pp. $1.50. GPO S/N 003-009-00445-4. (C 61.8:F 49/985) See the GPO order form.

Exporting Information Periodicals

Business America: The Magazine of International Trade

A biweekly publication designed to help American exporters penetrate overseas markets, *Business America* provides timely information on opportunities for trade and methods of doing business in foreign countries. A typical issue includes an analytical piece on current U.S. trade policy, a "how to" article for the novice exporter, a picture of the Nation's economic health, news of congressional and Government actions affecting trade, economic and market reports gathered by the Foreign Commercial Service, and other news generated by the International Trade Administration (ITA) and other U.S. Government agencies as well as foreign governments. The December 23, 1985, issue includes the annual "ITA Publications Checklist." Prepared by ITA, Department of Commerce. Subscription price: $57.00 a year. Single copy price: $2.50 a copy. GPO List ID CRTD. (C 61.18:) See the GPO subscription order form.

Export Administration Regulations, 1985

This comprehensive guide by the Export Administration Agency describes the policies controlling exporting and includes the official U.S. Government regulations. The regulations govern the export licensing of commodities and technical data. Subscription service consists of a basic manual, a set of dividers, and supplementary material issued as Export Administration Bulletins for approximately one year. Punched for 3-ring looseleaf binder. Subscription price: $86.00. GPO List ID EAR 85. (C 61.23:984) See the GPO subscription order form.

International Mail

A U.S. Postal Service manual that includes information on international postage rates, prohibitions, restrictions, availability of insurance and other special services. Also included is information on mailing to individual countries. Subscription service consists of a basic manual and changes for an indeterminate time. Punched for 3-ring looseleaf binder. Subscription price: $25.00. GPO List ID INTMA. (P 1.10/5:) See the GPO subscription order form.

Computerized Information Resources

The following are computer-based information systems that relate to this chapter. For more information on these and other online services, see Appendix D, "Computerized Information Resources."

BidNet

BidNet is a computerized database system that keeps track of Federal Government, State and city requests for bids on goods and services. When an appropriate bid notice appears, BidNet sends its customers a bid bulletin. BidNet, Inc., 5 Choke Cherry Road, Rockville, MD 20850; (800) 447-5837 or (301) 330-7000.

Commerce Business Daily

An electronic online version of the periodical by the same name (see first entry in the "Government Procurement Periodicals" section above) is available from a number of vendors. Consult a current issue of *Commerce Business Daily* for information on current vendors.

Procurement Automated Source System

The Procurement Automated Source System (PASS) program is a computerized matching system that puts Government procurement sources and major corporations in touch with small businesses capable of filling their contract and subcontract requirements. Participation in PASS is **FREE**. Operated by the Small Business Administration (SBA), PASS provides information on more than 145,000 small firms. Of these firms, more than 27,000 are minority-owned and more than 27,000 women-owned. Capabilities of each firm in the PASS database are identified by keywords. Whenever a Government agency or major corporation asks for a firm with certain capabilities, the system provides a listing of companies. The PASS system may be searched by geographic location, type of ownership, labor surplus area and other data elements. Registration with the PASS system should not preclude one from applying to individual Government agency procurement offices. Additional information and a registration form is available from any SBA field office or from the Office of Procurement Assistance (PASS), SBA, 1441 L Street NW, Washington, DC 20416; (202) 653-6586.

Subject Bibliographies

Most publications for sale by the Government Printing Office (GPO) that relate to Federal Government business may be identified using the following subject bibliographies (SB), available **FREE**. Use the GPO SB order form.

- Federal Government Forms (SB-90)
- Government Specifications and Standards (SB-231)
- How to Sell to Government Agencies (SB-171)
- Procurement, Supply Cataloging and Classification (SB-129)

Chapter 15
Mapping, Charting and Geologic Activities

The Federal Government is extensively involved in the production of maps, charts, aerial photographs and space imagery, geodetic control, digital and related cartographic data, and geological related information. This chapter presents descriptions of the principal types of materials published by Government agencies in this area and cites sources that provide more detailed information.

A complete list of types of maps, their publishing agencies, and sources from which they are sold appears in *Types of Maps Published by Government Agencies*, available **FREE** from the National Cartographic Information Center (NCIC). An excerpt from this publication is provided in Figure 15-1 to serve as an overview of the mapping and charting section of the chapter. The NCIC, a component of the Department of the Interior's U.S. Geological Survey (USGS), is the focal point for information on United States maps, charts and related information. It publishes the *NCIC Newsletter*, available **FREE**. Contact NCIC, USGS, 507 National Center, Reston, VA 22092; (703) 860-6045.

The Government Printing Office (GPO) makes available **FREE** three subject bibliographies (SB) of publications for sale by GPO: *Maps and Atlases (U.S. and Foreign)* (SB-102), *Surveying and Mapping* (SB-183) and *National Ocean Survey Publications* (SB-260). See the GPO SB order form.

The information resources described in this chapter are organized under the following headings.

- Policy Directive
- Map Collections
- Cartographic Data and Topographic Maps
- Nautical Charts
- Aeronautical Charts
- Defense Mapping Agency Products
- Geological Information

Policy Directive

Coordination of Surveying and Mapping Activities

This Office of Management and Budget (OMB) Circular No. A-16 describes the responsibilities of Federal agencies with respect to coordination of Federal

Type of Maps	Publisher	Source
Aeronautical Charts	DMA	NOS
Climatic Maps	NOAA	NCC
Geologic Quadrangle Maps	USGS	USGS
Nautical Charts of U.S. Coastal Waters	NOS	NOS
Great Lakes and Connecting Waters	NOS	NOS
Land Use and Land Cover Maps	USGS	USGS
Map Projections	NOS	NOS
Moon/Planetary Maps	USGS	USGS
Oil and Gas Investigations Maps & Charts	USGS	USGS
Space Imagery Maps	USGS	USGS
Time Zones of the World	DMA	DMA
Topographic Map Indexes	USGS	USGS
Water Resources Development Maps	USGS	USGS
World Maps	DMA	DMA

Legend:

```
DMA  = Defense Mapping Agency
NCC  = National Climatic Center
NOAA = National Oceanic and Atmospheric Administration
NOS  = National Ocean Survey
USGS = U.S. Geological Survey
```

Figure 15-1. Selected List of Types of Maps Published by Government Agencies

surveying and mapping activities. The directive covers all surveying and mapping activities financed in whole or in part by Federal funds that contribute to the National Topographic Map Series of the United States and outlying areas of sovereignty and jurisdiction, the *National Atlas of the United States of America*, the National Networks of Geodetic Control, or such other national geodetic control and topographic mapping programs that may be established. It further directs that the document shall apply to any product that results in cartographic representation of international boundaries, other than those of the United States with Canada or Mexico. 1967. 24pp. **FREE**. EOP Publications, 726 Jackson Place NW, Room 2200, Washington, DC 20503; (202) 395-7332.

Map Collections

Map Reference Libraries

Selected university and public libraries in all 50 States and Canada have been designated to serve as depositories for many of the maps published by the Department of the Interior's U.S. Geological Survey (USGS). This booklet is a list of the currently designated map reference libraries. 1984. 8pp. **FREE**. National Cartographic Information Center, USGS, 507 National Center, Reston, VA 22092; (703) 860-6045.

Map Collections in the United States and Canada

A directory that provides information on more than 800 map collections. The entries are arranged alphabetically by State (U.S.) and province (Canada). Included for each entry are the name of head of collection, address, telephone number, hours, size, geographic and subject specializations, and services available to users (e.g., copying). Compiled by David K. Carrington and Richard W. Stephenson of the Library of Congress, Geography and Map Division. 1985, 4th ed. 192pp. $35.00. ISBN 0-87111-306-5. (84-27571) Special Libraries Association, 1700 18th Street NW, Washington, DC 20009; (202) 234-4700.

Cartographic Data and Topographic Maps

National Cartographic Information Center

The National Cartographic Information Center (NCIC) of the Department of the Interior, U.S. Geological Survey's (USGS) National Mapping Program, exists to help find maps of all kinds—and much of the data and materials used to compile and print them. This leaflet describes the role of NCIC as the public's primary source of cartographic information. Overall, NCIC collects, sorts and describes all types of cartographic information from Federal, State and local government agencies and, where possible, from private companies in the mapping business. The leaflet provides addresses and telephone numbers of regional offices and an information inquiry card. **FREE**. NCIC, USGS, 507 National Center, Reston, VA 22092; (703) 860-6045.

NCIC Information Leaflets

The National Cartographic Information Center (NCIC), National Mapping Division, provides a variety of leaflets that describe elements of the National Mapping Program. A listing of the Division's leaflets—by subject category—follows. All leaflets are **FREE** from NCIC except if otherwise indicated. See entry above.

Educational Leaflets
- America's Place Names
- Measuring the Nation
- A Selected Bibliography of Maps, Mapping, and Remote Sensing

Information Systems
- Aerial Photography Summary Record System
- Using APSRS Microfiche
- Map Information

Mapping
- Map Scales
- Map Accuracy
- How to Order Maps on Microfilm
- Out-of-Print Maps
- Looking for an Old Map
- Advance Materials
- Finding Your Way with a Map and Compass
- Intermediate Scale Base Maps
- Selling US Maps
- MiniCatalog of Map Data
- Map Products
- Map Service

Satellite Imagery
- How to Order Landsat Images
- Manned Spacecraft Photographs and Major Metropolitan Area Photographs and Images
- Index of Earth Resources Observation Systems

Aerial Photography
- How to Order Aerial Photographs
- Micrographic Indexes
- Looking for an Old Aerial Photograph
- The Sky's the Limit (NHAP)

General
- Understanding Maps and Scale—$1.00

Digital Cartography
- US GeoData, 1:2,000,000-Scale, Planimetric Digital Data
- Digital Elevation Models
- 1:250,000- and 1:100,000-Scale Land Use and Land Cover and Associated Maps Digital Data
- 7.5- and 15-Minute Planimetric Digital Data
- Geographic Names Information System (GNIS)

Mapping, Charting and Geologic Activities 383

Map Data Catalog

Using text and illustrations, this book describes the products and services of the National Mapping Program for which specific information is available from the National Cartographic Information Center. It includes, but is not limited to, coverage of the following items: land-use and land-cover associated maps, manned spacecraft photos, aircraft photos, Landsat imagery, digital terrain tapes, slope maps, orthophotoquads, maps on microfilm, out-of-print maps, geodetic control data, photoindexes and geographic search and inquiry systems. 1984, 2nd ed. 48pp. $4.00. GPO S/N 024-001-03522-7. (I 19.2:M 32/13/984) See the GPO order form.

Maps for America

A comprehensive look at the history of mapping, different kinds of maps and map data, and the characteristics of U.S. Geological Survey (USGS) maps and maps produced by other sources. This USGS-prepared book also discusses the meaning of lines, colors, images, symbols and notes that appear on maps; the possible errors and anomalies affecting the reliability and interpretation of maps; and the various sources of maps and related information. 1981. 279pp. $15.00. GPO S/N 024-001-03449-2. (I 19.2:M 32/12/981) See the GPO order form.

Topographic Maps Indexes

Indexes showing topographic maps published for each State of the United States and its island territories are available **FREE**. Indexes for areas east of the Mississippi River, including Minnesota, Puerto Rico, and the Virgin Islands, may be requested from the Eastern Distribution Branch, U.S. Geological Survey, 1200 S. Eads Street, Arlington, VA 22202; (703) 557-2751. Indexes for areas west of the Mississippi River, including Alaska, Hawaii, Louisiana, Guam, and American Samoa, may be requested from the Western Distribution Branch, USGS, Box 25286, Federal Center, Denver, CO 80225; (303) 234-3832. The indexes contain lists of special maps, addresses of local map references libraries, local map dealers and Federal map distribution centers. An order blank and detailed instructions for ordering maps are supplied with each index.

Status of Orthophotoquad Mapping

Orthophotoquads are black and white photographic images in standard U.S. Geological Survey (USGS) quadrangle format. They may be used as map substitutes for unmapped areas and for areas in need of revision. They are valuable map complements and may be used as a base for special-purpose maps. They show detail that cannot easily be shown by map symbols. **FREE**. USGS, see addresses in entry above.

The EROS Data Center

The Earth Resources Observation Systems (EROS) Program of the Department of the Interior, administered by the U.S. Geological Survey, was established in 1966 to apply remote-sensing techniques to the inventory, monitoring and management of natural resources. Data from the EROS Data Center are available at nominal cost to scientists, resource planners, managers and the public. For further information, contact EROS Data Center, User Services Section, Sioux Falls, SD 57198; (605) 594-6151.

Nautical Charts

Nautical Charts Catalogs

Catalogs showing nautical charts, bathymetric maps and special-purpose charts published for the coastal areas of the United States and its island territories are available **FREE**. The following catalogs contain information on related publications and how to order the charts and publications. Distribution Branch, National Ocean Survey, Riverdale, MD 20737; (301) 436-6990.

> Catalog 1 Atlantic and Gulf Coasts, Including Puerto Rico and the Virgin Islands
> Catalog 2 Pacific Coast, Including Hawaii, Guam and Samoa Islands
> Catalog 3 Alaska, Including the Aleutian Islands
> Catalog 4 Great Lakes and Adjacent Waterways
> Catalog 5 Bathymetric Maps and Special Purpose Charts

Dates of Latest Editions—Nautical Charts & Miscellaneous Maps

Issued quarterly, this publication lists the latest date of charts and maps sold by the National Ocean Survey (NOS) of the Department of Commerce's National Oceanic and Atmospheric Administration. Charts with edition dates prior to those listed in the most current volume are considered obsolete for use in navigation. Natural and artificial changes—many of them critical—occur constantly; this source provides the means for navigators to locate the most up-to-date charts. Information in this publication may be updated between printings by referring to the *Notice to Mariners* published by the U.S. Coast Guard District Offices and the Defense Mapping Agency Hydrographic Center. **FREE**. NOS, see entry above.

Historic Nautical Charts Lithograhic Prints

A listing of lithographic reproductions of 19th century copperplate engravings available from the National Ocean Survey (NOS). It includes many reproductions that have not been printed since their original issue over a century ago. Order form included. **FREE**. NOS, see Nautical . . . entry above.

List of Educational Materials

A listing of National Ocean Survey (NOS) materials available for educational purposes. **FREE**. NOS, see *Nautical* . . . entry above.

Sales of Aerial Photographs

The National Ocean Survey (NOS) uses coastal aerial photography to produce its nautical charts. This information sheet provides details on what is available and how to get aerial photographs from NOS. **FREE**. Photogrammetry Branch, N/CG2314, Nautical Charting Division, NOS, Rockville, MD 20852; (301) 443-8601.

Aeronautical Charts

Catalog of Aeronautical Charts and Related Publications

The National Ocean Survey (NOS) of the Department of Commerce's National Oceanic and Atmospheric Administration (NOAA), publishes and maintains aeronautical charts and related publications designed for use in air navigation. These charts, in several series, depict the communication facilities, navigational aids, airport landing patterns, safe operating procedures and air traffic rules as determined by the Federal Aviation Administration (FAA). The aeronautical charts are divided primarily into two major series: visual charts and instrument charts. Published annually, this catalog includes descriptions, prices and ordering information on each series of aeronautical charts published by the NOS. Information on related publications of the FAA and the Defense Mapping Aerospace Center, which may be of interest to the civil aviation community, are also described. **FREE**. Distribution Branch, NOS, Riverdale, MD 20737; (301) 436-6990.

Defense Mapping Agency Products

Defense Mapping Agency Public Sale Catalog

This publication contains information on the types of maps and charts available to the public from the Department of Defense, Defense Mapping Agency (DMA) and how to obtain them. It includes a list of DMA U.S. sales agents and their addresses. **FREE**. DMA, Office of Distribution Services, Attn: DOCS, Washington, DC 20315-0010; (202) 227-2816.

Catalogs of Nautical Charts

These catalogs cover nine regions of the world. Each regional catalog contains titles and area coverage of the large and medium scale charts issued by the Defense Mapping Agency (DMA). The price is $2.25 per catalog; they may be purchased from DMA at the above address, Attn: DDCP. The regions and their respective areas of coverage are listed here.

1 United States and Canada
2 Central and South America and Antarctica
3 Western Europe, Iceland, Greenland and the Arctic
4 Scandinavia, Baltic and USSR

5 Western Africa and the Mediterranean
6 Indian Ocean
7 Australia, Indonesia and New Zealand
8 Oceania
9 East Asia
10 Miscellaneous and Special Purpose Navigational

DOD Glossary of Mapping, Charting and Geodetic Terms

Prepared under the direction of the Defense Mapping Agency (DMA), this Department of Defense (DOD) glossary provides a comprehensive source on current usage of mapping, charting and geodetic terms for all levels of users. Terms and definitions in this publication were selected from authoritative glossaries and dictionaries and from technical publications and papers concerned with the many disciplines associated with mapping, charting and geodesy. 1981, 4th ed. 204pp. $8.00. DMA stock number GLOSXMCGTERMS. DMA, Attn: DDCP, see entry above.

Geological Information

USGS Information Publications

Learning about the earth and its problems is the role of the U.S. Geological Survey (USGS) of the Department of the Interior. The USGS makes numerous publications available about geology, hydrology, topographic mapping and related earth sciences. Single copies of the following selected publications are available **FREE** from the Eastern Distribution Branch, USGS, 604 S. Pickett Street, Alexandria, VA 22304; (703) 756-6141. An annotated list of available titles of popular USGS publications may be obtained **FREE** from the distribution office by requesting a copy of *Popular Publications of the U.S. Geological Survey*.

EROS: A Space Program for Earth Resources
Elevations and Distances in the United States
Geologic Maps: Portraits of the Earth
Introduction to the U.S. Geological Survey's EROS Data Center
Land Use and Land Cover and Associated Maps
Map, Line, and Sinker
Motion Picture Film Services of the U.S. Geological Survey
NAWDEX: A Key to Finding Water Data
A Selected Bibliography on Maps and Mapping
Sources of Information, Products, and Services of the U.S. Geological Survey
State Hydrologic Unit Maps
Topographic Maps
Topographic Maps: Silent Guides for Outdoorsmen
Topographic Maps: Tools for Planning
Types of Maps Published by Government Agencies
The United States Geological Survey
The U.S. Geological Survey's Library
The U.S. Geological Survey: Earth Science in the Public Service
The U.S. Geological Survey's Photographic Library
U.S. Geological Survey Publications on Floods
The U.S. Geological Survey's Public Inquiries Offices: Focal Points for Information
WATSTORE: A WATer Data STOrage and REtrieval System

Guide to Obtaining Information from the USGS

The United States Geological Survey (USGS) produces and distributes information on a wide variety of earth science specialties such as geology, hydrology, cartography, geography and remote sensing, as well as information on land use and energy, mineral and water resources. This information is available in many forms, including books, maps, photographs and various other data formats. This publication describes the sources of USGS information and lists products and their sources. The descriptions of information sources are arranged by subject with USGS sources preceding others (e.g., other Federal, State or private organizations) and include addresses and telephone numbers. USGS products are organized in the following categories: catalogs and lists, indexes, book publications, periodicals, map publications, other USGS products and inactive report series. 1985. 35pp. **FREE**. Circular 900. Eastern Distribution Branch, USGS, 604 S. Pickett Street, Alexandria, VA 22304; (703) 756-6141.

Guide to USGS Geologic and Hydrologic Maps

Formerly called the *Guide to U.S. Government Maps, Geologic and Hydrologic Maps*, this guide covers more than 7,200 thematic or topical maps published by the United States Geological Survey (USGS) through December 1981. The *1984 Supplement* contains entries for maps issued by the USGS during 1982 and 1983. Entries and annotations have been taken from the USGS document *Publications of the Geological Survey*, 1879–1961, and their monthly lists of *New Publications of the Geological Survey* from January 1962 through December 1983. The entries include series number, title, author(s), date of publication, latitudes and longitudes, scale, contour intervals, map sheet size, and annotations for selected maps. Three indexes include: area-subject, subject-area and coordinate. 1983. 644pp. $120.00 (includes *1984 Supplement*), $115.00 prepaid. The *1984 Supplement* is sold separately for $45.00 ($40.00 prepaid). The indexes in the *1984 Supplement* have been merged to include both the 1983 basic volume and the 1984 supplement. Documents Index, P.O. Box 195, McLean, VA 22101; (703) 356-2434.

Bibliography and Index of Geology

This monthly periodical covers the earth science literature of the world, including the products of the Department of the Interior's U.S. Geological Survey (USGS). It includes books, serials, reports and maps. In 1969, it succeeded the *Bibliography of North American Geology*, a USGS publication. Each issue is divided into four sections: Serials (list), Fields of Interest, Subject Index and Author Index. Also included is a set of hardbound cumulative volumes for a year. The publication is photocomposed from citations in GeoRef, a machine-readable database produced at the American Geological Institute (AGI). ISSN 0098-2784. Subscription price: $1,100.00 a year. AGI, Customer Service Department, 4220 King Street, Alexandria, VA 22302; (703) 379-2480.

Part Three

Chapter 16
Government Printing Office

The Government Printing Office (GPO) serves as the principal publisher of documents for the Federal Government. Through a nationwide network of 24 Government bookstores and a direct mail program, the GPO sells more than 16,000 different publications, periodicals and subscription services that originate in various Federal agencies. On average, about 3,000 new titles enter the sales inventory each year, and a similar number of titles become outdated or superseded by revised editions. The GPO also administers the Federal Depository Library Program, through which selected U.S. Government publications are made available in nearly 1,400 libraries throughout the country. The day-to-day operations concerning the sale of publications by the GPO are directed by the Superintendent of Documents.

The GPO bookstores around the country are listed in Figure 16-1. Although each store carries only a small percentage of the many thousands of titles in the total sales inventory (those most in demand), it can accept orders for materials not stocked in that particular store. Single issues of some of the more popular periodicals are available in the stores for over-the-counter sales. The bookstores accept MasterCard, VISA, CHOICE or prepaid Superintendent of Documents deposit account charges.

In addition to the items cited in this chapter, the GPO makes available **FREE** the subject bibliography (SB) *Government Printing Office (U.S.) Publications* (SB-244) of publications sold by GPO. See the GPO SB order form.

The information resources described in this chapter are organized under the following headings.
- Publications Catalogs and Services
- Subject Bibliographies
- Federal Depository Library System

Publications Catalogs and Services

U.S. Government Books

A quarterly catalog containing information on nearly 1,000 of the most popular publications sold by the Government Printing Office. Publications are described under 26 subject headings, e.g., business and industry, diet and nutrition, inter-

TO SERVE YOU BETTER, the GPO operates 24 bookstores in 21 cities around the country. While the bookstores carry only a small percentage of the many thousands of titles in our active sales inventory, they do have the ones most in demand and can accept orders for any not carried in a store. Single issues of some of the more popular periodicals are available in the stores for over-the-counter sales.

The Retail Sales Outlet in Laurel, Maryland is a part of our Retail Distribution Division and has access to all titles currently in stock. Customers having an immediate need for one or more publications are encouraged to pick up their books at the Laurel Retail Sales Outlet where feasible. Before going to Laurel, please call our order desk at 202/783-3238 to check on the price, stock number, and availability of the publication(s) desired.

All of our bookstores and the sales outlet accept MasterCard, VISA, CHOICE, or prepaid Superintendent of Documents deposit account charges. If one of our bookstores or the Laurel outlet is convenient to you, why not stop in and get acquainted. Our managers and their staffs will be happy to assist you and answer any questions you may have about our many publications and services. The addresses and phone numbers of the bookstores and the retail sales outlet are listed below.

Bookstores

ATLANTA
Room 100, Federal Building
275 Peachtree Street, NE
Atlanta, Georgia 30303
(404) 221-6947

BIRMINGHAM
9220-B Parkway East
Roebuck Shopping City
Birmingham, Alabama 35206
(205) 254-1056

BOSTON
Room G25, Federal Building
Sudbury Street
Boston, Massachusetts 02203
(617) 223-6071

CHICAGO
Room 1365,
Federal Building
219 South Dearborn Street
Chicago, Illinois 60604
(312) 353-5133

CLEVELAND
First Floor, Federal Building
1240 East Ninth Street
Cleveland, Ohio 44199
(216) 522-4922

COLUMBUS
Room 207, Federal Building
200 North High Street
Columbus, Ohio 43215
(614) 469-6956

DALLAS
Room 1C50, Federal Building
1100 Commerce Street
Dallas, Texas 75242
(214) 767-0076

DENVER
Room 117, Federal Building
1961 Stout Street
Denver, Colorado 80294
(303) 837-3964

DETROIT
Federal Building
Suite 160
477 Michigan Avenue
Detroit, Michigan 48226
(313) 226-7816

HOUSTON
45 College Center
9319 Gulf Freeway
Houston, Texas 77017
(713) 229-3515/16

JACKSONVILLE
Room 158, Federal Building
400 West Bay Street
Jacksonville, Florida 32202
(904) 791-3801

KANSAS CITY
120 Bannister Mall
5600 East Bannister Road
Kansas City, Missouri 64137
(816) 765-2256

LOS ANGELES
ARCO Plaza, C-Level
505 S. Flower Street
Los Angeles, California 90071
(213) 688-5841

MILWAUKEE
Room 190, Federal Building
517 E. Wisconsin Avenue
Milwaukee, Wisconsin 53202
(414) 291-1304

NEW YORK
Room 110
26 Federal Plaza
New York, New York 10278
(212) 264-3825

PHILADELPHIA
Room 1214, Federal Building
600 Arch Street
Philadelphia, Pennsylvania 19106
(215) 597-0677

PITTSBURGH
Room 118, Federal Building
1000 Liberty Avenue
Pittsburgh, Pennsylvania 15222
(412) 644-2721

PUEBLO
World Savings Bldg.
720 North Main Street
Pueblo, Colorado 81003
(303) 544-3142

SAN FRANCISCO
Room 1023, Federal Building
450 Golden Gate Avenue
San Francisco, California 94102
(415) 556-0643

SEATTLE
Room 194, Federal Building
915 Second Avenue
Seattle, Washington 98174
(206) 442-4270

WASHINGTON, D.C. AND VICINITY
Government Printing Office
710 North Capitol Street, NW.
Washington, D.C. 20401
(202) 275-2091

Department of Commerce
14th and E Streets, NW.
Room 1604, First Floor
Washington, D.C. 20230
(202) 377-3527

Farragut West
Matomic Building
1717 H Street N.W.
Washington, D.C. 20006
(202) 653-5075

Pentagon
Main Concourse, South End
Room 2E172
Washington, D.C. 20310
(703) 557-1821

Retail Sales Outlet

LAUREL
8660 Cherry Lane
Laurel, Maryland 20707
(301) 953-7974

Figure 16-1. Government Printing Office (GPO) Bookstores

national topics and senior citizens. Order forms are included. **FREE**. ISSN 0734-2764. Write to New Catalog, P.O. Box 37000, Washington, DC 20013.

New Books

A bimonthly list that contains non-annotated listings of new publications placed on sale by the Government Printing Office. The list is organized into principal subject areas and then alphabetically within each category. **FREE**. ISSN 0734-2772. To add your name to the mailing list, write to New Books List, Superintendent of Documents, Washington, D.C. 20402.

GPO Standing Order Service

The Government Printing Office (GPO) has a "standing order" service for many of its recurring publications and publications issued in a series form. Essentially, a standing order allows you to place an order only once; you will automatically receive all subsequent editions or all subsequent issuances in the same series (e.g., Congressional Directory, budget documents, and the Statistical Abstract of the U.S.). For complete information about the standing order service and the necessary authorization form, contact the Order Division, Stop SSOP, Government Printing Office, Washington, DC 20402; (202) 275-3082.

GPO Priority Announcement Service

The Government Printing Office (GPO) Priority Announcement Service provides free announcements of new or revised publications in particular fields of interest and for certain annually issued publications that have wide demand. The more than 50 Priority Announcement Mailing Lists are identified in Figure 16-2. To be placed on one or more of these mailing lists for Priority Announcements in your interest area(s), send a letter or postcard to: Superintendent of Documents, Mail Stop SSOM, Washington, DC 20402. Please identify list by number and name.

Monthly Catalog of United States Government Publications

A subscription service that lists 2,000–3,000 publications issued each month, this catalog includes items sold by the Government Printing Office's Superintendent of Documents, those for official use and those sent to Depository Libraries. Bibliographic entries are arranged by Superintendent of Documents classification number and contain four indexes: author, title, subject and series report. In addition to 12 monthly indexes, a subscription includes two indexes and one periodicals supplement. The indexes are arranged by calendar year: all subscriptions are entered to begin with the January issue; back issues from the beginning of the year are furnished. Subscription price: $217.00 a year. Single copy price: $17.00. Semiannual Index, January–June: $46.00. Cumulative Index, January–December: $75.00. Periodicals Supplement: $15.00. GPO List ID MC86. (GP 3.8:) Microfiche (24X) subscription price: $59.00 a year. Single copy price: $3.75. Periodicals Supplement: $3.50. Semiannual Index: $5.50. Annual Index: $10.00. GPO List ID MCM. See the GPO subscription order form.

N-500	Letters of the Delegates of Congress, 1774–1789
N-502	Handbook of North American Indians
N-503	Computer Science and Technology Series
N-504	List of Proprietary Substances and Nonfood Compounds Authorized for Use Under USDA Inspection and Grading Programs
N-505	Construction
N-506	Yearbook of Agriculture
N-507	United States Postage Stamps
N-508	Education
N-509	Agriculture Publications (except N-504 and N-506)
N-510	Federal Communications Commission Publications
N-511	Naval Observatory Publications
N-513	State and Local Governments
N-514	State Department Publications
N-515	Smithsonian Institution Publications (except N-502)
N-516	NASA and Space Related Publications
N-517	Congressional Directory
N-518	Health and Health Related Publications
N-519	National Bureau of Standards Publications (except N-503)
N-521	Congressional Record (bound)
N-524	Exporting
N-525	Environment
N-526	Children's Bureau Publications
N-527	Social Security Publications
N-528	General Business
N-529	Securities and Exchange Commission Publications
N-530	Geological Survey Publications
N-531	Fish and Wildlife Publications
N-532	National Library of Medicine Publications
N-533	Public Papers of the Presidents
N-534	Military History
N-535	Housing and Urban Development Publications
N-538	Criminal Justice
N-539	National ZIP Code and Post Office Directory
N-540	Business Opportunities for Individuals
N-544	Veterans Administration Publications
N-545	Art, Audiovisual, Picture Sets and Posters
N-546	Initial Reports of the Deep Sea Drilling Project (National Science Foundation)

Figure 16-2. Priority Announcement Lists

N-548	Homeowners
N-554	Nuclear Regulatory Commission Publications
N-556	Treasury Department Publications (except IRS publications and N-920)
N-558	Directorate for Information Operations and Reports Administration Department of Defense Reports
N-559	Corps of Engineers Historical Publications
N-561	Register of Toxic Effects of Chemical Substances
N-562	Energy Publications
N-567	Banking and Financial
N-568	National Defense
N-569	Cancer Treatment Symposia
N-900	Defense Logistics Agency Publications
N-901	Budget Publications and Economic Report
N-903	Dangerous Cargoes and Hazardous Materials Regulations (will announce only those parts of the Code of Federal Regulations (CFR), Title 46, Shipping, and Title 49, Transportation, that include regulations on these subjects)
N-904	U.S. Codes and Statutes
N-905	United States Court of Appeals for the Federal Circuit Reports
N-906	Internal Revenue Service Cumulative Bulletins
N-907	U.S. Court of International Trade Reports
N-908	Decisions of the Comptroller General (bound and index-digest)
N-909	Federal Energy Regulatory Commission Publications
N-910	Federal Trade Commission Publications
N-911	The United States Government Manual
N-912	Interstate Commerce Commission Publications
N-903	U.S. Industrial Outlook
N-914	Internal Revenue Service and Related Publications (except N-906)
N-915	Labor and Labor Relations Publications
N-916	Patent and Trademark Publications
N-917	Statistical Abstract of the United States and Related Publications
N-918	United States Supreme Court Reports
N-919	United States Tax Court Reports
N-920	Customs Bulletin (bound)
N-921	Maritime Publications

Figure 16-2. Priority Announcement Lists—Continued

Periodicals Supplement

An annual supplement to the *Monthly Catalog of the United States Government Publications*, this is a compilation of those Federal publications issued three or more times per year and all publications sold on subscription by the Superintendent of Documents, Government Printing Office. The latter are described in *Government Subscription Services*, Price List 36, described below. The periodicals described in the supplement are arranged in an alphabetical list of documents issued by each specific agency. Entries in the main section are indexed by author, title, subject and series/report. January 1986. approx. 450pp. $15.00. GPO S/N 721-003-00000-1. (GP 3.8:) See the GPO order form.

Government Publications Index

A monthly microfilm subscription service that provides an index to Federal Government publications. The service cumulates and interfiles Government publications from 1978 to the present. The index interfiles authors, issuing agencies, titles and subjects into one alphabetical listing. Enquire for price information. Information Access Co., 11 Davis Drive, Belmont, CA 94002; (800) 227-8431 or (415) 591-2333.

GPO Monthly Catalog: Five Year Cumulated Index

Set 1 covers 1976–1980 and Set 2 covers 1981–1985—each including six volumes of printed indexes. Each set is to provide access to Government Printing Office (GPO) items through five indexes: author, subject, title, series, report, and GPO stock or classification numbers. Set 1 is planned for Spring 1986, $495.00. Enquire for price information on Set 2. Oryx Press, 2214 North Central at Encanto, Phoenix, AZ 85004; (800) 457-ORYX or (602) 254-6156.

Monthly Catalog on Microfiche 1895–1979

A collection on silver-halide microfiche of the *Monthly Catalog of United States Government Publications*, 1895–1979, that includes all indexes, supplements and appendices, this collection covers more than one million bibliographic entries. For information on individual volume prices, contact Information Interchange Corp., 3704 Shepherd Street, Chevy Chase, MD 20815; (301) 986-9551.

Popular Names of U.S. Government Reports

This catalog gives the commonly-used names of more than 1,500 Federal Government reports as well as the official titles used in library catalogs and bibliographies. Besides the reports issued by the Government Printing Office or specific Government agencies, private imprints issued for sponsoring agencies and commercial reprints are included. Each entry includes a bibliographic description—and in most cases a transcription—of the Library of Congress (LC) printed card. The index is comprised of entries for both corporate authors and subjects; corporate authors are also listed by subject to facilitate identification. Compiled by Bernard A. Bernier, Jr. and Karen A. Wood of the LC's Serial and Government Publications Division. 1984, 4th ed. 282pp. $12.00. GPO S/N 030-005-00012-1. (LC 6.2:G 74/984) See the GPO order form.

GPO Library Cataloging Transaction Tapes

This subscription service provides cataloging information for Federal Government documents cataloged by the Government Printing Office (GPO). It consists of 53 tapes, with weekly tapes that contain cataloging records in MARC II format entered or modified on the Online Computer Library Center (OCLC) System during a one-week period. One additional tape provides cataloging records for serials published three or more times a year. (The serials tape is available only as part of a subscription service.) Records from these tapes are edited to produce the *Monthly Catalog of United States Government Publications*. Subscription price: $3,975.00 a year. Single copy price: $75.00 per tape. GPO List ID GPOLC. (GP 3.8/4:) See the GPO subscription order form.

Guide to U.S. Government Publications

An annotated reference source of important series and periodicals published by various Federal Government agencies, as well as a complete listing of the Government Printing Office's Superintendent of Documents (SuDocs) Classification Scheme. Entry information includes the title, SuDocs classification number, frequency, International Standard Serial Number (ISSN) for periodicals, annotation, title changes, beginning and closing dates, and class number references to earlier and later classes. Available in hardback and microfiche. For more information, contact Documents Index, P.O. Box 195, McLean, VA 22101; (703) 356-2434.

Government Subscription Services

A quarterly catalog, also known as Price List 36, that describes nearly 600 periodicals and basic manuals with subscription supplements available from the Federal Government. **FREE**. See the GPO subject bibliography order form.

Index to U.S. Government Periodicals

An index to 185 U.S. Government periodicals containing articles of lasting research and reference value. Included are a few publications that are statistical or that contain updates of topical material needed to give more complete coverage to certain subject classifications in which articles of a textual nature are unavailable. Published quarterly in May, August, November and March (annual cumulative issue). Subscription price: $375.00 a year. ISSN 0098-4604. Beginning with January 1975, *Current U.S. Government Periodicals on Microfiche* is available. To be available from Bibliographic Retrieval Services, Inc. (BRS) in 1986, see Appendix D. Prices and availability of individual articles, issues, titles and subscriptions are available upon request. Infordata International Inc., 175 E. Delaware Place, Suite 4602, Chicago, IL 60611; (312) 266-0260.

GPO Sales Publications Reference File

The Government Printing Office (GPO) Sales Publications Reference File (PRF) is a catalog—issued only in microfiche (48X)—of all publications currently offered for sale by the Superintendent of Documents. The PRF is arranged in three sequences: GPO stock numbers; Superintendent of Documents classification numbers; and alphabetical arrangement of subjects, titles, agency series and report numbers, keywords and phrases, and personal authors. The complete file—300–350 fiche—is issued six times a year starting in January. Issued every other month is a single fiche supplement—not sold separately—to the PRF called "GPO New Sales Publications." It contains all new publications that have entered the sales inventory during the preceding month. Subscription price: $142.00 a year. Single copy price: $26.00. GPO List ID PRF. (GP 3.22/3:) A magnetic tape of the PRF is also available in EBCDIC, labeled and blocked up to 8,100 character records. Complete documentation is available upon request. Tapes are issued biweekly. GPO List ID GPRFT. (GP 3.22/3-2:) Subscription price: $850.00 a year. No single tapes are sold. See the GPO subscription order form.

GPO Sales Publications Reference File Online

The Government Printing Office (GPO) Sales Publications Reference File (PRF) is available to subscribers to the DIALOG Information Retrieval System. The PRF is a catalog of about 26,000 books, maps, posters, reports, microfiche and subscription services sold by the GPO's Superintendent of Documents. Users of the DIALOG file are able to perform online searches of GPO's sales inventory to determine if the publication is for sale, if the item is in stock, and the current price and stock number. DIALOG users also have access to the bibliographic data provided by the PRF. Users may also order available documents directly from GPO via the DIALORDER feature of the DIALOG system. This service eliminates most research required to fill customers' orders so order processing times is reduced. DIALOG Information Services, Inc., 3460 Hillview Avenue, Palo Alto, CA 94304; (800) 3-DIALOG.

Out-of-Print GPO Sales Publications Reference File

This publication is available only in microfiche (48X). It is a catalog of publications previously offered for sale by the Government Printing Office's (GPO) Superintendent of Documents, arranged in three sequences: GPO stock numbers; Superintendent of Documents classification numbers; and an alphabetical arrangement of titles, authors, subjects, keywords and phrases. It provides a reference to historical bibliographical data that may help identify out-of-print U.S. Government publications. The publications listed in this file became "out-of-stock" 1979–1984. Spring 1986. Price to be determined. A companion catalog covering the period 1972–1978 entitled *Exhausted GPO Sales Publications Reference File* is out-of-print, but may be available at depository libraries. See the GPO order form.

Subject Bibliographies

The more than 15,000 books, pamphlets, posters, periodicals, subscription services and other Government publications for sale by the Government Printing Office (GPO) are grouped into more than 240 subject bibliographies (SB). Each lists items on a single subject or field of interest. *Subject Bibliography Index* (SB-599) is available **FREE** to assist in identifying and ordering particular subject bibliographies. Figure 16-3 is a list of SBs in alphabetical order. To order, use the SB order form provided in the back of the book.

Title	SB#
Accidents and Accident Prevention	229
Accounting and Auditing	42
Adult Education	214
Africa	284
Aging	39
Agricultural Research, Statistics and Economic Reports	162
Agriculture Yearbooks (Department of)	31
Air Pollution	46
Aircraft, Airports and Airways	13
Airman's Information Manual	14
Alcohol, Tobacco, and Firearms	246
Alcoholism	175
American Revolution	144
Annual Reports	118
Anthropology and Archeology	205
Architecture	215
Armed Forces	131
Army Technical and Field Manuals	158
Art and Artists	107
Asia and Oceania	288
Astronomy and Astrophysics	115
Atomic Energy and Nuclear Power	200
Aviation Information and Training Materials	18
Background Notes	93
Banks and Banking	128
Birds	177
Board of Tax Appeals and Tax Court Reports	67
Budget of the United States Government and Economic Report of the President	204
Building Science Series	138
Bureau of Land Management Publications	256
Bureau of Reclamation Publications	249
Business and Business Management	4
Canada	278
Canning, Freezing, and Storage of Foods	5
Care and Disorders of the Eyes	28
Census of Agriculture	277
Census of Business	152
Census of Construction	157
Census of Governments	156
Census of Housing, Metropolitan Housing Characteristics	313
Census of Manufactures	146
Census of Mineral Industries	310
Census of Population and Housing	181
Census of Population and Housing, Block Statistics	311
Census of Population and Housing, Census Tracts	312
Census of Transportation	149
Child Abuse and Neglect	309
Children and Youth	35
China	299
Civil Aeronautics Board Publications	186

Figure 16-3. Subject Bibliographies

Civil and Structural Engineering	308
Civil Rights and Equal Opportunity	207
Civil War	192
Coins and Medals	198
College Debate Topic	176
Computers and Data Processing	51
Congress	201
Congressional Budget Office Publications	282
Congressional Directory	228
Conservation	238
Construction Industry	216
Consumer Information	2
Cookbooks and Recipes	65
Copyrights	126
Courts and Correctional Institutions	91
Crime and Criminal Justice	36
Customs, Immunization, and Passport Publications	27
Day Care	92
Dentistry	22
Digest of United States Practice in International Law and Digest of International Law	185
Directories and List of Persons and Organizations	114
Disarmament and Arms Control	127
Disaster Preparedness and Civil Defense	241
Diseases in Humans	8
Drug Education	163
Earth Sciences	160
Educational Statistics	83
Electricity and Electronics	53
Elementary Education	196
Employment and Occupations	44
Energy Conservation and Research Technology	306
Energy Management for Consumers and Businesses	303
Energy Policy, Issues, and Programs	305
Energy Supplies, Prices, and Consumption	304
Engineering Other Than Civil	132
Environmental Education and Protection	88
Europe (Including the United Kingdom)	289
Family Planning	292
Farms and Farming	161
Federal Aviation Regulations	12
Federal Communications Commission Publications	281
Federal Government	141
Federal Government Forms	90
Federal Trade Commission Decisions and Publications	100
Financial Aid to Students	85
Firefighting, Prevention, and Forest Fires	76
Fish and Marine Life	209
Food, Diet, and Nutrition	291

Figure 16-3. Continued

Foreign Affairs of the United States	75
Foreign Area Studies	166
Foreign Investments	275
Foreign Languages	82
Foreign Relations of the United States	210
Foreign Trade and Tariff	123
Fossils	143
Gardening	301
General Accounting Office Publications	250
General Services Administration Publications	247
Government Specifications and Standards	231
Grants and Awards	258
The Handicapped	37
Hearing and Hearing Disability	23
High School Debate Topic	43
Higher Education	217
Highway Construction, Safety, and Traffic	3
Historical Handbook Series	16
The Home	41
Home Economics	276
Hospitals	119
Housing, Urban, and Rural Development	280
How to Sell to Government Agencies	171
Immigration, Naturalization, and Citizenship	69
Insects	34
Insurance	294
Intergovernmental Relations	211
Internal Revenue Service Cumulative Bulletins	66
ICC Decisions and Reports	187
Irrigation and Drainage	94
Juvenile Delinquency	74
Labor-Management Relations	64
Latin America and the Caribbean	287
Law Enforcement	117
Laws and Statutes	293
Libraries and Library Science	150
Livestock and Poultry	10
Mammals and Reptiles	70
Maps and Atlases (United States and Foreign)	102
Marine Corps Publications	237
Marketing Research	125
Mass Transit	55
Mathematics	24
Medicine and Medical Science	154
Mental Health	167
Middle East	286
Military History	98
Minerals and Mining	151
Minerals Yearbooks	99
Minorities	6
Motion Pictures, Films, and Audiovisual Information	73

Figure 16-3. Continued

Motor Vehicles 49
Music 221
NASA Educational Publications 222
NASA Scientific and Technical Publications 257
National and World Economy 97
National Bureau of Standards Handbooks and Monographs 133
National Bureau of Standards Special Publications 271
National Bureau of Standards Technical Notes 148

National Defense and Security 153
National Park Service Folders 170
National Science Foundation Publications 220
Naval Facilities Engineering Command Publications 219
Naval Education Publications 173
Navigation 29
Noise Abatement 63
Nurses and Nursing Care 19
Occupational Outlook Handbook 270
Occupational Safety and Health 213
Oceanography 32
Office of Personnel Management Publications 300
Patents and Trademarks 21
Personnel Management, Guidance, and Counseling 202
Pesticides, Insecticides, Fungicides, and Rodenticides 227
Photography 72
Physical Fitness 239
Poetry and Literature 142
Postal Service 169
Posters, Charts, Picture Sets, and Decals 57
Presidents of the United States 106
Prices, Wages, and the Cost of Living 226
Printing and Graphic Arts 77
Procurement, Supply Cataloging, and Classification 129
Public and Private Utilities 298
Public Buildings, Landmarks, and Historic Sites of the United States .. 140
Public Health 122
Radiation and Radioactivity 48
Railroads 218
Reading 164
Recreational and Outdoor Activities 17
Retirement 285
Rural Electrification Administration (REA) Forms and Bulletins 168
School Administration, Buildings, and Equipment 223
Science Experiments and Projects 243
Secondary Education 68
Securities and Investments 295
Shipping and Transportation 40
Ships, Shipping, and Shipbuilding 225

Figure 16-3. Continued

Small Business	307
Smithsonian Institution Popular Publications	252
Smoking	15
Social Security	165
Social Welfare and Services	30
Soil and Soil Management	7
Solar Energy	9
Soviet Union	279
Space, Rockets, and Satellites	297
Spanish Publications	130
Statistical Publications	273
Stenography, Typing, and Writing	87
Subject Bibliography Index	599
Subversive Activities	259
Surveying and Mapping	183
Taxes and Taxation	195
Teachers and Teaching Methods	137
Telecommunications	296
Travel and Tourism	302
Treaties and Other International Agreements of the United States	191
Trees, Forest Products, and Forest Management	86
United States Air Force Manuals	182
United States Army Corps of Engineers	261
United States Coast Guard Publications	263
United States Code	197
United States Court of Claims Reports	174
United States Court of Customs and Patent Appeals Reports and United States Court of International Trade	52
United States Government Printing Office Publications	244
United States Intelligence Activities	272
United States Naval History	236
United States Postage Stamps	11
United States Reports	25
Veterans Affairs and Benefits	80
Vital and Health Statistics	121
Vocational and Career Education	110
Voting and Elections	245
Waste Management	95
Water Pollution and Water Resources	50
Weather	234
Weights and Measures	109
Wildlife Management	116
Women	111
Workers' Compensation	108

Figure 16-3. Continued

Federal Deposit Library System

The congressional Depository Library Program operated by the Government Printing Office (GPO) provides the public with **FREE** access to publications of the U.S. Government. There are nearly 1,400 designated depositories that include libraries of Federal and State governments, colleges and universities, special and public libraries. There are two categories of depositories: regional and selective. Regional Depository Libraries, listed in Figure 16-4, generally receive and retain one copy of every GPO publication—either in hardcopy or microform—for use by the general public. These libraries provide reference services and inter-library loans; however, they are not GPO sales outlets. Selective Depository Libraries receive only the publications chosen by their Depository librarians as appropriate to their collections, although they may choose to receive all Depository Library Program materials. Listed below are the titles maintained by each depository library in its basic collection.

Budget of the United States Government
Catalog of Federal Domestic Assistance
Census Bureau Catalog
Census of Housing (for State of Depository only)
Census of Population (for State of Depository only)
Code of Federal Regulations
Congressional Directory
Congressional District Data Book
Congressional Record
County-City Data Book
Federal Register
Historical Statistics of the United States
Monthly Catalog of United States Government Publications
Numerical Lists and Schedule of Volumes
Publications Reference File
Slip Laws (Public)
Statistical Abstract
Statutes at Large
Subject Bibliographies (SB Series)
Supreme Court Reports
United States Code
United States Government Manual
Weekly Compilation of Presidential Documents

A Directory of U.S. Government Depository Libraries

An annual Joint Committee on Printing publication, this listing provides the addresses and telephone numbers of the nearly 1,400 libraries in the Depository Library Program. It also presents an overview of the program, including early history of depository library legislation and laws currently in force relating to the program. June 1985. 48pp. **FREE**. GPO S/N 021-606-00010-3. See the GPO order form.

Government Printing Office's Depository Library Program

A General Accounting Office (GAO) report of the agency's audit of the Depository Library Program requested by the Joint Committee on Printing. GAO

ALABAMA

Auburn University at Montgomery
  Library
Montgomery, AL 36193
(205) 271-9650

University of Alabama Libraries
University, AL 35486
(205) 348-6046

ALASKA

Served by Washington State Library

ARIZONA

Department of Library, Archives
  and Public Records
State Capitol—3rd Floor
Phoenix, AZ 85007
(602) 255-4121

University Library
University of Arizona
Tucson, AZ 85721
(602) 621-6433

ARKANSAS

Arkansas State Library
One Capital Mall
Little Rock, AR 72201
(501) 371-2326

CALIFORNIA

California State Library
P.O. Box 2037
Sacramento, CA 95809
(916) 324-4863

COLORADO

Government Publications Library
University of Colorado at Boulder
Campus Box 184
Boulder, CO 80309
(303) 492-8834

Denver Public Library
1357 Broadway
Denver, CO 80203
(303) 571-2131

CONNECTICUT

Connecticut State Library
231 Capital Avenue
Hartford, CT 06106
(203) 566-7029

FLORIDA

University of Florida Libraries
Gainesville, FL 32611
(904) 392-0367

GEORGIA

University of Georgia Libraries
Athens, GA 30602
(404) 542-8949

HAWAII

Hamilton Library
University of Hawaii
2550 The Mall
Honolulu, HI 96822
(808) 948-8230

IDAHO

University of Idaho Libraries
Moscow, ID 83843
(208) 885-6344

ILLINOIS

Illinois State Library
Centennial Building
Springfield, IL 62756
(217) 782-5012

Figure 16-4. Regional Depository Libraries

INDIANA
Indiana State Library
140 North Senate Avenue
Indianapolis, IN 46204
(317) 232-3686

IOWA
University of Iowa Libraries
Iowa City, IA 52242
(319) 353-3318

KANSAS
Spencer Research Library
University of Kansas
Lawrence, KS 66045-2800
(913) 864-4662

KENTUCKY
University of Kentucky Libraries
Lexington, KY 40506-0039
(606) 257-3139

LOUISIANA
Middleton Library
Louisiana State University
Baton Rouge, LA 70803
(504) 388-2570

Prescott Memorial Library
Louisiana Tech Universtiy
Ruston, LA 71272-0046
(318) 257-4962

MAINE
Raymond Folger Library
University of Maine
Orono, ME 04469
(207) 581-1681

MARYLAND
McKeldin Library
University of Maryland
College Park, MD 20742
(301) 454-3034

MASSACHUSETTS
Boston Public Library
666 Boylston Street
Boston, MA 02117
(617) 536-5400, ext. 227

MICHIGAN
Detroit Public Library
5201 Woodward Avenue
Detroit, MI 48202-4093
(313) 833-1409

Library of Michigan
P.O. Box 30007
Lansing, MI 48909
(517) 373-1593, ext. 105

MINNESOTA
409 Wilson Library
University of Minnesota
Minneapolis, MN 55455
(612) 373-7870

MISSISSIPPI
University of Mississippi
University, MS 38677
(601) 232-5857

MONTANA
Mansfield Library
University of Montana
Missoula, MT 59812
(406) 243-6700

Figure 16-4. Continued

NEBRASKA

Love Library
University of Nebraska—Lincoln
Lincoln, NE 68588-0410
(402) 472-2562

NEVADA

University of Nevada Library
Reno, NV 89557-0044
(702) 784-6579

NEW JERSEY

Newark Public Library
5 Washington Street
Newark, NJ 07101-0630
(201) 733-7812

NEW MEXICO

General Library
University of New Mexico
Albuquerque, NM 86131
(505) 277-5441

New Mexico State Library
325 Don Gaspar Avenue
Santa Fe, NM 87503
(505) 827-3826

NEW YORK

New York State Library
Cultural Education Center
Empire State Plaza
Albany, NY 12230
(518) 474-5953

NORTH CAROLINA

Davis Library
University of North Carolina at Chapel Hill
Chapel Hill, NC 27514
(919) 962-1151

NORTH DAKOTA

North Dakota State University Library
Fargo, ND 58105
(701) 237-7008

Chester Fritz Library
University of North Dakota
Grand Forks, ND 58202
(701) 777-4630

OHIO

State Library of Ohio
65 South Front Street
Columbus, OH 43266-0334
(614) 462-7051

OKLAHOMA

Oklahoma Department of Libraries
200 Northeast 18th Street
Oklahoma City, OK 73105
(405) 521-2502, ext. 252

Oklahoma State University Library
Stillwater, OK 74078
(405) 624-6546

OREGON

Portland State University
P.O. Box 1151
Portland, OR 97207
(503) 229-3673

PENNSYLVANIA

State Library of Pennsylvania
Box 1601
Harrisburg, PA 17105
(717) 787-3752

Figure 16-4. Continued

TEXAS

Texas State Library
Box 12927 Capitol Station
Austin, TX 78711
(512) 463-5455

Texas Tech University Library
Lubbock, TX 79409
(806) 742-2268

UTAH

Merrill Library
Utah State University
Logan, UT 84322
(801) 750-2682

VIRGINIA

Alderman Library
University of Virginia
Charlottesville, VA 22903-2498
(804) 924-3133

WASHINGTON

Washington State Library
Olympia, WA 98504
(206) 753-4027

WEST VIRGINIA

West Virginia University Library
Morgantown, WV 26506-6069
(304) 293-3640

WISCONSIN

State Historical Society Library
816 State Street
Madison, WI 53706
(608) 262-4347

Milwaukee Public Library
814 West Wisconsin Avenue
Milwaukee, WI 53233
(414) 278-3065

WYOMING

Wyoming State Library
Supreme Court and Library Building
Cheyenne, WY 82002
(307) 777-5919

Figure 16-4. Continued

found that improvements have been made in the program and that the depository libraries are generally able to meet customer needs for Federal publications. Opportunities exist, the report notes, to improve the program's efficiency by developing better policies and procedures for selecting, classifying, cataloging and distributing publications. December 17, 1984. 23pp. **FREE**. GAO report number AFMD-85-19. See the GAO order form.

Depository Librarians' Views on GPO's Administration of the Depository Library Program

A report that summarizes the views of depository librarians on the Government Printing Office's (GPO) Depository Library Program as elicited from a 1983 questionnaire administered by the General Accounting Office (GAO). The study was requested by the Joint Committee on Printing. The body of the report consists of two appendices. The first discusses the librarians' responses to individual questions (tables reflecting these views are included) and summarizes the librarians' narrative comments. The second appendix is the actual survey questionnaire that notes the librarians' responses to each question. April 9, 1984. 40pp. **FREE**. GAO report number AFMD-84-50. See the GAO order form.

List of Classes of U.S. Government Publications Available for Selection by Depository Libraries

A quarterly publication containing the more than 3,800 classes of Government publications available for selection by member organizations of the Depository Library Program. Its primary division is by parent organization, then by subordinate bureaus and offices, followed by classes of documents. The subscription includes an annual supplement that lists inactive or discontinued items from the 1950 revision of the classified list. Subscription price: $24.00 a year. Single copy price: $6.00. Supplement issue: $2.50. GPO List ID LCGPD. (GP 3.24:) See the GPO subscription order form.

GPO Depository Union List of Item Selections

A periodic listing of more than 5,000 item number categories that represent U.S. Government documents distributed through the Federal Depository Program. It lists depository libraries that select each of the items. Available only in microfiche (48X). June 1985. 34 fiche. $5.50. GPO S/N 021-000-00127-9. (GP 3.32/2:) See the GPO order form.

Provision of Federal Government Publications in Electronic Format to Depository Libraries

A report of the Ad Hoc Committee on Depository Library Access to Federal Automated Data Bases to the Joint Committee on Printing, U.S. Congress, that presents the findings and recommendations resulting from a year-long investigation of Federal information programs, electronic distribution systems, automated databases and available databases. The Committee was asked to determine: what and how much Federal Government information is in electronic format? do depository libraries have the ability to access the new formats? what are the costs and benefits of providing information in electronic format? The report also outlines criteria for a proposed pilot program. 1984. 136pp. $5.50. GPO S/N 052-070-05970-2. (Y 4.P 93/1:P 96/2) See the GPO order form.

An Open Forum on the Provisions of Electronic Federal Information to Depository Libraries

The proceedings of a meeting held June 26, 1985, to let concerned parties comment on the report *Provision of Federal Government Publications in Electronic Format to Depository Libraries*, described above, and to solicit suggestions for possible pilot projects that can test the feasibility of the proposal. The report was compiled on behalf of the Joint Committee on Printing and the Ad Hoc Committee on Depository Library Access to Federal Automated Data Bases. 1985. 177pp. $3.75. GPO S/N 052-070-06066-2. (Y 4.P 93/1:E1 2/4) See the GPO order form.

Instructions to Depository Libraries

A manual of instructions that provides guidance regarding the duties and privileges of libraries designated as depositories for U.S. Government publications. Prepared by the Library Programs Service, Superintendent of Documents, Government Printing Office. 1984. 84pp. Available for review at depository libraries.

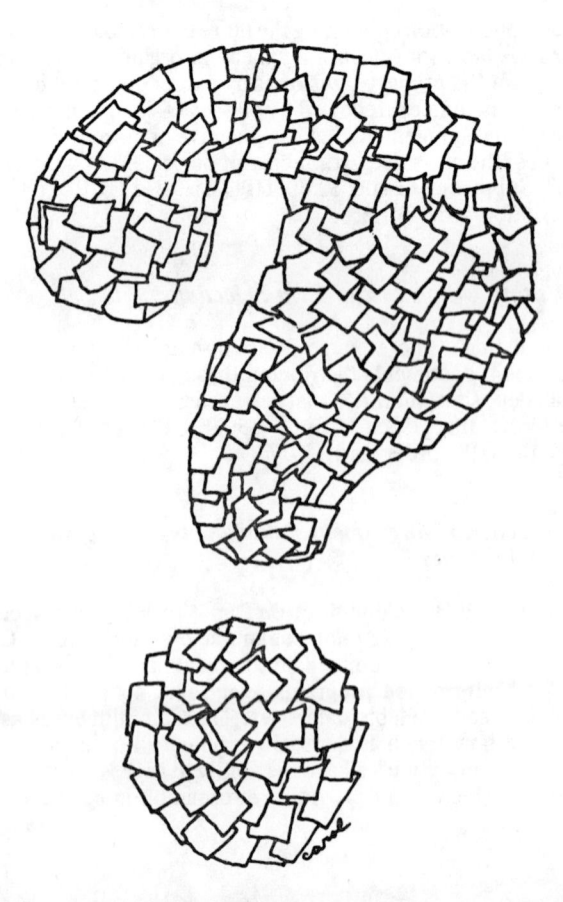

Chapter 17
National Technical Information Service

The National Technical Information Service (NTIS) is a self-supporting agency of the Department of Commerce. It is the central source for the public sale of U.S. Government-sponsored research, development and engineering reports, Government-owned patents, foreign technical reports and other analyses prepared by national and local governmental agencies, their contractors or grantees. It is also the central source for Federally-generated machine-readable data files, and manages the Federal Software Exchange Center for intergovernmental distribution.

NTIS acquires information from four separate sources: U.S. Government agencies; government-to-government agreements—e.g., NTIS' cooperating protocol with the People's Republic of China; NTIS cooperating agencies—private agencies in other countries with which NTIS has commercial agreements; and in-country acquisition representatives who contract to provide NTIS with information from other countries.

As of 1985, the NTIS collection approached two million titles, about 300,000 of which contain foreign technology or marketing information. All are permanently available for sale, either paper copy or microfiche. With 70,000 new reports added annually and the shipment of about 23,000 information products daily, NTIS is one of the world's leading processors of specialty information. Figure 17-1 shows the primary headings of the two subject classification schemes used to sort, selectively disseminate and search the NTIS bibliographic database.

The information resources described in this chapter are organized under the following headings.

- More About NTIS
- Current Awareness Products
- Annual Indexes
- Special Bibliographies
- Computer/Automation Related Products
- Federal Machine-Readable Data
- Specialized Programs and Products

In addition to the material described below, Chapter 13, Science and Technology, provides information on a number of NTIS scientific and technological resources.

Committee on Scientific & Technical Information (COSATI)

Aeronautics
Agriculture
Astronomy & Astrophysics
Atmospheric Sciences
Behavior & Social Sciences
Biological & Medical Sciences
Chemistry
Earth Sciences & Oceanography
Electronics & Electrical Engineering
Energy Conversion (Non-Propulsive)
Materials
Mathematical Sciences

Mechanical, Industrial, Civil, & Marine Engineering
Methods & Equipment
Military Sciences
Missile Technology
Navigation, Communications Detection, & Countermeasures
Nuclear Science & Technology
Ordnance
Physics
Propulsion & Fuels
Space Technology

National Technical Information Service (NTIS)

Administration & Management
Aeronautics & Aerodynamics
Agriculture & Food
Astronomy & Astrophysics
Atmospheric Sciences
Behavior & Society
Biomedical Technology & Human Factors Engineering
Building Industry Technology
Business & Economics
Chemistry
Civil Engineering
Combustion, Engines, & Propellants
Communication
Computers, Control, & Information Theory
Detection & Countermeasures
Electrotechnology
Energy
Environmental Pollution & Control
Government Inventions for Licensing
Health Planning & Health Services Research

Industrial & Mechanical Engineering
Library & Information Sciences
Manufacturing Technology
Materials Sciences
Mathematical Sciences
Medicine & Biology
Military Sciences
Missile Technology
NASA Earth Resources Survey Program
Natural Resources & Earth Sciences
Navigation, Guidance, & Control
Nuclear Science & Technology
Ocean Technology & Engineering
Ordnance
Photography & Recording Devices
Physics
Problem Solving Information for State & Local Governments
Space Technology
Transportation
Urban and Regional Technology & Development

Figure 17-1. Subject Classification Schemes

More About NTIS

The law that established NTIS as a clearinghouse for scientific, technical and engineering information requires that it recover its costs from the sale of its products and services. In this regard NTIS is a unique business-like organization. It is sustained only by its customers. All costs of its products and services, including salaries, marketing, promotion and postage, are paid from sales income and not by tax-supported congressional appropriations.

For details about NTIS, request a **FREE** copy of their *General Catalog of Information Services*, PR-154. See the NTIS order form.

FREE brochures, leaflets and other promotional pieces (see Figure 17-2) are available on request from NTIS, Promotion Division, 5285 Port Royal Road, Springfield, VA 22161. A number of selected products and services are described in the rest of this chapter.

A *Users' Guide to NTIS* designed for the convenience of users provides information on the effective and efficient use of NTIS products and services. A **FREE** copy of the guide, PR-786, is available from the Office of Customer Services, NTIS, 5285 Port Royal Road, Springfield, VA 22161; (703) 487-6424.

Prices for NTIS products are based on a number of criteria: contractual agreements, document length (for hard copy materials), number of reels in an order for tapes, delivery destination, etc. There are four Code Schedules: "A"—Standard Price Schedule; "E"—Exception Price Schedule; "T"—Computer Products, Software and Data Files; and "N"—NO1 covering Published Searches, NO2 for the Directory of Computerized Data Files and Directory of Computer Software. PR-360-3 gives the prices in dollars for all codes for products shipped to addresses in the United States, Canada and Mexico. PR-360-4 quotes prices for products to be shipped to all other destinations.

NTIS has representatives in a number of different countries; a list is provided in their *General Catalog of Information Services*, PR-154. Customers in the countries indicated may expedite service by transacting their NTIS business through these dealers.

Individuals interested in opening a deposit account with NTIS may request the brochure *Deposit Account*, PR-33. An NTIS deposit account holder may order by telephone, telegram or other means. Statements are rendered monthly when an account shows activity, charges or deposits. Purchases of documents or other services are automatically debited against an account, with the monthly statement showing all transactions and an account balance. This provides a record for tax deductible expenses, as appropriate. The NTIS deposit account holder may use American Express, VISA or MasterCard credit cards to replenish the account. These credit cards may also be used for the purchase of NTIS products.

To keep informed of product and procedure changes between issuances of the various NTIS catalogs, one may obtain **FREE** the NTIS *NewsLine*, issued four times a year. Request PR-660 to subscribe to this newsletter.

Abstract Newsletters, **PR-205**
Ada/Ed (software brochure), **PR-768**
Advanced Technology Reports, **PR-612B**
Bibliographic Databases Available From NTIS, **PR-717**
Bibliographic Database Files, **PR-446**
Bibliographic Database, Reference Guide to, **PR-253**
Cartographic Automatic Mapping Program, **PR-709**
CCITT Red Book Series, **PR-783**
Census Data 1980—Employment and Training Indicators, **PR-747**
Census Data 1980—Equal Employment Indicators, **PR-739**
Census Data 1980—Population & Housing Characteristics, **PR-726**
Census Data 1980—Social Indicators for Planning and Evaluation, **PR-748**
Centers for Disease Control (CDC) (brochure), **PR-565**
Center for Utilization of Federal Technology Catalog (CUFT) (brochure), **PR-732**
Center for Utilization of Federal Technology Catalog (CUFT) (pamphlet), **PR-734**
Computerized Data Files, Directory of (brochure), **PR-629**
Computer Software, Directory of (brochure), **PR-261**
Consumer Nutrition Center Data Sets, **PR-715**
Corporate Author Authority List (brochure), **PR-730**
Database Services & Federal Technology in Machine Readable Formats Catalog, **PR-595**
DATAPLOT—Graphics Software System, **PR-169-1**
Data Files Listing, **PR-700**
Data Files on Floppy Diskette, **PR-771-1**
Defense Logistics Services Center, Data Files, **PR-764**
Deposit Account (brochure and application), **PR-33**
Digest Catalog, **PR-755**
Energy Data Files on Magnetic Tape, **PR-712**
Energy Modeling Programs from EIA, **PR-705**
Energy Statistics, **PR-738**
EPA-NIOSH, **PR-719**
Environmental Health Data Files Brochure, **PR-758**
FCC Data Files on Magnetic Tape, **PR-718-2**
FCC Data Files on Microfiche, **PR-718-1**
Federal Energy Technology Catalog, **PR-593**
Federal Engineering Technology Catalog, **PR-596**
Federal Information Processing Standards (FIPS) Catalog (brochure), **PR-357**
Federal Reserve Board Data Files, **PR-790**
Federal Software Exchange Catalog, **PR-383**
Federal Technology Catalog (brochure), **PR-732**
Federal Technology Research Facilities, Directory of, **PR-746**
Federal Technology Transfer Online, **PR-725**

Figure 17-2. NTIS Promotional Items

National Technical Information Service

Foreign Broadcast Information Service/Joint Publications Research Service (FBIS/JPRS), **PR-376**
Foreign Technology Abstract Newsletter, **PR-731**
Foreign Technology Market Information Catalog, **PR-594**
Foreign Technology Program, **PR-724**
General Information Catalog, **PR-154**
Government Inventions for Licensing Newsletter, **PR-750**
Government Patents Catalog, **PR-735**
GRA&I (brochure), **PR-195**
GRA&I Annual Index (brochure), **PR-273**
Graphics Compatibility System (GCS), **PR-696**
Grazing Rental Flyer, **PR-766**
Integrated Library System (ILS), **PR-619**
International Technology Acquisition Program, **PR-687**
Manufacturers Catalog, **PR-612**
Medical Assistance, **PR-679**
Mine Rescue Brochure, **PR-759**
NASA Special Publications, **PR-655**
National Center for Health Services Research, Data Files, **PR-791**
National Center for Health Statistical Data Tapes, **PR-716**
National Fire Incidence Report, **PR-736**
NewsLine (quarterly newsletter on NTIS activities), **PR-660**
NTIS Library User Group Opportunities, **PR-778**
NTIS Computer Software Listing, **PR-260**
OKOCHI, **PR-676**
Partners in Information; SLA-NTIS Videotape, **PR-779**
Patent Catalog (brochure), **PR-278**
Patent Information Available from NTIS, **PR-694**
Patent Licensing, Office of Federal, **PR-751**
Patent Published Searches Title List, **PR-769**
Patent Technology Profile, **PR-661**
Price Code (Foreign), **PR-360-4**
Price Code (North American), **PR-360-3**
Published Searches Master Catalog, **PR-186**
Selected Research in Microfiche (SRIM) (brochure), **PR-270**
Selected Research in Microfiche (SRIM) Users' Guide, **PR-271**
Special Credit Account, **PR-220**
State Technical Assistance Centers and Federal Technical Information Centers (list), **PR-767**
Tech Notes, **PR-365**
Title Index, **PR-567**
UNAMAP—Air Pollution Modeling Software, **PR-710**
U.S. Government Information Standards and Classifications, Data Tapes, **PR-774**
World Bank Publications, **PR-722**

Figure 17-2. NTIS Promotional Items—Continued

Current Awareness Products

Government Reports Announcement & Index Journal

The *Government Reports Announcement & Index Journal* (GRA&I) is the all-inclusive biweekly journal that provides citations and abstracts of all publications received by NTIS. Each issue includes about 2,500 new entries. The abstracts are organized by the 22 Committee on Scientific and Technical Information subject categories (see Figure 17-1) and 178 subcategories. In addition, each issue provides five separate indexes: keyword, corporate author, personal author, Government contract number and NTIS accession (order)/report number. Biweekly. $379.00 per year in the U.S., Canada, and Mexico. For further information, request the GRA&I flyer, PR-195.

Selected Research in Microfiche

The Selected Research in Microfiche (SRIM) service enables customers to receive full-text copies of reports in specific areas of interest, as reports are announced by NTIS. Subscribers select from 41 major subject categories (see Figure 17-1, the NTIS List) and more than 355 subcategories. Reports from these categories, selected subcategories, or only those reports originating from specific Government departments or agencies may be obtained. The option of a cumulative quarterly index is available, as well as customized indexes for one's SRIM collection. Full details, including costs, are available in the *SRIM Brochure*, PR-270.

Annual Indexes

Government Reports Annual Index

The cumulation of the indexes from 26 issues of the biweekly *Government Reports Announcements & Index (GRA&I) Journal*. The Annual Index consists of six volumes with five indexed sections: keyword, personal author, corporate author, Government contract number and NTIS accession (order)/report number. The Index is used in conjunction with the GRA&I to obtain the complete report abstract and bibliographic data. For further information, request the *GRA&I Annual Index Brochure*, PR-273.

NTIS Title Index

The most comprehensive method for identifying previously published reports is the *NTIS Title Index*, available only in microfiche. This index is comprised of three sections: the Keyword-Out-of-Context (KWOC) Title Index, the Author Index and the Report/Accession (order) Number Index. The Retrospective Title Index, 1964–78, is available for $700.00. Beginning with 1979–1980, the Retrospective Updates are two-year cumulations, available at $120.00 each. The Retrospective Index Package, 1964–1984, may be purchased for $900.00—an overall savings of $160.00. The 1985–1986 Current Cumulative Index, a subscription product, is issued quarterly, $350.00.

Special Bibliographies

All the research summaries announced by NTIS are extracts from the complete NTIS Bibliographic Database. Customers may obtain information on research completed based on specific file elements: report title; report date; personal or corporate author; NTIS accession (order)/report numbers; contract/grant number; and subject, (using keywords, descriptors, subject codes). The NTIS Bibliographic Database may be used to create a wide variety of information products. To exploit this capability, the following items will be of interest.

A Reference Guide to the NTIS Bibliographic Database

This guide provides background material on the database that is helpful when working with NTIS files on a publicly available online service, personal computer system, or printed format. It provides information about file contents and bibliographic fields, as well as hints on doing online searches. The guide is available **FREE** by requesting PR-253. The NTIS Bibliographic Database is currently accessible through the following systems: DIALOG Information Services, Bibliographic Retrieval Services (BRS), SDC Information Services and Mead Data Central. Sample citations from these four systems are included in the guide.

Published Searches

Subject information specialists perform retrievals of the NTIS and 20 other databases to create Published Searches. More than 3,000 such search bibliographies are available and are specially priced at $45.00 each. Each covers a topic of special interest and consists of up to 200 or more research report summaries, including abstracts. In addition to the NTIS Bibliographic Database, the following sources are used in developing Published Searches: American Petroleum Institute, Engineering Information, Inc., Food Science and Technology Abstracts, International Aerospace Abstracts, RAPRA Life Sciences Collection and the Energy Data Base. A *Published Searches Master Catalog* is available **FREE**; request PR-186.

Custom Searches

Customized online searches may be conducted by working with NTIS information specialists to establish retrieval parameters tailored to a specific need. For more detailed information on this service, contact NTISearches order desk at (703) 487-4642.

Direct Leasing

Magnetic tapes of the NTIS Bibliographic Database may be leased annually. Files (back to mid-1964) may also be acquired. Current tapes are shipped biweekly to subscribers. Lease fees are negotiated, based on factors such as the number of citations displayed or searches performed and the possibility of third-party use. Contact the NTIS Office of Product Management at (703) 487-4929 for further information.

Computer/Automation Related Products

NTIS serves as the central source within the Federal Government for sale or lease of computer software, bibliographic databases, statistical databases and related technical reports. The present collection of products includes more than 2,500 computer programs and data files pertinent to business and scientific interests. The coverage of areas includes applied science, business, engineering, health and pollution.

Federal Information Processing Standards

The Federal Information Processing Standards (FIPS) are publications (including guidelines) developed by the National Bureau of Standards to facilitate computer compatibility, management, documentation and security. Many standards are the result of a consensus of industry, Government and academia—e.g., the Federal Government's issuance of American National Standards Institute (ANSI) standards. The specific categories of the documents are hardware, software, data and automatic data processing (ADP) operations standards. NTIS offers FIPS publications on demand and by standing order. With the standing order service, new and revised FIPS together with any change notices and associated industry (ANSI) standards issued during the year, are sent to subscribers automatically. For further information, request brochure PR-357. Annual subscription price: $150.00; back issues: $750.00 (includes the current FIPS documents with five specially labeled binders).

Federal Software Products

NTIS has established the Office of Product Management to facilitate access to computer-processible products produced by more than 100 U.S. Government agencies. The office is organized into four major product areas: bibliographic databases; computer software; numeric and textual source data files; and statistical services. A listing of hundreds of software products, together with more information about this program, is provided in PR-260.

Integrated Library System

The ILS software program was developed for the National Library of Medicine to improve its services, collection control and management, and resource sharing. It is available for sale by NTIS. The basic functional subsystems included in ILS are Master Bibliographic File and Bibliographic Control, Circulation, Public Catalog Access, Serials Check-In, and Administration. Enhancements are under development and include full serials control, acquisitions, enhanced cataloging capabilities and a generalized network access module. ILS software provided by NTIS includes user documentation that may be accessed online or via printouts. Additional information is available in PR-619, *The Integrated Library System (ILS)*, or by calling the NTIS Office of Product Management at (703) 487-4929.

Federal Machine-Readable Data

Various NTIS programs provide public access to machine-readable information products of Federal agencies. This effort includes access to scientific, technical and business information. The program's primary areas of concern include providing access to bibliographic data files produced by agencies other than NTIS, cataloging and indexing machine-readable statistical data files, and expanding the NTIS collection of available machine-readable data files and software. Machine-readable products and services currently available from NTIS are described in the booklet *Database Services and Federal Technology in Machine-readable Formats*, PR-595. For a listing of data files available, ask for PR-700 (magnetic tape) or PR-771-1 (floppy diskette).

Databases Available from NTIS

This promotional booklet (PR-717) provides basic information regarding Federal databases available for lease or access through commercial vendors. Databases included are the NTIS Bibliographic Database, the Energy Database, AGRICOLA (from the National Agricultural Library), Selected Water Resources Abstracts, among others.

Specialized Programs and Products

Federal Engineering Technology

A major portion of the NTIS technical information collection includes an interdisciplinary coverage of engineering information. The coverage includes six primary areas of engineering: aeronautical, mechanical, electrical, civil, industrial and chemical—but is not limited to these fields. Also included is information relating to ocean and marine engineering and human factors engineering. More information about access to the NTIS Bibliographic Database in engineering may be obtained by requesting the catalog on this subject, PR-596.

Federal Energy Technology

About a third of the information added to the NTIS Bibliographic Database each year relates to energy—24,000 documents. This includes thousands of documents of foreign origin. The catalog PR-593 describes associated information products and services, and provides details on locating and ordering the particular energy information. The energy topics covered include solar, nuclear, wind, geothermal, fossil and solid wastes. Some methods for obtaining information are to arrange for a standing order in microfiche distribution (information on specific subject interest is distributed as it is received at NTIS). You may subscribe to the weekly *Energy Abstract Newsletter* that identifies and summarizes new documents, or you may purchase selected Published Searches that contain research summaries of NTIS holdings in subject areas of particularly wide interest. For information on 25 different Department of Energy subscriptions, ask for *NTIS Subscription Digest,* PR-755.

Japanese Industrial R&D

The Okochi Memorial Foundation in Japan awards annual prizes to researchers and organizations judged to have made distinguished contributions to human knowledge in areas of industrial research and development (R&D). The 11 volumes documenting this R&D have been translated into English for the years 1970, and 1972 through 1981. Single volumes are $12.50 and the set is sold as PB82-232851/GBD for $110.00. The 1982, 1983 and 1984 editions are also available separately. A brochure describing the contents and prices of each volume is available; ask for PR-775.

Cancer Research Publications

The International Cancer Research Data Bank Program of the National Cancer Institute offers more than 150 cancer research publications. These publications provide comprehensive and convenient information on current cancer research. To assist in keeping up with this research, NTIS has developed a variety of products. A monthly current awareness bulletin, *Cancergram*, that contains abstracts of recently published articles in 66 areas of cancer research is available by subscription. Annual compilations describing ongoing unpublished projects in 55 areas of cancer research are available as *Special Listings*. Selected abstracts of high interest articles on cancer research topics in diagnosis and therapy; carcinogenesis; and cancer virology, immunology, and biology, are available in *Oncology Overviews*. Contact NTIS Subscriptions, (703) 487-4630, for further information.

Centers for Disease Control Information

The Centers for Disease Control (CDC), a Federal agency of the Public Health Service, is responsible for providing leadership and direction in the prevention and control of communicable diseases and other preventable conditions. Among its services, the CDC administers a nationwide program of research, information and education. It develops standards for safe and healthful working conditions. Selected reports are made available using the facilities of NTIS as a clearinghouse. An NTIS brochure describing a number of these reports, together with ordering information, is available in PR-565, *CDC Reports*.

Consumer Nutrition Data

Food consumption and nutrition data collected and compiled by the Consumer Nutrition Center of the Department of Agriculture are available on computer magnetic tapes and on diskettes through the NTIS. This includes the nationwide Food Consumption Survey conducted in 1977–78 by the USDA and (for comparison) the 1965–66 survey. The series provides such data as household food consumption, food and nutrient intake of individuals and nutritional composition of foods. An additional data set is available on food and nutrient intake for low-income individuals and households. For more information about these tapes, ask for the flyer PR-650.

Dental and Physician Assistant Self-Paced Curriculum Modules

This set of programmed-learning aids consists of 51 modules entitled *Competency-Based Dental Assistant and Physician Assistant Modules: A Conversion Project*. Based largely on Armed Forces training materials, the set is designed to give medical staff assistants state-of-the-art training to enhance their work with dentists and doctors. Material covered by the modules ranges from a unit that teaches the classification of dental instruments to one that details the psychology of stress. Modules are available both separately and at a special set price. A complete list of module titles and prices is available in the brochure PR-679.

NASA Special Publications

The National Aeronautics and Space Administration (NASA) special publications (SP) series includes a broad range of topics that include much of the agency's research and development work, space-exploration programs, work in advanced aeronautics technology, and associated historical and managerial efforts. In the two decades since 1961, some 1,200 titles have been issued in SP series. A booklet is available **FREE** from NTIS, PR-655 (NASA SP-449), listing all the SPs that have been released. Together with the title of the publication, a brief description is provided along with the original sales source and publication date. The publications are organized into nine categories: general, handbooks and data compilations, histories and chronologies, technology utilization, management evaluation and analysis standards, bibliographies, space vehicle design criteria, reference and conference publications.

Telecommunications Policy

The "Red Books," issued by the International Telecommunications Union (ITU), include the most recent reports, resolutions and approved recommendations of the International Telegraph and Telephone Consultative Committee (CCITT). These volumes are the official publications of the CCITT Eighth Plenary Assembly held in Malaga-Torremolinos, October 1984. These recommendations keep companies abreast of the rapid evolution in technology as it affects all aspects of telecommunications. Ask for PR-783.

Worldwide News Monitoring Services

Two news services are available from NTIS. The Foreign Broadcast Information Service (FBIS) includes news accounts, commentaries and government statements from foreign broadcasts, press agency transmissions, newspapers and periodicals. Coverage is from any one or combination of regions: People's Republic of China, Eastern Europe, Soviet Union, Asia and Pacific, Middle East and Africa, Latin America, Western Europe and South Asia. The Joint Publications Research Service (JPRS) is a standing order service for automatic receipt of political, economic and technical translations of communist media. It includes current subscriptions and single-copy back issues of more than 50,000 reports published since 1963. Detailed information on these two services is available in the FBIS/JPRS brochure PR-376.

420 FEDfind

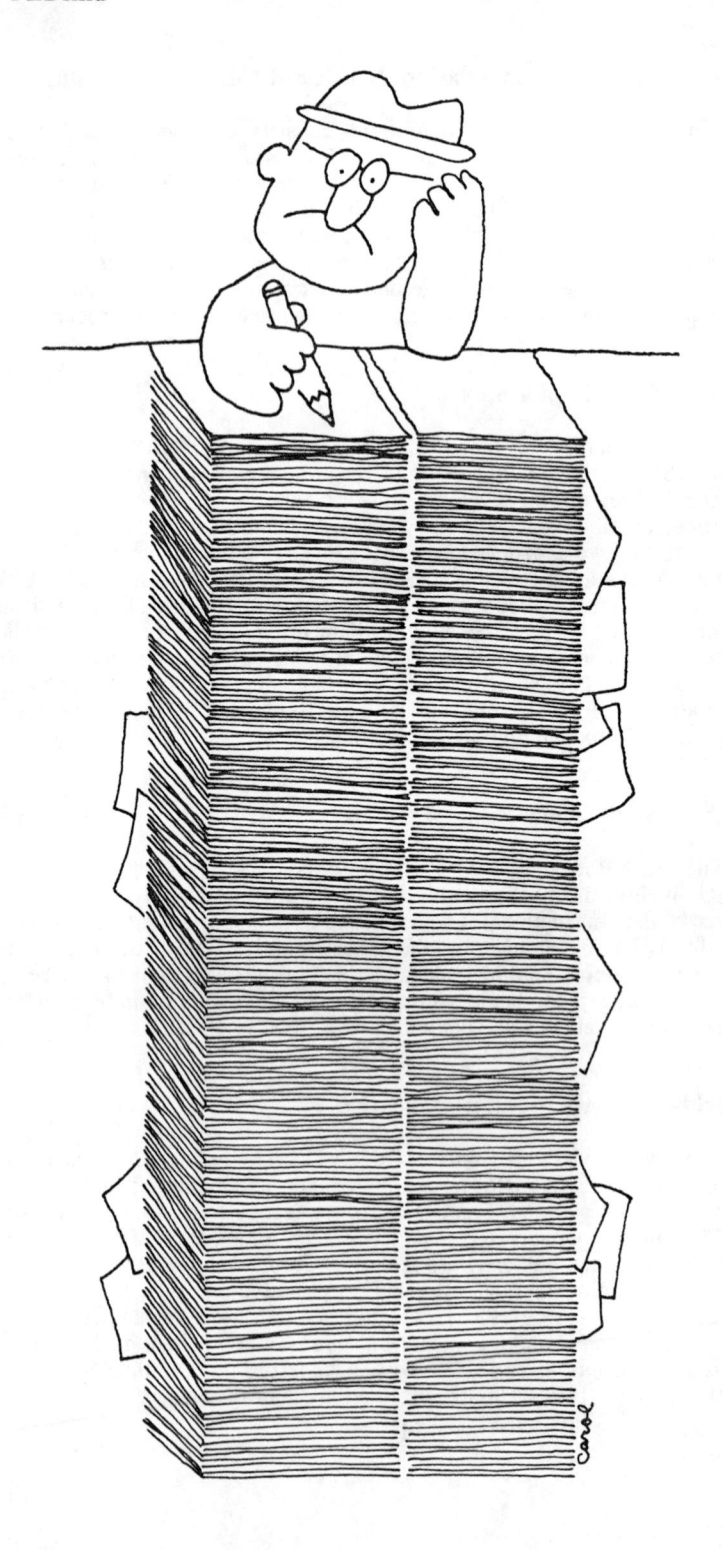

Chapter 18
General Accounting Office

The General Accounting Office (GAO), the investigative arm of Congress, is an independent, nonpolitical arm of Congress. GAO is charged with assisting the Congress, its committees and its Members in carrying out their legislative and oversight responsibilities; auditing and evaluating Government programs, activities and financial operations of Federal departments and agencies, and making recommendations for more efficient and effective operations. The GAO has no regulatory authority and may only bring problems to light and make recommendations. In Fiscal Year 1985 (October 1, 1984–September 30, 1985) alone, GAO issued 586 reports to the Congress and Federal agency officials, testified 117 times before congressional committees and provided legal opinions and written comments on proposed legislation 537 times.

The GAO is organized into operating divisions that concentrate on interagency and Government-wide programs and functions rather than on individual departments and agencies. Issue areas are specified for priority attention by designated lead divisions (see Figure 18-1). Each division takes the initiative in identifying specific matters to be examined, developing plans and formulating approaches. Within this context, GAO performs audits, investigations and evaluations of Federal organizations, programs, activities and functions. This work is either self-initiated or performed at the request of congressional committees or Members of Congress. GAO's findings, conclusions and recommendations are published in a "Report to the Congress"—often referred to as a "GAO report" or "GAO audit report." This chapter provides a framework within which the activities and products of GAO may be understood.

The information resources described in this chapter are organized under the following headings.
- Organization and Operations
- Identifying GAO Publications
- GAO Legal Decisions and Opinions
- GAO Bibliographies

Organization and Operations

United States General Accounting Office: Answers to Frequently Asked Questions

This booklet describes the objectives of the General Accounting Office (GAO) and answers 95 questions. The questions and answers are divided into the fol-

Lead Divisions	Issue Areas
Office Wide	Agency Management Reviews
Programming Divisions	
General Government Division	Financial Services Tax Policy & Administration Administration of Justice Federal Civilian Workforce Civil Procurement & Property Management
Human Resources Division	Income Security Health Financing Health Delivery & Quality of Care Employment & Education
National Security and International Affairs Division	Air Force Army Navy Research, Development, Acquisition & Procurement Logistics, Mobility & Sustainability Command, Control, Communications & Intelligence Security & Intl' Relations Manpr. & Reserve Affairs Development Assistance Intl' Trade/Commerce Policy
Resources, Community and Economic Development Division	Energy Food/Agriculture Transportation Housing & Community Devp. Environment Natural Resource Management

Figure 18-1. GAO Issue Areas by Lead Divisions

lowing groupings: purpose and responsibilities, organization, assistance to the Congress, auditing, accounting, legal services, settling claims, other responsibilities, Congressional Budget and Impoundment Control Act of 1974 and staffing. 1979. 39pp. **FREE.** See the GAO order form.

Annual Report: United States General Accounting Office

In accordance with the Budget and Accounting Act of 1921, this annual report summarizes the operations of the U.S. General Accounting Office (GAO) for a fiscal year ending September 30. The report is divided into chapters on highlights of activities, legislative recommendations and financial savings and other benefits. Included as appendices are a catalog of audit reports issued during the fiscal year and descriptions of major organizational units of GAO. January of each year. **FREE.** See the GAO order form.

GAO Manual for Guidance of Federal Agencies

This General Accounting Office (GAO) manual is the official medium through which the Comptroller General of the United States promulgates principles, standards and related requirements for accounting to be observed by Federal departments and agencies; uniform procedures for use by Federal agencies; and regulations governing the relationships of the GAO with other Federal agencies and with individuals and private concerns doing business with the Government. Subscription service for each title that follows consists of a basic manual and changes for an indeterminate period. Issued in looseleaf form with index dividers, punched for 3-ring binder. For each title the price and GPO List ID are provided. (GA 1.6/n:978) See the GPO subscription order form.

The United States General Accounting Office, $22.00, PPM01.
Accounting, $30.00, PPM02.
Audit, $8.00, PPM03.
Claims, $15.00, PPM04.
Transportation, $22.00, PPM05.
Pay, Leave and Allowances, $21.00, PPM06.
Policies and Procedures Manual, $44.00, PPM07.
Records Management, $22.00, PPM08.

GAO Review

A quarterly journal that contains articles on accounting generally, it focuses on accounting and audit activities of the General Accounting Office (GAO), its officials and staff employees. Subscription price: $12.00 a year. Single copy price: $3.25. GPO List ID GAOR. (GA 1.15:) See the GPO subscription order form.

Library & Information Services Handbook

A handbook that provides a description of the materials and services available from the General Accounting Office (GAO) Technical Information Sources and Services Branch. Though intended for GAO staff members, the handbook may be useful to non-GAO individuals since GAO facilities are open to the general public for in-house use of materials. 1981. 22pp. **FREE.** GAO report number OISS-81-09. See the GAO order form.

GAO 1966-1981: An Administrative History

The developments that shaped the role and operations of the General Accounting Office (GAO) during the term of Elmer B. Staats as Comptroller General of the United States are the focus of this book. The subjects covered include managing the agency, major organizational changes, developing an interdisciplinary staff and efforts to improve GAO's work products. Presented in three parts, the document first discusses GAO's external relationships with Congress and efforts to make the Government more effective and accountable. Covered next are internal management and organizational issues, such as managing the agency, GAO's legislative charter and audit program planning. Last are the operational matters affecting the scope, quality and impact of GAO's work, such as implementing the team concept, human resource management and the regional offices' role. Written by GAO staffers Roger L. Sperry, et al. 1981. 272pp. **FREE**. See the GAO order form.

Identifying GAO Publications

GAO Documents

A comprehensive monthly catalog of current General Accounting Office (GAO) publications and documents that includes audit reports, staff studies, letters, speeches, testimony, and legal decisions and opinions of the Comptroller General of the United States. The catalog is organized into two sections, index (yellow pages) and citations (white pages). The catalog may be used for in-depth research into a specific topic, searching for a particular document, maintaining current awareness on a given subject and general browsing. The index section is comprised of eight separate indexes that enable the user to search for information via any one or combination of the following items: subject, agency/organization, personal name, budget function, GAO issue area, congressional committee and Member, law/authority or document number. The citation section consists of brief descriptions of the documents and often includes an abstract. Some or all of the following information is contained in each citation, as appropriate: title/subtitle; type, date and pagination of the document; author/witness; GAO issue areas; agencies/organizations concerned; congressional committees/Members to whom the document is specifically relevant; law and/or related statutory/regulatory authorities on which the document is based; and GAO contact (the division/office for further information). Subscription price: $50.00 a year. Single copy price: $5.75. GPO List ID GAOD. (GA 1.16/4:) See the GPO subscription order form.

GAO Thesaurus

A listing of the terms that constitute the General Accounting Office (GAO) indexing vocabulary used to index all GAO documents and to store and retrieve information from the GAO Documents database. It provides complete cross-referencing for these terms, directing the user to synonyms and near-synonyms, to broader and narrower terms in the same area, and to otherwise related terms. 1985, 2nd ed. 113pp. FREE. GAO report number OIRM-85-3. See the GAO order form.

Monthly List of GAO Reports

A monthly listing that identifies all General Accounting Office (GAO) audit reports issued for the previous month, as well as congressional testimony by GAO officials. Reports are organized by broad subject headings (e.g., agriculture, national defense, general government, etc.). Under the subject headings, reports are listed by title and include an abstract, a report and accession number, and the date of the report. Abstracts are not provided for letter reports, but a descriptive subject is provided for each. An order form is included in each issue to facilitate obtaining desired GAO reports. There are no cumulative issues or indexes to this publication. FREE. See the GAO order form.

GAO Publications List

A semiannual catalog of General Accounting Office (GAO) publications, including unrestricted audit reports, congressional testimony by GAO officials, speeches by the Comptroller General of the United States and various other publications, including those of the Joint Financial Management Improvement Program. Addresses and telephone numbers are given for offices within GAO where selected publications may be obtained. Publications available from the Government Printing Office (GPO) have references to the GPO stock numbers and the prices in effect at the time of the publication. Audit reports and surveys for the six-month period ending as of the publication date are indexed under broad subject headings (e.g., defense procurement, foreign aid, housing, taxes and trade, etc.). There is also an index that identifies reports associated with departments or agencies. Issued semiannually: in September for the period January 1-June 30; in March for the period July 1-December 31. **FREE**. See the GAO order form.

GAO Legal Decisions and Opinions

The General Accounting Office (GAO) renders legal decisions to congressional committees and members on matters such as the legality or propriety of proposed expenditures of Federal funds. Bidders on Government contracts may ask GAO to review the procedures used in making awards to other parties. GAO may also be asked to grant relief to Government accountable and certifying officers; debtors and creditors of the Government who are dissatisfied with the handling of their affairs by other agencies may seek GAO reviews. The Comptroller General's ecisions on the legality of expenditures are binding on the executive branch; payments made contrary to them may be disallowed. In a typical year, GAO issues some 5,000 decisions in five major categories: general government matters, civil personnel, military personnel, transportation and procurement. Copies of individual decisions—published and unpublished—are available in person from GAO, 441 G Street NW, Room 1000, Washington, DC 20548. To order by mail, use the GAO order form.

The Index-Digest Section of GAO's Office of General Counsel may help individuals identify relevant decisions on specific subjects by using its filing system. Research services are available by telephone, (202) 275-5028. Individuals may conduct their own legal research by visiting the Index-Digest Section, GAO, 441 G Street NW, Room 7510, Washington, DC 20548.

Decisions of the Comptroller General of the United States

Each monthly issue contains the decisions of the Comptroller General on financial matters that involve Federal Government operations. Decisions are selected for publication on the basis of interpretation of new laws and regulations, widespread interest, discussion of important issues and modifications of previous decisions. The December, March and June issues include an index digest and legal tables; the September issue includes a cumulative table and index digests. Subscription price: $30.00 a year. Single copy price: $3.00. Index issue price (September): $5.50. GPO List ID DCG. (GA 1.5/a:) See the GPO subscription order form.

GAO Bibliographies

The General Accounting Office (GAO) compiles subject-matter bibliographies of GAO reports, testimony, legal decisions, speeches and other documents. Each bibliography is indexed by subject, Federal and nongovernmental agency, and relevant congressional committees and members. Brief abstracts are provided for each item included in the bibliography. **FREE**. Request bibliographies by number from the GAO. See the GAO order form.

ADP (Automatic Data Processing)
Volume I:	January 1976–December 1980	AFMD-81-85
Volume II:	January–December 1981	AFMD-82-50
Volume III:	January–December 1982	AFMD-83-53
Volume IV:	January–December 1983 (plus information resources management and telecommunications)	IMTEC-84-9
Volume V:	January–December 1984	IMTEC 85-9

Food
Volume I:	January 1973–September 1977	CED-78-37
Volume II:	January 1977–December 1980	CED-81-73
Volume III:	January–December 1982	RCED-83-110
Volume V:	January 1981–December 1983	RCED-84-130
Volume VI:	January 1981–December 1984	RCED-85-82

Health
Volume I:	January 1978–December 1980	OISS-81-8

Land Use Planning
Volume I:	January 1979–December 1982	RCED-83-134
Volume II:	January 1979–December 1983	RCED-84-153
Volume III:	January 1984–December 1984	RCED-85-119

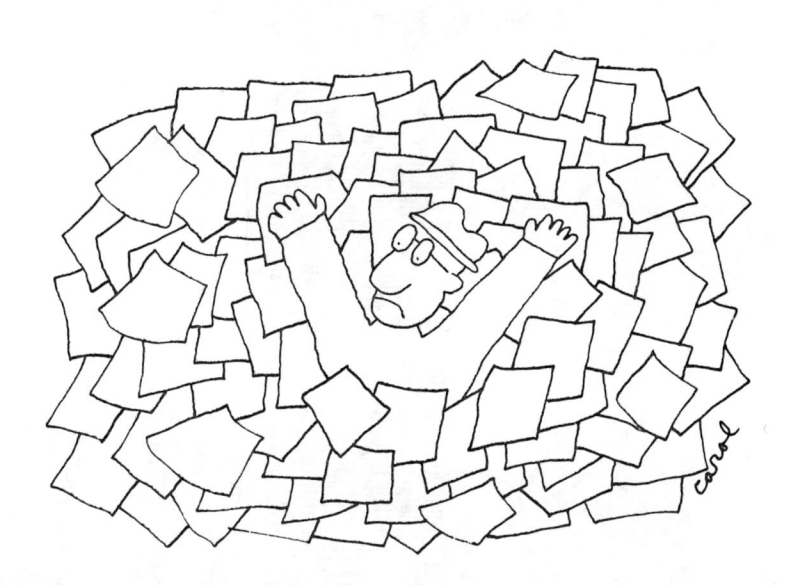

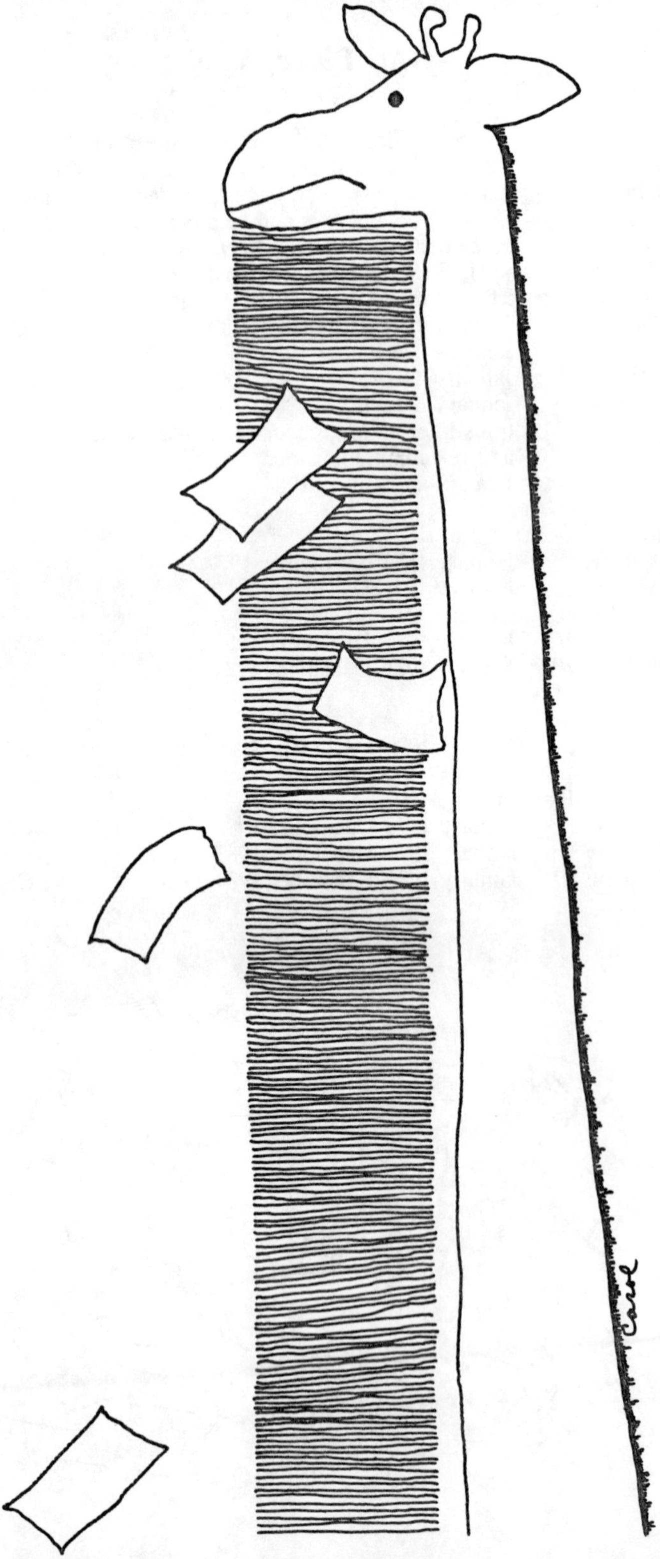
Carol

Chapter 19
Selected Private Sector Publishers

Selected publishers of material that relates to the Federal Government and its activities are described in this chapter. Among these organizations are major public policy "institutes." For each of the selected private sector publishers, this chapter provides general information, along with addresses and telephone numbers to enable you to contact organizations from which you would like additional information, including catalogs. The publishers described in this chapter are listed below.

American Enterprise Institute
The Brookings Institution
The Bureau of National Affairs, Inc.
Cato Institute
Center for Strategic and International Studies
Chamber of Commerce of the United States
Channing L. Bete Co., Inc.
Claritas Partners
Commerce Clearing House, Inc.
Common Cause
Congressional Information Service, Inc.
Congressional Quarterly Inc.
The Heritage Foundation
Hoover Institution
Institute for Policy Studies
The Lawyers Co-operative Publishing Co.
National Academy of Public Administration
Northeast-Midwest Institute
Prentice-Hall, Inc.
Public Citizen
The Rand Corporation
The Roosevelt Center
West Publishing Co.

American Enterprise Institute

The American Enterprise Institute (AEI) is a nonprofit, nonpartisan public policy research and education organization. Its purpose is to assist scholars, business leaders, policy makers, the press and the public by providing objective analysis of national and international issues. The periodicals of AEI—*Regulation*, *Public Opinion*, *The AEI Economist* and *AEI Foreign Policy and Defense Review*—present issues of national policy. AEI also publishes numerous books and working papers that are listed in its **FREE** *AEI Publications Catalog*. For further information, contact AEI, 1150 17th Street NW, Washington, DC 20036; (800) 424-2873 or (202) 862-5859.

The Brookings Institution

The Brookings Institution is a private nonprofit organization devoted to research, education and publication in economics, government, foreign policy and the social sciences. Its principal purpose is to bring knowledge to bear on current and emerging public policy issues facing the United States. Its activities are carried out through three research programs—economic, governmental and foreign policy studies—an advanced study program, a social science computation center and a publication program. For further information, request a copy of the **FREE** *Brookings Books* catalog. The Brookings Institution, 1775 Massachusetts Avenue NW, Washington, DC 20036; (202) 797-6254.

The Bureau of National Affairs, Inc.

The Bureau of National Affairs (BNA) provides research services for its subscribers in areas of Federal regulatory, judicial and legislative information. The scope of its information gathering and analysis services includes judicial decisions from Federal appellate courts, pending and current legislation, and proposed and adopted administrative rules and regulations. For further information, request a **FREE** copy of *Information Services from BNA*. BNA, 1231 25th Street NW, Washington, DC 20037; (800) 372-1033, (800) 352-1400 in Maryland, 258-9401 in Washington, DC. For a catalog of its books, contact BNA Books, 300 Raritan Center Parkway, C.N. 94, Edison, NJ 08818; (201) 225-1900.

Cato Institute

A public policy research foundation that publishes books, monographs and short studies that examine the Federal budget, social security, regulation, NATO, international trade and other policy issue areas. Major policy conferences are held throughout the year from which papers are published three times a year in the *Cato Journal*. For further information and a **FREE** *Publications Catalogue*, contact the Cato Institute, 224 2nd Street SE, Washington, DC 20003; (202) 546-0200.

Center for Strategic and International Studies

The Center for Strategic and International Studies (CSIS), a part of Georgetown University, is a nonprofit and bipartisan research institution to foster scholarship on and public awareness of emerging international issues on a broad and interdisciplinary basis. CSIS's agenda focuses on the following issues: energy and national resources, international business and economics, international communications, maritime studies, political-military studies, regional studies, and science and technology. For further information on CSIS and its publications, contact CSIS, 1800 K Street NW, Suite 400, Washington, DC 20006; (202) 887-0200.

Chamber of Commerce of the United States

An alliance of individuals and organizations representing the interests of the business community. This includes such areas as economic policy, consumer affairs, small business, Federal procurement, taxation and spending, and regulatory affairs. As such it produces publications, films, tape recordings and other communications tools that relate to the Federal Government. A **FREE** *Information Resources Guide* lists these products. For further information, contact Publications Fulfillment, Chamber of Commerce of the United States, 1615 H Street NW, Washington, DC 20062; (301) 468-5128.

Channing L. Bete Co., Inc.

This firm has developed a series of scriptographs that are designed to simplify the understanding of certain aspects of the Federal Government. Scriptography is a blend of key words, graphics and concise text to help effectively communicate a subject. The Congressional Research Service of the Library of Congress includes scriptographs in some of its "InfoPacks" on subjects related to Government institutions and operations. Of interest are the titles *About Congress*, *The Law and You*, *About the Constitution* and *About Government*. The **FREE** *Catalog of Scriptographic Booklets: For Educators Everywhere* includes information on these social studies booklets. Channing L. Bete Co., Inc., 200 State Road, South Deerfield, MA 01373; (800) 628-7733 or (413) 665-7611.

Claritas Partners

This organization processes Federal Government statistical data into information products and services for business, administrators and planners. Its specialty is the application of "small area" demography to marketing problems. Small area demography, also known as "geo-demography," involves the study of socioeconomic composition of populations residing in homogeneous, small neighborhoods and communities, as contrasted with less distinctive, more populous counties, Standard Metropolitan Statistical Areas (SMSA), states and regions. Geo-units of interest to geo-demographers include ZIP Code areas, school districts, retail trading areas, census tracts, census block groups and enumeration districts, and political precincts. For further information on Claritas' data publishing, systems and planning consultancy, request a copy of the corporate description and products brochure. Claritas Partners, 201 N. Union Street, 2nd Floor, Alexandria, VA 22314; (703) 683-8300.

Commerce Clearing House, Inc.

The Commerce Clearing House (CCH) is a publisher of topical tax and business regulatory law reports. CCH covers Congress, the courts and the Federal departments and agencies. The reports service is published, for the most part, in looseleaf form; it is designed for attorneys, accountants, business, finance, government officials and other specialists. Each service is devoted to a subject or grouping of allied subjects. For further information, request the **FREE** brochure *A Handy CCH Checklist*. CCH, 4025 W. Peterson Avenue, Chicago, IL 60646; (312) 583-8500.

Common Cause

A nonpartisan citizens' lobbying organization whose 255,000 members nationwide work toward making Federal, State and local governments function in a more efficient, responsive and honest manner. Current priority issues include campaign finance reform on the Congressional level, nuclear arms control, tax reform and ethics and accountability in government. Members receive the bimonthly *Common Cause Magazine* that includes major investigative pieces and political stories. Subscriptions are available to libraries at $12.00 a year. For further information, request a **FREE** copy of *Investigative Studies from Common Cause*, 2030 M Street NW, Washington, DC 20036; (202) 833-1200.

Congressional Information Service, Inc.

Congressional Information Service (CIS) is an indexer and micro-publisher of Government documents. CIS provides individuals and organizations various reference and retrieval services. In addition to the Federal Government, it covers State, municipal and foreign government sources and nongovernmental sources as well. For further information, request a copy of the **FREE** *CIS Catalog*. CIS, 4520 East-West Highway, Suite 800, Bethesda, MD 20814; (800) 638-8380 or (301) 654-1550.

Congressional Quarterly Inc.

Congressional Quarterly Inc. (CQ) is a news and research service providing coverage of Congress, the Federal Government, politics and national issues. CQ also publishes books, directories and newsletters; conducts seminars; produces online databases; and performs contract research. For further information, request a **FREE** copy of CQ's catalog *Book-News*. CQ, 1414 22nd Street NW, Washington, DC 20037; (202) 887-8620. For information on their computerized information service, Washington Alert Service, call (202) 887-6353 or write to the address above.

The Heritage Foundation

A public policy research institute that publishes books, monographs and studies. Regular publications include *National Security Record*, *Policy Digest*, *Education Update* and *Policy Review*, a quarterly journal of analysis and opinion. In addition the Foundation sponsors seminars, lectures, debates and briefings. For further information and a **FREE** publications catalog, contact The Heritage Foundation, 214 Massachusetts Avenue NE, Washington, DC 20002; (202) 546-4400.

Hoover Institution

A public policy research institute that publishes works on both foreign affairs and domestic issues. For further information, request a **FREE** copy of the publications catalog from the Hoover Institution Press, Stanford University, Stanford, CA 94305; (415) 497-3373.

Institute for Policy Studies

The Institute for Policy Studies (IPS) is a public policy research organization that studies and publishes material on peace and war, national priorities, the military budget, urban community development and other issues. For further information, request a **FREE** copy of *Books from the Institute for Policy Studies.* IPS, 1901 Q Street NW, Washington, DC 20009; (202) 234-9382.

The Lawyers Co-operative Publishing Co.

This firm is a publisher of legal reference materials in areas of Federal law, including principles of the law, analysis of points of law, substantive and procedural forms, and practice and trial aids. For further information, contact Lawyers Co-operative Publishing Co., Aqueduct Building, Rochester, NY 14694; (716) 546-5530.

National Academy of Public Administration

The National Academy of Public Administration (NAPA) is a nonprofit, nonpartisan organization, chartered by Congress, whose sole objective is improvement of the efficiency and effectiveness of government at all levels—Federal, State and local. The Academy's principal activity is the study of problems of government management. The 350 members of the Academy include past and present government officials—elected, appointed and career—and scholars in the field of public management. For further information on their studies, contact NAPA, 1120 G Street NW, Suite 540, Washington, DC 20005; (202) 347-3190.

Northeast-Midwest Institute

This nonprofit organization serves as an independent source of information concerning the economy of the 18-state region that forms the Nation's industrial heartland: Connecticut, Delaware, Illinois, Indiana, Iowa, Maine, Maryland, Massachusetts, Michigan, Minnesota, New Hampshire, New Jersey, New York, Ohio, Pennsylvania, Rhode Island, Vermont and Wisconsin. The Institute also provides nonpartisan research and analysis concerning the regional implications of a range of Federal policy alternatives. Its publications cover subjects such as defense, economic development, human services, energy, the Federal budget, rural policy, trade, transportation, urban policy and water resources. For further information, contact the Northeast-Midwest Institute, 218 D Street SE, Washington, DC 20003; (202) 544-5200.

Prentice-Hall, Inc.

Prentice-Hall provides publications on business, labor, legal and tax matters. The basic compilation usually includes laws, regulations, court cases and editorial explanation. A **FREE** catalog provides descriptions of the company's publications and looseleaf services. For further information, contact Prentice-Hall, Inc., Information Services Division, 240 Frisch Court, Paramus, NJ 07652; (800) 562-0245 or (201) 368-4517.

Public Citizen

A consumer rights organization, founded in 1971 by Ralph Nader, it champions the rights of consumers in the courts and in public forums. Its six divisions conduct programs to help achieve a healthier and safer America, and open, responsive government. The divisions of Public Citizen are: Congress Watch, Critical Mass Energy Project, The Health Research Group, The Litigation Group, The Tax Reform Research Group and Buyers Up. For further information and a publications list, contact Public Citizen, P.O. Box 19404, Washington, DC 20036; (202) 293-9142.

The Rand Corporation

An independent, nonprofit organization engaged in research and analysis of national security issues and the public welfare. The methods and findings of Rand research are reported chiefly in monographs published by the corporation. For further information, request a copy of Rand's publications catalog. Publications Department, Rand, 1700 Main Street, Santa Monica, CA 90406; (213) 393-0411.

The Roosevelt Center

A nonprofit, nonpartisan public policy research institute, the Roosevelt Center undertakes research in the areas of economic policy, social issues and international security. For further information on its projects and publications, contact the Center at 316 Pennsylvania Avenue SE, Suite 500, Washington, DC 20003; (202) 547-7227 or 250 S. Wacker Drive, Suite 1250, Chicago, IL 60606; (312) 876-1575.

West Publishing Co.

This company is a publisher of law books, subscription services and WESTLAW, a computerized information service. Built into its products and services are elements of its Key Number System, which cross-references West's law encyclopedia, reporters, digests and statutes to serve as a single law-finding unit. Catalogs of West's law books and the West library system are available **FREE** upon request. For further information, contact the West Publishing Co., P.O. Box 64526, St. Paul, MN 55164; (800) 328-9352 or (612) 228-2973. For WESTLAW-related questions, call (800) 328-0109 or (612) 228-2450.

Appendix A
Public Access Laws

This appendix provides an introduction to four Federal laws that set forth your rights to access U.S. Government information. Accompanying a summary of each law is a description of documents that provide detailed information on how to understand better the intent of each law and its use. The laws discussed are:

- Freedom of Information Act
- Privacy Act of 1974
- Government in the Sunshine Act
- Federal Advisory Committee Act

The following three publications include material on all four laws cited above.

Freedom of Information Case List

An annual publication prepared by the Office of Information and Privacy, Department of Justice. The principal component of the document is an alphabetical compilation of judicial decisions, both published and unpublished, addressing access issues under the Freedom of Information Act and the Privacy Act of 1974. Separate lists of cases arising under the Government in the Sunshine and the Federal Advisory Committee Acts appear following the main case list. Included also are the full texts of each of these Federal access laws, a list of related law review articles and a "Short Guide to the Freedom of Information Act." November 1985. 414pp. $9.00. GPO S/N 027-000-01247-7. (J 1.56:985) See the GPO order form.

Your Right to Government Information

An American Civil Liberties Union (ACLU) handbook written by Christine M. Marwick, this book sets forth an individual's rights under the present law to gain access to U.S. Government information. The guide tells you how to use the four laws listed above, what to expect and what legal steps you may take if the Government says no. It includes sample request and appeal letters, a listing of addresses for requests and appeals, and where to go for legal help. 1985. 252pp. $4.95, plus $1.00 for postage and handling. ISBN 0-553-24819-7. Literature Department, ACLU, 132 W. 43rd Street, New York, NY 10036.

ASAP News

A monthly newsletter of the American Society of Access Professionals (ASAP). It includes information on developments in access laws and other items of particular interest to the organization's membership. The newsletter is available as part of the Society's $20.00 a year membership dues. ASAP, P.O. Box 76865, Washington, DC 20013.

Privacy Times

A biweekly newsletter on the Freedom of Information Act, Privacy Act, computer and trade secrets, and associated law and policy. It includes coverage of congressional actions, court decisions, Federal agency policies and State laws. Subscription price: $225.00 a year. Privacy Times Inc., 2354 Champlain Street NW, Washington, DC 20009; (202) 265-6081.

Access Reports Reference File

A two-volume looseleaf service that provides documents and analysis to deal with the Freedom of Information Act (FOIA) and related laws. It includes the full text of the FOIA, a legislative history and an analysis of the case law for each of the FOIA's nine exemptions. It also presents the full text and/or summaries of agency regulations, the full text of all guidance issued by the Justice Department and the Office of Management and Budget, and the full text of selected major court decisions dealing with the FOIA, Government in the Sunshine Act and the Federal Advisory Committee Act. Subscription price: $350.00 a year. The Washington Monitor, Inc., 1301 Pennsylvania Avenue NW, Suite 1000, Washington, DC 20004; (202) 347-7757.

Freedom of Information Act

The Freedom of Information Act (FOIA) (5 U.S. Code 552) requires that information held by Federal agencies be made available to the public unless it comes within one of the specific categories exempt from public disclosure, such as matters involving an individual's right to privacy, national security or foreign policy interests, or the internal management of an agency. The Act provides for judicial review of agency decisions to withhold identifiable records requested under the law. Agencies of the executive branch of the Federal Government have issued regulations implementing the Act. These regulations inform the public where certain types of information may be readily obtained, how other information may be obtained on request, and what internal appeals are available if a member of the public is refused requested information. These specific agency regulations may be found in the *Code of Federal Regulations* index under "Freedom of Information."

Provided in Chapters 8 and 9—under "Key Offices and Telephone Numbers"—is the telephone number for the "Freedom of Information/Privacy Act" office for those departments and agencies that, as of 1986, had such an office.

How to Use the Federal FOI Act

A guide to the use of the Freedom of Information (FOI) Act as an investigative tool. The document was prepared by the FOI Service Center, a project of The Reporters Committee for Freedom of the Press. The guide includes sample letters, forms and directories. 1985, 5th ed. 24pp. $3.00. FOI Service Center, 800 18th Street NW, Suite 300, Washington, DC 20006; (202) 466-6313.

FOIA Update

A quarterly newsletter presenting current news pertaining to the Freedom of Information Act (FOIA). It is prepared by the Office of Information and Privacy (OIP), Department of Justice. Columns that appear in the newsletter include OIP Guidance, FOIA Counselor, Significant New Decisions, FOIA Focus and FOIA Training Opportunities. The Summer issue each year includes the "FOIA Legal and Administrative Contacts at Federal Agencies" list. Subscription price: $10.00 a year. Single copy price: $2.75. GPO List ID FOIA. (J 1.58:) See the GPO subscription order form.

Citizen's Guide on How to Use the Freedom of Information Act and the Privacy Act in Requesting Government Documents

A committee report based on a study made by the Government Information and Individual Rights Subcommittee of the House Committee on Government Operations. The report explains which act to use in obtaining documents and how to request records under both acts. It includes sample letters of request and appeal. 1977. 59pp. $4.50. GPO S/N 052-071-00540-4. (X 95.1 H Rpt 793) See the GPO order form.

Freedom of Information Guide

A guide to requesting documents under the Freedom of Information and Privacy Acts. It includes a discussion of major exemptions to release of information under these acts; sample request letters; names, addresses and telephone numbers of FOIA/Privacy Act officers; a survey of recent FOIA requests to major Federal agencies, including documents requested, who requested the information and the agency's response; and the full text of the acts. 1984. 116pp. $7.95. ISBN 0-942008-07-3. WANT Publishing Co., 1511 K Street NW, Washington, DC 20005; (202) 783-1887.

Access Reports/Freedom of Information

A biweekly newsletter that reports on developments in information law and policy. This includes coverage of Freedom of Information Act (FOIA) court decisions, congressional action, agency-wide guidance on the FOIA and Privacy Act, trends in information policy and agency proposals. Every three months an index is provided that includes a table of cases and subject matter index, cumulative from the beginning of the calendar year. Available electronically through NewsNet. Subscription price: $225.00 a year. ISSN 0364-7625. The Washington Monitor, Inc., 1301 Pennsylvania Avenue NW, Suite 1000, Washington, DC 20004; (202) 347-7757.

Privacy Act of 1974

The Privacy Act (Public Law 93-579, 5 U.S. Code 552a) provides a series of basic safeguards for the individual citizen to prevent the misuse of personal information by the Federal Government. The Act requires each executive agency to disclose to the public the existence and characteristics of all personal information systems the agency retains. It also permits an individual to have access to records containing personal information and to control the transfer of that information to other agencies for non-routine uses. The Act also requires each executive agency to keep records of transfers of personal information to other agencies and outsiders and to make the accountings available to the individual. Civil remedies are provided in the Act for individuals whose records are kept or used counter to the requirements of the Act. Agencies have issued implementing regulations. These regulations generally inform the public how to determine if a system of records contains information on themselves, how to gain access to such records, how to request amendment of such records, and the method of internal appeal of an adverse agency determination on such a request. A five-volume document entitled *Privacy Act Issuances, 1985 Compilation*, prepared by the Office of the Federal Register, includes descriptions of all the systems of records maintained by each agency of the Federal Government, the categories of individuals about whom each record system is maintained, and the agency rules and procedures whereby an individual may obtain further information. This compilation is available at Federal depository libraries, Federal Information Centers and at congressional offices.

Provided in Chapters 8 and 9—under "Key Offices and Telephone Numbers"—is the telephone number for the "Freedom of Information/Privacy Act" office for those departments and agencies that, as of 1986, had such an office.

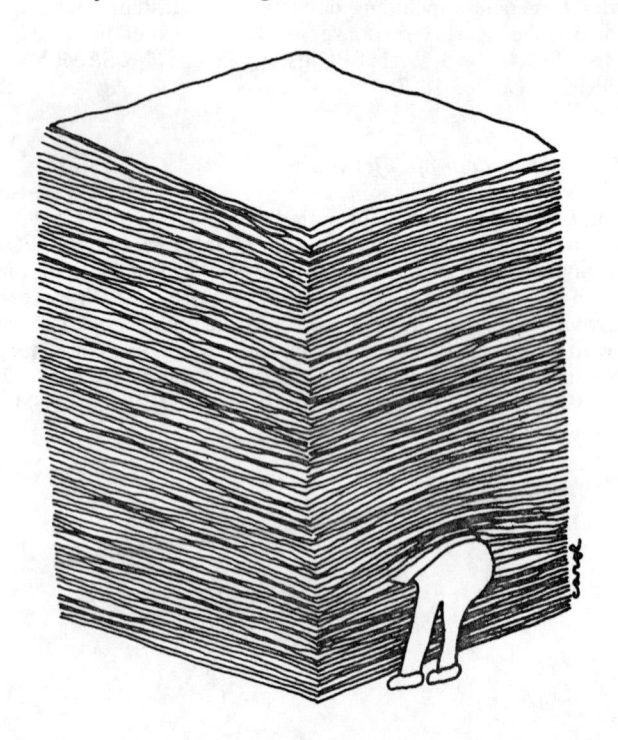

Government in the Sunshine Act

The Government in the Sunshine Act (Public Law 94-409, 5 U.S. Code 552b) establishes it to be the policy of the United States Government that the public is entitled to the fullest possible information about the decision-making processes of the Federal Government. The Act provides for making this information known by requiring that all meetings of executive agencies be open to the public unless they come within one of the specific categories exempt from public disclosure. These include not impairing an individual's right to privacy, the ability of the Government to carry out its responsibilities or national security interests. The Act requires each agency to make a public announcement of the time, place and subject matter of each agency meeting, whether it is open or closed to the public, and the name and telephone number of the official designated to answer questions about the meeting. Each issue of the Federal Register includes a section that lists agency notices of "Sunshine Act Meetings." Each agency must make a transcript of each meeting promptly and conveniently available to the public. Agencies have issued regulations to implement the Act, including procedures to be followed in closing meetings to the public.

An Interpretive Guide to the Government in the Sunshine Act

An examination of the principal questions that have arisen or appear likely to arise under the open meeting provisions of the Act. It is a publication of the Administrative Conference of the United States, Office of the Chairman. The organization of the guide follows the structure of the statute. Each chapter is headed by a subsection title and relates that subsection to both its relevant legislative history and sample agency regulations implementing it. 1978. 134pp. $5.50. Out-of-print. GPO S/N 052-003-00532-8. (Y 3.Ad 6:8 Su 7).

Federal Advisory Committee Act

The Federal Advisory Committee Act (FACA) (Public Law 92-463, 5 U.S. Code Appendix I) includes a provision that opens meetings of Federal advisory committees to the public. For the purposes of the Act, the term "advisory committee" means "any committee, board, commission, council, conference, panel, task force, or other similar group, or any subcommittee or other subgroup thereof . . . which have been established to advise officers and agencies in the executive branch of the Federal Government." The main focus of the FACA is the general regulation of such committees. The procedures for enforcing the open meeting provisions are weaker than those of the Government in the Sunshine Act, which goes into detail about open meetings and how they are announced to the public.

Provided in Chapters 8 and 9—under "Key Offices and Telephone Numbers"—is the telephone number for the "Agency Committee Management" office for those departments and agencies that, as of 1986, had such groups. The *Federal Advisory Committees—Annual Report* (described in Chapter 1) provides details. It is available **FREE** from the General Services Administration.

Less Paperwork Convention

Appendix B
Paperwork Reduction Act of 1980

The Paperwork Reduction Act of 1980 (Public Law 96-511, chapter 35 of title 44, U.S. Code) went into effect in April 1981. The Act was established in response to three concerns about the management of Federal Government information resources: (1) the increasing concern about the amount of paperwork the Government imposes on the public; (2) a perception that the Federal Government does not effectively manage information technology; and (3) an emerging view that information is a resource (like people, material and money) in that it has cost both to the public and the Government, and it should be managed. In response to these concerns the law provides for, among other things:

- a reduction in the paperwork burden imposed on the public by the Federal Government;
- a reduction in the cost of collecting, managing and disseminating information by Federal agencies;
- ensuring that Federal agencies collect only as much information as they need and can use effectively;
- the elimination of inconsistencies among Federal information policies by ensuring uniformity whenever possible;
- improving the efficiency of Government programs through the effective use of information technology; and
- the establishment of safeguards to protect the legitimate privacy and confidentiality concerns of individuals and enterprises.

Specifically, the Act created the Office of Information and Regulatory Affairs (OIRA) within the Executive Office of the President's Office of Management and Budget (OMB). OIRA is delegated the responsibility to review agency justifications of all reporting and record-keeping requirements and approve only those for which the information sought is needed by the Government, does not duplicate information already collected by the Government, and imposes the smallest burden on the public that is practicable and appropriate.

Primary responsibility for compliance with the Act is vested in the agencies and in a single official for information resources management (IRM) appointed by each agency. For purposes of the Act, IRM includes automatic data processing (ADP) and telecommunications, Federal statistical activities, records management, privacy of records, information policy, and paperwork and regulatory review.

Provided in Chapters 8 and 9—under "Key Office and Telephone Numbers"—is the "Paperwork Reduction Act (ADP/IRM)" office headed by each respective agency's designated official for IRM.

The OIRA-prepared *Managing Federal Information Resources: Fourth Annual Report under the Paperwork Reduction Act of 1980* provides a status report, as of April 1, 1985, on efforts to implement the IRM concept in the Federal Government. September 1985. 51pp. $2.25. GPO S/N 041-001-00297-9. (PrEx 2.25:985) Also compiled annually by OIRA is the *Information Collection Budget of the United States Government*. The *Information Collection Budget* (ICB) is a mechanism for measuring and controlling the costs of Federal information collections imposed upon individuals, businesses, and State and local governments. The fifth annual ICB or "paperwork budget" for fiscal year 1985 is dated April 1985. 103pp. $2.50. GPO S/N 041-001-00296-1. (PrEx 2.29:985) See the GPO order form.

The AFFIRMation

A monthly newsletter of the Association for Federal Information Resources Management (AFFIRM) that reports on information resources management (IRM) related regulations, publications and activities in the Federal Government. The Association is a nonprofit, professional organization whose purpose is to promote and advance the practice of IRM in the United States Government. The newsletter is one benefit available as part of AFFIRM membership. For further information, contact AFFIRM Membership, P.O. Box 28506, Washington, DC 20038.

Management of Federal Information Resources

This Office of Management and Budget (OMB) Circular No. A-130 establishes policy for the management of Federal information resources. Procedural and analytic guidelines for implementing specific aspects of these policies are included as appendices. The Circular rescinds OMB Circular Nos. A-71, *Responsibilities for the Administration and Management of Automatic Data Processing Activities;* Transmittal Memorandum No. 1 to Circular No. A-71, *Security of Federal Automated Information Systems;* A-90, *Cooperating with State and Local Governments to Coordinate and Improve Information Systems;* A-108, *Responsibilities for the Maintenance of Records about Individuals by Federal Agencies;* and A-121, *Cost Accounting, Cost Recovery, and Interagency Sharing of Data Processing Facilities.* 1985. 51 pp. **FREE.** EOP Publications, 726 Jackson Place NW, Room 2200, Washington, DC 20503; (202) 395-7332.

Appendix C
Ethics in Government Act

The Ethics in Government Act of 1978 (Public Law 95-521), as amended, is intended to preserve and promote public confidence in the integrity of Federal officials through financial disclosure, post-government employment restrictions and independent investigations of alleged wrongdoing by Federal Government officials.

The Federal executive branch developed its formal policy guidelines on conflict of interest and standards of ethical conduct in 1965. These guidelines, set forth in Executive Order 11222, serve as the foundation for the regulations that appear in Part 735 of Title 5 of the Code of Federal Regulations. Generally, they prohibit Government employees from soliciting or accepting gifts, loans or special favors from any party that may be economically, legally or otherwise substantially affected by either the employee's agency or the employee's official actions. The law further forbids employees to do anything that would result in, or appear to result in:

- using public office for private gain;
- giving preferential treatment to any organization or group;
- impeding Government efficiency;
- making a Government decision outside official channels;
- losing impartiality; or
- in any way undermining public confidence in the integrity of Government.

Figure C-1 presents a code of ethics posted in every executive branch office and post office where at least 20 Federal employees work. Congress exempted itself.

The 1978 Act created the Office of Government Ethics (OGE), a special unit within the Office of Personnel Management, charged with oversight responsibility for the executive branch ethical standards program. For further information about the Act and OGE functions, contact the OGE at P.O. Box 14108, Washington, DC 20044; (202) 632-7642.

Each agency has a designated agency ethics official, provided in Chapters 8 and 9 for each agency under "Key Offices and Telephone Numbers." These offices distribute new ethics information, answer questions concerning conflict of interest, and serve as a liaison with the Office of Government Ethics. Agency employees or members of the public with an ethics question involving a particular agency should first contact the agency's designated ethics official.

An assessment of Government ethics programs was published by Common Cause in November 1984, entitled *Bureaucratic Orphans: The Administration of Government Ethics Programs as Viewed by Agency Ethics Officials*. This 59-page report is available for $1.00 from Common Cause, 2030 M Street NW, Washington, DC 20036; (202) 833-1200.

Any Person in Government Service Should:

Put loyalty to the highest moral principles and to country above loyalty to persons, party, or Government department.

Uphold the Constitution, laws, and legal regulations of the United States and all governments therein and never be a party to their evasion.

Give a full day's labor for a full day's pay; giving to the performance of his duties his earnest effort and best thought.

Seek to find and employ more efficient and economical ways of getting tasks accomplished.

Never discriminate unfairly by the dispensing of special favors or privileges to anyone, whether for remuneration or not; and never accept, for himself or his family, favors or benefits under circumstances which might be construed by reasonable persons as influencing the performance of his governmental duties.

Make no private promises of any kind binding upon the duties of office, since a Government employee has no private word which can be binding on public duty.

Engage in no business with the Government, either directly or indirectly, which is inconsistent with the conscientious performance of his governmental duties.

Never use any information coming to him confidentially in the performance of governmental duties as a means for making private profit.

Expose corruption wherever discovered.

Uphold these principles, ever conscious that public office is a public trust.

Authority of Public Law 96-303, unanimously passed by the Congress of the United States on June 27, 1980, and signed into law by the President on July 3, 1980.

Your agency ethics official and Office of Government Ethics are available to answer your questions on conflicts of interest.

Figure C-1. Code of Ethics for Government Service

Appendix D
Computerized Information Resources

Presented in the body of this book are descriptions of selected "computerized information resources" that relate to a particular subject area or agency. The computer-based systems referred to are just some of the numerous services available from Federal Government and private sector sources. For further information about content and availability of these and other computer-based systems and online databases that relate to your specific agency or interest area, a list of directories and vendors is provided below. The listings include U.S. Government and/or commercial databases incorporating Government-originated information, along with addresses and telephone numbers of their publishers.

Complete Guide to Dial-Up Databases
Datapro Research Corp.
1805 Underwood Boulevard
Delran, NJ 08075
(800) 257-9406
(609) 764-0100 in New Jersey

Computer-Readable Databases: A Directory and Data Sourcebook
(Online access to the directory is available through DIALOG)
American Library Association
Publishing Services
50 E. Huron Street
Chicago, IL 60611
(312) 944-6780

DataBase Directory
(Online access to the directory is available through BRS)
Knowledge Industry Publications, Inc.
701 Westchester Avenue
White Plains, NY 10604
(800) 248-KIPI
(914) 328-9157 in New York State

Directory of Computerized Data Files
National Technical Information Service
Department of Commerce
5285 Port Royal Road
Springfield, VA 22161
(703) 487-4600

Directory of Online Databases
(Online access to the directory is available through WESTLAW)
Cuadra/Elsevier
P.O. Box 1672
New York, NY 10163
(212) 916-1010

Directory of On-line Services
Datapro Research Corp.
(see address above)

Encyclopedia of Information Systems and Services
Gale Research Co.
Book Tower
Detroit, MI 48226
(800) 223-GALE
(313) 961-2242 in Michigan, Alaska and Hawaii

The Federal Data Base Finder
Information USA, Inc.
4701 Willard Avenue, Suite 1707
Chevy Chase, MD 20815
(301) 657-1200

Federal Information Sources and Systems
General Accounting Office
(see Chapter 11, Program Administration and Evaluation, "Congressional Sourcebook Series" section)

Online Directory: Service Services Available in Metropolitan Washington
Metropolitan Washington Library Council
1875 Eye Street NW, Suite 200
Washington, DC 20006
(202) 223-6800 ext. 458

The following selected database vendors may be contacted for details on their U.S. Government-related products and services.

Bibliographic Retrieval Services, Inc. (BRS)
1200 Route 7
Latham, NY 12110
(800) 833-4707
(800) 553-5566 in New York

CompuServe Information Services, Inc.
Customer Service Ordering Department
Box L-477
Columbus, OH 43260
(800) 848-8199
(614) 457-8650

DIALOG Information Services, Inc.
3460 Hillview Avenue
Palo Alto, CA 94304
(800) 3-DIALOG

ITT Dialcom, Inc.
1109 Spring Street, Suite 410
Silver Spring, MD 20910
(301) 588-1572

LEGI-SLATE, Inc.
111 Massachusetts Avenue NW, Suite 520
Washington, DC 20001
(202) 898-2300

Mead Data Central
P.O. Box 933
Dayton, OH 45401
(800) 227-4908

NewsNet, Inc.
945 Haverford Road
Bryn Mawr, PA 19010
(800) 345-1301
(215) 527-8030 in Pennsylvania

Pergamon Infoline, Inc.
1340 Old Chain Bridge Road
McLean, VA 22101
(800) 336-7575
(703) 442-0900 in Virginia

SDC Information Services
2525 Colorado Avenue
Santa Monica, CA 90406
(800) 421-7229
(800) 352-6689 in California

The Source
Source Telecomputing Corp.
1616 Anderson Road
McLean, VA 22102
(800) 336-3366
(800) 572-2070 in Virginia
(703) 734-7500

Washington Alert Service
Congressional Quarterly Inc.
1414 22nd Street NW
Washington, DC 20037
(202) 887-6353

Washington On-Line
507 8th Street SE
Washington, DC 20003
(202) 543-9101

WESTLAW
West Publishing Co.
P.O. Box 64526
St. Paul, MN 55164
(800) 328-0109
(612) 228-2450 in Minnesota

Appendix E
Research and Document Retrieval Services

You may want specialized assistance in identifying and acquiring information from the Federal Government. In addition to **FREE** help available from professional personnel of the public and depository library systems, there are companies that—for a fee—will perform research and locate and retrieve information according to your specific requirements. It is beyond the scope of this book to list the companies available to do such work. In addition to help from your local library staff on leads to such services, two directories provide detailed information on hundreds of such companies.

For further information on these directories, contact the publishers directly.

Directory of Fee-Based Information Services
Burwell Enterprises
5106 FM 1960 W., Suite 349
Houston, TX 77069
(713) 537-9051

Document Retrieval: Sources & Services
The Information Store, Inc.
140 Second Street, 5th Floor
San Francisco, CA 94105
(415) 543-4636

450 **FEDfind**

Appendix F
Foreign Embassies

The following list provides the addresses and telephone numbers of foreign government embassies in Washington, DC and New York City. For descriptions of publications that include detailed information on personnel assigned to these and other locations, as well as foreign consular offices in the United States, see the "Foreign Affairs" section of Chapter 2, Directories.

Note: Two-letter license plate codes are included with the appropriate entries below (in parentheses) for 18 "criteria" countries that have been so designated by the Federal Bureau of Investigation (FBI). (Source: "New Game of Tag: Letter-Coded License Plates Help FBI Watch Diplomats," The Washington Post, July 5, 1985). Among other things, these codes help the FBI in its counterintelligence, counterespionage and antiterrorism mission. The codes appear on the red, white and blue U.S. diplomatic license plates issued by the U.S. Department of State as the second and third character. A vehicle with the license plate "DFC 203" would be that of a diplomat (D) from the Union of Soviet Socialist Republics (FC). (An initial letter "S" indicates staff; an initial "C" indicates consular. The characters appearing on license plates issued for vehicles owned by United Nations missions are reversed, with three digits first, followed by the two-letter country code and the single letter personnel designator, e.g., "203 FCD") If a vehicle whose license plates bear one of these designated codes is observed under suspicious circumstances, local FBI offices are open to hearing from citizens with details of those observations (license number, location, etc.). A list in alphabetical order by country code is provided here for easy reference.

AQ	Syria	GQ	North Korea
BL	South Africa*	KH	Hungary
BZ	Iraq	LD	Vietnam
CY	PRC (China)	ND	Romania
DC	Cuba	PH	Czechoslovakia
DM	Iran	QM	Bulgaria
FC	USSR	QU	Nicaragua
FM	Libya	QW	Poland
GP	Albania	TJ	East Germany

*The code for South Africa is listed because its own intelligence service is purported to closely monitor the activities of U.S. diplomats in that country.

Afghanistan
2341 Wyoming Avenue NW
Washington, DC 20008
(202) 234-3770

Albania (GP)
(No embassy)

Algeria
2118 Kalorama Road NW
Washington, DC 20008
(202) 328-5300

Antigua and Barbuda
3400 International Drive NW
Washington, DC 20008
(202) 362-5122

Argentina
1600 New Hampshire Avenue NW
Washington, DC 20009
(202) 939-6400

Australia
1601 Massachusetts Avenue NW
Washington, DC 20036
(202) 797-3000

Austria
2343 Massachusetts Avenue NW
Washington, DC 20008
(202) 483-4474

Bahamas
600 New Hampshire Avenue NW
Washington, DC 20037
(202) 338-3940

Bahrain
3502 International Drive NW
Washington, DC 20008
(202) 342-0741

Bangladesh
2201 Wisconsin Avenue NW
Washington, DC 20007
(202) 342-8372

Barbados
2144 Wyoming Avenue NW
Washington, DC 20008
(202) 939-9200

Belgium
3330 Garfield Street NW
Washington, DC 20008
(202) 333-6900

Belize
1575 Eye Street NW
Washington, DC 20005
(202) 289-1416

Benin
2737 Cathedral Avenue NW
Washington, DC 20008
(202) 232-6656

Bolivia
3014 Massachusetts Avenue NW
Washington, DC 20008
(202) 483-4410

Botswana
4301 Connecticut Avenue NW
Washington, DC 20008
(202) 244-4990

Brazil
3006 Massachusetts Avenue NW
Washington, DC 20008
(202) 745-2700

Brunei
2600 Virginia Avenue NW
Washington, DC 20037
(202) 342-0159

Bulgaria
1621 22nd Street NW
Washington, DC 20008
(202) 387-7969

Burkina-Faso
2340 Massachusetts Avenue NW
Washington, DC 20008
(202) 332-5577

Burma
2300 S Street NW
Washington, DC 20008
(202) 332-9044

Burundi
2233 Wisconsin Avenue NW
Washington, DC 20007
(202) 342-2574

Cambodia
(see Kampuchea)

Cameroon
2349 Massachusetts Avenue NW
Washington, DC 20008
(202) 265-8790

Canada
1746 Massachusetts Avenue NW
Washington, DC 20036
(202) 785-1400

Cape Verde
3415 Massachusetts Avenue NW
Washington, DC 20007
(202) 965-6820

Appendix F 453

Central African Republic
1618 22nd Street NW
Washington, DC 20008
(202) 483-7800

Chad
2002 R Street NW
Washington, DC 20009
(202) 462-4009

Chile
1732 Massachusetts Avenue NW
Washington, DC 20036
(202) 785-1746

China, People's Republic of (CY)
2300 Connecticut Avenue NW
Washington, DC 20008
(202) 328-2500

China (Taiwan) (see Taiwan)

Colombia
2118 Leroy Place NW
Washington, DC 20008
(202) 387-8338

Congo
4891 Colorado Avenue NW
Washington, DC 20011
(202) 726-5500

Costa Rica
2112 S Street NW
Washington, DC 20008
(202) 234-2945

Cuban Interests Section (DC)
2630 16th Street NW
Washington, DC 20009
(202) 797-8518

Cyprus
2211 R Street NW
Washington, DC 20008
(202) 462-5772

Czechoslovakia (PH)
3900 Linnean Avenue NW
Washington, DC 20008
(202) 363-6315

Denmark
3200 Whitehaven Street NW
Washington, DC 20008
(202) 234-4300

Djibouti
866 United Nations Plaza
New York, NY 10017
(212) 753-3163

Dominica
1629 K Street NW
Washington, DC 20006
(202) 467-5933

Dominican Republic
1715 22nd Street NW
Washington, DC 20008
(202) 332-6280

Ecuador
2535 15th Street NW
Washington, DC 20009
(202) 234-7200

Egypt
2310 Decatur Place NW
Washington, DC 20008
(202) 232-5400

El Salvador
2308 California Street NW
Washington, DC 20008
(202) 265-3480

Equatorial Guinea
801 Second Avenue
New York, NY 10017
(212) 599-1523

Estonia
9 Rockefeller Plaza
New York, NY 10020
(212) 247-1450

Ethiopia
2134 Kalorama Road NW
Washington, DC 20008
(202) 234-2281

Fiji
2233 Wisconsin Avenue NW
Washington, DC 20007
(202) 337-8320

Finland
3216 New Mexico Avenue NW
Washington, DC 20016
(202) 363-2430

France
4101 Reservoir Road NW
Washington, DC 20007
(202) 944-6000

Gabon
2034 20th Street NW
Washington, DC 20009
(202) 797-1000

Gambia
1785 Massachusetts Avenue NW
Washington, DC 20036
(202) 265-3252

German Democratic Republic (East) (TJ)
1717 Massachusetts Avenue NW
Washington, DC 20036
(202) 232-3134

Germany, Federal Republic of (West)
4645 Reservoir Road
Washington, DC 20007
(202) 298-4000

Ghana
2460 16th Street NW
Washington, DC 20009
(202) 462-0761

Greece
2221 Massachusetts Avenue NW
Washington, DC 20008
(202) 667-3168

Grenada
1701 New Hampshire Avenue NW
Washington, DC 20009
(202) 265-2561

Guatemala
2220 R Street NW
Washington, DC 20008
(202) 745-4952

Guinea
2112 Leroy Place NW
Washington, DC 20008
(202) 483-9420

Guinea-Bissau
211 East 43rd Street
New York, NY 10017
(212) 661-3977

Guyana
2490 Tracy Place NW
Washington, DC 20008
(202) 265-6900

Haiti
2311 Massachusetts Avenue NW
Washington, DC 20008
(202) 332-4090

Holy See
3339 Massachusetts Avenue NW
Washington, DC 20008
(202) 333-7121

Honduras
4301 Connecticut Avenue NW
Washington, DC 20008
(202) 966-7700

Hungary (KH)
3910 Shoemaker Street NW
Washington, DC 20008
(202) 362-6730

Iceland
2022 Connecticut Avenue NW
Washington, DC 20008
(202) 265-6653

India
2107 Massachusetts Avenue NW
Washington, DC 20008
(202) 939-7000

Indonesia
2020 Massachusetts Avenue NW
Washington, DC 20036
(202) 293-1745

Iran Interests Section (DM)
2139 Wisconsin Avenue NW
Washington, DC 20007
(202) 965-2050

Iraq (BZ)
1801 P Street NW
Washington, DC 20036
(202) 483-7500

Ireland
2234 Massachusetts Avenue NW
Washington, DC 20008
(202) 462-3939

Israel
3514 International Drive NW
Washington, DC 20008
(202) 364-5500

Italy
1601 Fuller Street NW
Washington, DC 20009
(202) 328-5500

Ivory Coast
2424 Massachusetts Avenue NW
Washington, DC 20008
(202) 483-2400

Jamaica
1850 K Street NW
Washington, DC 20006
(202) 452-0660

Japan
2520 Massachusetts Avenue NW
Washington, DC 20008
(202) 234-2266

Jordan
3504 International Drive NW
Washington, DC 20008
(202) 966-2664

Kampuchea (Mission to the United Nations)
212 East 47 Street
New York, NY 10019
(212) 888-6646

Kenya
2249 R Street NW
Washington, DC 20008
(202) 387-6101

Korea (North) (Mission to the United Nations) (GQ)
225 East 86 Street
New York, NY 10028
(212) 722-3589

Korea (South)
2320 Massachusetts Avenue NW
Washington, DC 20008
(202) 483-7383

Kuwait
2940 Tilden Street NW
Washington, DC 20008
(202) 966-0702

Laos
2222 S Street NW
Washington, DC 20008
(202) 332-6416

Latvia
4325 17th Street NW
Washington, DC 20011
(202) 726-8213

Lebanon
2560 28th Street NW
Washington, DC 20008
(202) 939-6300

Lesotho
1601 Connecticut Avenue NW
Washington, DC 20009
(202) 462-4190

Liberia
5201 16th Street NW
Washington, DC 20011
(202) 723-0437

Libya (FM) (No embassy)

Lithuania
2622 16th Street NW
Washington, DC 20009
(202) 234-5860

Luxembourg
2200 Massachusetts Avenue NW
Washington, DC 20008
(202) 265-4171

Madagascar
2374 Massachusetts Avenue NW
Washington, DC 20008
(202) 265-5525

Malawi
1400 20th Street NW
Washington, DC 20036
(202) 296-5530

Malaysia
2401 Massachusetts Avenue NW
Washington, DC 20008
(202) 328-2700

Maldives (Mission to the United Nations)
212 East 47 Street
New York, NY 10017
(212) 599-6195

Mali
2130 R Street NW
Washington, DC 20008
(202) 332-2249

Malta
2017 Connecticut Avenue NW
Washington, DC 20008
(202) 462-3611

Mauritania
2129 Leroy Place NW
Washington, DC 20008
(202) 232-5700

Mauritius
4301 Connecticut Avenue NW
Washington, DC 20008
(202) 244-1491

Mexico
2829 16th Street NW
Washington, DC 20009
(202) 234-6000

Mongolia (Mission to the United Nations)
6 East 77 Street
New York, NY 10021
(212) 861-9460

Morocco
1601 21st Street NW
Washington, DC 20009
(202) 462-7979

Mozambique
1990 M Street NW
Washington, DC 20037
(202) 293-7146

Nepal
2131 Leroy Place NW
Washington, DC 20008
(202) 667-4550

Netherlands
4200 Linnean Avenue NW
Washington, DC 20008
(202) 244-5304

New Zealand
37 Observatory Circle NW
Washington, DC 20008
(202) 328-4800

Nicaragua (QU)
1627 New Hampshire Avenue NW
Washington, DC 20009
(202) 387-4371

Niger
2204 R Street NW
Washington, DC 20008
(202) 483-4224

Nigeria
2201 M Street NW
Washington, DC 20037
(202) 822-1500

Norway
2720 34th Street NW
Washington, DC 20008
(202) 333-6000

Oman
2342 Massachusetts Avenue NW
Washington, DC 20008
(202) 387-1980

Pakistan
2315 Massachusetts Avenue NW
Washington, DC 20008
(202) 939-6200

Panama
2862 McGill Terrace NW
Washington, DC 20008
(202) 483-1407

Papua New Guinea
1330 Connecticut Avenue NW
Washington, DC 20036
(202) 659-0856

Paraguay
2400 Massachusetts Avenue NW
Washington, DC 20008
(202) 483-6960

Peru
1700 Massachusetts Avenue NW
Washington, DC 20036
(202) 833-9860

Philippines
1617 Massachusetts Avenue NW
Washington, DC 20036
(202) 483-1414

Poland (QW)
2640 16th Street NW
Washington, DC 20009
(202) 234-3800

Portugal
2125 Kalorama Road NW
Washington, DC 20008
(202) 328-8610

Qatar
600 New Hampshire Avenue NW
Washington, DC 20037
(202) 338-0111

Romania (ND)
1607 23rd Street NW
Washington, DC 20008
(202) 232-4747

Rwanda
1714 New Hampshire Avenue NW
Washington, DC 20009
(202) 232-2882

Saint Christopher and Nevis
1730 Rhode Island Avenue NW
Washington, DC 20036
(202) 833-3550

Saint Lucia
2100 M Street NW
Washington, DC 20037
(202) 463-7378

Saudi Arabia
601 New Hampshire Avenue NW
Washington, DC 20037
(202) 342-3800

Appendix F 457

Senegal
2112 Wyoming Avenue NW
Washington, DC 20008
(202) 234-0540

Seychelles
820 Second Avenue
New York, NY 10017
(212) 687-9766

Sierra Leone
1701 19th Street NW
Washington, DC 20009
(202) 939-9261

Singapore
1824 R Street NW
Washington, DC 20009
(202) 667-7555

Somalia
600 New Hampshire Avenue NW
Washington, DC 20037
(202) 342-1575

South Africa (BL)
3051 Massachusetts Avenue NW
Washington, DC 20008
(202) 232-4400

Spain
2700 15th Street NW
Washington, DC 20009
(202) 265-0190

Sri Lanka
2148 Wyoming Avenue NW
Washington, DC 20008
(202) 483-4025

Sudan
2210 Massachusetts Avenue NW
Washington, DC 20008
(202) 338-8565

Surinam
2600 Virginia Avenue NW
Washington, DC 20037
(202) 338-6980

Swaziland
4301 Connecticut Avenue NW
Washington, DC 20008
(202) 362-6683

Sweden
600 New Hampshire Avenue NW
Washington, DC 20037
(202) 298-3500

Switzerland
2900 Cathedral Avenue NW
Washington, DC 20008
(202) 745-7900

Syria (AQ)
2215 Wyoming Avenue NW
Washington, DC 20008
(202) 232-6313

Tanzania
2139 R Street NW
Washington, DC 20008
(202) 939-6125

Thailand
2300 Kalorama Road NW
Washington, DC 20008
(202) 483-7200

Togo
2208 Massachusetts Avenue NW
Washington, DC 20008
(202) 234-4212

Trinidad and Tobago
1708 Massachusetts Avenue NW
Washington, DC 20036
(202) 467-6490

Tunisia
2408 Massachusetts Avenue NW
Washington, DC 20008
(202) 234-6644

Turkey
1606 23rd Street NW
Washington, DC 20008
(202) 387-3200

Uganda 5909 16th Street NW
Washington, DC 20011
(202) 726-7100

Union of Soviet Socialist Republics (USSR) (FC)
1125 16th Street NW
Washington, DC 20036
(202) 628-7551

United Arab Emirates
600 New Hampshire Avenue NW
Washington, DC 20037
(202) 338-6500

United Kingdom
3100 Massachusetts Avenue NW
Washington, DC 20008
(202) 462-1340

Upper Volta
2340 Massachusetts Avenue NW
Washington, DC 20008
(202) 332-5577

Uruguay
1918 F Street NW
Washington, DC 20006
(202) 331-1313

Venezuela
2445 Massachusetts Avenue NW
Washington, DC 20008
(202) 797-3800

Vietnam (Mission to the United Nations) (LD)
20 Waterside Plaza New York, NY 10010
(212) 685-8001

Western Samoa
820 Second Avenue New York, NY 10017
(212) 599-6196

Yemen Arab Republic (North)
600 New Hampshire Avenue NW
Washington, DC 20037
(202) 965-4760

Yugoslavia
2410 California Street NW
Washington, DC 20008
(202) 462-6566

Zaire
1800 New Hampshire Avenue NW
Washington, DC 20009
(202) 234-7690

Zambia
2419 Massachusetts Avenue NW
Washington, DC 20008
(202) 265-9717

Zimbabwe
2852 McGill Terrace NW
Washington, DC 20008
(202) 332-7100

Publication Order Form

Order processing code: *** 6126**

1. Please print or type (Form is aligned for typewriter use.)

All prices include regular domestic postage and handling and are good through June 1986. After this date, please call Order and Information Desk at 202-783-3238 to verify prices.

Qty.	Stock Number	Title	Price Each	Total Price

Total for Publications

Foreign orders please add an additional 25%.

3. Please choose method of payment:
   - ☐ Check payable to the Superintendent of Documents
   - ☐ GPO Deposit Account ☐☐☐☐☐☐☐–☐
   - ☐ VISA, MasterCard or Choice Account ☐☐☐☐☐☐☐☐☐☐☐☐

   _____
   (Credit card expiration date)

   _____
   (Signature)

Please Type or Print

2. _____
   (Company or personal name)

   _____
   (Additional address/attention line)

   _____
   (Street address)

   _____
   (City, State, ZIP Code)

   ( ) _____
   (Daytime phone including area code)

4. **Mail To:** Superintendent of Documents, Government Printing Office, Washington, D.C. 20402

Thank you for your order!

Publisher Order Form 461

Subscriptions Order Form

Order processing code: *** 6127**

1. Please print or type (Form is aligned for typewriter use.)

All prices include regular domestic postage and handling and are good through June 1986. After this date, please call Order and Information Desk at 202-783-3238 to verify prices.

Qty.	List ID	Title	Price Each	Total Price

Total for Subscriptions

Foreign orders please add an additional 25%.

Please Type or Print

2. _____
   (Company or personal name)

   _____
   (Additional address/attention line)

   _____
   (Street address)

   _____
   (City, State, ZIP Code)

   (___) _____
   (Daytime phone including area code)

3. Please choose method of payment:

   ☐ Check payable to the Superintendent of Documents
   ☐ GPO Deposit Account ☐☐☐☐☐☐☐–☐
   ☐ VISA, MasterCard or Choice Account

   ☐☐☐☐☐☐☐☐☐☐☐☐

   ☐☐☐☐ _____
              (Credit card expiration date)

   _____
   (Signature)

   Thank you for your order!

4. **Mail To:** Superintendent of Documents, Government Printing Office, Washington, D.C. 20402

SUPERINTENDENT OF DOCUMENTS
U.S. GOVERNMENT PRINTING OFFICE
WASHINGTON, D.C. 20402

Telephone (202) 783-3238

Subject Bibliography Order Form

To order, indicate the quantity desired beside each SB number, complete the mailing label, and return to the address above.

SB No.	SB No.	SB No.	SB No.	SB No.	SB No.	SB No.
__ 2	__ 39	__ 85	__ 128	__ 168	__ 216	__ 260	__ 301
__ 3	__ 40	__ 86	__ 129	__ 169	__ 217	__ 261	__ 302
__ 4	__ 41	__ 87	__ 130	__ 170	__ 218	__ 263	__ 303
__ 5	__ 42	__ 88	__ 131	__ 171	__ 219	__ 267	__ 304
__ 6	__ 43	__ 90	__ 132	__ 173	__ 220	__ 270	__ 305
__ 7	__ 44	__ 91	__ 133	__ 174	__ 221	__ 271	__ 306
__ 8	__ 46	__ 92	__ 137	__ 175	__ 222	__ 272	__ 307
__ 9	__ 48	__ 93	__ 138	__ 176	__ 223	__ 273	__ 308
__ 10	__ 49	__ 94	__ 139	__ 177	__ 225	__ 275	__ 309
__ 11	__ 50	__ 95	__ 140	__ 181	__ 226	__ 276	__ 310
__ 12	__ 51	__ 97	__ 141	__ 182	__ 227	__ 277	__ 311
__ 13	__ 52	__ 98	__ 142	__ 183	__ 228	__ 278	__ 312
__ 14	__ 53	__ 99	__ 143	__ 185	__ 229	__ 279	__ 313
__ 15	__ 55	__ 100	__ 144	__ 186	__ 231	__ 280	
__ 16	__ 57	__ 102	__ 146	__ 187	__ 234	__ 281	
__ 17	__ 59	__ 106	__ 148	__ 191	__ 235	__ 282	
__ 18	__ 63	__ 107	__ 149	__ 192	__ 236	__ 284	
__ 19	__ 64	__ 108	__ 150	__ 195	__ 237	__ 285	

Publisher Order Forms 463

___ 21	___ 109	___ 151	___ 196	___ 238	___ 286
___ 22	___ 110	___ 152	___ 197	___ 239	___ 287
___ 23	___ 111	___ 153	___ 198	___ 241	___ 288
___ 24	___ 114	___ 154	___ 200	___ 243	___ 289
___ 25	___ 115	___ 156	___ 201	___ 244	___ 290
___ 27	___ 116	___ 157	___ 202	___ 245	___ 291
___ 28	___ 117	___ 158	___ 204	___ 246	___ 292
___ 29	___ 118	___ 160	___ 205	___ 247	___ 293
___ 30	___ 119	___ 161	___ 207	___ 249	___ 294
___ 31	___ 121	___ 162	___ 209	___ 250	___ 295
___ 32	___ 122	___ 163	___ 210	___ 252	___ 296
___ 34	___ 123	___ 164	___ 211	___ 256	___ 297
___ 35	___ 125	___ 165	___ 213	___ 257	___ 298
___ 36	___ 126	___ 166	___ 214	___ 258	___ 299
___ 37	___ 127	___ 167	___ 215	___ 259	___ 300

Missing numbers are obsolete or superseded by newer lists.

Please send me ___ additional copies of the Subject Bibliography Index.
Please send me ___ copies of Price List 36.

U.S. GOVERNMENT PRINTING OFFICE
SUPERINTENDENT OF DOCUMENTS
WASHINGTON, D.C. 20402

OFFICIAL BUSINESS
PENALTY FOR PRIVATE USE, $300

POSTAGE AND FEES PAID
U.S. GOVERNMENT PRINTING OFFICE
375

PRINTED MATTER

Name _____

Street address _____

City and State _____ ZIP Code _____

NTIS delivery and ordering options

Sales Desk Business Hours: 7:45 am-5:00pm Eastern Standard Time

Delivery Options	Class of Delivery	NTIS Inhouse Processing	Phone Numbers	Service Charge
Express	Overnight [1] Courier	Guaranteed [2] 24 hours	(800) 336-4700 VA (703) 487-4700	$20 per item
Rush	First Class or equivalent	Guaranteed [2] 24 hours	(800) 336-4700 VA (703) 487-4700	$10 per item
	Customer Pickup 8:00-4:00 VA 8:30-4:30 DC	Guaranteed [2] 24 hours	(800) 336-4700 VA (703) 487-4700	$7.50 per item
Regular	First Class or equivalent	Stocked Reports 2-3 days [3]	(703) 487-4650	$3 Shipping/ handling fee per order

[1] Express service guarantees overnight delivery. Express orders received by 1 pm (EST) on any working day are in your hands by 3 pm (local time) the following working day for *reports in stock*.

[2] Express and Rush handling guarantee same day processing on reports in stock and 24-hour processing on reports requiring printing. Toll free ordering is available for Express and Rush orders. All Express and Rush orders require NTIS Deposit Account, American Express, VISA, or MasterCard. Standard $3 NTIS Shipping and Handling fee is waived on all Express and Rush orders.

[3] Regular handling for reports not in shelf stock (requiring reproduction) normally takes 3 to 14 days to process.

Ordering Options Available 24 Hours A Day

Telex: 89-9405 or 64617 (international)
Telecopier: (703) 321-8547
Online: Dialog (Command: DIALORDER)
          SDC   (Command: ORDER NTIS)

Western Union:
$3.50 per item. Call NTIS
(703) 487-4650 for details.

NTIS Electronic Ordering Service:
Call (703) 487-4624 for details.
(Regular service only)

Code-A-Phone: (703) 487-4650
Available after business hours
and weekends to record your orders.

NOTE: Whether you request Express, Rush, or Regular service, your orders always receive prompt attention. NTIS is required by law to recover costs, and every order is important to us.

466 **FEDfind**

NTIS ORDER FORM

MAIL ORDER TO:

NTIS®
U.S. DEPARTMENT OF COMMERCE
National Technical Information Service
Springfield, VA. 22161

EXPRESS/RUSH   (800) 336-4700
                    (703) 487-4700
REGULAR SERVICE   (703) 487-4650
TELECOPIER   (703) 321-8547
TELEX   89-9405

For DTIC Users Only

DTIC User Code _____

Contract Number _____
(last 6 characters only)

Date _____

PURCHASER: _____

BILLING OFFICE TELEPHONE: (___) _____

ATTENTION: _____ _____
           (Last name)   (Initial)

_____
(company, university, agency)

_____
(bldg., suite, dept.)

_____
(street, P.O. Box)

U.S. _____ _____ _____
       (city)   (state)   (ZIP)

Foreign: _____
         (city, state or province, country)

SHIP TO: (Enter ONLY if different from address at left)

ATTENTION: _____ _____
           (Last name)   (Initial)

_____
(company, university, agency)

_____
(bldg., suite, dept.)

_____
(street, P.O. Box)

U.S. _____ _____ _____
       (city)   (state)   (ZIP)

Foreign: _____
         (city, state or province, country)

Publisher Order Forms

NTIS ORDER NUMBER/**GBD**	USER ROUTING CODE (see reverse)	QUANTITY Paper Copy	QUANTITY Micro-fiche	QUANTITY Other (specify)	UNIT PRICE	PRIORITY MAIL SERVICES	TOTAL PRICE
1.							
2.							
3.							
4.							
5.							
6.							
				Shipping and Handling Fee ($3 domestic/$4 foreign)			
				Grand Total			

METHOD OF PAYMENT

☐ Charge to NTIS Deposit Account No. _____

☐ Check/money order enclosed for $ _____

Charge to my ☐ American Express ☐ VISA ☐ MasterCard

Account No. _____ Expiration Date _____

Signature: _____

(Required to validate ALL orders)

USE MEDIA CODES

The two or three letters at the end of NTIS Order Numbers have been placed there to help NTIS marketers determine the most effective media in bringing various types of information to users' attention. **Please use the media codes when ordering.** The information they provide is very helpful to NTIS and to its user community.

(REV. 10-85)

Requests for copies of GAO reports should be sent to:

U.S. General Accounting Office
Post Office Box 6015
Gaithersburg, Maryland 20877

Telephone 202-275-6241

The first five copies of each report are free. Additional copies are $2.00 each.

There is a 25% discount on orders for 100 or more copies mailed to a single address.

Orders must be prepaid by cash or by check or money order made out the Superintendent of Documents.

Publisher Order Form 469

GAO Form 458 (Rev 3-80)
Report Order Form

HOW TO OBTAIN GAO REPORTS

Single copies of GAO reports are available free of charge. Orders should be sent to:

U.S. General Accounting Office
Post Office Box 6015
Gaithersburg, Maryland 20877

Telephone 202-275-6241

To order a GAO report, please use the accession number and date indicated in bold type after the title of each report.

ACCESSION NUMBER	REPORT NUMBER	DATE	ACCESSION NUMBER	REPORT NUMBER	DATE

Please check the appropriate boxes below:

☐ Member or Committee of Congress   ☐ College library, faculty, and students

☐ Government official   ☐ All other

☐ Member of press

☐ Please check here if you wish to receive microfiche rather than printed reports--there is no charge for microfiche.

☐ My address is incorrect, please change to the address listed below. (List old and new addresses)

NAME/OLD ADDRESS (Include ZIP Code)	NAME/NEW ADDRESS (Include ZIP Code)

☐ Please add my name to the distribution list for the Monthly List of GAO Reports (Requester completes "new address" block above.)

☐ Check this box if you no longer wish to receive the Monthly List of GAO Reports

Subject-Organization-Publisher Index

ABC-Clio, 109, 137, 138
ABMC, 234
Access laws, public, 435–39
Accounting Office, General, 97, 421–427
Acquisition Regulation, Federal, 369
ACDA, 298
ACIR, 231
ACS, 150
ACTION, 229
ADAMHA, 189
Administration (see other part of title)
Administration, Office of, 143
Administrative Conference of the United States, 230
Administrative laws, 113
Administrative Office of the United States Courts, 105, 107, 122
Advisory Commission on Intergovernmental Relations, 231
Advisory Committee Act, Federal, 439
Advisory committees and organizations, 33, 36
AEI, 429
Aeronautical charts, 385
Aeronautics and Space Administration, National, 265–66
AFFIRM, 442
Affirmative action, 62
Agency (see other part of title)
Agricultural Cooperative Service, 150
Agriculture, Department of, 147–57
Agricultural Library, National, 154
Agricultural Marketing Service, 150
Agricultural Outlook Board, World, 157
Agricultural Research Service, 153
Agricultural Service, Foreign, 153
Agricultural Stabilization and Conservation Service, 150
AID, 232–33
Air Force, Department of, 171
Alcohol, Drug Abuse and Mental Health Administration, 189
Alcohol, Tobacco and Firearms, Bureau of, 223
American Association for Budget and Program Analysis, 314
American Battle Monuments Commission, 234
American Civil Liberties Union, 435
American Enterprise Institute, 80, 133, 429–30
American Historical Association, 40
American Inheritance Press, 137
American Geological Institute, 388
American Library Association, 445
American Political Science Association, 80, 109
American Presidency, 135–38

American Society of Access Professionals, 435
American University, 80
AMS, 150
AMTRAK, 277
Amward Publications, Inc., 43
Animal and Plant Health Inspection Service, 151
Annual reports, 36
APDU, 345
Appalachian Regional Commission, 235
APHIS, 151
Appeals, Temporary Emergency Court of, 121
Appeals, U.S. Courts of, 119, 121
ARC, 235
Archives and Records Administration, National 267–68
A-R Editions, Inc., 108
Armed Services Information Service, 168
Arms Control and Disarmament Agency, United States, 298
Army, Department of, 172
Army Times Publishing Co., 73, 169
ARS, 150
Arts and the Humanities, National Foundation on the, 272
Arts, Commission of Fine, 239
Arts, National Endowment for the, 272–73
ASCS, 150
Association for Federal Information Resources Management, 442
Association of Public Data Users, 345
Atmospheric Administration, National Oceanic and, 163
ATSDR, 189
Audiovisual Center, National, 268
Audit standards, 331–32
Authority (see other part of title)
Aviation Administration, Federal, 217

Bank Board, Federal Home Loan, 254
Bank of the United States, Export-Import, 246
BATF, 223
Battle Monuments Commission, American, 234
BEA, 162
Benefit Guaranty Corporation, Pension, 288
Benton Foundation, 84
BIA, 196
Bibliographic Retrieval Services, Inc., 447
BidNet, Inc., 377
Bid protests, 368
Biographies, executive branch, 49, 133; legislative branch, 47–48, 92; judicial branch, 118

472 FEDfind

BJS, 200
BLM, 196
BLMRCP, 207
BLS, 207
BNA, 430
BNA Books, 64, 76
Board (see other part of title)
Book, Center for the, 100
Botanic Garden, United States, 102
Braddock Publications, Inc., 42, 49
Broadcasting, Board for International, 236
Brookings Institution, 430
BRS, 447
BSC, 362
Budget and Program Newsletter, 331
Budget Office, Congressional, 96
Budget, Office of Management and, 141
Budget process, 309–24; budget documents, 318–20; Congressional budget process, 321; executive branch preparation and submission, 314; implementation and control, 322–24; OMB technical staff papers, 317; policy directives, 314–16; review and audit, 324
Bureau (see other part of title)
Bureau of National Affairs, Inc., 117, 430
Burwell Enterprises, 449
Business Administration, Small, 295
Business Development Agency, Minority, 163
Business information resources, 371–73
Business Service Centers, 362

Cable Satellite Public Affairs Network, 84
Campaign & Elections, 90
Canal Commission, Panama, 285
Capital Planning Commission, National, 269
Capitol, Architect of the, 95
Capitol Hill employment, 72
Capitol Publications, Inc., 249, 370
Carroll Publishing Co., 39, 49–50
Cartographic data, 381–83
Cato Institute, 430
CBD, 369
CBO, 96
CBO Publications, 319
CCC, 151
CCH, 432
CCR, 238
CDC, 189
CEA, 142
Census, Bureau of the, 162
Center (see other part of title)
Central Intelligence Agency, 237
CEQ, 143
CFA, 239
CFR, 130–31
CFTC, 240

Chamber of Commerce of the United States, 47, 431
Channing L. Bete Co., Inc., 431
Chelsea House Publishers, 118
Child Support Enforcement, Office of, 188
CIA, 237
CIC, 262
CIS, 432
Citizens Against Government Waste, 333
Civilian personnel news, 73
Civilian personnel operations, 55–62
Civil Rights, Commission on, 238
Civil service law and procedures, 63
Claims Court, U.S. 121
Claritas Partners, 431
Classification decisions and opinions, 60
Coast Guard, U.S., 219
Code of Federal Regulations, 130–31
Columbia Books, Inc., 45
Commerce Business Daily, 369
Commerce Clearing House, Inc., 89, 94, 112, 431
Commerce Commission, Interstate, 263
Commerce, Department of, 159–65
Commission (see other part of title)
Committee Management Secretariat, 33
Committee on National Statistics, 345
Commodity Credit Corporation, 151
Commodity Futures Trading Commission, 240
Common Cause, 432, 443
Communications Commission, Federal, 248–49
Communications Service, 45
Community Services, Office of, 188
Comptroller General, 426
Comptroller of the Currency, Office of the, 224
CompuServe Information Services, Inc., 447
Computerized information resources, 445–48; databases, 343; Executive Office of the President, 141; judicial branch, 118; legislative branch, 93–95; procurement, 377; science and technology, 356
Conciliation Service, Federal Mediation and, 257
Congress, 75; biographies, 92–93; budget process, 321; computerized information resources, 93–95; congressional district information, 80–81; legislative coordination and clearance, 103; operation and organization, 76–80; organizations, 95–102; periodicals covering, 90–91; proceedings, 87–89; rules and procedures, 82–84
Congressional Budget Office, 96
Congressional Digest Corp., 90

Congressional Information Service, Inc., 76, 88, 129, 130, 339, 432
Congressional Management Foundation, 79
Congressional Quarterly Inc., 44, 50, 79, 81, 87, 89, 90, 92, 95, 110, 432, 448
Congressional Record, 87
Congressional Research Service, 100
Congressional Sourcebook Series, 327–28
Congressional Staff Directory, Ltd., 46, 48, 50
Conservation Service, Agricultural Stabilization and, 150
Conservation Service, Soil, 157
Consolidated Rail Corporation (Conrail), 307
Constitution, U.S., 108–9
Consortium of Social Science Associations, 345–46
Consumer Advisor, Office of, 155
Consumer Information Center, 262
Consumer Product Safety Commission, 241
Cooperative State Research Service, 151
COPAFS, 346–47
Copyright Royalty Tribunal, 97
COSSA, 345–46
Council (see other part of title)
Counsel, Office of the Special, 304
Court periodicals, 116–17
Court system, U.S., 105–7
Courts, Administrative Office of the United States, 122
CPSC, 241
CQ, 432
CQ Press, 76
Credit Administration, Farm, 247
Credit Corporation, Commodity, 151
Credit Union Administration, National, 271
Crop Insurance Corporation, Federal, 152
CRS, 100
CS, 179
CSIS, 430
C-SPAN, 84
CSRS, 151
Cuadra/Elsevier, 446
Currency, Office of the Comptroller of the, 224
Customs Service, U.S., 225

Databases, 417; directories, 445–46
Data Center Program, State, 339
Datapro Research Corp., 445, 446
Data Users, Association of Public, 345
DEA, 201
Defense agencies and joint service schools, 174–76

Defense, Department of, 167–76
Defense mapping, 385–86
Dembner Books, 137
Department (see other part of title)
Deposit Insurance Corporation, Federal, 250
Depository Library Program, 402–8
Development, Agency for International, 232–33
Development Cooperation Agency, U.S. International, 301
Development Program, Trade and, 301
DIALOG Information Services, Inc., 396, 447
Directories, 41–53; directories of directories, 53; executive branch, 49–51; foreign affairs, 52; judicial branch, 52; legislative branch, 46–48
Disarmament Agency, U.S. Arms Control and, 298
Disease Control, Centers for, 189
Disease Registry, Agency for Toxic Substances and, 189
Dissemination of Statistics, Interagency Committee on, 347
District Courts, U.S., 119
Document retrieval services, 449
Documents Index, 388, 395
DOD, 167
Dodd Mead, 330
DOE, 181–83
DOL, 205–9
DOT, 215–19
Drug Abuse and Mental Health Administration, Alcohol, 189
Drug Administration, Food and, 190
Drug Enforcement Administration, 201
DTIC, 174
Dun and Bradstreet, 368

Economic Advisors, Council of, 142
Economic Analysis, Bureau of, 162
Economic Development Administration, 162
Economic indicators, 340–41
Economic Regulatory Administration, 183
Economic Research Service, 152
Economics Management Staff, 151
EDA, 162
Education, Department of, 177–79
Education, National Institute of, 179
[Education] Statistics, Center for, 179
Educational Resources Information Center, 179
EEOC, 245
EIA, 183
Election Commission, Federal, 251
Electrification Administration, Rural, 156
Embassies, 451–58

Emergency Management Agency, Federal, 252
Employment and Training Administration, 207
Employment and Training Service, Veterans', 209
Employment information, Federal, 67–72
Employment Opportunity Commission, Equal, 245
Employment Standards Administration, 208
Endowment for the Arts, National, 272–73
Endowment for the Humanities, National, 272–73
Energy, Department of, 181–83
Energy Information Administration, 183
Energy, Office of, 155
Energy Regulatory Commission, Federal, 253
Engraving and Printing, Bureau of, 223
Environmental Protection Agency, 243–44
Environmental Quality, Council on, 143
EOP Publications, 33, 103, 140, 314, 326, 359, 380, 442
EPA, 243–44
Equal Employment Opportunity Commission, 245
ERA, 183
ERIC, 179
ERS, 152
ESA, 208
ETA, 207
Ethics in Government Act, 443–44
Ethics, Office of Government, 443
Exchange Commission, Securities and, 292–93
Executive Boards, Federal, 36
Executive branch agencies, 227–308
Executive branch overview, 125–33
Executive Office of the President, 135–44
Eximbank, 246
Export-Import Bank of the United States, 246
Exporting information references, 374–77
Extension Service, 152

FAA, 217
FACA, 439
Factor evaluation system, 59, 60
Facts on File, Inc., 110
FAR, 369
Farm Credit Administration, 247
Farmers Home Administration, 152
Farms and Farm Characteristics (see Agriculture)

FAS, 153
FBI, 201, 451
FCA, 247
FCC, 248–49
FCIC, 152
FDA, 190
FDIC, 250
FEBS, 36
FEC, 251
Fed, 258
Federal (see other part of title)
Federal Budget Report, 320
Federal Bureau of Investigation, 201, 451
Federal Employees' News Digest, Inc., 60, 73
Federal Jobs Digest, 71
Federal Managers' Association, 65
Federal Personnel Manual, 55–58
Federal Personnel Publications, 61, 73
Federal Register, 128–29
Federal Register, Office of the, 125, 127, 138, 139
Federal Register System, 125–27
Federal Reports Inc., 71
Federal Research Service, Inc., 68, 71, 73
Fed Facts, 61–62
Feistritzer Publications, 140
FEMA, 252
FERC, 253
FGIS, 153
FHLBB, 254
FHWA, 217
FIC, 261
Financial Management Improvement Program, Joint, 313
Financial Management Service, 224
Financing Administration, Health Care, 188
Fine Arts, Commission of, 239
Firearms, Bureau of Alcohol, Tobacco and, 223
Fish and Wildlife Service, U.S., 198
FJC, 133
FLC, 101
FLETC, 223
FLICC, 101
FLRA, 63, 255
FMA, 65
FMC, 256
FMCS, 257
FmHA, 152
FMS, 224
FNS, 153
Foggy Bottom Publications, 329
FOIA, 435–37
FOI Service Center, 436

Food and Drug Administration, 190
Food and Nutrition Service, 153
Food Safety and Inspection Service, 153
Foreign Agricultural Service, 153
Foreign Claims Settlement Commission of the U.S., 202
Foreign embassies, 451–58
Foreign Service, U.S., 213
Foreign technology, 355
Forest Service, 154
Foundation for Public Affairs, 43
Foundation Press, Inc., 108
FPDC, 363
FRA, 217
Franchising, 372–73
Freedom of Information Act, 435–37
FS, 213
FSIS, 153
FSLIC, 254
FTC, 259
Futures Trading Commission, Commodity, 240
FWS, 198

Gale Research Co., 36, 446
GAO, 97, 421–27
General Accounting Office, 97, 421–27
General Services Administration, 260–61
Geological information, 387–88
Geological Survey, U.S., 198
Government Data Publications, 370
Government Ethics, Office of, 443
Government in the Sunshine Act, 439
Government organization, Federal, 31–40
Government Printing Office, 98, 389–408
Government Sales Consultants, 368
GPO, 98, 389–408
Graduate School (U.S. Department of Agriculture), 154
Grain Inspection Service, Federal, 153
Greater Washington Society of Association Executives, 375
Greenwood Press, 39, 133
GSA, 260–61

Handbook X-118, 59
HCFA, 188
HDS, 188
Health Administration, Mine Safety and, 208
Health Administration, Occupational Safety and, 208
Health and Human Services, Department of, 185–92
Health Care Financing Administration, 188

Health Information Clearinghouse, National, 186
Health, National Institutes for, 191
Health Resources and Services Administration, 190
Health Review Commission, Occupational Safety and, 282
Health Service, Public, 189–91
Health Statistics, National Center for, 190
Heritage Foundation, 432
HHS, 185–92
Highway Administration, Federal, 217
Highway Traffic Safety Administration, National, 218
Hill and Knowlton, Inc., 42
Historical Office, U.S. Senate, 93
Historical programs, 40
Historical Publications and Records Commission, National, 267
HNIS, 154
Home Administration, Farmers, 152
Home Loan Bank Board, Federal, 254
Hoover Institution, 432
House of Representatives, U.S., (or: see Congress) rules and procedures, 83–84
Housing and Urban Development, Department of, 193–94
HRSA, 190
HUD, 193–94
HUD USER, 194
Hudson's Associates, 42–43
Human Development Services, Office of, 188
Humanities, National Endowment for the, 272–73
Humanities, National Foundation on the Arts and the, 272
Human Nutrition Information Service, 154
Human Services, Department of Health and, 185–92

IAF, 262
ICC, 263
IDCA, 301
Immigration and Naturalization Service, 202
Import Bank of the U.S., Export-, 246
Income Division, Statistics of, 224
Indian Affairs, Bureau of, 196
Infordata International Inc., 395
Information Access Co., 394
Information Administration, Energy, 183
Information Administration, National Telecommunications and, 164
Information Agency, United States, 299–300
Information and Regulatory Affairs, Office of, 336, 441

Information Center, Educational
  Resources, 179
Information Center Committee, Federal
  Library and, 101
Information Center, Consumer, 260
Information Center, Federal, 261
Information Center, Technical, 183
Information Clearinghouse, National
  Health, 186
Information Handling Services, 61
Information Interchange Corp., 394
Information resources management, 441
Information Science, National
  Commission on Libraries and, 270
Information Service, Human Nutrition,
  154
Information Service, National
  Technical, 164, 409-19
Information Service, U.S., 299
Information Store, Inc., 449
Information USA, Inc., 446
Innovation Research Program, Small
  Business, 357
INS, 202
Inside Washington Publishers, 141, 244
Inspection Service, Federal Grain, 153
Inspection Service, Food Safety and,
  153
Institute for Policy Studies, 168, 433
Insurance Corporation, Federal Crop,
  152
Insurance Corporation, Federal
  Deposit, 250
Insurance Corporation, Federal Savings
  and Loan, 254
Intelligence Agency, Central, 237
Interagency Committee on
  Dissemination of Statistics, 347
Inter-American Foundation, 262
Intergovernmental Relations, Advisory
  Commission on, 231
Interior, Department of the, 195-98
Internal Revenue Service, 224
International Broadcasting, Board for,
  236
International Cooperation and
  Development, Office of, 155
International Criminal Police
  Organization—United States National
  Central Bureau, 202
International Development, Agency for,
  232-33
International Development Cooperation
  Agency, United States, 301
International Policy, Office of Research,
  Statistics and, 192
International Studies, Center for
  Strategic and, 430
International Trade Administration, 163
International Trade Commission,
  United States, 302-3
International Trade, U.S. Court of, 121

INTERPOL-USNCB, 202
Interstate Commerce Commission, 263
Investigation, Federal Bureau of, 201,
  451
Investment Corporation, Overseas
  Private, 284
IPS, 433
IRM, 441
IRS, 224
ITA, 163
ITC, 302-3
ITT Dialcom, Inc., 148, 447

JFMIP, 313
Joint Financial Management
  Improvement Program, 313
Joint service schools, defense, 174-76
JSIA, 203
Judicial branch, 105-24; organizations,
  119-24; procedures and prosecution,
  113-14
Judicial Center, Federal, 123-24
Justice, Department of, 199-203
Justice Statistics, Bureau of, 200
Justice System Improvement Act
  Agencies, 203

Knowledge Industry Publications, Inc.,
  445

Labor, Department of, 205-9
Labor-management relations, 63-64
Labor-Management Relations and
  Cooperative Programs, Bureau of,
  207
Labor-Management Standards, Office
  of, 208
Labor Relations Authority, Federal, 63,
  253
Labor Relations Board, National,
  274-75
Labor Statistics, Bureau of, 207
Land Management, Bureau of, 196
Law Enforcement Training Center,
  Federal, 223
Lawyers Co-operative Publishing Co.,
  112, 116, 433
LC, 98
Legal employment, Federal, 71
Legal research guides, 108
Legal Services Corporation, 264
LEGI-SLATE, Inc., 94, 447
Legislative branch, 75-103
Legislative Information Group, 79
LEXIS, 118
Libraries and Information Science,
  National Commission on, 270
Libraries Unlimited, Inc., 53, 79
Library and Information Center
  Committee, Federal, 101
Library of Congress, 98-101

Loan Bank Board, Federal Home, 254
Loan Insurance Corporation, Federal Savings and, 254
Lobbyist Systems Corp., 93
LRP Publications, 63, 64
LSC, 264

Machine-readable data, 417
Macmillan Professional and Library Services, 80, 82
Management Agency, Federal Emergency, 252
Management and Budget, Office of, 141
Management, civilian personnel, 65–66
Management, Office of Personnel, 283
Mapping and charting, 379–86; aeronautical, 385; cartographic data, 381–83; collections of, 381; defense mapping, 385–86; nautical charts, 384; policy directive, 379
Marine Corps, 173
Maritime Administration, 217
Maritime Commission, Federal, 256
Marketing Service, Agricultural, 150
Marshals Service, U.S., 203
Martin Marietta Corp., 42, 148
Mass Transportation Administration, Urban, 219
MBDA, 163
McFarland & Co., 138, 298
McGraw-Hill, Inc., 253, 281
Mead Data Central, 118, 447
Mediation and Conciliation Service, Federal, 257
Mediation Board, National, 276
Medicine, National Library of, 191
Mental Health Administration, Alcohol, Drug Abuse and, 189
Merit systems protection, 64
Merit Systems Protection Board, United States, 304
Metropolitan Washington Library Council, 446
Micro Mega Corp., 94
Military Appeals, U.S. Court of, 122
Minerals Management Service, 197
Mine Safety and Health Administration, 208
Mines, Bureau of, 197
Minority Business Development Agency, 163
Mint, U.S., 225
MMS, 197
Monuments Commission, American Battle, 234
MSHA, 208
MSPB, 304

NAL, 154
NAPA, 433
NARA, 267–68
NASA, 265–66

National Academy of Public Administration, 433
National courts, 121–22
National Journal Inc., 41, 91, 92, 132
National Referral Center, 101
National Security Council, 142
National Standards Association, 87, 128
National Statistics, Committee on, 345
Nautical charts, 384
Navy, Department of, 173
NBS, 163
NCES, 179
NCHS, 190
NCIC, 381–82
NCLIS, 270
NCPC, 269
NCUA, 271
NEA, 272–73
NEH, 272–73
NewsNet, Inc., 447
NHIC, 186
NHPAC, 267
NHTSA, 218
NIE, 179
NIH, 191
NIJ, 203
NLM, 191
NLRB, 274
NMB, 276
NOAA, 163
Northeast-Midwest Institute, 433
NRC, 281
NSC, 142
NSF, 278–79
NTIA, 164
NTIS, 164, 409–19
NTSB, 280
Nuclear Regulatory Commission, 281
Nutrition Information Service, Human, 154
Nutrition Service, Food and, 153

OA, 143
OCA, 155
Occupational groups, 59
Occupational Safety and Health Administration, 208
Occupational Safety and Health Review Commission, 282
Oceanic and Atmospheric Administration, National, 163
Office (see other part of title)
OCS, 188
OCSE, 188
OGE, 443
OGPS, 155
OICD, 155
OIRA, 336, 441
OLMS, 208
OMB, 141

OMB Circulars, 140; No. A-10, 314; No. A-11, 314; No. A-12, 315; No. A-16, 379; No. A-19, 103; No. A-21, 360; No. A-31, 315; No. A-34, 315; No. A-49, 360; No. A-50, 326; No. A-64, 315; No. A-70, 315; No. A-73, 326; No. A-76, 360; No. A-89, 326; No. A-94, 316; No. A-102, 360; No. A-105, 33; No. A-109, 360; No. A-110, 361; No. A-112, 316; No. A-114, 361; No. A-119, 361; No. A-120, 361; No. A-123, 326; No. A-124, 361; No. A-125, 362; No. A-127, 316; No. A-128, 327; No. A-129, 316; No. A-130, 442
OMB Watch, 140
OPD, 142
OPIC, 284
OPM, 283
ORDP, 156
Organization, Federal Government, 31–40
ORSIP, 192
Oryx Press, 53, 340
OSHA, 208
OSHRC, 282
OSMRE, 198
OSTP, 143
OT, 156
OTA, 102
Overseas Private Investment Corporation, 284

Packers and Stockyards Administration, 156
PACs, 43, 251
PADC, 287
Panama Canal Commission, 285
Paperwork Reduction Act of 1980, 441–42
Park Service, National, 197
Parole Commission, U.S., 203
Passenger Corporation, National Railroad, 277
Patent and Trademark Office, 164
PBGC, 288
PCC, 285
PCPFS, 290
Peace Corps, 286
Pennsylvania Avenue Development Corporation, 287
Pension and Welfare Benefits Administration, 209
Pension Benefit Guaranty Corporation, 288
Pergamon Infoline, Inc., 448
Personnel Literature, 61
Personnel management, civilian, 55–73
Personnel Management, Office of, 283
PHS, 189–91
Physical Fitness and Sports, President's Council on, 290

Planning Commission, National Capital, 269
Plant Health Inspection Service, Animal and, 151
Plum Book, 35
Policy Analysis Co., Inc., 90
Policy and supporting positions, 35
Policy Development, Office of, 142
Political action committees, 43, 251
Political Profiles, Inc., 133
Position classification standards, 59
Postal Rate Commission, 289
Postal Service, U.S., 305–6
PRC, 289
Prentice-Hall, Inc., 433
President, Executive Office of the, 135–44
Presidential documents, 138–39
President's Council on Physical Fitness and Sports, 290
Printing, Bureau of Engraving and, 223
Printing Office, Government, 98, 389–408
Prisons, Bureau of, 200
Privacy Act of 1974, 438
Privacy Times Inc., 436
Private bills, 91
Private Investment Corporation, Overseas, 284
Procurement Data Center, Federal, 363
Procurement information, 359–70; 377–78; Business Service Centers, 362; periodicals, 369–70; policy directives, 359–62; references, 362–68
Professional Associations on Federal Statistics, Council of, 346–47
Product Safety Commission, Consumer, 241
Program administration and evaluation, 325–33; catalogs, 328–30; Congressional Sourcebook Series, 327–28; evaluation, 331–33; operations, 331; policy directives, 326–27
Project '87, 109
Prosecution, judicial, 113–14
Protection Board, United States Merit System, 304
PTO, 164
Public access laws, 435–39
Public Affairs Information, 94
Publications and Records Commission, National Historical, 267
Public bills and laws, 88, 91
Public Citizen, 434
Public Data Users, Association of, 345
Public Debt, Bureau of the, 223
Public Health Service, 189–91
Public interest groups, 43
PWBA, 209

Rail Corporation, Consolidated, 307
Railroad Administration, Federal, 217
Railroad Passenger Corporation, National, 277
Railroad Retirement Board, 291
Railway Association, United States, 307
Rand Corporation, 434
REA, 156
Reclamation, Bureau of, 197
Records Administration, National Archives and, 267–68
Records Commission, National Historical Publications and, 267
Referral Center, National, 101
Regional Commission, Appalachian, 235
Regional depository libraries, 403–6
Regional Operations, Office of, 36
Regulatory Administration, Economic, 183
Regulatory Affairs, Office of Information and, 336, 441
Regulatory Commission, Federal Energy, 253
Regulatory Commission, Nuclear, 281
Regulatory Information Service Center, 131
Research and Special Programs Administration, 218
Research Materials Corp., 137
Research Service, Agricultural, 150
Research Service, Cooperative State, 151
Research services, 449
Research, Statistics and International Policy, Office of, 192
Reserve System, Federal, 258
Retirement Board, Railroad, 291
Revenue Service, Internal, 224
Rights, Commission on Civil, 238
Roadmap program, 371
Roll Call, 91
Roosevelt Center, 434
RRB, 291
RSPA, 218
Rural Development Policy, Office of, 156
Rural Electrification Administration, 156

Safety Administration, National Highway Traffic, 218
Safety and Health Administration, Occupational, 208
Safety and Health Review Commission, Occupational, 282
Safety and Inspection Service, Food, 153
Safety Board, National Transportation, 280
Safety Commission, Consumer Product, 241

Saint Lawrence Seaway Development Corporation, 218
Savings and Loan Insurance Corporation, Federal, 254
Savings Bonds Division, U.S., 225
Savings Institutions, United States League of, 46
SBA, 295
SBIR, 357
Scarecrow Press, Inc., 112
Science and technology, 349–58; current awareness products, 353–54; foreign technology, 355; guides and catalogs, 349–52; innovation research, 357
Science and Technology Policy, Office of, 143
Science Foundation, National, 278–79
SCORPIO, 94
Scribner's Sons, Charles, 138
SCS, 157
SDC Information Services, 448
SEC, 292–93
Secret Service, U.S., 225
Securities and Exchange Commission, 292–93
Security Council, National, 142
Selective Service System, 294
Senate, U.S., rules and procedures, 82
Service (see other part of title)
Small Business Administration, 295
Smithsonian Institution, 296
Social List of Washington, Inc., 44
Social Science Associations, Consortium of, 345–46
Social Security Administration, 191
Society for History in the Federal Government, 40
Software, 352, 416
SOI, 224
Soil Conservation Service, 157
Source Telecomputing Corp., 448
Space Administration, National Aeronautics and, 265–66
Special Counsel, Office of the, 304
Special Programs Administration, Research and, 218
Sports, President's Council on Physical Fitness and, 290
SRS, 157
SSA, 191
Stabilization and Conservation Service, Agricultural, 150
Standard Federal Regions, 33
Standards Administration, Employment, 208
Standards, National Bureau of, 163
Standards, Office of Labor-Management, 208
State Data Center Program, 339
State, Department of, 211–14
State Research Service, Cooperative, 151

Statistical Policy Office, 336–37
Statistical programs, 335–47; central coordinating office, 336–37; future, present and past, 337–38; independent organizations, 345; information sources, 338–44
Statistical Reporting Service, 157
Statistics (see other part of title)
Stockyards Administration, Packers and, 156
Strategic and International Studies, Center for, 430
Subject bibliographies, 396–401
Sunshine Services Corp., 43
Supreme Court, U.S., 110–12, 119
Surface Mining Reclamation and Enforcement, Office of, 198
System (see other part of title)

Tax Court, U.S., 122
Tax Foundation, Inc., 324
TDP, 301
Technical Information Center, 183
Technical Information Service, National, 164, 409–19
Technology Assessment, Office of, 102
Technology Policy, Office of Science and, 143
Telecommunications and Information Administration, National, 164
Tennessee Valley Authority, 297
Tilden Press, 72
Tobacco and Firearms, Bureau of Alcohol, 223
Topographical maps, 281–83
Tourism Administration, U.S. Travel and, 165
Toxic Substances and Disease Registry, Agency for, 189
Trade Administration, International, 163
Trade and Development Program, 301
Trade Commission, Federal, 259
Trade Commission, United States International, 302–3
Trademark Office, Patent and, 164
Trade Representative, Office of the U.S., 143
Trades and labor occupations, 60
Trading Commission, Commodity Futures, 240
Traffic Safety Administration, National Highway, 218
Training Administration, Employment and, 207
Training Center, Federal Law Enforcement, 223
Training Service, Veterans' Employment and, 209
Transportation Administration, Urban Mass, 219
Transportation, Department of, 215–19
Transportation, Office of, 156
Transportation Safety Board, National, 280

Travel and Tourism Administration, U.S., 165
Treasury, Department of the, 221–25
TVA, 297
Tyson Capitol Institute, 81

UMTA, 219
U.N., 214
Uniform Services Almanac, Inc., 169
United Nations, 214
United States or U.S. (see other part of title)
University Publications of America, 112
Urban Development, Department of Housing and, 193–94
Urban Institute, 320
Urban Mass Transportation Administration, 219
USAF, 171
USCG, 219
U.S. Code, 114–16
U.S. Congress Handbook, 48
USDA, 147–57
USGS, 198
USIA, 299–300
USIS, 299
U.S. Organization Chart Service, Inc., 39
USPS, 305–6
USRA, 307
USTR, 143
USTTA, 165

VA, 308
Veterans Administration, 308
Veterans' Employment and Training Service, 209
VETS, 209
Vice President of the United States, Office of, 144
Viking Penguin Inc., 330

WANT Publishing Co., 44, 84, 107, 117, 437
Washington Alert Service, 95, 448
Washington Monitor, Inc., 48, 51, 436, 437
Washington On-Line, 93, 251, 448
Washington Researchers Publishing, Inc., 42, 43, 44, 49, 51
Welfare Benefits Administration, Pension and, 209
WESTLAW, 118, 448
West Publishing Co., 64, 110, 116, 118, 434
Westview Press, 109
White House, 140, 141
WHO, 141
Wildlife Service, U.S. Fish and, 198
Wiley Law Publications, 107
Wilson, H.W., Co., 137
Workbooks, Inc., 70
Workforce statistics, 33
World Agricultural Outlook Board, 157